Wagner's Melodies

Since the 1840s, critics have lambasted Wagner for lacking the ability to compose melody. But for him, melody was fundamental – "music's only form." This incongruity testifies to the surprising difficulties during the nineteenth century of conceptualizing melody. Despite its indispensable place in opera, contemporary theorists were unable even to agree on a definition for it, let alone formulate a stable basis for teaching it.

In *Wagner's Melodies*, David Trippett re-examines Wagner's central aesthetic claims. He places the composer's ideas about melody in the context of the scientific discourse of his age: from the emergence of the Natural Sciences and historical linguistics to sources about music's stimulation of the body, and inventions for "automatic" composition. Interweaving a rich variety of material from the history of science, music theory, criticism, private correspondence and court reports, Trippett uncovers a new and controversial discourse that placed melody at the apex of artistic self-consciousness, and generated problems of urgent dimensions for German music aesthetics.

DAVID TRIPPETT is Lecturer in Music at the University of Cambridge and a Fellow of Christ's College. His work on Wagner, the history of aesthetics, and theories of technology has appeared in various academic publications, and has earned him the Alfred Einstein Award of the American Musicological Society, and the Donald Tovey Memorial Prize of the University of Oxford. He has served as guest editor of *Musiktheorie*, and is editor and translator of Carl Stumpf's *The Origins of Music* (2012). He also performs regularly as a collaborative pianist.

Wagner's Melodies

Aesthetics and Materialism in German Musical Identity

DAVID TRIPPETT

CAMBRIDGE
UNIVERSITY PRESS

CAMBRIDGE UNIVERSITY PRESS
Cambridge, New York, Melbourne, Madrid, Cape Town,
Singapore, São Paulo, Delhi, Mexico City

Cambridge University Press
The Edinburgh Building, Cambridge CB2 8RU, UK

Published in the United States of America by Cambridge University Press, New York

www.cambridge.org
Information on this title: www.cambridge.org/9781107014305

First published 2013

Printed and bound in the United Kingdom by the MPG Books Group

A catalogue record for this publication is available from the British Library

Library of Congress Cataloguing in Publication data
Trippett, David, 1980–
Wagner's melodies : aesthetics and materialism in German musical identity / David Trippett.
    p.   cm.
Includes bibliographical references and index.
ISBN 978-1-107-01430-5
1. Wagner, Richard, 1813–1883 – Criticism and interpretation.   2. Music – 19th
century – Philosophy and aesthetics.   3. Melody.   I. Title.
ML410.W13T77   2013
782.1092–dc23

2012034001

ISBN 978-1-107-01430-5 Hardback

For Paula

Contents

Illustrations

Acknowledgements

On finishing his long essay *Oper und Drama*, Wagner admitted to a friend: "I have written the last pages of this in a mood I can intelligibly describe to no one." On completing the present book, I have some sympathy with Wagner's sentiment. But in my case, a raft of kind individuals have greatly eased and enriched the way. The subject of *Wagner's Melodies* has occupied me for a number of years, and during this time I have benefited from a wide circle of generous colleagues, friends, and relatives. I owe a debt of gratitude to all of these individuals for their contributions and input.

In its initial stage, this book began life amid discussion, debate, and vigorous cross-examination by Alex Rehding, whose dedication to and support of this project has been unfaltering. He has been a source of encouragement, prompting, and advice, and hence has been nothing short of Dante's Virgil to me. I also thank Carolyn Abbate, whose inspiring ideas and careful reading of chapters helped direct some of my ideas just when I needed it. And I thank Daniel Albright for sharing his inimitable gift for opening new intellectual corridors and for striding down them together with me.

In the later stages of this project, I imposed on the good nature of a number of colleagues, who generously gave up their time to read one or more chapters. My thanks go again to Carolyn Abbate, for the generous feedback and insight; John Deathridge, for the chats and the details; Dana Gooley, for the characteristically meticulous reading; Allan Keiler, for sharing expert thoughts on Wagner's often inexpert linguistics; Robin Holloway, for the conversations and the common sense; Roger Parker, for encouraging me to leave Germany once in a while; Matthew Pritchard, for the rapid readings; and my father, Christopher Trippett, for so much. I am grateful for all the ideas, cautions, prompts, and provisos, as well as the dexterous turns of phrase and otherwise helpful thoughts duly shared. Naturally, any remaining infelicities of language or argument are entirely my own.

At Christ's College, conversations with colleagues over lunch frequently prompted further reflection on my topic. I thank particularly the coterie of humanists, Gavin Alexander, Peter Agocs, David Irving, David Reynolds, David Sedley, and Carrie Vout. While in and around Cambridge more broadly,

x

I have benefited from contact with a range of scholars, some in the virtual realm, others in person. These include Nicholas Cook, Laurence Dreyfus, Thomas Grey, Kenneth Hamilton, Monique Ingells, Lewis Lockwood, Barry Millington, John Rink, Matthias Röder, Nicholas Vazsonyi, Egon Voss, and Benjamin Walton.

At Cambridge University Press, I am particularly grateful to Vicki Cooper, for believing in the project and for driving it forward so supportively, to Fleur Jones and Christina Sarigiannidou, for deftly bringing it to final production, and to Gwynneth Drabble for her meticulous copy-editing. I also thank the Readers for their helpful comments. My work would not have been possible without the assistance of Kristina Unger and Yvonne Jost at the *Nationalarchiv der Richard-Wagner-Stiftung*, Bayreuth, where Gudrun Föttingen was also extremely efficient in procuring materials; Evelyn Liepsch at the *Goethe- und Schiller-Archiv*, Weimar; Sarah Adams, Kerry Masteller, Liza Vick, and Andrew Wilson at Harvard's Isham and Loeb libraries; the director and assistants of the *Thüringisches Hauptstaatsarchiv* and the *Anna Amalia Bibliothek*, Weimar; those of the *Bayerischer Staatsbibliothek*, Munich, as well as the *Städtische Bibliothek* and *Universitätsbibliothek*, Leipzig. I also acknowledge with gratitude the financial assistance of the Krupp Foundation (Center for European Studies, Harvard University), the support of Adams House and the Music Department at Harvard, as well as that of Christ's College, Cambridge, the *Klassik Stiftung Weimar*, and most recently, the Donald Tovey Memorial Prize from the Faculty of Music at Oxford University, whose generous support allowed me to acquire all the required source material for publication.

Finally, this project would never have been completed without the love and support of my wife, Paula, to whom this book is dedicated. She has listened critically and supportively, and has shared the burden of late nights, overnights, and daylong sessions at the desk that have allowed me to complete this project. For her patience, encouragement, and fortitude I will always be indebted. Our daughter, Persephone, was born shortly after I completed Chapter 2. It is a curious measure of time passing that, four chapters on, she is now walking and talking, and has already helped to teach me anew just how important concise expression can be.

A note on presentation

All translations into English are my own unless otherwise stated. In the case of Richard Wagner's prose writings, letters, and opera poems, I have worked in consultation with published translations, where these exist. Since his collected letters and collected writings are widely available to readers, I do not reproduce his German text as a matter of course; where particular words or clauses are idiosyncratic I give these in parentheses in the main text. For clarity, I have opted to use Wagner's German titles throughout, for both his operas and his essays. For all other foreign language sources, I provide the original text in the footnotes, as this may be harder for readers to come by. To help readers locate sources with ease, I have chosen to use footnotes rather than the more aesthetically appealing endnote style.

Abbreviations

AmZ	*Allgemeine musikalische Zeitung*
BamZ	*Berliner allgemeine musikalische Zeitung*
CT	Wagner, Cosima. *Cosima Wagner's Diaries*. 2 vols., edited by Martin Gregor-Dellin and Dietrich Mack, translated and introduced by Geoffrey Skelton. New York: Harcourt Brace Jovanovich, 1978–80. The German edition on which this is based is *Die Tagebücher Cosima Wagner*. 2 vols. Munich and Zurich: Piper, 1976–77. References are by date to allow for easy cross-reference between the English and German editions.
FBfM	*Fliegende Blätter für Musik*
GSA	*Goethe- und Schiller-Archiv. Klassik Stiftung Weimar*
HSS	Hanslick, Eduard. *Eduard Hanslick – Sämtliche Schriften Historisch-kritische Ausgabe*. 6 vols. [to date], edited by Dietmar Strauß. Vienna: Böhlau, 1990–.
HSW	Herder, Johann Gottfried von. *Sämtliche Werke*. 33 vols., edited by Bernhard L. Suphan. Hildesheim: Olms, 1994.
ML	Wagner, Richard. *My Life*, translated by Andrew Gray, edited by Mary Whittall. Cambridge University Press, 1983. This translation is based on the authoritative German edition *Mein Leben*, edited by Martin Gregor-Dellin. Munich: List, 1963.
NA	*Nationalarchiv der Richard-Wagner-Stiftung Bayreuth*
NZfM	*Neue Zeitschrift für Musik*
PW	Wagner, Richard. *Richard Wagner Prose Works*. 8 vols., translated by William Ashton Ellis. London: Kegan Paul, Tench, Trübner & Co., 1892–99; reprinted by Lincoln and London: University of Nebraska Press, 1993–95.
SB	Wagner, Richard. *Sämtliche Briefe*. 34 vols. [projected] Edited by Gertrud Strobel and Werner Wolf (vols. 1–5), Hans-Joachim Bauer and Johannes Forner (vols. 6–8), Klaus Burmeister and Johannes Forner (vol. 9), Andreas Mielke (vol. 10), Martin Dürrer (vols. 11–13, 16–17), Andreas Mielke (vols. 14–15, 18), Margaret Jestremski (vol. 19). Leipzig: Deutscher Verlag für Musik, 1967–2000 [vols. 1–9]; Wiesbaden: Breitkopf & Härtel, 2000– [vols. 10–].

SLRW   Wagner, Richard. *Selected Letters of Richard Wagner*. Edited and translated by Barry Millington and Stewart Spencer. London and Melbourne: J. M. Dent & Sons Ltd., 1987.

SS   Liszt, Franz. *Sämtliche Schriften*. 9 vols. [projected] Detlef Altenburg general editor, edited by Rainer Kleinertz (vol. 1), Detlef Altenburg (vols. 3–4), Dorothea Redepenning and Britta Schilling (vol. 5). Wiesbaden: Breitkopf & Härtel, 1989–.

SSD   Wagner, Richard. *Sämtliche Schriften und Dichtungen*, 16 vols. Volks-Ausgabe (Leipzig: Breitkopf & Härtel and C. F. W. Siegel [R. Linnemann], 1911 [vol. 1–12], 1914 [13–16]). English translation by W. Ashton Ellis. *Richard Wagner's Prose Works*.

SW   Wagner, Richard. *Sämtliche Werke*. 31 vols. [projected] Egon Voss general editor. Mainz: B. Schott's Söhne / Schott Musik International, 1970–.

TMW   *The Musical World*

WWV   Deathridge, John, Carl Dahlhaus, Martin Geck, Egon Voss, and Isolde Vetter (eds.). *Wagner-Werk-Verzeichnis: Verzeichnis der musikalischen Werke Richard Wagners und ihrer Quellen*. Mainz, London, New York, Tokyo: B. Schott's Söhne, 1986.

Introduction

"Let us slander melody!" Nietzsche cried. "Nothing is more dangerous than a beautiful melody ... Let us dare to be ugly, my friends! Wagner dared!"[1] Written five years after Wagner's death, this was hardly an enviable epitaph for a composer of opera. Nietzsche's barb paraphrased the widely held view that the master of Bayreuth could not write melodies as such. It was a grave accusation. Music without melody was simply unthinkable for nineteenth-century aesthetics, like an opera staged without singers, or a language spoken without vowels. It was oxymoronic. And with it, Wagner's credibility was effectively being hollowed out to reveal a void at the center of his creative *métier*, for there was no strain of exaggeration when, in 1864, the Leipzig Thomaskantor Moritz Hauptmann dubbed melody simply the "alpha and omega of music."[2]

Yet against a hailstorm of criticism, Wagner agreed wholeheartedly with this view. "Music's only form is melody" he claimed while in exile at the age of forty-seven, "it is not even conceivable without melody."[3] Of the few genuine neologisms that the composer introduced in his extensive writings, "endless melody" (*unendliche Melodie*) perhaps best reflects this privileged status. But, coined in 1860, the term was also defensive: Wagner was anticipating the critical reception of his works in Paris, and arguably deployed it in response to the European-wide suspicion that his melodies were less than real – something of a fairy tale. The Danish author Hans Christian Andersen is one such critic[4] and, if we read literary texts and criticism as parallel discursive realms that offer ideas a different local habitation, the early reception of music

---

[1] Friedrich Nietzsche, "The Case of Wagner," *The Anti-Christ, Ecce Homo, Twilight of the Idols, and Other Writings*, ed. Aaron Ridley and Judith Norman (Cambridge University Press, 2005), 244.

[2] Moritz Hauptmann to Carl Kossmaly, September 9, 1864, Leipzig, in *The Letters of a Leipzig Cantor*, trans. A. D. Coleridge (London: Richard Bentley & Son, 1892), 2: 249.

[3] SSD 7: 125. Cf. PW 3: 333.

[4] After attending performances of *Tannhäuser* and *Lohengrin* in Weimar, Andersen described the central flaw consistently in his diary: "*Tannhäuser* (May 29, 1852): the music competent, but lacking in melody ... *Lohengrin* (June 5, 1852): well written, and the music is grand, but without melody – a barren tree without blossoms or fruit." Hans Christian Andersen, *Dagbøger 1825–75*, eds. Kåre Olsen and H. Topsøe-Jensen, 12 vols. (Copenhagen: Det danske Sprog- og Litteraturselskab/G.E.C. Gad, 1971–76), 4: 85, 89. For a full investigation of Andersen's musical leanings see Anna Harwell Celenza, *Hans Christian Andersen and Music* (Aldershot: Ashgate, 2005).

drama's thematic fabric has much in common with Andersen's story of the Emperor's New Clothes (1837), where an unusually beautiful cloth of silk and gold thread is apparently woven into an imperial costume with unprecedented industry and extravagance. The resulting gown is said to be magnificent. But the "magic property" of the fabric is its invisibility to idiots or those unequal to their office: a patently false claim that ridicules all pretenders once the fraud is exposed.[5]

Wagner himself understood the criticism only too well:

> The only thing the public seeks in opera, melodies, melodies – were downright not forthcoming in my operas; no, nothing but the most boring recitatives, the most incomprehensible musical gallimathias ... To say that a piece of music has no melody can only mean: the musician has failed to create a form that grips and stirs our feeling; a statement that simply announces the composer's lack of talent, his want of originality.[6]

What, then, was the problem? How could the central figure of nineteenth-century German opera have acquired an abiding reputation as an unmelodic pretender? For us today, such questions exaggerate Wagner's fragility as a cultural icon, and are deceptive in this sense. Against the metaphysics of transcendence in the libretto to *Tristan und Isolde*, completed shortly before this frank admission, Wagner would seem to be taunting his contemporary critics openly: "Friends! Look! / Do you not feel and see it? / Can it be that I alone / Hear this tune sounding ... so wondrously and softly around me?"[7] But the historical question remains: if he believed music was inseparable from the concept of melody, why were his melodies invisible – adapting Andersen's tale – to so many "idiots"?

In fact, we owe this assessment of Wagner to reactionary criticism that responded to his three major Zurich essays as much as his operas.[8] What is at stake in the discourse of melodic theory are differing understandings of the very fabric of opera itself, i.e. the mechanism of vocal expression through which emotion was thought to communicate between performing artist and sentient observer. This is the platform on which I shall investigate discourses about melody during the nineteenth century. In performance, melody becomes a medium: a channel of communication that maintains the

---

[5] Hans Christian Andersen, "The Emperor's new clothes" [1837], *The Complete Fairy Tales and Stories*, trans. Erik Christian Haugaard (New York: Anchor Books, 1974), 77–81.

[6] SSD 7: 116, 125. Cf. PW 3: 324, 333.

[7] See Isolde's transfiguration: "Freunde! Seht! / Fühlt und seht ihr's nicht? / Hör ich nur / diese Weise, / die so wunder-/voll und leise/ ... um mich klinget?" *Tristan und Isolde*, act 3, scene 3.

[8] *Die Kunst und die Revolution* (1849), *Das Kunstwerk der Zukunft* (1849), *Oper und Drama* (1851).

presence of numerous sensual stimuli in the transmission of a message. Quite what that message is, and how it came to assert itself over a listener's consciousness, prompted a good deal of speculation – and correspondingly few concrete answers – throughout the middle decades of the century.

The appeal of simply taking pleasure in melody's expressivity was never endangered, of course. In 1833, Schumann wryly invoked a chess analogy to reflect the disproportionate prominence melodic expression continued to have for dilettante listeners when compared to its formal dependence on harmonic structure: "The queen (melody) has the greatest power, but the king (harmony) decides the game."[9] Given its preeminence for listeners of all stripes, it may be no wonder that melody was such a problem for aesthetic and compositional theory at the time. Precisely because it was granted the freedom to express what language could not, melody became dauntingly indefinable, instilling anxiety in composers and theorists alike. The assumption that it could represent a seismographic register of emotional expression, and that melodic invention simply resided in the realm of the genius went hand in hand with accusations of melodic poverty in contemporary music, and of outright failure in contemporary theory. Two interconnected but conflicting forces perpetuated this situation. On the one hand, popular acclaim for melodic beauty was tied to its prestige as a product of nature; since it symbolized a fragment of a unified but unknowably magnificent and inscrutable cosmos, it was easily co-opted within the autopoietic system of *Naturphilosphie*, reinforcing Friedrich Schelling's belief that "the system of nature is at the same time the system of our mind."[10] On the other hand, the profound interest this inspired in the study of melody as the calling card of the natural genius led to attempts to probe and examine precisely that whose prestige depended on not being understood. The inhibiting factor for melodic theory, in other words, was contained in the very desire to understand melody.

---

[9] "Die Königin (Melodie) hat die höchste Gewalt, aber den Ausschlag gibt immer der König (Harmonie)." Schumann, *Gesammelte Schriften über Musik und Musiker*, ed. Martin Kreisig, 2 vols. (Leipzig: Breitkopf & Härtel, 1914), 1: 20. Translation taken from Robert Schumann, *On Music and Musicians*, trans. Paul Rosenfeld, ed. Konrad Wolff (Berkeley and Los Angeles: University of California Press, 1983), 40.

[10] F. W. J. Schelling, *Ideas for a Philosophy of Nature*, trans. E. E. Harris and P. Heath (Cambridge University Press, 1988), 30. In relation to Schelling's *Naturphilosophie*, autopoiesis refers to the circularity of a closed system as such, where no information passes between the system and its environment, and where the system's aim – were we, via cybernetics, to attribute agency to a system of ideas – is to perpetuate the organization of ideas that define it as a system. See Humberto R. Maturana and Francisco J. Varela, *Autopoiesis and Cognition: The Realization of the Living* (Dordrecht: D. Riedel, 1980), and later, Niklaus Luhmann, *Essays on Self-Reference* (New York: Columbia University Press, 1990).

The specific problem from the musical-theoretical side of this divide was not lack of theorists, it was a shifting ground of musical style coupled to the fact that prominent philosophers co-opted melody as a special category. There was no shortage of would-be music theorists in Germany; yet while a relatively large number of treatises on harmony were published during the course of the century, only a handful of German writers of any stature engaged with the concept of melodic pedagogy at length. (It is indicative that Franz Brendel's landmark competition in 1859 to celebrate the fiftieth issue of the *Neue Zeitschrift für Musik* solicited entries on "the transformation and progress of *harmony*" rather than melody.)[11] Approaches to melody were far from unimportant, but they failed to secure a tractable basis for analytical scrutiny, and therefore tended to be shunned in the public arena as partial or provisional.

Consider the first melodic treatise of the century: when the theorist and pedagogue Anton Reicha published his *Traité de mélodie* in 1814, boldly delimiting it to his consideration of phrasal metrical structure, François-Josef Fétis sneered that he "has not even touched upon the laws of melody in connection with tonality, modulation, harmony and aesthetics," concluding that "a good treatise on melody is yet to be written."[12] As it happens, the complaint was old. Similar calls for adequate *Melodik* had been voiced since Johann Mattheson's *Kern melodischer Wissenschafft* in 1737; even a year after Wagner's death, Friedrich von Hausegger still opined that "unfortunately, no one has taken the trouble to determine the laws of melodic composition in quite the same way as with harmony,"[13] and as late as 1945, Paul Hindemith would preface his discussion of melody by observing what was by now the "astounding fact that instruction in composition has never developed a theory of melody."[14] Even Hegel took a swipe at music theorists in 1830 when confessing his partial knowledge of "the rules of composition" in relation to melodic theory, protesting that "from real scholars and practicing musicians . . . we seldom hear anything definitive

---

[11] The full proposal of Brendel's competition reads: "Erklärende Erläuterung und musikalisch-theoretische Begründung der durch die neuesten Kunstschöpferungen bewirkten Umgestaltung und Weiterbildung der Harmonik." Brendel, "Zur Eröffnung des 50. Bandes der Zeitschrift," *NZfM* 50 (1859), 1.

[12] François-Josef Fétis' *Traité élémentaire de musique* (Brussels, 1831–32), reproduced in *Biographie universelle* (Paris, 1863), 7: 203.

[13] "Man hat sich leider noch nicht die Mühe gegeben, die Gesetze der Melodik in gleich eingehender Weise zu ermitteln, wie die der Harmonik." Friedrich von Hausegger, "Die Musik als Ausdruck," *Bayreuther Blätter* 10 (1884), 311.

[14] Paul Hindemith, *The Craft of Musical Composition*, trans. Arthur Mendel, 2 vols., revised edn. (New York: Associated Music Publishers, 1941–45) 1: 175.

and detailed on these matters."[15] But *Vormärz* music theorists were not negligent (as Hegel and Hausegger suggest), they were in an impossibly conflicted position, and given the degree of negative melodic criticism within German language journals and newspapers, this context of uncertainty only underscores Wagner's audacity in placing melodic theory at the center of a vision for opera in *Oper und Drama* (1851), the longest and most conceptually detailed of his theoretical essays.

Yet the significance of this single publication for Wagner's reception arguably belies its diachronic context. Wagner's life spanned nearly three quarters of a century in which considerable changes took place in the conception of musical sound. When he was born in Leipzig, an idealist metaphysics could still claim music as the metaphor of transcendence, something conceptual, disembodied and intangible; by his death, prominent figures within the natural sciences had argued that the entire basis of musical expression was explicable through mechanisms of sensation: in electrical nervous impulses and obedient muscular contractions. While this study of debates and tensions over melody cannot survey the breadth of the century in all its discursive richness, it is precisely an axis of idealist and materialist epistemologies that will structure my approach.

At the mid-century, materialism was less a new philosophy than a revival of an old one, one which Friedrich Lange in 1865 traced back to Democritus' belief in a world composed of physically indivisible atoms. Such a view quite literally anchored the present in the past, for Democritus' atoms could be neither created nor destroyed. They were responsible for all change and variety, governed by physical "cause and necessity," and constituted all that exists, including the soul as the seat of being and the essence of life, which – incidentally – "consists of fine, smooth, round atoms, like those of fire."[16] As Lange's genealogy revealed, nineteenth-century materialism also gave priority to matter over spirit, and shared with Democritus' atomism a view of matter that was conceived exclusively as material but with the crucial caveat (drawn from Newtonian physics) that it is subject to physical forces which regulate the mechanisms by which we perceive our environment. Occurring in the afterglow of Hegelian idealism, this latter outlook was typically cast negatively: as the rejection of an idealist worldview, the overthrowing of presumptive hypotheses based on disembodied or metaphysical prime causes. It is perhaps prudent to point out that this – the rejection of of idealism – is also a

---

[15] G. W. F. Hegel, *Aesthetics: Lectures on Fine Art*, trans. T. M. Knox (Oxford: Clarenden Press, 1998), 2: 930.

[16] Friedrich Albert Lange, *The History of Materialism and Criticism of its Present Importance* [1865], 3 vols., 2nd edn., trans. E. C. Thomas (London: Trubner & Co., 1877–81), 1: 19–36, here 28.

recurring stance I have adopted in this book with the intention of gaining perspective within the structures of knowledge that link contemporary criticism, literature, scientific thinking, and university curricula.

In Wagner's case, though he never attended university, his writings from Paris (1839–42) onward illustrate that he was an idealist by inclination (he would dismiss Lange's readership as "ignoramuses" in 1878, while in the same breath branding Humboldt and Helmholtz "Schopenhauerian 'donkeys'").[17] Against the drift among German academic writers towards a materialist philosophy, then, Wagner's formative years ensured that he never fully embraced materialist doctrine; they were years spent rather traditionally, absorbing – among other things – lengthy runs of Italian opera (as I explore in Chapter 3). In fact, while still an aspiring composer racked with insecurity over his artistic originality and prospects, he cited *Norma* as one of his favorite operas during the 1830s; the Italian flavor, though marginalized by an entire scholarly tradition following Hans von Wolzogen and Carl Friedrich Glasenapp in the late nineteenth century, plays an ever-present role in Wagner's aesthetics of expression, and can help to account for the unresolved tensions surrounding materialism in his writings. If Italy was the seat of song, and "music is not even thinkable without melody," it is unsurprising that a key concept for Wagner, that of *Sinnlichkeit* or sensuality (the aesthetic counterpart to pleasurable physical sensation), derives in large part from his engagement with the Italian tradition. Yet, at first glance, the ideology of Germany as a *Kulturnation* which Wagner courted so explicitly after 1842 through language as well as literary myth fails to mesh with this reading of his Italianate sensibility, an incongruity I explore in the short Excursus following Chapter 3. Moreover, ever since Rousseau's polemical appraisal of Italian melody in his *Lettre sur la musique française* (1753), melody had come to be understood principally as a *vocal* phenomenon among non-German critics, with language a latent presence. It was with the voice's innate semiotic capacity in mind that Wagner effectively adopted the Mediterranean priority of vocal melody over "pure" instrumental lines, declaring the voice "*the* organ to which our music exclusively owes its being."[18] This swept aside earlier German claims for instrumental melody, where purposively imprecise expression had pointed – for idealists – to a higher conceptual world accessible through the imagination (E. T. A. Hoffmann's "wondrous realm of the infinite" ["das wundervolle Reich des Unendlichen"]). Whereas a disagreement over mere melodic style might be considered insignificant, stylistic difference linked to language and its voices could readily be interpreted in terms of broader debates

---

[17] CT (June 12, 1878).   [18] SSD 4: 4. Cf PW 2: 122. Emphasis added.

over nationhood, particularly when allied to text-as-*Nationalsprache*. In this
respect the horizon against which the nineteenth-century melodic discourse
unfolds becomes overtly rather than merely implicitly political.

When Germany was finally unified in 1871, Wagner could look back on
six decades of ambivalent nationalism, reflecting upon the famous
Germanist Jacob Grimm: "of course, Grimm [in 1848] had given up all
hope of a German culture (and one can't blame him)."[19] Since the late
eighteenth century, liberal commentators from Johann Gottfried Herder to
Theodor Mundt had spelled out an ideology of nationhood that valued
linguistic unity above all, placing the sonority, syntax, and history of a
common tongue at the center of a project for national identity. The familiar
fallibility in this case is that the search for a persuasive identity in the present
was predicated on the assumption of a lost autochthony that could only be
reclaimed by drawing on the historical past. Indo-European philologists
such as Grimm and Franz Bopp were able to make astonishing claims for
etymological certainties in this respect, but the project of philology
also aspired to uncover the history of verbal *sounds*. This exercise in
historical imagination – a putative archeology of historical utterances –
effectively claimed to be holding a microphone to the *Germanen* or pre-
medieval German Goths (the earliest Germanic tribe to employ a written
literary language), simulating a kind of recording technology sensitized to
cultural need. Quite how a text vocalized in melody became synonymous
with national identity is a peculiarly German story.[20] Particularly within
Saxony and Prussia, the search for meaningful melodic content was defined,
in opposition to French and Italian operatic melody, and relatively few
composers pursued explicit links between music and German identity.
But Wagner was unequivocal in viewing melody as a signifier of the national
condition: "the national tendencies of melodic practice are *so telling*" he
explained, freely connecting melodic form to social identity and political
institutions.[21] However daring Wagner's semiotics may have appeared in

---

[19] CT (June 7, 1873).

[20] While links between the tonal elements of language and its signifiers of (national) identity
received a powerful framework in the work of Indo-European philologists, as I explore in
Chapter 5, the broader context for the association of German self-identity with musical traditions
is set out with enviable lucidity by Celia Applegate and Pamela Potter in "Germans as the 'People
of Music': Genealogy of an Identity," *Music and German National Identity*, ed. Celia Applegate
and Pamela Potter (Chicago: University of Chicago Press, 2002), 1–35. See also Applegate's
pioneering study, *A Nation of Provincials: The German Idea of Heimat* (Berkeley & Los Angeles:
University of California Press, 1990), and more recently, Abigail Green, *Fatherlands: State-
Building and Nationhood in Nineteenth-Century Germany* (Cambridge University Press, 2001).

[21] SSD 3: 259. Cf. PW 2: 50. Emphasis added.

1851, German commentators on vocal-melodic sounds had already opened wide a hermeneutic door. Hence the ensuing variety of interpretations of melodies often had little to do with music theory, but reflected correspondingly different epistemologies of sound that hinged between the aesthetic and the acoustic, between psychological reflection and somatic reflex.

Amid this expansion of "melody," the German quest for securely grounded melodic content was principally driven by one question: can melodic sounds carry a meaning that is intuitively comprehensible (*gefühlsverständlich*)? Brendel put this one way when he defined modern music's "developmental law" in 1852 as an increasing "particularity of expression."[22] Wagner put it slightly differently, however, emphasizing a cognitive process that governs "understanding." Indeed, for a time during the mid-century Wagner consistently defined his artistic aims as the avoidance of "misunderstanding" (in criticism) by accessing the listener's sensorium directly (in performance).[23] The belief that certain vocal-melodic sounds could not fail to be understood in their moment of delivery intrigued both aestheticians and their colleagues in the life sciences. The broken whimpering of a tearful utterance would seem unmistakable in the human empathy it elicits. Likewise the mimetic portrait of sexual desire in *Tristan*. But these primal vocalic sounds have more patterned, less characteristic cousins. Rossini's periodic phrase structures and standardized accompaniments famously disappointed Wagner for their lack of character (even if illustrating how a "pleasing" melodic line could serve as an amulet against criticism). The other side of the coin, however, is Wagner's incessant interest in performance aesthetics within these fixed lines – how such intervallic shapes are delivered. A pragmatist in matters of stage production, he complained throughout his life of inept singing and acting, notably citing this as a reason for what he took to be the poor reception of his vocal lines in *Lohengrin* when Liszt conducted the premiere in 1850. Was the reception solely down to the modest standard of the theater? The dull singers? Such questions raise the larger matter of why Wagner's vocal lines were so seemingly dependent on the singers' performances, a topic discussed in Chapter 4. One tantalizing hope for getting around this dependence on performers was to hit upon uniquely shaped phrases or interval structures that might establish a natural basis for expression, one effectively tending towards *qualia* (inherent properties of our mental lives perceived as lived

[22] Brendel, *Geschichte der Musik in Italien, Deutschland und Frankreich von den ersten christlichen Zeiten bis auf die Gegenwart* (Leipzig: Hinze, 1852), 338.
[23] SSD 4: 243. Cf. PW 3: 283.

experience, e.g. the whiteness of snow, the taste of liquorice, the consonance of perfect intervals). These aspirations entered the melodic discourse under the auspices of musical character, specifically, melody that was deemed *charakteristisch*. But like shot in game or sand in clams, gritty contortions of melodic line strewn throughout an opera were evidently hard to listen to, as Wagner's critics found ever new ways to explain.

For Nietzsche, the quest to find meaning in every sound merely desensitized listeners to a bombastic kind of music with "much greater volume, much greater 'noise'." This resulted in a twofold trend, he continued, in which a minority were "ever more attuned to 'what it means'" while the vast majority subsisted with dulled and weakened senses, leading to a physiologically inevitable appreciation of "the basely sensual."[24] Polemics aside, the possibility that a physiological explanation for how we perceive emotion might be attainable fired the imagination of researchers as diverse as Rudolf Hermann Lotze and Gustav Fechner. Accordingly, the historical belief in a "science of feeling" crystallizes towards the end of this study, and underpins the discursive network I trace in Chapter 6; it brought about uneasy compromises between monistic and old-school Cartesian doctrines, where the body's response to melody is no longer a literary metaphor (a phenomenon rapidly caricatured as a soul reduced to mere cerebral convulsion). While the opera house and the laboratory were quite separate spaces, curiosity about the potential of applied science established a conduit between the two in the writings of musical scientists and scientifically minded musicians, and audiences' critical reactions to melodic "stimuli" became something of a proving ground for physiological evidence about what was effective and ineffective in melody. Indeed, while the later field of experimental psychology and its associated empiricism emerged in Germany during the heyday of Wagnerism, many of its tenets are traceable earlier in the composer's reception, and it is indicative that the inauguration of psychophysics as a quantitative approach to mind–body relations is roughly coeval with this quasi-scientific reception of Wagner's music.[25]

Initially, the category of melodic expression most susceptible to this kind of explication was *Klangfarbe* (sound color), which promised to link the sonorities of instruments and voices directly to one another. But discussions of sound color soon raised the question as to whether "color" – like the body – was merely metaphorical, or whether in fact the literary comparison

---

[24] Nietzsche, *Human all too Human, Beyond Good and Evil*, trans. Helen Zimmern and Paul V. Cohn (Ware: Wordsworth Classics, 2008), 123.

[25] See Gustav Theodor Fechner, *Elemente der Psychophysik* (Leipzig: Breitkopf & Härtel, 1860).

of light and sound concealed a shattering literalism: a single, natural spectrum of wave forms whose differing lengths would determine whether pitch frequencies or colors are perceived. Fanciful though such theories turned out to be, the attractiveness of a scientific explication of melodic expression continued to besiege the imagination of writers, thinkers, and scientific researchers well into the twentieth century. In the margin alongside his list of the four "most fundamental features of melody," Arnold Schoenberg scribbled "what is water? H_2O," emphatically suggesting the possibility of getting at the essence of something – an objective knowledge of melody's elemental properties seemingly available to those with a mind to access them empirically.[26] And the mystique of melody's natural power survives comfortably into the digital age of videogame music, motivating figures such as Koji Kondo to explain that "for me it's the art of creating that one main melody that is the primary goal behind music composition."[27] Coming from the composer of *Legend of Zelda* and *Super Mario Brothers*, this illustrates the longevity of melody's appeal, for – oddly enough – Kondo's statement has a certain amount in common with Wagner's critical reception of Rossini 150 years earlier, wherein the popularity of a melodic line "that slips into your ear, although you don't know why, and that you sing to yourself, without knowing why" dominates all other compositional parameters.[28]

Remaining in the twentieth century, the suspicion that physical and chemical laws could explain what music theory could not finds perhaps its most fantastical outlet in the literary imagination rather than Wagner reception *per se*. Gilbert Lister, the fictional neuroscientist in Arthur C. Clarke's tale of *The Ultimate Melody* (1957), seeks out a tune that fits perfectly with "the fundamental electrical rhythms going on in the brain."[29] After researching the properties of all available hit tunes, he succeeds – we learn – and is promptly reduced to a catatonic state in which an endless melody monopolizes his brain function. A cautionary narrator explains why the resulting theme is so lethal: "it would form an endless ring in the memory circuits of the mind. It would go round and round forever, obliterating all other thoughts."[30] Needless to say, Clarke's modernist inversion of the hope for applied biologism, whether through a hit tune or a musical texture definitively saturated in melody – i.e.

[26] Arnold Schoenberg, *The Musical Idea and the Logic, Technique and Art of its Presentation* (Bloomington: Indiana University Press, 2006), 180.

[27] See Koji Kondo, "Interview with a legend" at http://uk.wii.ign.com/articles/772/772299p2.html.

[28] SSD 3: 252. Cf. PW 2: 42.

[29] Arthur C. Clarke, *The Collected Stories of Arthur C. Clarke* (London: Gollancz, 2001), 581–86, here 583.

[30] *Ibid.*, 585.

Wagner's *unendliche Melodie* – ultimately renders the project of a science of melodic expression distinctly ambivalent.

In this book, I ask what cultural circumstances allowed Wagner to arrive at his theory of melody as a means of communication. Each of the six chapters interrogates one aspect of the nineteenth-century melodic discourse: criticism; pedagogy; originality; voice; language; and sensory perception. These are presented neither chronologically nor with a sense of causal progression as such. Rather, they form a sequence of related tableaux organized around the book's central focus on Wagner's melodic composition. Broadly, Chapters 2–3 concern production; Chapters 1, 4–6 concern reception.

By way of sketching a map to help survey this territory, the principal topics addressed in each chapter might usefully be summarized as follows: (1) Wagner's early reception as a melodist and the pursuit of a specifying expression etched into intervallic shape; (2) psychological and pedagogical attempts to understand melodic invention as a cognitive process rather than occult inspiration; (3) Wagner's fear of copyright infringement set against his desire to learn from Bellini by imitation; (4) differing modes of listening to German singer–actors, and Wagner's desire to inscribe declamation as a means of controlling their performance; (5) Wagner's use of contemporary philological studies in the German language as a means of rendering vocal expression more denotative; and (6) materialist readings of melodic expression, stretched in the imagination of mid-century writers and scientists, where sound could convey color and ultimately semiotic meaning, becoming, that is, a fully embodied form of communication.

Such ideas were not part of a continuous discursive fabric, but emerged in clusters of overlapping beliefs, grouped aspirations, and convergent commentaries. In their terms of reference the discourses remained reflexive (meaning that definitions and concepts that were used to generate the discourse on melody were made to become part of the discourse generated), and hence inherently resistant to scrutiny. Yet this reflexivity is sublated by the concept of melodic form (as a function of expression); inserting "form" into the discourse had a stabilizing effect, as a kind of positive data that appears differently in different discursive formulations: simultaneously a music-theoretical category, a philosophical idea, an unwritable utterance, embodied sensuality, and a material emblem of sound waves. This approach to the concept of melody, in short, is neither substantialist (what Wagner's melodies *are*) nor hermeneutic (what they *mean*), but critical. I ask what enables Wagner's cultural position, and what makes his melodies possible in the form they take.

1 | German melody

PART 1

Monstrance

> Melody is the primary and most exquisite thing in music, that which
> grasps human sensibility with wonderful magical power.
>
> E. T. A. Hoffmann[1]

In many ways, melody is the bedrock of nineteenth-century German music
aesthetics. With its poetic claims to human subjectivity and inwardness –
the platform of voice, the soul, the "naked heart"[2] – melody would seem an
apt obsession for an age transfixed by concepts of the self: a vehicle
apparently given by "nature" for externalizing that hidden interiority so
prized by idealist philosophy.[3] But paradoxically, this dominant feature of
musical style was both its most celebrated and its most problematic aspect.
Far from being a self-evident musical category, melody turns out to be
something of a slippery conceptual problem, one that resists sustained
scrutiny, forever flitting in between definitions, never quite meshing with
any fixed schema of taste or identity.

  Such conceptual awkwardness arose partly through German anxieties at
the increasingly elaborate appropriation of melody by writers and thinkers.
Precisely because of its stylistic prominence in the early nineteenth century,
"melody" had gained considerable import in speculative philosophy. As the
most unmistakable part of a musical texture – the instinctive fixation point

---

[1] "Das Erste und Vorzüglichste in der Musik, welches mit wunderbarer Zauberkraft das
menschliche Gemüt ergreift, ist die Melodie." E. T. A. Hofmann, "Über einen Ausspruch Sachini's
und über den sogenannten Effekt in der Musik," E. T. A. Hoffmann's *Fantasiestücke in Callot's
Manier. Werke. 1814* (Frankfurt am Main: Deutscher Klassiker Verlag, 1993), 444.

[2] Peter Gay, *The Naked Heart* (New York: Norton, 1995).

[3] A range of historical definitions of melody are linked to concepts of nature, from melody as a
natural product – Roger North: "a sort of musick . . . [that] seems to flow from nature" [1710],
cited in Graham Strahle (ed.), *An Early Music Dictionary* (Cambridge University Press, 2009),
8b – to melody as a more essential part of nature – David Mollison: "this voice of nature" in
Melody: The Soul of Music (Glasgow: Courier Office, 1798), 17.

for listeners of all stripes – it became nothing less than a monstrance (Latin: *monstrare*, "to reveal"), i.e. the essential demonstration of a philosophical idea, where the limiting five-lined stave evaporated into the untrammeled space of the creative imagination. When seen specifically as one of nature's organizational secrets – a hidden parabola of forces regulating the archetype of any linear pattern – melody's pre-eminent status meant, in short, that the sound of a single, harmonically rounded, metrically balanced musical line was adopted as an emblem of man's integration in the universe, the locus of slippage between Romantic art and *Naturphilosophie* (that peculiar marriage of idealism and hard science – linked principally to Schelling – which asserts a continuum between the perceived organic world and the mind perceiving it).[4] This was a long way from the *melodia* that Johannes Burmeister first defined as a linear succession of tones and intervallic steps in 1601.[5] It meant, in practice, that melody became the metaphor of choice for speculative philosophers to insert as the representative keystone in their respective systems. Just how daunting, and perhaps irritating, this situation became for would-be melodists in the mid-century is apparent in frustrated protests such as: "Why all these authorities anyway? For every opinion, even the most absurd, there will always be at least *one* advocate!"[6] But if idealist authorities were drawn to melody, how specific were they in appropriating it?[7]

Just as the Jena Romantics documented an impulse to transcend the separation of artistic forms, so they also rendered the once-opaque mirror between music and philosophy increasingly transparent. In lecture notes compiled by his students between 1817 and 1829, Hegel – whose influence during the *Vormärz* is hard to overestimate – accorded melody a parallel status to the idealist notion of *Geist*, namely: "the free-sounding of the soul in the field of music."[8] It was, for him, that transport of freedom from within

---

[4] The rich interplay of literary metaphor and music across different historical periods has been treated most thoroughly by Michael Spitzer in *Metaphor and Musical Thought* (University of Chicago Press, 2003). On the specifically German metaphor of depth in Germanic music, see Holly Watkins' engaging study, *Metaphors of Depth in German Musical Thought* (Cambridge University Press, 2011).

[5] "Melodia dicitur carmen ex intervallis sonorum." Johannes Burmeister, *Musica autoschediastike* (Rostock: C. Reusnerus, 1601); see also *Musical Poetics* [1606], trans. Benito V. Rivera (New Haven: Yale University Press, 1983), 77ff.

[6] "Ueberhaupt, wozu den immer Autoritäten? Für jede Meinung, selbst die absurdeste, wird es immer wenigstens *einen* Gewährsinn geben!" Flodoard Geyer, "Kann und soll die Melodie gelehrt werden?" *Neue Berliner Musik-Zeitung* (October 10, 1860), 322.

[7] Wilhelm Heinrich Wackenroder, *Confessions and Fantasies*, trans. and ed. M. H. Schubert (University Park: Pennsylvania State University Press, 1971), 191.

[8] Hegel, *Aesthetics* 2: 930.

as "an apprehension of itself," expressed in language that was not literally *literal* as the "language of the soul" (*Seelensprache*).[9] Hegel, of course, privileged the concept of the spirit's striving for inner freedom elsewhere in his writing;[10] this striving was embodied for him in the concept of melody, where hope for socio-political freedom found an allegory in assumptions of musical freedom.

Certain professional musicians in Schumann's "new poetic age" were no less idealist, presenting readings of vocal as well as instrumental melody not as theory, but as allegory,[11] thereby establishing common ground with the discourse of a group of earlier German writers who situated the phenomenon of sounding melody squarely at a nexus of philosophy and music. Consider briefly the following quartet of idealists:

(i) In the 1790s Wilhelm Heinrich Wackenroder, who had received elite training as a musician, first explicitly anointed art in general and music in particular as a philosophical monstrance.[12] "Holiest Saint Cecilia!" he implored, "Ah! The wonder of your melody / To which I'm a slave enchantedly, / It has disarranged my soul,"[13] thus preparing the ground for an aesthetic of feeling (*Gefühlsaesthetik*), where human emotion is inscribed in or assumes semiotic coverage within musical form.

(ii) Friedrich Schlegel gave the metaphor its sharpest form, in which the composer in the act of composing melody actually becomes a philosopher: "There is a tendency of all pure instrumental music toward philosophy ... Is the theme in it not as developed, confirmed, varied and constrained as the object of meditation in a sequence of philosophical ideas?"[14] Schlegel's *Thema* alludes to the ancient rhetorical category of an idea apt for discursive treatment rather than a rounded instrumental melody *per se*; yet such distinctions were not firm in early

---

[9] *Ibid.*

[10] This he did perhaps nowhere more succinctly than in his *Philosophy of History* where freedom is posited as nothing less than the guiding aspiration of mankind: "The history of the world is none other than the progress of the consciousness of freedom." Hegel, *Lectures on the Philosophy of World History. Introduction: Reason in History*, trans. J. Sibree (New York: Dover, 1956), 19.

[11] Henri Blanchard, for one, declared in 1840 that Meyerbeer's melodies will remain "no less great" than Voltaire's poetry in this regard ["les mélodies de Meyerbeer ne resteront pas moins"]. Henri Blanchard, "Mélodies de Meyerbeer," *Revue et Gazette Musicale de Paris* 68 (November 29, 1840), 581.

[12] W. H. Wackenroder, *Werke und Briefe*, ed. Lambert Schneider (Heidelberg: Lambert Schneider, 1967), 207.

[13] Wackenroder, *Confessions and Fantasies*, 152.

[14] Friedrich Schlegel, *Kritische Schriften und Fragmente*, ed. Ernst Behler and Hans Eichner, 6 vols. (Paderborn: Schöningh, 1988), 2: 155.

nineteenth-century criticism (where "theme" had acquired the sense of distinctive, syntactically closed melodic material differentiated from the shorter "motif").[15] In his theory of the novel, moreover, Schlegel addresses the literary in musical terms, using instrumental music to substantiate the aesthetic autonomy of literature.[16] This idealist appropriation of "melody" gained sway from the ambiguity with which a non-semantic, linear succession of pitches was intrinsically linked to the heritage of rhetoric. Melody meant something profound without being clearly understood, in short, which amounted to having your rhetorico-melodic cake and eating it.

(iii) Schelling, in his *Philosophie der Kunst* (1802–03), celebrates the material impossibility and acoustic reality of melody – which is to say its metaphysics – as "the absolute informing of the infinite into the finite, and thus the entire unity."[17] Time is the "universal form of imagining the infinite in the finite," he explains, and music's quality of temporal "*succession*" is epitomized in melodic form.[18]

(iv) Schopenhauer, like Schelling, credited melody with daunting metaphysical prestige in 1819 as "the highest grade of the objectification of the Will, the intellectual life and endeavor of Man."[19] He pre-empted Hegel in postulating both a freedom of spirit and unity of idea for melodic construction, further emphasizing that melody's condition of "significant and intentional connexion from beginning to end" is analogous to reflecting forwards and backwards on the course of one's "actual life," which "is intellectual and is thus connected as a whole." As such, he concludes, melody "relates the most secret history of the intellectually enlightened will."[20]

While, in several instances here, melody is arguably a metonym for music proper, such consistently far-fetched claims in handling the concept indicate the extent to which it was idealist commentators rather than music theorists who controlled the rhetoric. When understood metaphorically, melody / music's power to inspire the monstrance writers was quite literally

---

[15] See Carl Dahlhaus, *Die Musiktheorie im 18. und 19. Jahrhundert*, 2 vols. (Darmstadt: Wissenschaftliche Buchgesellschaft, 1984), 2: 195ff.

[16] Schlegel, *Literary Notebooks 1797–1801*, ed. Hans Eichner (London: Athlone Press, 1957), 146ff.

[17] F. W. J. Schelling, *Philosophy of Art*, trans. Douglas W. Stott (Minneapolis: University of Minnesota Press, 1989), 113.

[18] *Ibid.*, 109, 114.

[19] Arthur Schopenhauer, *The World as Will and Representation*, 2 vols., trans. E. F. J. Payne (New York: Dover, 1969), 1: 259.

[20] *Ibid.*

unbounded, for it simply fed the appetite of an imagination, inviting commentators with varying degrees of musical literacy freely to broaden the scope of melody's metaphorical weight. It was not therefore *Weltanschauungsmusik* in Rudolf Stephan's sense, but its exact reversal: *Weltanschauung als Musik*, melody as illustrative metaphor for a disembodied view of the world.[21]

As literary praxis, this appropriation of melody draws on tropes of untranslatable musical language whose net effect was to render the gulf between philosophical idea and music-theoretical category utterly unbridgeable. Very few treatises on melody appeared (Riemann counts none between Anton Reicha [1814] and Ludwig Bußler [1879]), and given the impossible prestige melody commanded, it is no coincidence that Wagner's bold formulation of a vocal *Versmelodie* occurred only after the failed revolutions of 1848–49, when the dam of political optimism had broken and disillusionment had set in, thereby negating the earlier, largely unchecked aspirations that indirectly inhibited an adequate theory of melody.

Significantly for the perspective of melodic theory, the monstrance tradition decisively placed agency into the creative imagination of a beholder, implicitly shifting the concept of melody away from the status of a scrutable art "object" (with an independent ontic essence) towards that apprehended through the subjective screen of audition. The result? The concept changed from an objective compositional category into a floating signifier for listeners that fueled a freeplay of ideas; phenomenologically speaking, "melody" became synonymous with the power of a listening experience – subject to taste – which constituted something of a *carte blanche* of reception aesthetics. Hence its power as a prompt to introspection, evident in literary reactions from Schopenhauer to Bergson who, by the 1910s, would always represent inner consciousness as a metaphysical melody: "the continuous melody of our inner life, a persistent melody that will endure, indivisible, from the beginning to the end of our conscious existence."[22] In the early nineteenth century, the corollary turn towards a listening agent signals a shift away from the

---

[21] This marks a decisive break with Kant's critical philosophy, where music (as well as laughter) had been purely animal in nature: "a play with aesthetic ideas" causing gratification by "a motion of the intestines" that "furthers the feeling of health." Recent commentators, including Roger Scruton and Richard Mason, have simply concluded that Kant was "probably tone deaf." Immanuel Kant, *Critique of Judgment* [1790], trans. J. H. Bernard (New York: Haffner, 1951), §. 54 "Remark," 176–77; Scruton, "Musical Beauty: Negotiating the Boundary between Subject and Object," *British Journal of Aesthetics* 53 (2012), ays019; and Mason, *Understanding Understanding* (Albany: State University of New York, 2003), 31.

[22] "Il y a simplement la mélodie continue de notre vie intérieure, – mélodie qui se poursuit et se poursuivra, indivisible, du commencement à la fin de notre existence consciente." Henri Bergson, "La pensée et le mouvant," in *Oeuvres*, ed. André Robinet (Paris: Presses Universitaires de France, 1972), 1251–1484, here 1384.

hermeneutics implicit in Reicha's view from 1814 that one can recognize and teach "good and bad melodies, that is, those which express something and those which do not."[23] For a literary *Bildungsbürgertum*, then, German melody was now a central, yet centrally indistinct, undefined idea, the understandings of which slipped between two inversely related metaphors: at once a genius' Rosetta stone, melody had also now become a solipsist's blank slate for the transient inscription of illegible emotion.

Neurosis

It is not surprising, therefore, that German critics displayed an uncomfortable lack of consensus on the nature of desirable melodic composition during the 1830s and 1840s. Indeed, despite continuous musical output, a veritable neurosis surrounded the concept of melodic expression, in which critic chastised composer, composer ridiculed theorist, and theorist complained of composers' lack of adequate training in melodic composition (as well as critics' inability to judge). These roles were rarely mutually exclusive within professional music networks: the respected Leipzig-based theorist Johann Christian Lobe complained in 1852 about Schumann's *Genoveva* that "the main deficiencies of his opera are the utter lack of concise, comprehensible, melody that could be sung back."[24] For his part, Schumann had criticized the critic Eduard Sobolewski's melodic poverty a decade earlier in a review of the latter's new oratorio cycle *Die Erlöser*:

One thing is entirely missing, we must announce beforehand; a natural melody. Yet in the most artificially interlaced forms of Sebastian Bach, a mysterious melody floats and melody is to be found in everything of Beethoven's! This our intelligent composer also knows, surely; but an immense abyss lies between knowing and creating, and it is only after many hard battles that a mediatory bridge can be built between these.[25]

And none other than Sobolewski had Wagner in his sights when he declared that criticism concerning melody was the "real *casus belli*" that was bringing about the present upheaval in the musical world. After explaining that

---

[23] Anton Reicha, *Treatise on Melody* [1814], trans. Peter M. Landey (Hillsdale: Pendragon, 2000), 3.

[24] "Die Hauptmängel seiner Oper sind das gänzliche Fehlen der prägnanten, faßbaren, nachsingbaren Melodie." J. C. Lobe, "Robert Schumann," *Musikalische Briefe. Wahrheit über Tonkunst und Tonkünstler. Von einem Wohlbekannten*, 2nd edn. (Leipzig: Baumgärtner, 1860), 270.

[25] Schumann, "Eduard Sobolewsky," *NZfM* 15 (1841), 2–4. Quoted here in translation by Fanny R. Ritter in Schumann, *Music and Musicians*, 3rd edn. (London, 1880), 35. Sobolewski's oratorio *Die Erlöser* was comprised of three separate compositions: *Die Prophezeiung, Heilige Nacht*, and *Der Retter*.

Example 1.1 *Lohengrin*'s "series of intervals" that Eduard Sobolewski finds unmelodic, from *Lohengrin*, act 1, scene 3, mm. 1155–58.

Wagner "never sought anything so eagerly as melody" in his operas, he lambasts *Lohengrin* for its vocal writing, scoffing that "to find any expression . . . in the series of intervals (for it cannot be called melody) of *Lohengrin*, from the passage 'Den Sieg hab' ich errungen [*sic*]' . . . would require the imagination of a Brendelist."[26] These "intervals" are reproduced in Example 1.1. The invocation of Franz Brendel's *Zukunft* aesthetics is apt for discussion, for Wagner himself was certainly not above the fray, condemning his contemporaries en masse: "most Germans who compose operas" he summarized in 1843, are simply incapable of writing "an independent free melody."[27]

Ironically, this very coherency of disagreement underscored the German experience through a form of what Michael Herzfeld calls "cultural intimacy," namely a communal recognition of those "aspects of a cultural identity that are considered a source of external embarrassment but that nevertheless provide insiders with their assurance of common sociality."[28] Enabling such prickly "intimacy" was the fact that the definition of melody was so contestable, and the manner of listening to melody so varied, that criticism could not assess the quality of melodic composition in new works with any respectable consensus or authority.

Indeed, already by the early twentieth century this had become a defining characteristic of the period for several commentators. Reflecting during the First World War, the musicologist Oscar Bie declared simply that "every definition [of melody] falsifies."[29] And an entire book on "[t]he melody

---

[26] Sobolewski, "Reactionary Letters IV," *TMW* 33 (1855), 70.

[27] "in den einzelnen Gesangsstücken fehlte die selbständige freie Melodie . . ..[d. h. ein] Übelstand der meisten Deutschen, welche Opern schreiben." Wagner, "Autobiographische Skizze," (February 1 and 8, 1843) *Zeitung für die Elegante Welt*, rpt. SB 1: 100. Wagner cut this sentence from his *Gesammelte Schriften* of 1871.

[28] Michael Herzfeld, *Cultural Intimacy: Social Poetics in the Nation-State* (New York: Routledge, 1997), 3.

[29] His survey of concepts easily demonstrated that the narrow sense of a tonal succession was a fallacy of convenience, one that Bie – on offering his own proto-Wagnerian definition – felt obliged to expand into a vast "melody-element." See Oscar Bie, "Melody," trans. Theodor Baker, *Musical Quarterly* 2 (1916), 402–17, here 402.

problem" appeared in 1910, seeking a remedy for the imbroglio of criticism in the data-rich methods of experimental psychology.[30] Amid the semantic tangles, however, the mid-nineteenth-century discourse nevertheless congealed around a stable opposition: that between Italian and German cultural hegemony. Yet melody skewers the easy binary here. It reframes the national antithesis of superficiality / depth, sensation / spirit, sugar / nourishment, as a question of aesthetic and – by other coordinates – semiotic structure. This chapter, accordingly, relates a story of tensions and conflicts within German criticism about melodic form and the discourses surrounding its comprehensibility, principally in terms of predefined continuity and the lack thereof; turning to the concept of forms of expression, the second part of the chapter uncovers the framework of philosophical ideas underpinning these discourses, and specifically centers on the linkage between idealist critics' only partially anti-Italian stance and the difficult reception of *Tannhäuser* and *Lohengrin* as melodic opera.

Reflecting on a decade of debate in the German press over Wagner's melodies, the *Berliner Musik-Zeitung Echo* in 1859 called melody the "acid test" that every composer must endure, but complicates the effectiveness of any such test by adding that "it is harder to argue about the absence or presence of a melody than anything else."[31] Indeed, this view was not limited to Wagner criticism, but was echoed by the Italian critic and Verdi supporter, Filippo Filippi, who simply declined to comment on the melodies in *Don Carlos* because: "of this essential musical element, there are so many diverse concepts that, when judging an opera, it is impossible ever to ascertain or deny whether melody is present or lacking." Instead, Filippi cited three pervasive kinds of melodic taste – reifiable as those of the transnational dilettante, the Italian, and the German – making little attempt to disguise his preference:

For some [dilettantes], melody is the trivial motif that tickles the ear and for which is reserved the final honor [of being played] on hurdy-gurdies; for others [Italians], melody is any musical phrase that penetrates the fiber of the heart, that touches them and makes them cry – and those are the ones with a better concept; for Wagner, melody is infinite, the murmur of the forest, melopoeia without rhythm,

---

[30] Walter van Dyke Bingham, *Studies in Melody* (Baltimore: Review Publishing Company, 1910).

[31] "Über keinen Gegenstand ist wohl schwerer zu streiten, als über Mangel oder Dasein einer Melodie ... Es ist und bleibt die Feuerprobe, die jeder Componist und je geistreicher er ist, nur um desto gewisser wieder durchmachen muss, dass die Welt seinen schönen Gedanken die künstlerische Existenz abspricht." in "Die Aufführung der Wagner'schen Opern auf dem Dresdner Hoftheater," *Berliner Musik-Zeitung Echo* 38 (1859), 300.

without proportions, without returns, that wanders and digresses, and that can produce a metaphysical excitement, leaving the ear dissatisfied and the heart arid.[32]

The positive (Italianate) conception of melody in this typology "penetrates . . . the heart," i.e. eliciting a visceral emotional response, but the question of *how* this actually happens – i.e. the question German theorists (fired by idealist visions of the will) urgently wanted to answer – remained unasked.

Writing more broadly about the problem of melodic competency in opera, Lobe identified the predicament in 1852 ("our modern German composers have no sense of simple *volksmäßige* melody; they neither want nor are able to invent any"), and drew a tripartite distinction similar to Filippi by way of articulating future options.[33] In a telling difference of national approach, Filippi organizes his melodic typology by listener response while Lobe does so in terms of differing commitments to a text: first, by simply declaiming the words with orotund vocal intonation; second, by grasping onto a poem's overall meaning and resultant feeling; or third, by discarding the text's relation to musical character altogether in favor of the ear's pleasure, and deferring responsibility to the singer for "giving the vocal work expression and character."[34] Tensions between pleasure and comprehension when listening go back at least to the debates over periodic syntax between J. N. Forkel and H. C. Koch, yet Lobe's ostensibly critical description of the Franco–Italian (third) model betrays a revealing ambivalence.[35] Although wholly inappropriate dance rhythms express "sad, impetuous, wild passions," these "lovely melodies" nevertheless remain alluring and "snare the ear with sweet magic bands and find great applause . . . [among those] who only want to sway and bathe in flatteringly caressing waves of tone."[36] It remains genuinely unclear whether Lobe was, is, or would like to be among the swimmers. Irrespective, the regional indexing of melodic style

---

[32] Filippo Filippi, "Studio analitico sul *Don Carlos* di Giuseppe Verdi," *Gazetta musicale di Milano* 24 (1869), 35. Cited in Andreas Giger, *Verdi and the French Aesthetic* (Cambridge University Press, 2008), 46.

[33] "unsere jetzigen deutschen Componisten haben keinen Sinn für einfache volksmäßige Melodie; sie wollen oder können keine schaffen." Lobe, "Die deutsche Oper der Gegenwart im Allgemeinen," *Musikalische Briefe*, 37.

[34] "man bemüht sich nur angenehm ansprechend für das Ohr zu sein, kümmert sich um die Worte, um den Sinn und den Charakter des Stückes wenig oder gar nicht und überläßt die Sorge, dem Gesangstücke Ausdruck und Charakter zu geben, ausschließlich dem Sänger." *Ibid.*

[35] On the topic of late eighteenth-century listening, specifically the concern for pleasure and comprehensibility of periodic form among theorists, see Matthew Riley, *Musical Listening in the German Enlightenment* (Aldershot: Ashgate, 2004), 17ff.

[36] "das Ohr mit süßen Zauberbanden umstricken und großen Beifall bei allen Denen finden, welche *nur* Melodie suchen und . . . in den schmeichelnd kosenden Tonwellen eben nur behaglich sich wiegen und baden wollen." Lobe, *Musikalische Briefe*, 37.

functioned as a means of categorizing listeners' perception of melodic beauty negatively: as satiation (Lobe's Italian style) or unsatisfied hunger (Filippi's Wagner). Neither critic seemed able to affirm their native style directly in this respect, though it was only German melodic criticism that was reflexively self-deprecating.

So what exactly did German critics perceive as the poverty of their native melodists? Historiographically, broken lines voided melody of the aesthetic principle of unity, by now a century-old notion that had been applied to melodic theory since Jean-Jacques Rousseau's *unité de mélodie* of 1753 where melody in the uppermost voice – as the sovereign, consolidating element – becomes an arbiter of form, and which entered German discourse a year later under Friedrich Marpurg's corrective notion of a principal voice synonymous with "unity of the whole" (*Einheit des Ganzen*).[37]

Again, it is Lobe – himself a Weimar-born, Weimar-trained composer and flautist – who stared most searchingly into the national mirror. He lists a series of mistaken attitudes as the causes for contemporary compositional problems that give rise to fractured melodic lines. His diatribe is representative of a body of criticism so is recounted here in all its confessional zeal: composers pay too little attention to the human voice, treating it as a ripieno instrument, he argues, and ignoring "the public's demand for beautiful, melodies that ring out clearly." Consequently one hears "mere notes, no closed melodies," since German melodic attempts are "ripped apart" between singer and orchestra. The use of harmony is also culpable for atomizing expression, we learn, for Germanic melodists set almost every note to a different chord, and make way for a different key in every measure; their melodies are therefore "too modulatory and harmonically rich," which destroys their sense of unity and prevents listeners from gaining a "meaningful conception" of their line. All hope is forlorn, he despairs, for even if singers "really do once take up a full melody," the accompaniment is invariably "too thick," daubing "dense tonal color" over the melody and thereby obscuring it. Reaching his acerbic height, Lobe likens "recent composers" to murderers, whose "immature melodic embryos" tend to fracture any melodic continuity into lifeless micro phrases:

An eight-measure, forward-moving melody appears to them as too "usual" a form, as one that is too clear, too simple – horror! And to think that there could even be a second

[37] Friedrich Marpurg (ed.), *Historisch-Kritische Beyträge zur Aufnahme der Musik*, 5 vols. (Berlin: J. J. Schützens selige Witwe, 1754), 1: 63. Rousseau's *unité de mélodie* appears in the *Lettre sur la musique françoise*, see Rousseau, *Oeuvres complètes*, 5 vols. (Paris: Gallimard, 1959–95), 5: 289–328, esp. 305ff.

part [to the melody]! If they are ever moved to write anything melodic, they cannot shake it off fast enough in order to return to their unmelodic academic clutter. *They are true child killers*, for hardly has a melodic infant been wrested from them, they strangle and choke it.[38]

Infanticide notwithstanding, such charges were not in fact limited to German melody, but – as Andreas Giger has pointed out – were also leveled at French melodists by Italian critics, where cries of "frasi spezzate" or "frasi truncate" indicated a corruption of the "melodie lunghe, lunghe, lunghe," that for Verdi defined Bellinian style.[39] A satirical anecdote in the recently founded *L'Art musical* from 1861 underscores the view that Italian melodic talent is verifiable by "a short aria accompanied on the piano by only two chords, the chord of the tonic and the chord of the dominant."[40] Cast as an unlikely dialogue between (an unnamed parody of) Berlioz and Rossini, it sees the former approaching the latter for compositional mentoring, contrasting the apprentice's "grand work for double choir and double orchestra called *The Last Judgment*" (bloated by eight-part brass, eight piccolos and eight sets of timpani, as well as a chorus of three hundred children), with Rossini's advice to prove one's authenticity of talent by means of simple melody, tonic and dominant: *simplex sigillum veri*. Within the tale, natural invention is posited as a signifier both of true compositional ability and as a universalized Italian style. In other words, charges of composing "fractured" melodic lines that required expansive orchestral effects to compensate for a perceived lack of continuity and coherence were essentially criticisms of non-Italian style, not just of German ineptitude.

A useful illustration of this principle occurs in a critical review of Meyerbeer's *Le Prophète* from 1855, where the Italian composer and singing teacher Alberto Mazzucato exemplifies the well-established view that

---

[38] "Eine achttactige fortgeführte Melodie erscheint ihnen als eine zu 'gewöhnliche' Gestalt, als ein zu klarer, einfacher – Gräuel. Und gar einen zweiten Theil dazu zu bringen! Wandelt sie einmal eine melodische Regung an, so können sie dieselbe nicht schnell genug von sich abschütteln, um in ihren unmelodischen gelahrten Wirrwar zurückzukehren. Sie sind wahre Kindesmörderinnen, denn kaum hat sich ein Melodiekind von ihnen losgerungen, so erwürgen und ersticken sie es." Lobe, *Musikalische Briefe*, 39–40. Emphasis added.

[39] Verdi to Camille Bellaigue, May 2, 1898, see Alessandro Luzio, *Carteggi verdiani*, 4 vols. (Rome: Reale accademia d'Italia, 1935–47), 2: 312.

[40] Cited in Giger, *Verdi and the French Aesthetic*, 73. We should bear in mind that the real Berlioz disliked Rossini with a passion ("S'il eût été alors en mon pouvoir de mettre un baril de poudre sous la Salle Louvois et de la faire sauter pendant la représentation de la Gazza ou du Barbiere avec tout ce qu'elle contenait, à coup sûr je n'y eusse pas manqué"). This appeared in the *Gazette musicale de Paris* in 1834. See Berlioz, *Critique musicale I: 1823–1834*, ed. H. Robert Cohen and Yves Gérard (Paris: Bucht/Chastel, 1996), 443.

architecturally rounded Italian melody contrasts with the stunted, deformed vocal lines of non-Italian opera:

Our [Italian] melody is smooth, fluid, composed of proportions that are said to be architectonic; it is symmetrical, respondent in its various phrases, rounded, periodic, concluding. It has a homogenous beginning, middle, and end. In short, it flows naturally in carrying out its two elements, that is, tonality and rhythm.

Melody north of the Alps shuns this naturalness, this spontaneity with study, almost (as it seems) with affection, even repugnance ... But when it comes to rhythm, and specifically its natural vehicle, the musical period, the whole thing proceeds very differently. In the melodies of *Le Prophète*, with a few exceptions, there is no ordinary regularity, no rigor of proportions, no symmetry, no rhythmical correspondence of phrases, no roundedness of periods, no natural conclusions. More often than not, the melody stops, breaks off, is truncated; and if not always at the beginning, then certainly in the middle or unfailingly toward the end.[41]

With his differentiation of melodic structure, Mazzucato neatly summarizes a body of European opinion.[42] Yet along with the few attempts during this period to construct a typology of melody, it occurred in the context of journalistic reviews where value-laden categories such as naturalness, beauty, and expression were themselves ill-defined and subject to criticisms of national bias. German "art" melody was thought more ambiguous in this respect than that of Italy, for it was hampered by a musical heritage more closely linked to late eighteenth-century collections of folk melody, notably by such luminaries as Johann Gottfried Herder and Johann Friedrich Reichardt, both of whom had explicitly recommended folksong as a model for melodic composition.[43] The synthesis of dialectical categories such as art and folk, as Matthew Gelbart has argued, was expressed in terms of a literal overlap, in which composers aestheticized putative folk melodies, incorporating them into compositions by an individual.[44] But it also meant that composed "art" melody carried the burden of both individual and national

---

[41] Alberto Mazzucato, "Il profeta," *Gazetta musicale di Milano* 13 (1855), 187. Cited in *Verdi and the French Aesthetic*, 45. In fact, Lobe put forward a strikingly similar assessment of Italianate melody in 1854, but judged it was the librettist who must first enable the rounded, symmetrical forms of music. See Lobe, "Bellini," *FBfM* (1854), 262–80. Rpt. "Vincenzo Bellini," *Musik-Konzepte* 46 (1985), ed. Heinz-Klaus Metzger and Rainer Riehn (Munich: Edition Text + Kritik, 1985), 50.

[42] See commentators from Stendhal, *Vies de Haydn, de Mozart et de Métastase* (1814), ed. Daniel Muller (Geneva: Slatkine, 1986) to Abramo Basevi, *Studio sulle opera di Giuseppe Verdi* (1859).

[43] See Margaret Mahony Stoljar, *Poetry and Song in Later Eighteenth Century Germany: A Study in the Musical Sturm und Drang* (London: Routledge, 1985), 194.

[44] See Matthew Gelbart, *The Invention of "Folk Music" and "Art Music"* (Cambridge University Press, 2007), esp. 197–205.

expression, resulting in tropes of public embarrassment from theorists such as Lobe, who vociferated about his "true child killer" compatriots, whose feral, fragmented progeny constituted "*un*melodic academic clutter." Eduard Hanslick summed up the gloomy situation in 1846, musing: "it almost seems as if we had entered upon a period of poverty and impotence, a state of barrenness after an ample harvest." With overtones of national shame, he asked with exaggerated pathos: "Is German opera entirely widowed? Is there no one else? No one?"[45]

Within this discourse, the point of structural difference between Italian "architectonics" and German "clutter" uncovers a site of tension within a far older dialectic of formal beauty and expression. In contrast to Lobe's aversion to fractured *Vormärz* opera, Mazzucato's description of the "homogenous beginning, middle, and end" of Italian melodic proportions fulfills a key criterion of beauty dating back at least to Aristotle's *Poetics*, namely magnitude and ordered arrangement: that which the eye can easily apprehend in its entirety, that which can be grasped as a whole.[46] It is for this reason, as Friedrich Kittler has argued, that the story of *Oedipus* is beautiful for Aristotle, because – like Mazzucato's architectonic Italian melodic form – it "fulfills the temporalized optical requirement of having a beginning, a middle, and an end."[47] The significance of this for melodic theory is that expression *of* a (socially distasteful) content, whether scenes of incest and patricide or arias of vampires and vengeance, was a problem for an aesthetics defined in opposition to Italianate form. Kittler's insight was that the operative principle of pre-Baumgartenian aesthetics was simply: *pattern recognition*.[48] The signified of melody thus remained racked between the semiotics of formal beauty and expressive truth, a condition (to which we will return) that can be abstracted in terms of a dialectic of pattern and chaos, "architectonics" and "clutter."

Wagnerian melody: infinite criticism

It was Wagner, more than any other mid-century German composer, who was subject to the severest public attacks as a "fanatic of melodic absence."[49]

---

[45] Ironically, of course, in 1846 it was none other than Wagner that the 22-year-old law student had in mind to play the role of champion in this history of German opera. Eduard Hanslick, "Tannhäuser," *Music Criticisms*, trans. Henry Pleasants (London: Penguin, 1950), 33–34.

[46] Aristotle, *The Poetics*, 1995, 1450b–1451a.

[47] Friedrich Kittler, "The World of the Symbolic – A World of the Machine," *Literature, Media, Information Systems*, ed. John Johnston (Amsterdam: G+B Arts International, 1997), 130.

[48] *Ibid.*   [49] "Fanatiker der Melodielosigkeit." Eduard Hanslick, HSS, I/4: 347.

Ironically, as a respected conductor and aspiring composer in the 1830s, he was drawn to Mazzucatoean "architectonics" through Bellini, engaging closely with the discourse on Italian melodic style throughout his twenties. This resulted in a battery of critical, often mocking, anti-German sentiments that surface particularly in the essays: "Die deutsche Oper" (1834), "Der dramatische Gesang" (1837), and "Bellini: Ein Wort zu seiner Zeit" (1837). As late as 1872, Cosima dictated what would become his well-known *mot juste* that "Bellini wrote melodies lovelier than one's dreams,"[50] and as a young man, he had indeed dreamt of being an Italian composer: "surely it would not be a sin if, before going to bed, we prayed that heaven would one day give German composers such melodies and such a mode of handling song."[51] The joke was on him, however, when the tease of his compatriots was inverted as a criticism of his own melodic poverty. Since the premiere of *Tannhäuser* on October 19, 1845, discourses of German music criticism had targeted Wagner's perceived weakness in melodic invention. It would prove a durable accusation in the nineteenth century, and even become a historical verdict in the twentieth, with writers such as Paul Bekker, who cited moments of lyrical climax as the points where Wagner's "weakness as a melodic writer is at its most apparent,"[52] and Theodor W. Adorno, who echoed Nietzsche in speaking of Wagner's melody as an objective lack, calling *unendliche Melodie* "a bombastic term [that] covers up a weakness."[53] Yet as Paul de Man once observed, whenever Romantic attitudes are implicitly or explicitly under discussion, "a certain heightening of tone takes place, an increase of polemical tension develops, as if something of immediate concern to all were at stake,"[54] and a full anatomy of discourse since *Tannhäuser* would unhelpfully merge personal and often political hostility with partisan quarrels, clouding the present inquiry. I therefore present a representative sampling from the 1850s to illustrate the fault lines along which criticism of Wagner's melodies extended.

Before *Das Kunstwerk der Zukunft* (1849) and *Oper und Drama* (1851) began circulating, two of the heavyweight organs of the German musical press, the *Allgemeine musikalische Zeitung* and the *Neue Zeitschrift für Musik*, spoke of the *Tannhäuser* overture as a musical void that was

---

[50] CT (August 3, 1872).   [51] SSD 12: 20. Cf. PW 8: 68.

[52] "Wo er sie [die Gesangmelodie] in einzelnen Fällen noch anwendet, weil der Augenblick ein lyrisch liedmäßiges Auschwingen erfordert . . . da erscheint er als Melodiker am schwächsten." Paul Bekker, *Wagner: Das Leben im Werke* (Berlin and Leipzig: Deutsche Verlags-Anstalt Stuttgart, 1924). English translation by M. M. Bozman. *Richard Wagner: His Life in His Work* (New York: Norton & Co., 1931), 177.

[53] Theodor W. Adorno, *In Search of Wagner*, trans. Rodney Livingstone (London: Verso, 2005), 44.

[54] Paul de Man, *Romanticism and Contemporary Criticism* (Baltimore: Johns Hopkins University Press, 1996), 3.

inadequately concealed by "instrumental effects."[55] These were not unusual objections. Similar critiques would be made of Berlioz's *Benvenuto Cellini* in 1851, and we even find the future doyen of *Zukunft* (later: *Neudeutsch*) ideology, Franz Brendel, cautioning Wagner: "interesting instrumental combinations, specifically an interesting violin effect, do not compensate for a lack of inner content."[56] It was a rare occasion on which the trope of musical "emptiness" was levelled at Wagner by a would-be advocate.

Following these mild beginnings, Wagner's Zurich essays sent a shot of adrenaline into the body of melodic criticism. By rendering his aesthetic aspirations verbally tangible, Wagner made them susceptible to close scrutiny by German literati with varying degrees of professional musical education. In particular, his claims that music should be considered a mere means for the purposes of drama stuck in the throat, as did his attack on the most celebrated living melodist of his age: he dandified Rossini pejoratively as an "uncommonly handy modeler of *artificial flowers* [aka melodies]" that were drenched in fake scent ("narcotizing melody"), while rolling his eyes at Weber for having plucked a genuine melodic flower from the meadow of German *Volksmelodie* – killing it dead: "the flower bloomed no more!"[57] As an unemployed political refugee, Wagner was in a weak position to make such claims, and only the memory of *Rienzi*'s success in 1842 prevented them from appearing as idle provocation. But Wagner's perceived temerity riled conservative critics such as Ludwig Bischoff, whose descent to a mocking, personal level in the *Niederrheinische Musik-Zeitung* from 1858 is not untypical:

Richard Wagner despises melody and does not care much about her. The feeling appears reciprocal, and it is, perhaps, out of mere spite that R. Wagner speaks so rudely about the gentle virgin in his books. Let's leave aside for once the misused, even equivocal expression "Melody." Melody or no melody: we don't want to argue about that. What we require from every work of art . . . are well-defined, palpable, I want to say, plastically perceptible forms . . . We regret having to confess that scarcely the slightest trace of such forms and thoughts was visible to our weak mind, during the four hours *Lohengrin* took in performance . . . this continuous,

---

[55] "Finden sich auch darin manche interessante Instrumentaleffecte, so fehlt es doch überall an der Hauptsache: an Melodie, Einheit, künstlerischer Ruhe und Mässigung," in "Nachrichten," *AmZ* 7 (February 18, 1846), 125.

[56] "Interessante Instrumentalcombinationen, insbesondere ein interessanter Geigeneffect, entschädigt [*sic*] nicht für Mangel an innerem Gehalt," in Franz Brendel, "Leipziger Musikleben," *NZfM* 18 (March 1, 1846), 72.

[57] SSD 3: 251–52, 261. Cf. PW 2: 41, 43, 52.

eternal psalmodically reciting, musically unmusical declamation bored us, it bored us indescribably.[58]

Responding to the same run of *Lohengrin* at Vienna's Hof-Operntheater, a reviewer from the *Monatschrift für Theater und Musik* characterized Wagner's monotony as a historical misstep, roundly contradicting the assertive stance his writings had adopted on melodic innovation:

If opera is indeed to be only a succession of *recitatives*, without a resting point – a mere musical intoning of the dramatic dialogue, without any specific musical aim and substance . . . Wagner is no *reformer*, but the most violent artistic *reactionary*, who ignores the progress made since *Rameau* and *Lully*, and in a most unpractical way and in place of the *cultivated dramatic music* we have had for eighty years, wants to re-establish *recitative*, the exclusive predominance of whose quintessence would form the worst monotony.[59]

Inevitably, critics uncomprehending of Wagner's reforms suspected an ulterior motive. Namely, that Wagner's extensive individuation of "melody" in *Oper und Drama* must conceal ineptitude. Hanslick articulated this view most clearly – following his warm reception of *Tannhäuser* in 1846[60] – in a review of the same production of *Lohengrin* in Vienna:

---

[58] "Richard Wagner mißachtet die Melodie, will wenig von ihr wissen. Das Verhältnis scheint ein gegenseitiges zu sein, und es ist vielleicht bloße Rancune, wenn R. Wagner in seinen Büchern von der zarten Jungfrau 'Melodie' so unglimpflich spricht. Lassen wir einmal den durch Missbrauch allerdings zweideutig gewordenen ausdruck 'Melodie' bei Seite. Melodie oder nicht Melodie: darüber wollen wir nicht streiten. Was wir aber von jeglichem Kunstwerke verlangen . . . das sind feste, greifbare, ich möchte sagen: plastisch anschauliche Gestalten . . . Es thut uns leid, bekennen zu müssen, dass unseren schwachen Sinnen von solchen Gestaltungen und Gedanken in der vier Stunden spielenden Oper Lohengrin kaum das Mindeste wahrnehmbar geworden ist . . . ja, dieses endlose, ewige psalmodistisch recitirende, musicalisch–unmusicalische Declamiren langweilte uns, langweilte uns unsäglich," in Ludwig Bischoff, "Richard Wagner's Lohengrin," *Niederrheinische Musik-Zeitung* 38 (1858), 299–300.

[59] "Soll die Oper nichts sein, als eine Reihe von *Recitativen*, ohne Ruhepunct, – eine bloße musikalische Betonung der drammatischen Rede, ohne specifisch musikalischen Zweck und Gehalt . . . *Wagner* ist dann kein *Reformator*, sondern der ärgste *Reactionär* im Gebiete der Kunst, der die seit *Rameau* und *Lully* gemachten Fortschritte mißachtet und, höchst unpractischer Weise, an die Stelle der *ausgebildeten dramatischen Musik*, wie wir sie seit achtzig Jahren besitzen, das *Recitativ* wieder herstellen möchte, dessen Alleinherrschaft den Inbegriff ärgster Monotonie bilden würde." W. M. S., "*Lohengrin in Wien*," *Monatschrift für Theater und Musik* (1858), 437.

[60] Contrary to clichéd views of his antagonism towards Wagner, in 1846 Hanslick inserted *Tannhäuser* into a succession of great operas, as one he regarded as "the finest thing achieved in grand opera in at least twelve years . . . just as epoch-making in its time as were *Les Huguenots* [1836], *Der Freischütz* [1821], and *Don Giovanni* [1787], each for its respective period of music history." ["ich [bin] der festen (wenn auch unmaßgeblichen) Meinung, daß der 'Tannhäuser' das Vorzüglichste sei, was seit wenigstens 12 Jahren in der großen Oper geleistet wurde . . . ebenso epochemachend, dem Geiste der Zeit entsprossen, und hervorragend über die

The [master composers] knew and respected very well the demands of poets, but they were also musicians, they were inventors. The strength is proper to them that Wagner wants to deny because it is lacking in him: the strength of melody, of independently beautiful *musical thoughts*. It is a great error to portray melody-in-itself and nothing more as the enemy of those dramatic traits; one only does that when one is by nature without melody, [and] instructed by clever effects to small profit ... [A]s long as there has been a history of music, contempt for melody has been identical with melodic impotence.[61]

But the flipside to such criticism of Wagner's apparently disingenuous theorizing was his commercial gain from the media exposure. As Lobe pointed out in 1852, it was precisely the controversy over Wagner's theory that began to expand his audience. Or as he put it: Wagner's operas were to *Oper und Drama* what heavily laden sailing ships stuck at port (in windless weather) are to a billowing breeze; the essay whipped up such a "wind" that his fleet of dramatic works now "float with full sail on the sea of his fame."[62] (Although only 500 copies of *Oper und Drama* were printed in 1851, the content of the essay was propagated further afield by the German press, albeit with varying degrees of accuracy.[63])

The trouble, however, was that most writers had read the essays before hearing the operas, and *Tannhäuser* and *Lohengrin* were now being received proleptically as "music drama," when, as one informed commentator

dazwischenliegenden (wenngleich trefflichen) Bestrebungen auf die *Hugenotten* folgt, wie diese nach dem *Freischütz*, und dieser nach *Don Juan*."] The serialized review appeared in the *Wiener Allgemeine musikalische Zeitung* (1846) and is reprinted in Eduard Hanslick, *Sämtliche Schriften: Historisch-kritische Ausgabe*. 6 vols., ed. Dietmar Strauß (Vienna: Böhlau, 1993), I/1: 62. In a reassessment of Hanslick's view of "criticism *as an institution*" in the second half of the nineteenth century, Dana Gooley argues that recent musicology has tended to place disproportionate emphasis on *Vom Musikalisch-Schönen*, which has exaggerated Hanslick's opposition to Wagner. See "Hanslick and the Institution of Criticism," *Journal of Musicology* 28 (2011), 289–324.

[61] "Die letzteren kannten und achteten die Forderungen des Dichters sehr wohl, aber zugleich waren sie Musiker, sie waren Erfinder. Ihnen eignete die Kraft, die Wagner leugnen möchte, weil sie ihm fehlt: die Kraft der Melodie, des selbständig schönen *musikalischen Gedankens*. Es ist ein großer Irrthum, die Melodie an sich und ohneweiteres als Feindin jeder dramatischen Charakteristik darzustellen; das thut nur, wer von Natur melodielos, auf die kleinen Gewinne durch geistreiche Effecte angewiesen ist. Vielmehr kann in dem gegliederten musikalischen Gedanken, in der *Melodie selbst* eine dramatische Kraft wohnen, die das declamatorische Pathos und aller Instrumentalwitz der Welt niemals erreichen ... denn so lange es eine Geschichte der Musik gibt, war Verachtung der Melodie und Mangel an Melodie identisch." Eduard Hanslick, "Die Oper *Lohengrin*," *Niederrheinische Musik-Zeitung* 47 (1858), 371. Rpt. in Hanslick, HSS I/4, 337, 343.

[62] "Seine Opern lagen lange Zeit wie schwer befrachtete Segelschiffe bei gänzliche Windstille im Hafen fest gebannt. Da fuhr er mit seinen Schriften auf, und die erregten einen solchen Wind, daß seine kleine dramatische Flotte in Bewegung kam und jetzt mit vollen Segeln auf dem Meere des Ruhmes dahin schwimmt." Lobe, *Musikalische Briefe*, 277.

[63] See Wagner to Eduard Avenarius, May 31, 1851, Zurich, SB 2: 567.

explained, the operas "have little or nothing in common" with the theoretical essays.[64] Wagner tried to clear up the confused chronology in both *Oper und Drama* and *Eine Mitteilung* but a majority of German critics continued to judge his most recent operas as exemplifications of the tenets laid down in his Zurich essays, adding to the "misunderstandings" that Wagner privately dubbed "the depths of the most utter mindlessness."[65] Literary networks, in other words, controlled the flow of critical persuasion. If we choose to view literature in this way, as a channel of communication, as an information system that processes, stores and transmits data, the 1850s emerge as a site of heightened interference, where the traditional rhetoric of physical presence and persuasion became reliant on more anonymous technologies of mass communication. The high frequency of start-up journals, limited print runs and fractured distribution networks expedited the disintegration of signifiers such as "melody" into their diverse symbolic values, provoking contrasting significations, misunderstandings and communication gaps.[66] And we should not underestimate the more devious, wilful desire for misunderstanding. Wagner admitted to Fédéric Villot in 1860 that "when all is said and done [an artist's theories] can only expect to be understood by one who already shares his artistic standpoint."[67] (This was not mere egotism: Wittgenstein would begin his *Tractatus* in much the same fashion.)[68] After a decade of partisan criticism, Wagner recognized that being understood in print was particularly difficult since "understanding" – in his sense of self-effacing assent – required agreement among politicized factions that often had little desire to see eye to eye.

In the same publication (introducing the French translation of his Romantic operas), Wagner responded most publicly to the welter of melodic criticism, coining the term *unendliche Melodie* a year before the planned Parisian premiere of *Tannhäuser* in 1861. His explanation of the music's melodic form as totalizing rather than absent, and his move to characterize this as unending (between orchestral parts) rather than fragmented (within

---

[64] "die Opern [waren] lange vor den Schriften erschienen, und mit den in den letzteren dargelegten Theoremen wenig oder Nichts gemein haben." Raff, *Die Wagnerfrage: Kritisch Beleuchtet* (Brunswick: Friedrich Vieweg und Sohn, 1854), 5.

[65] "in der absoluten gedankenlosigkeit." Wagner to Theodor Uhlig, July 27, 1850, Zurich, SB 3: 363.

[66] On the fragmentation of discourse, see David Pavón Cuéllar, *From the Conscious Interior to an Exterior Unconscious: Lacan, Discourse Analysis and Social Psychology* (London: Karnac, 2010), 296ff., and on the broader topic of the influence of music criticism on listening practices, see Benjamin Korstvedt, "Reading Music Criticism beyond the Fin-de-siècle Vienna Paradigm," *Musical Quarterly* 94 (2011), 156–210.

[67] SSD 7: 113. Cf. *Three Wagner Essays*, trans. Robert Jacobs (London: Eulenburg, 1979), 29.

[68] Ludwig Wittgenstein, *Tractatus Logico-Philosophicus* [1921], trans. D. F. Pears and B. F. McGuinness (London and New York: Routledge, 2010), 3.

phrasal sections), arguably anticipated French reactions to those very melodies that had been mauled in the German press over the previous decade, as well as warning listeners of what was to come in *Tristan*.[69] Ironically, one critic anticipated and dismissed this very strategy in 1854, complaining that the principal theme of the *Tannhäuser* overture "is varied to infinite length in such a way that gifted listeners grow tired of it, at least [they] long for something 'truly new' – which unfortunately never appears."[70]

As a republican agitator, Wagner's compromised political profile meant that critics with an interest in devaluing his art had little difficulty; "melody" served this purpose well since it was already a magnet for controversial opinion. This complicated what Mary Sue Morrow has called the "us against them" mentality in German criticism, a rhetorical strategy that involved "positing a superior Germanic Chosen in opposition to an inferior musical 'Other.'"[71] On one hand, the dominance of Italian opera within German theaters – "a quantitative menace to the claim of German hegemony,"[72] as Gundula Kreuzer puts it – supports Morrow's second criterion for dualistic criticism, namely that "the Other . . . be held responsible for some injury or wrong to the Chosen."[73] On the other hand, (i) Wagner's exile meant that, politically speaking, he was not wholly one of "the Chosen" (Liszt had to draw his attention to this fact in 1849),[74] and (ii) the traditional Germanic ground for unified opposition to Italian aesthetics was instrumental music based on the paradigm of mimesis, not vocal melody. Since the early eighteenth century, moreover, a coalition of theorists including Brossard, Walther, Rameau, and Heinichen began to define melody itself principally as a vocal aesthetic (a process capped by Rousseau's *Lettre* of 1753).[75] Wagner's two caveats thus ran contrary to the established terms on which German criticism had functioned since the

---

[69] On this point, see also Thomas Grey, *Wagner's Musical Prose: Texts and Contexts* (Cambridge University Press, 1995), 249.

[70] "Dieses Thema wird jedoch in unendlicher Länge dergestalt variirt, dass begabte Hörer überdrüssig werden, mindestens sehnsüchtig nach 'wahrhaft Neuem' – was denn leider nicht erscheint." See "Richard Wagner" in *Niederrheinische Musik-Zeitung* 8 (1854), 59.

[71] Mary Sue Morrow, *German Music Criticism in the Late Eighteenth Century* (Cambridge University Press, 1997), 46.

[72] Gundula Kreuzer, *Verdi and the Germans* (Cambridge University Press, 2010), 13.

[73] Morrow, *German Music Criticism*, 46.

[74] Liszt to Wagner, October 28, 1849, Bückeburg, in *Correspondence of Liszt and Wagner* (Vols. 1 and 2), trans. Francis Hueffer (Cirencester: The Echo Library, 2005), 39

[75] Sébastien de Brossard, "Mélodie" in *Dictionnaire de Musique* (Paris: Ballard, 1703), 43; J. G. Walther, *Praecepta der musikalischen Composition* [1708] rpt. in *Jenaer Beiträge zur Musikforschung*, ed. Peter Benary (Leipzig: Breitkopf, 1955), 2: 10; J.-P. Rameau, *Nouveau Système de Musique Théorique* (Paris, 1726), 1; J. D. Heinichen, *Der General Bass in der Composition* (Dresden: Bey dem Autore, 1748), 543.

late eighteenth century. It was partly for this reason that German critiques of Wagner's melodies were unusually cannibalistic, so to speak. They can be broken down into three broad complaints: (i) fragmentation of pre-formed melodic units; (ii) incomplete compositional working; (iii) pretentions towards melodic "character."

The lack of a single perceptible cantabile line led to objections that Wagner fractured melodic continuity. Some, like the archeologist and philologist Otto Jahn, heard a concatenation of pre-formed melodic–motific segments in *Lohengrin* that lacked integration; it was "as though one wanted to hurl completed pieces into a mass in flux . . . [W]e find only the raw materialism of external signs, which moreover pretend to be ingenious."[76] Others felt Wagner's disjointed melodic working was inherently incomplete, even sloppy in its craftsmanship. In 1853, for example, August Hitzschold dubbed him a *Prosaiker* whose "mosaic of tones" betrayed an internal battle between graphic artist and painter, in which the constructional labor of the former is clearly revealed in the final product of the latter:

We miss here and there the law-governed order, the transparency and the equilibrium. Wagner's melodies are like paintings, in which the painter had left the lines that he particularly liked when he proceeded to the coloring stage. There they are now, the abrupt, angular outlines, perceptible and graspable while the mellow, fragrant, even *sensory* hue – cut through everywhere by those lines – now becomes faint and ineffective. But the [pencil-wielding] *graphic artist* is victorious; he, the main artist – the painter may only follow as a second – looks forth everywhere out of the work, and the tracks of the all-powerful pencil, of the fashioner, remain unsmudged . . . and the illusion? Yes, fortunately it would be destroyed."[77]

Hitzschold implies that such melodic forms rely by their nature on a deceptive *Schein* in which "higher dramatic truth [is supposedly clothed]

---

[76] "wie wenn man in eine im Fluß begriffne Masse schon fertige Stücke hineinwerfen wollte . . . [W]ir [finden] aber nur den rohen Materialismus äußerlicher Kennzeichen der noch dazu prätendirt geistreich zu sein." Otto Jahn, "*Lohengrin*. Oper von Richard Wagner," first published in *Die Grenzboten* (1854); rpt. in Jahn, *Gesammenlte Aufsätze über Musik* (Leipzig: Breitkopf & Härtel, 1866), 149.

[77] "dort die gesetzmässige Ordnung, hier die Durchsichtigkeit und das Ebenmaass vermissend. Wagner's Sang-Melodieen gleichen Gemälden, in welchen der Maler die Linien der Zeichnung, die ihm besonders gelungen, hat stehen lassen, als er an die Farbengebung ging. Da stehen sie nun, die schroffen, kantigen Umrisse, fühlbar und handgreiflich, aber der weiche, duftige, zugegeben *sinnliche* Farbenton wird nun, überall von jeden Linien durchschnitten, matt und wirkungslos. Aber der *Zeichner* hat gesiegt; er, der Hauptkünstler – der Maler darf ihm ja stets nur in zweiter Linie folgen – blickt überall aus dem Werke hervor, und die Spuren des allmächtigen Bleistiftes, des gestaltenden, bleiben unverwischt . . . Und die Illusion? Ja, die wäre glücklich vernichtet." In August Hitzschold, "Zur Physiologie des musicalischen Drama's," *Niederrheinische Musik-Zeitung* 23 (1853), 177.

in music," but the constant failure of this illusion – revealed by those "abrupt, angular outlines" – results only in his disappointment at the tonal mosaic with its "mangle of connections" that Hitzschold hears as musically and dramatically arbitrary.[78] (Curiously, Wagner as "graphic artist" actually inverts later definitions of his techniques of phantasmagoria as "the product [that] presents itself as self-producing,"[79] replacing what Adorno – and before him, Mann and Nietzsche – regarded as a sinister anonymity of underlying forces with outright incompetence: Wagner's failure to conceal his modes of melodic production.)

Seeking an explanation for why audiences seemed unable to make sense of Wagnerian melody, the pedagogue Carl Alberti cited Wagner's dominant metaphor – of a vast ocean of harmony on which the dinghy of melody floats – to argue that a certain amount of confusion is inevitable because Wagner sets out from the principle of total melodic freedom. He wants to characterize the "finest nuances" in every progressive emotional step, Alberti explains, through "swerves and transitions in all conceivable keys," but "the harmonic motion of his melody is restricted mostly to triads because these alone can lie immediately next to each other; and moreover a monotony emerges, induced especially by the uninterrupted use of the diminished seventh chord, which . . . allows endless turns."[80] These ambiguities in Wagner's expression thus implied a hermeneutical problem where listeners were simply unable to follow the alleged meaning of the shifting harmonic terrain.

Following such incomprehension, accusations of ineptitude were quick to set in, and Wagner could be charged with a scandalous lack of creative power. While such criticism reflected conservative interests within the atmosphere of disillusionment pervading *Nachmärz* criticism, it also presented Wagner's case as a renegade burner of world orders, whose credibility had been lost

---

[78] "der Hörer . . . wird mit unbefriedigtem Verlangen nach diesem Mosaik der Töne hin horchen und für die mangelnde Verbindung derselben, die fehlende Abrundung der Perioden, wenig Trost und Entschädigung in der schweren Harmonieenfolge [u. s. w.] . . . finden." *Ibid.*

[79] Adorno, *In Search of Wagner*, 74.

[80] "Die Harmonie ist ihm [Wagner] eigentlich nur ein unendliches Meer, auf dem sich der Nachen der Melodie gewegt; er geht aus von der vollkommenen Freiheit der Melodie, will mit ihr jeden Fortschritt der Empfindung bis in die feinsten Nuancirungen durch Ausweichungen und Uebergänge in alle erdenklichen Tonarten begleiten und bezeichnen. Dabei sind Verirrungen unvermeidlich; die harmonische Bewegung seiner Melodie beschränkt sich meist auf Dreiklänge, weil nur diese unvermittelt neben einander stehen können; und es entsteht daraus eine Monotonie, die ausserdem noch besonders durch die unausgesetzte Anwendung des verminderten Septimen-Accords herbeigeführt wird, der . . . unendliche Wendungen zulässt." C. E. R. Alberti, *Richard Wagner und seine Stellung in der Geschichte der dramatischen Musik* (Stettin: Müller, 1856). Quoted in "Stimmen der Kritik über Richard Wagner," *Niederrheinische Musik-Zeitung* 38 (1856), 303.

when the destruction of world order had failed to come to pass in 1848–49, and, specifically, whose melodic charisma had been swallowed up as part of what the socialist philosopher Moses Hess called the old "epoch of illusions."[81] A typical line of criticism found in Bischoff's *Rheinische* and *Niederrheinische Musik-Zeitungen* in 1853–54 argues doggedly that the melodies of *Lohengrin* show "no great and especially no free invention,"[82] and that, although Wagner evidently tried to compose melodically, in *Tannhäuser* the protagonist's narration betrays the fact that "Wagner lacks the actual creative power of musical invention, and that whenever melody comes to the fore in his music, it can make no claims … to novelty and originality."[83] It was hardly a stretch, then, when Hanslick summarized the general belief in Wagner's inherent "thematic poverty" with the claim that in the whole of *Lohengrin* he was unable to find an eight-measure theme that could only have been written by a "first rate musical genius."[84] Such damning conclusions were echoed abroad, notably by the Englishman Henry Chorley, who disdainfully stated: "no opera existed before *Tannhäuser* – since the cradle-days of Opera – so totally barren of rhythmical melody." With outspoken loathing of the "insulting" piece, he reveals how quickly rational objection to melodic fragmentation could tip over into vitriolic projections of a composer "more poor in melodic inspiration than any predecessor or contemporary," one who gropes in vain for tunes: "when [they] would not come, he forced his way along by a recitative as uncouth and tasteless as it is ambitious."[85]

To be sure, the negative impulse behind such hyperbolic criticism was self-reinforcing, generating a momentum of opinion against Wagnerian melody that had little to do with score analysis or even the relatively few performances of his operas that took place. The only serious mid-century defense of Wagner as an architectonic melodist picked up on this. Lobe quoted

---

[81] Moses Hess, *Judgement dernier du vieux monde social* (Geneva: F. Melly, 1851).

[82] keine grosse und namentlich keine freie Erfindung." See "Lohengrin, Oper von Richard Wagner," *Niederrheinische Musik-Zeitung* 6 (February 11, 1854), 42.

[83] "[Es] wird uns auch klar, dass es Wagner an eigentlich schöpferischer Kraft der musicalischen Erfindung fehlt und dass, wenn Melodie bei ihm zum Vorschein kommt, sie gerade auf nichts weniger Anspruch machen kann, als auf … Neuheit und Originalität," in "Tannhäuser und der Sängerkrieg auf Wartburg. Romantische Oper in drei Akten von Richard Wagner. IX," *Rheinische Musik-Zeitung* 138 (February 19, 1853), 1097.

[84] "Ich habe bei wiederholtem aufmerksamsten Studium des *Lohengrin* inmitten der geistreichsten Intentionen und Züge nicht ein Thema von acht Tacten auffinden können, von denen sich sagen ließe, diese acht Tacte kann nur ein musikalisches Genie ersten Ranges geschrieben haben," Eduard Hanslick, "Die Oper *Lohengrin*," *Niederrheinische Musik-Zeitung* 47 (1858), 371–72. Rpt. in Hanslick, HSS I/4: 338.

[85] Henry Chorley, "Glimpses at Dresden," *Modern German Music: Recollections and Criticism* (London: Smith Elder & Co., 1854), 1: 362–63.

extensively from Wagner's vocal scores (presented as a kind of hard data) in his analyses to argue, for instance, of Lohengrin's *Verbot*: "there is rhythmic balance, simplest construction, referentiality, unity and a rounding off of the whole form."[86] Such views are anomalous, however, because very few critics had a vested interest in defending Wagner's specific ability as a German melodist in terms of Italianate construction.

Even those commentators who admired his thematic construction and accepted his tendency to obviate periodic syntax still conveyed a sense of bewilderment at the scarcity of demonstrable thematic material. George Eliot once deduced, in an attempt to remain objective about her disappointment over *Lohengrin*, that Wagner's "exclusion of melody" must follow from one of two possible suppositions: "either that Wagner is deficient in melodic inspiration, or that his inspiration has been overridden by his system, which opposition has pushed to exaggeration."[87] Yet Eliot's conundrum ultimately takes on a charitably Hegelian slant:

As to melody – who knows? It is just possible that melody, as we conceive it, is only a transitory phase of music, and that musicians of the future may read the airs of Mozart and Beethoven and Rossini as scholars read the *Stabreim* and assonance of early poetry. We are but in "the morning of the times," and must learn to think of ourselves as tadpoles unprescient of the future frog.[88]

But whether because of Wagner's participation in violent political reforms, or because of his call for sweeping aesthetic reforms in opera, few writers were willing to give him the benefit of the doubt in this way.

It is indicative that even the traditional defense of German melody – a careful portrait of dramatic character – was inverted as a further criticism. The critic and iconoclast Eduard Krüger vociferated in 1856 over "a boundless monotony of stereotypical phrases [in *Lohengrin*] that one habitually calls *Charakteristik*."[89] The aesthetic category of *das Charakteristische / die*

---

[86] "Da ist Eurhythmie, einfachste Konstruktion, Bezüglichkeit, Einheit und Abrundung der ganzen Form," in J. C. Lobe, "Briefe über Richard Wagner an einen jungen Komponisten: Zwölfter Brief," *FBfM* 2 (1855), 29.

[87] Eliot's 1855 essay was written for *Fraser's Magazine* and followed the London concert series between May and June, where Wagner directed the New Philharmonic Society; it forms one of the earliest documents about Wagner reception in Victorian England. See George Eliot [Mary Anne Evans], "Liszt, Wagner, Weimar," *Selected Critical Writings* (Oxford University Press, 1992), 87.

[88] *Ibid.*

[89] "Die Folge ist eine gränzenlose Monotonie stereotyper Sätze, die man *charakteristisch* zu nennen beliebt." Eduard Krüger, "Zerstreute Anmerkungen zu Wagner's *Lohengrin*," *Niederrheinische Musik-Zeitung* 1 (January 5, 1856), 5.

Charakteristik was ostensibly linked to tropes of serious, closely crafted German expression in opposition to formulaic Italianate melody, but it could equally be used as a by-word for forced originality, i.e. contorted, inexpressive melody justified by the promise of dramatic expression that voided the listening experience of pleasure.[90] In Wagner's case, the Emperor's characteristic clothes were clearly invisible for a number of commentators; Otto Jahn, whom we met earlier, judged that "the striving to be characteristic allows for no calm flow and no harmonic development ... In Wagner, melodies are not rare that are completely crooked just so that they appear to mean something, and thereby become entirely unsingable."[91] His two examples of this – both instrumental lines, incidentally – are reproduced in Examples 1.2a and 1.2b. The former illustrates how elements such as syncopated or fractured rhythms, harmonic ambiguity (centering here on different diminished 7ths), and amodular construction defined the trope of empty melodic character for disbelieving ears. Typically known as the "revenge" motif, Example 1.2b is rhythmically patterned and metrically balanced, which leads one to suspect Jahn may have disliked its intervallic play between minor, major, and augmented seconds, the irregular phrase units (2 + 2 + 3), and the range that is racked across two octaves, as well as the sudden Neapolitan jolt at the clarinet's peak pitch. There were plenty of pro-Wagner articles that made contrary observations about his melodic portrait of character[92] (several citing the need for multiple hearings as a prerequisite for true appreciation),[93] but I have found none from the 1850s that engaged in an extended defense of Wagner's specific ability as a melodist.

---

[90] For an elaboration of this point, see the summary of Franz Grillparzer's critique of Weber's *Euryanthe* in Jacob de Ruiter, *Der Charakterbegriff in der Musik: Studien zur deutschen Ästhetik der Instrumentalmusik 1740–1850* (Stuttgart: F. Steiner Verlag, 1989), 241ff.

[91] "das Bestreben, charakteristisch zu sein, läßt keinen ruhigen Fluß und keine harmonische Ausbildung zu ... Melodien, die vollständig verschroben sind, damit sie nur etwas zu bedeuten scheinen, und daher ganz unsangbar werden, [sind] nicht selten. " Jahn, "*Lohengrin*. Oper von Richard Wagner," 151. Cited in "Richard Wagner," *Niederrheinische Musik-Zeitung* 6 (1854), 42.

[92] One example from a journal otherwise hostile to Wagner concerns the oboe melody immediately prior to Elsa's first entry: "Elsa erscheint, der lebendige Gegensatz der Anklage, hehr, rein, keusch; das Orchester wandelt seine stürmischen Klänge in eine liebliche Melodie (*As C*, Oboe und englisch Horn) um, und lässt die Jungfrau in ihrer Reine und Hehre erscheinen." See Anon., "Richard Wagner's *Lohengrin*," *Rheinische Musik-Zeitung* 165 (1853), 1287.

[93] Here we remain with the critic of footnote 92: "diese Oper [*Lohengrin*] will oft gehört sein, bevor man ihre Schönheiten erfassen kann ... Wundervoll sind in der ganzen Oper die Modulationen; sie sind so originell, so überraschend schön und doch so natürlich; die Melodien, ohne diese gehört, bleiben gänzlich unverstanden." See Anon., "Richard Wagner's *Lohengrin*," *Rheinische Musik-Zeitung* 170: 1307.

Example 1.2 Two characteristic melodies singled out by Otto Jahn in *Lohengrin*.

(a) The cello melody from act 2, scene 1, mm. 3–17.

(b) The bass clarinet melody from act 1, scene 2, mm. 533–41.

From this sampling of critiques it seems clear that the anti-Wagner discourse rested principally on the fact that his melodies did not sound Italianate. Felix Draeseke, an astute voice within Wagner's circle, even suggested in 1856 that the entire debacle over Wagner's lack of melody rests on this: "the nonsensical demand that poetry in music drama ought to be accompanied by melodies from Italian opera."[94] Despite such awareness, and the fact that Wagner's negative status was driven by a politicized identity that galvanized reactionary criticism to his Zurich essays, the net result was a series of damning judgments about his basic creative faculties, manifest as melodic poverty or vacuity. Lobe's perverse defense of Wagner's melodic structures demonstrated how easily these could be refuted, but given the Italianate associations of the concept of melody, it simply did not serve anyone's critical interest to claim Wagner as a "melodist" as such. Though it will certainly serve our interests to see where this critical impasse would lead.

At an archeological level, the tensions within German melodic criticism just examined are superficial to the extent that they are structured by a broader philosophical ground of expression, character, and "Germanness." It was this ground that effectively determined the lines along which critical discourse could extend. Uncovering this deeper matrix involves pursuing several concepts back to the eighteenth century but along philosophical rather than critical tracks. Accordingly we will now revisit some familiar voices, but with the new purpose of detecting their grounding in concepts somewhat deaf to immediate temporal events.

PART 2

Forms of expression

> Anyone who studies composition – what does he want to learn? The *forms* of melody!
>
> Flodoard Geyer[95]

Imagine a perfect melodic expression: a one-to-one correspondence between units of expression and units of content that leaves no space for mystery (hermeneutic or semiotic), and hence rules out "misunderstanding." This hermetic concept was centuries old by the time it reached writers of Wagner's generation; having first been posited by such English linguists

---

[94] "Ein weiterer Vorwurf nennt Wagner *melodielos* . . . er [beruht] auf der sinnlosen Anforderung, daß in einem Musikdrama der Dichtung musikalisch durch italienische Opernmelodien begleitet werden solle." Felix Draeseke, "Richard Wagner, der Componist," *NZfM* 13 (1856), 135.

[95] "Ein Jeder, der Composition studirt, – was will er lernen? Die *Formen* der Melodie!" Geyer, "Kann und soll die Melodie gelehrt werden?" 338. Emphasis added.

as John Webster and Francis Bacon on discovering Chinese ideograms (whose putatively precise signifiers contrasted with the diverse meanings extractable from Egyptian hieroglyphs), it aspired to dissect words into their constituent "simple notions" and assign symbols to these, which "will be extremely few ... the reason of their composition easily known, and the most compounded ones at once will be comprehended ... so to deliver the nature of things."[96] In the nineteenth century, Schleiermacher decried the enterprise of universal language as an inevitable failure because "agreement about the universal language is itself subordinated to particular languages."[97] The diversity of linguistic systems did not apply to the relatively delimited tradition of a "developing musical language"[98] in early nineteenth-century Germany, however, and compositional hopes for determining general melodic signifiers persisted, even if the results were often ridiculed, i.e. "mincing the [musical] impression into little details and detailed littleness."[99]

The German problem, Wagner had specified in 1834, was over-zealous attention to the minutiae of melodic expression: "What splitting of hairs in the declamation," he vociferated about *Euryanthe*, "what fussy use of this or that instrument to emphasize a single word!"[100] His insight was the difficulty of a break with Italianate style. The intractable dilemma for German melodists was how to convey a specific emotional content, yet adhere to principles of formal beauty considered by a majority of contemporary theorists to be subject to inviolable universal laws: "the true and the beautiful."[101] This contradiction initiated a shift away from the conception of melody as an abstract "plastic" shape onto which specific content was applied through *text* (i.e. Hegel's sensuous embodiment of the idea, after Leibniz – in his critique of Locke – had asserted the intellect as prior to sensation), to a shape itself as the load bearer *and* signifier of a content, i.e. as a kind of perfect physiognomy, whose limited meaning

---

[96] Seth Ward, *Vindicae academiarum* (Oxford: Leonard Litchfield, 1654), 21.

[97] Friedrich Schleiermacher, *Hermeneutics and Criticism*, ed. Andrew Bowie (Cambridge University Press, 1998), 274.

[98] Charles Rosen, *Sonata Forms* (New York and London: Norton, 1988), 366.

[99] SSD 12: 2. Cf. PW 8: 56.   [100] *Ibid.*

[101] Lobe is a good example of this: "Man will frei sein und hält jede Regel für eine Fessel. Man wirft nicht nur die ältere Theorie bei Seite ... man lehnt sich auch auf gegen die ewigen Gesetze des Wahren und Schönen." Lobe, *Musikalische Briefe*, 26.

is innate. The writer Theodor Mundt captured something of this ambition in a corrective from 1845:

[W]e may occasionally have just a suspicion that this or that succession of tones [*Tonreihe*] would equally well express a serious or tragic idea as a serene or jovial one. This tendency . . . is not part of the nature of music itself. It always results, in fact, from imprecision or from the defects of a particular musical composition.[102]

Hanslick would cite Gluck's *Che farò senza Euridice!* precisely in order to argue that vocal melodies do not distinguish joy from grief, Orpheus' loss from his hypothetical reunion with Euridice, that without text melodies become "like silhouettes whose originals we cannot recognize."[103] But the logic of geometric semiosis, i.e. the interpretive criterion that equates melodic form monogamously with expressive content, could go much further. It would achieve an objective sphere for art that Kant had sought, but without presupposing a consent (beauty as universally pleasing) that is subordinate to social convention.[104] Otherwise expressed, it marked a drive among German composers to individualize melodic expression, thereby increasing the degree to which melody could differentiate between content on the basis of its geometric and harmonic properties.

In response to this impulse the unflattering suspicion arose that density of expressive effect concealed an inadequacy of simple beauty of invention in German music, as noted above. The Swiss essayist and novelist Germaine de Staël lifted the curtain on this judgment when she observed in her cultural profile of German Romantic thought "De L'Allemagne" (1807) that: "everything which tends to particularize the object of melody must necessarily diminish its effect."[105] This is a key statement and a portentous problem; it is worth backtracking to uncover the circumstances that brought it about.

---

[102] "[E]s hat zuweilen den Anstrich, als ob diese oder jene Tonreihe, z.B. ebenso gut einen ernsten, tragischen, wie einen heitern und scherzhaften Gedanken ansdrücken könne . . . [Das] wird immer nur die Fehlerhaftigkeit und der Mangel der besondern musikalischen Composition sein." Theodor Mundt, *Aesthetik: Die Idee der Schönheit und des Kunstwerks im Lichte unserer Zeit* (Berlin: M. Simion, 1845), 352–53.

[103] Eduard Hanslick, *On the Musically Beautiful*, trans. Geoffrey Payzant (Indianapolis: Hackett, 1986), 18.

[104] Theodor W. Adorno elaborates on the latter point in *Aesthetic Theory*, trans. Robert Hullot-Kentor (London: Continuum, 2002), 218ff.

[105] Germaine de Staël, "On German Music" [1807], rpt. *TMW* (February 18, 1841), 103–04. See also Stendhal, *Vies de Haydn, de Mozart et de Métastase*, who, in publishing a collection of letters from Haydn, Mozart, and Metastasio, glorified Italian music with melody at its fountainhead in 1814. Yet as late as 1879, Saint-Saëns would declare Stendhal culpable – as a melody-monger of simple "vulgar" tunes – for the still-widespread attitude that complicated melodic

Since the mid-eighteenth century, a dialectic of beauty and expression had become deeply rooted in the structure of aesthetic discourses. It was given its characteristic formulation by Johann Joachim Winckelmann in 1764, whose study of human forms in Greek sculpture led him to contrast their undistorted, natural beauty with those same forms when they "expressed" a particular emotion, objectifying the predicate of expression with formerly untroubled limbs and unfurrowed brows:

Expression is an imitation of the active and suffering states of our minds and our bodies and of passions as well as deeds. In both states, the features of the face and posture of the body changes, and thus the forms that constitute beauty change, and the greater this change is, the more disadvantageous it is to beauty.[106]

A paradigmatic example of Winckelmann's distinction – made famous by Lessing – was the statue of Laocoön (*ca.* 200 BC; Figure 1.1), the Trojan priest from book two of the *Aeneid*, whose anguished expression and torturously mutilated body is graphically depicted as the two serpents of Minerva tear at his flesh and devour his two sons, while he curses and snorts in animalistic death throes. This statue, for Winckelmann, shows:

a being in the greatest pain . . . swell[ing] his muscles and tens[ing] his nerves . . . The fearful groan he draws in and the breath he takes empty the abdomen and hollow out the sides, exposing to our view the movement of his entrails . . . [Yet] the father's heart is manifested in the wistful eyes, and his compassion seems to float over them like a cloudy exhalation. His face is plaintive rather than agonized; his eyes are turned toward the higher power."[107]

In other words, even though the expression of Laocoön's pain is mediated by the symbolic functions of his facial expression – which otherwise ought to maximize distension (paradoxically, "where the greatest pain is expressed, the greatest beauty is also to be found") – the contortions distorting his "natural" state mark the statue less as beautiful, more as expressive art – a contentious description that would initiate one of central aesthetic debates of the later eighteenth century.[108]

---

configurations must be "learned music, and the composer [must be] a pedant who does not know how to conceal his learning – he [must be] a pretentious nincompoop, an algebraist, a chemist, a what you will." Camille Saint-Saëns, *On Music and Musicians,* trans. Roger Nichols (Oxford University Press, 2008), 23.

[106] J. J. Winckelmann, *History of the Art of Antiquity,* trans. Harry Francis Mallgrave (Los Angeles: Getty Research Institute, 2006), 204.

[107] *Ibid.,* 313.

[108] Prominent contributions to this debate include Goethe, "Über Laokoön" [1797] in *Kunsttheoretische Schriften und Übersetzungen,* Berliner Ausgabe (Berlin: Aufbau, 1985), 19:

1.1 *Hagesandros, Athenedoros, and Polydoros [Laocoön and his sons].* Marble copy of the original, from *ca.* 200 BC; discovered in the Baths of Trajan in 1506. Musei Vaticani, Museo Pio-Clementino, Octagon, Laocoön Hall.

In respect of these categories, Winckelmann's argument bears comparison with the debate over German melodic structure. Writing of "melodic speech" in 1813, the musically trained writer (and Goethe student) Heinrich August Kerndörffer argued that "absolute beauty" means declamation "without approaching consideration of the content of the speech," i.e. without contorting sonorous beauty for the purpose of expression, while declamation substantively linked to the semantic content of what is said is what "we call *relative beauty*."[109] Yet the discourse of melodic structure was complicated by the fact that "form" implied both musical form as a compositional parameter and plastic form as an aesthetic category. These overlapped in the imagination of certain writers, but were never properly synonymous (E. T. A. Hoffmann, for one, emphatically rejected any such

129–41; Aloys Hirt, "Laokoön," in *Die Horen*, ed. Friedrich Schiller (1797), 3: 1–26; and Friedrich Schlegel, "Fragmente," in *Athenaeum* 1 (1798), 261–63.

[109] "Unter absoluter Schönheit verstehen wir diejenige, welche der Declamation ohne Rücksicht auf den Inhalt der Rede zukommt; diejenige, welche ihr in Beziehung auf den Inhalt der Rede angehört, nennen wir relative Schönheit." Heinrich August Kerndörffer, *Handbuch der Declamation. Ein Leitfaden für Schulen und für den Selbstunterricht zur Bildung eines guten rednerischen Vortrags* (Leipzig: Fleischer, 1813), 5. Emphasis added.

comparison).[110] More than half a century after Winckelmann had died, Hegel associated plastically perceptible form principally with classical sculpture and architecture as the second of his three epochs delineating the history of aesthetics: Symbolic, Classical, and Romantic. The ideal of Classical form, as articulated in his *Aesthetics*, was nothing less than the "free and adequate embodiment of the Idea in the shape peculiarly appropriate to the Idea itself in its essential nature."[111] That is, a perfect expression. More specifically, its historical occurrence in Ancient Greek statues represented a coincidence of *Geist* as both content and form, without engaging only the consciousness (Symbolic art) and without divorcing idea from shape (Romantic art):

[C]lassical art actually attains and sets forth what constitutes its innermost concept and essence. At this point it lays hold of the spiritual as its *content*, in so far as the spiritual draws [the reality of] nature and its power into its own sphere and so is represented otherwise than as pure inwardness or as dominion over nature.[112]

When transferred to melody, the philosophical apex this represented was twofold: first, it completed the unity of the idea in its reality – i.e. unifying sensuous and spiritual existence – wherein the only defect became "the restrictedness of the sphere of art [itself]";[113] second, in terms of the compositional process, it synthesized the dialectic of conscious and unconscious cognition, since classical art – being generated by the spirit – originated "in the most inward and personal being of poets and artists who have [nevertheless] created it with clear and free deliberateness, consciously aiming at artistic production."[114] Within *Vormärz* discourses on aesthetics that emerged in the afterglow of Hegel, therefore, self-contained plastic form acquired status as the signifier of highest attainment, as well as of beauty: whether in terms of melodic composition, plastically three-dimensional sculpture, or historical aesthetics.

Whether by design or by accident, Hegel thereby gave Italianate melodic syntax a learned underpinning. As noted earlier, he employed the concept of melodic form as a metaphor for freedom – "the free-sounding of the soul" – that is, analogous to the central organizing concept, and ethical–historical

---

[110] See E. T. A. Hoffmann, "Beethovens Instrumental-Musik," in *Fantasiestücke*, 52.

[111] Hegel, *Aesthetics*, 1: 77.

[112] *Ibid.*, 1: 476. Such was the desire to see Classical art as unsurpassed, the very perfection of the marble's whiteness reinforced the essential connection between material and artistic form, for Hegel, becoming the focus of a bitter debate over whether or not the statues had originally been brightly painted. See Patrik Reuterswärd, *Studien zur Polychromie der Plastik. Griechenland und Rom* (Stockholm: Almqvist & Wiksell, 1960), 1–34.

[113] Hegel, *Aesthetics*, 1: 79.   [114] *Ibid.*, 1: 477.

telos, of his social philosophy. The melodies he had in mind when writing these words were almost certainly Rossini's. Citing a pantheon of historically Italianate composers, he expounds that "nature has bestowed on the Italians above all the gift of melodic expression,"[115] later justifying his preference for Rossini's melodies as music that is "full of feeling and genius, piercing the mind and heart [cf. classical architecture's unity of spiritual and sensuous], even if it does not have to do with the sort of characterization beloved of our strict German musical intellect."[116] By connecting the category of melody to closed, proportionate, symmetrical qualities, i.e. a classical formalist beauty later adduced in Mazzucato's vocabulary for Italianate melody, Hegel thereby reduces the opposition of melody and musical portrayal of character quite precisely to Winckelmann's dichotomy of beauty and expression, where expressive motion effectively *hinders* the free and purely resounding soul. The continuity of symmetrically balanced, rounded melodic form – the aesthetic against which Wagner's vocal lines were measured during the 1850s – thus found its idealist description, as well as its historically aesthetic justification, in what Hegel had ascribed to classical beauty.

Unsurprisingly, his musical rationalization of this view appealed to nature:[117]

The bird on the bough or the lark in the air sings cheerfully and touchingly just in order to sing, just as a natural production without any other aim and without any specific subject-matter, and it is the same with human song and melodious expression. Therefore, Italian music, where in particular this principle prevails, often passes over, like poetry, into melodious sound as such and may easily seem to sacrifice, or may actually sacrifice, feeling and its definite expression because it looks only to the enjoyment of art as art, to the melodious sound of the soul in its inner satisfaction.[118]

But musical "freedom" is not innocent here. The concept easily splits apart into its opposing elements along the performance network: to sing on a whim, to improvise; to piece together expression through increasingly unregulated configurations of pitch and rhythm; to hear melody abstractly as a mirror of the "right of subjective freedom."[119]

Recall that the critic Alberti understood "total melodic freedom" – in pitch, meter and rhythm – as the premise for Wagner's melodic characterization of "every step of emotion up to the finest nuancing."[120] The paradox

---

[115] Hegel, *Aesthetics*, 2: 939.   [116] *Ibid.*, 2: 949.

[117] Specifically, Hegel's reference is to the still-prevalent, Rousseauian construct of melody as the representation of nature and genius, harmony of skill and artifice.

[118] *Ibid.*, 2: 940.   [119] Hegel, *Philosophy of Right*, § 124.

[120] "Er [Wagner] geht aus von der vollkommenen Freiheit der Melodie, will mit ihr jeden Fortschritt der Empfindung bis in die feinsten Nuancirungen." Alberti, *Richard Wagner und*

was that Hegel's rigidly architectonic Italian form allowed the singer's line to ring out as a "free-sounding soul." Wagner's melodic expression was itself compositionally "free"; Hegel's conception of melody was that it expressed freedom in performance. A seeming tension nevertheless arises between the freedom that Hegel cherishes, and the symmetrically determinate, "unfree" melodic forms generated by this gift for freedom. He would likely respond that within a dialectic of nature and freedom, the latter is the self-transcending of the former,[121] but the ambiguity of melodic freedom vis-à-vis predefined shape functions as a nodal point in the discourse that finally undoes the eighteenth-century dichotomy of formal beauty and expression. Just as Italianate structure was not without expression, so the expressionism within Germanic melodic shape must by definition determine an array of forms. But what were they? Wagner pointed out the critical orientation of such a question in 1857, arguing that critics cry out "in agony" for form, while "the carefree artist – who could no more exist without form than [critics] – doesn't worry himself about it in the least while engaged in the task of creation. How can that be? Probably because the artist, without knowing it, is always creating forms."[122] When seen as a false dichotomy, form / expression emphasizes the lack of conscious formal principles available for melodic expression, that is, the absence of recognizable criteria by which to determine how expressive melody should be formed. From which building blocks? Measured by whose criteria?

While Wagner's writings did not provide an explicit answer, certain critics used him as the *auctoritas* against seemingly invariant menus of "pleasing" melody. Draeseke backed *Tannhäuser* in this respect, for "suddenly it is possible to express in melody that which is magnificent, sublime, deeply serious, and majestic, and to present it to the masses in graphic vividness."[123] And Bekker, reflecting in 1924, even felt Wagner had provided a historical answer to the problem of expression, namely as an "expressionist" whose earliest identification with music amounted to "gesture in sound." What Bekker was actually describing (biographically,

---

seine Stellung in der Geschichte der dramatischen Musik. Quoted in "Stimmen der Kritik über Richard Wagner," 303.

[121] Hegel's argument relates specifically to the finite and the infinite, but can be applied by extension to such dialectics as nature and freedom, individual and universal. See Hegel, *The Science of Logic*, trans. A. V. Miller (Atlantic Highlands, N. J.: Humanities Press International, 1969), 146ff.

[122] SSD 5: 187. Cf. PW 3: 242.

[123] Felix Draeseke, "Franz Liszt's neun symphonische Dichtungen II. Artikel," *Anregungen für Kunst, Leben und Wissenschaft* 2 (1857), 298–316; trans. Susan Hohl, in *Franz Liszt and his World* (Princeton University Press, 2006), 496.

genetically) as the basis for Wagner's art – "neither formal design in tone nor the natural pleasure of the ear, but a music with an expressive significance as precise as that presented by the visual concept"[124] – was in essence the aesthetic category mobilized in response to a shift away from forms of the dramatically generic toward the painterly specific: *das Charakteristische*.

Das Charakteristische / Die Charakteristik

Since the seventeenth century, the concept of character had been part of "the historical development of an anthropology of difference," i.e. the index for contradistinguishing members of a common group.[125] As such it can be considered part of the emergence of the notion of the individual within society. In one of the earliest references to this, Bacon describes going behind the social mask that disguises individual nature with etiquette and mores: "A man's *Nature* is best perceived in Privatenesse, for there is no Affectation; In passion, for that putteth a Man out of his Precepts; And in a new Case or Experiment, for there Custome leaveth him."[126] While the *Deutsches Wörterbuch* of the brothers Grimm and the later *Goethe-Wörterbuch* emphasize the variety of meanings this Greek loanword had acquired by the early nineteenth century,[127] both articulate its central split between "particular features, individualizing as well as typifying,"[128] i.e. between the sense of an individual trait and a basic (generic) disposition. It is the former that pervades definitions given in nineteenth-century conversation lexicons, one of which even specifies six categories by which to differentiate character according to its constituent elements.[129] Within aesthetics, already by the middle of the

---

[124] Paul Bekker, *Richard Wagner: His Life in his Works*, trans. M. Bozman (New York: Norton, 1931), 5.

[125] "[die] Entwicklungsgeschichte einer Anthropologie der Differenz." Thomas Bremer, "Charakter / Charakteristisch," *Ästhetische Grundbegriffe*, 7 vols. (Stuttgart and Weimar: J. J. Metzler, 2000), 1: 773.

[126] Francis Bacon, *The Essayes or Councele, Civil and Morall* (1597–1625), ed. Michael Kiernan (Oxford: Clarendon Press, 1985), 120.

[127] J. and W. Grimm, *Deutsches Wörterbuch*, 2: 611ff, see http://woerterbuchnetz.de/DWB/; Goethe, *Wörterbuch*, 2: 980ff, see http://gwb.uni-trier.de/Projekte/WBB2009/GWB/wbgui_py?lemid=JA00001

[128] "Die Möglichkeit bestimmt, sowohl individuierende wie typisierende Merkmale zu erfassen." Goethe, *Wörterbuch*, 2: 980.

[129] The six categories are: disposition; temperament; mind; heart; sensibility; and how personal freedom animates the aforementioned assemblage of traits. See *Conversations-Lexicon oder encyclopädisches Handwörterbuch für gebildete Stände* [Stuttgart, 1816], in Roland Kanz and Jürgen Schönwälder (eds.), *Ästhetik des Charakteristischen: Quellentexte zu Kunstkritik und Romantik* (Göttingen and Bonn: V&R unipress / Bonn University Press, 2008), 169.

eighteenth century *das Charakteristische* had become established in a field of conflict midway between the beautiful–ideal and the ugly (*das Häßliche*), but this often involved a convoluted negotiation: writers such as Christian Gottfried Körner felt it was possible to retain the beautiful in music by obviating individual, momentary passion (pathos), and portraying human character (ethos) instead, for in this way music "can sensualize what is infinite within human nature: moral freedom," as Jacob de Ruiter puts it.[130] For some writers, this even made musical character and beauty synonymous. But in terms specific to *vocal*, rather than instrumental, melodic composition, the historical emergence of *das Charakteristische* as part of a larger impulse toward realist forms of expression is best traceable through its cardinal properties: particularity of identity and physicality of expression.

German critics were united in proclaiming characteristic expression distinctly un-Italian.[131] But it seems a post-Hegelian aesthetics came to terms only uneasily with its drive toward specificity. In 1849, Brendel declared the elapsed decade unfavorable to "dramatic characterization and objective portrayal,"[132] while Lobe, in 1855, claimed defiantly that all musical content is verbally nameable or it "is not content."[133] A year later the aesthetician and art historian Josef Bayer sought to address this issue by updating Hegelian doctrine for the modern age. Labeling melody "the *pure median of musical beauty* [between harmony and rhythm], as it were, a reproduction of the *plastic ideal* in the sphere of tones,"[134] he recast Hegel's defunct tripartite division of fine art as the historical ages of the archaic, the classical, and the modern, onto which he mapped the sublime, the beautiful, and *das Charakteristische* (which take their paradigmatic forms

---

[130] "weil [die Musik, wenn sie einem menschlichen Charakter darstellt] auf diese Weise das Unendliche in der menschlichen Natur, die sittliche Freiheit versinnlichen kann." De Ruiter, *Der Charakterbegriff in der Musik*, 13.

[131] Two prominent examples are Lobe: "Auf tiefere Charakteristik, auf jene Individualisirung ieder Person . . . richten die Italiener ihr Streben nicht, weil das Verlangen danach bei dem italienischen Publikum in der Oper nicht vorhanden ist." Lobe, "Bellini," 50; and Hanslick: "Ich will gar nicht von den modernen Italienern reden, deren ganzes Opernwesen eine große Gewohnheit ist." Hanslick, HSS I/1: 78.

[132] "Die neueste Zeit ist dramatischer Charakteristik und der Objektivität der Darstellung nicht günstig." Franz Brendel, "Das Bewußtsein der Neuzeit, das moderne Ideal," *NZfM* 30 (1849), 233–34, 237–39, here 237.

[133] "Und ein Inhalt, der sich 'nur fühlen' und nicht in Worten wiedergeben läßt, ist freilich kein Inhalt." Lobe, "Gegen Dr. Hanslick's *Vom Musikalisch-Schönen*," *FBfM* 2: 2, 65–105, here 103.

[134] "Wenn die Melodie sich mit der Harmonie und dem Rhythmus ins Gleichgewicht setzt, so erzeugt dies die *reine Mitte der musikalischen Schönheit*, gleichsam eine Reproduction des *plastischen Ideals* im Reiche der Töne." Josef Bayer, *Aesthetik in Umrissen: Zur allgemeineren philosophischen Orientirung auf dem Gebiete der Kunst*, 2 vols. (Prague: Mercy, 1856), 2: 92.

in architecture, plastic arts, and painting, respectively). Thus Bayer accommodates precisely what Hegel rejects, namely characteristic expression as a higher, historico–aesthetic development that "gives back the [lost] bodily side of the poetic worldview."[135]

For present purposes, Bayer's clearest definition of *das Charakteristische* occurs within his discussion of the visual arts. As the most representative form of the characteristic style, painting:

> raises itself from the portrayal of a plastic generic picture [*Gattungsbild*] to that of a worked-through form of character [*Charakterform*], from the typical form that a whole should conceive for itself to the significant individuality which, striving, acting, or conniving, refers to an intellectual whole.[136]

As an aesthetic category, however, *das Charakteristische* remained unstable (even by the end of the century the philosopher Eduard von Hartmann concluded that it was still ill-defined).[137]

In defining a move from the generic to the individual, it held a similarly equivocal status within music criticism. The aesthetician Friedrich Theodor Vischer spoke in 1857 of music's characteristic style as a "portraying, painting style," noting that: "Here music progresses right up to the most extreme boundaries possible, it becomes portraying, objectifying, it becomes epic, dramatic, orchestrating."[138] If this drive to render music a fully semiotic language sounds implausible, it is worth remembering that this was exclusively a debate between German aestheticians, whereas a similar debate was almost inconceivable in the intellectual traditions of England, France, or Italy.[139]

As we noted earlier, the descriptive power of this aesthetic came to be associated directly with Wagnerian melody. Joachim Raff even held that a dialectic of form and character structured Wagner's entire approach to

---

[135] "Beim charakteristischen Styl angelangt, giebt sie gleichsam die *körperliche* Seite des poetischen Weltbildes wieder." *Ibid.*, 2: 90.

[136] "So erhebt sie sich von der Darstellung des plastischen *Gattungsbildes* zu jener der durchgearbeiteten *Charakterform*, – von der typischen Gestalt, die ein Ganzes für sich vorstellen soll, zu der bedeutenden Individualität, die sich strebend, handelnd oder duldend auf ein geistiges Ganze bezieht." *Ibid.*

[137] Eduard von Hartmann, *Die deutsche Ästhetik seit Kant*, 12 vols. (Leipzig: Friedrich, 1886), 1: 376.

[138] "Hier schreitet die Musik bis zu den äussersten Grenzen des ihr Möglichen fort, sie wird darstellend, objektivierend, sie wird epische, dramatische, orchestische." Friedrich Theodor Vischer, *Aesthetik oder Wissenschaft des Schönen*, 2nd edn. (Munich: Meyer & Jessen, 1923), 5: 242. Dahlhaus points out that this paragraph was actually written by Karl Köstlin, see Dahlhaus, "Die Kategorie des 'Charakteristischen' in den Ästhetik des 19. Jahrhunderts," *Klassische und romantische Musikästhetik* (Laaber, 1988), 286fn.

[139] On the German identity of the debate, see Roland Kanz, *Ästhetik des Charakteristischen*, 7ff.

melodic composition, continuing: "If melody makes use of the same material as recitative in respect of outward portrayal, we must first begin here to observe inner characterization in the most fundamental melodic moments." He nuanced Liszt's public claim that *Tannhäuser*'s motifs depict emotions so "vividly" they require no text to be understood,[140] in concluding: "It cannot be denied that these motifs [in *Lohengrin*] are very concise and characterizing [*kennzeichnend*] in a melodic, rhythmic, and harmonic respect."[141] Wagner would gently disagree with Liszt in 1857,[142] and even Raff felt obliged to point out potential problems in coding melodic material in this way: it renders opera plots incomprehensible without the aid of portraying, melodic signs, and subordinates musical style to a dramatic context (the heroic, noble material of *Lohengrin*, he instances, ensures the music is almost entirely restricted to elementary rhythms and 4/4 meter, meaning that a feeling of monotony is unavoidable in an opera lasting three and a half hours).[143] Other critics argued more practically that Wagner was restricting himself to a string of unpleasant instants, for he could only characterize "fleeting situations, agitated moments etc." with no allowance for graceful figures.[144]

To be sure, Wagner's music was not generating a new debate, but being inserted into an existing one.[145] Yet *das Charakteristische* had achieved more than a degree of legitimacy within German aesthetics by the mid-

---

[140] See Liszt, "Lohengrin et Tannhäuser de Richard Wagner par Franz Liszt" trans. John Sullivan Dwight, in *Wagner and his World*, 257–58.

[141] "Wenn in Hinsicht der äußeren Darstellung die Melodie sich derselben Mittel zu bedienen hat, als das Recitativ, so muß hier zunächst die Betrachtung der inneren Charakteristik in den wesentlichsten Momenten des Melodischen beginnen . . . Es ist nicht zu leugnen, daß diese Motive in melodischer, rhythmischer und harmonischer Hinsicht sehr prägnant und kennzeichnend sind." Raff, *Die Wagnerfrage*, 100, 109–10.

[142] Referring to the mental images of Orpheus and Prometheus, Wagner argues euphemistically that one "may still point to the difficulty of extracting an intelligible form for musical composition out of such exalted representations." SSD 5: 192. Cf. PW 3: 247.

[143] Raff, *Die Wagnerfrage*, 111.

[144] "er charakterisirt immer nur einzelne vorübergehende Situationen, unruhige Momente u. dergl." [Julian Schmidt], "Stimmen der Kritik über Richard Wagner," *Niederrheinische Musik-Zeitung* 11 (March 17, 1855), 83–84.

[145] This goes back at least to 1805 when Goethe translated Diderot's unpublished satirical dialogue *Le Neveu de Rameau*, explaining in a postscript that northern composers' "peculiar harmonies, interrupted melodies, forcible deviations and transitions" cannot but "insult" the ear. He explains that, for northern composers in competition with poetic expression: "Seltsame Harmonieen, unterbrochene Melodieen, gewaltsame Abweichungen und Übergänge sucht man auf, um den Schrei des Entzückens, der Angst und der Verzweiflung auszudrücken. Solche Componisten werden bei Empfindenden, bei Verständigen ihr Glück machen, aber dem Vorwurf des beleidigten Ohres . . . schwerlich entgehen." Goethe, "Anmerkungen über Personen und Gegenstände, deren in dem Dialog: *Rameau's Neffe* erwähnt wird," *Goethes Sämmtliche Werke* (Stuttgart: J. G. Cotta, 1874), 13: 467. Equally, Friedrich Schlegel had spoken

nineteenth century. After Körner's pioneering essay *Über Charakter-Darstellung in der Musik* (1795) had been "barely noticed"[146] by his contemporaries, later applications of *das Charakteristische* to music were mostly left to professional theorists, who remained ambivalent about its perceived destruction of unity. Brendel simultaneously legitimized and rebuked the modern *Lied* aesthetic in this respect, where a drive "towards sharper characterization"[147] forms part of a narrative of decline: "every expansion, every progression, by devaluing art, is also a backward step."[148] But in a self-serving move, he later alluded to Marx for the view that some harmonic progressions cannot be explained through normative theory and must be interpreted by the ear in conjunction with an *Idee*. This uncoupling of grammar and sensation was enlisted to interpret the more outlandish harmonic maneuvers in Liszt's Symphonic Poems:

> The sensory point of view [*Sinnlichkeitsstandpunkt*] is the Marxian principle of the characteristic . . . on this footing it can therefore certainly happen that a [harmonic] combination is justified not merely through technical harmonic analysis, rather directly through the idea . . . [W]here the ear is the judge, other laws are in force than where the characteristic principle appears.[149]

This occasional incongruence between pleasing, euphonious sensations and *das Charakteristische* explains why, for Bayer, "plastic and music [are] completely opposite," effectively dashing any lingering hopes to merge Italianate and Germanic aesthetics. But consider the specious dialectics needed to transcend this impasse: Bayer's melodic ideal is defined precisely as a *"plastic ideal in the sphere of tones"* where one must regard beauty itself as *"doubly*

---

of "artistic chaos" in his critique of modern literature, where the "total predominance of what is characteristic, individual and interesting" was leading to a "restless, insatiable striving for what is new, piquant and striking," an outcome – he felt – of an aesthetics of innovation engaged in an empty process of continually outdoing itself. See Friedrich Schlegel, "Über das Studium der griechischen Poesie" [1795–97], *Kritische Friedrich-Schlegel-Ausgabe*, 35 vols., ed. Ernst Behler (Munich: F. Schöningh, 1958–) 1: 224, 228.

[146] de Ruiter, *Der Charakterbegriff in der Musik*, 13. But see also Matthew Pritchard's counter-case in "'The Moral Background of the Work of Art': 'Character' in German Musical Aesthetics 1780–1850," *Eighteenth-Century Music* 9 (2012), 63–80.

[147] *"zu schärferer Charakteristik."* Brendel, "Zur Einleitung," *NZfM* 22 (1845), 8.

[148] "Jede Erweiterung, jede Fortschritt ist beim Sinken der Kunst zugleich ein Rückschritt." *Ibid.*, 9.

[149] "[Die Sinnlichkeitsstandpunkt] ist das Marxsche Prinzip des Charakteristischen . . . Auf diesem Wege kann es demnach auch wohl geschehen, dass nicht mehr bloss durch technisch harmonische Analyse, sondern durch die Idee unmittelbar eine Kombination zu rechtfertigen ist . . . Wo das Ohr der Richter ist, gelten andere Gesetze, als da, wo das Charakteristische als Prinzip auftritt." Franz Brendel, "Franz Liszt als Symphoniker," *NZfM* 49 (1858), 73ff. For an examination of Brendel's position, see Berthold Hoeckner, *Programming the Absolute* (Princeton University Press, 2002), 161–67.

formed"[150] since the visual arts and music more or less isolate two sides of the beautiful against each other: "the visible and the audible, appearance and movement, form and life."[151] This confrontation of silent matter and sounding motion can only be unified in poetry, Bayer claims optimistically, and, anticipating the final telos of modern art, he alludes to physiology – implicitly disagreeing with Brendel – where the sheer pleasure of any sonic stimulation makes up for the lack of beautiful forms in visually specific characterization.

In terms of Winckelmann's category of expression, the resulting compromise Bayer comes up with invokes music through classical sculpture in a grand bargain:

> The [modern] artistic genius is that Pygmalion who wants to give soul to and imbue with his innermost life the form that he has created. But this form disappears disembodied in his arms as soon as he tries to embrace it with rising feeling. Here enters, instead of beautiful form that delighted the *eye*, the inner euphony of harmonic existence that fills the *ear* with delight. The former *silent* beauty must part from the realms of the visible, in order to make *audible* the deeper fullness of its being.[152]

Pygmalion – that Cypriot sculptor whose ivory female statue came to life at the amorous touch of his lips – is an apt analogy, both in breathing animate, particularizing life into inanimate, sculptural beauty and in requiring divine intervention in the process. (Wagner had spoken similarly of "liberating" human sculpture into the reality of the mimetic dancer, where "the illusion of plastic art turns to truth in drama."[153]) It is the movement of music, whose corollary is the physical pleasure of sound, that makes up for any loss of visual specificity, the amputated "realms of the visual" that Bayer allied to the emergent category of *das Charakteristische*. Briefly stated, he wants to safeguard the category of the beautiful as a higher sphere, while welcoming the characteristic as a quintessentially modern form of art. Again, however,

---

[150] "So sind *Plastik* und *Musik* völlige Gegensätze; wir müssen die eine über der anderen vergessen, um uns dem vollen Genusse der Schönheit hingeben zu können, die hier *doppelgestaltig* erscheint: einmal als ein Zauber für das Auge, das anderemal als ein Zauber für das Ohr und die Seele." Bayer, *Aesthetik in Umrissen*, 2: 300.

[151] "Die bildende Kunst und die Musik haben mehr oder weniger zwei Seiten des Schönen gegen einander isolirt: Das Sichtbare und das Vernehmbare, die Erscheinung und die Bewegung, die Gestalt und das Leben." *Ibid.*

[152] "Der künstlerische Genius ist jener Pygmalion, welcher die Gestalt, die er geschaffen hat, auch beseelen und mit seinem innersten Leben durchdringen möchte. Aber diese Gestalt verschwindet ihm körperlos in den Armen, sobald er sie mit gesteigertem Gefühl zu umfassen sucht. Da tritt an die Stelle der schönen Form, die das *Auge* entzückte, der innere Wohlklang der harmonischen Existenz, der den *Lauscher* beseligt; die früher *stumme* Schönheit muß aus dem Bereiche des Sichtbaren scheiden, um die tiefere Fülle ihres Seins *vernehmbar* zu machen." *Ibid.*

[153] SSD 3: 155. Cf. PW 1: 189.

the means for achieving this was not melody, but harmony ("the inner euphony of harmonic existence") where melody becomes an incidental remainder. Such convoluted dialectics signal a decidedly reluctant acceptance of the historical agency propelling a painterly manifestation of the characteristic, namely "a realism having arrived at its true goal."[154]

Perhaps melody played no part in this compromise because it had already been co-opted in an alternative drive for artistic realism. One of the reasons Nietzsche described Wagner as "the Victor Hugo of music as language" is that, even by the age of 25, Hugo had gone further than Bayer would in outlining an aesthetic capacity for portraying the real, for expressing atomized particularities that contravened classical aesthetics.[155] Since real life is "ugly" in its endless diversity, Hugo argues, suspicions about the infinite complexities of reality actually support the aesthetic integrity of ugliness:

From the human point of view, beauty is none other than form seen in its most elementary relationships, in its most absolute symmetry, and in its deepest harmony with our organism ... what we call ugly, on the other hand, is a detail from a great whole that eludes us, and that harmonizes not so much with man alone but with all of creation. That is why ugliness constantly reveals new, but incomplete aspects of it.[156]

Nachmärz criticism frequently cited Wagner's harmonic freedom and melodic disintegration as wearisome, which surely figures as "ugly" in Hugo's sense of that which appears constantly new, but irredeemably fragmentary.[157] "His reckless melody mocks our logical reflection," Friedrich Hindrichs slammed *Lohengrin* in 1854.[158] Indeed, for all the charges of *Melodielosigkeit*, very few critiques of Wagner's music during the 1850s actually labeled his melodies by their aesthetically accurate term: *ugly*. Nietzsche's finger-waving quip about Wagner's "gymnastics of ugliness on the ropes of the enharmonic. Let us dare to be ugly my friends! Wagner

---

[154] "Mit Hilfe dieser geistvollen [painterly] Technik, dieses zu seinem wahren Ziele gelangten Realismus folgt jetzt die Malerei dem psychologischen Ausdruck auf seiner leisesten Spur." Bayer, *Aesthetik in Umrissen*, 2: 90.

[155] Nietzsche, *Basic Writings of Nietzsche*, trans. Walter Kaufmann (New York: Vintage Books, 2000), 629.

[156] Hugo, "Preface" to *Cromwell*. Cited in Umberto Eco, *On Ugliness*, trans. Alastair McEwen (London: Harvill Secker, 2007), 281.

[157] Eduard Sobolewski writes on this topic with his customary ebullience: "when, in 60 bars [Wagner] treats us to about 56 bars of chords of the seventh, minor, major, and diminished, so that, in order to satisfy our desire of dissolution, we would fain be changed into a piece of butter upon a hot tub – then we are not at all for Wagner." Sobolewski, "Reactionary Letters. III," *The Musical World* 33 (January 27, 1855), 68.

[158] Friedrich Hinrichs, *Richard Wagner und die neuere Musik. Eine Skizze aus der musikalischen Gegenwart* (Halle: Schrödel and Simon, 1854), 63. Cited in Grey, *Wagner's Musical Prose*, 246.

dared!" was not entirely hyperbolic.[159] Even the broader discourse that
defined German melody negatively, in opposition to that of Italy, finds a
new frame in this sense; the Christian philosopher Johann Dursch thought of
ugliness in 1839 as an unnatural distortion of some natural, primary state:
"something [melody] is ugly if it doesn't emerge in accordance with its nature
[periodic, rounded, Italianate], i.e. if it appears in a form not determined
by its essence, or in which that essence or being vanishes."[160] Hugo's notion
of isolated elements reflecting an elusive whole allows us to reread
his claims specifically in light of the melodic debate: "beauty has only
one type [Italianate architectonics], ugliness has thousands [Wagnerian
expressionism]."[161] Far from a negative aesthetic category, then, the ugly
pervaded the nineteenth century – a period Umberto Eco recently termed
"the redemption of ugliness" – denying the expectation that its art will be
pleasurable, yet affirming its fractured realism as an object of fascinated
contemplation.[162]

The principal mid-century German monograph on the subject was Karl
Rosenkranz's *Ästhetik des Häßlichen* (1853), which – with echoes of
Aristotle – drew on Winckelmann's 1764 treatise to argue that unity is
"the basic condition of all beauty."[163] Beauty requires "restriction," he
continues (in silent analogy to Italianate style), because only in restriction
lies the power of differentiation, and differentiation is impossible without
isolated unity. Rosenkranz thus formulates his theory of ugliness by inverting the principle of beauty, i.e. as negative beauty:

1. [Ugliness] represents disunity, incompleteness, uncertainty of form;
2. [Ugliness] elicits difference, if it clarifies it, either as false irregularity or
   as false equality and inequality;

---

[159] Nietzsche, *The Anti-Christ*, 244.

[160] "Ein Ding ist Häßlich, wenn es nicht seinem Wesen gemäß in die Erscheinung tritt, wenn es also
in einer Gestalt erscheint, die durch das Wesen desselben nicht bedingt ist, oder in welcher das
Wesen oder Seyn verschwindet." Johann Georg Martin Dursch, *Aesthetik; oder die Wissenschaft
des Schönen auf dem christlichen Standpunkte* (Stuttgart and Tübingen: J. G. Cotta, 1839), 426.

[161] Victor Hugo, *Cromwell* (Paris: Garnier, 1968), 71.   [162] Eco, *On Ugliness*, 271.

[163] "Die abstrakte Grundbestimmung alles Schönen ist . . . die Einheit." Karl Rosenkranz, *Ästhetik
des Häßlichen* (Königsberg: Gebrüder Bornträger, 1853); rpt. (Leipzig: Reclam, 1996), 62. It
seems likely that Rosenkranz based his definition of ugliness on Winckelmann's influential
treatise of 1764: "All beauty is heightened by unity and simplicity . . . Everything which we must
consider in separate pieces, or which we cannot survey at once, from the number of its
constituent parts, loses thereby some portion of its greatness . . . From unity proceeds . . . the
absence of individuality; that is, the forms of it are described neither by points nor lines other
than those which shape beauty merely, and consequently produce a figure which is neither
peculiar to any particular individual, nor yet expresses any one state of the mind or affection of
the passions." J. J. Winckelmann, *The History of Ancient Art Among the Greeks*, 43–44.

3. Instead of the reunification of form with itself, [ugliness] engenders, on the contrary, the transition to divisiveness in the fogginess of false contrasts.[164]

The three Greek terms Rosenkranz uses to identify these subdivisions are: *amorphousness, asymmetry*, and *disharmony*. Recall that Filippi described Wagner's melodies in 1869 as: "melopoeia without [formed] rhythm, without [symmetrical] proportions, without [harmonious] returns," and Hanslick thought *Die Meistersinger* was simply a "boneless tonal mollusk float[ing] on towards the immeasurable."[165] Without needing to engage in a close reading, the overlap between the discourse on ugliness and Wagner's critical reception would seem evident both at the level of vocabulary and of concept.

Ugliness in *Das Rheingold* (1854)

If we step outside the discourse linking *Tannhäuser* and *Lohengrin* to idealist criticism, Wagner's composition most contemporary with Rosenkranz's treatise was *Das Rheingold* (1853–54). By way of exploring Wagner's claims for *unendliche Melodie*, Thomas Grey once linked the aesthetic of ugliness to the "interior musical logic" of the fragmented instrumental prelude to *Siegfried*, act II (illustrating what Charles Stanford criticized as "ugly characters" portrayed by unnecessarily "ugly music").[166] Building on this effective comparison, it would seem the primary domain of *melodic* ugliness was vocal, not instrumental, at least when conceived as a realist, literary aesthetic: cries, saliva, panting, and clamour disfigure a "singing" voice more palpably than the still refined playing of instrumental motifs. As Example 1.3 shows, the third scene from *Das Rheingold*, set in Nibelheim, presents mimetic chromatic lurches and syncopated twitches in a series of one-measure instrumental fragments whose rising chromatic sequencing is void of harmonic logic (until m. 1903 when the dominant is tentatively established). Its pictorial logic is vividly onomatopoeic – Alberich dragging a shrieking Mime on stage by the ear, pinching him, Caliban-like – and continues through a series of stunted motific gestures that become the figures for the nine-measure vocal line, where Alberich's

---

[164] "1. die Nichteinheit, Nichtabgeschlossenheit, Unbestimmtheit der Gestalt ausmacht; 2. daß es den Unterschied, wenn es ihn setzt, entweder als eine falsche Unregelmäßigkeit oder als eine falsche Gleichheit und Ungleichheit hervorbringt; 3. daß es statt der Wiedereinheit der Gestalt mit sich vielmehr den Übergang der Entzweiung in die Verworrenheit falscher Kontraste erzeugt." Rosenkranz, *Ästhetik des Häßlichen*, 62.

[165] Taken from Hanslick's 1874 review of *Die Meistersinger*. See *Vienna's Golden Years*, trans. Henry Pleasants (New York: Simon and Schuster, 1950), 127.

[166] Grey, *Wagner's Musical Prose*, 287; for Stanford's comments see Robert Hartford (ed.), *Bayreuth: the Early Years* (London: Victor Gollancz, 1980), 106.

Example 1.3 Different instances of Karl Rosenkranz's aesthetic of "ugliness" within Wagnerian melody. (a) *Das Rheingold*, scene 2, mm. 1894–1910.

voice – between a snigger and disgusted shout – characterizes the heaving exhalation of his physical supremacy written into the downbeats of each utterance. The pervasive half step motion in the instrumental fragments then transmutes into Mime's first notated cries, whose own rising and falling half step (F–G♭ / G♭–F) mocks the heritage of the *pianto* / *Seufzer* – so

Example 1.3 (Cont.)

(b) *Das Rheingold*, scene 3, mm. 2175–81.

earnestly adopted for Fricka's cries of "Wehe!" earlier in scene 2 – with a realist prerogative. But beyond mimesis, Mime's stuttering monotony (given in Example 1.3b) as he relates how the magic tarnhelm outwitted him indicates that Rosenkranz's ugly aesthetic need not only apply thematically: to physical pain, deformity, and fractured movement. The tarnhelm's *Leitmotiv* itself rocks back-and-forth between common-tone chords with no sense of progression (A♭ / F♭), which along with Mime's "melody" presents the zero-degree of melodic invention if we insist that melody consists of balanced form, phrasal contour, and harmonic closure, to paraphrase Charles Rosen.[167] Viewing Wagnerian melody in reductionist terms as decisively deformed, the negative or inverse of Italian melody, is helpful in that it structures the critical debate around a polarity of predefined formal continuity and its absence. In itself this is hardly new to Wagner scholarship, but as Rosenkranz explains: "Asymmetry is not simple shapelessness, it is an un-shape [*entschiedene Ungestalt*]."[168] The aesthetic platform that Hugo provided for Rosenkranz here found visual expression early on in Theodor Géricault's oil *A Study of Severed Limbs* (1818–19) – reproduced as Figure 1.2. It is mutilated man: expressing either an assemblage of incomplete parts or elements ripped apart from an absent whole i.e. literalizing the shredding of the bourgeois subject whose unity was predicated on, and found its aesthetic mirror in, the work of art.[169] Never had the nascent *Leitmotiv* technique found such an ambivalent visual analogue.

In this respect, it is perhaps no coincidence that Rosenkranz cites *melody* as the most apparent site of the destruction of perceptible unity:

---

[167] Charles Rosen, *The Romantic Generation* (London: Fontana, 1999), 492.

[168] "Die Asymmetrie ist nicht einfache Gestaltlosigkeit, sie ist entschiedene Ungestalt." Rosenkranz, *Ästhetik des Häßlichen*, 76.

[169] Jacob de Ruiter specifically discusses critics' perception of fractured melody during the early nineteenth century in *Der Charakterbegriff in der Musik*, 241ff.

1.2 Theodor Géricault, *A Study of Severed Limbs* (1818–19) © Musée Fabre de Montpellier Agglomération – Photograph by Frédéric Jaulmes.

With music the ease of production increases, and with it the possibility of the ugly, like with that of this art-specific subjective inwardness. Although in its abstract form – in meter and rhythm – this art rests on arithmetic, it is nevertheless subject to the greatest indefiniteness and randomness in that which first preserves its true soulful expression of the idea, in *melody*, and the judgment about what is beautiful and what is not beautiful therein is often infinitely difficult. Therefore the ugly is able to gain here still more ground than in painting because of the ethereal, volatile, mysterious, symbolic nature of tones and the uncertainty of criticism.[170]

At least one music journalist made essentially these connections between music, melody, ugliness, and Wagner. Reviewing *Lohengrin*, Bischoff worried that "[m]usic is just as free as a bird. It has absolutely no rules, not even acoustic rules that the artist must respect; Wagner's scores announce this

---

[170] "Mit der Musik steigert sich die Leichtigkeit der Produktion und mit ihr sowie mit der dieser Kunst eigenen subjektiven Innerlichkeit die Möglichkeit des Häßlichen. Obwohl nämlich diese Kunst in ihrer abstrakten Form, im Takt und Rhythmus, auf der Arithmetik beruhet, so ist sie doch in dem, was sie erst zum wahren, seelenvollen Ausdruck der Idee macht, in der Melodie, der größten Unbestimmtheit und Zufälligkeit ausgesetzt und das Urtheil, was schön, was nicht schön sei, in ihr oft unendlich schwer. Daher denn die Häßlichkeit vermöge der ätherischen, volatilen, mysteriösen, symbolischen Natur des Tons und vermöge der Unsicherheit der Kritik hier noch mehr Boden als in der Malerei gewinnt." Rosenkranz, *Ästhetik des Häßlichen* [1853], 47.

principle 'loud and clear.'"[171] In this respect, Wagner's approach to melodic freedom, viewed by some critics (though not by Wagner himself)[172] as part of a characteristic aesthetic, exemplifies the shifting condition of melody from a metaphysically plastic form governed by metrical and harmonic organization, to a deliberately disfigured, fragmentary form expressive of some level of specifiable reality that was officially beyond the grasp of fine art (Hugo's universal harmony). Among the spectra of shaded meanings "melody" had acquired in this discourse, the term's mid-century position in Germany can be summarized under the category of a geometric semiosis defined as melodic, but voided of melodious continuity.

Between symbolism and realism

> Germany, land of harmony, of symphonists; Italy, land of melody, of singers.
>
> Victor Hugo[173]

> And here you still speak of Italy, of Bellini and the land of song. When will we have done with the naïve superstition that we could learn something about song from them?
>
> Robert Schumann[174]

Predictably, perhaps, a backlash against the validity of pro-Italian aesthetics[175] catalyzed the embrace of "ugliness" (if not always under that

---

[171] "Die Musik ist eine völlig vogelfreie Kunst. Es gibt in ihr keinerlei, auch nicht akustische Gesetze, welche der Künstler zu respectiren hätte; dieses Princip verkünden Wagner's Partituren 'laut und hell.'" Bischoff, "Richard Wagner's *Lohengrin*," 299.

[172] For a discussion of the differences between Wagner's critical application of the term "charakteristik" to Weber and Meyerbeer in *Oper und Drama*, see Dahlhaus, *Klassische und romantische Musikästhetik*, 228–30.

[173] "L'Allemagne, terre de l'harmonie, a des symphonistes; l'Italie, terre de la mélodie, a des chanteurs." Victor Hugo, "Post-scriptum de ma vie," in Hugo, *Oeuvres complètes*, "Philosophie II: William Shakespeare et Post-scriptum de ma vie" (Paris: Albin Michel, 1937), 512.

[174] "Und ihr sprecht noch immer von Italien, von Bellini und dem Lande des Gesanges? Wann endlich wird jener Köhlerglaube aufhören, wir könnten im Gesange von dorther lernen?" Schumann, *Gesammelte Schriften über Musik und Musiker*, 2: 250.

[175] The *Niederrheinische Musik-Zeitung* directly challenged the indigenous argument in 1855, namely the "great prejudice" that melody is created in Italy. It was not native Italians, the paper argues, who first gave Italian composers the impulse "we now call melodic," but "German (Dutch) masters" since they first taught at the music academies of Rome and Venice. Appealing to remote levels of ethnographic realism, the paper seeks to undermine the myth of congenital melodic talent further by reversing the clichéd roles of German and Italian opera: contemporary Venetian gondoliers do not sing "plastically formed" themes or "rounded, closed melodies," the paper retorts, instead they sing *declamatorische Recitative*. As if citing a conclusive proof, the article declares that none of the

name), where critics sought to gain a legitimate role for musical complexity within the prevailing *Gefühlsaesthetik*. This demanded a creative response from music theory. The challenge, in short, was not only how to systematize melodic expression adequate to (non-Italian) *Vormärz* opera, but to conceive of a kind of "grammar of expression" that reflected a worldview at once limited and universal. (Much the same problem had dogged the British search for a universal language during the seventeenth century, where "inventors of philosophic *a priori* languages needed to invent characters that referred to things or notions: this meant that their first step was to draw up a list of notions and things," Eco explains. "This was not an easy task."[176])

It dissuaded some. Writing in 1774, Johann A. P. Schulz asserted that "the essence of melody consists in expression" but he remained skeptical of an expansion of this knowledge into formulaic phrases or plastically finite shapes.[177] Any rigid itemizing of expression is doomed, he asserted:

It would be a ridiculous task to want to stipulate to the composer particular formulae or small melodic phrases that truly express every particular emotion, or even to say how he should invent such forms or phrases.[178]

Forty years after Schulz's skepticism, the implicit onus was precisely on achieving systematic melodic expression. By 1852 it formed one part of what Brendel called music's "law of development" (*Entwicklungsgesetz*), namely an ever greater "particularity of expression" (*Bestimmtheit des Ausdrucks*).[179] The closest a music theorist from Wagner's formative years came to objectifying melodic intervals in this sense was A. B. Marx, whose first book *Die Kunst des Gesanges* (1826) is a philosophical and pedagogical study of singing and vocal composition.[180] Towards the end of the text, after

---

older Italian folk melodies exist in the sense of "our *plastische* Lied form." See "Vorbeifliegende Gedanken," *Niederrheinische Musik-Zeitung* 22 (June 2, 1855), 172.

[176] Umberto Eco, *The Search for the Perfect Language*, trans. James Fentress (London: Fontana, 1997), 222.

[177] "Das Wesen der Melodie besteht in dem Ausdruck." Johann Georg Sulzer, *Allgemeine Theorie der schönen Künste in Einzeln*, 2nd edn. (Leipzig: Weidmannschen, 1793), 3: 371. (J. A. P. Schulz wrote the music entries in Sulzer's edition.)

[178] "Uebrigens würde es ein lächerliches Unternehmen seyn, dem Tonsetzer besondere Formeln, oder kleine melodische Sätze vorschreiben zu wollen, die für jede Empfindung den wahren Ausdruck haben, oder gar zu sagen, wie er solche erfinden soll." *Ibid.*, 3: 379.

[179] Brendel, *Geschichte der Musik in Italien, Deutschland und Frankreich*, 338.

[180] Published in 1826, two years after Marx co-founded and began editing the *BamZ*, the book analyzes many aspects of vocal production, providing detailed discussions with examples for a musically educated readership in the Prussian capital. It comprises three sections: rudiments of music theory, vocal training, and vocal performance. These structured Marx's putatively encyclopedic commentary on the history and notation of vocal music, the variously differentiated compositional structures and their aesthetic properties, the teaching and training of singers, as well as national styles and linguistics.

Marx declares that "one must follow faithfully the witty [German] composer in each individual situation, and in each configuration keep in mind his essential intention in order to be adequate to his works,"[181] he proceeds to examine tonal intervals as finite entities, categorizing them according to their apparently inherent emotional properties for listeners. The paradox of a "limited universality," then, was to be resolved through the equal-tempered chromatic keyboard. Marx begins from the essentializing premise that not only the rising or sinking of human utterances, but "all intervals" in which the voice rises or falls "each have their necessary meaning," and proceeds to the more general assertion that "all tonal relationships desire an inherent particular, special meaning."[182] While acknowledging that it is difficult fully to grasp such meanings, and that comparisons of the symbolic (*sinnbildlich*) representation of ideas have led to "*apparent* differences of opinion" in this matter, Marx proceeds to outline his view of the "underlying truth" of each relationship with startling candor:[183]

Minor 2nd	= calm but powerless, faint movement
Major 2nd	= calm, secure movement
Augmented 2nd	= painfully felt movement
Minor 3rd	= ascertainment, but without the awareness of power and of success
Major 3rd	= firm ascertainment, with the awareness of accomplishment
Perfect 4th	= the accomplished, decisive stepping out
Perfect 5th	= yearns for another, unspecified point to the first tone
Augmented 5th	= expects the unknown so violently that the fixed relation to the first tone is lost
Major 6th	= pronounces the need for outside reassurance
Diminished 7th	= soft, but hopeless longing
Minor 7th	= character of powerfully felt, painfully urgent desire mixed with a related but weaker, hopeful longing etc.
Major 7th	= the painful, lively desire for satisfaction[184]

[181] "Man muß dem geistreichen Künstler in jede einzelne Situation treu folgen und in jeder seiner Gestaltungen seine wesentliche Intention vor Augen behalten, um seinen Werken zu genügen." Marx, *Die Kunst des Gesanges: theoretisch-praktisch* (Berlin: A. M. Schlesinger, 1826), 232.

[182] "[A]lle Intervalle, in denen sie [die Stimme] steigt oder fällt, haben jedes seine nothwendige Bedeutung ... allen Tonverhältnissen [möge] eine bestimmte besondere Bedeutung inwohnen." *Ibid.*, 257.

[183] "eine *anscheinende* Meinungsverschiedenheit ... [D]ie verschiedenen und dennoch unter sich stets verwandten Darstellung [deuten] auf eine ihnen allen zum Grunde liegende Wahrheit." *Ibid.*

[184] Marx orders his intervals by major and minor, diminished and augmented categories, which I reorder to form the chromatic scale in my translation. Here, I quote Marx's original ordering of intervals: "Von den innerhalb der Oktave liegenden großen Intervallen stellt die Sekunde – c d – die ruhige, sichere Bewegung, die Terz – c e – feste Bestimmung mit dem Bewußtsein des

Though putatively abstract, this relies partly on the imagination of a human voice, and, of course, a harmonic context (to distinguish an augmented 2nd from a minor 3rd; a diminished 7th from a major 6th). Indeed, later attempts at similar intervallic maps made this explicit, from Paul Hindemith (where harmonic tension is empirical, based on acoustics)[185] to Arthur C. Edwards (where it is psychological, based on perception).[186] Needless to say, all typologies differ, anachronisms notwithstanding. In 1848, a pseudonymous Anglo-German theorist named *Teutonius*[187] would reassert Marx's principle of intervallic correlates, though less systematically, declining to specify each interval's putative character.[188] Raff similarly shied away from

---

Vollbringens . . . die Quarte – c f – das vollbrachte, entscheidende Hinaustreten dar . . . Die Quinte – c g verlangt vom Anfangstone nach einem andern, unbestimmten Punkte hin, . . . die Sexte – c a – spricht das Bedürfniß nach Beruhigung von außen, die Septime – c h das schmerzlich lebhafte Begehren dieser Befriedigung aus . . . So ist die Sekunde – c des – eine ruhige aber unkräftige, matte Bewegung; die Terz – c es – Bestimmung, aber ohne jenes Bewußtsein der Kraft des Gelingens; die Septime – c b – hat den Karakter kräftig empfundenen, ja schmerzlich dringenden Begehrens mit dem verwadten aber schwächern einer weichen hoffenden Sehnsucht vertaucht u. s. w. Die *verminderte* Septime – cis b – wird dagegen zur weichen, aber hoffnungslosen Sehnsucht . . . Daher wird schon die Sekunde – c dis schmerzlich empfundene Bewegung, die Quinte – c gis – verlangt so heftig in das Unbestimmte, daß das feste Beruhen auf dem Aufangstone verloren geht." *Ibid.*, 258–59.

[185] Hindemith, *The Craft of Musical Composition*, 1: 87–89, 175–201.

[186] Arthur C. Edwards, *The Art of Melody* (New York: Philosophical Library, 1956), 145ff.

[187] The pseudonymous identity of this writer was never publicly revealed. He appears to have been a Bristol-based correspondent for *The Musical World* and writer for the *Bristol Times*, contributing letters, reviews, and reports between 1848 and 1849. His review of one particular concert [*TMW* 36 (1848), 572–73] garnered controversy from local musicians for its apparently disrespectful and erroneous reportage [See "Original Correspondence" *TMW* 38 (1848), 604–05], which Teutonius rebutted [*TMW* 39 (1848), 612–13], and after which he continued to review concerts and engage in journalistic ping-pong with local Bristol musicians. Towards the end of 1848, he published six *Letters to a Music Student* in *The Musical World*: (i) "On the Tonal System," *TMW* 44 (1848), 689–91; (ii) "The Origin and Fundamental Laws of Harmony," *TMW* 45 (1848), 709–11; (iii) cont., *TMW* 46 (1848), 729–31; (iv) "The Study of Musical Composition," *TMW* 48 (1848), 762–64; (v) "Melody and Melodious Combination," *TMW* 49 (1848), 773–75; (vi) cont., *TMW* 50 (1848), 792–96. Teutonius continued to receive criticism that speculated on his identity [*TMW* 40 (1848), 636–37], and it was alleged that he was not actually German as his name suggests. His reference to "Dr. A. Mara" in the sixth letter probably refers to Adolph Bernhard Marx, and suggests that he could not read Fraktur well; his translation of Marx's title *Die alte Musiklehre im Streit mit unserer Zeit* (Leipzig: Breitkopf & Härtel, 1841) as "the present musical instruction a contradiction to the spirit of our age" similarly shows a very dubious grasp of German. See "The Study of Musical Composition," 763.

[188] "When . . . a feeling, or sensation, is already firmly rooted in the soul, and has obtained a considerable degree of intensity, it will manifest its decided character by such a lever motion [of intervals] of the melody." Teutonius adds that every intervallic progression "has its own peculiar character," and that, given more time and space, it "would not be difficult to distinguish and define" each interval's character. See Teutonius, "Letters to a Music Student: VI. Melody and Melodious Composition," *TMW* 47 (1848), 795.

illustrating his assertion that "every impression is essentially the result of the change of consonant and dissonant intervals."[189] Marx's concrete descriptions of intervals are on the cusp of a semantic melodic theory, one that would utilize what Wackenroder had called "the inexplicable sympathy . . . between the individual, mathematical, tonal relationships and the individual fibers of the human heart," though this can hardly be considered practical from a compositional standpoint.[190] With palpable disappointment, Marx later conceded as much. Music and drama, expression and meaning, "ought to blend together with equal right and equal share of effect," he maintained in 1855. "But this is impossible. The wavy line of melody and the being-in-itself of feeling run directly counter to the sharpness of character and quick-wittedness of action."[191]

But what about the original desire to circumscribe expression that is inherent in melodic configurations, i.e. to identify some part of melody's "essence" that could be objectified? The standard response to this was either to argue that listeners' tastes were too mobile (or fickle) and therefore not stable enough to build a theory that allied plastic shape with specific expression, or to protest that this real correlation of shape and expression existed, but would forever remain beyond human comprehension. Lobe opted for the latter view in 1844, as had Reicha thirty years earlier when he posited the shape of musical figures as that which truly defines melodic character or characteristic expression in a phrase of identical proportions, key, meter, dynamics, and length; these figures, he asserts, "must [actually] be created," and cannot be taught. Backing away from the implications of this arguably naïve admission, Reicha continues that:

[Figures are] the product of feeling, taste, intelligence, and finally of genius. It would be absolutely useless to wish to determine the means by which and principles for creating the figures of an aria, for this would be overly prescriptive, and cannot be done with impunity.[192]

---

[189] "Jener Eindruck ist wesentlich das Resultat der Abwechselung consoner und dissoner Intervalle." Raff, *Die Wagnerfrage*, 59.

[190] Wackenroder, *Confessions*, 188.

[191] "Drama und Musik sollten . . . in gleichem Recht und gleichem Wirkungsantheil sich verschmelzen. Allein das ist unmöglich. Die Wellenlinie der Stimmung und das Insichhineinleben des Gefühls sind der Schärfe des Karakters und der Schlagfertigkeit der Handlung stracks entgegengesetzt." Marx, *Die Musik des neunzehnten Jahrhunderts und ihre Pflege* (Leipzig: Breitkopf & Härtel, 1855). English translation by August Heinrich Wehrhan and C. Natalia Macfarren. *The Music of the Nineteenth Century and Its Culture* (London: Robert Cocks & Co., 1854), 111.

[192] Reicha, *Treatise on Melody*, 62–3.

The hope for a different answer persisted, however, and it is indicative of the longevity of the hermetic concept that Reicha's dismissal reflected the same skepticism Schutz had voiced forty years earlier, and presaged Marx's dispirited comments forty-one years hence.

To generalize for a moment, most aesthetics of this period taught that art was to express in outward, sensibly perceptible forms the inward spiritual life of human beings.[193] Wagner interpreted this pragmatically as the need for shape-giving structures of some kind: "music can be perceived only in forms which were originally foreign to it, forms derived from external aspects of human experience."[194] Beyond dyadic units, the assumed form through which this was to be accomplished is a basic equation of linear shape and emotion. This involved a visual conception of musical line as a topographical register of emotion, or what an anti-idealist might term the seismographic tracing of feeling (rendered objective by its implied mechanism).[195] Since we are now dealing with conceptions of sound structure that put the psyche in dialogue with the external world, we are breaking out of the idealist tradition that we have been revisiting hitherto, and will draw on a slightly different set of concepts; here, a distinction between symbolic and realist orders of perception will be useful in structuring this closing analysis of the historical discourse under discussion.

Briefly, melody as a symbolic representation of feeling is shape that acquires signification by association (tradition) and context. It involves the formation of arbitrary musical signifiers that have no intrinsic connection with what is signified, and are without inherent meaning but acquire this through their interrelation with an immediate harmonic context, or, more distantly, with the muffled heritage of *Figurenlehre*, and can be categorized by such properties as dyadic intervals and short formulae (their patterning, durational extension, and repetition). Realist melody, by contrast, is iconic, intuitively comprehended as being "real" in relation to some order of our experience of the external world. It is that emotive unity

---

[193] Precisely this definition is given in a discussion of the pedagogy of music composition by "Teutonius." See "Letters to a Music Student: V. Melody and Melodious Combination," *TMW* 47 (1848), 774. See also the broader definition of "Ausdruck" in Schilling's *Encyclopädie* as the "vividness of inwardness through outwardness, the powerful and lively emergence of the mental within the corporeal" ["die Anschaulichkeit des Innern im Aeußern, das kräftige und lebendige Hervortreten des Geistigen im Körperlichen."], *Encyclopädie der gesammten musikalischen Wissenschaften*, 336.

[194] SSD 5: 192. Cf. PW 3: 246–47.

[195] Adorno's use of the metaphor of music as a seismographic register of social conditions is quite different (pointing towards a concealed social meaning of musical works), and carries none of the literalism that "seismographic melody" can in the present context. See, Adorno, "Schubert" (1928), *Musikalische Schriften*, 4 vols., ed. Rolf Tiedemann (Frankfurt am Main, 1982), 4: 18–33.

of sound and expression that resists representation. By definition, this kind of vocal melody must be performative (in the Austinian sense of not saying something, but accomplishing an action), for it does not represent emotional content, but transmits it directly to a recipient, stamping it directly inside the cochlea. Thus there is no space in realist melody between positive content and form. In this sense, the media theorist Friedrich Kittler has aligned the Lacanian real with the "physiology of voice"[196] reproduced by the gramophone as a paradoxical writing system that eschews legible signification, but that makes the real accessible in the sense of actual, physical sound waves.

A cluster of German writers argued that linear melody could function as a real register of emotion, eliciting a mirror response from listeners by essentially tracing the topography of one's inward feelings across the stave. In 1837, Gustav Schilling's *Encyclopädie* is unequivocal:

Just as every feeling does not linger for long at the same level, and never inwardly makes rhythmically disjointed leaps . . . so its vehicle of expression – melody – in order to gain necessary satisfaction demands not an arbitrary ascent and descent through larger or smaller, consonant or dissonant intervals, but [motion that is] alternately rising or falling, moving easily or with difficulty in joy or pain like emotion itself.[197]

This belief in the absolute correlation of feeling and melodic trajectory had traction.[198] It was effectively reasserted in 1848 by Teutonius, who stated that "a rising melody always expresses and excites a growing intensity of feeling . . . whilst a falling one depicts a relaxation . . . from the climax of excitement";[199] and by Lobe[200] who argued further that stirrings in the "soul of our spiritual perception" are a linear wave play (*Wogenspiel*) that is

[196] Friedrich Kittler, *Gramophone, Film, Typewriter*, trans. Geoffrey Winthrop-Young and Michael Wutz (Stanford University Press, 1999), 82.

[197] "Denn so wie jedes Gefühl nicht auf gleicher Höhe lange verweilt, und wie es niemals innerlich rhythmisch unverbundene Sprünge macht . . . so fordert auch sein Ausdruck, die Melodie, wie aber auch um des nöthigen Wohlgefallens an dieser willen, ein nicht willkürliches Aus- und Absteigen durch größere oder kleinere, consonirende oder dissonirende Intervalle, sondern wie die Empfindung selbst abwechselnd steigt oder fällt, sich leicht oder mühsam in Freude oder Schmerz bewegt." Gustav von Schilling, "Melodie," *Encyclopädie der gesammten musikalischen Wissenschaften*, 644.

[198] As late as 1882, Riemann essentially repeats this definition in his dictionary. See "Melodie" in Riemann, *Musik-Lexikon* (Leipzig, 1882), 568a.

[199] Teutonius, "Letters to a Music Student: VI. Melody and Melodious Composition," *TMW* 50 (1848), 794.

[200] "[Eine Tonfolge] bleibt nicht auf gleichem Niveau, sie steigt von e bis h höher, und *kann* eine sich steigernde Empfindung analogisiren," in Lobe, "Aesthetische Briefe. Dritter Brief. *Die Tonfolge,*" *FBfM* 1 (1854), 328.

"alternately rising, sinking and lingering, now fast, violent . . . now slow, lethargically creeping and then rippling more narrowly." The metaphorical movements of a composer's soul "can and must mould themselves onto the [literal movements of the] tone sequence as faithfully as possible" he continues, "when they deliver their elementary contribution to the truth of musical expression."[201] But, for Lobe, this analogy is only capable of explaining the likeness, not of generating any self-recognition or empathy. In other words, it remained symbolic.[202]

Why not realist? Simply put, melodic realism could go too far, whether in the service of *das Häßliche* or indeed of any geometric semiosis. That theorists had begun to caution against incorporating direct realism into melodic expression indicates that it was a conceivable threat. Lobe himself argued that music could not truly express the real world: "Art remains art and can never become actuality," he retorts:

Full realism destroys art . . . no one actually *sings* his fury, his desperation . . . But if one could force a man actually to sing of his fury, his desperation, and one wanted – in order to be true to nature – to copy such singing exactly on the stage, everyone would rightly laugh at *such* natural realism. / Germans take *too little* heed of this.[203]

Yet claims for melodic realism encroached by other means. In 1880, the psychologist Edmund Gurney offered a Darwinian rationale for the sympathetic sensation of emotional rising and falling in terms of a learned response. Higher vocal registers are always used "to attract attention or to give force and wide reach to the utterance of vocal sound," he explains.[204]

---

[201] "die Regungen [erscheinen] in unserem Gemüth unserer geistigen Wahrnehmung im Ganzen als ein Wogenspiel . . . als ein Wechselsweises Heben, Senken und Verweilen, bald rasch, heftig . . . bald langsam, träge schleichend und dann geringere Kräuselungen nur auftreibend . . . jenes Steigen und Fallen und Verweilen der Regungen und Regungstheilchen der Gefühle aber kann und muß die Tonfolge überall so treue wie möglich verähnlichen, wenn sie ihren Elementarbeitrag zur Wahrheit des musikalischen Ausdrucks liefern soll." *Ibid.*, 330.

[202] Other, more nebulous orders of symbolism have been proposed, such as Alfred Cramer's claim for a structural link between the contours of calligraphic writing and melodic expression, even likening Wagnerian melody to cursive script with the argument that "melodic shapes could evoke voice because similar shapes had this effect in handwriting." Alfred Cramer, "Of Serpentina and Stenography: Shapes of Handwriting in Romantic Melody," *19th-Century Music* 30 (2006), 163.

[203] "Die Kunst bleibt Kunst und kann niemals Wirklichkeit werden. Volle Naturwahrheit vernichtet die Kunst . . . Kein Mensch *singt* in der Wirklichkeit seinen Zorn, seine Verzweiflung . . . Könnte man aber einen Menschen zwingen, in der Wirklichkeit seinen Zorn, seine Verzweiflung auszusingen und man wollte, um naturwahr zu werden, auf der Bühne einen so Singenden genau copiren, so würde Jedermann mit Recht über *solche* Naturwahrheit lachen. / Das beachten die Deutschen *zu wenig*." Lobe, "Vierter Brief. Deutsche Musik," *Musikalische Briefe*, 22–23.

[204] Edmund Gurney, *The Power of Sound* (London: Smith, Elder & Co., 1880), 140.

1.3 The modest wavy line ("V") to indicate Brangäne's scream in Wagner's *Orchesterpartitur* for *Tristan und Isolde*, NA A III h 7, p. 235. Reproduced by permission of the *Nationalarchiv der Richard-Wagner-Stiftung*, Bayreuth.

More developed claims linking melodic pitch and evolutionary context appear well into the twentieth century,[205] but it was Herbert Spencer's materialism from the 1850s that helped render such views plausible by claiming that music originated on just this basis, that the raw "musical" expression of high-pitched cries and yells were a response to noxious stimuli of the musculature.[206] And it is in this sense that, for Kittler, Wagner could allow Brangäne "to utter a scream whose notation cut straight through the score"[207] in a moment of totalizing realism, i.e. a "melody" that finally dared entirely to annul melody's symbolic form, while still maintaining its identity as an expressive utterance. In fact, Wagner did not actually write a descending wavy line to indicate this "piercing scream" (*greller Schrei*), rendering the seismographic register of emotion more conceptual, less literal. The symbol "V" (Figure 1.3) was a common notational shorthand for him and sits alongside his numerous other prescribed screams, wails, cries, and laughter (mostly unnotated), which, in *Parsifal*, turn melody's most literal, "ugly" realism into Kundry's characteristic mode of utterance: animalistic sounds that only humans can utter.[208]

[205] A prominent example is Arthur Edwards, who argued in 1956: "the fluctuation of sounds in the crude emotional vocalizations of primitive man had several characteristics which carried over naturally into the musical movements of tones. With an increase in intensity of emotional expression, the voice would ascend, and the speed quicken; conversely, with a decrease in intensity of emotional expression, the voice would descend and the speed slacken. This emotional wave-expression took on definite melodic patterns in primitive melodies and realistically recalled the savage shouts of joy or rage." Edwards, *The Art of Melody*, 140.

[206] Herbert Spencer, "The Origin and Function of Music" [1857], *Essays, Scientific, Political, and Speculative* (New York: D. Appleton & Co., 1907), 358–84.

[207] Kittler, *Gramophone, Film, Typewriter*, 23.

[208] See also Philip Friedheim's study of this phenomenon in Wagner's compositions, "Wagner and the Aesthetics of the Scream," *19th-Century Music* 7 (1983), 63–70.

But irrespective of the merits of Spencer's or Gurney's claims, pitch-continuous screaming epitomizes inarticulate expression, a form too crude, and ultimately had little to offer opera (or drama) beyond a momentary effect. Against such imprecision, hopes for the precise correlation of emotion and melodic shape fell to speech physiognomy as the alternative to plastic shape for approaching an Hugoean realism. The hope, specifically, was that by positing individual units of speech as metaphysical objects of utterance parallel to melodic expression, a *Gefühlsaesthetik* could be sharpened semantically by accessing impulses prior to their semantic utterance.

Some of the leading European music journals had carried articles on this linguistic turn in melodic theory. Two of the most important contributions to the discourse come from critics Stephan Schütze and Gustav Nauenburg. In 1830, Schütze had peddled the old line that "in declamation lies the nucleus of melody," but he cautioned readers of *Caecelia* that music should not blithely mirror declamation, but completely transform it into melody.[209] Drawing on the Jena Romantics' argument that through music, a far wider realm of feelings opens up than through language, Schütze believed that although melodic composition is outwardly structured by a text's physiognomy, it should "turn immediately to the inner stirring itself, and create the inspiration of heaven from this source, which the human heart transfigures."[210] While this lofty manifesto for pre-linguistic impulses remains a poetic abstraction, Schütze fleshes it out in terms of a compromise that would be echoed by a generation of aestheticians:

The art [of melodic composition] consists in bringing each accent into a melodic course [*Gang*] so that a really beautiful melody results, so that it sounds as though the text had only given the opportunity for a beautiful melody, while the feeling therein believes only to be examining the text, and to understand it completely. Strictly, the text is never reproduced in the music, rather only the feeling on which it is based.[211]

Written without any music examples, such rhetoric remained defensively abstract. The postulate of subvocal feelings that acquire their outward form

---

[209] "*[I]n der Deklamation liegt der Keim der Melodie.*" Stephan Schütze, "Über Gefühl und Ausdruck in der Musik" *Caecelia* 12 (1830), 253.

[210] "[Ein rechter Meister wird] sich lieber unmittelbar an die innern Regungen selbst wenden, und aus dieser Quelle die Eingebungen des Himmels schöpfen, die das Herz des Menschen verklären." *Ibid.*, 254.

[211] "Die Kunst besteht eben darin, Accente so in einen melodischen Gang zu bringen, dass eine wirklich schöne Melodie entsteht, so dass es klingt, als ob der Text nur Gelegenheit zu einer schönen Melodie gegeben hätte, während doch das Gefühl darin nur den Text zu vernehmen, und ihn so erst ganz zu verstehen glaubt. Streng genommen wird eigentlich nie der Text in der Musik wiedergegeben, sondern nur das Gefühl, das demselben zum Grunde liegt." *Ibid.*

in German poetry would prove the fulcrum around which the debate over German melodic expression turned. Poetic metaphor did a lot of heavy lifting in making such claims persuasive, though, as Gustav Nauenburg, the last of our melodic witnesses, illustrates in the *Neue Zeitschrift* from 1843:

> Real German vocal music is a fragrant bridal gown, which the composer wraps around the genius of language; where the musical garment nestles *supplely* up to the body of speech, there *singable* melody has melded with the poem, there melodic expression runs *parallel* with declamatory expression, *there the basis for real German vocal melody is to be found.*[212]

By placing a dress code of text loyalty at the heart of a melodic theory, Nauenburg could argue pragmatically that vocal composers simply need to be taught text-emphasis just as instrumental composers are taught harmony and counterpoint. But by comparison with Schütze, this was simplistic, deceptively impractical, and hardly new.

The concept was in fact borrowed from dramatic theorists, such as Heinrich Theodor Rötscher, who, only two years earlier, had posited a direct correlation between the shape of the melodic waveform emitted by verbal speech and the quality of emotional effect perceived, that is, effectively an emotional seismograph for language:

> *Beauty* first permeates the expression of human speech when the tone in itself is able to generate different vibrations which, notwithstanding the purity of sound and word accent, resound in our ear, and through their rising and sinking move the emotions in equal alternation. This is the musical element of tonal formation [*Tonbildung*]: *height and depth, slowness and rapidity, strength and weakness.*[213]

The centrality of language here, the linguistic turn, is indicative of the strengthening bond between a culture of literary *Bildung* within German self-identity, and is prognostic of the future directions for melodic theory during the 1850s. To be sure, the nationalist argument also allowed German critics to rationalize a flawless skepticism at Italy's "content-less" musical

---

[212] "Echt deutsche Gesangmusik ist ein duftiges Brautgewand, welches der Tondichter um den Genius der Sprache hüllt; wo sich das Tongewand *geschmeidig* an den Sprachkörper anschmiegt, da ist *sangbare* Melodie dem Gedichte entquollen, da läuft der Melodieausdrück *parallel* mit dem Declamations-ausdrucke, *da ist die Basis für echt deutsche Vocal-Melodik gefunden.*" Nauenburg, "Kritische Mischlinge," *NZfM* 18 (January 26, 1843), 30.

[213] "Die *Schönheit* dringt erst in den Ausdruck der menschlichen Rede, wenn der Ton in sich selbst verschiedene Schwingungen zu erzeugen vermag, welche unbeschadet der Reinheit des Lauts und des Wortaccents an unser Ohr klingen und durch sein Auf- und Absteigen die Empfindung in gleichen Wechsel versetzen. Dies ist das musikalische Element der Tonbildung; *die Höhe und Tiefe, die Langsamkeit und Schnelligkeit, die Stärke und Schwäche.*" Heinrich Theodor Rötscher, *Die Kunst der dramatischen Darstellung*, 3 vols. (Berlin: Wilhelm Thome, 1841), 1: 137–38.

style that seemingly used poetic text only as a "starting point."[214] (Schumann quipped you could recognize an Italian melody even before it started.) If the search for semantic melodic shapes and intervals had failed, the tentative coalescing of text and melodic line opened up the possibility for nascent disciplines such as *Philologie* (historical linguistics) to enter the fray as fresh nourishment for those anticipating the establishment of a more precise melodic expression.

* * *

We have tracked a shift in the discourse on melody from "plastic" form to linguistic physiognomy; from (classical) beauty to the "relative" beauty of characteristic shapes; from a plastically generic, to the dramatically specific form. Following the decisive, reactionary break of post-Hegelian German aestheticians with the prestige of Italianate idiom, the two forms of positive data they drew upon as the basis for melodic structure were the image of linear, seismographic emotion and text physiognomy. Both remained vaguely defined, however, leading Brendel to complain in 1845 that even the better music critics are idle, and allow "Italian meaninglessness" (*italiänische Sinnlosigkeiten*) to dominate German theaters without once finding it necessary "to develop the laws of dramatic music."[215] Beyond the interrelation of melodic theory and linguistics, the stakes underlying the enterprise of systematizing melodic expression were high enough to subject Wagner to ridicule for his "illogical," incomprehensible fragmentation of melodic material. They were predicated, needless to say, on the assumption that melody rather than harmony is the vehicle of choice for communicating comprehensible emotional experience in operatic scenarios. For German critics, the mid-century debate over Wagner's melodic material can therefore be construed not so much as to whether it was "beautiful" or why it was "ugly," but the extent to which it could be understood.

---

[214] "Anknüpfungspunct." Brendel, "Zur Einleitung," 7. While many Italian composers did of course seek to couple text and music closely, and rejected their German labels as cavalier text setters, the view that they disregarded textual subtleties was catalyzed by the fact that foreign opera was frequently performed in translation within the German states. Under such circumstances, the integrity of syllabic enunciation was perilously susceptible in performance to disconnection from the metrics and pitch assignment of a musical line. As Simon Maguire points out, one of Bellini's teachers, Girolamo Crescenti (1762–1846), writes in the preface to his treatise *Raccolta di essercizi* (1811): "il canto deve essere un'imitazione del discorso" and closes with the observation that: "Good taste in singing lies solely in the expression of the words, and in those appropriate inflections that are mentioned in paragraph 8." Cited in Maguire, *Vincenzo Bellini and the Aesthetics of the Early Nineteenth-Century Italian Opera* (New York and London: Garland, 1989), 45.

[215] "doch hatte [die bessere Kritik] gar nicht einmal nötig, die Gesetze dramatischer Musik zu entwickeln." Brendel, "Zur Einleitung," 6.

2 | *Melodielehre?*

I feel it, and yet can't fathom it;
can't retain it – and yet can't forget it;
and were I to grasp the whole thing, – I couldn't
   measure it!
But then, how should I measure that
which seemed immeasurable to me?
No rule would fit here,
and yet there was no error in it.

Ich fühl's und kann's nicht versteh'n; –
kann's nicht behalten, – doch auch nicht vergessen;
und fass' ich es ganz, kann ich's nicht messen!

Doch wie wollt' ich auch fassen,
was unermesslich mir schien?
Kein' Regel wollte da passen,
und war doch kein Fehler drin.

Hans Sachs, *Die Meistersinger*[1]

> The genius does not know himself how he has come by his ideas; and he
> has not the power to devise the like at pleasure or in accordance with a
> plan, and to communicate it to others in precepts that will enable them to
> produce similar products.

Immanuel Kant[2]

Lightning bolts

Goethe said it first: the ideas of a creative genius are as bolts of lightning
whose heavenly origin remains unknown, but whose otherworldly brilliance
illuminates our earthly travails. His oft-quoted letter from June 6, 1810
speaks of Beethoven's music in this vein:

> To think of teaching him would be an insolence even in one with greater insight
> than mine, since he has the guiding light of his genius, which frequently illuminates
> his mind like a stroke of lightning while we sit in darkness and scarcely suspect the
> direction from which daylight will break upon us.[3]

---

[1] Act 2, scene 3 of *Die Meistersinger von Nürnberg*.   [2] Kant, *Critique of Judgment*, 151.
[3] "[I]hn belehren zu wollen, wäre wohl selbst von einsichtigern, als ich, Frevel, da ihm sein
Genie vorleuchtet, und ihm oft wie durch einen Blitz Hellung giebt, wo wir im Dunkel sitzen und
kaum ahnen von welcher Seite der Tag anbrechen werde." J. W. von Goethe to Bettina von
Brentano, June 6, 1810, *Goethes Briefwechsel mit einem Kinde* (Berlin: Ferdinand Dümmler,
1835), 202.

With all the claims for sublime natural power, instantaneous invention, and unpredictability this simile projects, the flipside of such appreciation is the blinding "darkness" of pedagogy, of knowing that systematic learning is "insolent" in the presence of musical genius.

Of course, the poetic equation of light with knowledge had informed French Enlightenment projects since the mid-eighteenth century; by blurring the differentiated metaphors of sun and lightning, and thus the creative sources of systematic knowledge and immediate inspiration, the model of genial invention to which Goethe alludes became ambiguous for a generation of would-be lightning rods. (By 1838, Liszt's inference of "momentary flashes" could refer to either.)[4] How could you know when lightning will strike, or if it will choose you? Would it be better first to absorb the sun's "daylight" through disciplined music-theoretical study and later hope melodic lightning will strike in your hour of need? At the other end of the century, Nietzsche confirmed such occult fears when he described the ecstatic power of inspiration with Goethe's simile, but emphasized there can be no wilful candidacy in the act:

If one had the slightest residue of superstition left in one's system, one could hardly reject altogether the idea that one is merely incarnation, merely mouthpiece, merely a medium of overpowering forces. The concept of revelation, in the sense that suddenly, with indescribable certainty and subtlety, something becomes *visible*, audible, something that shakes one to the last depths and throws one down, that merely describes the facts. One hears, one does not seek; one accepts, one does not ask who gives; like lightning, a thought flashes up, with necessity, without hesitation regarding its form, – I never had any choice.[5]

Given the neurosis surrounding melodic expression in Germany that we saw in Chapter 1, it was not merely problematic that John Gregory's classic assertion – "musical genius consists in the invention of melody"[6] – still held sway a century on. "[Melody] is a gift of nature" Berlioz shrugged in 1837.[7] More than ever, it was melody's apparent autogenesis that poetic commentators equated with those mysterious origins that fulfilled a primary criterion for

[4] Franz Liszt, *Artist's Journey: lettres d'un bachelier ès musique, 1835–1841*, trans. Charles Suttoni (University of Chicago Press, 1989), 66.
[5] Friedrich Nietzsche, "Also Sprach Zarathustra," in *Philosophical Writings*, ed. Reinhold Grimm and Caroline Molina y Vedia, trans. Walter Kaufmann and R. J. Hollingdale (New York: Continuum, 1995), 219.
[6] John Gregory, *A Comparative View of the State and Faculties of Man with those of the Animal World*, 4th edn. (London: J. Dodsley, 1767), 148.
[7] "C'est un don de la nature." Berlioz, "De la musique en général I" [1837], *Revue et gazette musicale de Paris* IV (1837), 407a.

Kantian genius, otherwise construed as "that innate mental disposition (*ingenium*) *through which* nature gives the rule to art."[8] At stake, then, is the function of music theory in its pedagogical application with respect to melody as a product of nature. That constituted a stark oxymoron.

Melody's special status rested precisely on the long-standing belief that it could not be taught, as well as the fact that – in liturgical chant repertories – it sat at the fountainhead of Western musical practice itself. Eighteenth-century theorists such as Daube, Riepel, and Koch had addressed the design of melodic units at the phrasal level, but this was remote from the stylistic and expressive demands of German opera in the new century.[9] While only a few nineteenth-century theorists broached the prestigious but inherently thorny topic of melodic pedagogy, the pressing need brought its own neologism: *Melodik*, first defined by Gottfried Weber in 1821, referred to the teaching of voice-leading within a succession of notes.[10] The controversy of *Melodielehre* came to a head in the infamous quarrel about compositional pedagogy between A. B. Marx and G. W. Fink in 1841–42.[11] While Fink maintained the traditionalist view that *General-Baß* (thoroughbass, incorporating harmony and counterpoint) sufficed for training composers, Marx sought dedicated studies in melody, harmony, rhythm, counterpoint, and form. "One should at least hope now to find a theory of melody," he vociferated in 1841, "for melody is the simpler substance and precedes and is primary to harmony, which cannot form an artwork by itself, as melody is famously able to do (e.g. in unaccompanied song). But a theory of melody is lacking altogether."[12] The hope was not, therefore, that young composers might learn their craft exclusively by using a textbook, an unlikely scenario for any period, but that such studies could provide a modern understanding of melodic function and working. Uncertainty about the place and function of *Melodielehre* within music theory doubtless contributed to the difficulties of outlining a persuasive melodic

---

[8] Kant, *Critique of Judgment*, §. 46.

[9] Regardless of stylistic differentiation, Thomas Grey insightfully links the move from smaller to larger melodic units in eighteenth-century theory to Wagner's conception of form as an expansion of melody (*Ausdehnung der Melodie*). See Grey, *Wagner's Musical Prose*, 274.

[10] Gottfried Weber, *Versuch einer geordneten Theorie der Tonsetzkunst*, 4 vols. (Mainz: Schott, 1824), 1: 136.

[11] The most comprehensive study of this is still Kurt-Erich Eicke, *Der Streit zwischen Adolf Bernhard Marx und Gottfried Wilhelm Fink um die Kompositionslehre* (Regensburg: Gustav Bosse, 1966). See also Scott Burnham's translation of Marx, *Musical Form in the Age of Beethoven* (Cambridge University Press, 1997), 1–34.

[12] "Nun sollte man wenigstens hoffen, die Lehre von der Melodie zu finden, da Melodie die einfachere Substanz ist und der Harmonie vor- und vorangeht, die für sich allein kein Kunstwerk bilden kann, wie es die Melodie (z. B. Im Naturgesang) bekanntlich vermag. Aber – die Lehre von der Melodie fehlt überall," in *Die alte Musiklehre im Streit in unserer Zeit* (Leipzig: Breitkopf & Härtel, 1841), 16.

theory. Quantitatively, *Harmonielehren* dwarfed their melodic counterparts during the nineteenth century, indicating that Marx's reversal of hierarchy proved more problematic than perhaps it seemed at first. Eyeing the historical failure of *Melodielehre*, Carl Dahlhaus could argue comfortably in 1972 that it had been an "error" to regard melody as "elementary and fundamental" to music theory, that such a belief rested on a restriction of the concept of harmony (echoing Hindemith),[13] and tended to invalidate harmonically oriented approaches to the study of counterpoint with the spurious logic that counterpoint is a polyphony of melodies and therefore "would have, for its part, to be founded on a theory of melody."[14] Instead, the teaching of counterpoint is far better suited to *Harmonik*, he reflected, and always assumes a harmonic basis.

Whereas *General-Baß* had served as the foundation of compositional pedagogy since a cluster of treatises explicated *la règle de l'octave* in the early eighteenth century, neither harmony nor counterpoint formed the central category of musical expression a century later. "In song ... the listener's attention should not be wasted on harmonic art," explained Friedrich August Kanne, the leading critic of the *Allgemeine musikalische Zeitung* in 1821.[15] Yet as late as 1851 Emil Grimm (younger brother to the Brothers Grimm) could still caricature the "musical madness of the nineteenth century" (Figure 2.1) with a regime of merciless schooling in *General-Baß* for girls, seemingly from cradle to social eligibility. In contrast to such comfortable satire, the seemingly unbridgeable gulf between idea and exemplification in *Melodielehre* meant that almost all attempts were cast defensively, and begin with nervous provisos that they could not open a gateway to genius.[16] *Melodie* had become radically overdetermined – overloaded with expectations of expressive truth, emotional intensity, and natural form – and it is perhaps no coincidence that Marx and Johann Christian Lobe both chose to use the synonym *Tonfolge* in their respective *Treatise on Musical Composition* (1837) and "Aesthetic Letters"

---

[13] Paul Hindemith had argued in 1937 that it is "not practicable" (*nicht ausführbar*) to construct melody without harmonic grounding. See *Unterweisung im Tonsatz: Theoretische Teil* (Mainz: Schott's Söhne, 1937), 206.

[14] Carl Dahlhaus and L. U. Abraham, *Melodielehre* (Cologne: Hans Greig, 1972), 11.

[15] "beym Gesang ... darf also die Aufmerksamkeit des Hörers nicht durch Verschwendung harmonischer Künste abgezogen werden." A. F. Kanne, "Der Zauber der Tonkunst," *Allgemeine musikalische Zeitung, mit besonderer Rücksicht auf den österreichischen Kaiserstaat* 69 (August 29, 1821), 547.

[16] Reicha's *Traité* calls explicitly for three unteachable attributes – "perfect feeling, an exquisite taste, and finally genius" – as the prerequisites to avoid melodic monotony, and Teutonius declared openly that "you cannot expect ... to see me develop a complete system or theory of melody, or to put down certain abstract rules. Such a thing is out of the question." See Reicha, *Treatise on Melody*, 64; Teutonius, "Melody and Melodious Combination," 774–75.

2.1 Emil Grimm, *Musikalischer Wahnsinn des 19ten Jahrhundert* (1851) © Museumslandschaft Hessen Kassel.

(1854) when addressing the topic. Back in 1821, Kanne's bathos highlighted the gulf between poetic description and music-theoretical category:

Melody is . . . [i] the inner thread through which the human creative sprit forms a soulful web, invisible to the eyes, that glides over the enraptured ears with its magic world, and penetrates the soul with such omnipotence that the outside world surrounding it disappears before it, and lets itself delightedly bear part of the tonal vibrations through all pain and bliss of the earth. It is [ii] the language of the spirit that finds its echo in every disposition, although it will not at all be understood by reason – that rouses all feelings from their slumber, and simultaneously wraps the sharply seeing eye of reason in mist – it is [iii] the ideal and invisible embodiment of all feelings and passions because on reviving their first breath, the related spiritual elements are awoken in the souls of the listeners – it is [iv] the successive wave play [*Wellenspiel*] of all lines of beauty that float on the coexisting basis of harmony, on the fixed construction of its inner organism – *it is (for mere musicians) the stepwise progress of tones according to the rules of beauty.*[17]

---

[17] "Die Melodie ist . . . der geistige Faden, durch den der menschliche Schöpfergeist das seelenvolle Gewebe bildet, das unsichtbar dem Auge, mit seiner Zauberwelt vor dem entzückten Ohre vorübergleitet, und mit solcher Allgewalt die Seele durchdringt, dass die sie umgebende Aussenwelt vor ihr verschwindet, und sie sich entzückt auf den Schwingen der Töne mittragen lässt, durch alle Schmerzen und Wonnen der Erde. Es ist die Geistersprache, die in dem Gemüthe allen Wiederhall findet, indessen sie vom Verstande gar nicht begriffen wird – die alle Gefühle aus dem Schlummer ruft, und die scharfblickenden Augen des Verstandes gleichsam in Nebel hüllt – es ist die ideale, und unsichtbare Verkörperung aller Gefühle und Leidenschaften, weil bey Belebung ihrer ersten Hauche schon die verwandten geistigen Elemente in der Seele des Hörenden

With four poetic metaphors stacked against one bland theoretical description, the gap between "melody" and *Melodik* was unmistakable.

As one might expect, the exclusionist cult of genius garnered a number of detractors as well as a majority of blithe advocates. Anton Reicha initiated a limited succession of theorists who countermanded the aesthetics of mystery in composition by emphasizing the constructedness of melodies, alongside the industry and training composers needed to produce them. Table 2.1 lists the principal German contributors up to 1862, cites their definitions of melody, and gives the musical elements they believed to be fundamental to understanding and teaching melody.

But a counterimpulse against these attempts, nourished on an aesthetics of inspiration, invalidated systematic attempts at melodic theory. A representative voice in this regard was the Königsberg-based Kapellmeister Eduard Sobolewski, who affirmed in 1855 that "*Melody cannot be taught* ... We may criticize it here and there, but we cannot improve it, or it is no melody."[18] To support this judgment, Sobolewski relates a cautionary tale of an aspiring composer in Dresden – with unintentional overtones of Wagner – who was deficient in melody, and who sold everything he owned to pay for lessons and advice, begging every composer who visited the city to remedy his affliction: "Nothing, however, availed him," Sobolewski concludes bleakly.[19]

The skepticism underpinning Sobolewski's tale, i.e. the hierarchical division of *poiesis* into unthinking inspiration and conscious artifice, goes back at least to Plato's *Ion*. While its full history cannot be traced here, it rests on a somewhat schematic opposition between divine power and human artifice, where genius is merely a vessel through which celestial agency channels artistic inspiration.[20]

---

erwachen – es ist das *successive* Wellenspiel aller Schönheitslinien die auf der coexistirenden Basis der Harmonie, auf dem festen Baue ihres inneren Organismus dahinschweben – es ist (für blosse Musiker) die secundenweise Fortschreitung der Töne, nach den Gesetzen der Schönheit." Kanne, "Der Zauber der Tonkunst," *AmZ* 64, 507. Emphasis added.

[18] Eduard Sobolewski, "Reactionary Letters II," *TMW* 33 (1855), 45.

[19] Sobolewski, "Reactionary Letters I," *TMW* 33 (1855), 19.

[20] Plato's Socratic dialogue *Ion* sees a rhapsode (actor) interrogated by Socrates about his recitations of Homer. Divine inspiration or possession, the latter deduces, are the origins of all beautiful poetry; the rules of art, by contrast, are only a means of deception, of expressing something disingenuously: "[T]he poet is a light and winged and holy thing, and there is no invention in him until he has been inspired and is out of his senses, and the mind is no longer in him: when he has not attained to this state, he is powerless and is unable to utter his oracles ... for *not by art does the poet sing, but by power divine ... God takes away the minds of poets*, and uses them as his ministers ... in order that we who hear them may know them to be speaking not of themselves who utter these priceless words in a state of unconsciousness, but that *God himself is the speaker, and that through them he is conversing with us.*" See Plato, *Ion*, trans. Benjamin Jowett at: http://classics.mit.edu/Plato/ion. Emphasis added.

Table 2.1 Nineteenth-century theoretical approaches to *Melodik*

Theorist	Publication	Definition	Fundamental *Melodik*
A. Reicha (tr. Czerny)	*Traité de mélodie* (1814)	Melody is a succession of tones, just as harmony is a succession of chords, or as discourse is a succession of words[a]	Musical rhythm; "symmetry of ideas" as the basis for periodic structure
F. A. Kanne	"Der Zauber der Tonkunst," *AmZ* 68 (1821)	Melody (for mere musicians) is the stepwise progress of tones according to the rules of beauty[b]	Wave motion (*Wellenspiel*) of rising and falling lines
A. B. Marx	*Die Lehre von der Komposition* (1837)	A tonally and rhythmically ordered series of tones is called melody[c]	major scale; rest – motion – rest
J. C. Lobe	*Compositions-lehre* (1844); "Aesthetische Briefe," *FBfM* 1 (1854)	[Melody is a] sequence of tones in a certain order, relation, symmetry[d]	Thematic working (*thematische Arbeit*) within 8-measure periods
Teutonius	"Letters to a Music Student: Melodies and Melodious Combination," *TMW* 47 (1848)	Melody is a succession of different sounds expressing a certain feeling or sensation in a beautiful form[e]	Scale; truth of expression corresponding to a particular psychological character
R. Wagner	*Oper und Drama* (1851)	Melody is the redemption of the poet's endlessly conditioned thought into a deep-felt consciousness of emotion's highest freedom[f]	Root syllables; vowels; breath; assonance and alliteration in archaic poetry; poetic–musical period
J. Raff	*Die Wagnerfrage* (1854)	Melody is a crookedly inflected line in space and time simultaneously[g]	Speech inflection in tandem with consonant / dissonant intervals
F. Geyer	*Musikalische Compositions-lehre* (1862)	Melody is a succession of tones governed by rhythmic, scalic, and harmonic order[h]	Rhythmicized scale (cf. Marx)

[a] Reicha, *Treatise on Melody*, 9.

[b] "[Melodie] ist (für blosse Musiker) die secundenweise Fortschreitung der Töne, nach den Gesetzen der Schönheit." A. F. Kanne, "Der Zauber der Tonkunst," *AmZ* 64 (1821): 507.

[c] A. B. Marx, *School of Composition*, 4th edn., trans. Augustus Wehrhan (London: Robert Cocks and Co., 1852), 1: 21.

[d] J. C. Lobe, "Aesthetische Briefe. Dritter Brief: Tonfolge," *FBfM* 1 (1854): 326.

[e] Teutonius, "Letters to a Music Student," *TMW* 44 (1848): 774.

[f] "Die Melodie ist die Erlösung des unendlich bedingten dichterischen Gedankens zum tiefempfundenen Bewußtsein höchster Gefühlsfreiheit." Wagner, SSD 4: 142. Cf. PW 2: 281.

[g] "Die Melodie ist eine krumme inflexionsvolle Linie in Raum und Zeit zugleich." Joachim Raff, *Die Wagnerfrage* (Brunswick: Vieweg, 1854), 58.

[h] "Jedenfalls ist sie ein Aufeinanderfolge von Tonen. Doch wird derjenige . . . bald genug innewerden, dass hierbei in vieler Hinsicht Ordnung herrschen müsse, wie auch, welche andere Einflüsse geltend werden. Der Rhythmus ist das Erste . . . der Tonleiter . . . ist das Zweite, . . . Harmonie . . ., dies ist das Dritte." F. Geyer, *Musikalische Compositions-Lehre* (Berlin: A. Vogel & Co., 1862), 15.

Even into the 1850s – ostensibly encroaching on a post-Romantic age in which Jochen Schmidt finds a proliferation of cracks in the history of the *Genie-Gedanke*[21] – this paradigm continued to lay siege to the poetic imagination. It is precisely a clairvoyant state of altered consciousness, for instance, that allows Eduard Mörike's Mozart – in *Mozart auf der Reise nach Prag* (1855) – to conceive a melody for Zerlina (in *Don Giovanni*) while simultaneously stealing Edenic fruit from an orange grove in an instance of blatantly adjusted biblical symbolism.[22] Without delving into the cobwebbed contradictions of contemporary writing on genius,[23] the nodal point in this discussion, that which fueled the inhibiting factor for a pragmatic approach to melodic pedagogy, was the inverse of unconscious invention, namely paralyzing *self-consciousness*, the burden of reflecting – in solitude – on one's self-awareness as an impudent double, all the while being consciously aware of the idealist mantra that melody could not truly be invented through conscious awareness.

Explanations for this logical bind relied on the incompatibility of categories of activity and observation. For Hegel's dialectic, the condition of being trapped observing oneself in the act of observation "is a [mental] battle … a life and death struggle" that splits apart orders of experience and perception.[24] Analytical psychologists would clarify during the 1830s that two states of mind – direct experience (inspiration) and assimilative monitoring (theorizing scrutiny) – cannot be simultaneous, and that the one must necessarily inhibit the other,[25] while more poetic commentators had addressed the tricky

---

[21] "In der nachromantischen Zeit ist die Geschichte des Genie-Gedankens voller Verwerfungen." Jochen Schmidt, *Die Geschichte des Genie-Gedankens in der deutschen Literatur, Philosophie und Politik*, 3rd edn. (Heidelberg: Universitätsverlag Winter, 2004), 2: 63.

[22] In Mörike's narrative, Mozart: "was seized by an idea, which he immediately and eagerly pursued. Unthinkingly, he again grasped the orange … He saw this happen and yet did not see it; indeed so far did the distraction of his creative mood take him as he sat there twirling the scented fruit from side to side under his nose, while his lips silently toyed with a melody, beginning and continuing and beginning again, that he finally, instinctively … cut through the yellow globe of the orange from top to bottom." In a reflexive move, Mörike even scripts a jest about Mozart's Edenic fall in a paradisiacal grove (p. 19), but the manual "mischief" here could just as well be writing down the freshly captured tune as stealing the fruit, presenting an ambiguity that links Mozart's theft structurally to his creativity in a resounding endorsement of the divinely inspired genius model. See Eduard Mörike, *Mozart's Journey to Prague and a Selection of Poems*, trans. David Luke (London: Penguin, 2003), 17–18, 31–32.

[23] The classic account of the historical *Genie-Gedanke* within German-speaking territories remains Jochen Schmidt, *Die Geschichte des Genie-Gedankens in der deutschen Literatur, Philosophie und Politik*.

[24] Hegel, *Philosophy of Mind*, trans. A. V. Miller (Oxford: Clarendon Press, 1971), §431–32.

[25] See the review-article "Mr Mill's Analysis of the Mind," in *The Westminster Review* 36 (1869), 148–79, here 165. The book under review is James Mill's *Analysis of the Phenomena of the Human Mind*, ed. John Stuart Mill (London, 1869), which was originally published in 1829 (2 vols.), but reprinted by the author's son in 1869.

specter of a (Fichtean) mind only too aware of itself thinking by arguing that to become capable of beautiful art the mind must first pass through an infinity of consciousness, which is to say, rendering man either "a marionette or a god."[26] Thus, in the same year as Mörike's novella, Wagner was not alone in wishing that "I could have lost my private consciousness, and hence my *consciousness in general*, in that refining fire."[27] This broad condition was witness to a uniquely Romantic exploration of what Geoffrey Hartman has called "the dangerous passageways of [an artist's] maturation,"[28] and speaks to a fundamental condition of aesthetic modernity. The knowledge that even asking the question of how to write melody would dispel any chance that it could be achieved unselfconsciously was a matter of some despair. It was against this despair that composers and melodic theorists staked their art and, to some extent, their sanity.

Following the vigorous melodic debates of the 1850s, the *Neue Berliner Musik-Zeitung* carried an article by the Berlin-based professor of music, Flodoard Geyer, that asked just that question. Boldly entitled "Can and Should Melody be Taught?" it parodied the usual skepticism by lampooning Johann Mattheson's antique sentiment (from 1739) that melody is given "only through God's grace,"[29] labeling him as "one of the first satirists, a delightful rapier wit and main cock, an original, a 'Bonmotist.'"[30] While

[26] Heinrich von Kleist, *Selected Writings*, trans. and ed. David Constantine (Indianapolis and Cambridge: Hacket Publishing, 1997), 412.

[27] Wagner to Liszt, June 7, 1855, Weimar, in SB 7: 205.

[28] Geoffrey H. Hartman, "Romanticisim and Anti-Self-Consciousness," in *Romanticism and Consciousness: Essays in Criticism*, ed. Harold Bloom (New York: Norton, 1970), 47.

[29] "Melodiker werde nur von Gottes Gnaden," quoted in Flodoard Geyer, "Kann und soll die Melodie gelehrt werden?" 321.

[30] "Mattheson in Ehren: es ist einer der ersten Satiriker, ein ergötzlicher Klopffechter und Haupthahn, ein Original, ein Bonmotist," in *Ibid.*, 322. Geyer was evidently unsympathetic to Mattheson's treatise on the topic. Two years before penning his more famous *Der vollkommene Capellmeister*, Mattheson had published a treatise entitled *Kern melodischer Wissenschaft* (Hamburg: Christian Herold, 1737) with detailed chapters on a variety of aspects pertaining to melodic composition: intervallic construction; differentiation of style (church, theater, chamber); melodic character (light, lively, clear, flowing); distinctions between vocal and instrumental melody; the rhetoric and syntax of melodic speech; melodic differentiation by genre (both vocal and instrumental); and the "dispositon, development and ornamentation" ("Einrichtung, Ausarbeitung und Zierde ... *dispositio*, *elaboratio*, and *decoratio*") of linear phrases. The inclusion of three letters of support entitled "Gültige Zeugnisse über die jüngste Matthesonisch-Musicalische Kern-Schrift" as an appendix to editions from 1738 onwards suggests that Mattheson's attempt to codify melody in all its elements met with a certain amount of resistance. At fifty-six, and with fifteen music-theoretical publications behind him, Mattheson's decision to append letters of support from Johann Paul Kuntzen and Johann Adolph Scheibe (as well that of an aristocrat from the Schleswig-Holstein court) to his treatise is perhaps indicative of its controversial status. Though aspects of this earlier treatise on melody were later incorporated into Mattheson's "Von der wircklichen Verfertigung einer Melodie" from *Vollkommene Capellmeister*, it is noteworthy that he

Geyer – a student of Marx and C. F. Zelter – actually argues for the possibility of systematically teaching "melodic form" through model-based studies of counterpoint and sonata movements, he summarizes the widespread doubt surrounding his titular question:

Surely, readers want to answer with great unanimity: "No; melody cannot be taught! If it could – then we would at least like you to show us how we could write something similar to, say, Schubert's 'Lob der Thränen' or an andante like that of Beethoven's C-minor symphony. We would readily pay large sums for this skill!"[31]

When Geyer's satire later extends specifically to the melodists of the recently formulated *neudeutsche Schule*, however, it acquires a more mocking tone as an ironic dialogue between the learner and the learned:

STUDENT: Look, there is little Müller; he composed such a nice Waltz. I really want to compose a Waltz just like that for my small cousin . . .
TEACHER: [D]on't you know yet, or don't you believe me: Melody comes from God's grace! . . . Melody cannot and should not be taught now or ever. Some have tried it – this Marx, this Lobe and now even this Geyer – but the desire to teach has had the opposite effect and the whole "music of the future" of our present age is completely devoid of melody. The music is without melody in spite of the fact that one teaches melody. Heaven forbid . . . that it may ever become so with us.[32]

Such parody is accurate in a double sense: the New Germans were criticized with remarkable consistency – Wagner in particular – for an inability to invent melody; in this, Geyer's "teacher" is not merely satirical, becoming an ironic parody in stating exactly what his author intends to say.

states: "es sey fast unmöglich, gewisse Regeln davon [about composing melody] zu geben," in Mattheson, *Der Vollkommene Capellmeister*, ed. Friederike Ramm (Kassel: Bärenreiter, 1999), 219.

[31] "möchten freilich mit grosser Einmüthigkeit die Leser wohl antworten: 'Nein; die Melodie kann nicht gelehrt werden! Könnte sie es – dann wünschten auch wir wenigstens uns zeigen zu lassen, wie wir so Aehnliches, als z. B. Lob der Thränen von Schubert oder ein Andante, wie das der C-moll-Symphonie Beethoven's schaffen könnten. Wir wollten das gern theuer bezahlen!'" See Geyer, "Kann und soll die Melodie gelehrt werden?," 321.

[32] "'Sehen Sie, da ist der kleine Müller, der hat einen so netten Walzer geschrieben. Ich möchte doch gar zu gerne auch einen solchen Walzer für meine kleine Cousine componieren...' weisst Du denn noch nicht oder glaubst Du mir nicht: Melodiker ist ja von Gottes Gnaden! . . . Die Melodie kann und soll nun und nimmermehr Jemand lehren. Es haben zwar Einige versucht – dieser Marx, dieser Lobe und nun dieser Geyer, – aber das Lehrenwollen hat gerade den entgegensetzten Erfolg gehabt und die ganze gegenwärtige Zukunftsmusik ist der Melodie vollkommen baar. Die Musik ist trotzdem, dass man Melodie lehrt, ohne Melodie. Gott behüte . . . so soll es mit uns nimmermehr werden!'," *Ibid.*, 338.

What, then, was the solution to the problem of inhibiting self-consciousness and melody's putative autogenesis? In the end, it rests on an epistemological shift between thought as disembodied imagination, and quantifiable, material substance. Discourses on the materiality of melodic invention typically involved two beliefs: that plastic melodic shape is a crafted, constructed object; and that the process of composition is cognitive and, to some extent, determined by physical and electro-chemical forces. These beliefs were not mutually dependent. Melody as an ideal construct of the listener was entirely different to the crafting of a musical line *qua* material shape, as Kanne made clear in 1821; and the task of modern melodic theorists was principally to *objectify* or desubjectify melody without annulling its poetic content, to render it unthinkingly systematic so that it functioned like "a marionette or a god" – flowing from an absence or totality of consciousness – both unaware or self-forgetful of its coming into being and yet directed unwittingly by an background agency of knowledge. In light of this, the present chapter pursues three aims: to examine the ways in which creative thought, and melody in particular, could be objectified or otherwise rendered material; to counterpoint the nineteenth-century residue of earlier philosophical ideals of originality and natural genius against the compositional aspirations of music theorists during the 1830s and 1840s; and to interrogate – among others – the two chief theorists of the *Vormärz*, Marx and Lobe, through their responses to the problem of *Melodik* and their attempts to retool German musicians with melodic capability during a period heavily stigmatized for its lack of melodic beauty. This chapter is not therefore a survey of "how it was done," how pedagogical approaches might potentially relate to actual compositional practice in the nineteenth century. It is a study of ideas; specifically, the shift between conceptions of melody as an intangible and tangible phenomenon.

While the transition to a fully "desubjectified" melody would ultimately fail, the enterprise of rationalizing melodic content sheds light on the broader scene of music pedagogy as it adapted to the shifting philosophical ground of the 1840s and 1850s. The Janus-faces of theorists such as Lobe – looking back to eighteenth-century theories of mechanical invention while anticipating a post-Romantic age of materialism – has some resonance even today in the implicitly wide-ranging reach for systematic approaches to melody. One of the challenges of modern melodic genres, from 8-bit video game music to big budget film scores, is precisely the commercial demand for memorable melodic material that is stylistically restricted yet original (Koji Kondo, the composer behind *Super Mario Brothers* and *Legend of Zelda*, is unequivocal: "for me it's the art of creating that one main melody that is the primary goal behind music composition"),[33] suggesting that the need to get around self-consciousness in composing melody and puncture idealist assumptions remains the same; and so – one imagines – do the attendant economic and psychological struggles.[34]

Associationism

Nature and Nature's laws lay hid in night
God said: "Let Newton be" and all was light.

Alexander Pope[35]

The laws of the phenomena of mind are sometimes analogous to mechanical, but sometimes also to chemical laws.

John Stuart Mill[36]

In the German counter-revolution against the Enlightenment, divine inspiration – as a concealed positive faculty[37] – was inverted to become an acknowledged void, a kind of quantified ignorance or "negative greatness"[38] – as J. G. Hamann put it – that could explain what aestheticians felt ill-disposed to address. By the nineteenth century, this acknowledged void expressed the need for perfect ignorance of nature's "workshop," and would become strongly associated, as Jennifer Ann Bates summarizes, with "the realm of magic" for the simple reason that "genius is located in the movement of

---

[33] See "Interview with a legend" at http://uk.wii.ign.com/articles/772/772299p2.html

[34] See John Seabrook's assesment of the economic imperative driving musical style in the modern record industry, "The Money Note," *The New Yorker* (July 7, 2003): www.newyorker.com/archive/2003/07/07/030707fa_fact_seabrook

[35] Alexander Pope, "Epitaph. Intended for Sir Isaac Newton, in Westminster-Abbey" [1730], *The Poems of Alexander Pope*, ed. John Butt (London: Methuen, 1963), 808.

[36] John Stuart Mill, *The Logic of the Moral Sciences*, excerpted from *A System of Logic*, vol. 2, bk. 6 [1843]; rpt. (London: Open Court, 1994), 39.

[37] Eduard Young, *Conjectures on Original Composition in a Letter to the Author of Sir Charles Grandison* (London: A. Millar, R. and J. Dodsley, 1759), 31ff. Young saw creative genius in religious terms back in 1759 as an inwardly divine secret: "God within," that remained foreign to the human nature of its bearer, i.e. a "stranger within."

[38] Johann Georg Hamann's term: "eine negative Größe." From "Hamburgische Nachricht. Berlinische Beurtheilung der Kreuzzüge des Philologen" [1763], in J. G. Hamann, *Sämtliche Werke*, ed. Josef Nadler (Vienna: Thomas-Morus-Presse, 1950), 2: 260.

a merely subjective soul ... [which] in itself it is not sufficient for a science of experience."[39] Yet, as noted earlier, attempts at *Melodielehre* needed a degree of rational stability to approach a pedagogical application. As it turns out, the drive to objectify creative invention drew on none other than the eighteenth-century principle of mechanical associationism (the involuntary connection of ideas wherein "the simple ideas generate ... the complex ones"),[40] which stemmed, as M. H. Abrams reminds us, from the attempt "to import into the psychical realm the explanatory scheme of physical science, and so to extend the victories of mechanics from matter to mind."[41] This parallelism between mental activity and elementary concepts of Newtonian physics held that the creative association of disparate ideas in the brain becomes an introspective correlate to the operation of the mechanical laws of motion in the electrical nervous system, and would provide a key link between the eighteenth-century belief in a mechanical imagination and the automatic cognitions required, for instance, by Lobe's melodic theory in 1844 (which we will examine presently). The Aberdeen-based philosopher Alexander Gerard offers a detailed account of artistically applied associationism in his *Essay on Genius* (1774). The imagination's associative principle forms the "origin of genius," for him, but if it was to avoid arbitrariness, a governing "design" must regulate it in the same way that a magnet will sort ferruginous items according to the laws of magnetism or a sequence of interconnected water ducts will direct the water down the path of least resistance according to Newton's law of gravity. An overarching design doubles the strength of certain associative links, allowing relevant ideas to overrule their irrelevant rivals. Genius in this sense is merely a superior pathway complex of interconnected associations that regulates the imaginative process. It is a more efficient mechanism, a finer filterer of unwanted ideas, a better algorithm, and Gerard can thus claim quite logically that "[t]he extent of Homer's imagination is not more remarkable than its regularity."[42] Just as associationism could regulate the functioning of an unconsciously inventive mind, so by extension it could be deployed to objectify the functioning of unconsciously inspired acts of melodic composition: the association of tonal succession, thematic permutation, modular phrasal syntax, and rhythmic patterning were all amenable to mechanism in this

---

[39] Jennifer Ann Bates refers specifically to Hegel's conception of genius in the Preface of the *Phenomenology of Spirit*. See Bates, *Hegel's Theory of Imagination* (New York: State University of New York Press, 2004), 140.

[40] Mill, *The Logic of the Moral Sciences*, 40.

[41] M. H. Abrams, *The Mirror and the Lamp* (Oxford University Press, 1971), 159.

[42] Alexander Gerard, *Essay on Genius* (London: Strahan and Cadell, 1774), esp. 39–70, here 48.

sense. By offering a means of circumventing conscious deliberation, it proved to be the Trojan horse that pedagogy needed to breach the gates of divinely inspired genius, at least in the discourse of nineteenth-century *Melodik*.[43]

If we accept that the principles of mechanical association continued to dominate the psychology of the age (as late as 1890 William James would characterize associationism as our elementary "law of neural habit"),[44] how exactly did they interrelate with melodic theory? In one reading, analogical laws were originally nothing more than a means of regulating failures in our memory: the imprecision of our recollections resulted in the invention-by-substitution of seemingly new phenomena.[45] Far from an arbitrary or lawless faculty, then, the temporal and spatial reordering of images in the mind's eye (or inner ear) becomes the elementary process by which items lacking a precedent in sense (mythological grotesqueries, for example, or "original" melodic shapes) enter our thoughts, or are "created" by the imagination according to the laws of association. Distinct objects are diversified by the varying combinations into which they are instinctively associated, thus poetic imagination feeds off real sensory input, rearranging its elements into irreal compounds (as in, for example, a hybrid between a lion and eagle, a gryphon; or between a man and bull, a minotaur). This stickle-brick conception of imaginative invention would essentially form the basis of Lobe's justification for *thematische Arbeit* in 1844, as well as the rationale for piecing together complex thematic units mechanically from simple fragments.

Nineteenth-century devices for enforcing mechanical learning were long familiar in German territories. J. B. Logier's "Chiroplast," which regulated the finger movement of aspiring piano virtuosos, was endorsed by the Prussian government in 1821 when funds were created to set up the first

---

43 The nineteenth-century afterlife of associationism was secured through the widespread influence of such concepts as Kant's basic "analogical laws" and Coleridge's "mechanical fancy" (defined in opposition to the "organic imagination"), which occurs in the thirteenth chapter of the latter's *Biographia Literaria* [1817], ed. George Watson (London: J. M. Dent & Sons, 1975). See also Kant, *Critique of Judgment* § 49.

44 William James, *The Principles of Psychology*, 2 vols. (New York: Henry Holt, 1890), 1: 566

45 Alongside comments in Gerard's *Essay on Genius*, 38ff, it is arguably his *Essay on Taste* (1759) that offers the clearest articulation: "when *memory* has lost [the] real bonds of union [between ideas], *fancy*, by its associating power, confers upon them new ties, that they may not lie perfectly loose, and it can range them in an endless variety of forms [cf. 'original' melodic shapes]. Many of these being representations of nothing that exists in nature; and therefore whatever is fictitious or chimerical is acknowledged to be the offspring of this faculty, and is termed imaginary." Gerard, *Essay on Taste*, 3rd edn. [1780], rpt. ed. Walter J. Hipple Jr. (Gainsville: Scholars' Facsimiles & Reprints, 1963), 153–54.

of several academies for "chiroplastic" instruction, while rote-learning of literature – its mental analogue – remained commonplace in German grammar schools.[46] Marx was quick to give a patriotic stamp of approval: "So in Germany, [Logier's chiroplastic method] received its scientific acceptance and basis, its general adoption in the science of sound."[47] On this basis, Myles Jackson has argued that "musicians used machines and mechanical principles to teach the skills normally taught by masters, and . . . some musicians, rather controversially, saw physicists as possible allies in pedagogical matters."[48] Beyond the measurable physical practices Jackson illuminates, however, this principle plausibly extended to understandings of compositional pedagogy. It is arguably in this sense of physical mechanism, for instance, that the second volume of Heinrich Christoph Koch's *Versuch einer Anleitung zur Komposition* (1793) could speak of the "mechanical rules of melody" which regulate the piecing together (*Zusammenzetsung*) of melody as opposed to its invention (*Erfindung*).[49]

While originally driven by associationism, the nineteenth-century incarnation of a mechanical mind placed emotion at its center, a move that allowed for an unequivocal link between *Melodik* and the scientific discourse. In 1833, John Stuart Mill had proposed "feeling" as the organizing principle of poetic invention, to which are indebted "all the combinations which the mind puts together, all the pictures which it paints, the wholes which Imagination constructs out of the materials supplied by [mechanical] Fancy."[50] Lobe similarly would argue that unlearnable "inner emotion" remained the source for all melodic expression, and that the training he advocates was to ensure the smooth transmittance of emotion into melody

---

[46] See David Blackbourn, *History of Germany, 1780–1918*, 2nd edn. (Oxford: Blackwell, 2003), 228ff.

[47] Marx, "Zusatz aus andrer Feder," *BamZ* 2 (1825), 58–60, 65–67, 73–75, here 60.

[48] M. W. Jackson, "Physics, Machines and Musical Pedagogy in Nineteenth-Century Germany," *History of Science* 42 (2004), 371–418, here 374.

[49] "Von den mechanischen Regeln der Melodie," in H. C. Koch, *Versuch einer Anleitung zur Komposition* [1787], 2: 6, 135.

[50] Mill's full statement reveals his rationale: "Thoughts and images will be linked together, according to the similarity of the feelings which cling to them. A thought will introduce a thought by first introducing a feeling which is allied with it. At the center of each group of thoughts or images will be found a feeling; and the thoughts or images are only there because the feeling was there. All the combinations which the mind puts together, all the pictures which it paints, the wholes which Imagination constructs out of the materials supplied by Fancy, will be indebted to some dominant *feeling*, not as in other natures to a dominant *thought*, for their unity and consistency of character – for what distinguishes them from incoherencies." J. S. Mill, "The Two kinds of Poetry," *Early Essays*, ed. J. W. M. Gibbs (London: George Bell & Sons, 1897), 225. This was first published in *Monthly Repository* n.s. (1833), 714–24.

as part of a mechanical operation.[51] While the link between Mill and Lobe remains indirect, Mill's psychology mirrored eighteenth-century melodic theorists in arguing the basic principle that complex (cognitive / phrasal) units must result from the association of smaller units, but questioned whether this was a mental or a physical process, whether "the association did not exist between the two thoughts, but between the two states of the brain or nerves, which preceded the thoughts."[52] Receptive to such materialist sympathies, Lobe conceived melody as an object, and would draw on mechanical-associative principles within the governance of "feeling" a year later to outline a pedagogical strategy, in which, paradoxically, theories of a mechanical mind could be employed to subjectivist ends.

The psychograph, or *Lohengrin* as "unconscious consciousness"

> These pages . . . contain a soul in its entirety. Is it my own, or is it the soul of someone else? . . . The soul stirred the pen and overwhelmed it. / I prefer to leave all that in the realm of mystery and conjecture.
>
> Gustave Flaubert (1838)[53]

This need to objectify the creative flow of thought returns us to our starting point. If we revisit Goethe's stroke of lightning with materialist spectacles, his metaphor no longer appears entirely poetic, perhaps not even entirely metaphorical. Corresponding with the same interlocutor, Bettina von Brentano, Goethe also spoke of: "the electric shocks of your inspiration" after which Brentano herself ventured: "electricity excites the spirit to musical, fluent, streaming production. / I am of electric nature."[54] It had been sixty years since Benjamin Franklin and Thomas-François Dalibard had proven that lightning was in fact a giant electrostatic spark, a discovery that led Kant – defender of an aesthetics of mystery in the natural genius – to dub Franklin "the modern Prometheus" who had brought down

---

[51] Lobe, *Compositions-Lehre oder umfassende Theorie von der thematischen Arbeit und den modernen Instrumentalformen* (Weimar: Bernhard Friedrich Voigt, 1844), 42; rpt. (Hildesheim: Georg Olms, 1988), 37.

[52] Mill, *The Logic of the Moral Sciences*, 36.

[53] Gustave Flaubert, *Mémoires d'un fou* [1838], trans. Timothy Unwin, www.liv.ac.uk/soclas/los/madman.pdf, 3.

[54] "die elektrischen Schläge Deiner Begeisterungen." *Goethes Briefwechsel*, 1: 278; "Alles elektrisches regt den Geist zu musikalischer, fließender, ausströmender Erzeugung. / Ich bin elektrischer Natur." *Ibid.*, 2: 199.

fire from the heavens.[55] Theological fears as to the implications of channeling "natural" electricity or "tinkering with God's messaging system"[56] were registered widely both in Europe and the American colonies,[57] and in the early nineteenth century, Kant's epithet was used as the subtitle for one of the most famous novels capturing the popular fascination with the secret of a galvanic vital force within human forms. The promise of electricity in Mary Shelley's imagination was precisely that Frankenstein's monster could receive a divine spark. Structurally, the playful affinity between this and Goethe's Beethoven is more than coincidental. If we pursue the idea of electrophysiology further, then the metaphor for inspiration reads increasingly as scientific description.

Half a century after Luigi Galvani had used electric current to induce twitching from the legs of dead frogs via the sciatic nerve, an altogether different implication for human cognition arose from his concept of an endogenous "animal electricity":[58] that electrical impulses from the cerebrum could be decoded to create art. Alexander von Humboldt's experiments in Jena during 1797 had seemingly verified Galvani's view that electrical current had an internal source in the nerves and brain.[59] During the 1850s, this suspicion was embodied most notably in an invention called the "psychograph" or "thought indicator" whose sole agency was given as "nervous electricity." The patent, registered on January 23, 1854, reads as follows:

A Psychograph, or Apparatus for Indicating Persons Thoughts by the Agency of Nervous Electricity:

The apparatus consists of a combination of rods or pieces of wood joined so as to permit of free action in all the parts. From one of the legs of the instrument hangs a tracer; on one or more of the other extremities is fixed a disc, upon which the operator is to place his hand, and from this extremity or these extremities depends

---

[55] Immanuel Kant, *Kant's Werke*, Prussian Academy Edition, 29 vols. (Berlin: Reimer, 1910–), 1: 472.

[56] Michael Brian Schiffer, *Draw the Lightning Down: Benjamin Franklin and Electrical Technology in the Age of Enlightenment* (Berkeley and Los Angeles: University of California Press, 2006), 189.

[57] See, for instance, Reverend Thomas Prince. "Appendix Concerning the Operation of GOD in Earthquakes by Means of the Electrical Substance," in *Two Boston Puritans on God, Earthquakes, Electricity and Faith*, 1755–1756, see http://nationalhumanitiescenter.org/pds/becomingamer/ideas/text1/godlightningrods.pdf. For a summary account of reactions to Franklin's lightning conductors in the wider context of his experiments, see Schiffer, *Draw the Lightning Down*, 188–93.

[58] Luigi Galvani, *De viribus electricitatis in motu musculari commentarius* (Bononiae: Ex Typographia Instituti Scientiarium, 1791), 15ff.

[59] Alexander von Humboldt, *Versuche über die gereizte Muskel- und Nervenfaser nebst Vermuthungen über den chemischen Process des Lebens in der Thier- und Pflanzenwelt*, 2 vols. (Berlin: Heinrich August Rottmann, 1797–99).

another tracer. The other parts of the apparatus consist of a glass slab or other non-conductor, and of an alphabet and set of figures or numerals. Upon a person possessing nervous electricity placing his hand upon one of the discs the instrument will immediately work, and the tracer will spell upon the alphabet what is passing in the operator's mind.[60]

A colleague of the inventor, Freiherr von Forstner, reports that several such devices were sold in California, and to advertise the sale, Forstner published no fewer than four psychographically induced poems; these were attributed to supposedly inartistic and not especially literate Prussian citizens (a first lieutenant in the Prussian army, and a 12-year-old girl).[61] While hardly a challenge to the literary elite, psychographically induced literature offered the promise of socializing genial invention. Indeed, the appeal of the psychograph for early commentators rested partly on the assumption that anyone could tap into their "genius" to some extent.

As one of the more philosophically intriguing inventions of the 1850s, this contrivance can be viewed as an expression of a larger materialist trend whose quest for the "real" vacillated between embodied and disembodied entities, where ostensibly intangible phenomena such as thought and sound courted the suspicion of harboring a substantive, physical "reality" which could be harnessed, channeled, and quantified.[62] In this sense, it is not surprising that

---

[60] See patent no. 173 from 1854 in the London Patent Office, also listed in *Patents for Inventions: Abridgements of Specifications, Patent Office, Great Britain* (Patent Office, 1859), 382–83. References to the device appear in *The Mechanics Magazine: Iron* 60 (1854), 107; *Arthur's Home Magazine*, May 1854 (T. S. Arthur & Co., 1854), 398; *Journal of the Proceedings of the Assembly of the State of California* (California Legislature Assembly, 1854), 434; *The Mechanic's Magazine* (Robertson, Brooman & Co., 1854), 142; *Newton's London Journal of Arts and Sciences: Being Record of the Progress of Invention as Applied to the Arts* 44 (William Newton, 1854), 231.

[61] A. Freiherr von Forstner, *Der Psychograph oder Seelenschreiber des Herrn Musikdirektor A. Wagner in Berlin* (Berlin: A. Wagner, 1853), esp. 15–16.

[62] An entire industry of occult literature thrived on the belief that scientific breakthroughs could transgress laws that separated consciousness from non-consciousness, or even the living from the dead. The pseudo-scientific basis for this was the phenomenon of animate polarities within inanimate objects. In addition to electricity, magnetism was co-opted in a number of fantastical claims about communicating with dead figures. One such example purported to use a psychographic apparatus to talk to Heine and printed the transcripts, see D. Hornung, *Heinrich Heine, der Unsterbliche: Eine Mahnung aus dem Jenseits. Nur Thatsächliches, keine Dichtung* (Stuttgart: J. Scheible, 1857). Other texts in this vein include: Louis Alphonse Cahagnet, *Blicke in das Leben der Todten. Die Lehre von Gott und den Geheimen Kräften der Natur* (Leipzig: Edmund Stoll, 1853); Pater Lacordaire, *Die enthüllten Geheimnisse des Magnetismus und des der Electrizität* (Leipzig: Edmund Stoll, 1853); August Debay, *Die Mysterien des Schlafes und Magnetismus, oder Physiologie des natürlichen und magnetischen Somnambulismus in Erzählungen und Anekdoten*, and *Die Physik des Tischrückens* (Stuttgart: J. Scheible, 1855); Ferdinand Santanelli, *Geheime Philosophie oder magisch-magnetisch Heilkunde. Eine Erklärung der wunderbaren Erscheinungen des Magnetismus und Einleitung in die verborgensten Geheimnisse der Natur* (Stuttgart: J. Scheible, 1855).

the invention was patented in London by a *music* professional, the Berlin-based professor of music Adolphus Theodore Wagner (no relation). While there is no evidence to suggest that it was conceived in relation to any specific theory of mind – whether associationist, materialist, or mechanistic – among the range of available theories at the time, its initial plausibility rests on the idea that it obeyed a set of electrochemical forces, utilizing their material interconnections. Hence it can be seen as an anti-metaphysical statement that embodied the *desire* to conceive of thought as a material process.[63]

Skeptical commentators protested, notably within Humboldt's circle, that the psychograph was only the latest of a string of "monstrous absurdities"[64] of the age, and by the 1890s its proto-scientific claims for electrical agency were replaced by "spirits" as it definitively entered the realm of occult fantasy.[65] (Its quack-phrenology would become a precursor to both the lie detector and the Ouija board.) Though recent medical technologies *have* decoded speech from brain synapses,[66] at the time this "invention" was clearly a scam, forming part of what James Sheehan has termed an age of "eccentric theories and fashionable fakery."[67] At an archeological level, though, it also emblematized the desire to tap inventive faculties by reifying thought as a material substance: ostensibly offering a failsafe solution to the problem of inhibiting self-consciousness. Beyond Forstner's unscientific propaganda, mentioned above, the specific belief that processes of cognition could be reified as such, and that electricity carried these, whether as fluid or synaptic impulse, throughout the nervous system – the belief, that is, that enabled the psychograph to appear

[63] There were philosophical precedents. Kant, notably, suggested to Samuel Thomas Sömmerring that neural impulses cause electrolysis to occur within the cerebrospinal fluid linking spinal nerves with the brain, Because this watery conduit "would not only allow nerves to perceive the sensory world, but also to 'react back on it,'" Veit Erlmann sees in this "Kant's cautious turn towards the materiality of thought . . . by transforming the production of ideas into a form of data processing." See Erlmann, *Reason and Resonance* (New York: Zone books / Cambridge, MA: MIT Press, 2010), 181–83; and Kant to Sömmerring, August 10, 1795, in *Soemmerring und die Gelehrten der Goethezeit*, ed. Gunter Mann and Franz Dumont (Stuttgart: Fischer, 1985), 33.

[64] "solche Ungeheuerlichkeiten." K. A. Varnhagen to A. von Humboldt, July 8, 1854, Berlin. See *Briefe von Alexander von Humboldt an Varnhagen von Ense aus den Jahren 1827–1858*, 5th edn. (Leipzig: F. A. Brockhaus, 1860), 288.

[65] In Rudolf Eisler's philosophical dictionary from 1899, spirits rather than electricial energy moved the machine, and the whole operation was now merely "alleged." ["Psychograph: Name eines von den Spiritisten benutzten Apparates, der angeblich durch 'Spirits' in Tätigkeit versetzt wird."] See Rudolf Eisler, *Wörterbuch der philosophischen Begriffe*, 2nd edn. (Berlin: Ernst Siegfried Mittler und Sohn, 1904), 2: 151.

[66] B. Pasley, S. David, N. Mesgarani, A. Flinker, S. Shamma, N. Crone, R. Knight, and E. Chang, "Reconstructing Speech from Human Auditory Cortex," *PLoS Biology* 10 (2012), e1001251, doi:10.1371/journal.pbio.1001251.

[67] James Sheehan, *German History 1770–1866* (Oxford University Press, 1994), 809.

plausible – was given empirical credence in the 1850s by a circle of academic materialists associated with the Prussian Academy of Sciences. First to put the case among them was Carl Vogt, a professor of zoology at the University of Geneva, who declared in his *Physiological Letters* of 1854: "all those capabilities that we understand by the term activities of the soul [*Seelenthätigkeiten*] are just functions of brain substance ... thoughts in themselves stand in relation to the brain as gall to the liver or urine to the kidney."[68] Jacob Moleschott, a prominent colleague at Heidelberg, regarded such comparative logic as "incontestable," adding that "[t]hought is movement, a conversion of brain substance; the activity of thinking is just as necessary, just as inseparable a characteristic of the brain as any material will always possess agency [*Kraft*] as an inner, inexpressible feature."[69] Such ideas had already percolated into musical discourse. Gustav Nauenburg, the aesthetician and pedagogue we met in Chapter 1, declared himself "a warm, if *not an absolute* admirer of phrenological science" to readers of Brendel's *Neue Zeitschrift*. He related how different areas of the brain correspond to different musical aptitudes, continuing that "mental, immaterial force acts *from* the sensory organ [brain], like magnetic or electrical force; it appears as the *expression* of the material's *activity*."[70] During the 1850s, moreover, the dominant

[68] "alle jene Fähigkeiten, die wir unter dem Namen der Seelenthätigkeiten begreifen, [sind] nur Funktionen der Gehirnsubstanz ... die Gedanken [stehen] in demselben Verhältniß etwa zu dem Gehirne ... wie die Galle zu der Leber oder der Urin zu der Nieren." Carl Vogt, *Physiologische Briefe für Gebildete aller Stände*, 323. In her study of materialist thinking within the German natural sciences, Annette Wittkau-Horgby has emphasized that it was principally Vogt whose arguments led to the view that a materialistic interpretation of the connection between brain and consciousness (or "soul" as he put it) was the logical necessary outcome of the study of natural science. See Wittkau-Horgby, *Materialismus: Entstehung und Wirkung in den Wissenschaften des 19. Jahnhunderts* (Göttingen: Vandenhoeck & Ruprecht, 1998), 77–95, here 85. With this view, Vogt was only reformulating a statement by the physiologist Pierre Jean George Cabanis (1757–1808), who had spoken in 1802 of "la sécrétion de la pensée" from the brain. See Cabanis, *Rapports du physique et du moral de l'homme*, 2 vols. (Paris: Crapart, Caille and Ravier, 1802), 2: 137–38.

[69] "Der Vergleich ist unangreiflbar ... Der Gedanke ist eine Bewegung, eine Umsetzung des Hirnstoffs, die Gedankenthätigkeit ist eine eben so nothwendige, eben so unzertrennliche Eigenschaft des Gehirns, wie in allen Fällen die Kraft dem Stoff als inneres, unveräußerliches Merkmal innewohnt." Quoted in *Ibid.*, 324.

[70] "ich bin jetzt ein warmer, wenn auch *nich unbedingter* Verehrer der phrenologischen Wissenschaft ... Die geistige, immaterielle Kraft wirk *aus* dem sinnlichen Organe; wie, z.B. die magnetische, electrische etc. Kraft; sie erscheint als *Thätigkeitsäußerung* der Materie." Nauenburg, "Die Phrenologie in ihrer Beziehung zur Tonkunst," *NZfM* 2 (1851), 13–16, here 13. Nauenburg also recommended that, by identifying and distinguishing musical faculties within the brain, composers could determine their most favorable stylistic aptitudes (and parents, those of their children) without the painful experience of trial and error. This appears not to have provoked much discussion in the *Neue Zeitschrift*.

metaphor for communication within human neural networks was an alternative mechanism for transmitting ideas. In the same year as Nauenburg's article, the widely respected experimental physiologist Emil du Bois-Reymond suggested that:

the wonder of our time, electrical telegraphy, was long ago modeled in the animal machine. But the similarity between the two apparatuses, the nervous system and the electric telegraph, has a much deeper foundation. It is more than similarity, it is a kinship between the two, an agreement not merely of the effects, but also perhaps of the causes.[71]

Just as the invention of telegraphy could transmit literal coded (Morse) signals through electrical cable from 1837, the psychograph claimed to simulate the mysterious transmission of actual creative thought, albeit coded through the Roman alphabet.[72] Its very conception demonstrates the extent to which it became unproblematic, even desirable, that human self-consciousness could be bypassed in favor of a conductor of "nervous energy" that transmitted an original idea, transforming it into symbolic graphics. Humboldt, accordingly, once described telegraphy to Werner von Siemens as *Gedankendrahtung* (wiring thoughts), i.e. an embodied form of information that characterizes an entanglement of signal and materiality.[73]

Such materialism held an artistic appeal. Writing about the process of drafting his realist novel *Effi Briest*,[74] Theodor Fontane claimed to have finished it "as in a dream and almost as if I were using a psychograph."[75] This creative process appealed for its absence of mundane labor; but like Fontane's novels, the statement was actually a fiction based on putative reality (he in fact spent years revising and redrafting). His claim nevertheless appeals to the styling of a writing process that is subjective to the point of becoming unthinking, "as if" a machine were giving voice to and transcribing pre-linguistic thoughts immediately as they occurred in a pure

---

[71] Emil du Bois-Reymond, *Reden*, 2 vols. (Leipzig: Veit, 1887), 2: 51, cited in Laura Otis, *Networking: Communicating with Bodies and Machines in the Nineteenth Century* (Ann Arbor: University of Michigan Press, 2001), 11.

[72] Samuel Finley Breese Morse first built a telegraphic conductor in 1835; the patent followed in 1837. A summary of the genesis of this device is given in Anton A. Huurdeman, *The Worldwide History of Telecommunications* (Hoboken: Wiley, 2003), 55ff.

[73] See Laura Otis' rich exploration of the metaphors, experiments and writings surrounding the theory of communication within neural networks in the nineteenth century, in *Networking*, 1.

[74] Theodor Fontane, *Effi Briest* [1894]. Rpt. trans. Hugh Rorrison and Helen Chambers (London: Penguin, 2000).

[75] "Vielleicht ist es mir so gelungen, weil ich das Ganze träumerisch und fast wie mit einem Psychographen geschrieben habe." Fontane to Hans Hertz, March 2, 1895, in *Briefe an Wilhelm und Hans Hertz 1859–1898*, ed. Kurt Schreinert (Stuttgart: Ernst Klett, 1972), 356.

state to the author, who is now reduced to an origination function and stripped of any formative, revisionary, or calligraphic craft. This is where the historical psychograph becomes dislocated from the discourse it tapped into, for there is a sharp distinction between the conscious, unspoken thoughts putatively transcribed by it, and its broader artistic appropriation as a mechanism for *unconscious* invention that fed into a far longer tradition of automatic writing. A century earlier, Voltaire had pretended to marvel that Virgil's hand just happened to write the *Aeneid* at precisely the time that his soul produced it: "even though his hand in no way obeyed the intention of the author."[76] Decades later, E. T. A. Hoffmann captured essentially the same principle in the sphere of fiction with *The Golden Pot* (1814), when the exotic Serpentina turns the bourgeois Anselmus into an unconscious writing machine who transcribes her spoken story unawares into Sanskrit.[77] And in the realm of autobiography, Gustave Flaubert fictionalized his writing process similarly as the involuntary transmission "of a madman" directly from soul to pen. Giving voice to the narrative agency's ambivalence, Flaubert's fictional author cautions right at the outset: "I know no more than you [the reader] of what you are going to read,"[78] thereby replicating the desired condition of would-be writers of melody.

The literary topos had rich musical resonances. For his part, Wagner's appeal to a creative dream state in *Die Meistersinger*, where "man's truest madness is disclosed to him in dreams: all poetry and the art of verse is nothing but true interpretation of dreams"[79] essentially rewords the aspiration to tap the unconscious. Fitting within the Enlightenment (but anti-rationalist) dichotomy of (natural) genius and (schooled) scientist, such comments inscribe a valuation system into modes of artistic production. The mode of literary production embodied in Fontane's psychograph,

---

[76] "Ainsi l'âme de Virgile produisait l'Enéide, et sa main écrivait l'Enéide, sans que cette main obéît en aucune façon à l'intention de l'auteur." Voltaire, "La Métaphysique de Neuton ou parallèlle des sentiments de Neuton et de Leibnitz" [1740], *Oeuvres complètes de Voltaire* (Oxford: Taylor Institution, 1992), 15: 229.

[77] E. T. A. Hoffmann, *The Golden Pot and Other Tales*, trans. and ed. Ritchie Robertson (Oxford University Press, 1992), 1–84.

[78] Gustave Flaubert, *Mémoires d'un fou* [1838], 3. This resolution of dream and reality would of course later come to define the aesthetic of surrealism: "psychic automatism in its pure state, by which one proposes to express – verbally, by means of the written word . . . the actual functioning of thought," and its architect – André Breton – argued accordingly that good writing from Swift to Roussel had always been surreal in its coming-into-being. See Breton, "From the First Manifesto of Surrealism 1924," in *Modernism: An Anthology of Sources*, ed. Vassiliki Kolocotroni, Jane Goldman, and Olga Taxidou (University of Chicago Press, 1998), 309.

[79] "des Menschen wahrster Wahn / wird ihm im Traume aufgetan: / All' Dichtkunst und Poeterei / ist nichts als Wahrtraumdeuterei." Act 3, scene 2, *Die Meistersinger von Nürnberg*.

suggested by Flaubert's autobiographical "madman," and reinforced by Hans Sachs is unsettling in part because it both mystifies and mechanizes the creative process by transgressing Cartesian oppositions of outer and inner, mechanical sequence and organic causality, thereby also weakening such dichotomous constructs as labor and inspiration, layman and genius, activity and feeling.[80] This slackening of antagonistic categories was essential for the achievement of an adequate melodic theory, where melody had to be understood systematically in terms of a rational pedagogical application. Devices such as the psychograph, in short, can be read as materializing a conception of automatic creation through a concealed process of ideation that remained mechanic–systematic: this was precisely the task of melodic theory during the nineteenth century.[81]

In a sense, German idealism had always constituted a systematic attempt to legitimize creative subjectivity and to understand this at the same time as an organ for portraying the absolute.[82] But mid-century materialism remains an autonomous concept here; it does not necessarily go hand in hand with the belief that mind is irreducibly mechanistic.[83] Nor are the associationist psychologies of the previous section necessarily materialist, even though the metaphorical and analogical thinking that was often used to chart those psychologies frequently resorted to materialist imagery (e.g. Mill's mental chemistry). For music theorists, aligning non-conscious cognition with materialist philosophy could arguably be just as impractical and inhibiting as idealist models of genius. Under the changing skies of the *Nachmärz*, then, the implicit question for an aesthetics of *Melodik* is

---

[80] Here I take the distinction between mechanical and organic expressed by Marshall McLuhan: "mechanization is achieved by fragmentation of any process and by putting the fragmented parts in a series ... there can be no principle of [organic] causality in a mere sequence." McLuhan, *Understanding Media: The Extensions of Man* (Cambridge, MA: MIT Press, 1994), 11–12.

[81] Far from a trivial toy, the psychograph can be understood as a simulacrum whose very existence offered tangible proof, more so than any theory, that the natural universe of physics and human biology was susceptible to mechanistic explication. In this sense, the psychograph can be viewed much like the eighteenth-century automata of inventors such as Henri Maillardet, Pierre Jacquet-Droz, and Jacques de Vaucanson. Helmholtz, for one, explained that it would be incomprehensible for men like Vaucanson and Droz to spend so much time in the construction of these figures "if they had not hoped in solemn earnest to solve a great problem." Hermann von Helmholtz, "On the Interaction of the Natural Forces," in *Popular Lectures on Scientific Subjects*, trans. E. Atkinson (New York: Dover, 1962), 138.

[82] For an investigation of this definition in the wider context of post-Enlightenment German aesthetics, see Jochen Schmidt, "Die intellektuale Anschauung als ästhetische Genialität," in *Die Geschichte des Genie-Gedankens*, 1: 415.

[83] A prominent contemporary example would be Rudolf Hermann Lotze's comments on "physical–mental mechanisms." See *Medicinische Physiologie, oder Physiologie der Seele* (Leipzig: Wiedmann, 1852), 66ff.

"why the *Romantic* reaction to the problem of self-consciousness should be in the form of an aggrandizement of art," as Hartman puts it.[84] Wagner's reaction in these terms is revealing, for it illustrates his engagement with the problem of a supremely self-conscious model of unconscious creativity. Nine years before his desire to lose his "private consciousness," he advised Hanslick that art of the most modern period "can only be produced by a process of conscious creation,"[85] yet he vacillated, telling Liszt in 1851 that his expository discourse in *Oper und Drama* was merely a conscious means to unconscious ends: "the beautiful unconsciousness of artistic creation."[86] This debate did not remain a private matter. The protean symbolism of *Lohengrin* was seen by Wagner's most prominent journalistic spokesperson as an explicit dramatization of the antagonism between creative acts and self-conscious knowledge thereof. "*Lohengrin is the representative of Genius, of artistic genius*," Franz Brendel explained in 1859, "and the opera depicts the conflicts in which this genius – with his opposite, otherworldly and simultaneously earthly double-nature – gets caught through his relations to the world."[87] Following its Vienna premiere in 1858, widespread criticism of the opera impelled Brendel to clarify, on Wagner's behalf, the curious taciturnity and aloofness of the undercover grail knight.[88] Although he was extrapolating freely from Wagner's more nuanced programmatic explanations, his insight is that the value of an artwork (still) depended on its mysterious creation, both for audience and artist. Mystery is classed as a fundamental enabler of appreciative perception. That his hermeneutics may appear naïve to us is less important than his implicit belief that this clarification of *Lohengrin*'s meaning would garner public sympathy against a deepening tide of anti-Wagner criticism, especially the journalistic vortex encircling Wagner's melodic writing:

Any artistic creation [such as melody] is rooted in a mysterious workshop, from which the veil of mist may not be cleared away if the creation is not to be profaned; and only

---

[84] Hartman, "Romanticism and Anti-Self-Consciousness," 52.

[85] Wagner to Hanslick, January 1, 1847, Dresden, in SB 2: 538. In view of the pragmatic decisions an operatic composer must make, Wagner's assertion suggests less a negation of the inexplicability of natural genius, and more the view that this genius must also be conjoined to conscious decision-making as operatic projects are conceived, planned, and executed.

[86] Wagner to Liszt, November 25, 1850, Zurich, in SB 3: 467.

[87] "*Lohengrin ist Repräsentant des Genius, des künstlerischen Genius, und das Werk stellt die Conflikte dar, in die dieser Genius mit seiner jenseitigen, außerweltlichen und zugleich irdschen Doppelnatur in seinen Beziehungen zur Welt geräth.*" Franz Brendel, "Einige Worte über Lohengrin zum besseren Verständniß desselben," *NZfM* 8 (February 18, 1859), 91.

[88] See also "Lohengrin als dramatischer Charakter," *Anregungen für Kunst, Leben und Wissenschaft* 4 (1859), 265–73.

as long as this workshop is removed from profane eyes, is it the creative property out of which the forms of imagination arise aloft. Every really great artist possesses this sacred awe that warns him to tread at his peril on his inner self and thereby to blurt out the most inward secret . . . He may not sever the mysterious threads that bind him to a higher world if he does not want to betray his genius; he may not give himself completely to the world, he may not even make this sacrifice for his beloved wife, as in fact no genius has done . . . So we see brought to portrayal the pain that the divinely sent feels in his relation to the world, his tragic fate, to have to drag through the world in his most inner essence the misunderstood urge to communicate.[89]

In the context of materialist perspectives on cognition, the "mysterious workshop" Brendel posits functions almost as a synonym for the psychograph's "rods and pieces of wood" in that the latter sought to lay bare the workshop's mechanism in an act of "profane" afflatus.

The character Lohengrin, we remember, bans Elsa from asking after his name or provenance as a condition of his service to her. Given that Brendel made his claims amid the full force of criticism over Wagner's melodic ineptitude we saw in Chapter 1, *Lohengrin*'s mystification of artistic invention suggests that this *Verbot* can be read, not so much in the dramatic sense of "where does he come from," but more allegorically, as the composer's arch psychological weakness: "where do melodies come from?" Brendel's conclusion was indeed that Wagner's *Verbot* was "psychologically grounded,"[90] making him the last scion, and first psychologist, of Wagner reception.

Wagner's own reading of his opera was explicitly self-reflexive in these terms. The fantasy of an idealized unconscious creative process implied by A. T. Wagner's patent had been one of the composer's allegories for the relationship between Elsa and Lohengrin in 1851 ("Elsa is the unconscious, the involuntary, into which Lohengrin's conscious, deliberate being yearns

---

[89] "Jedes künstlerische Schaffen wurzelt in einer geheimnißvollen Werkstätte, von der der Schleier nicht hinweggezogen werden darf, wenn dasselbe nicht profanirt werden soll, und nur solange als diese Werkstätte profanen Blicken entzogen bleibt, ist sie der schöpferische Grund und Boden, aus dem die Gebilde der Phantasie emporwachsen. Jeder echte große Künstler besitzt diese heilige Scheu, die ihn warnt, zersetzend an sein Innres heranzutreten und damit das innerste Geheimniß auszusprechen . . . Er darf die geheimnißvollen Fäden, die ihn an eine höhere Welt ketten, nicht zerreißen, wenn er seinen Genius nicht verläugnen will, er darf sich nicht vollständig hingeben an die Welt, selbst dem geliebten Weibe darf er dieses Opfer nicht bringen, wie es in der That auch noch kein Genius gebracht hat; . . . So sehen wir den Schmerz zur Darstellung gebracht, den der Gottgesandte empfindet in seinen Beziehungen zur Welt, sein tragisches Geschick, im Drange nach Mittheilung in seinem innersten Wesen unverstanden durch die Welt ziehen zu müssen." Brendel, "Einige Worte über Lohengrin zum besseren Verständniß desselben," 91.

[90] "So ist das Verbot psychologisch begründet." *Ibid.*

to be redeemed") as well as – like Fontane's fictive realism – a description of R. Wagner's own mind in the act of composition:

> Through the capability of this "unconscious consciousness," such as I myself now felt alike with Lohengrin, the nature of Woman also … came to ever clearer understanding in my inner mind … But this blessedly felt knowledge lay hidden at first … only slowly did it ripen into loud acknowledgement.[91]

In other words, according to Wagner, the ideal, androgynous unity of conscious and unconscious allegorized in the dramatic relationship at the center of *Lohengrin* is a description of the state of mind that allowed him to write the opera in the first place, a state of "unconscious consciousness" seemingly manifest technologically in the material transmissions of the psychograph.[92] Other speculations about *Lohengrin* couched this opposition more explicitly in terms of divine knowledge and mortal ignorance (Jupiter and Semele),[93] and whether or not Wagner's remarks represent a cart-before-horse scenario not untypical of his self-styling practices, it at least articulates a creative process he publicly aspired to at this time.

Musically, one can extrapolate from his comments about the redemption of consciousness into unconsciousness that the psychic meeting point, i.e. the wakeup call, then becomes Lohengrin's alarmed repetition of his interdiction up a half step in act 1 (A♭ → A; see Example 2.1), which follows Elsa's "quiet, almost unconscious" ascent to his first *Verbot*.[94] Thus, before this explicit awakening, in Elsa's ethereal dream from act 1 we arguably hear Lohengrin's music in a finer state than Lohengrin himself can sing it later in the act, i.e. Elsa's unconscious vision – as a musical way station between the celestial Prelude and Lohengrin's bombastic earthly arrival – thematizes the purity of pre-conscious creation in the human realm. The vocabulary of Liszt's propagandistic description glimmers with this possibility: "[delivered] as if in a state of somnambulism … Elsa's song … loses itself in the infinite, and touches upon an unattainable ideal."[95] But as we have seen, hopes for attaining this kind of artistic ideal were grounded in decidedly

---

[91] SSD 4: 301–2. Cf. PW 1: 346–48.

[92] By invoking androgyny, I refer particularly to Jean-Jacques Nattiez's extensive work into this question in *Wagner Androgyne: A Study in Interpretation*, trans. Stewart Spencer (Princeton University Press, 1993).

[93] See Eduard Kulke, "*Semele* und *Lohengrin*. Eine Parallele," *Anregungen für Kunst, Leben und Wissenschaft* 6 (1861), 41–6, 77–90.

[94] Wagner's stage direction for Elsa's first response to the *Verbot* is: "leise, fast bewußtlos." See *Lohengrin*, WWV75, ed. John Deathridge and Klaus Döge (London and Mainz: Eulenburg, 2007), 104.

[95] "[C]omme dans un accès de somnambulisme … [s]on chant … se perd dans l'infini, et touche à un insaisissable idéal." Liszt, SS 4: 38, 80.

Example 2.1 Lohengrin's repetition of his *Verbot* to Elsa; *Lohengrin*, act 1, scene 3, mm. 777–**96**.

finite mental processes that were frequently deemed automatic, and sometimes mechanical.

The "melograph" as mindless composing

Machines that simulate psychic processes implicitly assert the objectivity of those processes. In the second decade of the nineteenth century, the desired process of automatic–unconscious melodic invention was seemingly modeled in a mechanical device called the "Componium" or "mechanical improviser" that generated melodic variations. Invented in 1821 by Diederich Nicolaus Winkel, it was a sophisticated orchestrion (a clockwork musical instrument whose components created the aural impression of a performing orchestra), but outstripped related devices of the period in that its mechanism feigned automatic, unceasing improvisation without repetition of material.

When exhibited at Paris' Wenzel Pavilion late in 1823, it was advertised as an *improvisateur musical*, and the *Journal de débats* marveled misleadingly at its ability to improvise instantly on a given theme from the audience.[96] In fact, the theme had to be pre-programmed, and the music was restricted to aleatoric permutations and combinations of melodically and harmonically predefined segments. Every two measures the "improvisation" alternated imperceptibly between the pins of two simultaneously rotating barrels, each of which could offer eight different musical segments at any one time, and whose selection was determined by a random sequencer. While the principle is essentially that of mere musical dice games, Philippe van Tiggelen estimates the combinatorial potential of the componuim's seven barrels at 14.513 quintillion variations.[97] In 1865 François-Joseph Fétis cited an official report from the Institut de France to predict that "thousands of years could pass without the same variation occurring exactly."[98] The sequencer, pin, and rotation mechanism which seemed to embody this ceaselessly inventive automation is shown in Figure 2.2.

Gustav Schilling's *Encyclopädie* classed this as a species of *melograph*, an automaton that improvises mechanically on a given theme by itself using wheel and clock mechanisms set in motion by spring tension: "for the sake of its mechanical performance" he explains, this "is more correctly called an

---

[96] See Philippe Van Tiggelen, *Componium: The Mechanical Musical Improvisor* (Louvain-la-Neuve: Institut supérieur d'archéologie et d'histoire de l'Art, 1987), 199ff.

[97] *Ibid.*, 325.

[98] "il est dit que des milliers d'années pourraient se passer sans que la même variation se produisit exactement." F.-J. Fétis, *Biographie universelle des musiciens*, 8th edn. (Paris: 1865), 447.

2.2 The internal mechanism for Diederich Nicolaus Winkel's
Componium (1821) © Musée des Instruments de Musique, Brussels.

extemporizing machine, *Fantasirmaschine* or improvising machine."[99]
It represented a kind of unthinking creation "where nothing is lacking
but imagination [*Fantasie*]," Schilling explained, and each theme is
worked according to extant rules of inversion and imitation in a predefined
manner so that it "runs around in a circular line like a ball in roulette."[100]
The medium of performance is centrally implicated in the discourse,
and if these clockwork machines lack original ideas, their capacity to
generate melodies without conscious cognition (and thus inhibiting self-
consciousness) once thematic material was entered into them allegorizes the

---

[99] "eine Art Automat, der um seiner mechanischen Verrichtungen willen richtiger auch
      Extemporirmaschine, Fantasirmaschine und Improvisirmaschine heißt." Gustav von Schilling,
      *Encyclopädie der gesammten musikalischen Wissenschaften, oder Universal-Lexicon der
      Tonkunst* (Stuttgart: Franz Heinrich Köhler, 1837), 4: 651
[100] "weiter nichts fehlt als die Fantasie." *Ibid.* Schilling's description is suggestive of the melodic
      discourse in this sense. While the *Fantasirmaschine* is mechanically fascinating, on the whole it
      has "absolutely no value from a musical or artistic point of view" ["so hat sie im Ganzen doch in
      musikalischem oder künstlerischem Betracht gar keinen Werth."] because it cannot generate
      original ideas, and lacks any feedback loop coupled to aesthetic sense with which to hear and
      correct itself. *Ibid.*, 651–52.

unconscious mind that is all rule application.[101] This essentially rewords the "mental disposition ... through which nature gives the *rule* to art" that Kant equated with the faculty of genius. And intriguingly, Lobe's stylized "conversation" with Hummel essentially recounts the melographic principle as compositional method:

First I search for some interesting opening measures for a passage. That is its melodic material; I need nothing more from the direct inventive power of imagination, for ... the majority of passages are just a continuation of the same opening measures with different progressions, which is already more a matter of exercise [*Uebung*].[102]

For the melograph, such development of a theme – i.e. "composition" – simply happens automatically according to predefined mechanical laws (cf. "associative laws"); an original theme, weights and spring tension are all that is required to begin the process: no (self-) consciousness necessary.

This aesthetic is heir to the kind of "mechanical sublime" that Annette Richards has identified in Mozart's F minor Fantasie K. 608 – "an organ piece written for a clock" – whose variation set and intricate fugal permutations redouble the signifiers of an "automatic genius."[103] It is not hard to see how the debate over *Melodik* stoked arguments over the desirability of such "mindless" automation. And during the early nineteenth century, the principal exemplar for this was the received *idea* of Mozart. As we saw in Möricke's novella, German criticism vaunted Mozart as the paradigmatic musical genius under the cult of individualism. For Jean Paul Richter, he embodied the combination of "blindness and security of instinct" with the supremacy of a particular organ and creative power.[104] The *Mozartbild*, primarily propagated by Johann Friedrich Rochlitz's forged letter from August 23, 1815,[105] was classic romanticized Kant and constructed the

[101] Even though the machine is all rule-application, the allegorical reading of unconscious mind holds, for as we shall see with Lobe it is precisely the inculcation of mechanical rules to unconscious levels the enables melodic pedagogy.

[102] "Erstens suche ich nach interessanten Anfangstakten der Passage. Das ist ihr melodisches Material; mehr brauche ich von der unmittelbaren Erfindungskraft der Phantasie nicht, denn wie Sie sehen, ist ein großer Theil der Passage nur Fortführung derselben Anfangstakte über andere Harmoniefolgen, was schon mehr Sache der Uebung ... ist." J. C. Lobe, *Aus dem Leben eines Musikers* (Leipzig: J. J. Weber, 1859), 75–76.

[103] Annette Richards, "Automatic genius: Mozart and the mechanical sublime," *Music and Letters* 80 (1999), 366–89, here 366, 389.

[104] "die Oberherrschaft *eines* Organs und *einer* Kraft, z. B. in Mozart, wirkt alsdann mit der Blindheit und Sicherheit des Instinktes." Jean Paul Richter, *Vorschule der Aesthetik*, ed. Norbert Miller (Munich: Carl Hanser, 1974), 56.

[105] Mozart's frequently reprinted (and inauthentic) letter about his compositional process first published in the *AmZ* (1815), in tandem with F. Rochlitz's criticism from 1820 in the same

composer as a psychographic *Kopfkomponist* who "completed entire works in his head"[106] where "the finding and working out takes place as it were in a dream."[107] Amid a rationalist confrontation between natural aptitude and deliberate hard work, the latter – conceived as a sure path to diminishing returns – could continue to rehearse the notion that unthinking creation is authentic, while conscious, deliberate construction is artificial.[108] One of the most frequently cited similes for this was somnambulism, where straining to compose beautiful melodies is like trying hard to fall asleep: it is by definition counterproductive, though it is precisely the confidence of the sleepwalker that the composer constantly seeks.[109]

In an article on the essence of *Phantasie*, Sobolewski (the Kapellmeister we met earlier who emphatically upheld an antinomy of melody and pedagogy) argued simply that "our greatest composers were generally bad theorists,"[110] and, by alluding to Schiller's conception of the naïve genius, turned it into a stick with which to beat Wagner:

There will always be a great difference between the kind of intelligence which calculates and that which really creates; the last is what is properly called Genius! Should we not hold it to be the sign that a person is somewhat deficient in this

paper, and A. Oulibicheff's 1843 biography reinforced the *Mozartbild* as an exemplar of a *Kopfkomponist*. Recent commentaries on this aspect of Mozart reception have emphasized the constructedness of the composer's image. See Ulrich Konrad, "Friedrich Rochlitz und die Entstehung des Mozart-Bildes um 1900," in *Mozart – Aspekte des 19. Jahrhunderts* (Mannheim: Hoschulschriften, 1995), 1–22; and Torstend Brandt, "Mozart," in *Johann Christian Lobe* (Göttingen: Vadenhoeck and Ruprecht, 2002), 126–53.

[106] "So machte [Mozart] ganze Musikstücke im Kopfe fertig." F. Rochlitz, "Mozarts guter Rath an Componisten," *AmZ* 22 (1820), 299.

[107] "Alles das Finden und Machen gehet in mir nur, wie in einem schönstarken Traume vor." See "Schreiben Mozarts an den Baron von . . ." *AmZ* 34 (1815), 564. This statement is from the spurious letter, published by Rochlitz in 1815, pertaining to Mozart's compositional process. While broadly adhering to the *Kopfkomponieren* thesis, Georg Niklaus von Nissen's early biography of Mozart (1828) appears to lend the discourse flavor realism by referencing Mozart's minor corrections and a protracted working out period, while nevertheless reinscribing the primacy of *Kopfkomponieren* for the composer's most valued works. See Georg Niklaus von Nissen, *Biographie W. A. Mozart's* [1828], rpt. (Hildesheim and New York: G. Olms, 1972), 649.

[108] Kant, *Critique of Judgment*, 151.

[109] Two diverse examples are J. F. Unger, author of the most extensive treatise on the *Notensetzer*, and Arthur Schopenhauer in his discussion of "the invention of melody" (§52). See Unger, *Entwurf einer Maschine, wodurch alles was auf dem Clavier gespielt wird, sich von selber in Noten setzt* (Brunswick: Waisenhaus, 1774), 5; Arthur Schopenhauer, *The World as Will and Idea*, trans. E. F. J. Payne, 2 vols. (New York: Dover, 1969), 1: 260.

[110] "Unsere größten Componisten waren in der Regel schlechte theoretische Schriftsteller." Eduard Sobolewski, "Phantasie," *NZfM* 5 (December 24, 1839), 202.

quality when we perceive but too clearly the immense labor expended in seeking for means of expression.[111]

While such ideas seemed trapped in a penumbra cast by the moon of thirty years past, in other quarters, a deepening apostasy in the guise of realism signalled a turn away from this model of creative invention. In the same year as Sobolewski's antique comments, Klaus Ziegler set out the Marxist position with wry humor in his biography of the dramatist Christian Dietrich Grabbe:

[T]he period in which one went on bended knee before men of genius is already long past . . . On the whole, one no longer loves geniuses since the recent discovery that they are none other than the organs of the time, that the spirit of God hides in the masses, and that only the masses move the course of history forwards. If in fact men of genius have bad habits and weaknesses to boot, one easily takes a dislike. In this context, one asks why the genius can't behave as well as every other reasonable person.[112]

In this antagonistic atmosphere, the fact that the only true "living" exemplars of the ageing principle of natural melodic genius were mechanical simulacra gave pause. Pedagogically minded music critics such as Marx took issue with the "myth" on principle, directly contradicting it in his *Streit* with Fink.[113] While unthinking creation remained a durable belief, then, the desire to puncture it was more in sync with a crystallizing spirit of realism grounded in scientific materialism.[114]

---

[111] This comment occurs in the context of a criticism of Wagner's charlatanism, where he uses "scales" – perhaps a euphemism for melody – that are only employed by "beginners or bunglers, or by careless persons, and such as are hard of hearing." E. Sobolewski, "Reactionary Letters, VII" *TMW* 33 (1855), 114.

[112] "[D]ie Periode, wo man vor den Genies auf den Knien lag, [ist] schon lang vorüber . . . Im Ganzen liebt man die Genies nicht mehr, seit dem man in neuerer Zeit die Entdeckung gemacht hat, daß sie nichts anderes als die Organe der Zeit sind, daß der Geist Gottes in der Masse steckt, und daß nur die Masse den Lauf der Geschichte fortbewegt. Haben sie sogar noch Unarten und Schwächen, so gewinnt man leicht eine Abneigung. Man sagt sich in dieser Beziehung, warum können sich die Genies nicht ebenso gut gebehrden, wie jeder andere vernünftige Mensch." Klaus Ziegler, *Grabbes Leben und Charakter* (Hamburg: Hoffmann, 1855), 2.

[113] See Marx's comment from *Die alte Musiklehre im Streit mit unserer Zeit* (1841) that: "if anyone still desired to return to that old misunderstanding about the dreamlike unconsciousness of genial creativity, he would find himself corrected not only by words of a Goethe but by the works and words of the musical masters, namely by Mozart himself – who reveals a remarkably clear consciousness of his intentions and their execution in his letters," in Marx, *Musical Form in the Age of Beethoven*, 19.

[114] For a study of the educational ideal of genius during the later Enlightenment, see Christoph Hubig, "Genie – Typus oder Original? Vom Paradigma der Kreativität zum Kult des Individuums," in *Propyläen-Geschichte der Literatur*, ed. E. Wischer (Berlin: Propyläen, 1983), 4: 207–10.

Let me summarize the matrix of *Genie-Gedanke* laid out so far in relation to melodic theory: simulacra of musical invention such as the melograph – propped up during *Vormärz* aesthetics by the *Mozartbild* – embodied an inventive process that obviated inhibiting consciousness by seemingly materializing processes of mechanical associationism theorized within 1830s psychology. The cognitions central to this model were utilized fraudulently in the 1850s by devices such as the psychograph which aspired to harness creative inventiveness itself as "nervous electricity," i.e. as literalized material thought. While this move was decidedly monistic and coincided with a wider realist turn that was increasingly skeptical of genius, the belief (among philosophers of mind as well as music theorists) in emotion as both the origin and coordinating agent of mechanically inventive cognition meant that an aesthetics of inspiration still retained a vestige of mystery in the concept of feeling (a nodal concept for Wagner, explored in Chapter 6).

The question of whether it matters that man can conceive himself in mechanical terms provoked a number of satirical responses during the eighteenth century,[115] but it applies equally to nineteenth-century melodists: namely, does it still matter if we conceive melodic structure as a mechanical assemblage, a constructed imitation of something more genuine? Whether or not this was thought injurious to beauty, there were few alternatives for a self-aware theoretical approach. *Lohengrin* – in Brendel's reading – had seemingly forbidden any such questing, at least in the eyes of self-conscious composers, and in this sense the project of a material melodic

---

[115] Writing satirically on the ambivalence within this uneasy transcendence, Jean Paul's narrative voice in *Menschen sind Maschinen der Engel* (1785) disabuses the reader of the assumption that the world exists for mankind, and explains that angels are the real inhabitants of the earth; humans are merely their tools, toiling on their behalf as automata to serve "all [their] needs." The "bleak, naked truth," he concludes, is that humans are "mere *machines*." ["Denn es ist keine poetische Redensart, sondern kahle nakte Wahrheit, daß wir Menschen blosse *Maschinen* sind, deren sich höhere Wesen, denen diese Erde zum Wohlplatz beschieden worden, dienen."] Jean Paul applies a second layer to the narrative by citing machines of angels (humans) who also build machines, and thus "mimic the angels in the machine-building process." Since the writer references well-known, actual (chess-playing, piano-playing) automata of the eighteenth century, the discourse enters a new level of realism that plays ambiguously on the boundaries of his metaphor, and is now fully reflexive for the reader: "this woman who plays the piano is at most a fortunate copy," he claims slyly, "of those female machines who play the piano and who accompany the music with [bodily] motions, which clearly seem to betray emotion." ["ienes [sic] Frauenzimmer z. B., das Klavier [spielt], ist höchstens eine glückliche Kopie der weiblichen Maschinen, die das Klavier schlagen und die Töne mit Bewegungen begleiten, die offenbar Rührung zu verrathen scheinen."] Such satirical rhetoric exploits ambivalence over the desirability of the mechanical in acts of expression (of which melody must count as one) by deliberately blurring the status of man-made automata with biological humans. Jean Paul, *Sämtliche Werke*, pt. 2 (Munich: Carl Hanser, 1974), 1: 1028, 1031.

theory risked a willing act of masochism, one that would finally short circuit the divine spark.

(Failed) attempts at *Melodik ca.* 1840–50

The two major *Vormärz* theorists writing about melodic invention were Marx and Lobe. As we have seen, both opposed the notion that melodic structure was inscrutable; Marx, in particular, is bluntly combative. "The lament is old," he carped in 1841, "so too is its answer: melody is a matter of talent; one is born with it; it cannot be taught and exercised."[116] In his *Compositions-Lehre* four years earlier, he had praised Reicha for rebuffing the "old-school" doctrines,[117] and alluded to models of cognition to argue that modern science "would be hard pressed to concede such a thing as innate melody or a specific mental faculty for tone succession and rhythmic motion."[118] Instead, the ability to discover melody is universally innate, he argues, and extends to "most well-constituted children." This facility is only blunted in adults, he qualifies, through "dry rules," "eternal prohibitions," and stifling "rows of chords" handed down from the desk of dry theory.

This was a distinctly modern approach to melody (and genius). Back in 1814, Reicha's commonplace distinction between genius ("a favorable natural aptitude") and talent ("acquired only through strict, assiduous, painstaking application") had already begun to dissolve the monolith of the Kantian genius by inverting its normative hierarchy, claiming that talent is actually far more useful than genius, which "amounts to little" without the means provided by the former.[119] But Marx and Lobe went a stage further. They finally annulled Kant's original distinction between (mechanical) talent and (organic) genius[120] by arguing that "genius" itself is in fact an aptitude that must be developed, i.e. a product of hard work. In this respect, the mechanical aspect of study – including the assimilation of patterns,

---

[116] Burnham, *Musical Performance in the Age of Beethoven*, 20.

[117] Marx, *The School of Musical Composition*, x.

[118] Burnham, *Musical Performance in the Age of Beethoven*, 21. Translation modified.

[119] Reicha, *Treatise on Melody*, 3.

[120] While arguing for the possibility of a mechanical understanding of art produced by natural genius, Kant maintains the division between talent and genius in terms of artistic invention itself: "Although mechanical and beautiful art are very different, the first being a mere art of industry and learning and the second of genius, yet there is no beautiful art in which there is not a mechanical element that can be comprehended by rules and followed accordingly." See Kant, *Critique of Judgment*, 153.

the repetition of models, and the absorption by constant practice of principles of motific variation – effectively recasts the genius of melodic invention as a mechanical–associative faculty predicated on the postulate of associative laws.

Within this realist awakening, what were the strategies for objectifying melody that began to make this shift towards rigorous study plausible? I briefly summarize four representative examples.

Rhythm

Musical rhythm – i.e. periodicity and proportion – was at the very center of Reicha's *Traité* (1814). After subordinating harmony to melody "entirely," he declares that, first and foremost, melody "requires a theory of rhythm,"[121] which is later defined simply as "*musical symmetry*."[122] The interrelation and metric balance of periods according to cadence type, measure count, and phrasal symmetry provide the analytical means for him to interrogate eighteenth-century melodic models with empirical certitude. This methodology was drawn from Reicha's Enlightenment belief in the centrality of reason ("the sun in the system of the world"),[123] and enables his radical stance against the mystery of melody: "the composer is either a skillful architect, or a simple workman ... Music is either good or bad and the reasons for this difference are indisputably demonstrable."[124]

After chastising the "vague arguments" of earlier attempts at melodic theory for their lack of rigor and amenability to proof, he allies the metrical scrutability of melody with the study of poetic rhythm and oratory to argue that if melody:

is only the fruit of genius, or more precisely an outpouring of feeling and its various forms, it must be conceded that it holds this in common with poetry and oratory.[125]

But if the metrical scrutability of language and the rules of oratory are both Reicha's initial justification for approaching melody quantatively, they are also his closing confirmation that such an approach to melodic theory is valid. The comparative logic argues that like alcaic and iambic feet, melody can be measured and assessed, but whereas these meters measure "only the syllables," true musical rhythm measures "ideas."[126]

In a further expansion of the definition of rhythm, Reicha posits the symmetry of ideas, not of periods or figures, as the defining element of good

---

[121] Reicha, *Treatise on Melody*, 13.   [122] *Ibid.*, 94.   [123] *Ibid.*, 120.   [124] *Ibid.*, 119.
[125] *Ibid.*, 3.   [126] *Ibid.*, 97.

melody. His final sentence poses a question that brings the argument full circle, where melody becomes didactic for the very linguistic elements that enabled Reicha's scrutiny of it in the first place:

> Could not the principal rhythmic procedures, as important for both poetry and oratory, be discovered by strictly imitating the best melodies with poetic phrases, rendering them as well rhythmicized as melodic phrases?[127]

Irrespective of whether this reinstates a degree of mystery over melodic origins, reviews of Czerny's German translation of the *Traité* in 1824 admired the audacity with which Reicha tackled "music's most essential element, about which no treatise has yet appeared."[128] But the ostensibly narrow insistence on rhythm earned Reicha's treatise an abrupt dismissal by its most influential reviewer. François-Josef Fétis regarded it as inferior to its precursors because Reicha "has considered his topic in only one respect, that of rhythm and melodic phraseology," and leaves out such central parameters as "tonality, modulation, harmony and aesthetics."[129] The controversy over this point was still being discussed as late as 1850 by the *Gazzetta musicale di Milano*,[130] but in fact, Fétis only identified what Reicha himself openly acknowledged: that two arias sharing the same meter and key, and with the same modulations, rhythm, and form – i.e. exhausting the scope of his investigation – "may nevertheless be entirely opposite in character."[131]

Wellenspiel

Rather than isolating the temporal properties of melodic form, Kanne's brief excursus into melody sought a way of objectifying the poetic idea of melody's linear motion. Like Reicha, Kanne pursues a means of giving

---

[127] *Ibid.*, 98.

[128] "[Reicha bietet ein Werk an,] ueber dessen Gegenstand, als den wesentlichsten in der Musik, bisher noch gar keine Abhandlung erschienen ist." *Caecilia* 8, Supplement "Intelligenzblatt zur Caecilia" (1825), 57.

[129] "A l'égard de son livre en lui-même, on peut dire qu'il est imparfait, en ce que l'auteur n'y a considéré son sujet que sous un seul aspect, celui de rythme de la phraséologie mélodique, et n'a pas même entrevu les lois de la mélodie sous les rapports de tonalité, de modulation, d'harmonie et d'esthétique." Fétis, *Traité élémentaire de musique* (Brussels, 1831–32), rpt. *Biographie universelle* (Paris, 1863), vii: 203.

[130] See G. V., "Del 'Trattato di melodia' di Antonio *Reicha*," *Gazzetta musicale di Milano* 42 (October 20, 1850), 180–81.

[131] Reicha, *Treatise on Melody*, 62.

form to melody. He acknowledges rhythm as a primary factor, and symmetry as "just as essential for music as superior architecture."[132] But unlike Reicha, Kanne's simile for symmetry is the imperfect human body, and his fundamental law of melodic succession is wave motion, which he likens emphatically to the ocean:

Who will think me wrong for seeking a relationship in great nature that is entirely analogous in its puzzling organization to that which I am endeavoring to analyze here in music? . . . / With her gentle movements, the surface of the sea is like the primal key of C major. The [musical] scale recurs on it like a measure of tones, except that the latter accumulates more precisely and does so in the smallest relationship of the tapering scale [of proportions], namely in the shortening strings and in the higher octaves. / But even this relationship finds its likeness, namely by means of one's perspective wherein every more distant wave appears like a higher octave that permits smaller vibrations, and yet it has the same nature as the larger wave – just in a greater magnitude . . . / It is certain that there is no relationship to be found in all the grandeur of nature that would be more similar to the melodic scale through its inner essence and lively nature than the moving surface of the sea! / What can better help explain the embodied picture of all feeling and passion, music, than this symbol of all rest and movement, all gentle feelings and stormy passions, all change of calm stillness and of furious struggle? / Morally the similarity would be undeniable.[133]

There is a literal quality to this simile. For Kanne, all melodic motion is fundamentally stepwise, and intervals larger than a second merely leave out an original composite of second steps through "an act of freedom that the sense of beauty demanded."[134] The proof thereof lies in nature, in the

---

[132] "Denn die Symetrie ist in der Musik so unerlässlich, als in der höheren Architectur." Kanne, "Der Zauber der Tonkunst," *AmZ* 65 (August 15, 1821), 514.

[133] "Wer wird es mir übel nehmen, dass ich ein Verhältniss in der grossen Natur aufsuchte, das in seiner räthselhaften Eintheilung ganz analog dem ist, welches ich hier in der Musik zu analysiren bemüht bin? . . . / Die Fläche des Meeres in ihrer sanften Bewegung ist gleich der Urtonart C-dur, und in ihr wiederholt sich die Scala wie im Tonmass, nur dass sie in letzterem spitziger und in das kleinste Verhältniss des verjüngten Massstabes ausläuft, nähmlich in den kürzer werdenden Saiten, und den höheren Octaven? / Jedoch auch diess Verhältniss findet seine Vergleichung. Nähmlich durch die Perspective erscheint jede entferntere Welle gleichsam als eine höhere Octave, die also kürzere Schwingungen zulässt, und doch dieselbe Natur hat, wie die grosse Welle, nur in höherer Potenz . . . / Soviel ist wenigstens gewiss, dass kein Verhältniss in der ganzen grossen Natur aufzufinden, das dem der melodischen Scala durch sein inneres Wesen und lebendige Natur ähnlicher wäre, als die bewegte Meeresfläche! / Was kann mehr das verkörperte Bild aller Gefühle und Leidenschaften, die Musik, erläutern helfen, als dieses Sinnbild aller Ruhe und Bewegung, aller sanften Gefühle und stürmischen Leidenschaften, alles Wechsels der ruhigen Stille und des wüthendsten Kampfes? / Moralisch wäre die Ähnlichkeit unläugbar." Kanne, "Der Zauber der Tonkunst," *AmZ* 68 (August 25, 1821), 538–39.

[134] "Ich sage die secundenweise Fortschreitung, weil alle bey Terzen-, Quarten-, Quinten und anderen Sprüngen ausgelassenen Secunden doch ursprünglich mit gedacht, und nur durch

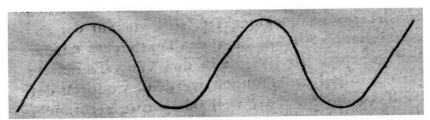

2.3a F. A. Kanne's illustration of melodic wave motion in imitation of water, *AmZ* 68 (1821), 537.

Volk ("e.g. farmers, old wives, children, shepherds") who fill in intervening intervals because they cannot actually manage leaps, and because their "instinct for symmetry and order forces them spontaneously to fill in the gaps."[135] (Marx went the other way and, five years later, would associate such vocal fill-ins with the original impulse for virtuosic embellishment in Italian singers.[136])

On the basis of this speculation, an unbroken chain of seconds in every melody is able to mirror the undulating waves of the ocean with tactile literalism since every melodic leap implies a "wave" in one direction and must then be balanced in the other. As Figure 2.3a shows, graphic wave motion was also pictorial for Kanne, and in Examples 2.2a and 2.2b, he illustrates how actual melodic lines become, as it were, a reduction of implied linear motion.

More specifically, the octave is split at the fifth into two halves. Melodic "waves" rise up to the fifth, and fall in tension as the line continues to the tonic. In other words, in ascending $\hat{1}$–$\hat{5}$ we increase tension, and as we continue $\hat{6}$–$\hat{8}$ we return to repose. The scale can incline entirely, if rising to a new key, as Figure 2.3b shows.

But here "the calm is abolished" and the fixed trajectory destroys the "wonderful circle of scales rising and returning to repose."[137] As Figure 2.3c shows, the movement often rises and forms a new "circle" (i.e. tonicizes the

---

einen Act der Freyheit, den das Gefühl der Schönheit geboth, weggelassen sind." A. F. Kanne, "Der Zauber der Tonkunst," *AmZ* 42 (May 26, 1821), 508.

[135] Kanne's full justification for a folk-reading of melodic seconds is: "Daher zieht der Naturalist im Gesange (z. B. Bauern, alte Weiber, Kinder, Hirten etc.) die Secunden auch alle durch, und nimmt selten einen Sextensprung ohne die inmitten liegenden Secunden mit anzuschlagen … der gemeine Mann [singt so] weil er erstlich die Sprünge oft nicht treffen kann, aber (2) weil ihm da Lücken zu seyn scheinen, die das jedem Menschen innewohnende Wohlgefallen zu Symetrie und Ordnung, ihn unwillkürlich auszufüllen zwingt." Kanne, "Der Zauber der Tonkunst," *AmZ* 65 (August 15, 1821), 513.

[136] Marx, *Die Kunst des Gesanges, Theoretisch–Praktisch* (Berlin: A. M. Schlesinger, 1826), 261.

[137] "Durch eine solche Scala wäre der Aufschwung fortgesetzt, aber auch alle Ruhe aufgehoben, und der wunderbare Zirkel der steigenden und wieder zur Ruhe zurückkehrenden Scala zerstört." Kanne, "Der Zauber der Tonkunst," *AmZ* 68 (August 25, 1821), 538.

Example 2.2a F. A. Kanne's sample Lutheran melody, *AmZ* 65 (1821), 513.

Example 2.2b F. A. Kanne illustrates an underlying melody, composed only of seconds, *AmZ* 65 (1821), 537.

2.3b F. A. Kanne's scale, rising by 5th to modulate, *AmZ* 68 (1821), 538.

2.3c F. A. Kanne's melodic "whirlpools," centered around each station of the cycle of fifths, *AmZ* 68 (1821), 538.

dominant) where the "concrete particularity of the wave circle" can relocate its center like a series of whirlpools. In Figure 2.3d, Kanne illustrates the kinship between graphic wave motion and non-modulating melodic scales, i.e. the "vividness of the first plastic line of oceanic waves applied to music."[138]

One wonders why Kanne's illustrative sine waves do not demand non-discrete intervals, i.e. glissandi, or vocal portamento. Though this may be implied by the continuous topography of water, the practical impossibility of justifying such anti-grammatical lines – essentially: pitch-continuous cries – in compositional terms perhaps rendered the full implications of this principle of motion unrealizable in 1821.

---

[138] "Wir wollen der Anschaulichkeit wegen die erste plastische Linie der Meereswellen, welche oben abgegeben ist, auf die Scala der Musik angewendet, hier aufzeichnen." *Ibid.*

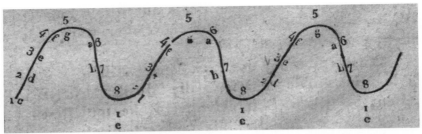

2.3d F. A. Kanne's graphic register of tension within non-modulating (C major) melodic scales, *AmZ* 68 (1821), 538.

Parameters of expression

In seeking to fulfill the idealist criterion where "the beauty of melody depends solely upon the truth of its expression,"[139] the Anglo-German theorist Teutonius spelled out two objectives for melodic material:

[1] to give a characteristic expression to certain feelings, and to raise the same or similar feelings in the heart of the listener
[2] to do this in a manner pleasing to the human ear.[140]

His ensuing approach to *Melodik* advances little beyond unconvincing generalities, indicating how difficult it remained to identify melodic objects analytically. All melody is essentially vocal and must reside within a given key, he argues, while a melody's character is determined by:

● ambitus[141]
● relation to the tonic scale degree[142]
● intervallic motion[143]

---

[139] Teutonius, "Melody and Melodious Combination," 795.   [140] *Ibid.*, 774.
[141] A determined or violent character requires larger; more passive or quieter feelings require smaller range. *Ibid.*, 794.
[142] Melodies beginning on the tonic exhibit a decisive, definite character; those beginning on other scale degrees are unsettled, "expressive of feelings [and] float on trembling waves." *Ibid.*, 793.
[143] Stepwise melodies are "more natural in accordance with the way feelings arise . . . [and] typical for singing the praise of nature, innocence, domestic happiness, tenderness . . . or any other *quiet* feeling"; but melodies characterized by leaps express "greater boldness and decision" proportionately to the frequency and size of the leaps. *Ibid.*, 795.

- relation to the tonic scale[144]
- choice of key and tonality[145]

Such unhelpfully broad categories underscore a general disappointment over attempts to quantify "true" melodic expressivity through the objectification of discrete analytical parameters.

Plural listening

An intractable problem – foregrounded by Teutonius – in this questing for objectified expression was that "[a]mong a thousand hearers perhaps not two agree in opinion of the outward beauty of any musical production."[146] Musical beauty was in fact commonly defined only as "the effect produced upon the organ of hearing," he asserts, and, by broadening the scope of *Melodik* to the effects of sound on sensory perception, his approach to expression becomes inherently unstable because no two listeners are identical (as he admits) and, furthermore, any auditor's perception cannot be measured remotely, it can only hypothesized vicariously by a composer.[147]

One response to this indeterminacy of expression was a pragmatic recourse to recurrent structure. While addressing thematic development as an essential ingredient of melody, Kanne sets up a listening perspective wherein the varied repetition and recurrence of thematic material is demanded by the nature of music's transience; if a theme is heard only once and disappears, it "scarcely leaves behind a lasting impression on the listener's soul." This condition is not true of poetry, Kanne qualifies, since semantic concepts are clearer and more distinct than melody in what they express, and therefore easier to grasp and retain mentally. Kanne thus articulates a "law of

---

[144] Remaining in a scale's tonal orbit creates "a feeling or sensation [that] is already rooted in the soul . . . [such as] faith, courage, enthusiastic love . . . [it is typical for] songs of war and hymns of praise"; while the incorporation of foreign notes, particularly by leap "always express[es] an excited state of mind, and progressions to strange sounding intervals, indicate always a sudden change, or the unexpected appearance of a new emotion in the heart of the singer." *Ibid.*

[145] All of which have "distinctive characters" which Teutonius does not specify. Teutonius, "Melody and Melodious Combination," 774–75, 792–95.

[146] *Ibid.*, 795.

[147] Paradoxically, Teutonius accounts for this difficulty by embracing the illimitability of renditions for each melody under observation, i.e. by embracing the diversity of the listening subjects. He asserts that the integrity of the "spiritual idea" behind each melodic expression determines the perception of beauty irrespective of who is listening: "the nearer [a melody] approaches this ideal, the greater is the beauty of its [material] production." *Ibid.*

recurrence" as a distinguishing feature (and basic condition) of music in general, and melody in particular:

> Does music not rush ... so quickly before our souls that hardly any thought of it remains in our memory unless the composer was accustomed to leading his wonderworld into new shapes and shining colors? ... With the wonderful forms of melody our memory tries in vain to hold on to certain main moments ... He who follows the whole is unable to hold on to ragged moments and individual beauties in his soul ... the rapid rushing by of sounds has made the repetition of phrases an essential postulate of music.[148]

In a sense, Kanne's observation is only that we are slow on the uptake, and that composers must account for this in their melodic structure. But the direct, causal connection he establishes between listener and compositional theory was new, and distantly foreshadows Wagner's later aspiration for a sound mass that would be intuitively comprehensible (*gefühlsverständlich*) for a listener, whether or not fractured through multiple perspectives.

Marx's organicism

With a slightly different pedagogical purpose in mind, Marx brushed aside concerns over the signified of melody – the heritage of seventeenth-century *Figurenlehre* – arguing contrariwise that composers should let go of their aesthetic inhibitions and stop fretting about the quality of a theme and its expression. In a drive to shake off the collective neurosis surrounding melodic poverty in the German states, he explains that "any combination of two or more sounds ... may serve as a motif," at least for pedagogical purposes.[149] The innate quality of a combination of two or more notes is not that important, since – unlike periodic structures – it can be developed and manipulated indefinitely through continual permutation. (Citing the first movement of Beethoven's Fifth Symphony, he is entirely serious when

---

[148] "Denn rauscht nicht die Musik ... so schnell vor der Seele vorüber, dass von ihr kaum ein Gedanke in der Erinnerung bleibe, wenn nicht der Tonsetzer seine Wunderwelt in neuer Gestalt und Farbenglanz wieder vor die Seele zu führen gewohnt wäre? ... indess bey den wunderbaren Formen der Melodie das Gedächtnisse vergeblich sich bemühen würde, gewisse Hauptmomente festzuhalten ... Denn wer das Ganze verfolgt, kann unmöglich abgerissene Momente und einzelne Schönheiten in seiner Seele auffassen und festhalten ... Denn das schnelle Vorüberrauschen der Töne hat die Wiederholung der Sätze als ein unerlässliches Postulat in der Tonkunst aufgestellt." Kanne, "Der Zauber der Tonkunst," *AmZ* 66 (August 18, 1821), 522–23.

[149] Marx, *The School of Musical Composition*, 27.

stating that even "apparently the most insignificant" motifs can be used to great effect.)[150]

If the task of *Melodielehre* had once been the systematization of melodic expression, Marx's four-volume treatise of 1837 – which went through six full or partial editions during his lifetime – returned the debate to modes of construction and fluent productivity. He elaborates a theory of melodic–motific germination based, as we know, on principles of homology derived from Goethe's *Versuch die Metamorphose der Pflanzen zu erklären* (1790), where the motif – as he clarified in 1856 – corresponds to "the germinal vesicle, that membranous sac filled with some fluid element . . . the *Urgestalt* of everything organic – the true primal plant or primal animal."[151] This raises the question as to whether Marx's purpose was actionable pedagogy or more a philosophical validation of the compositional process through organicism.[152]

With this in mind, here is a brief reminder of Marx's approach to melody. His paradigm for all melodic construction was the major scale in a single octave, which – like Kanne's *Wellenspiel* of repose rising to tension and falling back to repose – embodies his mantra of *Ruhe – Bewegung – Ruhe* as it rises and falls (see Example 2.3a). Thus, the formal principle from which Marx derives all the genres of modern instrumental music is, for him, equally embedded in the nature of melody's fundamental formation. Not surprisingly, the scale is also implicit in the origin of periodic form, which Marx casts as a literal peak; that is, an "elevation from repose and intensification in tone succession and rhythm up to a natural *high point*; *return*, likewise with intensified motion . . . to the true *tone of repose*." He denies that the seven degrees of the major scale are restrictive, calling them simply "the most natural model for the formation of tonal succession."[153] But they are unequal, he explains, even in purely melodic terms, for tetrachordal structure requires that G rise to C, F fall to C, as illustrated in Example 2.3b. Though it is not substantiated, the implication is that hierarchies of harmonic function influence all melodic motion.

While Marx discusses four types of melodic motion – ascending, descending, wandering, and repeating – only the first two constitute genuine motion for him, and awaken predictably contrary feelings (of excitement

---

[150]　*Ibid.*, 28.

[151]　Marx, "Die Form in der Musik," in *Die Wissenschaften im neunzehnten Jahrhundert*, ed. J. A. Romberg (Leipzig: Romburg, 1856), 2: 21–48, here 29.

[152]　A thorough account of organicist models of theories of invention during the eighteenth and nineteenth centuries is given in Abrams, *The Mirror and the Lamp*, 198–225.

[153]　Marx, *The School of Musical Composition*, 17.

Example 2.3a A. B. Marx's complete periodic melody based on the scale.

Example 2.3b A. B. Marx's examination of the scale.

and calm) in the listener.[154] The need for the first and last sounds of a melody to fall on the principal parts of the measure entails Marx's different rhythmicizations of the scale, where the beginning and end must be "sufficiently energetic." Over and above this highly systematic approach to a melody-as-scale (which Marx admits is "of no artistic value"[155]), his interest in the actual germination of thematic motifs enters regions that earlier theorists, wary of being seen to prescribe and thereby reify genius, could not access. In doing so, he begins to articulate the territory of what could be called the Romantic–mechanic genius. The rationale for needing such a concept is clear:

> We may, perhaps, be so fortunate as to possess some good [melodic] ideas. But this alone would be of little use. We must be *certain* that we shall *always* be able to produce something new; our productive power must not depend upon the accidental occurrence of a happy idea.[156]

Marx's veiled play with two of Goethe's more influential metaphors – organic growth ("produce something new") and a lightning strike of inspiration ("accidental occurrence of a happy idea") – encapsulates his solution to the difficulties of other melodic theorists. By ignoring rather than directly contradicting an aesthetics of inspiration, Marx sidesteps the doctrine of genius and replaces it with a theory at once organically conceived and mechanically modeled, as well as foregrounding the imperative of a work ethic.

Such an attitude risked appearing dismissive of expression, which Schilling's *Encyclopädie* regarded "solely and exclusively" as the "real

---

[154] With ascent comes "the feeling of intensification, elevation, and tension"; descent brings "feelings of slackening, depression, and the return to rest"; and roving motion has no decided character. Burnham, *Musical Form in the Age of Beethoven*, 38.

[155] Marx, *The School of Musical Composition*, 26.   [156] *Ibid.*

essence of every melody."[157] If Marx's *Melodielehre* marked a watershed in the history of melodic theory, how was it received? While the next generation of German critics such as Joachim Raff tended to laud "Marx's excellent composition treatise,"[158] an émigré organist and composition teacher – Max Braun – demonstrates that twenty years after its initial publication it still courted controversy, at least from the safe distance of New York.[159] Writing in the *New York Musical World*, Braun charged that Marx was "falsely representing the character of melody in general."[160] He systematically disputes every step of Marx's process for generating melodic forms, protesting against the theorist's specious tools in a pyrrhic reassertion of the old school of natural genius:

Will the reader even get a distinct idea of the character of a sound and good melody? Must not this method of inciting to "artistic activity" give him the idea that composing a melody consists merely in filling up four or eight bars in a rhythmical manner? Is not such treatment simply detestable note-making in its most horrible shape?[161]

Though riddled with the rhetorical excess of polemics, Braun's line of criticism evidently proved hard to refute. Marx's original compositions – both within and without his theoretical writings – would seem to have been a prime opportunity to dismiss such attacks. But press reviews only served to reinscribe suspicions of Marx's creative monotony. Even August Kahlert, a staunch advocate of Marx's theoretical writings, conceded in the *Neue Zeitschrift* that he was divided over the professor's 1841 oratorio *Moses*, equivocating politely that "the musical invention appeared to me not always to be on the same level as the poetic inspiration that distinguishes the composer overall."[162] And looking purely at Marx's theoretical writings, Gustav Prinz reviewed the second edition of the *Compositions-Lehre* warmly in the *Allgemeine Wiener Musik-Zeitung*, but requested that, in future, Marx direct his "mental energy" (*geistige Thatkraft*) more towards

---

[157] "denn das eigentliche Wesen einer jeden Melodie besteht einzig und allein im Ausdruck." Schilling, *Encyclopädie*, 4: 644.

[158] "Marx's vortrefflicher Compositions-Lehre." Raff, *Die Wagnerfrage*, 57.

[159] Max Braun's primary professional identity appears to have been as the organist at St. Francis Xavier's College, New York.

[160] Max Braun, "Max 'versus' Marx: Critical analysis of A. B. Marx's 'Musical Composition' with additional commentary on music training," *New York Musical World* 18 (1857), 533.

[161] *Ibid.*

[162] "die musikalische Erfindung schien mir nicht überall auf der Höhe der poetischen Begeisterung, die den Componisten in seinem ganzen Wirken auszeichnet, zu stehen." August Kahlert, "Aus Breslau," *NZfM* 16 (1842), 116.

examples of "authentic folk melody" (*das wahre Volkslied*), thereby implicitly belittling Marx's examples.[163]

Nevertheless, as Example 2.4 illustrates, Marx demonstrates a painfully incremental approach to melodic germination, indicating that he is aspiring to create neither expressive natural gestures (Kahlert) nor *volkstümliche Melodie* (Prinz), but rather is illustrating the paradigmatic construction of melody from a single motif. It is a *tour de force* of Goethean organicism, and very much illustrative of a process, not a product. "A piece of gold which I find," Marx exhorts professorially, "is worth only so much as its value in money; but a skill which I have acquired, may be a source of constant profit." This skill – of inventing melody from a motific fragment – is bravely exemplified in his own procedure.

Of course, it remains rooted in the C major scale and consequently "partakes in a general monotony of expression."[164] Not only does the approach therefore require a leap of faith from readers that such a method could yield beautiful, expressive melodies, but Marx also cautions against consciously striving for originality, which he felt would always be forced unless it arises spontaneously when a composer is in the right state of mind (this is the closest Marx comes to a Goethean view of melodic lightning).[165]

But Braun continues to lampoon the artifice in Marx's modern methodology, quipping that his means of spinning out a melody to infinite lengths could provide a "musical submarine telegraph around the globe."[166] (The metaphor was *a propos*: a first attempt at laying a transatlantic cable took place that same year, 1857.)[167] Braun's accusation is that, in practice, no genuine composition or beautiful melody is derived from germinal motifs in this way; he likens Marx's organicist language ironically to that of a producer of artificial flowers, who instructs his apprentice: "Here is a leaf, and here is a stem; nurse them; apply them, etc. Make a bouquet!" This results, he continues sarcastically, in "splendid bouquets, which would look [as good] . . . as Marx's *designs sound!*"[168] Artificiality of means and materials thus underpin Braun's critique and, with overtones of *Tristan avant la lettre*, the notion that Marx – "a first rate necromancer" – utilizes the major

---

[163] Gustav Prinz, "Musikalische Literatur," *Allgemeine Weiner Musik–Zeitung* 4 (1843), 119.

[164] Marx, *The School of Musical Composition*, 34.

[165] Marx states that a student should not search for that "which he fancies to be most interesting or unusual," – continuing that – "such things cannot even be discovered by being purposely sought for, but arise spontaneously, when the mind is fully engrossed in the development of an artistic idea." *Ibid.*, 35.

[166] Braun, "Max 'versus' Marx," 615.

[167] Huurdeman, *The Worldwide History of Telecommunications*, 130ff.

[168] Braun, "Max 'versus' Marx," 567.

Example 2.4 A. B. Marx's illustration (adapted) of how to derive melodic phrases from a two-note motif; *The School of Musical Composition*, pp. 30–32.

scale – "his magic musical bottle" – to provide the melodic material for all sorts of motifs – *"all sorts of drinks"*[169] – provokes a positively glandular response:

[S]hould [a composer] wish to *invent* a melody of eight bars, to fit to a long or a short meter, he will find, at last, that his carefully nursed [motific] germs will forsake him in the hour of necessity, and he will be thrown back, musically poverty-stricken, upon his barren Marx again. I speak from experience … The whole of Marx's treatment … consists merely of making notes, and it is, for this reason, the most objectionable method that an extravagant mind could put forth. It stupefies and kills."[170]

Marx's necromantic "drinks" are noxious, Braun implies, because they do not work – a placebo exposed as such – requiring not even an "antidote for evil poisons" (*für böse Gifte Gegengift*); by contrast, Wagner's lovers in *Tristan* pursue their sexual destiny precisely because their potion *does* work, even though, dramatically, we understand it as a functioning placebo, as Thomas Mann first argued.[171] According to his own ironic conceit, Braun desires a state of altered consciousness through the "secret arts" in order to compose melodies; but when this is denied him, the *Compositions-Lehre* becomes merely another redundant prop, and the mystery of melodic invention torments him into publishing his black review.

Such visceral anger stems from Braun's frustration at being duped, as he sees it, into believing that a system could generate melodies. The logical problem he identifies is that Marx derives his motifs from the scale, encouraging his readers to imitate the procedures by which such motifs are generated. As a final *jeu d'esprit*, Braun gripes that an aspiring composer would have first to invent an original melody for the derivative motifs to be possible. Without a melody or scale from which to take motific fragments in the first place, there can be nothing to develop: "Just like the man who cannot find the matches in the dark, and strikes a light to seek them!"[172] Thus, the underlying theoretical construct that serves in place of original melody, the C major scale, is both the source and predicate of Marx's "barren" and "unnatural" examples, in this reading, as well as the proof that – from Braun's perspective – Marx is not addressing original composition *per se*.

---

[169] *Ibid.*, 615. Emphasis added.   [170] *Ibid.*, 567.

[171] "[the lovers] might as well have been drinking water." Thomas Mann, "The Sorrows and Grandeur of Richard Wagner," in *Pro and Contra Wagner*, trans. Allan Blunden (University of Chicago Press, 1985), 105.

[172] Braun, "Max 'versus' Marx," 567.

J. C. Lobe and the human melograph

While no theorist risked citing their own melodies exclusively as exemplars, Lobe's *Compositions-Lehre* (1844) avoided paradigmatic scales, relying instead on a combination of borrowed melodies of the First Viennese School and thematic deconstruction to move beyond such criticism. It propounds a methodology in which the mechanical assimilation of prized melodic models is a prerequisite for any composer (alongside the ability to correct and improve one's original melodies). As a means of composition, such inculcation resonates with the mechanical melograph we saw earlier in that it ultimately aspires to foster the ability to formulate expressive melody without conscious intervention because of an internalized associative mechanism – a learned mental process (substituting for an intricately designed mechanical assemblage) – that makes invention possible.

Lobe is explicit about this: the student's objective is "to internalize the purely technical means [of expressive melody] so that he does not have to think about them, at least not at moments of invention."[173] Though ostensibly commonsensical, this registers an unequivocal point of contact between pedagogy and unconscious creation. Where sublimation is the aim, the purpose of studies in melody – Lobe continues – is:

to fathom and bring to consciousness in the most particular and clearest way which tempo, which meter, which kind of notes, which kind of rising and falling from a tonic, which kind of articulation, and which accent to apply and which would be suitable to elicit the desired expression in the listener.[174]

Once this special knowledge has been fully absorbed and its "technical means" operate unconsciously within the composer's mind (i.e. the laws of associating the means of expression have been inculcated), a composer ought to be able to invent expressive melodies without needing "to think about" the means, Lobe argues. In this context, he proceeds to a decidedly practical definition of genius that moves dialectically between conscious (study) and unconscious (inspiration) before being sublated as a higher state of consciousness (revision):

---

[173] "Vorausgesetzt wird, dass er (der Schüler) die rein technischen Mittel bereits so durchgeübt und in sich aufgenommen habe, um an sie nicht mehr besonders denken zu müssen. Im Momente der Erfindung wenigstens nicht." Lobe, *Compositions-Lehre*, 42.

[174] "*bei den Uebungen*, auf's Schärfste und Klarste zu ergründen und in sein Bewustseyn zu bringen, welches Tempo, welche Taktart, welche Notengattungen, welche Art von tonischem Steigen und Fallen, welche Stricharten und welche Accente anzuwenden und geeignet seyn möchten, den bezweckten Ausdruck bei dem Hörer hervorzubringen." *Ibid*.

As a master, he will no longer need these [technical melodic] procedures. Then he exercises zeal [*Begeisterung*] in invention, and notates what this provides him. But in this zeal all the elements that he had consciously practiced affect him, admittedly more mysteriously in that instant, in a more dreamlike manner, but nevertheless operating more securely and with more accomplishment; and altogether they bring him his due. To be sure, the glowing stream of zeal also carries cinders with it, at least it rarely flows in a pure way onto the paper. But then in the cool moments following, the entire, lucid knowledge of various artistic means learned earlier come to consciousness, and where, on looking over his creation, his feeling notices something that does not belong, this knowledge tells him where the foreign element lies, how he might cut it out and replace it with something authentic and correct.[175]

The intricate cog mechanisms of the melograph can be seen as a material analogue for the first stage of this *Melodik* in its embodiment of the agency of unconscious, systematic processing.[176] Recall that this embodied the hope to obviate inhibiting self-consciousness. Perhaps it was on this basis that the pedagogue Julius Becker dubbed Lobe's approach "synthetic" in a review from 1844.[177] Unlike other experts – Becker continues – who "first discover a half-measure, then become aware of a way to a way to a distant lying error, and finally perhaps even are embarrassed by a school-masterly, pedantic method, and want to ascribe genius to what appears to them as unattainable by an arithmetic example," Becker cites Lobe's unrelenting, systematic strictness as laudable, labeling his approach "just as necessary as of essential benefit."[178]

---

[175] "Als Meister wird er dieser Proceduren nicht mehr bedürfen. Dann läßt er bei der Erfindung die Begeisterung walten, und zeichnet hin, was sie ihm eingibt, aber in dieser Begeisterung wirken alle die früher mit Bewusstseyn durchgeübten Elemente ein, zwar ihm in Augenblicke dunkler, traumumfangener, aber dennoch sicherer und wohlerzogener Thätigkeit, und bringen ihm im Ganzen das Rechte. Allerdings führt der glühende Strom der Begeisterung auch Schlacken mit sich, wenigstens wird er sehr selten durchaus rein auf das Papier fliessen. Dann kommt ihm aber in den nachherigen kühlen Augenblicken die ganze früher gewonnene hellere Erkenntniss der mannichfaltigen Kunstmittel in's Bewusstseyn, wo sein Gefühl bei'm Ueberschauen des Erfundenen ihn auf etwas Ungehöriges aufmerksam macht, sagt ihm auch diese Erkenntniss, worin das Ungehörige liege, wie es ausschneiden und durch Aechtes und Rechtes ersetzen könne." *Ibid.*, 42–43.

[176] Lobe's reference to cinders curiously modifies Shelley's metaphor – in *A Defence of Poetry* (1821) – of the mind in creation as burning coals glowing according to an inconstant wind. By inserting dirtying cinders into the creative flow, Lobe appears inadvertently to critique Shelley's belief in the purity of unconscious invention.

[177] "Der Verfasser geht nun in seinem Werke den synthetischen Weg. . ." Julius Becker, "Theorie: J. C. Lobe, 'Compositions-Lehre'," *NZfM* 25 (1844), 97.

[178] "Wenn im flüchtigen Durchblicken der Sachverständige bei einzelnen Bemerkungen, Erörterungen und Regeln bald eine Halbheit entdeckt, bald einen Weg zu einem Weg zu einem entfernt liegenden Irrthume gewahrt, bald vielleicht sogar da von einem schulmeisterlichen pedantischen Verfahren unangenehm berührt wird, wo er dem Genius anheim gegeben wissen

In answer, then, to the perennial question of whether melody can be learned, Lobe asserts that it *must* be learned. "No skill exists from birth," he warns, adding for good measure that "no skill would develop by itself along with the growing human [either]."[179] The evidence for this is conveniently close at hand: if German composers had been directed to melodic exercises early on "we would not have so many melody-less composers"; and if the striving for expressive melody were part of those exercises, "there would not be so many expressionless compositions that say nothing."[180] His emphasis on expressivity demands that he foreground expressive motifs themselves as the foundation of a melodic pedagogy. Accordingly, this dominates his analytical approach to musical models within the framework of the 8-measure period. Specifically, it is the interrelation, frequency, and repetition of motifs within a period that interests him, i.e. a governing principle of *thematische Arbeit* – defined as "the art of being able to repeat a musical thought, yet always altered, always metamorphosed so that it always appears as *the same*, but then also as *always different*."[181] This mechanism for generating motific variants further reinforces the common ground with the melograph's mechanical permutation, under-scoring the extent to which the treatise and the machine represented two sides of the same philosophical coin, even though, as noted earlier, such devices bore no explicit connection to any individual theories of mind.

Stylistically, Lobe's models (and the Componium) are rooted in the late eighteenth century, however, and may seem a long way from the fleshy bodies and expressive voices of mid-nineteenth-century Wagnerian opera, around which the debate over melody raged most vehemently. But Wagner's famous comment on Beethovenian sonata allegro forms (from 1860) establishes an elective sympathy with Lobe's mechanical project. It was precisely through the principle of motific permutation that Wagner envisaged the crystallization of motific fragmentation into a single unified melodic sense, that is, the principle of a proto-*unendliche Melodie*. His

möchte, was ihm auf dem Wege eines Rechenexempels nicht erreichtbar scheint, so bemerken wir, daß die Strenge, mit welcher der Verfasser in seiner Entwickelung vorschreitet und den Schüler an den Weg fesselt, welchen er ihn führt, eben so nothwendig als von wesentlichem Nutzen sei." *Ibid.*

[179] "Kein Können kommt mit dem Menschen auf die Welt; kein Können bildet sich etwa mit seinem körperlichen Wachsthum von selbst in ihm aus." Lobe, *Compositions-Lehre*, 36.

[180] "Wenn des Compositions-Schülers Streben frühzeitig auf technische Bildung von Melodieen gerichtet würde, so hätten wir nicht so viele melodielose Componisten; und wenn damit bald das Streben nach ausdrucksvollen Melodieen verbunden würde, so gäbe es gewiss nicht so viele ausdruckslose, nichtssagende Compositionen." *Ibid.*, 39.

[181] "die Kunst, einen musikalischen Gedanken vielmals wiederholen zu können, aber immer verändert, immer verwandelt, dergestalt, dass er stets *als derselbe*, aber doch zugleich *immer als ein anderer erscheint.*"*Ibid.*, 29.

description pertains to Beethoven, but could almost be read in relation to the Componium's putative improvisation:

The fragments are continually being reassembled in different formations – coalescing in a logical succession which here pours forth like a stream, there disperses as in an eddying vortex. Throughout one is riveted by their vivid expressiveness, absorbed by the excitement of sensing melodic significance in every harmony . . . [T]he completely novel outcome of this procedure was the expansion of a melody, through the rightly various development of all its constituent motifs, into a continuous large-scale piece of music, which itself constituted no less than a single, perfectly coherent melody.[182]

With Beethoven in mind, Lobe encourages his students to use their own motifs and copy the procedure through which he develops and varies his motifs, as well as the order in which he introduces motifs where more than one is used within a period. Aesthetics is "guilty" of not being able to explain why some motifs are "more interesting" than others, he argues, but melodies with fewer basic motifs are perhaps generally more comprehensible than those with many, and the use of only one motif in a melody may lead to monotony, he continues, adding that: "monotony and incomprehensibility may, however, be reduced or totally quashed by other elements" listed simply as rhythm, tonal structure, meter, and tempo.[183]

  Lobe's achievement, in short, was to apply principles of systematic learning to model-based pedagogy with a mandate for uncovering expressive "mechanisms." In a sense, this merely reverses the direction of stylistic composition or pastiche: instead of copying generic models within a given style to learn their expressive grammar, a student dismantles a particular model to discover the causes of its expression. But since the listening subject must register the changes in expression precisely and individually in Lobe's process, he is forced to argue that the "main condition" of an aspiring composer is simply "constant observation of the essence of the stirrings, feelings, affects, and passions in one's breast as well as of the ways in which others express the same."[184] In other words, the composer-as-listener is now to become the expressive register of his own melody, which in a feedback loop then educates him cumulatively as to the emotional properties of melodic expression.

---

[182] Wagner, "Music of the Future," *Three Wagner Essays*, 38.

[183] "Doch mag die Monotonie, so wie die Umfasslichkeit durch eine Menge anderer, günstig hinzutretender Umstände . . . sehr gemildert oder ganz verbannt werden." Lobe, *Compositions-Lehre*, 35.

[184] "Unausgesetzte Beobachtungen des Wesens der Regungen, Gefühle, Affecte und Leidenschaften in seiner eigenen Brust sowohl, als in den Aeusserungsweisen derselben bei Anderen, ist Haupbedingung eines Jeden, der ein ächter Componist werden will." *Ibid.*, 39–40.

In this respect, Lobe – after Kant – conjoins natural aptitude with rational expertise without philosophical trauma or contradiction.[185] This is only made possible by ascribing both mechanical and organic functions to a composer without a preference for the priority of either. Within the broader discourse on genius, such rhetoric was decidedly unusual. Whereas the organic imagination of genius was effectively lawless and expressly unregulated, it must also – in Lobe's reading – be a product of systematic cognitive construction. Lobe holds these two properties in equilibrium (as complementary) in his discussion of utilizing melodic inspiration. Here, as we have seen, the processes of automatic recall are educated to function according to a centrally governing emotion or design:

In all real artistic creation, there is inner emotion or thought, and the artist portrays both externally through the medium of art. The warmth of emotion or the depth of thought cannot be learned, although it can be very much educated and increased through learning and individual study; contrariwise, the still warm emotion or still deep thought cannot emerge from the head and heart without complete technical training. Melodic construction has such technical training, and this can be learned and improved with exercises.[186]

Mechanism is most evident in Lobe's illustration of how to compose a symphonic theme. In fact, it is an artificial reconstruction of the first theme from the fourth movement of Haydn's Symphony No. 104, even though reversing his dissection of Haydn's theme into its rhythmic and tonal parameters would seem far from a normative compositional process. Example 2.5 gives the five-part derivation. The zero-degree of melodic invention in Lobe's point of departure (Example 2.5i), the "primal figure of all possible themes," which he labels "monotonous – a dead thing," suggests that every melody can be created by building up rhythmic and tonal motion mechanically – step by step – from the underlying *Urgestalt*.[187] Had Lobe used his own melody, the derivation process would have succeeded or failed according to the quality of

---

[185] See Kant's counterpoint of genius with taste as the "disciplining (or training) of genius," in *Critique of Judgment*, § 50.

[186] "Bei allem ächten Kunstschaffen wirkt ein innerlich Empfundenes oder Gedachtes, und beides stellt der Künstler ausser sich dar durch das Medium seiner Kunst. Die Wärme der Empfindung oder die Tiefe des Denkens kann nicht erlernt werden, obgleich sehr ausgebildet und gesteigert durch Lehre und eigenes Studium; dagegen kann auch das noch so warm Empfundene und noch so tief Gedachte nicht heraus aus Kopf und Herz, ohne vollendete technische Ausbildung. Einen solchen technischen Theil hat auch die Melodiebildung, und dieser lässt sich erlernen und durch Uebung fördern." Lobe, *Compositions-Lehre*, 37.

[187] "Ich nehme . . . als Urgestalt aller möglichen Thema's, ja aller musikalischen Gedanken überhaupt, eine Melodie von acht Takten an . . . Folgender achtaktige Gedanke . . . ist . . . monoton – ein todtes Ding." *Ibid.*, 3.

Example 2.5 J. C. Lobe's process of thematic derivation, "Das Thema," *Compositions-Lehre* (1844), pp. 3–4.

the resulting melody; by relying on Haydn's reputation and working backwards, he merely underscores the artificial mechanism of the process.

The painterly practice of copying models was familiar in eighteenth-century compositional treatises, of course, where it had been quite explicit about melody. Daube recommended that budding composers adopt one or two pieces and write them out, adding: "It simply cannot fail, the benefits must follow. To work with good examples always remains praiseworthy."[188] That Geyer in 1860 would parody his readers who doubted they could learn to compose in this manner indicates a failure to persuade, suggesting not so much a methodological weakness, but rather that by the middle of the nineteenth century the method was out of sync with the aesthetic moment.

As mentioned above, Lobe did not accept the reasoning that held this process to be artificial, mechanical and therefore worthless; instead, he defended elementary illustrations of recomposition (such as those in Example 2.5) as those which develop and explain the melodic, thematic, periodic and formal designs "of all possible pieces of music."[189] Only by internalizing the technical means through such exercises, he countered, will students become able to wield

---

[188] "Man nehme sich vor, auf ein oder zwei Stücke Achtung zu geben, sodann sich solche aufschreiben . . . Es kann gar nicht fehlen, der Nutzen muß nachfolgen. Nach guten Mustern arbeiten, bleibt allezeit lobenswürdig." Johann Friedrich Daube, *Anleitung zur Erfindung der Melodie und ihrer Fortsetzung* (Vienna: Christian Gottlob Täubel, 1797), 58.

[189] "alle melodischen, thematischen, periodischen und formellen Gestaltungen aller möglichen Tonstücke. . ." Lobe, *Compositions-Lehre*, 3.

their own inspiration. To this end, he seeks in a later example to demonstrate a middle ground between this mechanical reconstruction of Haydn and actual original composition; this takes the form of an organic dissection of Mozart. If the one appears to piece together a Frankensteinian monster from "dead" melodic matter (or *Urgestalt*), the other dissects living melodic tissue with the scalpel of music analytical parameters, as it were, testing – as though galvanic current were being passed through the various neural networks – what expressive movement sparks into life. The former enlivens melody, the latter dismembers it: processes of simulated composition, and musical autopsy, respectively. In this second approach, given in Example 2.6, Lobe disrupts different musical elements one by one in Zerlina's aria "Batti, batti o bel Masetto" from act 1 of *Don Giovanni*, and asks rhetorically how Mozart created the "coaxing–asking" expression.[190]

The notion that melodic expression can only be revealed in its moment of destruction – i.e. as *apophasis*, only definable obliquely by its absence rather than directly by its presence – suggests that Lobe regards it as fundamentally concealed, in line with Hamann's definition of genius as a "negative greatness." The laws by which "every affect, every feeling, every passion" appears recognizably formed in melodic expression encompass for Lobe the "laws of motific formation and rearrangement."[191] But despite his pedagogical urge to show how these can be explored, he ultimately hints at the blasphemy in a student's desire to know and understand them directly. In other words, the natural, systematic mechanism of expression exists, but is safely beyond conscious comprehension:

[I]t is granted to no mortal to understand these laws exactly, to enumerate them in detail, and to bring them to recognition. One can only intimate the points on which one's mind fixes, drawing attention to what we expect and desire it to deliver to us. What it delivers to us, to examine the extent to which it corresponds to what is desired, is for the moment something of our feelings and our taste.[192]

While Lobe does not pursue his veiled reference to genius, he finally frees himself from "slave-like imitation," and composes an original melody (see Example 2.7) through the mechanical permutation and rearrangement of a

---

[190] "schmeichelnd-bittender Ausdruck," *Ibid.*, 40.

[191] "jeder Affekt, jedes Gefühl, jede Leidenschaft . . . tragen ihre Gesetze der Motivgestaltung und Umgestaltung in allen bisher gezeigten Verhältnissen ihrem Wesen gemäss in sich." *Ibid.*, 43.

[192] "[D]em Verstand aber diese Gesetze bestimmt und im Detail aufzuzählen und zur Erkenntniss zu bringen, ist keinem Sterblichen vergönnt. Nur andeuten kann man die Punkte, auf die man seinem Geist zu fixiren hat, gleichsam ihn aufmerksam machen, was wir verlangen und wünschen, das er uns liefern soll . . . Was er uns aber liefert, zu prüfen, in wie weit es dem Gewünschten entspricht, ist zunächst Sache unseres Gefühls und unseres Geschmacks." *Ibid.*

Example 2.6 J. C. Lobe's thematic deconstruction, "Aesthetic tips on melodic formation," *Compositions-Lehre* (1844), pp. 40–42.

(a) *Mozart's original.*

(b) *Rhythmic alteration*: the expression is "destroyed." *Deduction*: "a simple note type is a basic condition to every expression."[193]

(c) *Pitch alteration*: the original feeling is again "destroyed."
Deduction: "the gentle, stepwise falling and rising of tones in the . . . [original] melody awakens the coaxing–asking feeling most perceptibly," and larger intervals modify this expression, but cannot increase or enhance it.[194]

(d) *Metric alteration 1*: the original expression is essentially maintained in common time, "although a quiet change to the delicate feeling cannot be avoided."[195]

---

[193] "Wir folgen daraus . . . dass zu jenem Ausdrucke eine einfache Notengattung wesentliche Bedingung ist." Lobe, *Compositions-Lehre*, 40.

[194] "Wir folgen daraus . . . dass das sanfte, stufenweise Fallen und Steigen der Töne in dem ersten Abschnitte obiger Melodie das Schmeichelnd-Bittende am empfindsarsten weckt." *Ibid.*, 41.

[195] "eine leise Veränderung [mag] dem feinen Gefühle nicht entgehen." *Ibid.*

(e) *Metric alteration 2*: the change of expression "stands out more" in triple meter, but rhythmic modifications also contribute to this.[196]

(f) *Articulation alteration*: accents and other aspects of performance articulation "smudge or entirely alter" a melody's expression.[197]

(g) *Dynamic and articulation alteration*: "again the expression is different" to Mozart's original.[198] *Deduction*: The degree of this difference is directly proportional to the degree of alteration, leading ultimately to "an entirely different" kind of expression which at times can even become unrecognizable.

virgin arpeggiated motif, examining its aesthetic balance with a second contrasting motif, and the expressive conditions under which they function symbiotically as an expressive whole. This is the closest any response to the oxymoron of *Melodielehre* came to a concrete application.

* * *

The story of mid-nineteenth-century *Melodielehre* is an epic rather than a novella. The mystique of unthinking creation had underpinned melody's pre-eminence since the early eighteenth-century discourses on genius, but after Galvani animated dead matter, its idealist footing was undermined by creative speculation into the mechanisms of human biology. Once thought itself could be deemed material (electrochemical), the principle of vital materialism afforded modern aestheticians a more tactile grasp of processes of "genius." Hence, unconscious melodic invention was no longer absolute,

---

[196] "Hier wäre aber freilich nicht blos diese, sondern auch das Rhythmische verändert." *Ibid.*
[197] "den Ausdruck einer Melodie verwischen oder ganz umwandeln." *Ibid.*
[198] "Wieder anders wird der Ausdruck." *Ibid.*, 42

Example 2.7 J. C. Lobe's exercises in original melodic composition ("Reshuffling of 8-measure melodies"), *Compositions-Lehre* (1844), ex. 146, 156–**62.**

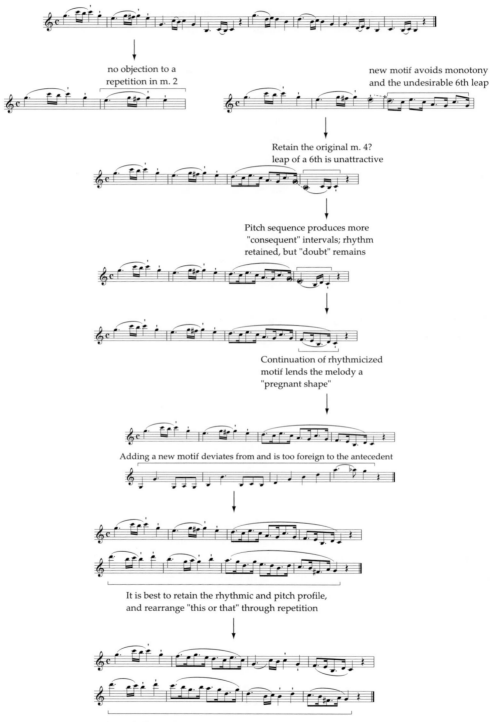

no objection to a
repetition in m. 2

new motif avoids monotony
and the undesirable 6th leap

Retain the original m. 4?
leap of a 6th is unattractive

Pitch sequence produces more
"consequent" intervals; rhythm
retained, but "doubt" remains

Continuation of rhythmicized
motif lends the melody a
"pregnant shape"

Adding a new motif deviates from and is too foreign to the antecedent

It is best to retain the rhythmic and pitch profile,
and rearrange "this or that" through repetition

The melody can be recast in terms of the order and sequence
of the motifs (because it is bound to no particular model)

and even appeared susceptible to scientific explication through the mechanical permutations of melographic automata, leaving only the conundrum of systematic or simulated melodic *expression*. But broadening our horizon somewhat, for Baudrillard (quoting Ecclesiastes), simulacra "never conceal the truth – it is the truth which conceals the fact that there is none. The simulacrum is true."[199] Was original melody an idealist hoax, with no truth to it? The mechanical simulation of musical cognition effectively challenged a faculty of modern melodic genius to reveal itself. Beyond the *Mozartbild*, narratives of German criticism prevented any show-and-tell, however, leaving only the "truth" of simulated expression within treatises such as Lobe's, whose very existence served to conceal the absence of more authentic invention. Numerous eighteenth-century definitions of genius allowed for such rule-bound practice, and it was only when *a priori* rules became conscious precepts that they constituted the simulation of something deemed more genuine. Precisely the accusation of dull mechanism was leveled at Lobe and Marx. Even half a century later, the same halo of doubt surrounded self-aware melodic composition: "Is the invention of melody unique and merely an expression of the unconsciously creating imagination of the composer," the theorist Salomon Jadassohn asked sixteen years after Wagner's death, "or is [conscious] musical artistic sense also already active in this process? / We are unable to answer even this question, for we are unable to separate these two activities."[200] Of course, it was theoretically possible to teach schematic dance melodies in various genres and "imitation" folk melodies by principle or by copying models, but what remained out of reach was the assumed source of melody's essential expressivity. On a shifting stylistic platform, earnest attempts to bridge the gap between emotional response and tonal configurations never reached a state of readiness for practical application in composition. Lobe held that laws governing melodic expression did exist, but as we have seen, urges and pledges in this direction were not followed with actionable theory, and Lobe had to compromise that while such laws could be assimilated mechanically they were not consciously knowable. This effectively marks the failure of pedagogical approaches to the elusive source of melody's expressiveness.

[199] Jean Baudrillard, *Simulacra and Simulation*, trans. Sheila Faria Glaser (Ann Arbor: University of Michigan Press, 1994), 1.

[200] "Ist nun die Erfindung der Melodie einzig und allein eine Äusserung der unbewusst schaffenden Fantasie des Tonschöpfers, oder ist auch hierbei schon der musikalische Kunstverstand mitthätig? / Auch diese Frage vermögen wir nicht zu beantworten, da wir überhaupt diese beiden Thätigkeiten nicht in der Weise trennen können." Salomon Jadassohn, *Das Wesen der Melodie in der Tonkunst* (Leipzig: Breitkopf & Härtel, 1899), 80.

Perhaps this was inevitable. Kanne had poeticized in 1821 that mystery is basic to the condition of Romanticism:

Melody ... will not at all be understood by reason ... Who can have an inkling, for example, of what is Romantic if he does not know that precisely this magic spurns the sharpness of contours and that character that is clearly defined in dazzling light ... rather its spirits always enter in the twilight of moonlight, or allow themselves to develop from the silver veil of mist.[201]

Against this validation of a "twilight" whose only illumination could take the form of unpredictable electrostatic sparks, Lobe's *Melodik* provided a model for inculcated "mechanical" learning that was expressly to be sublimated, supposedly allowing for emotion to be converted – via this internalized, now unconscious process – into expressive music, or true German melodic invention.

While it is difficult to know whether these different strands of thought interacted, and how many student composers in the 1840s and 1850s actually adhered successfully to a Lobean approach, the latter's intersubjective conceptualization of the aesthetic of inspiration has lent itself readily to mechanical explication in this study. If the melograph offered a framework for understanding unconscious melodic creativity, it also cast a dark shadow over claims for melody's teachability, for it is *expression* – the signal (human) quality of melody for many observers – that is lost when machines generate melody. Whether the creative mind – conceived mechanically – arrives at the same lack must remain undecidable within the semiotics of organic and mechanic. The fact that the melograph still needed an initial theme to be programmed also meant that the device had not solved the problem of autogenesis, but merely defined the problem of *Melodik* in terms of scientific agency: mechanical invention needs an *a priori* inventor of devices to function (for melody was never literally autogenetic); hence the discourse of melodic theory is forever retrospective.

Ultimately, this condition shares an affinity with one aspect of Fichte's *Wissenschaftslehre*. If the Fichtean ego only knows itself in the act of philosophizing, the logic of melodic expression similarly is only created

---

[201] "[Melodie wird] vom Verstande gar nicht begriffen ... Wer kann aber eine Ahnung z. B. vom Romantischen haben, wenn er nicht weiss dass gerade diese Zauberwelt die Schärfe der Conturen und die in zu grelles Licht tretende Bestimmtheit der Charaktere verschmäht, ... sondern stets in der Dämmerung des Mondlichtes ihre Geister hervortreten, oder aus den silbernen Schleyern des Nebels sich entwickeln lässt." Kanne, "Der Zauber der Tonkunst," *AmZ* (August 22, 1821), 507, 529.

and perhaps conceivably "understood" in the moment of its creation: its action and existence are the same, that is, it can have no quality of self-awareness, which lends credence to Jean Paul's statement that "[t]he genius of the moment alone gives a law of melody to music; what an aesthetic theorist can provide to this end is itself [nothing but] melody."[202] The pedagogical response was to work on constructing the composer's *mind*, rather than melody itself. At root, however, this equates mind with melody in what was ultimately a failed coupling made plausible by belief in the tangibility of creative thought processes.

---

[202] "Eine Melodestik gibt der Ton- und der Dichtkunst nur der Genius des Augenblicks; was die Ästhetiker dazu liefern kann, ist selber Melodie." Jean Paul, *Vorschule zur Ästhetik*, 25.

3 | Wagner in the melodic workshop

Plagiarism . . . exalteth the lowly, it enricheth those who are of poor estate; it purchaseth respect and reverence from the ignorant and oftentimes winneth the applauses of the learned . . . O Divine Sovereign and Omnipotent *Plagiarism*, who, like Midas, canst transmute all thou touchest into pure gold, or at least an admirable semblance of the same . . . thou hast been the resource . . . of all the poor in spirit, the mean in capacity, the pigmy in intellect, the deficient in ability, and the weak in imagination! Thou canst lend the bright sunbeam Fancy to the darkest souls, and the gem Learning to the duskiest understandings! . . . Thou art equally the goddess of the rich and poor, of Parnassus and of Grub Street . . . With solemn awe we contemplate so potent a divinity.

Francis Mahony, 1849[1]

Even in his old age, Wagner remained insecure about matters of originality and imitation. With the external trappings of success behind him – international fame, royal sponsorship, a network of eponymous societies, an army of articulate propagandists, as well as the egoist's dream of Bayreuth replete with distinguished, pilgrim-like followers – his remarks to Cosima as late as 1880 indicate the degree of self-consciousness and moral ambivalence that continued to color his views on melodic invention and its flipside: the "unmelodic" or inexpressive.

On June 20, 1880, Giovanni Sgambati, an Italian symphonist (who composed no operas), gave a private performance of his recently completed piano concerto at Wahnfried. Cosima reports Wagner's frank assessment the morning after:

Music has taken a bad turn; these young people have no idea how to write a melody, they just give us shavings, which they dress up to look like a lion's mane and shake at us! *It's as if they avoid melodies, for fear of having perhaps stolen them from someone else.* It is always as if the world is having to be created anew, so forceful, so pompous, while I am always looking for melody. In painting, one still has the advantage of

[1] Francis Mahony, "Moore's Plagiarisms," *TMW* 48 (December 1, 1849), 764.

shape and form: when a painter paints a rooster and does it badly, it still remains a rooster, but here I do not even have a rooster.[2]

The freedom of form in abstraction could evidently become as much a burden for Wagner's melodic imagination, as it was a liberation from "dance melody, sternly chained to certain rhythmic and melismatic conventions."[3] Melodic originality appears decidedly self-conscious territory for him to the extent that the "fear of having perhaps stolen [melodies] from someone else," occurring in his autumn years, can be read self-reflexively in terms of the caustic criticism to which he himself had been subject in earlier compositions. The suspicion arises, namely, that the older Wagner is projecting the fears of the younger Wagner onto other composers.

With all the accoutrements of his Bayreuth *éclat*, why would this be the case? What did he have left to prove? Perhaps because Wagner's renown was coupled to the excesses of a drawn-out propaganda war in the German press, he was subject to accusations of plagiarism as late as 1870. Two instances detail charges both of general imitation and of specific hack work. The *Niederrheinische Musik-Zeitung* regarded such practice as un-German in a post-concert report from Paris:

What brutish, base materialism! I had expected to be introduced to newly created music, and was astounded to find nothing but a shallow plagiarism of Berlioz! – Berlioz must consider himself unlucky to see such imitation and caricature. – I cannot possibly explain how such idiocy can arise in Germany.[4]

In more measured tones, Eduard Hanslick had made the same argument of the melodies in *Lohengrin*, which he found "conspicuously reminiscent of Carl Maria von Weber."[5] This trope of Wagner criticism was pre-empted in 1854 by the London *Times*, where J. W. Davison groused that the *Tannhäuser* overture "is a weak parody ... not of M. Berlioz, but of his imitators," illustrating the degree of imitation in such claims themselves.[6]

But rebuttals are equally informative: with a certain political savvy, the composer and conductor Heinrich Dorn laughed off an accusation – circulating

---

[2] CT (June 21, 1880). Emphasis added.   [3] SSD: 3: 285. Cf. PW 2: 78.

[4] "Welch ein roher, niedriger Materialismus! Ich hatte erwartet, eine Musik von neuer Erfindung kennen zu lernen, und erstaunte, nichts zu finden, als einen *flachen Plagiarius* Berliozs! – Berlioz muß sich unglücklich fühlen, sich so nachahmen und karikieren zu sehen. – Eines kann ich mir nicht erklären, wie solche Niaiserie in Deutschland hat aufkommen können." This relates to a concert in Paris on January 25, 1860, see "Stimmen aus Paris von R. Wagners erstes Konzert," *Niederrheinische Musik-Zeitung* (February 11, 1860), 11.

[5] "theils ganz alltäglich, theils auffallende Reminiscenz an C. M. v. Weber" [1858]. Edward Hanslick, HSS I/4: 344.

[6] J. W. Davison, "New Philharmonic Society," *The Times* (May 3, 1854), 9.

in 1870 – that Wagner had borrowed a musical phrase from Otto Nicolai's *Lustige Weiber* in his *Meistersinger*:

> If one depicts the *plagiarist* Wagner with tender, monumental concern for wooing the artistic comradeship of Otto Nicolai, that is just childish. Wagner and Nicolai in one breath: I reckon Richard would laugh himself to death and Otto would turn in his grave.[7]

What matters here are the implications of an attitude in which accusations of melodic borrowing were either scandalous or ridiculous. Within the ethics of borrowing, in other words, there was no middle ground. In a familiar cyclic trap, the would-be melodist's desire to compose "original" melodies means in this case avoiding normative "melodic" patterns, which casts Wagner's composer-by-composer denunciation of almost all prior operatic melody in *Oper und Drama* in a new, defensive light. Avoiding melodic cliché was a prevalent criticism of both German and Italian opera at the time,[8] and Hanslick's review of *Tannhäuser* from 1846 makes this very point in relation to Wagner's own "melodic habits." The rising sixth to the submediant or mediant, Hanslick worried, is a vocal phrase that had almost become an obsession for Wagner. After citing examples from *Rienzi* and *Tannhäuser*, reproduced as Examples 3.1, the 22-year-old critic explains soberly:

> [N]othing becomes more damaging and restrictive for a composer over time than a melodic habit which is often much harder to give up than a moral habit. ... [Elisabeth's cantilena *Der Sänger klugen Weisen lauscht'*] is indeed impeccable, but not innovative enough, too *habitual*, and reminds one of so many routine composers who believe they have done everything if they bind together the text before them with appropriate notes. A mediocre opera would still be graced by the cantabile, in *Tannhäuser* it is a shadow."[9]

---

[7] Heinrich Dorn: "Wenn jemand den *Plagiarius* Wagner als einen in zärtlicher monumentaler Besorgnis für Otto Nicolai schwärmenden Kunstgenossen darstellt, so ist das kindisch. Wagner und Nicolai in einem Atem: ich glaube, Richard lacht sich zu Tode und Otto dreht sich im Grabe." (May 2, 1870). Cited in Wilhelm Tappert, *Richard Wagner im Spiegel der Kritik* (Leipzig: C. F. W. Siegel, 1915), 66.

[8] See, for example, Berlioz's complaint in an obituary about the monotony of Bellini's recitative based on motifs centered on the fifth and sixth scale degrees. See Berlioz, "Notes nécrologiques," *Les Musiciens et la musique* (Paris: Calmann-Lévy, 1903), 167–79.

[9] "Nichts kann einem Componisten mit der Zeit schädlicher und hemmender werden, als eine melodische Gewohnheit, indem eine solche wirklich oft schwerer abzulegen ist, als moralische. Ich will gar nicht von den modernen Italienern reden, deren ganzes Opernwesen eine große Gewohnheit ist ... Der Gesang [von Elisabeth] ist durchaus tadellos, aber zu wenig neu, zu *gewöhnlich*, und mahnt an so manche routinirte Componisten, die Alles gethan zu haben glauben, wenn sie den vorliegenden Text mit passenden Noten zusammenbinden. In einer mittelmäßigen Oper wäre das genannte Cantabile noch eine *Zierde*, im *Tannhäuser* ist es ein Schatten." Hanslick, "Richard Wagner, und seine neueste Oper *Tannhäuser*," *Wiener allgemeine musikalische Zeitung* (December 17, 1846); rpt. in Hanslick, HSS I/1: 78–79.

Example 3.1 Eduard Hanslick's illustrations of Wagner's *Manie* for rising 6ths in his review of *Tannhä*user (1846).

But as Roman Jakobson argued long ago, all human communication (whether linguistic–phonological or pitch–timbral) is based on a principle of common coding, hence "the originality of the [art] work finds itself restricted by the artistic code which dominates during a given epoch and in a given society."[10] By renouncing imitative "shadows" completely, and valuing amorphousness as a first principle for beginning composition, the danger is that a Wagner figure would begin to undermine the aim of comprehensible expression when he renounces those very modes of expression that made a line "melodic" in the first place.

At root, such logic is self-defeating, for it posits an antithesis of expressivity and originality. Eighteen years earlier, Wagner acknowledged the selfsame antithesis, confessing to Mathilde Wesendonck that, as a young man, he had grave doubts about his capacity for original expression. Reflecting on the period in which he premiered *Rienzi* and *Der fliegende Holländer*, his oft-quoted confession invokes a veritably Bloomian anxiety:

> I well remember how, when I was about thirty, I used to ask myself whether after all I had the stuff in me to do really original work. I could still see influence and imitation in everything of mine, and could only venture an anxious hope that I might someday develop as a truly original artist.[11]

Twelve years later, Nietzsche would share (though did not publish) Wagner's concern, placing it in a negatively charged context fully four years before his official "break" with the composer: "None of our great composers was still such a bad composer as [Wagner] when he was 28 years

---

[10] Roman Jakobson, *Language in Literature*, ed. Krystyna Pomorska and Stephen Rudy (Cambridge, MA: Harvard University Press, 1987), 451; see also "Linguistics and Communication Theory," *Selected Writings II: Word and Language* (The Hague: Mouton & Co., 1971), 570–79.

[11] Wagner to Mathilde Wesendonck, June 9, 1862, Biebrich, in SB 14: 176–77.

old."[12] Beyond the basic autobiographical reading of a young composer
thirsty for success, whose financial privation and professional circumstance
compelled him frequently to make musical arrangements, Wagner's
"anxious hope" rhymes with his inhibiting fear in 1880 that "the world is
[always] having to be created anew." (He told Cosima "with splendid high
spirits" in 1878 that he had "'stolen' so much from [Liszt's] symphonic
poems"; but this relaxed confession belies an irremediable condition of
self-awareness.[13] Witness Wagner's continuing magpie practice at this
time in his well-documented borrowing of the opening theme and Holy
Grail March for *Parsifal* from Liszt's secular oratorio *Die Glocken des
Strassburger Münsters*, which he checked against Liszt's score "to make
sure he has not committed a *plagiarism*," and which Liszt re-incorporated
into a poetic benediction for his late son-in-law: *Am Grabe Richard
Wagners*.[14]) It seems that even later in his life, such fatalism appears
inevitable, reinscribing a psychology in which every attempt to find a
substitute for the "original" melody, theme, or expression pivots uncomfortably between a benign displacement – a melody among "friends" – and
yet only another culpable trespass.

Plagiarism and originality

To be sure, Wagner's insecurity over melodic originality was fueled in part by
a new legal milieu. For almost two decades before his birth, under

---

[12] Nietzsche, *Unpublished Writings from the Period of Unfashionable Observations*, trans. Richard
T. Gray (Stanford University Press, 2000), 346. In a study of the shifting relationship between
Nietzsche and Wagner, Dieter Borchmeyer argues that "the 'break' with Wagner was hardly so
rigorous as it has long been represented," in Borchmeyer, "Critique as Passion and Polemic:
Nietzsche and Wagner," *The Cambridge Companion to Wagner*, ed. Thomas Grey (Cambridge
University Press, 2008), 192–202, here 192.

[13] CT (August 27, 1878).

[14] CT (December 27, 1877). Liszt's inscription on his manuscript for *Am Grabe Richard Wagners*
(1883) reads: "Wagner once reminded me of the similarity between his *Parsifal* motifs and my
earlier composition – 'Excelsior' – (Introduction to the *Bells of Strasbourg*). May these
remembrances live on here. He achieved the great and the sublime art of the present." ["Wagner
erinnerte mich einst an die Ähnlichkeit seines *Parsifal* Motivs mit meinem früher
geschriebenen – 'Excelsior' – (Einleitung zu den *Glocken von Strassburg*). Möge diese Erinnerung
hiermit verbleiben. Er hat das Grosse und Hehre in der Kunst der Jetzt-zeit vollbracht."] The
quotation by Wagner of "Excelsior" was first pointed out in print by Hans Redlich, *Parsifal*
(London: Boosey and Hawkes, 1951), and the "re-quotation" by Liszt in his late piano works
began to receive attention in 1953 from Arthur Marget. See Marget, "Liszt and Parsifal," *Music
Review* 14 (1953), 107–24. The most recent assessment of mutual borrowing between Liszt and
Wagner is Kenneth Hamilton, "Wagner and Liszt: Elective Affinities," in *Wagner and his World*,
44–54.

the *Allgemeines Landrecht für die Preußischen Staaten* of 1794 (ALR), plagiarism had in principle been a form of property theft, and protected publishers' (rather than authors') rights, including specifically the reprinting of "musical compostions."[15]   An unsuccessful claim brought by Adolph Martin Schlesinger against the Viennese publisher of a piano arrangement of *Der Freischütz* being sold in Berlin during 1822 illustrates that, under the ALR, reprinting referred to specific arrangements and not an abstract musical work. E. T. A. Hoffmann – a trained lawyer and Prussian civil servant – served as an expert witness on this point, arguing that "it is impossible to extract musical compositions in the same way as can be done with books. The reprint of a composition would only occur where an original is 're-engraved' [*nachgestochen*] and reprinted identically with the original."[16] But on July 11, 1837 – shortly after Wagner turned twenty four – laws specifically pertaining to copyright (*Urhebergesetz*) were first passed in Berlin to protect citizens against theft of intellectual property, including music in the sense of abstract works, thereby making imitation-bordering-on-plagiarism a potentially criminal as well as an ethical matter.[17] The 1837 Act gave Prussia the most modern legal protection of the age for intellectual property. Regarding musical arrangements, it dictated:

It is regarded as an infringement if somebody publishes an excerpt, any instrumental arrangements, or other adaptations which cannot be considered as an original composition.[18]

[15] See ALR, part 1, no. 11, § 997. The *Allgemeines Landrecht für die Preußischen Staaten* became law on February 5, 1794. The entire legal document is reproduced at www.smixx.de/ra/Links_F-R/PrALR/pralr.html. For a study of the legal and political apparatus during the first half of the nineteenth century in Germany see Reinhart Koselleck's classic study, *Preußen zwischen Reform und Revolution. Allgemeines Landrecht, Verwaltung und soziale Bewegung von 1791 bis 1848* (Stuttgart: Klett, 1967).

[16] See Friedemann Kawohl, "Music Copyright and the Prussian Copyright Act of 1837," *Nineteenth-Century Music. Selected Proceedings of the Tenth International Conference*, ed. Jim Samson and Bennett Zon (Aldershot: Ashgate, 2002), 269.

[17] This was the *Gesetzt zum Schutz der Wissenschaft und Kunst gegen Nachdruck und Nachbildung*. An account of the details is given in Elmar Wadle, "Das preußische Urheberrechtgesetz von 1837 im Spiegel seiner Vorgeschichte," in *Woher kommt das Urheberrecht und wohin geht es?*, ed. Robert Dittrich (Vienna: Manz, 1988), 55–98. The wider context is given in Friedemann Kawohl's study, *Urheberrecht der Musik in Preussen (1820–1840)* (Tutzing: Hans Schneider, 2002).

[18] § 20. "Einem verbotenen Nachdruck ist gleich zu achten, wenn Jemand von musikalischen Kompositionen Auszüge, Arrangements für einzelne Instrumente, oder sonstige Bearbeitungen, die nicht als eigenthümliche Kompositionen betrachtet werden können, ohne Genehmigung des Verfassers herausgiebt." The complete text of the 1837 Act is given in Elmar Wadle, "Das preußische Urheberrechtgesetz von 1837 im Spiegel seiner Vorgeschichte," 55–98. This translation is taken from Kawohl, "Music Copyright and the Prussian Copyright Act of 1837," 284.

In addition to overt borrowing, the *Paulskirchenverfassung* or constitution of fundamental rights from the Frankfurt assembly in 1849 would refer directly to the protection of artistic works against *imitation*.[19]

The point at which legitimate stylistic imitation becomes illegal copying was not subject to uniform principles, however.[20] On the one hand, Paul Daude, surveying the legal territory of intellectual property in 1888, confirmed that "the labor of a composer does not need to consist in the production of new material, but can also express itself in the artistic arrangement of already extant musical compositions or in the peculiar use of foreign melodies in a completely independent manner."[21] In addition to orchestral and piano arrangements that occupied Wagner during his tenure at Riga, Magdeburg, and Königsberg, as well as "all manner of instrumental arrangements" for Maurice Schlesinger in Paris, the individuation of borrowed melodic material also has direct implications for his more stylistically "imitative," early scores.[22] Daude's viewpoint might have mollified Wagner's fears, as he continues that any judgment as to whether such an arrangement or individuation constitutes "independent usage" of the material must be left to the judicial assessment of individual cases, but

---

[19] Article VII, § 40 of the *Paulskirchenverfassung* stated: "State power also exclusively legislates against the reprinting of books, every unauthorized imitation of art works, factory signs, models and forms, and against other infringements of intellectual property." ["auch steht der Reichsgewalt ausschließlich die Gesetzgebung gegen den Nachdruck von Büchern, jedes unbefugte Nachahmen von Kunstwerken, Fabrikzeichen, Mustern und Formen und gegen andere Beeinträchtigungen des geistigen Eigenthums zu."] Cited in E. R. Huber (ed.), *Dokumente zur deutschen Verfassungsgeschichte*, "Deutsche Verfassungsdokumente 1803–1850," 3rd edn. (Stuttgart: Kohlhammer, 1978), 377.

[20] The *Staatsvertrag zwischen Hannover und Großbritannien* of August 4, 1847 indicates simply that such questions: "shall be decided in all cases through the courts of justice in the respective states according to their extant laws." ["Die Frage, ob ein Werk als Nachahmung oder als unerlaubte Vervielfältigung zu betrachten ist, soll in allen Fällen durch die Gerichtshöfe der respektiven Staaten nach deren bestehenden Gesetzen entschieden werden."] This is reproduced in Paul Daude, *Lehrbuch des Deutschen litterarischen, künstlerischen und gewerblichen Urheberrechts* (Stuttgart: Ferdinand Enke, 1888), 184.

[21] "Im übrigen braucht auch das Schaffen des Komponisten nicht notwendig in der Produktion eines neuen Stoffes zu bestehen, sondern kann sich auch in der künstlerischen Verarbeitung bereits vorhandener musikalischer Kompositionen oder in der eigentümlichen Benutzung fremder Melodien auf eine vollkommen selbständige Weise äußern." Daude, *Lehrbuch*, 81.

[22] Wagner notes with disdain in his autobiographical sketch from 1842 that: "now I found myself forced to renounce all creative activity for some time while I had to produce for Schlesinger all manner of instrumental arrangements, including even some for the *cornet à pistons*. This work provided some slight amelioration of my circumstances. Thus I subsisted through the winter of 1841 in a most inglorious manner." See Wagner, "Autobiographische Skizze," *Zeitung für die elegante Welt* (February 1–8, 1843). Translation adapted from Thomas Grey, "Richard Wagner: Autobiographical Sketch (to 1842)," *The Wagner Journal* 2 (2008), 42–58, here 58.

reminds readers that "the law itself . . . does not forbid the use of a foreign composition out of hand."[23]

On the other hand, it seems that one reason for Wagner's sustained anxiety over original melodic composition was that, by the early 1830s, melody was recognized in Germany as the main protectable "object" of a musical work. A Leipzig publisher's agreement on May 12, 1831[24] – an *Erweiterungsakte* to the Saxon *Erläuterungsmandat* which itself had expanded on the so-called *Konventionalakte* (May 23, 1829) – penned by Heinrich Dorn stipulated that:

Melody will be recognized as the exclusive property of the publisher, and every arrangement that reproduces the composer's notes and is only based on mechanical workmanship should be seen as a reprint and be subject . . . to a fine of 50 Louis d'or.[25]

In England, similarly, a judgment from the Lord Chancellor, Lord Lyndhurst, in the case of D'Almaire vs. Boosey (1835) specified that "it is the *air or melody* which is the invention of the author, and which may in such cases be the subject of piracy."[26] Wagner was well aware of such legal battles. In a haughty complaint about them – written for Schumann's *Neue Zeitschrift* – he gave a witty account of a lawsuit between publishers, Troupenas and Schlesinger, over the rights to Rossini's *Stabat Mater*, closing:

That dreadful word: *copyright* – growls through the scarce pacified breezes. Lawsuit! Lawsuit! Once more, lawsuit! And money is fetched out to pay the best of lawyers, to have documents produced, to enter caveats. Oh, you foolish people, have you lost your love of gold? I know someone who, for five francs, will compose five waltzes for you, each of which is better than the wealthy master's [Rossini] miserable specimens![27]

Rossini-envy aside, Wagner's ridicule of court action in 1841 was grounded on the fact that the legal arguments had nothing to do with the composers

---

[23] "Ob eine solche künstlerische Verarbeitung oder selbständige Benutzung vorliegt, muß der richterlichen Beurteilung des einzelnen Falles überlassen bleiben, soweit nicht das Gesetz selbst . . . die Benutzung einer fremden Komposition überhaupt verboten hat." Daude, *Lehrbuch des Deutschen litterarischen, künstlerischen und gewerblichen Urheberrechts*, 81.

[24] The publishers who signed were all from the larger houses, indicating that this was a powerful business agreement: Friedrich Hofmeister, Wilhelm Härtel (Breitkopf & Härtel), H. A. Probst, H. Simrock, C. H. Hartmann (Wolfenbüttel), C. C. Lose, G. M. Meyer (Brunswick), Schuberth & Niemeyer, Cosmar & Krause, Friedrich Laue, Friedrich Ph. Dunst, Schott Söhne.

[25] "§ 5. Die Melodie wird als ausschließliches Eigenthum des Verlegers anerkannt und jedes Arrangement, daß die Töne des Componisten wiedergibt und nur auf mechanischer Verarbeitung beruht, soll als Nachdruck angesehen und der Strafe von 50 Louis d'or . . . unterworfen sein." The full text of this Act is reproduced in Friedemann Kawohl, "Die Erweiterungsakte," in *Urheberrecht der Musik in Preussen*, 239–41. Emphasis added.

[26] Cited in W. A. Copinger, *The Law of Copyright in Works of Literature and Art* (London: Stevens and Haynes, 1870), 159. Emphasis added.

[27] SSD 1: 193. Cf. PW 7: 149.

who actually created the melodies, and monies paid benefitted dispropor-
tionately an elite commercial circle (which excluded him).

But there was also a more ideological objection to the new legislation.
Wagner may well have become familiar with Pierre-Joseph Proudhon's
leftist manifesto *What is Property?* (1840) while based in Paris
(1839–42);[28] Proudhon, whom Wagner later credited as the only man in
France to know "that we are *human*,"[29] famously argued that all property is
"theft" and should be abolished, that (compositional) talent is the product of
"universal intelligence" and accumulated knowledge across generations,
meaning that, in reality, artists and poets "do not labour for themselves
but for society, which creates them."[30] Nobody has the right to own the
means of (melodic) production, in other words. The argument is bolstered
by witty rhetoric: "Should the vase say to the potter, 'I am what I am, and I
owe nothing to you'?" and leads Proudhon to conclude that: "all capital,
whether material *or mental*, is the result of collective labour and so is
collective property."[31] Wagner was drawn to such egalitarian logic. He
would identify Proudhon's ideas with the Nibelungen hoard at the end of
his 1848 scenario *Die Wibelungen: Weltgeschichte aus der Saga*, and with his
negational supplement to "Thou shalt not steal" in *Jesus von Nazareth*;[32]
and of course, Proudhon's marked influence on Wagner's subsequent
revolutionary texts is not in question.[33] Yet the contrast between a utopia
of common ownership – that must include melody – and Wagner's penny-
counting correspondence at the time with his publisher Schlesinger is
glaring.[34] It seems Wagner remained pragmatic while dreaming of the
abolition of debt: whether monetary or artistic.[35]

[28] Speculation on this point comes from Mitchell Cohen, "To the Dresden barricades: the
genesis of Wagner's political ideas," in *The Cambridge Companion to Wagner*, 51–52; and
Barry Millington, *Wagner* (London: Dent, 1992), 26.

[29] Wagner to Ernst Benedikt Kietz, December 30, 1851, Zurich, in *Letters of Richard Wagner.
The Burrell Collection*, ed. John N. Burk (London: Gollancz, 1951), 258.

[30] Pierre-Joseph Proudhon, *What is Property?*, ed. and trans. Donald R. Kelley and Bonnie
G. Smith (Cambridge University Press, 2004), 111.

[31] *Ibid.*, 111, 114. Emphasis added.

[32] SSD 2: 152–55. Cf PW 7: 295–98. After condoning the commandment "du sollst nicht
stehlen," Wagner continues: "but . . . do not store up treasures for yourself, whereby you steal
from your neighbor and cause him to starve." SSD 11: 290–91. Cf. PW 8: 303–04.

[33] See Grey, *Wagner's Musical Prose*, 133fn, and Mark Berry, *Treacherous Bonds and Laughing
Fire: Politics and Religion in Wagner's* Ring (Aldershot: Ashgate, 2006), 38ff.

[34] See especially the itemized billing and advances of Wagner to Schlesinger, April 27, 1841,
Paris, in SB 1: 478–80.

[35] Unsurprisingly, this attitude to debt was set out explicitly by Proundhon: "A peasant
admitted one day at confession that he had destroyed a document by which he admitted
being a debtor to the amout of 300 francs. / Said his confessor, 'You must return these

While the legal injunctions mentioned earlier sought to prevent publishers from stealing each others' wares, a debate in the Berlin press mere months before Wagner's courtroom sarcasm about Rossini specifically addressed *authorial* rights concerning melody, and sheds light on contemporary attitudes to musical originality at the time that Wagner was engaged with his closest imitation of Bellini's *Norma*, as we shall see. The interlocutors were Karl Gaillard, a 30-year-old poet and dramatist, who would found and edit the *Berliner Musikalische Zeitung* (1844–47), and Friedrich Hofmeister, a 59-year-old Leipzig publisher who, in 1829, had established the association of German music publishers (*Verein der deutschen Musikalienhändler*).[36] Whereas Hofmeister, concerned about printing rearrangements, argued that these "require[ed] mere mechanical skills"[37] to alter an original, and asserted that offending publishers would be sued only if the *name* of the composer is used to advertise the borrowed melodic material, Gaillard argued for a more essentialist conception of original melody, and retorted eloquently:

As Shakespeare put it: "What's in a name? That which we call a rose by any name would smell as sweet." So it seems to me that it is not only a matter of justice but also of duty that an artist who borrows from another has to quote his source. If he does not, he is robbing him of his most noble richness.[38]

Commercially, Breitkopf would later force Wagner to realize that he did not even own his own "name" in this sense,[39] but ethically, Gaillard's

---

300 francs.' 'No,' replied the peasant, 'I will return two pennies to pay for the paper.'" Even if the dreamt-of utopia never came to pass, such anecdotes would seem to have characterized Wagner's view of artistic borrowing at the time as well as, more obviously, his oft-cited financial irresponsibility. See Proudhon, *What is Property?*, 83–84.

[36] See Max Schumann, *Zur Geschichte des deutschen Musikalienbuchhandels seit der Gründung des Vereins der deutschen Musikalienhändler 1829–1929* (Leipzig: Verband der Deutschen Musikalienhändler, 1929), 15ff.

[37] Cited in Kawohl, "Music Copyright and the Prussian Copyright Act of 1837," 291.

[38] "Shakespeare dagegen: 'Was ist ein Name? Was uns Rose heißt, wie es auch heiße, würde lieblich duften.' So will es mir denn auch scheinen, daß es nicht nur ein Act der Gerechtigkeit, sondern einer der Pflicht ist, daß der Künstler, der etwas von einem andern entlehnt, auch seine Quelle angiebt, denn sonst betrügt er diesen um seinem edelsten Reichtum." Karl Gaillard, "Über das Eigenthum an einer musikalischen Composition," *Allgemeine Press-Zeitung* 80 (1841), 757. In his study of copyright, Kawohl summarizes the exchange as "a shift of the work's essential factors from 'melody plus author's name' to 'melody plus form.'" See Kawohl, "Music Copyright and the Prussian Copyright Act of 1837," 294.

[39] The publishing house reissued Wagner's 1831 piano sonata in B-flat major (WWV 21) in 1862 without consulting the composer, later citing public demand as the reason. Curiosity had been aroused over the composer of the sonata after Selmar Bagge, editor of Vienna's weekly *Deutsche Musik-Zeitung*, had published the opening of the Minuet and Trio on February 1, 1862 without naming the composer, but instead challenging readers to name the contemporary composer to whom it belonged. A week after Bagge's challenge, entitled "Rätsel," he revealed

point that melodic form itself is a "most noble" authorial property rapidly gained ground, and by 1847, concerns about a veritable *Reminiscenzenjägerei* began circulating in the largest papers.[40] In 1855, the *Berlin Musik-Zeitung Echo* complained that now every kind of melodic reminiscence is regarded as thievery, that "one sometimes hunts with raging fury for any melodic similarity which finds its way more or less unconsciously with new composers into their works from those of predecessors."[41] The resulting mania for uncovering illicit borrowing makes it far harder for young composers to actually create, the article continues, discouraging, exhausting, and suffocating them as they "wriggle between the search for novelty and the fear of getting into a fight with an already very famous maestro over the [musical] expression, and thus in the most characterless way continually end up writing the most knotty, most ridiculous leaps in order to get away with it, to get over all obstacles of reminiscence."[42] Wagner's ascription of the "fear of having perhaps stolen [melodies] from someone else" was thus part of a wider discourse protesting at a detrimental situation whereby the idealist belief in original invention fuels a legalistic awareness of property ownership, inserting composers such as Sgambati – and no doubt Wagner too – into a minefield of potential infringements. (A genre of literary plagiarism even became a vehicle for character assassination when mid-nineteenth-century Irish writers such as William Maginn and Francis Mahony – cited in the epigraph above – produced works artfully modeled on some

---

the answer, no doubt to the great surprise of his readers. The episode coincides with Wagner's preparation in Vienna for the planned premiere of *Tristan und Isolde*, and seems clearly to have been intended to damage the composer's reputation. Wagner would surely not have given permission for the reprint, describing the sonata as "scanty work" [*dürftiges Werk*] and the republication without his permission as an "indiscretion" [*Indiskretion*]. A full account is given in WWV 83; see also Egon Voss, *Richard Wagner und die Instrumentalmusik. Wagners symphonischer Ehrgeiz* (Wilhelmshaven: Heinrichshofen, 1977), 20–22.

[40] See "Über Reminiscenzenjägerei," *AmZ* 49 (1847), 561–66; L. A. Zellner, "Über Plagiat," *Blätter für Musik, Theater und Kunst* 1 (November 27, 1855).

[41] "man [macht Jagd] . . . zum Theil mit wahrer Wuth . . . auf jegliche melodische Aehnlichkeit, welche sich bei neuen Componisten, mehr oder weniger unbewußt, in ihren Werken mit denen ihrer Vorgänger vorfindet," in "Über Plagiate und Reminiscenzen," *Berlin Musik-Zeitung Echo* 7 (February 18, 1855), 49.

[42] Here I quote the phrases in full from which I part paraphrased and part quoted in the main text: "Diese vielseitig sanctionirte Reminiscenzenjägerei hat manchem aufkeimenden Talente das Leben recht schwer gemacht, ja dasselbe wohl ganz entmuthigt, ermattet, erstickt. Oder, was noch schlimmer, sie hat eine Literatur erzeugt, die nicht süß nicht sauer, nicht warm nicht kalt, in kläglicher Weise in der Luft herumzappelt zwischen Neuerungssucht und der Angst, in die Wendungen irgend eines schon zu sehr bekannten Maestro hineinzugerathen, und deshalb in der charakterlosesten Weise fortwährend die verzwicktesten, lächerlichsten Sprünge macht, um über alle Reminiscenzenklippen mit heiler Haut hinwegzukommen," in *Ibid.*, 50.

literary text by a famous author, which they then claimed audaciously to be the lost original that the author had plagiarized.[43])

While very few prosecutions of composers took place during Wagner's lifetime, Christopher Reynolds in his study of musical allusion in this period states explicitly what was at stake beyond a jail term and a shared pitch content:

Notions of creativity, inspiration, and originality; the constraints of tradition and innovation; musical listening and the audience for allusion; the relationship between criticism and composition; and musical symbolism.[44]

What Reynolds leaves out – because it is not strictly part of allusional practice – is pedagogy. Categories of borrowing and learning overlap in the modeling of compositions when the later work is intended for professional performance and publication. A legal distinction between what could be called "artistic" and "didactic" borrowing – allusion that is elective, incidental as opposed to instructive, structural – did not exist, and as the contemporary critic Wilhelm Tappert observed in his pioneering study of melodic borrowing, *Wandernde Melodien* (1868): "there are no music police who ask for birth certificates and certificates of conduct!"[45] On occasion, press skirmishes did debate melodic ownership publicly, however, illustrating that although the boundaries of musical allusion, quotation, and plagiarism may be decidedly fuzzy (for the salient *varia* Reynolds lists), such acts of borrowing remained an acknowledged fact.[46] "Melodies roam," Tappert exclaims, "They are the most tireless tourists on earth! They cross raging rivers, pass the Alpine mountains, emerge beyond the ocean, and nomadize in the desert."[47] Example 3.2, taken

---

[43] See Terry Eagleton, *Figures of Dissent* (London: Verso, 2003), 240ff.

[44] Christopher Reynolds, *Motives for Allusion: Context and Content in Nineteenth-Century Music* (Cambridge University Press, 2003), xi.

[45] "Es giebt ja keine musikalische Polizei, welche nach Geburtsschein und Führungsattest früge!" Wilhelm Tappert, *Wandernde Melodien: eine musikalische Studie* [1868], 2nd edn. (Berlin: Brachvogel & Ranft, 1889), 5.

[46] One such instance is a letter from J. B. Sale (an English organist at St. Margaret's, Westminster) to the editor of *The Musical World* in which he denies having borrowed from a melody of J. Dair for his duet *The Butterfly*, stating flatly: "I never was aware, until the present moment, of the existence of Mr. Dair's Song ... *The Butterfly*, such as it is, is my own unassisted production." See "Correspondence: Mr. J. B. Sale, and Mr. J. Dare," *TMW* 15 (February 18, 1841), 105.

[47] "Die Melodien wandern, sie sind die unermüdlichsten Touristen der Erde! Sie überschreiten die rauschenden Ströme, passiren die Alpen, tauchen jenseits des Oceans auf und nomadisiren in der Wüste." Tappert, *Wandernde Melodien*, 5.

There is a vast literature on musical borrowing and influence expressed in the form of quotation, allusion or other traceable incorporation of a certain musical material from one composer's work into another's. For an overview, see the extensive bibliography maintained by Peter Burkholder at

Example 3.2 Wilhelm Tappert's illustrations of Wagner's melodic borrowing in *Wandernde Melodien: eine musikalische Studie* (1868).

from Tappert's study, illustrates the kind of shared linear contour and harmonic kinship that he believed constituted melodic borrowing.

As we have seen, suspicions of plagiarism clung to Wagner in less charitable criticism. But pragmatism led the debate in a different direction. J. C. Lobe suggested publicly that blatant melodic commonalities between *Tannhäuser* and Meyerbeer's *Robert* were real, but unwitting musical adoptions. "Do not think I want to indict Wagner as a deliberate plagiarist," he cautions diplomatically. "That would be more than ridiculous, it would be slanderous. Less injustice would be done were one to think: Meyerbeer's phrase emerged from Wagner's quill unconsciously through memory while he worked, and he regarded it as his own invention."[48] But legalistic rhetoric aside, the argument finally reaches the nub of the issue in Lobe's next letter, which states that "no single measure [in anything] is absolutely new."[49] The implications of this were equally injurious to a composer's reputation (by contradicting the legal and idealist criterion of originality), and as Tappert's single use of the word *Plagiat* indicates, musical "rights" remained a thoroughly ambiguous issue in professional criticism.[50] Acknowledging the

Indiana University: www.chmtl.indiana.edu/borrowing/. For nineteenth-century borrowing in particular, see Reynolds, *Motives for Allusion*; Charles Rosen, "Influence: Plagiarism and Inspiration," *19th-Century Music* 4 (1980), 87–100; Kevin Korsyn, "Towards a New Poetics of Musical Influence," *Musical Analysis* 10 (1991), 3–72; Raymond Knapp, "Brahms and the Anxiety of Allusion," *Journal of Musicological Research* 18 (1998), 1–30; Paul Thissen, *Zitattechniken in der Symphonik des 19. Jahrhunderts* (Sinzig: Studio, 1998); W. C. Petty, "Chopin and the Ghost of Beethoven," *19th-Century Music* 22 (1998), 281–99.

[48] See "Letters to a Young Composer about Richard Wagner" in *Wagner and his World*, 280.

[49] *Ibid.*, 283.

[50] Speaking of Lucien Grison's oratorio *Esther*, Tappert explains: "The opening is formed in such a way that one could even (and with much greater justification!) speak of [Grison] having committed plagiarism from Mozart's *Zauberflöte*." ["Der Anfang ist so gestaltet, dass man auch

truism that melodic originality remained endlessly discoverable and debatable, Lobe publicly cast absolute originality as a false idol; it seems the case of Wagner was merely the means by which this Kantian myth could best be exploded. Suffice to conclude that while Wagner's self-consciousness about melodic invention stemmed primarily from his belief in the prestige of idealism, it must also be seen against a background of the juristic principles of material property ownership as they expanded into the sphere of intellectual property.

Given this context, we may suspect that Wagner's insistence in the Zurich essays on the historical unprecedentedness – i.e. total originality – of his music is an exaggeration that conceals an insecurity.[51] Human credulity is elastic, but not endless. The disbelief inspired by Wagner's claim received a certain historiographic reinforcement when his early operas re-emerged after his death. Carl Dahlhaus' assessment of them as mere "Kapellmeistermusik," i.e. the product of a parasitic musical mind, able to imitate styles and construct forms, but otherwise devoid of original creativity, essentially reworded Hanslick's withering critique of *Die Feen* from 1888, after Franz Fischer had directed a popular performance of the opera in Munich on June 29 of that year:

The Fairies is a caricatured imitation of Weber . . . Not one strong original thought, not one alluring melody, not one note emerging from the bottom of the heart interrupts the monotony of this factory work. One could ascribe this work less to an as-yet-unskilled young genius, and much more to a run-of-the-mill old *Capellmeister*, to whose mind nothing occurs anymore."[52]

(Wagner remarks blithely in *Mein Leben* that the same label – *Kapellmeisteroper* – was applied to *Der fliegende Holländer* by the managers of the Berlin Court Theater in 1844; and of course he himself devalued his

---

(und zwar mit viel grösserem Rechte!) von einem Plagiat, an Mozart's *Zauberflöte* begangen, reden könnte"], *Wandernde Melodien*, 61.

[51] Lobe disputed Wagner's claims as early as 1854. He criticized the Zurich essays for their bluster about the historically unprecedented nature of Wagner's music, scoffing that the composer "appears to be congenitally blessed in the highest degree with the belief that he is absolutely original, that he creates everything purely from his spirit." ["Wagner glaubt er sei durchaus original, schöpfe alles rein nur aus seinem Geiste, schon von Haus aus in hohem Grade gesegnet zu sein scheint."] Lobe, "Briefe über Rich. Wagner an einen jungen Komponisten. Fünfter Brief," *FBfM* 1 (1854), 427.

[52] "*Die Feen* sind eine carikirte Nachahmung Webers . . . Nicht ein starker origineller Gedanke, nicht eine reizvolle Melodie, nicht ein aus dem Herzensgrund aufquillender Ton unterbricht das Einerlei dieser musikalischen Fabriksarbeit . . . Man könnte diese Musik weniger einem noch ungeschickten jungen Genie zuschreiben, als vielmehr einem routinierten alten Capellmeister, dem nichts mehr einfällt." Hanslick, *Musikalische und Litterarisches. Kritiken und Schilderungen*, 2nd edn. (Berlin: Allgemeiner Verein für Deutsche Litteratur, 1889), 54.

early works in later years, remarking "how bad" *Das Liebesverbot* was: "[w]hat phases one goes through! It is hard to believe it is the same person."[53])

But Hanslick's view is less a verdict on the young Wagner than a validation of the later criticisms of his mature output. In other words, it is not that the early works are inexplicable in relation to the later works, but that "the criticism of the mature Wagner receives its confirmation through the early Wagner," as Ludwig Holtmeier put it.[54] The comments about melodic habits in Hanslick's 1846 review of *Tannhäuser* indicate that the seeds of this criticism were sown early on, and that the Viennese critic sowed them even under the best of circumstances.

Shadowing Bellini: Wagner's armature

Given that some critics heard Wagner's works as aesthetically barren as early as 1844, it would surely not be specious to draw parallels with the critiques of melodic training we encountered in Chapter 2. Recall how, on the way to his fully fledged pedagogy of melodic expression that same year, Lobe admitted that certain products of the training are "still worth nothing in terms of *aesthetics*."[55] At the risk of an overly schematic perspective, might this apply to Wagner's *Kapellmeistermusik*? To what extent did Wagner's "apprenticeship"[56] – as Thomas Grey recently dubbed the period from 1833 to 1840 – in fact follow a clear pedagogical methodology that would later be codified in Lobe's *Compositions-Lehre*?[57] If we accept that such a view brings together the pedagogical approach of analytical, model-based compositional practice with Wagner's acknowledged tendency towards imitation during this period, this would lead us to reassess aspects of his pre-1849 melodies.

---

[53] ML 263; and CT 2: 263 (February 1, 1879).

[54] "[D]ie Kritik des reifen Wagner erfährt durch das Frühwerk Bestätigung." Ludwig Holtmeier, "Von den *Feen* zum *Liebesverbot*," in *Richard Wagner und seine Zeit*, ed. Eckehard Keim and Ludwig Holtmeier (Laaber: Laaber, 2003), 34.

[55] "In *ästhetischer* Hinsicht ist sie [eine aus eigen erfundenen Motiven nachgebildete und ausgesponnene Melodie] noch nichts wert." Lobe, *Compositions-Lehre*, 38.

[56] Thomas Grey, "*Meister* Richard's Apprenticeship: The Early Operas (1833–1840)," in *The Cambridge Companion to Wagner*, 18–46. See also Cooke, "Wagner's Operatic Apprenticeship," *The Musical Times* 106 (1965), 103–05.

[57] See also Nicholas Baragwanath's detailed study of the interwoven practices of vocal pedagogy and compositional training in nineteenth-century Italy, which provides a complementary instance wherein compositional method cannot meaningfully be extracted from its context of performance practice and training in music theory. See Baragwanath, *The Italian Traditions and Puccini: Compositional Theory and Practice in Nineteenth-Century Opera* (Bloomington: Indiana University Press, 2011), esp. 256–312.

So what, or who, did Wagner imitate? "How little we are really convinced by our pack of [German] rules and prejudices!" he chided his fellow countrymen:

Let us drop for once the jest, let us spare ourselves for once the sermon, and ponder what it was that so enchanted us; we then find, especially with *Bellini*, that it was the limpid melody, the simple, noble, beauteous Song . . . Song, song, and a third time Song, ye Germans! For Song is once and for all the speech in which man should musically express himself.[58]

It was between 1834 and 1839 – the period in which he radicalized his pro-Italian position – that Wagner's public engagement with Bellini's operas reached its height: he first conducted *I Capuleti e i Montecchi*, *La straniera*, *Norma*, and *I puritani* between 1834 and 1836, including no fewer than six performances of *Norma* in Bad Lauchstädt, Rudolstadt, and Magdeburg;[59] in 1837–38, he directed eight performances of the opera in Riga, and even selected it for his first benefit concert there as musical director of the theater (December 11, 1837),[60] for which he adjusted the wind parts to suit the smaller forces available to him.[61] Though Wagner's appointment in the German-colonized Latvian town would be short-lived, it had promised to keep his spiralling debt at bay and allow his wife, Minna, to return after she had left him for her parents (he was to receive all proceeds from the event).[62] It was correspondingly important – personally and professionally – that his initial performance of *Norma* was well received, and in seeking to draw an audience, Wagner's notice in the *Neue freie Presse* alluded principally to the power of melody: "Of all Bellini's creations [*Norma* is] the richest in the profoundly realistic way in which true melody is united with intimate

---

[58] SSD 12: 20. Cf. PW 8: 67–68.

[59] A complete list of Wagner's operatic repertory in the 1830s is given in *The Wagner Compendium*, ed. Barry Millington (London: Thames & Hudson, 1992), 69.

[60] See Egon Voss, "Wagner und Rossini," *'Wagner und kein Ende': Betrachtungen und Studien* (Zurich: Atlantis, 1996), 359–76.

[61] The resulting orchestral retouchings are listed as WWV 46A, but are not contained in the New Wagner Edition because "Wagner's alterations to Bellini's score are too slight to justify printing the musical score." Furthermore, Egon Voss explains that Wagner based his arrangement not on Bellini's original score, but on "a version which differs from it, particularly as regards the orchestration, and that is probably an arrangement by somebody else." Further information on this source is not forthcoming, though the full score with Wagner's handwritten alterations is housed in the Zentralbibliothek in Zurich. See SW 20: viii.

[62] Natalie Planer, who believed she was Minna's sister, remembers from 1894 how Wagner "made Minna's life a veritable hell through his unjust, immoderate and violent jealousy . . . Minna could stand it no longer. And so . . . on the last day of May or June 1837 . . . she left Königsberg with me . . . not stopping till she was back with our parents." See *Wagner Remembered*, ed. Stewart Spencer (London: Faber, 2000), 22–23. Wagner's correspondence reveals the role that financial circumstances played in this. See especially Wagner to Minna, June 20, 1837, Berlin, in SB 1: 331.

passion."[63] It was a failsafe play to popular taste, but remained true to his own deep-seated musical interests at the time.[64]

It was on the basis of such close engagement with Italianate musical grammar that Holtmeier muses: "[p]erhaps in the Wagner biography, Bellini approaches the role that Vivaldi played in Johann Sebastian Bach's life."[65] While Bach's numerous concerto transcriptions tip the numerical balance of such a relationship heavily in favor of the baroque pair, Wagner's single recomposition of a Bellini aria from 1839 – "Norma il predisse, o Druidi" – nevertheless provides a lens through which to focus his quasi-Oedipal engagement with one of the nineteenth century's most famed Italian melodists. With Lobe's *Compositions-Lehre* in the background, then, there is good reason to consider the view that, as with the privately didactic partnerships peppered throughout music history, Wagner's borrowings functioned partly as a pedagogical tool. Equally, Wagner was expressly imitating Bellini as a model (and insertion arias rarely matched their surroundings in this way);[66] over and above any pedagogical purpose, he nevertheless intended the work to be performed in Paris, resulting in a complex claim to its originality and his own creative agency.

But before examining Wagner's Italian aria it will be helpful first to consider the changing status of artistic imitation alongside what, for Wagner, became a nodal point in the debate over originality: borrowed poetry. The eighteenth-century heritage of mimesis – epitomized in Winckelmann's 1755 prediction that "the only way for us to become great, and indeed (if this is possible) inimitable, is by imitating the ancients"[67] – represented a weighty historical double bind because it prevented a modern

---

[63] "*Norma*, tra le creazioni di Bellini, è quella che è più ricca di vera melodia unita, con profondo realismo, all passione intima." Quoted in Giampiero Tintori, *Bellini* (Milan Rusconi, 1983), 176.

[64] It was also to inspire interest in this performance that Wagner wrote his essay on "Bellini, a word about his time," which appeared in Riga's main newspaper, *Der Zuschauer*, mere days before the performance. See "Bellini: Ein Wort zu seiner Zeit," *Der Zuschauer* (December 7, 1837), reprinted *Dichtungen und Schriften*, 10 vols., ed. Dieter Borchmeyer (Frankfurt am Main: Insel, 1983), 5: 25–27.

[65] "Vielleicht kommt Bellini in der Wagnerschen Biographie die Rolle zu, die Vivaldi in Johann Sebastian Bachs Leben gespielt hat." Ludwig Holtmeier, "Von den *Feen* zum *Liebesverbot*", 59.

[66] To cite one example, John Ebers, manager of the King's Theatre in London 1820–27, explained: "Let a new opera be intended to be brought forward. Signor This will not sing his part, because it is not prominent enough; so to enrich it, a gathering must be made of airs from other operas, no matter whether by the same composer or not, nor whether there be any congruity between the style of the original piece and the adventitious passages introduced." See Ebers, *Seven Years of the King's Theatre* (London: Cary, Lea & Carey, 1828), 82–83.

[67] This statement from *Gedanken über die Nachahmung der griechischen Werke* is given in *German Aesthetic and Literary Criticism: Winckelmann, Lessing, Hamann, Herder, Schiller, Goethe*, ed. H. B. Nisbet (Cambridge University Press, 1985), 33.

worldview from being free from restrictive self-identification with a different culture. Thirty-five years after this staunch Philhellenism, and in the context of a long and complex debate, the Kantian position where "everyone is agreed on the point of complete opposition between [original] genius and the spirit of imitation" marks a significant delegitimization of mimesis in the sphere of German idealism.[68] Imitation appears as a negative absolute in Kant's value-laden categories, and, of course, informs most readings of Wagner's early stylistic dependency.

On closer inspection, however, we see that Kant's position is not absolute. His statement is incomplete because he later insists that works of genius must be received as models which awaken the younger genius "to a feeling of his own originality."[69] Such a reading of this passage is based on Kant's distinction between "original sense" and "original nonsense," where the former establishes a new sense or rule for art that others can follow, while the latter, remaining inherently incomprehensible, makes no such sense, creates no such rule and cannot therefore be imitated despite being original. Kant is clear: "Since there may also be original nonsense, [works of genius] must at the same time be models, i.e. be *exemplary*."[70] Was the possibility of "original nonsense" in this specific sense of not being received as an exemplary work, was this the cause of Wagner's fear that "the world is [always] having to be created anew"? If so, Sgambati's self-conscious melodicizing would count as nonsensical, and the legitimacy of working with (melodic) models is revealed as basic to Wagner's compositional *Weltanschauung*, for the matrix just outlined situates his artistic endeavors in a reflexive discourse on invention that is self-aware of creating its own "original sense." As we saw in Chapter 2, musical genius was no longer defined exclusively by an aristocracy of natural talent, but by studiously cultivated – mechanically inculcated – aptitude, after Lobe, who continued to condone the use of stylistic models; thus, within this discourse, "genius" and "didactic imitation" become two sides of the same coin.

(To an extent, this was also indicative of a shift in the model of the German genius away from the *Kopfkomponist*, towards the studious, struggling, refining, revising composer: the *Skizzenkomponist*. As concerns over

---

[68] Kant, *Critique of Judgment*, 151.

[69] Another term for this would be inspiration, which differs from imitation ethically, in terms of its motives. "[T]he product of a genius (as regards what is to be ascribed to genius and not to possible learning or schooling) is an example, not to be imitated (for then that which in it is genius and constitutes the spirit of the work would be lost) but to be followed by another genius, whom it awakens to a feeling of his own originality and whom it stirs so to exercise his art in freedom from the constraint of rules, that thereby a new rule is gained for art; and thus his talent shows itself to be exemplary." Kant, *Critique of Judgment*, 162.

[70] *Ibid.*, 150.

German melody continued to trickle corrosively over the pages of music journals, in other words, the *Mozartbild* was increasingly replaced with the *Beethovenbild*. "Many 'new geniuses' will think: what a vulgar realistic view of the procedures of genius!" Lobe parodies, acknowledging that in the old view, education ought simply to come "like pure revelation."[71] But in 1844, he drew explicitly on Anton Schindler's creative biography of Beethoven [1840] to back up his claim that Germany's *Riesengeist*[72] thoroughly revised parts of *Fidelio* "three or four times."[73] Schumann would make a similar point about Beethoven's working habits to a student in 1848, later encouraging them: "above all, you must strive [*suchen*] to write new and beautiful melodies."[74] But overturning the entrenched idol of natural genius was slow, and Lobe's treatise was no silver bullet; arguably the construct was never fully invalidated in the field of modern German music, and as late as 1947, Thomas Mann's most famous fictional composer ambivalently reinscribes the concept: Adrian Leverkühn must still make a pact at the cost of deadly syphilis for his *geniale Zeit*.[75] Back in 1844, such was the anticipated resistance and need for proof of Beethoven's work ethic that Lobe even included an expensive lithograph of his revisions to the passage "Freude schöner Götterfunken" in the first edition of the *Compositions-Lehre*, asking with duplicitous disbelief: "But *Beethoven* was certainly a genius, right?"[76])

---

[71] "Das Genie ist eben Genie dadurch, dass ihm seine herrlichen Bildung wie reine Offenbarung kommen." Lobe, *Compositions-Lehre*, 48.

[72] Lobe's pronoun of choice for Beethoven. See *Musikalische Briefe*, 24.

[73] "Drei-, vier-mal hat er ganze Nummern in seinem Fidelio total umgearbeitet." Lobe, *Compositions-Lehre*, 48.

[74] For Schumann's comments about Beethoven as a model for the constantly revising composer see his letter to Ludwig Meinardus, September 16, 1848. For his comment to Meinardus about striving hard to achieve his own melodies, see Schumann to Meinardus, December 28, 1853. Translations are taken from Schumann, *On Music and Musicians*, 78–79.

[75] Thomas Mann, *Doktor Faustus. Das Leben des deutschen Tonsetzers Adrian Leverkühn erzählt von einem Freunde* (Frankfurt am Main: S. Fischer, 1947).

[76] "*Beethoven* war doch wohl ein Genie?" Lobe, *Compositions-Lehre*, 48. We should remember, however, that the status of the Ninth Symphony was contested during the 1840s, even by such eminent composers as Louis Spohr. Lobe's publication of the Beethoven facsimile in effect forms part of the pre-history of Beethoven sketch studies, and predates Gustav Nottebohm's revelatory article on the composer's studies (in species counterpoint, figured bass, and fugue) in the *AmZ* by some nineteen years. The first of Nottebohm's volumes on Beethoven's sketchbooks appeared only in 1865. Gustav Nottebohm, *Ein Skizzenbuch von Beethoven* (Leipzig: Breitkopf & Härtel, 1865). Two years earlier, he had probed Beethoven's formative studies in: "Beethoven's theoretische Studien," *AmZ* 41 (October 7, 1863), 685–91.

Cementing the link between model-based pedagogy and contemporary melody, Lobe's 1854 letter on *Tonfolge* analyzes the arhythmic pitch sequence from nothing but the first movement of Beethoven's Fifth Symphony. His strategy, in short, was to reorient what he saw as misdirected energy and overturn an inhibiting aesthetic belief in the instantaneous birth of works of "nature." Against doctrines of natural genius and legal protectionism, this reflected a broader project to legitimize both creative struggle as compositional praxis ("the materialist version of subjective agency")[77] and imitation as compositional method, respectively.

The assault on Kant was blunt. But as late as January 1844, Wagner articulated his own proudly retrograde genial self-assessment to Karl Gaillard, the very interlocutor of the legal debate over melodic property in 1841 we met earlier. Following the Berlin production of *Der fliegende Holländer* on January 7, 1844, Wagner invoked his own mysteriously instantaneous invention thereby aligning himself explicitly with the *Kopfkomponist* tradition:

[E]ven before I begin writing a single line of the text or drafting a scene, I am already immersed in the musical aura of my new creation, I have the whole sound and all the characteristic motifs in my head so that when the poem is finished and the scenes are arranged in order the actual opera, for me, is already completed.[78]

Given Gaillard's well-publicized legalistic opinion that melody is a composer's "most noble richness" and property, where not only justice but duty dictates that any borrowing must be acknowledged, Wagner's comments glimmer with self-awareness – awareness about his status as a melodist, confirming his later remarks to Mathilde Wesendonck that positively document his insecurity.

The letter to Gaillard has typically been celebrated by Wagner scholars as "one of the most valuable documents we possess in connection with Wagnerian aesthetics."[79] Since – in addition to binding dramatic character genetically to musical themes – it aligns Wagner with tenets of the Kantian genius, it serves the agenda of confirming his creative prowess. The context of its inception suggests, however, that this may have been precisely Wagner's intention, and we might consider taking a more circumspect view of this document, particularly given that Wagner would squarely

---

[77] David Wellbery, "Forward" to Friedrich Kittler, *Discourse Networks 1800–1900* (Stanford University Press, 1990), xv.

[78] Wagner to Karl Gaillard, January 30, 1844, in SB 2: 358.

[79] Ernest Newman, *The Life of Richard Wagner*, 4 vols. (New York: Alfred Knopf, 1966), 1: 453.

contradict it twelve years later.[80] Gaillard had recently established one of the most significant music journals in Berlin, the weekly *Berliner musikalische Zeitung* (1844–47), and pledged his emphatic admiration for Wagner, which elicited Wagner's self-elucidatory response, that is, his first communication with this well-disposed public defender of melodic originality. Why was Wagner's unsolicited, rare self-assessment of his creative process sent to a complete stranger? While Wagner's later comments in *Mein Leben* are dismissive of Gaillard's own talents, they emphasize his disappointment that the journalist was unable to help him professionally in Berlin, hinting that Wagner calculated somewhat in his first letter.[81] The tendency remains to accept Wagner's comments on faith, perhaps because we too want to believe their claims. Yet rather than any methodological veracity, it seems more likely that the remarks testify to Wagner's awareness of his need to be seen as original, i.e. at root, an enterprising attempt to insert himself into narratives of the natural genius.[82]

Contrafacta and confessions of melodic failure

Praise for Wagner's melodies that expressly contravened the composer's aesthetic vision outlined to Gaillard illustrates that more was at stake here than merely a quarrel over creative aptitude: it was a conflict over creative method. In his serialized "Letters to a Young Composer about Richard Wagner," published as part of the *Fliegende Blätter* between 1854 and 1855, Lobe offered one of the most articulate mid-century defenses of Wagner's vocal melodies but rejected his *poiesis* (the inner conflation of word and tone) as a "regrettable error!" (*Bedauerlicher Irrthum!*), explaining: "[i]n no way does Wagner practice what he preaches."[83] Lobe's analysis, accordingly, disentangles Wagner's melodies from their orchestral and poetic context. As Examples 3.3a and 3.3b show, the

---

[80] "Sonderbar! erst beim Komponiren geht mir das eigentliche Wesen meiner Dichtung auf: überall entdecken sich mir Geheimnisse, die mir selbst bis dahin noch verborgen blieben." Wagner to Liszt, December 6, 1856, Zurich, in SB 8: 219.

[81] "Only my poor friend Gaillard stuck by me through all the unpleasantness, but was entirely powerless to do anything about it. His . . . music periodical had already perished: thus he could help me solely in very small matters." ML 350.

[82] This would form an early instance of the kind of behavior Nicholas Vazsonyi has characterized more broadly as Wagner's "marketing strategies" wherein the composer "pioneered his own merchandizing . . . [and] presented his works as distinct creations unlike all others." See Vazsonyi, *Richard Wagner: Self-Promotion and the Making of a Brand* (Cambridge University Press, 2010), 1ff.

[83] "Was aber Wagner lehrt, übt er keineswegs konsequent praktisch aus." Lobe, "Briefe über Rich, Wagner an einen jungen Komponisten. Dreizehnter Brief," *FBfM* 2 (1855), 37.

Example 3.3a Wolfram's lyric song for the *Sängerkrieg* from *Tannhäuser*, act 2, scene 4, mm. 664–96.

Example 3.3a (cont.)

Example 3.3b Lohengrin's repetition of his *Verbot* from *Lohengrin* act 1, scene 3, mm. 789–96.

two melodies he cites are purposively formulaic, with patterned repetitions that have little or nothing to do with the "musical prose" Wagner had outlined in 1850–51. "Melodies," Lobe explains "must have simple construction out of truth of expression, they must allow themselves to be grasped easily as musical periods and groups."[84] As the theorist observes, Wolfram's melody (Example 3.3a)

---

[84] "Melodien . . . müssen außer der Wahrheit des Ausdrucks, auch einfache Konstruktion haben, müssen sich als musikalische Periode und Gruppen leicht auffassen lassen." *Ibid.*, 29.

shows a triple repetition: the second period (b) repeats the first (a), the fourth (d) repeats the third (c), and the final period (e) is a varied repeat of the opening (a). In other words, the form is: a a' b b' a" which corresponds precisely to basic mid-century lyric form, common in lyrical passages throughout contemporary Italian opera, as Lobe well knew. In another example (which we encountered in Chapter 1), Lobe cites the double repetition in Lohengrin's interdiction (Example 3.3b) to sum up his endorsement with a claim to formal organization: "there is rhythmic balance, simplest construction, referentiality, unity and a rounding off of the whole form."[85] By ignoring the poetic text, Lobe was constructing Wagner as a defensible melodist emphatically against the tide of criticism. Had Wagner written nothing but these two melodies, he continues, the notion that he lacked the ability to compose melody "would be incomprehensible, or – there are no melodies in any operas at all."[86]

Of course, in what would become a famous protest, Wagner complained to Theodor Uhlig in 1852 that "[t]he person who, in judging my music, divorces the harmony from the instrumentation does me as great an injustice as the one who divorces my music from my poem, my vocal line from the words!"[87] Lobe would actually support the composer's claims as a melodist by arguing the reverse, that "one need only sing Wolfram's and Lohengrin's melody *without text* and they are and remain music because they have comprehensible phrase and periodic structure, and also express without words a certain feeling."[88] At root, such comments merely co-opted Wagner (as a self-styled genius and victim of sustained criticism over *Melodielosigkeit*) to make a larger point during the *Nachmärz* that (Wagner's) compositional work defeats (his) merely

---

[85] "Da ist Eurhythmie, einfachste Konstruktion, Bezüglichkeit, Einheit und Abrundung der ganzen Form." in Lobe, "Briefe über Richard Wagner an einen jungen Komponisten. Zwölfter Brief," *FBfM* 2 (1855), 29.

[86] "Hätte Wagner nichts als diese beiden Melodien geschrieben, der obige Ausspruch wäre darnach schon ein unbegreiflicher, oder – es gibt in keiner einzigen Oper Melodie." *Ibid.*, 28. Admittedly, this was not the fragmentary, recitational stichomythia that the majority of critics associated with Wagnerian melody from the mid-1840s. Indeed, in his study of Wagner's stylistic development, Lippman tacitly implies that Lobe was on the wrong side of history when he characterized the particular nature of Wagner's development during the 1840s as "a transition from symmetrical melody and balanced melodic phrases to a freely constructed continuity." See Edward A. Lippman, *The Philosophy and Aesthetics of Music* (Lincoln and London: University of Nebraska Press, 1999), 203. And yet, by rejecting Wagner's *poiesis*, Lobe consciously interprets Wagner's melodies against the doctrine of continuity laid out in *Oper und Drama*, that is, as "absolute" melody (in Wagner's use of the term).

[87] Wagner to Theodor Uhlig, May 31, 1852, Zurich, in SB 4: 386.

[88] "Man singt die Melodie 'Wolfram's' und 'Lohengrin's' *ohne Text*, beide sind und bleiben gute Musik, weil sie verständlichen Satz- und Periodenbau haben, und auch ohne Worte eine Gefühlstimmung ausdrücken," in Lobe "Briefe über Richard Wagner an einen jungen Komponisten," *FBfM* 2 (1855), 30.

ambitious, wishful thinking. But as we shall see presently, Lobe had good reason to misread Wagner in the case of Lohengrin's *Verbot*. His position vis-à-vis Wagner's vocal melody, in short, is that Wagner was a *bone fide* melodist in spite of himself.

On the few occasions that Wagner speaks about his compositional process, it is not musical but *poetic* originality that he regards as the inhibiting factor in melodic composition. In the same letter to Gaillard in which Wagner divulged his putative creative process, he explains that "it would now be totally impossible for me to set another's text to music."[89] But aside from suspected acts of borrowing from Weber or Meyerbeer, it is the specter of self-borrowing, of Wagner setting different texts to the same "original" melody (and regretting it), that finally renders his claims plausible for an inseverable bond between original melody and poetry after the mid-1840s. Even the most famous line from *Lohengrin* is derivative.[90] Far from a theft from his contemporaries (or their publishers), this was self-theft. The *Verbot* was borrowed from a sketch for an earlier, incomplete, perhaps incidentally accompanied theatrical work in 1837 that appears on the reverse side of the manuscript for Wagner's overture on *Rule Britannia* (the redoubtable Tappert first pointed out the correspondence in 1887).[91] The repetitious phrase structure of Wagner's *Verbot* bears a striking similarity to his unpublished sketch – a little over two leafs – of a scene about *Percunos* drafted in Riga. Examples 3.4a and 3.4b present the music in question, and the extant text for this scene is provided below.

Extant text to *Percunos* (square boxes mark the lines set in A minor to Wagner's later *Verbot*; dotted lines mark the same music in F major)

Chor der Priester	*Chorus of Priests*
Hört der Götter Spruch!	Hear the word of the Gods!
Fühlet ihren Fluch!	Heed their curse!
Auf blut'gem Throne herrscht Picullos,	Picullos reigns on a bloody throne,
die Feuerkrone trägt Percunos,	Percunos wears a crown of fire,
doch Glück zum Lohne	Potrimpos, however, grants
schenkt Potrimpos	happiness as reward

---

[89] Wagner to Karl Gaillard, January 30, 1844, in SB 2: 358–59.

[90] It was not entirely unusual for Wagner to salvage thematic material from earlier works for use in later projects. In another instance, Deryck Cooke pointed out in 1965 the self-borrowing of the Nuns' *Salve Regina* from *Das Liebesverbot* for use as the motif for the "Feast of Grace" in *Tannhäuser*. See Cooke, "Wagner's Operatic Apprenticeship," 104.

[91] Wilhelm Tappert, "Percunos und Lohengrin," *Musikalisches Wochenblatt. Organ für Musiker und Musikfreunde* 35 (August 25, 1887), 413–15. The manuscript in question is in the Nationalarchiv (NA B I c 4) along with Tappert's transcription (NA B I g 3).

Jünglinge

Percunos! Percunos!

Nimm auf blutigem Alter

Unser Opfer gnädig wahr!

Leih' uns Deiner Schrecken Macht,

Stärke uns in wilder Schlacht!

Jungfrauen

Potrimpos! Potrimpos!

Nimm auf Deinem Weihalter

Unsers Opfers gnädig wahr!

Sende Deines Segens Macht,

Strahle Licht in unsre Nacht!

Tutti

Für die Opfer, die wir bringen,

Steht mit Eurer Macht uns bei,

Dass im Kampfe wir bezwingen

Feindes Macht, Tyrannei!

Chor der Priester

Die Flamme sprüht,

Der Holzstoss glüht;

Percunos, Blutgott, gib ein Zeichen,

Wer Dir zum Opfer soll erbleichen!

Young men

Percunos! Percunos!

Receive our sacrifice mercifully

On the bloody altar!

Lend us your terrible power,

Strengthen us in ferocious battle!

Virgins

Potrimpos! Potrimpos!

Receive our sacrifice mercifully

On your consecrated altar!

Send us the power of your blessing,

Shine a light into our night!

Tutti

For the sacrifices that we bring,

Stand by us with your power,

So that in battle we conquer

the tyranny of enemy power!

Chorus of priests

The flame flickers

the pile of wood glows;

Percunos, God of blood, give us a sign

Who shall be your sacrifice!

Example 3.4a Sacrificial song from Wagner's aborted sketch for *Percunos* (1837), *Nationalarchiv der Richard-Wagner-Stiftung*, Bayreuth NA B I c 4.

Example 3.4b Sacrificial song in canon, from Wagner's aborted sketch for *Percunos* (1837), *Nationalarchiv der Richard-Wagner-Stiftung*, Bayreuth NA B I c 4.

Beyond the musical correspondence, there also appears to be a topical connection with *Lohengrin*, suggesting that rather than text physiognomy, it was the dramatic scenario that determined his choice. So who was Wagner's *Percunos*? *Percunis* is the Old Prussian name for thunder (Latvian: *Pērkons*; Lithuanian: *Perkúnas*), as recorded in the Elbing glossary (a Middle Low German glossary which contains some 802 Old Prussian words; dated *ca.* 1300). This mythical Percunos, the pagan god of thunder, would later be refashioned as Donner in *Das Rheingold*,[92] and in his *Geschichte der deutschen Sprache* (1848), the eminent philologist Jacob Grimm would characterize the three deities Wagner adduces (the three "chief divinities" of the ancient Prussians or *Pruzzi*, according to James Bell's 1832 account)[93] as archetypal powers within different pre-Christian cultures: military, creative, and thunderous (earth fertilizing) power, respectively:[94]

Latin	Mars	Mercurius	Jupiter
Greek	Ἄρης	Ἑρμῆς	Ζεύς
Celtic	Hesus	Teutates	Taranis
Old High German	Zio	Wuotan	Donar
Old Norse	Týr	Odinn	Thôrr
Slavic	Svjatovit	Radigast	Perun
Lithuanian	Pykullas	Potrimpos	Perkunas
Indian	Siva	Brahma	Vishnus

While residing in Riga during 1837, Wagner evidently planned to use the Lithuanian names for his narrative of sacrifice, but switched to Old High German for divinities in *Lohengrin* and the *Ring*.

Thus, at precisely the time Wagner was immersed in themes of druidic rebellion while conducting and arranging Bellini's *Norma*, his mythic allusion to *Percunos* established a point of contact between a repetitious A-minor melody, themes of sacrifice, and pagan gods, all of which would be duly recycled in *Lohengrin* where his "composition" of the *Verbot* was seemingly driven by dramatic association. Wagner's 1837 text even provides a tentative thematic link to the "sacrifice" of knowledge and temptation that Elsa must

---

[92] Percunos is a god to whom life is sacrificed for rain, while also being called upon to spit fire (bolts of lightning) and kill devils. He is closely associated with the oak tree, which he strikes with his lightning, and which accordingly stores up (the potential for) fire. For a brief account of the different connotations associated with the god *Perkunas*, see Martin West, *Indo-European Poetry and Myth* (Oxford University Press, 2007), 239–40.

[93] Percunos was worshiped, Bell explains, under the venerated oak: "the monarch of the wood." See James Bell, *A System of Geography, Popular and Scientific: Or A Physical, Political, and Statistical Account of the World and Its Various Divisions* (Glasgow: Archibald Fullarton, 1832), 473.

[94] Jacob Grimm, *Geschichte der deutschen Sprache* [1848], 4th edn. (Leipzig: S. Hirzel, 1880), 84.

Example 3.4c J. C. Lobe's contrafactum of the well-known *Verbot* in *Lohengrin*, act 1, scene 3, from Lobe's *Briefe über Rich. Wagner an einen jungen Komponisten* (1855). [Trans. "Here lies she whom you have slandered; I have killed her / and you have stolen all my happiness."]

Hier liegt die du ver leum - det;   ich   ha-be sie ge - tö - tet   und du hast mir   ge   raubt all'mei-nes Le - bens Glück!

endure in order to gain Lohengrin as her champion. As the extant text for this scene shows, Wagner's three substantive references to sacrificial offerings (for Potrimpos and Percunos) are accompanied by the proto-*Verbot* motif. This motif also accompanies the chorus as they implore Percunos in exchange to "stand by us with your power," mirroring Elsa's desperate plea for "my knight [who] will fight for me!" to whom she "sacrifices" her hand, soul, and body: "to him I'll give everything I am!"[95] But in all this, the connections remain topical, not textual. Unaware of the likely origin of the motif, Lobe illustrated his point in 1855 by supplying an entirely new text (Example 3.4c), which becomes all the more salient in light of the *Percunos* sketch.[96]

That Wagner interpreted such accusations of melodic–poetic inter-changeability as an attack on his originality belies his most severe criticism, a charge that brings together many of the threads in the discourse I am uncovering, and which he explicitly articulated in 1860 in answer to a decade of vigorous debates over melody:

to say that a piece of music has no melody – taken in its highest sense – can only mean: the musician has failed to create a form that grips and stirs our feeling; a statement which simply announces the composer's *lack of talent*, his *want of originality*, compelling him to *cobble together his piece from melodic phrases often heard before*, which therefore leave the ear indifferent.[97]

But if Wagner was setting the same tunes to different texts, yet consistently lauded melody as "music's [very] nature" and "only form," to what extent did he secretly agree with the criticisms about the *Melodielosigkeit* of his own music before his exile in 1849?[98] In 1851, Adolph Stahr had published a

---

[95] "Des Ritters will ich wahren / er soll mein Streiter sein!" and "geb' ich ihm was ich bin!" *Lohengrin*, Act 1, scene 2. Intriguingly, in some accounts, Percunos' car is drawn by a male goat, which if not quite the white swan of Lohengrin, nonetheless offers a vague correspondence of bestial transport. See J. Balys, *Tautosakos darbai* (Kaunas: Lietuvie Tautosakos Archyvas, 1937), 3: nos. 316f. See also West's brief discussion of "Perkunas" in relation to thunder in *Indo-European Poetry and Myth*, 240.

[96] Lobe, "Briefe über Rich. Wagner an einen jungen Komponisten," *FBfM* 2 (1855), 31.

[97] SSD 7: 125. Cf. PW 3: 333. Emphasis added.

[98] SSD 3: 309. Cf. PW 3: 103; and SSD 7: 125. Cf. PW 3: 333.

review of the fifth performance of *Lohengrin* in Weimar, comparing Wagner's "rigor against melody, his rhythmic monotony, his disregard for the most virtuosic elements of artful singing, with the zealous severity of Lutheranism."[99] Wagner, of course, was not consciously practicing melodic asceticism. But in a letter to Stahr three days later, his response tacitly accepts the implied criticism:

I know what you mean when you speak of monotonous, unrhythmical melody [in *Lohengrin*] . . . The reason lies not in the music but – since music after all can only ever be language developing to its fullest potential – in the language itself, in the verse. At present we have only inadequately formed verse, not the real thing. My musical expression, moreover, continues to be related only supersensually to language: a substantial, sensual [*sinnliche*] relationship between the two has escaped me until now.[100]

Under pressure of Stahr's scrutiny (and without ever having heard a performance of *Lohengrin*), Wagner silently concedes his earlier ideal of perceptibly melodic composition, which is to say the "clear, graspable melody" that he lauded in Bellini, and sublimates this to a "sensualized" relation between verse and melody.[101] The realization that *Lohengrin*'s melodies had failed entailed a forcible recasting of Wagner's erstwhile aspirations; thirteen years after praising Bellini's "limpid melody, the simple, noble, beauteous song," Wagner now decried how modern "ploughboys march to Bellinian Arias to the murder of their brothers," perhaps the most politically negative allusion to Bellini ever to flow from Wagner's pen.[102] In contrast to Wagner's ebullient rebuttals of criticism over what Nietzsche would mockingly call his "infinity: but without melody," he expressed a different view in private to Stahr. In light of the *Percunos* sketch, i.e. after borrowing his own melody, he invokes an inseverable, sensory bond between poetry and melody to account for what he acknowledged, for the first time, as his melodic *insufficiency*.[103]

---

[99] "In diesem Betrachte möchte man Wagner mit seinem Rigorismus gegen die Melodie, seiner rhythmischen Eintönigkeit, seiner Vernachlässigung der virtuosistischen Elemente im Kunstgesange vergleichen mit der eifervollen Strenge des Lutherthums." Rpt. *Frankfurter Zeitung und Handelsblatt*, August 17, 1901, "Erstes Morgenblatt." Quoted in SB 4: 59.

[100] Wagner to Adolph Stahr, May 31, 1851, Zurich, in SB 4: 59. The fifth performance of *Lohengrin* at the Weimar Hoftheater took place on May 11, 1851. Stahr's review was printed in the Berlin *National-Zeitung* on May 27–28, nos. 243 and 245.

[101] SSD 12: 20. Cf. PW 8: 68. Wagner first heard a performance of *Lohengrin* at the dress rehearsal in Vienna on May 11, 1861. See his letter to Minna Wagner on May 13, 1861.

[102] SSD 3: 261, Cf. PW 2: 52.

[103] Nietzsche's quip was that the term *unendliche Melodie* merely concealed an absence. See Nietzsche, "The Case of Wagner" [1888], in *The Anti-Christ, Ecce Homo, Twilight of the Idols and Other Writings*, ed. Aaron Ridley & Judith Norman (Cambridge University Press, 2005), 243.

Wagner redoubled his protest about borrowed text while in exile. In response to Liszt's suggestion that he publish a volume of vocal compositions to alleviate his financial dependence on the Weimar Kapellmeister, an increasingly beggarly Wagner confesses that "it would be absolutely impossible for me simply to write music to another man's poems, not because I consider this beneath me, but because I know, *and know by experience*, that my music would be bad and meaningless."[104] Beckmesser's feeble attempt to sing the words of Walther's song in act 3 of *Die Meistersinger* would appear to dramatize this sentiment, and is preceded in act 2 by Hans Sachs' general warning: "Don't you care about the melody? / Methinks tone and word should fit."[105] Although the opera's poem was only completed in 1862, the first prose scenario was finished less than eighteen months after Wagner's first complaint to Gaillard (August 3, 1845); if Sachs counts as one of several acknowledged musical self-portraits, so too must Beckmesser, whose actions aptly stylize Wagner's fear of embarrassment at mid-century.

If we take Wagner's numerous comments about setting the poetry of others at face value, what "experience" before *Lohengrin* is he talking about? What had conditioned such inadequacy in 1849, inadequacy he confessed to Wesendonck in 1862, and projected onto Sgambati in 1880? John Deathridge's study of the sources for *Rienzi* revealed that the musical revisions correspond, in the majority of cases, with alterations in the verse draft (i.e. in the text itself), suggesting that "Wagner was already on the verge of challenging the notion of music as an autonomous mode of expression."[106] Deathridge's insight is that "when deprived of dramatic movement and a workable text," Wagner's "purely musical moments [show him] at his weakest and most imitative."[107] The years during which he composed the music for his aria "Norma il predisse, o Druidi" (1839), in other words, during which text and musical originality were still officially separated in his mind, form a crucible of Wagner's attitude toward imitation, melodic originality, and original verse. They also indicate the centrality of borrowed Italianate melody to him within this formative period.

The crux is that Wagner valued Bellinian melody above all others during the 1830s, but feared his own attempts at melodious composition were correspondingly derivative. His mid-century reassessment of vocal melody – well within memory of composing his most explicit pastiche aria – was seemingly

---

[104] Wagner to Liszt, December 5, 1849, Zurich, in *Correspondence*, 41.

[105] "Ist Euch an der Weise nichts gelegen? / Mich dünkt, sollt' passen Ton und Wort." *Die Meistersinger*, Act 2, scene 6.

[106] John Deathridge, *Wagner's Rienzi. A Reappraisal based on a Study of the Sketches and Drafts* (Oxford: Clarendon Press, 1977), 141.

[107] *Ibid.*

driven by his belief that a sensory (*sinnlich*) relation between text and music was what ensured melody would communicate with a listener's "feelings." Hence, poetic text was vital for a non-derivative melody; but this belief meant something different to Wagner in 1839 and 1849.

Norma "simuliamo" and the pedagogy of remodeling

> Far be it from me to regard and recommend Bellini as a model for us . . . To invite imitations of his operatic style? Certainly not! But I want to induce the German artist to investigate and to consider whether some of his maxims could not be developed with German spirit and German thoroughness so that German opera might also win a large public and a long life?
>
> J. C. Lobe (1854)[108]

On numerous occasions Wagner did set relatively short texts by other poets (see Table 3.1), producing a number of Lieder and one insertion aria for Bellini's *Norma* while in Paris in 1839.[109] The first problem he encountered in composing this aria was his poor Italian. Dictating *Mein Leben* in 1866, he explains: "[Samuel] Lehrs was obliged to dig up an Italian political refugee to extract from him the text for such an aria. This was done, and I executed an effective composition in Bellini's style."[110] The resulting ersatz aria with chorus documents Wagner's most explicit musical engagement with *bel canto* melody. It was most likely intended to supplant Oroveso's "Ah! del Tebro al giogo indegno" in act 2 and Wagner presented it to the famed bass Luigi Lablache in October 1839 for performance at the Théâtre Italien that season.[111] Whereas

---

[108] "Ich bin daher weit entfernt, Bellini als Muster für uns zu betrachten und zu empfehlen . . . Zur Nachahmung seiner Opernweise auffordern? Gewiß nicht! Aber ich möchte die deutschen Künstler veranlassen, zu untersuchen und zu überlegen, ob nicht manche seiner [Bellini's] Maximen, mit deutschem Geiste und deutscher Gründlichkeit so auszuprägen wären, daß auch die deutschen Opern sich ein größeres Publikum und ein längeres Leben erringen könnten?" Lobe, "Bellini," rpt. *Musik Konzepte 46: Vincenzo Bellini* (Munich: Edition Text + Kritik, 1985), 48, 63.

[109] Wagner wrote his own text for his only other insertion aria "Doch jetzt wohin ich blicke, umgibt mich Schreckensnacht" in Marschner's *Der Vampyr*. This dates from Wagner's time at Würzburg (1833) and is not a complete aria but rather a new Allegro section to be appended to Marschner's Andantino "Wie ein schöner Frühlingsmorgen." See SW 15: 55–81.

[110] ML 173.

[111] Competing theories exist as to the intended placement of Wagner's aria: the New Wagner edition indicates the likely location as Oroveso's modest recitative "Invan di Norman la mente investigai," in act 2, scene 5; whereas the *Verzeichnis der musikalischen Werke Richard Wagners und ihre Quellen* (WWV) suggests that the aria was intended for act 1, to be inserted between Norma's and Aldagisa's first scenes. See WWV, 195–96. The manifest musical misreadings of Oroveso's "Ah del Tebro" in act 2, however, along with the strong textual correspondence between this and Wagner's Italian text, leads me to believe that it was in fact intended to replace Oroveso's aria in act 2. That there remains a sense of ambiguity over this question would seem – at one level – a testament to Wagner's camouflaging of any overt borrowing.

Table 3.1 Original compositions by Wagner that set texts by other poets

Date	WWV	poet	comp. / singer / wk	title	status
1831	15	Goethe	7 pieces for Goethe's *Faust*	*i. Lied der Soldaten*	Lied
–	–	Goethe	–	*ii. Bauer unter der Linde*	Lied
–	–	Goethe	–	*iii. Branders Lied*	Lied
–	–	Goethe	–	*iv. Es war einmal ein König*	Lied
–	–	Goethe	–	*v. Was machst du mir vor Liebchens Tür*	Lied
–	–	Goethe	–	*vi. Gretchen am Spinnrade*	Lied
–	–	Goethe	–	*vii. Gretchen*	melodrama
1832	30	Theodor Apel	*Abendglocken*	*Glockentöne*	Lied (lost)
1834	41	J. Singer	"Die letzte Heidenverschwörung in Preussen"		theater music (127 mm. sketch)
1837	43	Karl von Holtei	Blum (*Mary, Max u. Michel*)	*Sanfte Wehmut will sich regen*	Lied
1837	45	I. F. Castelli	Joseph Weigl (*Die Schweizerfamilie*)		aria (comp. sketch)
1838	50	Georg Schuerlin		*Der Tannenbaum*	Lied
1839	52	?	Bellini (*Norma*)	*Norma il predisse, o Druidi*	insertion aria
1839	54	Victor Hugo	"Les orientales"	*Extase*	Lied (19 mm fragment)
1839	55	Victor Hugo	"Les orientales"	*Attente*	Lied
1839	56	Victor Hugo	"Les voix intérieures"	*La tombe dit à la rose*	Lied (31 mm. sketch)
1839	57	Pierre de Ronsard		*Mignonne*	Lied
1839	58	Jean Reboul		*Tout n'est qu'images fugitives*	Lied
1839	60	Heinrich Heine (trans. F.-A. Loeve-Veimar)		*Les deux grenadiers*	Lied
1840	61	Pierre Jean de Béranger		*Adieux de Marie Stuart*	Lied
1841	53	?		*Dors mon enfant*	Lied
1857–58	91	Mathilde Wesendonk		*Der Engel; Stehe still Im Triebhaus; Schmerzen Träume*	Concert Lieder
1858	92	Baron E. von Feuchtersleben		*Es ist bestimmt in Gottes Rat*	Lied (13 mm. draft)

the use of insertion arias was common practice during the later eighteenth and early nineteenth centuries, copyright laws limiting the liberties that could be taken with a score began to appear in 1840,[112] and as Hilary Poriss points out, even by the early 1830s contracts began to forbid singers from interpolating arias on their own volition.[113] Whether by contract or caprice, Lablache declined Wagner's entreaty on the grounds that the Parisian public knew Bellini's opera too well and would expect the customary (authentic) melodies. Evidently, he did not want to disappoint them.[114]

As a result, Wagner's aria was never performed during his lifetime, and warrants examination because of the light it sheds on him as a neophyte Italian melodist and advocate of Bellini shortly after the Italian's death in 1835, about which time Wagner later confessed he was striving for originality.[115] It can be viewed as a musical counterpart to the early pro-Bellinian essays, in which – as we read in Chapter 1 – Wagner chastised his fellow Germans for "our pack of rules and prejudices," dreaming instead of awaking as an Italian composer ("surely it would not be a sin if, before going to bed, we prayed that heaven would one day give German composers such melodies and such a mode of handling song").[116] In this context, the aria becomes something of an "Italian confession" that essentially admits what the coeval melodic idiom of *Rienzi* implies, namely that Wagner actively sought to insert himself into this sphere of culturally appealing melodic expression. The key difference for Wagner's development is that he penned the text for his opera, but not for the aria.

There is little need in this case to establish covert correspondences between Wagner's and Bellini's arias because the former is already an

---

[112] See Julian Budden, *The Operas of Verdi* (Oxford: Clarendon Press, 1992), 1: 5.

[113] In her enlightening study of operatic perforance practice, Hilary Poriss cites the example of Giuditta Grisi's contract for the 1833 carnival season at La Fenice, whose third article set a trend in declaring: "It is forbidden for Signora Grisi to insert pieces of music without special permission from the impresario." See *Changing the Score: Arias, Prima Donnas, and the Authority of Performance* (Oxford University Press, 2009), 18.

[114] "Er [Wagner] berichtet, daß ihm Lablache bedauernd erklärt hatte, sich weigern zu müssen, eine Wagner'sche Komposition bei der Aufführung einer schon oft gespielten Oper einlegen zu lassen. Er bedauert den Rat Anders['] nicht befolgt zu haben, sich vorher Lablache vorstellen zu lassen." Jacob Levi, Wiesbaden, Autographen-Anzeiger, No.1, p. 21, No. 228, quoted in SW 15: 22.

[115] For mention of recent performances of this aria, see John Deathridge, "Reminiscences of *Norma*," in *Das musikalische Kunstwerk: Geschichte – Ästhetik – Theorie: Festschrift Carl Dahlhaus zum 60. Geburtstag*, ed. Hermann Danuser, Helga de la Motte-Haber, Silke Leopold and Norbert Miller (Laaber: Laaber, 1988), 225.

[116] SSD 12: 20. Cf. PW 8: 67–68.

explicit surrogate, and was written – almost as historical revisionism made manifest – for performance: to out-sing, out-maneuver Bellini's original, and otherwise woo the Parisian *beau monde*. This actually reverses the Bloomian critic's strategy to uncover borrowings or other relational arcana, and the new onus is to establish *difference* in the sense both of creating new benchmarks for Bellini's popularity, and of Wagner's failure to hide behind a seamless stylistic mask. For, if we ignore those aspects of his aria that exceed mere imitation, the danger is to think of him in 1839 as a benign chameleon, where his ambitions towards Meyerbeer and Scribe at the Opéra suggest he was far more predatory in daring Europe's musical mecca to shift – or at least share – its allegiance.[117]

The respective recitative and aria texts both concern Oroveso's rage at the Roman oppressors and his bidding to the druid troops to remain patient until Norma decrees the time for uprising. Both texts are provided in Table 3.2. While a comparative reading would only compare the poets Felice Romani and Wagner's unknown Italian refugee, we might note that Wagner chose to set a moment of repressed revolutionary ambition amid druid worship of pagan gods (a topic that resonates with his 1837 *Percunos* sketch as well as Ortrud's entire persona), and pays particular attention to Bellini's setting of the line "simuliamo" (we shall pretend, from *simulare*: to fake, feign, or simulate), as we shall see. We cannot know whether Wagner intended a double meaning encompassing the *Norma* plot and his pretensions towards Bellini's style, but these remain enticing possibilities, as does the idea that it was a double-edged in-joke for Lablache who would have sung the simulated Bellini on behalf of an ascendant German revolutionary rather than a reigning Italian melodist.

---

[117] Wagner desperately wanted a Parisian success with *Rienzi*, for the French capital was unquestionably Europe's musical mecca. Owing to the fact that Paris paid continuous royalties to the composers of works performed, a successful opera premiere meant not only fame, but fortune. Wagner was optimistic in 1839 and pursued a collaboration with Scribe and support from Meyerbeer to this end; in Wagner's retrospection, both were ill-fated. His aspirations, frustrations, and debts in Paris between 1839 and 1842 are very well documented in the literature. Two specific accounts of Wagner's literary activities are Philippe Reyna, "Richard Wagner als Pariser Korrespondent 1841: Neun Pariser Berichte für die Dresdner Abend-Zeitung – Reportage oder Vorwand?," *'Schlagen Sie die Kraft der Reflexion nicht zu gering an!' Beiträge zu Richard Wagners Denken, Werk und Wirken*, ed. Klaus Döge, Christa Jost, Peter Jost (Mainz: Schott, 2002), 21–31 and Bernard Schulé, "Wagner, Paris et la musique française: Jeux d'influences," *Revue musicale de Suisse romande* 37 (1984), 72–78.

Table 3.2 The texts for Bellini's "Ah! Del Tebro" (1831) and Wagner's insertion aria (1839).

Wagner	Bellini (Italian)	Bellini (English)
Norma il predisse, o Druidi. Ancor non fulse il giorno di vendicar lo scorno, che sulle Gallie stà.	O: Invan di Norma la mente investigati. C: E che far pensi?	I questioned Norma to no avail. What do you think we should do?
Ma già gli dei preparano terribile vendetta; come del ciel saette sugli empi scoppierà! Ratti dell'armi al sonito dè boschi uscite, o Forti, chè dio à più liete sorti v'apella e a libertà!	O: Al fato piegar la fronte, separarci, e nulla lasciar sospetto, del fallito intento. C: E finger sempre? O: Cruda legge! Il sento.	Bow to fate, separate, and arouse no suspicion of our failed intention. Must we always pretend? It is a cruel command. I feel it.
Sulle Gallie alfin risplenda al nemico il di d'orror, e sull'armi nostre scenda la vittoria e lo splendor! E voi tremate, o barbari, dell'aquil vostre il volo fia tronce e infranto al suolo, il giogo vil cadrà!	O: Ah! del Tebro al giogo indegno fremo io pure, all'armi anelo; ma nemico è sempre il cielo, ma consiglio è simular. C: Ah sì, fingiamo, se il finger giovi; ma il furor in sen si covi.	I too rage at being under the Roman yoke, and long for battle. But heaven is always against us, And pretence is advised. Yes, we shall pretend if we must; But let's cultivate anger in our breasts.
	O: Divoriam in cor lo sdegno, tal che Roma estinto il creda. Di verrà, sì, che desto ei rieda più tremendo, sì, a divampar. C: Guai per Roma allor che il segno dia dell'armi il sacro altar! Sì, ma fingiam, se il finger giovi, ma il furore in sen si covi. O: **Simuliano**, sì, ma il consiglio è il simular. O / C: Ma fingiamo, è consiglio il simular, Sì, fingiamo.	Let us swallow the anger in our hearts so that Rome thinks it has died. But the day will come when it will waken and return blazing more fiercely. Heaven help Rome when the altar gives the signal for battle! But yes, we shall pretend if we must, Yet anger will be hidden in our breasts. **We shall pretend**, yes, pretence is advised. But we shall pretend, pretence is advised, yes, we shall pretend.

O = Oroveso
C = Chorus of Druids

In many respects Wagner's and Bellini's aria themes share the hallmarks of early nineteenth-century Italianate shaping: periodic phrasing,[118] patterned rhythmic profile, and a balanced pitch contour comprised mostly of stepwise motion and gap-filling. Correspondingly, Wagner's 1837 essay emphasizes broad melodic outline over constituent details:

[T]he instantaneous, clear apprehension of a whole passion on stage is made far easier when, with all its allied feelings and emotions, that passion is brought by one firm stroke into *one* clear, comprehensible melody, than when it is obscured by a hundred tiny commentaries, with this and that harmonic nuance . . . until at last it is doctored out of sight.[119]

In the context of a discourse hostile to borrowing, Wagner's statement can be read as profoundly anxious in that it postulates an *a priori* stroke of natural melodic genius. Criticisms of overly nuanced harmonic expression were commonplace, and it was probably with this in mind that Wagner composed his melody in 1839. Examples 3.5a and 3.5b compare the principal themes.

Wagner's use of angular rising minor sevenths and a rising perfect fourth and fifth distinguishes his melodic intervals from Bellini's sixths and thirds, establishing difference, yet he studiously adopts his model's gap-filling technique, alternating leap with contrary step in almost academic fashion. There are notable correspondences between the themes: the anacrusis, maintaining d^1 as the peak pitch, an almost identical, fifth-based harmonic vocabulary, use of formulaic accompanimental patterns (though these are different enough to avoid thoughts of plagiarism and monotony, such as Fétis had leveled at Verdi's accompaniments),[120] maintenance of a pervasive dotted rhythm, and

---

[118] It was the subtle periodicity in *Norma* that Wagner praised above all in a review of a performance in Königsberg on March 8, 1837. "It is this very merit – there is *style* in this music – that makes it so important in our age of confusion and formlessness. The musical periods are built along assured and measured lines, agitation is followed by calm; and even if the manner of all Italian opera composers suited Bellini, too, so that each aria and each duet has its regular periodic structure, we must recognize all the more clearly that a manner that had become stuck in a rut thanks to Rossini was ennobled in this work." The German text is printed in Friedrich Lippmann, "Ein neuentdecktes Autograph Richard Wagners: Rezension der Königsberger 'Norma'-Aufführung von 1837," in *Musica scientiae collectanea: Festschrift Karl Gustav Fellerer zum siebzigsten Geburtstag*, ed. H. Hüschen (Cologne, 1973), 373–79. It is unknown whether the review was actually ever published in 1837.

[119] SSD 12: 20. Cf. PW 8: 68–69.

[120] "If the fashionable maestro [Verdi] lacks originality and invention in melody, his imagination is no richer in the orchestration and rhythm of his accompaniments. There is only one manner, one formula for each thing, and from his first score to the latest, he shows himself everywhere the same, with a desperate obstinacy. For his arias and duets, he seized a form of accompaniment for the themes put in use by Bellini and Donizetti." Fétis, "Verdi," *Revue et gazette musicale de Paris* 17 (1850), 323. Cited in Giger, *Verdi and the French Aesthetic*, 74.

Example 3.5a The principal theme from Oroveso's aria "Ah del Tebro" in Bellini's *Norma* (1831).

Example 3.5b The principal theme from Wagner's insertion aria for Oroveso in "Norma il predisse, o Druidi" (1839).

Table 3.3 Structural comparison of the aria themes (Arabic figures indicate number of measures; Roman numerals indicate harmony)

Wagner	4 / 4	4 / 4	4 / 8
	I / I→V	III / IV	V / V→I
Bellini	4		4
	I		vi. . .→I

the use of a chromatic neighbor (Bellini = C – C♯ – D; Wagner = C – B♮ – B♭) to characterize vocal lightness. Such correspondences speak to a compositional pre-history where Wagner *worked* with the details of Bellini's aria in the manner suggested by theorists such as Lobe where autodidactic composers were encouraged to dissect and reconstruct models to study melodic composition. Did he alter Bellini's parameters of musical expression in the same way as Examples 2.5–2.6? We may never know, but the residual thematic affinities between the two arias indicate a similarly close engagement.

Wagner begins to emerge as a distinct melodist through a larger ambitus (a major ninth rather than Bellini's major sixth)[121] and an expanded thematic structure, as Table 3.3 shows. He repeats both the antecedent (mm. 5–8) and consequent phrases (mm. 29–32), before proceeding to an eight-measure dominant prolongation. The net effect is to more than double the length of the thematic material used by Bellini, arguably overbalancing the *scena* into which the aria was intended to fit. To regard this as insensitive would be to confuse analytical perspectives, however. The advantage of thinking of Wagner's aria as compositional training, as a fragment from an absent whole, is that it obviates the need to find compelling logic and unity in it or its relation to the opera. (One might simply observe, of course, that Wagner had to persuade Lablache to accept his aria in the first place, and that appeals to Lablache's ego motivated its larger scale, not to mention that Wagner was salivating for a *coup de théâtre* in Paris.)

But the flipside of the didactic element in Wagner's imitation is its confrontationalism. The very act of seeking to perform a melodic imitation within its original context is itself antagonistic to the extent that it reveals

---

[121] Henry Chorley reports that in 1830 Lablache's range was "about two octaves – from E to E." Wagner's aria employs this almost entirely, spanning F to e', whereas Bellini's aria has a compass of just c to d'. See Chorley, *Thirty Years' Musical Recollections* [1862], ed. Ernest Newman (New York: Vienna House, 1972), 12.

Bellini can be successfully imitated, i.e. it becomes a form of reification and prosthesis. By humanizing a formerly divine melodist, Wagner effectively reduces the composer to "prosthetic Bellini," which arguably entails a loss of status in the formerly untouchable melodies of the precursor. This reading supports the view stated earlier that the ersatz Italian aria is not what it seems, it is not "mere" imitation.

With overtones of the *Percunos* contrafactum, Wagner's metaphor for degrading one's capacity to express through melody was the absolute musician who is forced to discard "all [original] emotional expression" inherent in the natural form of that emotion by "counterfeiting some outward object" for the vehicle of that expression. His key statement reads: "Music thus resembled the good God of our legends, who came down from Heaven to earth, but, to make himself visible there, must assume the shape and outward appearance of a common, everyday man."[122] To clarify Wagner's slightly awkward biblical conceit: (infinite) God is to (finite) Jesus what true emotional expression is to a predefined "object" of musical form (such as Bellini's aria). In appropriating Bellini's melodic idiom, i.e. humanizing the divine, Wagner engages in a particular kind of musical metonymy in which the basic external aspect of a thing is substituted for the thing itself: such as Bellini's chromatic neighbor figures, harmonic rhythm and vocabulary, gap-filling patterns, and periodicity. Structurally, Wagner's act of imitation is ominously close to his subsequent critique of inadequate musical expression. Both take an idealized, fluid original and house it in a restrictive, received, artificial shell. As unintentional autobiography, the deep homology between overt imitation and meaningless expression is telling for Wagner's understanding of melody: the logical trap in which he is snared is that deriving material of any kind only results in a cynical reduction to nothingness.

Beyond the thematic correspondences, his decision to incorporate Bellini's most unmelodic material from the original as his only direct borrowing seems counterintuitive, aesthetically. For a quintessential melodist who became synonymous with nineteenth-century melody in the strong sense of the term, Wagner's interest in four unison chromatic half notes nevertheless seems odd at first. Yet it makes perfect sense in the post-1837 legal context where melody was an abstraction of property. This is reproduced in Example 3.6.

---

[122] SSD 4: 139–40. Cf. PW 2: 278.

Example 3.6 Bellini's chromatic descending minor third on Oroveso's text "Simuliamo."

This passage is striking as the first strict unison passage in Bellini's aria, played *tutti* (except for the flutes) in its steady descent to C.[123] Recall that Marx (and Lobe) both argued that "any combination of two or more sounds, of equal or unequal durations, may serve as a motif" for melodic development.[124] Before seeking to answer the question of why Wagner was attracted to this chromatic lead weight on the verb "to pretend or simulate," let us first explore how and to what extent it becomes an operative melodic cell in Wagner's aria.

As Example 3.7 shows, the first allusion occurs in the introduction (mm. 1–15), where Wagner repeats the opening phrase on C up a tone (on D), finally rising to E♭ before outlining Bellini's full chromatic descending minor third. The effect is an expansion and reinterpretation of these anti-melodic pitches. Arguably, Bellini's unison texture is acknowledged and deliberately modified by Wagner in mm. 10–12, where he first adopts unison octaves (m. 10), but then fully harmonizes the movement from D♭ to C with a French sixth to dominant progression (mm. 11–12).

Whereas Bellini's chromatic octaves interrupt the otherwise diatonic flow of his melody, Wagner introduces a full chromatic scale gradually (see

---

[123] It is underscored by the *subito pianissimo* appearance of the trombones, the usage of which David Kimbell finds "bizarrely reckless" in Bellini's operas, underscoring the singularity of this passage. See Kimbell, *Italian Opera* (Cambridge University Press, 1991), 523.

[124] "Jede Notenzeile bietet deren, jede Verbindung von zwei oder mehr beliebigen Tönen in beliebiger Geltung kann als Motiv dienen." Marx, *Die Lehre von der musikalischen Komposition, praktisch theoretisch*, 3rd edn. (Leipzig: Breitkopf & Härtel, 1868), 33.

Example 3.7 Wagner's first use of Bellini's chromatic figure, mm. 9–12.

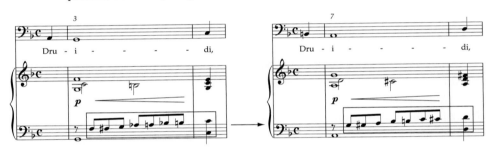

Example 3.8 Wagner's two initial chromatically rising 5ths in "Norma il predisse, o Druidi" (1839), mm. 3, 7.

Example 3.8). Viewing Wagner's heightened use of chromatic motion as an outgrowth, expansion, or intensification of Bellini's smaller motif is supported by the fact that Wagner moves progressively away from the limiting dimensions of his four-note model: the full scales first emerges as an extension of a chromatically rising fifth (mm. 11–12); as Example 3.9 shows, it reappears as an accompaniment to the thematic consequent (Example 3.9a); and finally, as the bass soloist's accompanimental line (Example 3.9b). This progressive extension and melodicizing of the chromatic unit would seem reminiscent of Lobe's advice that "there can really be no bad melody that cannot be improved by this or that alteration, or be transformed into a better melody through a simultaneous combination."[125]

By emancipating the unmelodic material that Bellini had used to contrast with his otherwise mellifluous tunes, Wagner reinterprets Bellini's half steps, raising the figure to new independence in a moment of chromatic hyperbole. By taking an expressly un-mellifluous figure and using it to forge

---

[125] "es [könne] eigentlich gar keine schlechte Melodie geben . . ., die nicht durch diese oder jene Umbildung, oder durch mehrere zugleich in eine bessere zu verwandeln sey." Lobe, *Compositions-Lehre*, 47–48,

Example 3.9a Wagner's full chromatic scale as instrumental accompaniment to Oroveso's vocal line, "Norma il predisse, o Druidi" (1839), mm. 29–32.

Example 3.9b Wagner's chromatic scale as vocal accompaniment itself, "Norma il predisse, o Druidi" (1839), mm. 50–52.

melodic material, Wagner recasts the concept of operatic melody negatively, as that which is not noticeably borrowed (a procedure that chimes guiltily with his 1880 dismissal of Sgambati's concerto as the fear of "perhaps having stolen [melodies] from someone else"). In antagonistic terms, Wagner's action suggests Bellini's relative weakness for not utilizing the potential of the figure, but he purchases this only at the cost of an individuating withdrawal from his melodic self in the first place, a process Wagner began simply by deciding to write an aria in Bellini's style.

But ironically, Wagner makes as much "original sense" (to borrow Kant's term) out of the chromaticism as possible. Consider two further

Example 3.10 Wagner harmonizes (mm. 44–45) his chromatic motif from its initial unison (mm. 37–39).

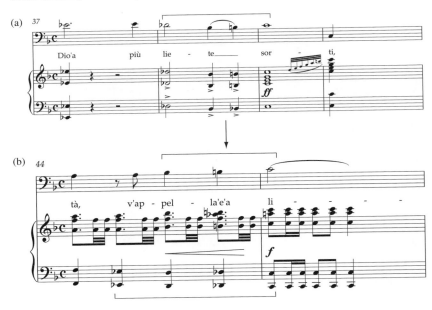

instances in which he engages with Bellini's unharmonized unison octaves. The first – Example 3.10a – is a striking unison between trumpet, horn, and soloist (mm. 38–39), which plays with a variant of Bellini's chromatic figure and leads – like Bellini – to a dominant prolongation. Later in the aria (m. 44), Wagner reinterprets the absent harmony of Bellini's unison by harmonizing the chromatic progression with a German sixth (Example 3.10b), thereby perhaps rendering it more outwardly "German" in its enriched harmonic palette. As if to underscore a corrective need, the need for harmony, the aria returns to this progression, but – as Example 3.11 shows – seems to become stuck on the unison octaves between B♮ and C (prepared through prior phrasal repetitions on the chromatic neighbors A♮ and B♭), thereby heightening the precadential tension through the "mistakenly" bare octaves, before the requisite dominant prolongation is resolved.

Wagner's second engagement with Bellini's octaves, given as Example 3.12, concerns the repeated peak pitch (E♭). This is the highest point in the original aria (sung by the chorus of druid soldiers) as well as the immediate preparation for the chromatic descent examined above. Wagner almost quotes Bellini's dotted rhythm verbatim when he repeats the note for the second

Example 3.11 Wagner's chromatic octaves, which become "stuck," delaying the harmonic resolution, "Norma il predisse, o Druidi" (1839), mm. 77–85.

Example 3.12 Wagner's peak pitch (E♭–E♮) contest with Bellini, "Norma il predisse, o Druidi" (1839), mm. 108–10.

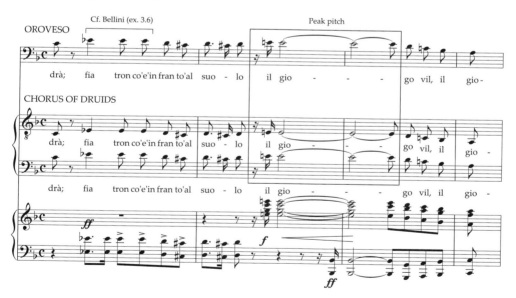

Example 3.13 Wagner's over-rhetorical close.
(a) Bellini's final measures.

(b) Wagner's final measures.

time (m. 108), but he exceeds it with a revisionist prerogative, rising to a sustained E♮ so as to trump his model as though in corrective "hyperbole" of its perceived weaknesses.

The close of Wagner's aria operates in much the same fashion. As Example 3.13 shows, Wagner reproduces Bellini's ending exactly in pitch, rhythm, and orchestration (the only difference being the timpani register and the presence of trombones and serpent in the orchestra), but again exceeds it by adding two further chords, alluding to a more Beethovenian close.

And one final instance of Wagner's part agonistic, part didactic interaction with Bellini's original concerns the accompaniment. For eighty-four measures Wagner avoids triplets / sextuplets. It is a loud absence given that pizzicato triplets are the main signifier of Bellini's accompaniment, permeating all but six measures of the original aria. After Oroveso's emphatic chromatic octaves (Example 3.11), Wagner finally does include sextuplets in the lower strings creating a climactic effect in which "Bellini" returns as though his voice had somehow been lost, and yet the material is singularly different: arco, accented, forte not piano, performed by the violas and cellos rather than the violins. It is the fitting climax to Wagner's strategy of self-effacing difference through simulation.

Let us return briefly to the puzzling chromaticism of "simuliamo." Holtmeier's study of *Das Liebesverbot* sheds further light on Wagner's chromatic tendencies in the 1830s. Drawing on Ernst Kurth's concept of melodic chromaticism,[126] he argues that "the harmonic basis of Italian opera

---

[126] Ernst Kurth, *Romantische Harmonik und ihre Krise in Wagners Tristan* (Berlin: Hesse, 1920), 44. Only excerpts are available in translation. See Kurth, "Romantic Harmony and its

is fundamentally of 'melodic chromaticism,' which German Romantic opera and 'German' instrumental music appropriated as 'harmonic chromaticism.'"[127] However generalized, Holtmeier's insight is the existence of a structural link between Italian and German melodic traditions. This rests on a distinction, drawn from Kurth's analysis of *Tristan*, between melodic (kinetic) and harmonic (potential) motion as the arbiter of chromatic forms: (i) where a melodic factor, i.e. the constant stepwise ascent or descent "is already the bearer of the harmonic development ... melodic energy is the primary feature, the impelling content that causes the manner and order of the harmonic progressions";[128] and (ii) where harmonic shading by chromatic voice-leading produces "effects of luminescence ... [which] are not at all actually *kinetic* motion in the larger melodic current but rather their mere *urge* toward motion."[129] In his Bellini aria, Wagner clearly retained melodic chromaticism in Kurth's first sense (witness the phrasal repetitions up a semitone alongside the explicit, snaking chromatic scales); but this stepwise ("Italianate") chromatic motion arguably also becomes a source, as it were, in Kurth's second sense, for chromatic voice-leading in Wagner's later works. Either way, some listeners continued to respond skeptically to Wagner's chromatic innovations; in the case of *Tristan*, they would be dubbed "the spasmodic strife to be original in music," a charge whose veracity would seem rooted most evidently in Wagner's magnification of "simuliamo" in his Bellini pastiche from 1839.[130]

Chromatic continuations

By the early 1850s, one of the paradigmatic melodies associated with Wagner's Dresden years was Wolfram's cavatina "O du mein holder Abendstern" from *Tannhäuser* (given as Example 3.14) popularized in part through Liszt's finger-friendly piano transcription from 1849.[131] The harmonic motion between II–$^\flat$III–V^7–VI in which the arrival on $^\flat$III pivots between the implied chromatic motion in the bass between A–B$\flat$, as well as preparing the actual chromatic motion between D and E$\flat$ – all in contrary motion to Wolfram's stepwise chromatic descent – would seem to strike a

crises in Wagner's *Tristan*," in *Ernst Kurth: Selected Writings*, ed. and trans. Lee A. Rothfarb (Cambridge University Press, 1991), 97–150.

[127] "Die Harmonik der italienischen Oper ist grundsätzlich von 'melodischer Chromatik,' die der deutschen romantischen Oper, der 'deutschen' Instrumentalmusik von 'harmonischer Chromatik' bestimmt." Holtmeier, "Von *den Feen* zum *Liebesverbot*," 54.

[128] Kurth, "Romantic Harmony and its Crises in Wagner's *Tristan*," 136.   [129] *Ibid.*, 106.

[130] Anon, "Symphony Concerts," *Dwight's Journal of Music* 34 (January 9, 1875), 366–67, here 367.

[131] As Liszt notes in a letter to Wagner: "the scene of the 'Abendstern' should be within easy reach of second-class pianists." Liszt to Wagner, February 26, 1849, in *Correspondence*, 19.

Example 3.14 The principal theme from Wolfram's cavatina "O du mein holder Abendstern," from *Tannhäuser*, act 3, scene 2, which was received as Wagner's quintessential chromatic melodic of the 1850s.

balance between Kurth's two senses of melodic chromaticism, without quite falling under the terms of either.

Taking a step back, we might wonder to what extent a causal relation exists between Bellinian Italian melody and the chromatic intensification between the ersatz aria (1839) and Wolfram's cavatina (1845). While the tendency toward increasing chromatic *harmony* – documented most publicly in Brendel's 1859 competition in the *Neue Zeitschrift* for new approaches to harmonic analysis[132] – took impetus from a *Neudeutsch* aesthetic as well as increasingly theoretical investigations into chromatic chordal functions, melodic chromaticism itself remained relatively uncharted as a theoretical principle. This was not for lack of chromatic melodies. Other notable examples exist such as the principal theme of Liszt's "Dante" sonata (premiered in the same year Wagner worked up his Bellini aria), and the topic of chromatic

---

[132] The full proposal of Brendel's competition reads: "Erklärende Erläuterung und musikalisch-theoretische Begründung der durch die neuesten Kunstschöpferungen bewirkten Umgestaltung und Weiterbildung der Harmonik." Franz Brendel, "Zur Eröffnung des 50. Bandes der Zeitschrift," *NZfM* 50 (1859), 1. The most celebrated entrants to the competition were Carl Friedrich Weitzmann and Ferdinand Graf Laurencin. Between 1853 and 1854, Weitzmann published three studies: on the augmented triad, the seventh, and the diminished seventh chord, *Der übermässige Dreiklang* (Berlin, 1853), *Geschichte des Septimen-Akkordes* (Berlin, 1854), and *Der verminderte Septimen-Akkord* (Berlin, 1854). Formal studies of Weitzmann's work have appeared in several articles within the last decade, but there remains no single extended study. See Robert Wason, "Progressive Harmonic Theory in the Mid-Nineteenth Century," *Journal of Musicological Research* 8 (1988), 55–90; Richard Cohn, "Weitzmann's Regions, My Cycles, and Douthett's Dancing Cubes," *Music Theory Spectrum* 22 (2000), 99–104; R. L. Todd, "Franz Liszt, Carl Friedrich Weitzmann, and the Augmented Triad," in *The Second Practice of Nineteenth-Century Tonality*, ed. W. Kinderman and H. M. Krebs (Lincoln: University of Nebraska Press, 1996), 153–77. The beginnings of a biographical study appeared a century ago (i) in *Allgemeine deutsche Biographie* 41 (Leipzig: Duncker & Humblot 1896), 635; and (ii) in Paul Bekker's "Zum Gedächtnis K. Fr. Weitzmann," *AmZ* 35 (1908), 577.

(a) recto

(b) verso

3.1 Berlioz's two-page entry in the Album of Marie von Sayn-Wittgenstein, entitled *Valse chanté par le vent dans les cheminées d'un de mes châteaux en Espagne* (1855). Reproduced by permission of the *Goethe- und Schiller-Archiv*, Weimar (GSA 60/Z 170). Photo: Klassik Stiftung Weimar.

melody even formed the basis of self-deprecating humor, as in Berlioz's ironic composition for Liszt's *de facto* stepdaughter, Marie von Sayn-Wittgenstein, in 1855: "Waltz sung by the wind in the chimneys of one of my castles in Spain" (Figures 3.1a–b), on the manuscript of which Berlioz jokes that "Liszt is requested to provide the bass line!!"[133]

To be sure, definitions of melody were expanding in this direction. The critic J. B. Allfeld, in a review of *Tristan und Isolde*, recalled the complaints of an "enharmonic cry of pain" from the Munich audience in 1855 when they first heard Wolfram's opening half steps; nowadays, Allfeld shrugs in 1865, it is accepted as a *bona fide* melody.[134] By 1899 Wolfram's cavatina had even become a paradigm of melodic chromaticism, and at least one theorist described it as a model of the limits of acceptable chromatic construction, where any "greater extension of a chromatic sequence of tones, even with correct voice-leading . . . will not make for effective melody either in a calm or still less in a lively tempo."[135] It is tempting to view the opening gambit of Wolfram's main theme in light of Wagner's curiously original borrowing from Bellini. It became quintessential Wagner, though it is rooted in Bellini in more than one sense. The simultaneously didactic engagement with Bellini as a model, and competitive recasting of his aria in aggrandized terms, outlined above, point to a deeper antagonism within the surface imitation that can be interpreted as more than admiration for the Italian.

* * *

Wagner's earnest endeavors in the melodic chromaticism of "Norma il predisse" would seem to offer a singular instance of the merger of Italian influence with a systematic approach to melodic pedagogy by imitation. As unequivocal *Stilübung*, it initiates a discursive network of transnational, musical signifiers through borrowings that were stylistically overt, though concealed in their details. Did this concealment reflect a legal awareness? We may never know. But in this vein, the *Berliner Musik-Zeitung Echo* asked in 1855 what would happen if a celebrated composer was inspired by Bach's *Matthäus Passion*, and wanted to create "similar effects." To stamp his own invention on the music and avoid actually copying Bach, the composer might give the Evangelist part

---

[133] The title is given as "Valse chantée par le vent dans les cheminées d'un de mes châteaux en Espagne" and Berlioz's quip reads: "Liszt est prié d'écrire la basse!!" This whimsical two-page composition is written into the Album of Marie von Sayn-Wittgenstein, see GSA 60 / Z 170, Weimar.

[134] J. B. Allfeld, *Tristan und Isolde von Richard Wagner. Kritisch beleuchtet mit einleitenden Bemerkungen über Melodie und Musik* (Munich: C. Fritsch, 1865), 10–11.

[135] "Grössere Ausdehnung von chromatischer Tonfolge wird aber selbst bei korrekter Stimmführung . . . weder im ruhigen und noch weniger im belebten Zeitmasse in der Melodie gute Wirkung machen." Jadassohn, *Das Wesen der Melodie in der Tonkunst*, 16–17.

"to a *female* voice!" Equally, an opera composer inspired by the storm from Beethoven's Pastoral Symphony might situate his imitation in the overture, to mark a point of difference. "These would be examples," the article concludes:

of appropriating foreign material without any real reason, in spite of all individual melodies and thoughts in it being perhaps [the composer's] own invention. Even so, these would more rightly and by greater standards deserve to be held up as *plagiarism* than all of the often unavoidable 'reminiscences,' provided that the latter emerge from the context, and the character of the intended sentiment is reproduced completely and unalloyed.[136]

Under the terms of this apologia for melodic reminiscence, Wagner's aria remains overt plagiarism, not of phrasal details, but of "foreign material" regarded abstractly as an overall source of inspiration. The discrepancy with Gaillard's 1844 description of melodic form as a composer's "most noble richness" – precisely its copyrightable phrasal details – underlines the inconsistency and contingencies pervading the contemporary journalistic debate.

In some ways, a legal mentality is beside the point. A few months after composing "Norma il predisse," Wagner's comments "On the essence of German greatness" (1840) link the weakness of invention-by-imitation to weak nationalism among German composers. Like earlier German critiques of Mozart, he ascribes universality to the German genius only when a composer retains their national identity having absorbed foreign elements:

the German genius would almost seem predestined to seek out among its neighbors what is not native to its motherland . . . and thus make something universal for the world. Naturally, however, this can only be achieved by he who is not satisfied to ape a foreign nationality deceitfully [*sich in eine fremde Nationalität hineinzulügen*], but keeps his German birthright pure and unspoilt, and that birthright is purity of feeling and chasteness of invention.[137]

This dialectic of national style, with its emphasis on the final integrity of invention, would seem an apt statement for Wagner wanting to "move on," after having failed to secure a performance of his aria for *Norma*.

But perhaps we are focusing too narrowly on a small piece of juvenilia. In 1980, Charles Rosen was skeptical about the merits of studying immature

---

[136] "Dies wären Beispiele von Aneignung eines fremden Stoffes, ohne recht eigentliche Begründung, welche, trotzdem vielleicht alle einzelnen Melodieen und Gedanken in denselben eigner Erfindung sind, dennoch gewiß mit mehr Recht und in großartigerem Maaßstabe verdienen, als Plagiate hingestellt zu werden, als alle oft unvermeidlichen 'Reminiscenzen,' so lange dieselben aus dem Zusammenhange hervorgehen, und den Charakter der beabsichtigten Stimmung vollständig und ungestört wiedergeben . . . geworden sind." In "Über Plagiate und Reminiscenzen," 59. Emphasis added.

[137] SSD 1: 160. Cf. PW 7: 95.

works. "In discussing Influence in music," he explained, "it would be wise to refuse in advance to consider the work of adolescent composers ... a very young composer has no style of his own, and he is forced to get one some-where else."[138] This would seem to apply to almost all Wagner's works before *Der fliegende Holländer* (1843); the peculiarity of Wagner's situation is that he was an extraordinarily late bloomer whose doubts about his capacity for original expression continued to plague him even into his Dresden period, and, as witnessed by the Sgambati episode, the painful memory of his early struggles evidently stayed with him into his final years.[139]

It seems that Wagner's stylistic imitations defined a protracted "adoles-cence" which led critics such as Lobe and Hanslick to argue that imitation was more germane to his basic compositional aesthetic than Wagner was willing to admit. After all, it contradicted the "complete opposition between genius and the spirit of imitation" disseminated by Kant. By yielding to the popular attraction of Italian song during the 1830s, Wagner monumental-ized the problem of German melodic composition for his epoch. Yet he increasingly rejected the notion that musical imitation – however small-scale – could be adequately expressive. After April 1842 when he returned to Saxony, his environment (bifurcated by Dresden's heritage of Weber's German, and Morlacchi's Italian opera companies) was suffused by atti-tudes that defined melody according to a pedagogical license to imitate model compositions, and a Beethovenian authority to work at melodic invention. The resulting clash – between the national impulse to character-ize German *Melodik* by poetic declamation, and an abiding desire to retain the sensuous expressivity widely attributed by German critics to Italian opera – forced the composer into new aesthetic territory. In acknowledging the want of expressivity of both his overt Bellinian imitation and his dry speech mimicry in *Lohengrin*, Wagner explains he was led to the sensuality of language as the central problem for expressive melody. Hence, a dialectic of nationalism and Italianate imitation in Wagner's *Melodik* ultimately gave some ground to the former as the compositional category of "melody" expanded exponentially in the direction of verbal language and philology. And we will explore the two different sides of this development in Chapters 4 and 5.

Rosen – alluding to Kantian "original sense" – argued paradoxically that "the most important form of influence is that which provokes the most

---

[138] Rosen, "Influence: Plagiarism and Inspiration," *19th-Century Music* 4 (1980), 88.

[139] Wagner was 26 when he composed "Norma il predisse"; he had already lived a year longer than had John Keats (1795–1821), and was fully ten years older than Mendelssohn when the latter composed his Octet in 1825.

original and most personal work."[140] As Wagner's experience with Bellini's aria from *Norma* shows, he was guided in 1839 both by a natural tendency toward chromatic forms of expression and by a desire to imitate. The result thus documents perhaps his most slavish and yet paradoxically his most self-consciously original composition.

[140] Rosen, "Influence: Plagiarism and Inspiration," 88.

Excursus: Bellini's *Sinnlichkeit* and Wagner's Italy

> Bellini wrote melodies lovelier than one's dreams.
>
> Richard Wagner (1872)[1]

In 1880, Bellini's close Neapolitan friend, Francesco Florimo, reports Wagner's profession of sustained infatuation for the Italian's music:

> They all think me an ogre with regard to Italian music and place me in opposition to Bellini. But no, no, a thousand times no. Bellini is one of my predilections: *his music is all heart, closely, intimately linked to the words.* The music I hate is that vague, indeterminate music which laughs at the libretto and at the situation![2]

Far from the quirk of a "rebellious phase"[3] of pro-Italian sentiments during the 1830s, then, the longevity of Wagner's attachment to Bellinian melody would seem assured, at least in part, because of his perception of a special bond between text and music. As is well known, however, by the mid-1840s his allegiance had shifted somewhat. During Wagner's tenure at Dresden, and a decade after Bellini's death, his new stance was quite different:

> The downfall . . . [of sacred polyphony] in Italy, and the simultaneous rise of opera melody among Italians, I can call nothing but a relapse into Paganism . . . Italian opera melody has contented itself with such a cheap periodic structure . . . that the educated musician of our times stands sorrowfully astonished before this threadbare, almost childish art form, whose narrow confines condemn even the most talented composer . . . to total formal–metrical stability.[4]

---

[1] CT (August 3, 1872).

[2] "Tutti mi credono un orco in riguardo alla musica italiana, e mi pongono in antitesi con Bellini. Ma no, no, mille volte no. Bellini e una delle mie predilezioni: la sua musica e tutta cuore, legata stretta intimamente alle parole . . . La musiche io abomino e quella vaga, sconclusionata, che si ride del libretto e della situazione." Francesco Florimo, *La Scuola musicale di Napoli* (Naples, 1881–82), 3: 198–99. Emphasis added.

[3] Thomas Grey's apt description of Wagner's pro-Italian years during the 1830s, in Millington, *The Wagner Compendium*, 67.

[4] SSD 7: 107. Cf. PW 3: 314–15.

This set the tone for what became a common perception of Wagner's cultural Italianophobia during the late nineteenth century. Elsewhere, Wagner appends complaints about Italian audiences who "seek nothing but sensuous distraction,"[5] and protests that Italian vocalism has transformed music into "an *art of sheer agreeableness*."[6] Such humorlessness reached its zenith when Wagner forcibly excised his earlier literary self, editing out a number of pro-Italian comments from his earlier essays for publication in 1871 as part of his collected writings;[7] equally, the three explicitly pro-Italian essays of the 1830s – "Die deutsche Oper" (1834), "Der dramatische Gesang" (1837), and "Bellini: ein Wort zu seiner Zeit" (1837) – were silently excluded, not considered part of his intellectual corpus. By the decade of German unification, such infractions of national identity had simply become incongruous with his public image.

When, shortly after Wagner's death, these early pro-Italian essays were reprinted in the *Bayreuther Blätter*, and news broke of his deep admiration for Bellinian melody, it sent a seismic shock through the critical orthodoxy of Wagnerism by undermining both his famed anti-Italianism and supposed lack of melody.[8] "We now, therefore, stand face to face with the fact, on Wagner's own showing, that the protoplasm of some portion of the charm of his music is to be found in the Italian style of its melody," balked *The Musical Times* in 1886. Following nearly half a century of diatribes against Wagnerian melody, this revelation initiated a renewed consideration of the opposite, his *melodiousness*:

[O]f all the many constituents which together go to make up the complex of a Wagner Opera, is it not principally due to the melodiousness – we will not say the set tunes, for these are few and far between – by which each is pervaded, that Wagner's music has gained so strong a hold upon the public ear?[9]

The implications of this historic reversal have arguably not been fully explored. The pro-Bellini essays were issued only with explanatory disclaimers by Hans von Wolzogen and Carl Friedrich Glasenapp.[10] And as late as 1971, we read Herbert Weinstock reflecting a certain strand of received

---

[5] SSD 5: 26. Cf. PW 3: 31.   [6] SSD 8: 255. Cf. PW 3: 116.

[7] For further comment on this, see Deathridge, *Wagner Beyond Good and Evil* (Berkeley and Los Angeles: University of California Press, 2008), 12ff.

[8] "Pasticio von Canto Spianato (1834)," *Bayreuther Blätter* 11 (1884), 337–42; "Bellini (1835)," *Bayreuther Blätter* 12 (1885), 363–64.

[9] "Wagner on Bellini," *The Musical Times and Singing Class Circular* 27 (1886), 67–68.

[10] "Admittedly, he still did not possess the saving sword of the new, dramatic style that he had first to weld from pieces of noble ancestors – a community of heroes; he still didn't know from plainly obvious examples what 'melody' actually and completely *should be*, which would achieve musical, i.e. ideal *expression* for the *German* spirit." ["Noch freilich besass er nicht das Rettungsschwert des neuen, dramatischen Styls, das er selbst erst aus Stücken edler

mid-nineteenth-century opinion, namely that: "Wagner attacked bitterly almost all Italian opera."[11] While Wagner undoubtedly posited Rossini's music negatively, as the archetype of absolute melody, and lamented a reliance on formulae in Bellini,[12] it is striking that, in his voluminous literary output, Wagner appears never to have criticized Bellini's melodic expression. Whether or not his scattered pejorative comments indicate he was in two minds on the matter, Bellini's melodies seem to have occupied a privileged – if discreet – seat in his pantheon of forebears, one that was awkwardly implicated in the normative politicized hierarchy of a German *Kunstreligion* defined in opposition to the "ear-tickling" of Italian opera.[13]

This knowledge has implications for how we understand the unicum of Wagner's "Norma il predisse, o Druidi." If he sought to simulate Bellini in 1839 as part of a didactic strategy for improving his "melodic" composition, what was the worth of that strategy? What did Bellini's identity signify to Wagner in this context? We can begin to answer these questions by returning to the occasion on which Wagner confessed to melodic inadequacy in *Lohengrin*. Wagner rarely admitted such weakness. It was alien to the immense energy of his character. His singular confession to Adolf Stahr in 1851 about the opera's "monotonous, unrhythmical melody" points to a problem that could ostensibly be remedied by "a substantial, sensory [*sinnliche*] relationship" between musical expression and language. If, in the Wagner biography, a familiar solution was alliterative verse, the vocabulary of his confession – invoking *Sinnlichkeit* – offers a glimpse of another aspect easily overlooked in the heady nationalism of the *Wagnerbild*: the German reception of Italianate identity.[14] If we dig through the sedimented

---

Ahnen – Heldenschaft sich schweissen musste; noch wusste er nicht vom sinnlich offenbar gewordenen Beispiele her, was die 'Melodie' wirklich und völlig *sei*, welche dem *deutschen* Geiste im Drama den musikalischen, d.h. idealen *Ausdruck* schaffen werde."] In Wolzogen, "Nachwort," *Bayreuther Blätter* 8 (1885), 365–67; and Carl Friedrich Glasenapp explained that "only beyond his de-Germanified floor did he find the power and strength in himself to renew [German theater] from the very bottom up. All the consequence of these approaches occurred because of the greater distance from our public art institutions." ["Nur abseits von seinem entdeutschten Boden fand er sich in sich selbst Kraft und Stärke, um es von Grund aus zu erneuen. Jede folgende dieser Annäherungen geschah aus grösserer Entfernung von unseren öffentlichen Kunst-Anstalten."] See Glasenapp, "1834–1884. Ein Nachwort," *Bayreuther Blätter* 7 (1884), 343–47.

[11] Herbert Weinstock, *Vincenzo Bellini: His Life and Operas* (New York: Alfred Knopf, 1971), 447.

[12] CT (March 22, 1880).

[13] Wagner's reference to clichéd German complaints about Italian opera, which he counterpoints – tongue-in-cheek – with the "eye-ache" ["Augenjucken"] of staring at dry German opera scores. SSD 12: 19. Cf. PW 8: 67.

[14] Following Friedrich Lippmann's pioneering "Wagner und Italien," *Analecta Musicologica* 11 (1972), 200–47, more recent scholarship that has begun to address this blind spot includes

discourse, an archeological perspective would suggest, in short, that Wagner's Bellinian ideal of a "clear, graspable melody" and sensualized melodic verse were connected.

Writing in the conservative Prussian capital, A. B. Marx equated the essence of Italian opera in 1826 with the principle of sensuality (*Sinnlichkeit*). Back in 1784, Herder had cited the capacity for sensory perception as part of a common humanity, yet drew upon *Sinnlichkeit* as a variable within human physiognomy to differentiate race according to climate.[15] Marx adheres to Herder's environmental determinism, where the "hotter sun, radiating . . . has given the Italian a lighter, more excitable, but also less fixed and imitative [*widerhaltige*] nature,"[16] to claim that "the Italian composer . . . gives nothing but the expression of his own individuality, of the sensual nature of his fellow countrymen in his works,"[17] a view in dialogue with his second principle for Italian opera – after *Sinnlichkeit* – namely "the most total *freedom* in performance."[18] For Marx, this willing absorption of the sensorium into the performer's ego dominates and subordinates "a higher principle" that German readers would have understood as truth of expression, but, in dialectical fashion, he later admits that "[i]n the highest expression of sensual passion, the Italian principle then [itself] becomes raised to another and higher sphere."[19] Both Wagner's 1837 essay on Bellini and his review of *Norma* from Königsberg earlier that year underline his attraction to the sensual power of Bellini's melody built on the security of uninhibiting periodic construction. If *Lohengrin*'s melodies failed for want of a "substantial, *sinnliche* relationship" between tone and word, it would seem that Marx's Italian principle – *Sinnlichkeit* – functioned here as something of a cementing agency by which the two spheres of text and music,

Kreuzer, *Verdi and the Germans*; "Wagner und Italie" special issue of *Wagner Spectrum* 1 (2010); and John Baker, *Wagner and Venice* (University of Rochester Press, 2008). See also my study, "Defending Wagner's Italy," in *The Legacy of Richard Wagner*, ed. Luca Sala (Turnhaut: Bropols, 2012), 363–98.

[15] "Die Sinnlichkeit unsres Geschlechts verändert sich mit Bildungen und Klimaten; überall aber ist ein menschlicher Gebrauch der Sinne das, was Humanität führet." Herder, *Werke in zehn Bänden*, "*Ideen zur Philosophie der Geschichte der Menschheit*," ed. Martin Bollacher (Frankfurt a. M.: Deutscher Klassiker Verlag, 1989), 6: 286.

[16] "Die heißere Sonne, die durchglühtere . . . hat dem Italiener eine leichtere, erregtere, aber auch weniger befestigte und widerhaltige Natur gegeben." Marx, *Die Kunst des Gesanges* [1826], 196. This comment was reprinted from *BAmZ* 20 (1825), 158.

[17] "Der italische Komponist . . . giebt in seinen Werken nichts, als den Ausdruck seiner eigenen Individualität, des sinnlichen Naturells seiner Landsleute." *Ibid.*, 196.

[18] "Eine zweite Bedingung vollkommenen Erfolges ist, aber die vollkommenste *Freiheit* der Leistung." *Ibid.*, 203.

[19] "In dem höchsten Ausdruck sinnlicher Leidenschaft wird dann das italische Princip einer andern und höhern Sphäre nahe gehoben." *Ibid.*, 204.

regarded independently, were to be sealed together. That is, a quality of sensation would collapse any lingering distinctions between the two, where – in media-historical terms – *Sinnlichkeit* is nothing but the carbon-based reception of stimuli.

This noun – *Sinnlichkeit* – is of course something of a floating signifier. In his discourse on the nature of music and sensuality, Søren Kierkegaard clarified the relationship Wagner felt he had failed at in *Lohengrin*, namely that "in language the sensual is, as medium, reduced to the level of mere instrument and constantly negated."[20] On the other hand, music itself, Kierkegaard argues, can express the "sensual erotic" for it is the art form predisposed to evoke desire within us "in all its immediacy."[21] In these terms Wagner's mid-century project becomes explicitly the sensualizing of language and it is no coincidence that Kierkegaard's exemplary instance of the sensual erotic is one of Mozart's *Italian* operas. Just as for him, *Don Giovanni* enacts narratives of seduction, so Marx visualized the principle of Italian vocal melody embodied in the physical presence of its female singers. Unlike "prudish" German dismissals of "ear-tickling," Marx regarded Italianate sensuality as palpably somatic and inherently audio-visual in performance, where its "sensual passion" was gendered female within patriarchal Prussian narratives of Italian identity:

For female singers who evidently devote themselves to performance, especially on the stage, it must be said that *youth and external beauty are almost indispensable*, if the highest peak of Italian artistic achievement and the song as the most individual subjective expression of a *fresh, sensory beauty* and of rich nature is to be established – wherewith the public's general preference for younger and more beautiful female singers over musically able ones appears completely justified in the context of the Italian essence.[22]

By coupling the sexual imagination of a listener with the principle of Italian opera, Marx sublimates the spectacle of feminine erotic appeal within German notions of Italian singing. This is none other than the sexual gaze of psychoanalytic theory – sexual because the spectator imagines possessing

---

[20] Søren Kierkegaard, *Either / Or*, trans. Alastair Hannay (London: Penguin Classics, 1992), 78.

[21] *Ibid.*, 75.

[22] "Ja, für Sängerinnen, die sich öffentlichen Leistungen, zumal auf der Bühne widmen, muß ausgesprochen werden, daß Jugend und äußerliche Schönheit fast unerläßlich sind, wenn der höchste Gipfel italischer Kunstleistung erreicht und der Gesang als eigenste subjective Aeußerung eines frischen, sinnlich-schönen und reichen Naturells aufgenommen werden soll: womit denn die allgemeine Vorliebe des Publikums für jüngere und schönere Sängerinnen vor musikalisch-fähigern, im Gebiete des italischen Wesens vollkommen gerechtfertigt erscheint." Marx, *Die Kunst des Gesanges*, 203. Emphasis added.

the object of his gaze, only this is not the beauty of a young female body as such, but an embodiment of the sensual principle enacted within the music.[23]

As Marx's formulation suggests, the spectator needs to be in direct scopophilic contact with the female body for the "essence" of Italian music to be experienced, connoting a role of looking that Laura Mulvey defines starkly as "pleasure in using another person as an object of sexual stimulation." She continues:

[T]he determining male gaze projects its fantasy onto the female figure, which is styled accordingly . . . [and] coded for strong visual and erotic impact so that they can be said to connote *to-be-looked-at-ness*.[24]

In this context, it is suggestive that Wagner repeatedly confessed he was singularly drawn to Bellini's music by a "wonderful woman,"[25] Wilhelmine Schröder-Devrient, about whom he later admitted to Cosima: "she was no longer very reputable when I started to associate with her, but for a person possessing such tremendous talent, there was only one compensation, and that was her sexual allure [*Sinnlichkeit*]."[26] And of course, music itself – like the sensual "essence" of Italian opera – is emphatically gendered female for Wagner. In light of this sensual–sexual frame of reference, his complaint that "we [Germans] are too intellectual and much too learned to create warm human figures" appears in a slightly different light, reinforcing almost with sexual envy his statements about the "sensuously warm" beauty that German singers lacked. Accordingly, in a letter to Theodor Uhlig from 1852 Wagner aligns himself unequivocally with Italy, as a "hot-blooded son of the south."[27]

Reading these statements archeologically in this way is not arbitrary. The Viennese physician Heinrich Kaan argued as early as 1844 that "the sexual instinct governs all physical and mental life."[28] His Latin treatise *Psychopathia sexualis* observed further that the sexual instinct overflows its natural end, and does so naturally. The displacement of sexual instinct into Italianate "sensuality" thus potentially becomes a fact of reception.[29]

---

[23] This principle entered the psychoanalytic discourse after Sigmund Freud's "Three Essays on the Theory of Sexuality" (1905), see *Standard Edition of the Complete Psychological Works of Sigmund Freud*, ed. James Strachey (London: Hogarth Press, 1959), 7: 125–244, esp. 149–59.

[24] Laura Mulvey, *Visual and Other Pleasures* (Basingstoke: Palgrave Macmillan, 2009), 18–19.

[25] SSD 9: 219. Cf PW 5: 218.   [26] CT (December 9, 1869).

[27] Wagner to Theodor Uhlig, July 22, 1852, Lugano, in SB 4: 419.

[28] Cited in Michel Foucault, *Abnormal: Lectures at the Collège de France 1974–1975*, trans. Graham Burchel, ed. Valerio Marchetti and Antonella Salomoni (New York: Picador, 2003), 282–83.

[29] In using the term "fact," I allude to epistemological distinctions made by Mary Poovey between interpretation and description of knowledge in the use of statistics, where numerical forms of representation gain authority by their duplication (as in double book-keeping) but remain

In a lecture from 1975, Michel Foucault identified Kaan's work as the point when sexuality first emerged in the psychiatric field because it established a direct link between the imagination and sexual instinct, where the former functions as the site that makes sexual aberration possible.[30] The "fresh sensory beauty" that Marx attributes to young female singers of Italian opera can be read as a displacement of desire; that is, as part of what Foucault terms "rituals of confession" that enacts the "transformation of sex into discourse."[31]

This slippage, though newly framed, is not entirely new to the Wagner literature. Thomas Mann regarded Nietzsche's question – "who dares to speak the word, the *real* word to describe the *ardeurs* of the *Tristan* music?" – as "old-maidish" in 1933; his blunt answer establishes a correspondence with the critical vocabulary assigned to Italianicity a century earlier: "*Sinnlichkeit*, unbounded, spiritualized *Sinnlichkeit*, raised to a mystical order of magnitude and portrayed with the utmost naturalism, *Sinnlichkeit* that will not be appeased by *any* gratification."[32] Thus, while not constituting tangible or even conscious knowledge, the flipside of Marx's critique of "the Italian principle" and Wagner's effusive embrace of the same during the 1830s is a confession about projected desire. It was a displacement of sexual instinct (as Nietzsche and Mann recognized) that one could argue infiltrated Wagner's imagination and, at an interpretive push, finally migrated to depictions of eros in his musical composition. Reading Italian opera as the fount of Wagner's musico–erotic sensual imagination complements the notion, recently advanced by Laurence Dreyfus, that Wagner's depiction of desire and sexual fantasy was quite deliberate: "in composing music representing 'sensuality' . . . [i]t seems Wagner knew exactly what he was doing."[33] In light of the melodic chromaticism we saw in Wagner's Bellini aria, it is surely no coincidence that the desire motif of *Tristan* – G♯–A♮–A♯–B♮– is also a

contingent and have not "always seemed free of an interpretive dimension"; and to Dahlhaus' distinction between historical facts and data. Whereas data (*datum*) are given, facts (*factum*) are made, hence Dahlhaus' warning is that the word "fact" does not refer to something tangible but: "is nothing more than an hypothesis." See Mary Poovey, *A History of the Modern Fact* (University of Chicago Press, 1998), xiiff; and Carl Dahlhaus, *Foundations of Music History*, trans. J. B. Robinson (Cambridge University Press, 1983), 35.

[30] Foucault, *Abnormal*, 278–87.

[31] *Ibid.*, 167; and Foucault, *The History of Sexuality: An Introduction*, trans. Robert Hurley (New York: Vintage Books, 1990), 28ff., esp. 58–63.

[32] Mann, "The Sorrows and Grandeur of Richard Wagner," 130. Here I substitute Mann's "Sinnlichkeit" for Blunden's "sensuality."

[33] Laurence Dreyfus, *Wagner and the Erotic Impulse* (Cambridge, MA: Harvard University Press, 2010), xi.

linear chromatic minor third, inverting that of 1839; now no longer treated as a melodic cell, it appears as the quintessential mimetic depiction of melodic yearning, or as Berlioz would have it: "a kind of chromatic moan" atop its unresolved harmonies.[34] Irrespective of the difficult brevity of this argument, the salient point is that, for the mature Wagner, Bellini's vocal-melodic sensations transgressed the semantic divide: "all heart, closely, intimately linked to the words." That is, within this discursive hypertrope linking nubile bodies, German constructs of Italian opera and climate, and sexual desire, text–melody relations figure as a wholly sensory phenomenon. (It may be worth recalling here that it was to his *librettist*, Carlo Pepoli, that Bellini related the physical effect of vocal–verbal sound, imploring: "Grave on your mind in adamantine letters: the [opera] must make people weep, shudder and die through the singing."[35]) In short, it would seem to be the sensory quality Wagner ascribed to Italian melody that permanently welded together vocal text, melody, and displaced sexual–sensuality in his imagination.

To be sure, it was *only* in the imagination. Wagner did not physically set foot in Italy until August 1853. His trip that summer to the cities of Turin, Genoa, and La Spezia would assume official status as "*my* Italian journey" (a sarcastic reference to Goethe),[36] and, prior to setting off, the composer was bubbling with expectation: "a great deal, I expect a great deal from Italy,"[37] he remarked, later reflecting in *Mein Leben* over the "indescribable visions of what was awaiting me and the manner in which my hopes would be fulfilled."[38] So what horizon of expectation informed that ardour?

It seems Wagner read travel literature on Italy with a certain envy during his 20s. As a young man, he could not afford an Italian *Kavalierreise* in the manner of Goethe, Byron, or Mendelssohn; during the 1830s he was neither inclined to elope, as Liszt, nor did he receive the *Prix de Rome*, as Berlioz. Thus, he never initiated himself in this cultural rite of passage, relying instead on the travel writings of Goethe and Germaine de Staël, among others. Taking de Staël as an example, her novella *Corinne ou d'Italie* (1807) concerns the experiences of Oswald Lord Nelville, a Scottish peer, as he witnesses Corinne – a celebrated poet, "the image of our beautiful Italy . . . an admirable product of our climate and of our arts" – return triumphantly to Rome, meets her and is enchanted by her poetry and physical beauty, takes her for a mistress and explores the history and art of Italy with her, but finally abandons her for another, less independent

---

[34] "une sorte de gémissement chromatique." Hector Berlioz, *A travers chants*, ed. Léon Guichard (Paris: Gründ, 1971), 327.

[35] Cited in Weinstock, *Vincenzo Bellini*, 170.

[36] Richard Wagner to Franz Liszt, September 12, 1853, Zurich, in SB 5: 424.

[37] Wagner to Otto Wesendonck, July 13, 1853, Zurich, in SB 5: 356.   [38] ML 498.

woman.[39] The nubile poetess is an allegory for Italy, and throughout the narrative female beauty is equated with Italy's superiority within the aesthetic sphere in general. De Staël's emphasis is backed up in this regard by numerous other texts concerning Italy. Stendhal's *Rome, Naples et Florence* (1826) constructs Italy as an earthly, carnal paradise, deploying the male gaze through voyeuristic fantasies of Italian women;[40] Goethe's *Roman Elegies* and *Venetian Epigrams* evoke similar situations, all of which arguably fed Wagner's imagination. He brazenly remarked en route to Italy in 1852 that "there are gorgeous women here ... but only for looking at."[41] (It was of course an age-old association, inscribed in the palindrome *Roma tibi subito motibus ibit Amor* ["Rome, to you love will suddenly come with its tumults"], which appeared fragmentarily as graffiti during the second century A D in such disparate places as Ostian and Aquincum, while the play on Roma–Amor exists even on coins of the Constantine period.[42])

Back in the nineteenth century, congruent readings of Italianicity led to a degree of stereotyping; the specific equation of Italian femininity with European ideals of beauty arguably intensified during the 1840s, that is, just as Wagner was achieving a degree of professional stability.[43] Artists such as Francesco Hayez adopted female figures of Italy, similarly depicted as sensuously beautiful, and posed his subjects as allegories for the nation's condition, manipulating their iconographic status. Figure 3.2, *Meditations on the History of Italy* (1850) – originally called *Meditations on the Old and New Testament*, but renamed according to the book in the subject's hands, clearly entitled "Histories of Italy" – reveals the aesthetically beautiful but disheartened, crest-fallen female form, following the failure of the first war of Italian independence (1848–49). Her partial nakedness, in reference to Delacroix's iconic *La Liberté guidant le peuple*, now suggests vulnerability rather than power; a violated, rather than a

---

[39] Germaine De Staël, *Corinne, or Italy*, trans. Avriel H. Goldberger (New Brunswick and London: Rutgers University Press, 1987), 25.

[40] "Cette jeune femme si tendre a pu connaître les passions, mais n'a jamais perdu la pureté d'âme d'une jeune fille." Stendhal, *Rome, Naples et Florence*, 3rd edn. (Paris: Delaunay, Libraire, Palais-Royal, 1826), 1: 143.

[41] Wagner to Theodor Uhlig, July 15, 1852, Meiringen, in SB 4: 409.

[42] On the coins, see H. Dressel, "Numismatische Analekten," *Zeitschrift für Numismatik* 23 (1900), 36ff. Regarding the palindrome, see M. Guarducci, "'Il misterioso 'quadrato magico': l'interpretazione du Jérôme Carcopino, e documenti nuovi," *Archeologia Classica* 17 (1986), 219–70, here 249; and J. Szilagyi, "Ein Ziegelstein mit Zauberformer aus dem Palast des Statthalters in Aquincum," *Acta Antiqua* 2 (1953–54), 305–10.

[43] See Isabel Skokan, *Germania und Italia: Nationale Mythen und Heldengestalten in Gemälden des 19. Jahnhunderts* (Berlin: Lukas 2009), 71ff. For a broader discussion of paradigms within de Staël's writing, see Robert Casillo, *The Empire of Stereotypes: Germaine de Staël and the Idea of Italy* (New York: Palgrave Macmillan, 2006).

3.2 Francesco Hayez, *Meditations on the History of Italy / Meditations on the Old and New Testament* (1850), Galleria Civica D'Arte Moderna E Contemporanea Di Palazzo Forti.

revolutionary, female form. Responding to this image in 1850, the Verdi librettist Andrea Maffei maintains a strictly religious interpretation of Hayez's subject, but the popular, emotive political reading was never officially denied.[44]

What does all this have to do with Wagner? We know from *Mein Leben* and from Cosima's diary that his reading of Goethe and de Staël informed his conception of Italy.[45] So the composer's exposure to literary

[44] "Cara angelica donna, in qual pensiero / Hai tu la sconsolata anima assorta? / Che ti afflige così, che ti sconforta / Nel lieto fior degli anni tuoi?. . . mistero. / Quella croce che stringi e quel severo / Volume, ove il mesto occhio si porta / Dicono che per te la gioia è morta, / Né t'offre il mondo che il suo tristo vero. / Sì, la bibbia e la croce! util consiglio / All'età sventurata, in cui sul buono / L'impudente cervice alza il perverso. / Ferma in que' segni di riscatto il ciglio, / Cara, angelica donna; essi ti sono / Un rifiuto al dolor dell'universo." *Gemme d'Arti Italiane*, 5 (1852), 37; See http://gemmedartitaliane.com/texts/Andrea%20Maffei/La%20Meditazione.pdf.

[45] Following Wagner's failure to secure funding to improve the municipal orchestra in Zurich, the composer draws on Goethe's *Briefe aus der Schweiz* to express his chagrin: "And the Swiss call

projections and allegorical images of Italy, the continuity between de Staël's *Corinne* and the stereotypes embraced by nineteenth-century travel writers, is unquestioned. While the tracing of influence always remains contestable, two related points of contact between Wagner's aesthetics and German Italianism are suggestive for his early pro-Italian stance: first, the primacy of an instinctive–emotional trigger and delegitimizing of intellectual reflection in artistic conduct; second, the female gendering of *Sinnlichkeit* as a privileged mode of communication within the nexus of art as a corporeal, quasi-Dionysian experience. Wagner's writings indicate he saw the two as interdependent. The necessity of "physical realization" (*sinnliche Erscheinung*) was precisely its capacity to access feelings directly: "the very essence of every physical portrayal [*sinnliche Darstellung*] consists in this, that it should exert a sure and definite impression upon the feeling." In other words, Wagner's belief in the priority of sensory experience over ideation – i.e. in sensory melodic verse – bears a structural relation to received ideas of Italianicity.

It will be helpful here to trace a genealogy of Wagner's ideas. First, recall the lengthy theoretical exposition of "sensory feeling" from *Oper und Drama*:

Feeling grasps nothing but the actual [*das Wirkliche*], what is physically enacted, perceivable by the senses: to *it* one can only impart the complete, the concluded, what is just entirely that, which it can be at this moment ... [W]hatever is at variance with itself, what has not yet reached an actual and definite manifestation confuses feeling and makes thought necessary, leading to a combined act which negates feeling. / In order to convince it, the poet who turns towards feeling must already be so at one with himself that he can dispense with any help from the mechanism of logic, and address himself with full consciousness to the unmistakable receptive agency [*Empfängniss*] of unconscious, pure human feeling. With this message of his he has therefore to proceed as plainly and (in view of sensory perception) as unconditionally as *feeling is addressed by actual phenomena – such as warmth*, the wind, the flower, the animal, the man.[46]

Now consider Wagner's earlier, less abstract statements of the same from the mid-1830s, specifically framed as a battle between German and Italian identity. In such a reading, *Sinnlichkeit* equates to warmth (just as Goethe had referred to the "sensual people" of a "warm and beautiful country"),[47] and Wagner specifically prioritizes warmth as the first example of that which "touches" human feeling:

themselves free! These smug bourgeois shut up in their little towns, these poor devils on their precipices and rocks, call themselves free!" ML 531; and Cosima confirms that Wagner read de Staël, see CT (June 29, 1870).

[46] SSD 4: 69–70. Cf. PW 2: 198–99.

[47] Johann Wolfgang von Goethe, *Italian Journey*, trans. W. H. Auden and Elizabeth Mayer (Middlesex: Penguin, 1962), 29, 35.

We [Germans] are too intellectual and much too learned to create warm human figures ... The Italians have an immeasurable advantage over us ... their creations are ... sensuously warm.[48]

And later:

Why is it that no German opera composer has come to the fore of late? ... *because none has grasped true warm life as it is* ... Give us *passion!* Man is only drawn to what is human; the dramatic singer can only represent what is humanly tangible [*das menschlich Fühlbare*].[49]

Though Wagner's emphasis on the physical–sensory basis of any artistic understanding undoubtedly draws on the materialist doctrines of Germanic figures such as Ludwig Feuerbach and Johannes Müller (as our final chapter will explore), his belief in "feeling" as the requisite currency of sensory perception finds an earlier analogue in the superiority of Italianate "warm human figures" and "sensuously warm" artistic creations, i.e. properties of a physical existence, a pathos of the body.

With this association in mind, Wagner's chauvinistic musical metaphors now come into focus. In a familiar alliance between music and femininity, he pointedly invokes biology as a medicalization of sexuality where the poetic aim quite literally inseminates music as "the womanly, bearing element."[50] "Melody" is quite logically then fertilized by the procreative seed of the word. While more properly dependent on discourses of bourgeois health – what Foucault called "the menaces of heredity"[51] – Wagner's conceit segues immediately into a description of Italian opera as a prostitute, thereby drawing on a further construction of femininity associated with Italy, which by older customs of cicisbeism, and the mid-century perception that Italian cities "were being swamped with prostitutes" had lent the *Kavalierreise* an element of sexual tourism.[52]

But Wagner's metaphors do not always interlock, suggesting his displacement of desire was not specifically aimed at forming a calculated, gendered conceit. His characterization of the historic commingling of music and drama as a quasi-sexual union follows a more overt fantasy of the "three primeval sisters" representing the individual arts of music, poetry and dance. This ostensibly invokes the three ancient muses of Plutarch, but arguably derives its imagery more immediately from Italian representations

---

[48] SSD 12: 1. Cf. PW 8: 55.   [49] SSD 11: 11–12. Cf. PW 8: 65–66.
[50] SSD 4: 155–56. Cf. PW 2: 296.   [51] Foucault, *The History of Sexuality*, 125.
[52] Mary Gibson, *Prostitution and the State in Italy, 1860–1915*, 2nd edn. (Columbus, OH: Ohio State University Press, 2000), 3.

of the three Graces, leaving a decidedly Italianate trace of his metaphor-driven imagination. Might these merit consideration as prompts to his imagery? Over and above Botticelli's *Primavera* (1482) with its daintily touching finger-tips, the interlocking embraces of naked female forms in Antonio Canova's *Three Graces* was a widely disseminated image, appearing in engravings and periodicals during the early nineteenth century (Figure 3.3). Stendhal refers to it as "the three sisters, gently interlacing their arms with each other" in *Promenades dans Rome* (1830), claiming this as an unforgettable visage of Italy, and his sole reason for visiting Rome.[53] Wagner himself described his melody for the three Graces in *Tannhäuser* (Paris revisions) as "sensuousness transformed into beauty,"[54] and it is certainly plausible that he was similarly acquainted with Canova's sculpture prior to conceiving his own metaphor:

> As we gaze on this entrancing round dance of the . . . Muses of artistic man, we now see the three stepping forward, each with her loving arm curled around her sister's neck; then, first this one and now that, loosing herself from their interlocked embrace – as though to show the others her beauteous form in full autonomy – and only just brushing with her very finger-tips the others' hands . . . until at last all three, tightly embracing, breast on breast, and limb to limb, grow together in amorous love kisses into a single, sweetly undulating [*wonnig-lebendige*] form.[55]

As Mary Ann Smart has emphasized, the dancing body itself – whether fantasized naked sisters or actual danseuses – figures as a sexual signifier in the Wagner discourse. Pushing Marx's "sexual gaze" to its logical extension, Wagner characterized the animated stage bodies of the Parisian cancan as "the immediate act of procreation . . . symbolically consummated,"[56] while the poet Pierre Louÿs – as Smart points out – projects Wagner's representation of movement onto a vision of ballerinas intimately engaged "in imaginary intercourse with Wotan" behind the curtains of the Opéra.[57] If these allegories yield little specific to Italy, Wagner's infamously

---

[53] "Avant-hier nous sommes venus à Rome tout exprès pour voir *Les Graces*, groupe célèbre de Canova . . . Je n'ai pas recontré dans tout notre voyage d'Italie, de statue qui m'ait fait l'impression du groupe des trois *Graces* de Canova . . . Les trois soeurs, légèrement enlacés dans les bas l'une de l'autre." Stendhal, *Promenades dans Rome* (Brussels: Louis Hauman, 1830), 1: 150–51. It is also true, however, that Wagner never commented on specific representations of the Graces. Any hypothesis of a connection between Canova and Wagner's "primeval sisters" must remain tenuous, therefore, in light of Wagner's admission that he "would never be worth anything as a judge of paintings, for once the subject matter reveals itself to me clearly and agreeably, it settles my view and nothing else counts." Wagner, ML 584.

[54] CT 2 (January 8, 1880).   [55] SSD 3: 67–68. Cf. PW 1: 96.   [56] SSD 9: 53. Cf. PW 5: 48.

[57] Mary Ann Smart, *Mimomania* (Berkeley and Los Angeles: University of California Press, 2004), 167, 163.

3.3 Antonio Canova, *The Three Graces: Aglaia, Euphrosyne, and Thalia*
(1815–17) © National Gallery of Scotland, Edinburgh, and Victoria and Albert
Museum, London.

explicit metaphors for differentiating operatic nationalities are more infor-
mative. Before labeling Italian opera a prostitute (*Lustdirne*), he dubbed
French opera a coquette (*Kokette*), and German opera a prude (*Prüde*).[58]
The sexist elaboration of the Italian role parallels Wagner's comments above

---

[58] SSD 3: 317–18. Cf. PW 2: 111–13.

on sensuous physicality (*Sinnlichkeit*) as the primary condition of all art that communicates to "feeling." It therefore seems, on this reading, that the rhetoric of Wagner's images of music, women, and Italian opera may be more intimately bound up than previously assumed.

Gutrune's phoney union with Siegfried in *Götterdämmerung* depicts a purely sensuous–physical relationship: their love is chemically induced by Hagen's potion. Wagner ventriloquizes his view in Brünnhilde's righteous assertion: "you [Gutrune] were never truly [Siegfried's] wife; you only served him as a paramour [*Buhlerin*]."[59] While Siegfried and Gutrune never have sex, Wagner clarifies in *Oper und Drama*:

> In the embraces of a paramour [*Buhlerin*] the woman is not present, but only a part of her physical [*sinnliche*] organism: she conceives no individuality by loving, but gives herself in general to the general world. Thus the paramour [*Buhlerin*] is an undeveloped, neglected woman: yet she at least fulfills the physical functions of the female sex, by which we can still – albeit regretfully – detect the woman in her.[60]

Extrapolating back to music, the empty physicality of such an embrace is the necessary but insufficient condition of Wagner's "realizing moment of an artwork," i.e. a literal, sensory existence. It is corporeality *in excelsis* and nothing else. At a reductive extreme, Wagner's music, as "a woman," requires a sensory–physical reality – "the embraces of a paramour" – to communicate or function. Whereas music and "women" are typically enlisted to signify an alternative or unstable discourse, they nevertheless tend, as Susan Berstein has noted, "to reinstate stability at the very moments when they are enlisted to undo it."[61] This seemingly is the rhetorical function of Wagner's Italian "prostitute"; it stabilizes the discourse of music's most extreme form of sensuousness as a stereotype of Italianicity.

The radicalism of Wagner's position, as a Saxon born and bred, is highlighted by Marx's suggestion that Germans may be congenitally predisposed to dislike the sensuous nature of Italian opera: "we should not forget that much of what appears to us Germans as luxuriance, dissipation, overload, in other words as unhealthy and improper, may be entirely natural for the more excitable and weaker southerners."[62] Decades before the degenerationists,

---

[59] "Sein Ehrweib warst du nie, als Buhlerin bandest du ihn." *Götterdämmerung*, Act 3, scene 3.

[60] SSD 3: 317–18. Cf. PW 2: 112

[61] Susan Bernstein, "Fear of Music?" in *Nietzsche and the Feminine*, ed. Peter J. Burgard (University of Virginia Press, 1994), 104–34, here 106.

[62] "Auch sollen wir nicht vergessen, daß manches, was uns Deutschen an ihm und sonst am italischen Gesange als Üppigkeit, Ausschweifung, Überladung, also als ungesund und ungehörig erscheint, im erregtern und – schwächlichern Süden ganz naturgemäß sein mag." Marx, *Die Kunst des Gesanges*, 198.

this discrepancy assumed a racial, quasi-biological rationale in Marx's read-ing: "There are those – without a rich, powerful, and agreeably formed *sensory organization* and without a consolidation in the sensory element – in whom pure subjectivity and sensuality [*Sinnlichkeit*] cannot achieve anything significant."[63] Thus, where Wagner aspires to simulate, and ultimately, to master "the Italian principle" or "the good Italian cantabile style" that in 1834 he held as necessary to "re-establish ... the shattered unity of poetry and song," Marx acknowledges its contingent merits, but declares it alien to the German condition.[64] Wagner, it seems, was altogether more pragmatic.

His hint at the need for a "sensory relationship" between melody and verse is far from a banal comment on text setting, then; a single adjective – *sinnlich* – offers us a glimpse through this historical keyhole. It implicates a network of associations within the literary imagination that characterize the German etic construction of Italy and thereby perhaps encapsulate part of Bellini's enduring relevance for Wagner.

---

[63] "Es wird jedoch in jenem, der reinen Subjektivität und der Sinnlichkeit eigenen Gebiete ohne eine reiche, kräftig und wohlthuend gestaltete *Sinneorganisation* und ohne eine Vertiefung in das Element der Sinnlichkeit nichts Bedeutendes geleistet werden können." *Ibid.*, 203.

[64] SSD 12: 9. Cf. PW 8: 64

4 | Hearing voices: Wilhelmine Schröder-Devrient and the *Lohengrin* "recitatives"

PART 1

Adolescent ears

Wagner must have been a good listener. "The ear is no child," he declared in 1851.[1] Embracing the psychology of cognition, he clarified that listening to alliterative verse is not merely a passive reception of sound, but an active task that depends on an inherent human ability to organize sound information. "The capacity of immediately receptive hearing is so unbounded," he explains, "that it knows to connect the most diverse sensations as soon as they are brought into physiognomic resemblance, and to assign them to feelings for the purposes of all-encompassing absorption as related, purely human emotions."[2] In this process the ear transforms the raw sound data from something particular into something universally human. That is, in addition to the semantic sense transmitted in melodicized poetic verse, a second layer of sensation crystallizes as collective emotion within the listener. Rather than resembling a prosthetic microphone, Wagner's "completely *understanding* ear"[3] is closer to a body-generic processor that transforms sounds – seemingly randomized within the phonemic matrix of language – from signifying patterns into emotion according to their inherent similitude. This attributes considerable agency to ears confronted by art, in effect an art that endlessly solicits cognitive persistence.

Wagner's claims don't stop there. The "all-embracing, all-uniting power"[4] of the ear does not even require alliterative patterning to transform linguistic sound into emotion. Corrupted modern prose is good enough:

[The ear] can take the subversive understanding's millionfold tatters and severed strands, remake them as purely human, as an original unity, and evermore unified, and offer them to our feeling for its highest, most ravishing delectation.[5]

---

[1] SSD 4: 133. Cf. PW 2: 271.   [2] SSD 4: 132. Cf. PW 2: 270.   [3] SSD 4: 136. Cf. PW 2: 274.
[4] SSD 4: 132. Cf. PW 2: 270.   [5] SSD 4: 132–3. Cf. PW 2: 274.

At stake in Wagner's interest in sensory mediation is the transmission that takes place in live performance between creative activity and active observer. His comments in *Oper und Drama* betray a desire to take total control of this transmission as a means of fulfilling the rhetorician's primary task: to persuade.

But this chapter is not about Wagner's theory of language, it is about his theory of hearing and the tensions between this and his attempts to transcribe what is accomplished by the ear. Making sense of – i.e. "knitting together" – the sounding "physiognomic resemblance" of alliterative verse on hearing it spoken or sung, demands a theory of communication based on the aural recipient, in which the listener realizes the sound, as well as the sound itself being – in some measure – a realization of Wagner's text (or score). "I am concerned here only with the impression ... melody must make upon the listener," he explained in 1860 of the later principle of endless melody.[6] Far from obeying a one-way circuit between performer and listener, this theory destabilizes the concept of a musical signifier because what is signified is not static, but becomes absorbed dialectically as "purely human" emotion by the interpretant. Listening, in such a theory, is explicitly a two-way street (though as we shall see, Wagner's calls for freedom are covertly built on close monitoring and control. So here, for all his rhetoric, Wagner ends up *dictating* meaning rather than allowing for its construction by the listener).

To reinforce his communicative model, Wagner co-opts a second sense, arguing for the need to persuade both "the eye and ear of hearing," which is less a claim for synæsthesia than a belief that seeing alphabetic letters affects the way we hear and recite text.[7] The "physiognomic resemblance" of alliterative consonants is also a visual cue for the eyes, in other words. With this, Wagner effectively distinguishes a Lacanian visuality ("a screen of signs [inserted] between the retina and the world"[8]) from unmediated vision in the reception of sound. If vision usually dominates perception,[9] its ancilla

[6] SSD 7: 131. Cf. *Three Wagner Essays*, 40–41.   [7] SSD 4: 136. Cf. PW 2: 274.

[8] Norman Bryson, "The Gaze in the Expanded Field," in *Vision and Visuality*, ed. Hal Foster (Seattle: Bay Press, 1988), 91.

[9] For a historical account of visuality in the nineteenth century see Jonathan Crary, *Techniques of the Observer: On Vision and Modernity in the Nineteenth Century* (Cambridge, MA: MIT Press, 1992). Debates over the historical priority of senses continue today with Paul Virilio's pioneering work on the primacy of vision in modern culture on the one hand (*War and Cinema: The Logistics of Perception*, trans. Patrick Camiller [London: Verso, 1989], 7ff), and recent volumes redressing a perceived ocular dominance, on the other, including Veit Erlmann, *Reason and Resonance*; Viet Erlmann (ed.), *Hearing Cultures: Essays on Sound, Listening and Modernity* (New York: Berg, 2004), and Michael Bull and Les Black (eds.), *The Auditory Culture Reader* (New York: Berg, 2003).

role (as handmaiden) to audition here can perhaps be explained by the fact that nineteenth-century German infants, schooled in reading through the emergent science of phonetics by their mothers, "would not see letters [when they read silently] but hear, with irresistible longing, a voice [*her* voice] between the lines," as Friedrich Kittler famously argued.[10] Accepting this, the intimacy of the experience serves to demote letters as textual signifiers below both the sound of a voice and the new image of an enunciating mouth. The outcome, put in its most radical terms, is a situation where "only the mother's pointing finger retained any relation to the optic form of the letter."[11]

If we take Wagner's ear-dominated "eye of hearing" seriously, it is no surprise that musical notation and handwriting – the demoted signifier – formed something of a *bête noire* for Wagner. In a letter to Robert Franz, he complained of the lifelessness of *Lohengrin* as a printed score, explicitly bemoaning the inadequacy of notation as "something which no one feels more keenly than I . . . [for] even a printed drama or an engraved opera score is, after all, simply an example of the written word."[12] In this mind-set, he simply refused to send Liszt the verse draft of *Siegfrieds Tod* because he feared it could only be misunderstood as writing. "But if I could recite it to you full voiced, suggestively, as I intend," Wagner qualified, "then I would be satisfied as to the desired impression of my poem on you . . . The written word is . . . entirely insufficient for my intention."[13] At this time of controversial operatic reforms, eradicating a listener's misunderstanding was precisely the point for Wagner. Irrespective of whether scores or written script are at stake, the principle of a listening perspective, or "recipient epistemology," remains. In both instances the listener remains the agent and, to a disproportionate extent, the arbiter of melodic "sense."

---

[10] Kittler, *Discourse Networks 1800–1900*, 34. Kittler compares philosophical assessments of stenography at the turn of the nineteenth century to critique "a metaphysics of silent reading" in which, he claims, the written word triggers in the reader the aural sensation of hearing speech: "A voice, as pure as it is transcendental, rises from between the lines . . . the hallucination becomes optical as well as auditory . . . It is not hard to say to whom it belongs. The only alphabetization technique in which one seems to hear what has been read is the phonetic method from the Mother's Mouth." Kittler, *Discourse Networks 1800–1900*, 65. Attempts to apply this to melodic theory include Alfred Cramer, who claimed that for Berlioz, Schumann, Mendelssohn, and especially Wagner: "melodies evoked pen strokes, and . . . they evoked meanings and images much as pen strokes did." With specific reference to Wagner's melodies, Cramer's claim is daring: "that music created a sense of voice using gestures and shapes, and that in nineteenth-century culture melodic shapes could evoke voice because similar shapes had this effect in handwritings." See Cramer, "Of Serpentina and Stenography," 135, 163.

[11] Kittler, *Discourse Networks 1800–1900*, 34.

[12] Wagner to Robert Franz, October 28, 1852, Zurich, SB 5: 87.

[13] Wagner to Liszt, June 29, 1851, Enge/Zurich, SB 4: 67.

So far so good. But consider a foil to Wagner's model of sensory mediation. The literary theorist Wolfgang Iser has supplied a framework for literature whose "sense" congeals between writing and reading. What he terms the "artistic" and "aesthetic" poles of *Konkretisation* refer respectively to a text created by the author, and the realization accomplished by a reader. While an irreconcilable difference of medium between sound and text undermines their structural comparison, Iser's notion of a convergence between text and reader is useful for Wagner's theory of listening because the convergence Iser intimates "can never be precisely pin-pointed, but must always remain virtual, as it is not to be identified either with the reality of the text or with the individual disposition of the reader."[14] In other words, it sits inscrutably between immanent knowledge and epistemology as a structurally indeterminate site. The aim of Iser's phenomenological approach is to vary each text in the imagination until we discover what is invariable about it, abstracting what Husserl – after Plato – termed its *eidos* (type), or in this case, its frame of convergence. But where Iser rejects both poles *in extremis* – artistic and aesthetic – in favor of a dynamic merging of author–reader imagination, Wagner's model traces convergence back to an ill-defined *eidos* of primordial Teutonic sounds. Both concern imagination, but Wagner's is considerably less democratic: he pinpoints the convergence with old-fashioned *auctoritas* by claiming that listeners must "'feel back' [the words'] sensations," sensations that *he* intuited and orchestrated, and "reach their original truth ... [in order] to grasp the sensuous substance of our roots of speech."[15] By alluding to an unknowable historical mode of listening, Wagner brings the site of convergence securely into his own audio-visual imagination; it is a panopticon of authorial perception (though Wagner would probably have seen this in terms of the Fichtean universal mind). I am arguing, in a nutshell, that – unlike Iser's inscrutable convergence – Wagner models how to listen to his verse by dictating how he wants to be heard according to his beliefs about the origins of language. Paradoxically, for Nietzsche this resulted in a kind of magical incomprehensibility, a powerful, "unexpected and utterly unintelligible effect" that never quite reaches conscious, conceptual comprehension: "like a mysterious star, [the feeling] expired after a moment's gleaming."[16]

---

[14] Wolfgang Iser, "The Reading Process: A Phenomenological Approach," *Reader–Response Criticism: From Formalism to Post-Structuralism*, ed. Jane P. Tompkins (Baltimore and London: Johns Hopkins University Press, 1980), 50.

[15] SSD 4: 127. Cf. PW 2: 264.

[16] Friedrich Nietzsche, *The Birth of Tragedy out of the Spirit of Music* [1872], trans. Shaun Whiteside (London: Penguin, 2003), 109.

Why does this matter? Rather than dismissing another act of Wagnerian tendentiousness, two related questions arise: first, Wagner's emphasis on the sensory, communicative capacity of alliteration was a singular mid-century response to preceding, beleaguered attempts at melodic theory; but why did an intuitive connection between verbal sounds suddenly appear to offer an answer, a way out of what had become an extraordinary aesthetic quagmire of German text setting? Second, at the level of his verse composition, Wagner decisively factored the listener into his musical equations, but when did the master of Bayreuth first draw a distinction – adapting Iser – between "artistic" and "aesthetic" listening, between aurally receiving a composer's music and the cognitive task of making sense of it? When did he first awaken into an adolescence, that is, in which the ear is "no child"?

Die richtige Sängerin

Wagner's own ears had only made sense of Bellinian melody on June 10, 1834 through the voice of Wilhelmine Schröder-Devrient, a German "dramatic soprano" whose influence on Wagner's career is well documented.[17] Before her guest appearance in Leipzig as Romeo (*I Capuleti e i Montecchi*), Wagner's autobiographical sketch recounts that he had heard the Italian's music as trivial. As a listener, he reports being taken aback by the soprano's "extraordinary achievement" given Bellini's "thoroughly insignificant music." It was evidently an awakening of sorts:

I was far from granting Bellini any great merit; nonetheless, the material out of which his music was crafted appeared to me more successful and more suitable to radiate warm life than the anxiously concerned conscientiousness with which we Germans mostly brought about only a tormented semblance of truth.[18]

Later, in *Mein Leben*, Wagner openly characterized the experience as a prompt "to ruminate on the causes of the ineffectuality of . . . German music used hitherto in drama."[19] This included his own music. If a

---

[17] Two relatively recent studies of Schröder-Devrient are: Karl-Josef Kutsch and Leo Riemens, *Großes Sängerlexikon*, vol. 2 (Bern and Stuttgart: Franke 1987–1994), 2670–72; and Stephen Meyer, "*Das wilde Herz*: Interpreting Wilhelmine Schröder-Devrient," *Opera Quarterly* 14 (1997), 23–40. A similar claim to Wagner's experience of Bellini concerns Schröder-Devrient's role in the reception of *Fidelio*. According to Alfred von Wolzogen, it was only after German critics heard her sing Leonora in November 1822 that the formerly "frosty coldness" of Beethoven's music was accorded "more and more effusive praise," leading Wolzogen to assert that "she created the role" [*créer un rôle*] in the truest sense. See Alfred von Wolzogen, *Wilhelmine Schröder-Devrient* (Leipzig: F. A. Brockhaus, 1863), 54–55.

[18] SSD 1: 9. Cf. PW 1: 8.   [19] ML 81.

particular performer allowed him to "hear" Bellini's melodies as compelling rather than crass, to what extent had Schröder-Devrient become, in effect, Wagner's signifier for performative melody, i.e. melody that only truly realizes its identity in the act of its delivery? On that night in Leipzig his ears made sense of Bellinian "sensations" seemingly for the first time through a voice type, not a verse type. We may wonder how measurably this led him to factor the performer's melodic delivery into his melodic composition. This would seem what the final act of *Meistersinger* thematizes all too openly when Walther trumps Beckmesser's feeble attempt with ostensibly the same poem:

MEISTERSINGER: Yes, indeed! I see, it makes a difference if one sings it wrong or right.
VOLK: That's something else, who'd have thought it?
   What a difference the right words and the proper delivery make![20]

In reality, of course, Beckmesser is not just singing Walther's composition badly, he is actually singing a different "text" – both words and music are different from the Prize Song. This would seem Wagner's way of presenting, *to the ears of the theater audience only*, an experience of "Beckmesser singing Walther's exact composition, but badly" that is audible only in the stage world. Adopting Carolyn Abbate's terms, it is a scene of "phenomenal" performance – singing heard by its singer – but one contrived to distort the sound for listeners in the theater in order to illustrate the absence of "proper delivery."[21]

We can first begin to address this topic through a recollection. It is likely that a cryptic entry in Cosima's diary as late as March 7, 1878 refers back to Schröder-Devrient's importance for Wagner's hearing of "Bellini" in 1834:

R. played various Italian themes, from Bellini's *I Capuleti e i Montecchi*, *La Straniera* and *Norma*, and said: "For all the poverty of invention, there is real passion and feeling there, and the right singer has only to get up and sing it for it to win all hearts. I have learned things from them which Messrs. Brahms & Co. have never learned, and they can be seen in my melodies" . . . After playing the C-sharp Minor Prelude [WTC I], he observes, with reference to the Italian melodies . . . "That is *pour le monde*, but this (the Prelude) is the world itself."[22]

---

[20] "[Meistersinger]: Ja wohl, ich merk', 's ist ein ander Ding, / ob falsch man oder richtig sing'. / [Volk] Das ist was andres, wer hätt's gedacht; / was doch recht Wort und Vortrag macht!" Act 3, scene 5.
[21] See Carolyn Abbate, *Unsung Voices* (Princeton University Press, 1991), 5ff.
[22] CT (March 7, 1878).

The anecdote reveals a fracture in Wagner's musical *Weltanschauung* that relates to different ways in which music can be heard. Bach's *Prelude* is cast as a composer's inner musical world, central and all-encompassing, entirely complete in itself (redolent of Wagner's ecstatic claim for his lovers' unity in *Tristan*: "Selbst dann bin ich die Welt");[23] Bellini's themes, by contrast, communicate to the outer world by actively enrapturing an audience. The one is self-contained and inert, the other is an open, dynamic process; at root their contrast articulates a broad distinction between the assignment of meaning to a state of being or an act of conveying, conditions of status and passage. This raises doubts about the extent to which it is the themes themselves – melodies as inert, "plastic" shapes – that communicate or are innately beautiful (an idea defeated by the melodic theorists who accepted notions of plural listening), and lends a new dimension to Wagner's intended criticism of "absolute" melody: "fine art can only display the finished, i.e. the motionless; it can never make of the beholder a convinced witness to the becoming of a thing."[24]

This division assumed national connotations as part of a wider discourse on the split between the composition of melodic shape and an aesthetics of singing we saw in Chapter 1. For some critics, Italianate music posited an antithesis between predefined melodic structure and the singing voice, where the former is self-sufficient and independent of the latter's spontaneous freedom to communicate to an audience. "Italian song . . . [is] always beautiful in its substance," Pietro Siciliani declared in 1868, "whether you hear it sung by the uncouth voice of a yokel or by the most able artist."[25] German melody, by contrast, typically posited a dependence between these two, a synthesis of expression and compositional work where the predefined melodic shape contains its characteristic expression within it, permitting considerably less freedom in performance.[26]

---

[23] Tristan and Isolde sing this iconic line together in *Tristan*, act 2, scene 2, mm. 1188–93.

[24] SSD 4: 192. Cf. PW 2: 337. It was Wagner, of course, who first coined the term "absolute melody." A recent, historiographic study of the term is Sanna Pederson, "Defining the Term 'Absolute Music' Historically," *Music and Letters* 90 (2009), 240–62; see also Carl Dahlhaus and L. U. Abraham, *The Idea of Absolute Music*, trans. Roger Lustig (University of Chicago Press, 1989).

[25] "il canto italiano . . . [e] sempre bello nella sua sostanza, sia che lo sentiate modulato dalla rozze voce del bifolco, sia dal più abile artista." Pietro Siciliani, *Sulla differente ragione estetica nell'indole della musica tedesca e della musica italiana: Dialogo fra un critic ed un filosofo* [1868], quoted in Mazzucato's review of the book in the *Gazzetta musicale di Milano* 23 (1868), 209–10.

[26] Lobe's *Musikalische Briefe* offers an animated discussion of these alternative principles. See in particular the chapters "Deutsche Musik" and "Die neuern deutschen Componisten im Allgemeinen," *Musikalische Briefe*, 2nd edn. (Leipzig: Baumgärtner, 1860), 16–32.

In the lecture notes for his *Aesthetics*, Hegel couched this in terms of producing (Rossinian), and *re*producing (Weberean) melody in performance:

When it is said, for instance, that Rossini makes things easy for the singers, this is only partly correct. Indeed he makes it really difficult for them by so often referring them to the activity of their own musical genius. If this really is genius, the resulting work of art has a quite peculiar attraction, because we have present before us not merely a work of art but the actual production of one.[27]

This also implies that a melody created in the moment of its delivery becomes increasingly unwritable: its intricate, improvisatory means of expression are sensible to the listening ear, but largely illegible to the eye presented with the dyslexic imprecision of a five-line stave. Notation, we recall, was "entirely insufficient" for Wagner, and in arguing that the German mistake is to prescribe all raw musical expression exclusively for the orchestra, the Leipzig-based music theorist Lobe thinks it a "hugely obvious fact" that "passion can only be truly, movingly portrayed in opera through the human voice."[28] Schröder-Devrient is again his exemplar of choice.[29] Since her performances function not as a detail, but as a mighty hinge for the German discourse on vocal melody, the criticism surrounding her reception bears closer scrutiny.

We tend to think of her as a card-carrying German artist whose combination of mimetic stage talents and vocal idiosyncrasies embodied the modern goal of unifying tragic acting and modern opera – a figure who comfortably flitted between speaking and singing at decisive moments in performances that were always driven by the portrayal of character. This certainly describes her ideological reception in mid-century Germany. Reviewing her performance as Leonore (*Fidelio*) from 1831, the German poet and critic Ludwig Rellstab illustrates this familiar reading. Like many others, he interpreted the disconnect between her charismatic acting and poor vocal timbre and technique as an educational deficiency. But he went further in claiming that her early training as an actress and lack of

---

[27] Hegel, *Aesthetics*, 2: 957.

[28] "Die Leidenschaft kann in der Oper *nur durch die menschliche Stimme* wahrhaft ergreifend dargestellt werden." Lobe, *Musikalische Briefe*, 40.

[29] In her prime, Schröder-Devrient was reputedly without equal as Leonore, a role with which she was most closely associated and received her greatest acclaim after she first sang the part in November 1822. Lobe's adulation therefore reinscribes a link between her artistry, the reception of *Fidelio*, and the *Beethovenbild*: "Many have heard the great Schröder-Devrient in *Fidelio* where in the dungeon scene, with a mostly silent orchestra, she hurls out the words: 'Tödt' erst sein Weib!' and each who hears this surely shivers through the soul still with the memory of the extraordinary effect of these few sung notes." See Lobe, *Musikalische Briefe*, 40.

sheer vocal prominence rebalanced her stage presence between the kindred institutions of opera and theater, leading to an embodied artistic unity, a kind of realist *Gesamtkunstdarstellung* which admittedly played into existing models of artistic synthesis, but which also had obvious connotations for Wagner's future:

> Never have we seen an artist unite all the various aspects of her performance like this one did. Dialogue, pantomime, gesture, song all lift up and inform each other … It will never be the natural power of the tone itself that enraptures us, indeed, we often even see her struggle with hindrances in her technique that are not inconsequential. And yet she creates a soul for the sound, gives it a heart, so that, flowing out from the innermost recesses of her breast, it irresistibly penetrates into the deepest depths of her heart.[30]

As Stephen Meyer has argued, this unified performance aesthetic reflected a new "spiritual outlook" for liberal criticism and became a trope of Schröder-Devrient's reception in Germany in the 1830s,[31] with the contemporary critic Heinrich Laube even claiming for her a revolutionary status as "truly the prototype of a new era of Art; her Fidelio is the enchanting bright night, when the old god Poesis, in his eternal youth, presses Music, the euphonious lotus flower, in his immortal arms."[32] A review of her opera debut from January 20, 1821 in the *Allgemeine musikalische Zeitung* set a prognostic tone, describing her creation of "a pure ideal-poetic side from prosaic poetry,"[33] an accolade that resonates with none other than Wagner's project for *Versmelodie*. And with unambiguously rhyming rhetoric, the mythology surrounding Wagner's debt to Schröder-Devrient spawned many fanciful accounts of his "decisive" artistic encounters with her.

---

[30] "Noch nie sahen wir eine Künstlerin so die Gesammtheit aller Mittel zu einer Leistung vereinigen wie diese. Dialog, Mimik, Plastik, Gesang, Alles hebt und trägt sich gegenseitig … Niemals wird es die Naturgewalt des Tones an sich sein, womit sie uns hinreißt, ja wir erblicken sie sogar häufig im Kampfe mit nicht unbedeutenden Hindernissen in ihren Mitteln; allein sie schafft dem Klange eine Seele, gibt ihm ein Herz, und so, aus dem Innersten der Brust entquollen, dringt er unwiderstehlich in ihre tiefsten Tiefen ein." Ludwig Rellstab, *Musikalische Beurteilungen* [1848]; rpt. (Leipzig: Brockhaus, 1861), 172.

[31] Meyer, "*Das wilde Herz*," 32ff.

[32] "Sie ist wirklich der Prototyp einer neuen Aera der Kunst, ihr Fidelio ist die reizende Brautnacht, wo der alte Gott der Poesis in seiner ewigen Jugend die klingende Lotusblume Musik in seine unsterblichen Arme drückt." Heinrich Laube, "Wilhelmine Schröder-Devrient," *Zeitung für die elegante Welt* 6 (1833), 21.

[33] "[es] gelang vielleicht noch nie einer Mime, der prosaischen Poesie eine rein idealisch-poetische Seite [abgewonnen hat], wie dieser hoffnungsvollen Schülerin." *AmZ* (January 20, 1821), quoted in Claire von Glümer, *Erinnerungen an Wilhelmine Schröder-Devrient* (Leipzig: Johann Ambrose Barth, 1862), 23.

By far the most adventurous anecdote – given by the (occasionally unreliable) biographer and theater critic Carl Hagemann – purports to quote Wagner's sister-in-law, Cäcilie Avenarius, who recounts a visit by Schröder-Devrient to the Geyer family in Leipzig when Wagner was a teenager. There is no evidence that such a visit took place, though it remains possible, for Wagner does mention in *Mein Leben* that famous singers visited their household while his younger sister, Clara, sang at the Leipzig opera. Whether or not parts of the story are fact, Avenarius' account sits at the apex of creative Wagner–Devrient mythology and is worth quoting at length:

[The famous female guest singer] came and sang quite incomparably. Albert, the older brother, accompanied her, and leaning silently in the deep window balustrade, Richard Wagner stood motionless and let the entire magic of the tones act upon him. It was as though a veil fell from before his eyes . . . for the first time he felt the essence and effect of dramatic expression. He was awoken from an unconscious dream. His eyes gleamed and his slim delicate face was deadly pale from excitement. He crept from the room as though anesthetized and hid for the rest of the evening. While the wondrous singing resounded, he sat in his small room with eyes wide open: and his artistic path rose before him . . . Now he saw clearly and purely for the first time what he ought to – must do in the world. Not only the artist but the prophet was awoken in him. The deeply powerful experience of these few minutes and the ensuing terrible night gave birth to the music dramatist, the new value of German opera theater . . . and this was achieved by the rare art of Wilhelmine Schröder-Devrient.[34]

While a claim of such magnitude almost certainly belongs to the hyperbole of a wishful historian, it probably alludes to Wagner's own apocryphal claims that after hearing her *Fidelio* aged sixteen, he wrote a succinct but effusive letter explaining "that my life had henceforth found its meaning . . . that she had on this evening made of me that which I now vowed

---

[34] "Und sie kam und sang ganz unvergleichlich. Der älteste Bruder Albert begleitete, und still in die tiefe Fensterbrüstung gelehnt, stand unbeweglich Richard Wagner und ließ den ganzen Zauber der Töne auf sich einwirken. Es war, als ob ein Schleier von seinen Augen fiel . . . Zum erstenmal fühlte er das Wesen und die Wirkung des dramatischen Ausdrucks. Er war aus einem unbewußten Traum erwacht. Seine Augen glänzten und sein schmales, zartes Gesicht war vor Erregung totenbleich. Wie betäubt schlich er aus dem Zimmer und ließ sich für den Abend nicht mehr sehen. Während der wundervolle Gesang weitertönte, saß er mit groß geöffneten Augen in seinem kleinen Stübschen: und seine künstlerische Lebensaufgange stieg vor ihm auf . . . Jetzt sah er zum erstenmal deutlich und rein, was er in der Welt sollte – mußte. Nicht nur der Künstler, auch der Seher war in ihm erwacht. Das tief-große Erlebnis jener wenigen Minuten und die darauf folgende furchtbare Nacht hatte den Musikdramatiker, den Neuwerter des deutschen Opernhauses geboren . . . Und die dies mit ihrer seltenen Kunst vollbrachte, war Wilhelmine Schröder-Devrient." Carl Hagemann, *Wilhelmine Schröder-Devrient* (Berlin and Leipzig: Schuster & Loeffler, 1904), 6–7.

to become."[35] In light of this, the association of her performance aesthetic with the cliché of *Gesamtkunstwerk* was as easy for uncritical biographers of the last century as it was simplistic. Against such conformism, I will seek in part to reset her cultural memory with the argument that she principally affected the way Wagner heard and notated voices.

Revising the Wagner–Devrient relationship

Both Wagner's divided world and his acknowledgement of the *richtige Sängerin* recognize the imperative of performance acts in communicating "real passion and feeling" through melody. Was this what he learned that "Messrs. Brahms & Co." apparently did not? If so, it underscored his view that the impulse to communicate dramatic feeling was bound to the structuring of melody, conceived as an active process between singer and listener; as such, it was not entirely written down, which is to say, not entirely in the hands of the composer.

In this reading, Wagner's melodies were intricately bound to the voices that would sing them, not in the sense of composing parts for a particular voice (Handel's Cuzzoni, Mozart's Constanze) but of conceiving – and subsequently composing – a vocal aesthetic according to the experience of a prior performance by a particular voice. Of course, I rehearse a commonplace to state that Wagner (and his uncritical biographers) consistently claimed Schröder-Devrient's 1834 performance as Romeo made an "overwhelming impression" on him.[36] If we put some pressure on this reading, however, it turns out that Wagner mostly discusses his changed opinion of Bellini in that passage from the *Autobiographische Skizze*. Indeed, on closer inspection, all sorts of cracks begin to appear in the Schröder-Devrient myth: less than a year after hearing Schröder-Devrient's Romeo, Wagner had relativized her achievement, comparing it to Amalie Planer's

---

[35] ML 37. On the basis of strong documentary evidence, John Deathridge doubts this performance actually took place, while Klaus Kropfinger points out equally that "there is no positive proof that it never happened." Complicating our credence in Wagner's claims, *Mein Leben* reports that Schröder-Devrient recited the teenage Wagner's letter "word for word" during rehearsals for *Rienzi*. This would have required her to recall or file away this fan mail from an unknown boy for some fourteen years, which is possible but unlikely. See Dahlhaus and Deathridge, *The New Grove Wagner* (New York: Norton, 1984), 7; Kropfinger, *Wagner and Beethoven: Richard Wagner's Reception of Beethoven* [1974], trans. Peter Palmer (Cambridge University Press, 1991), 32–33; Wagner, ML 37.

[36] Ernest Newman's description in *Wagner as Man & Artist* (New York: Alfred A. Knopf, 1924), 157.

performance of the same role;[37] his tendency during the early 1840s, furthermore, was to refer to Schröder-Devrient together with her operatic partner, Josef Tichatschek, indicating that her artistic significance was equatable with his for Wagner at this time.[38] Though he certainly had hailed her (as Romeo, Norma, and Amina) in 1837 as "the greatest living German dramatic singer,"[39] by 1843 he aligned her efforts with more nationalistic German taste, speaking of the "forced enthusiasm" with which she portrayed these same Bellinian heroines that inspired his initial endorsement;[40] it was only after her death in 1860, moreover, that Wagner began to posit her real causality, namely "a magic that was to determine the whole direction of my career," wherein "there arose in me a consistent image, not only of what a singing and acting performance should be, but also of the poetic and musical shape of a work of art."[41] While she was still alive, albeit retired, Wagner barely mentions her in his Zurich essays, and it is not until *Mein Leben* (1865–80) that he actually specifies in detail her performances of Beethoven and Bellini as artistic epiphanies for his life's work. The construct, in other words, was fully realized more than three decades after the original "moment of intensity," to borrow Hans Ulrich Gumbrecht's phrase.[42]

---

[37] "Rarely can a débutante have caused such a great sensation as she did [Amalie Planer as *Romeo* in Bellini's *I Capuleti e i Montecchi*]; people were beside themselves with enthusiasm; the opera had to be repeated immediately afterwards, and the house was once again packed to the rafters, and the noise was as deafening as that which normally greets Devrient." Wagner to Theodor Apel, October 26–27, 1835, Magdeburg, in SB 1: 225–26.

[38] "Tichatschek & Devrient are well-suited to their parts [in *Rienzi*]." Wagner to Apel, September 20, 1840, Leipzig, SB 1: 410. Writing to Tichatschek himself, Wagner engages the tenor for *Rienzi* as part of a required *duo*: "the opera's success lies principally in the best possible casting of the two main roles (and in no other theater in the world do I know artists whom I would be more justified in expecting to fulfill the boldest wishes I entertain for the success of the opera than Mad. Schr.-Dev. and you yourself – my very dear Sir." Wagner to Tichatschek, September 6–7, 1841, Dresden, in SB 1: 506. Both in preparation for, and following the success of, *Rienzi*, Wagner continued to think of the pair as an artistic unit: "of Devrient I need only say that I am assured she has never studied la rôle with such enthusiasm, since she almost always finds it uncommonly difficult to familiarize herself with anything new straightaway: at the very end of the opera she intends to come galloping onto the stage on horseback, riding *cross-saddle!* – Tichatschek has given up the holiday in Salzburg on my account: vocally he is made for the part." Wagner to Ernst Benedikt Kietz, September 6, 1842, Dresden, SB 2: 147; "The performance was *ravishingly* beautiful – Tichatschek – Devrient – everything – everything was more perfect than has ever been seen here previously!" Wagner to Eduard and Cäcilie Avenarius, October 21, 1842, Paris, in SB 2: 167–68.

[39] SSD 12: 17.   [40] Wagner to Robert Schumann, February 25, 1843, Dresden, in SB 2: 221.

[41] SSD 7: 97. Cf. Jacobs, *Three Wagner Essays*, 19.

[42] Hans Ulrich Gumbrecht, *The Production of Presence* (Stanford University Press, 2004), 97ff.

What scant evidence exists about their actual contact during artistic collaborations supports this reinterpretation. Despite the fact that Schröder-Devrient created the roles of Adriano, Senta, and Venus under Wagner during the 1840s, there is little reason to suspect that she advocated his music or associated her national loyalties with his. Indeed, after being unable to master a section from the role of Adriano in 1842, she reputedly threw the score of *Rienzi* at the composer's feet during a rehearsal, saying: "You can sing your own crap!"[43] Wagner himself indicates in *Mein Leben* that Schröder-Devrient often did not see eye to eye with him. During rehearsals for the premiere of *Tannhäuser*, they specifically disagreed on the possibility of inscribing declamation into the plastic form of a melody. After declaiming the text aloud "with great feeling and force," Schröder-Devrient called Wagner naïve (he reports) and explained that Tichatschek would be quite incapable of learning this manner of delivery:

I tried to bring her attention and my own to bear upon the nature of the music, which was written so clearly in order to bring out the necessary accent that, in my opinion, the music actually spoke for him who interpreted the passage, even if he were only a musical singer and nothing more. She shook her head, saying that this would [only] be all right in the case of an oratorio.[44]

Wagner's implied response – tucked away in his 1872 essay on acting – was that "the *Tannhäuser* I myself conceived has never been performed at all," and that "whoever may choose to think that I meant to fetter the life of a spirited performance by mechanical minutiae ... [is wrong because] those marks are but the picture I hold up to [singers] to follow."[45] This robust disagreement over notation also informs the first section of his 1852 essay "On the Performance of *Tannhäuser*," suggesting that it was precisely at this time, in the wake of his Zurich essays (1849–51) and the aborted musical sketches for *Siegfrieds Tod* (1850), that her influence on him is traceable, specifically in relation to vocal notation.

[43] "Singe er seinen Quark selber!" The anecdote is recorded in Glümer, *Erinnerungen an Wilhelmine Schröder-Devrient*, 121.

[44] ML 367. In the same passage, Wagner seeks to vindicate his own views on prescribing vocal declamation by recounting his success in tutoring Anton Mitterwurzer, the baritone who created Wolfram for the 1845 premiere: "During several rehearsals he [Mittelwurzer] only sang in a whisper in order to get over the difficulty [of adopting Wagner's explicit declamatory intonation], but at the last rehearsal he acquitted himself so admirably of his task, and threw himself into it so heartily, that his work has remained to this day as my most conclusive reason for believing that, in spite of the unsatisfactory state of the world of opera today, it is possible not only to find, but also properly to train, the singer whom I should regard as indispensable for a correct interpretation of my works." *Ibid.*, 370–71.

[45] SSD 9: 212–3. Cf. PW 5: 211.

Celebrated idealist commentaries about Schröder-Devrient suddenly speaking the words "Tödt' erst sein Weib!" in *Fidelio*, or suddenly laughing convulsively, tend to obscure the fact that it was only after hearing Schröder-Devrient *fail* in this trademark strategy of breaking operatic codes – Wagner explains – that he realized the significance of her earlier impression on him. Her later efforts as Julia in Spontini's *La Vestale*:

> frequently led to some exaggeration and at one crucial point even to a truly deplorable instance of over-acting . . . [With] . . . the words "Er ist frei!" she let herself be tempted into speaking the words instead of singing them. She had often previously demonstrated what overwhelming effect can be produced by tones approaching pure speech in *Fidelio* . . . The tremendous effect, to which I, of all people, was particularly sensitive, was derived from the strange shock, like the blow of an executioner's axe, which I received at being abruptly brought down from the exalted sphere into which music lifts even the most gruesome situations to the bedrock of harshest reality . . . [I]n recalling this feeling, I can only describe the instant like a flash of lightning . . . The tremendous significance of such a moment, and the fact that there should be no trifling with it, was revealed to me in this performance by the complete failure of this great artist to produce the desired result.[46]

The changing reality of her ageing vocal cords is multiplied by the "harshest reality" that Wagner (wanted to have) heard in her earlier utterances. The claim for an epiphanic bolt of lightning, in other words, is *retrospective* and can therefore appear to us as self-serving.

Consider the following: Wagner continued to laud Schröder-Devrient's stage talents for a suspiciously long time (given his mutable aesthetic priorities since Magdeburg and her vocal decline from *ca.* 1840 onward), right up to 1872 in fact, when he dedicated the essay "Über Schauspieler und Sänger" to her memory, thereby associating her *imago* with the moral authority of his call for theatrical reform. By this stage, twelve years had passed since her death on January 26, 1860, allowing Wagner to preserve the pure memory because there was nothing to disturb it.[47] Under these circumstances, Wagner could safely make his most decisive claim: "she had the gift of teaching a composer how to compose."[48] The sincerity we ascribe to this and similar retrospective comments must remain an open question. By contrast, the effect of Liszt's longevity on his once-white-hot relationship

---

[46] ML 285.

[47] The scandal of her three husbands, double bankruptcy, staunch liberalism, and brief imprisonment had faded, while her apocryphal pornographic memoirs were so salacious that the question of their authenticity was simply not taken seriously, however much they fascinated readers. Anon., *Aus den Memoiren einer Saengerin* (Altona: n.p., 1862).

[48] SSD 11: 221. Cf. PW 5: 219.

with Wagner was quite different because Liszt subsisted and continued to compose new music, becoming "just like King Lear, his acquaintances the one hundred knights, and his arrangements the Learisms,"[49] whose latest works amounted to "budding insanity."[50] Not coincidentally, Wagner's sustained estimation of "this wonderful woman"[51] parallels his admiration for Bellini (post-1834), as mentioned in Chapter 3: both were lifelong and, despite some occasional harsh words about Bellini, both remained unqualified to the extent they were self-serving.[52] To my knowledge, there were no other living contemporary musicians – Liszt and Tichatschek included – about whom these conditions held true for Wagner.

The power of literary memory organizing Wagner's understanding of past performances plays into a trope of Romantic autobiography predicated on the concept of continual reassessment through the passage of time. Wordsworth opined that it is nearly impossible to extricate "the naked recollection of [past] time" from the incursions of "after-mediation,"[53] making it quite literally poetic, therefore, that Wagner's actual correspondence with Schröder-Devrient is lost. As Deathridge first pointed out, moreover, *Mein Leben* notoriously refers to a fictional performance by Schröder-Devrient of *Fidelio* in Leipzig during 1829.[54] It seems Wagner backdated his first real experience of her singing (from 1834 in Bellini's *I Capuleti e i Montecchi*), and switched the composer from an Italian fop to a Germanic titan, comparing the imaginary musical epiphany of a sixteen-year-old boy's understanding of Beethoven only to his later experience of the Ninth Symphony under François-Antoine Habeneck in Paris (*ca.* 1840), another event Deathridge has shown to be more wishful than real.[55] Rather than

---

[49] CT (November 29, 1883).   [50] CT (June 1, 1883).   [51] SSD 9: 219. Cf. PW 5: 218.

[52] Typically, even Wagner's harshest criticism of Bellini's music allows for its improvement through Schröder-Devrient's performance. See, for instance, his statement in 1871 that: "We only need recall the performance, surely unforgettable by many still alive, once given by Schröder-Devrient of 'Romeo' in Bellini's opera. Every fiber of the musician's being rebels against acknowledging any kind of artistic value in the poor, utterly threadbare music here hung upon an opera poem of grotesque barrenness; but ask anyone who saw it what impression he received from the 'Romeo' of Schröder-Devrient as compared with the Romeo of our very best actor in even the great Briton's piece?" SSD 9: 140. Cf. PW 5: 141.

[53] Wordsworth, "The Prelude," III 644–68. This work proved unfinishable; see particularly Susan Wolfson's argument for a decentered *Prelude* in a study of its dynamic, fragmentary status, in "Revision as Form: Wordsworth's Drowned Man," in *William Wordsworth's The Prelude*, ed. Stephen C. Gill (Oxford University Press, 2006), 73–122.

[54] See Deathridge, "Early Life" in *The New Grove: Wagner* (New York: Norton, 1984), 7.

[55] "[T]here is no evidence that Wagner heard Beethoven's Ninth when he said he did." Deathridge argues that it was most likely Berlioz's *Roméo et Juliette* overture that influenced Wagner's composition of the *Faust* overture, which Wagner wanted to posit as "a profoundly 'German' work." See *Ibid.*, 20. For Wagner's claims, see ML 174–75.

outright deceit, this properly accords with Wagner's tendency publicly to construct symbols of his life, a tendency characterized by the creative interplay of memory and imagination that uncovers and expands on the perceived significance of life events. In a discussion of "the crisis autobiography," M. H. Abrams captures this nexus of recollection and revisionism:

In such a recovery of former experience [the narrator / Wagner] not only has the power to live and enjoy the essence of things "entirely outside of time," but also to create a new world, an eternal world of art, out of the "resurrection" of his fugitive time-bound past. Only now is he able to recognize that an implicit design had been silently governing his seemingly haphazard and wasted past . . . art is "the genuine Last Judgment," for by extricating essence from time, it is able to recover the past in a new creation – an aesthetic world which is a regained paradise.[56]

Whether or not we ascribe agency to the "implicit design" governing Wagner's "seemingly haphazard" early development, this remains a retrospective "new creation," and the construct must remain a type of revisionism.

We have seen Wagner's fascination with manipulating the process of translating sound into sentient response, and the fact that Schröder-Devrient's importance to Wagner's "aesthetic world" therefore lies arguably outside the familiar twentieth-century readings of "the most powerful [artistic] impression he ever received."[57] Let us replace a hermeneutical question with a substantialist one, asking not what she "means," but what she "is" to Wagner's *Melodik*.

Expressing with "no 'voice'"

In the very essay Wagner dedicated to his *richtige Sängerin*, his irritation at suspicions about her innate vocal quality suggests a misalignment of perspective, which is to say, an inappropriate question:

Concerning this artist I have again and again been asked if her *voice* was really so remarkable, since we glorified her as a singer . . . It constantly annoyed me to answer this question, for I was incensed at the thought of the great tragedian being in a hierarchy with the female castrati of our opera. Were I asked again today, I should answer somewhat as follows: No! She had no "voice" at all; but she knew how to use her breath so beautifully, and to let a true womanly soul stream forth in such wondrous sounds, that we thought neither of voice nor of singing![58]

---

[56] M. H. Abrams, *Natural Supernaturalism: Tradition and Revolution in Romantic Literature* (New York: Norton, 1973), 81–82.
[57] Bekker, *Richard Wagner: His Life in his Works*, 80.   [58] SSD 9: 221. Cf. PW 5: 219.

By reluctantly disclosing a fissure between voice, singing, and breath, Wagner compensates by foregrounding the impression of her unified subjectivity on stage ("true womanly soul"), allowing breath, diction, and enunciation to paper over the absent qualities of cantabile song. But this is an unwilling exchange that plays on a somewhat fraught eighteenth-century cooperation between speaking and singing that continually called the unified subjectivity of a voice into question; like oil and water, *Atem* and *Gesang* were constituted and behaved similarly, yet they did not mix, except perhaps at very high temperatures.[59]

Descriptions of such unusual vocal expressivity play into a mid-nineteenth-century discourse of what the Dresden novelist and playwright Otto Ludwig termed "poetischer Realismus," whose combination of verisimilitude and idealized detailing of the real world can function for our purposes as a synonym for Schröder-Devrient's expressive utterances.[60] In his *Dramaturgische Aphorismen*, Ludwig defined this oxymoronic concept as a heightened or corrected vision of reality that would include the naturalist's objective reality and the idealist's ethical, morally ideal content; implicit in this was the *realist*, "concrete portrayal" of character, rather than "reflections on it," which entailed a "dramatic objectivity," in which – by extrapolating to the stage – inner feelings would be acted out through seemingly unfeigned gesture, utterance, and action. In principle, Ludwig explains, this entails a reconciliation of opposites: "Naturalists are more concerned with plurality; Idealists more with unity. These two directions are partial, *artistic realism* unifies them in one artistic center."[61] This reconciliation forms part of a shift in attitudes to literature, and

---

[59] Historically, even when reduced to a division between enunciating and intoning, the fissure was uncomfortable enough for Christoph Martin Wieland to renounce the possibility of overcoming the divide in *Singspiel*; instead he advocated simply the abandonment of speech. For Wieland, the problem of juxtaposing speech and singing was obsolete by 1775, and he advocated instead fully musical opera in German "because in *Singspiel* everything is music" ["weil im Singspiel *Alles* Musik ist"]. See Wieland, *Versuch über das teutsche Singspiel und einige darin einschlagende Gegenstände* (first published in: *Der Teutsche Merkur* 1775), in: Christoph Martin Wieland, *Sämtliche Werke*, 52 vols. (Leipzig: G. J. Göschen, 1824–28), 38: 126–53.

[60] The term "poetic realism" was itself first applied to literature in this sense by Per Daniel Amadeus Atterbom ("poetisk realist") in 1838; it entered the German discourse via Carl August Hagberg seven months later. For a detailed critique of the concept in the nineteenth century, including Ludwig's position in a canon of authors espousing the term (beginning with Friedrich Schlegel in 1802), see Roy C. Cowen, *Der Poetische Realismus: Kommentar zu einer Epoche* (Munich: Winkler, 1985). See also Clifford Bernd, "The Emergence of *Poetischer Realismus* as a term of Literary Criticism in German," in *Thematics Reconsidered*, ed. Frank Trommler (Amsterdam: Rodopi, 1995), 229–36.

[61] "Dem *Naturalisten* ist es mehr um die Mannigfaltigkeit zu thun, dem *Idealisten* mehr um die Einheit. Diese beiden Richtungen sind einseitig, der *künstlerische Realismus* vereinigt sie in einer künstlerischen Mitte." Otto Ludwig, *Gesammelte Schriften*, 6 vols. (Leipzig: Fr. Wilh. Grunow, 1891), 5: 458–62, here 459. For a study of Ludwig's novels and other writings from the 1830s–50s,

by extension, to acting. Wagner explicitly cited Schröder-Devrient's occasional switch between song and speech as a migration between the ideal and the real in this sense; the moment of changeover is then a "flash of lightning, a glimpse into the nature of both spheres at once ... Obviously, for an instant the ideal was unable to bear a certain load, and discharged it onto other."[62] In more measured tones, Laube observed that Schröder-Devrient "is not a singer who acts, but an actress who sings. We no longer detect the artificiality of opera."[63] With Ludwig, then, a circle of writers and dramatists in Dresden found a term for the heightened mimicry on stage of what was considered to be "real" life speech that gifted the accolade of dramatic "expressivity" to a voice that was neither beautiful nor inherently musical. (Of course, terms such as "real" and "expressive" are to some extent floating signifiers with no objective status in the discourse of dramatic theater, but the positively conceived dyad "real–expressive" remains broadly defined in opposition to "ideal–representational" in Ludwig's aphorisms.) But from a listener's perspective, the realist voice – as a lone aural medium – also *created* (rather than reflected or expressed) a reality for its auditors. As Gary Tomlinson points out, "voice" connects its bearers and hearers "to ordinarily supersensible realities"[64] and, phenomenologically speaking, in spoken theater it effectively constitutes the perceptible reality it is supposed to express. In this realist portrayal of character, then, an uncertainty remains over artistic origins: if the speaking, declamatory voice of poetic realism constitutes the very "reality" it purports to express, it simultaneously negates the poetic origin of that expression, leaving a void at its center that could never be filled, only concealed. This, however, is nothing but a sonorous excess, in which the sensuality of vocal sound itself becomes the medium of the poetic realist.[65]

Spearheading the impetus toward realist acting in Dresden was Bogumil Dawison (1818–72),[66] a Polish-born German character actor, championed by Laube in Vienna, and whom the contemporary commentator Robert

---

see William McClaine, *Between Real and Ideal: the Course of Otto Ludwig's Development as a Narrative Writer* (Chapel Hill: University North Carolina Press, 1963).

[62] SSD 9: 152. Cf. PW 5: 152,

[63] "Sie ist nicht eine Sängerin, welche spielt – sie ist eine Schauspielerin, die singt ... Man kann die Unnatur einer Oper nicht mehr erkennen." Laube, "Wilhelmine Schröder-Devrient," *Zeitung für die Elegante Welt* 6 (1833), 23.

[64] Gary Tomlinson, *Metaphysical Song: An Essay on Opera* (Princeton University Press, 1999), 4.

[65] Of course, the historical opposition to poetic realism on stage was embodied in the socially and politically idealized *Tendenzdramen* (topical, often explicitly political plays), for which the stage functioned only as a means, and whose crafted "messages" reinforced a link between what was commonly understood to be falsified life and art.

[66] A brief biographical entry by Josef Kürschner for Dawison can be found in the *Allgemeine deutsche Biographie*, 56 vols. (Leipzig: Duncker & Humblot, 1875–1912) 4: 787–89. The most

Prölss credited as bringing a "new manner of acting" to the Dresden stage, one that contrasted with the outgoing producer and actor, Eduard Devrient (Wilhelmine's brother-in-law):

Dresden had not seen such daring of actor's intuition for a long time, perhaps never before . . . [Dawison's] face was not pretty, not even noble, his frame, his walk hardly raised him above the norm – but what was he not able to do with these materials through the wealth of his creative power of embodiment![67]

Descriptions of how exactly Dawison spoke or declaimed the *Trauerspiele* of Tieck, Shakespeare or Ludwig parallel Wagner's descriptions about Schröder-Devrient using her "breath so beautifully," underscoring the shared critical goal of excising artificiality from a self-identifying "German" stage. Like the dramatic soprano, Dawison – the dramatic actor – apparently lacked an innately sonorous voice ("when passionate, his tone was very powerful and dreadfully energetic, though far more sharp and cutting than round and full"),[68] but this only emphasized its function as a signifier of dramaturgical expressivity:

His speech was not completely free from foreign Slavic echoes; at first there was hardly anything appealing about the tone of his voice, but what riches of color he was able to display, how compellingly he harnessed this, enrapturing through the magic, through the energy, through the dialectical power of eloquence and of dramatic expression! . . . This was so different from that which one previously regarded as beautiful and great that one had to throw out the question in astonishment: which of the two is now correct?[69]

Leaving aside the concept of "correct" declamation for the moment, the paradox of singing with "no 'voice'" became quite literal for Schröder-Devrient

extensive study is Peter Kollek, *Bogumil Dawison: Porträt und Deutung eines genialen Schauspielers* (Kastellaun: A. Henn, 1978).

[67] "Seit lange nicht, vielleicht selbst noch nie hatte Dresden einen Darsteller von dieser Kühnheit der schauspielerischen Intuition . . . Sein Gesicht war nicht schön, ja nicht einmal edel, seine Gestalt, sein Gang hoben ihn für gewöhnlich kaum über das Gewöhnliche hinaus – allein was vermochte er in der Fülle seiner Gestaltungskraft aus diesem wiederstrebenden Material nicht zu machen!" Prölss, *Geschichte des Hoftheaters zu Dresden von seinem Anfängen bis zum Jahren 1862* (Dresden: Wilhelm Baensch, 1878), 565.

[68] "in der Leidenschaft [war sein Ton] zwar von großer Kraft und furchtbarer Energie, aber viel mehr scharf und schneidend, als rund und voll." An anonymous review cited in Kollek, *Bogumil Dawison*, 154.

[69] "Seine Sprache war nicht ganz frei von fremden, slavischen Anklängen, der Ton seiner Stimme hatte zunächst kaum etwas Anziehendes, aber welchen Reichtum der Farbe vermochte er darin zu entfalten, wie unwiderstehlich durch den Zauber, durch die Energie, durch die dialektische Kraft der Beredtsamkeit und des dramatischen Ausdrucks zu fesseln und hinzureissen! . . . das Alles war so verschieden von dem, was man bisher für schön und gross hier gehalten hatte, dass man erstaunt die Frage aufwerfen musste, welches von beiden nun wohl das Richtige sei?" Prölss, *Geschichte des Hoftheaters zu Dresden*, 566.

shortly before she died. After the end of her public career in 1847 she returned to the stage in autumn 1858 to sing Schubert's "Der Wanderer." Listening to this, the dramatist and biographer Claire von Glümer reported being "deeply shocked" by the experience because Schröder-Devrient "cannot sing anymore! . . . the sound was faint, with no body, no metal." Crucially (and like descriptions of Dawison), this appeared not to affect her capacity to express, and Glümer proceeds to draw an obvious though counterintuitive conclusion that corroborates Wagner's own judgment: "even without a voice, she would have remained the greatest singer."[70]

Henry Chorley's remarks about her emotive performance of *Fidelio* in London during 1833 locate her reception firmly within the category Ludwig would call poetic realism: "It was impossible to hear the 'Prisoners' Chorus' . . . to *see* the eager woman as she unclosed cell after cell . . . questioning face after face, all in vain, without tears."[71] In separating the ocular and aural, the Englishman mobilizes a tension between acting and singing, judging each aspect independently in a dislocation that contravened Wagner's "eye and ear of hearing" and would antagonize his stance in 1872. Yet it was a resolute dislocation; Beethoven's very deafness offered a site for Romantic authors to write the division of seeing and hearing *into* the composer's response to Schröder-Devrient's Leonore, constructing an idealist melodic synesthesia in their assessments: "[Beethoven] *saw* his Fidelio before him as he had pictured to himself in his melody-filled dreams."[72]

The cold reality, however, was that listening to Schröder-Devrient was very different to seeing her, as Chorley explains:

Such training as had been given to [her voice] belonged to that false school which admits of such a barbarism as the defence and admiration of "nature-singing." . . . A more absurd phrase was never coined by ignorance conceiving itself sagacity . . . [A] woman, supposing she can correctly flounder through the notes of a given composition, has been allowed, too contemptuously, to take rank as a singer. Such a

---

[70] Glümer's full statement reads: "Sie kann nicht mehr singen! Dachte ich – der Ton war matt, ohne Fülle, ohne Metall – aber . . . hatte sie gesiegt . . . so darf von *Wilhelmine Schröder-Devrient* behauptet werden, daß sie auch ohne Stimme die größte Sängerin geblieben wäre." Glümer, *Erinnerungen an Wilhelmine Schröder-Devrient*, 2.

[71] Chorley, *Thirty Years' Musical Recollections*, 39. Elsewhere, Chorley corroborates Wagner's reluctant disclosure about Schröder-Devrient, placing emphasis on her ability to convey pathos, not through "*canto*," but through *parlando* enunciation, crafted gestures, and intensity of physical expression. His animated descriptions are often explicitly visual. For intensity of physical expression, he records, Schröder-Devrient drew on her "superb figure," and "profuse fair hair" which – the critic indulges – in moments of heightened emotion she would "fling loose with the wild vehemence of a Moenad." *Ibid.*

[72] Karoline Bauer, *Memoirs of Karoline Bauer*, 4 vols. (London: Remington & Co.: 1885), 4: 104.

woman was not [Henriette] Sontag – neither, of later days, [Jenny] Lind. The two had learned to sing; Madame Schröder-Devrient *not*. Her tones were delivered without any care, save to give them due force. Her execution was bad and heavy. There was an air of strain and spasm throughout her performances, of that struggle for victory which never conquers.[73]

Over and above the rhetorical excess of Chorley's polemic, later biographers indicate that Schröder-Devrient was well aware of her vocal deficiency and considered it a problem. Writing in 1904, Hagemann explains that whenever she returned to Dresden from guest appearances elsewhere and tours, she continued to take lessons from Johann Aloys Miksch, the choral director; and that, where possible, she tried to meet visiting Italian colleagues to "learn what she herself was lacking."[74]

In 1853, Friedrich Wieck similarly describes Schröder-Devrient's diligent attitude to study, as well as ascribing to her the great singer cliché of tracing a lineage back to the castrati:

She was not at all surprised when [J. A.] Miksch called her attention to this deficiency [in German vocal education]. She devoted herself thoroughly to the primary formation of the tone under the instruction of Miksch, and must still remember the old master, and his extraordinary practice in this particular. Miksch learned it from [Vincenzo] Caselli, a pupil of [Antonio] Bernacchi."[75]

But several of Schröder-Devrient's surviving part books reveal the extent of her technical shortcomings; most of the more florid, vocally challenging passages were simplified or eliminated altogether.[76] This formed the very antithesis of popular expectations regarding Italian prima donnas. Then again, it is precisely coloratura passages wherein *logos* is notoriously absent from singing, for they offer no opportunity for melody conceived as a heightened delivery of speech. Irrespective of whether the simplified music in fact reflected Schröder-Devrient's modest technique, it projected her theatrical orientation. Despite this, even comparisons with native

[73] Chorley, *Thirty Years' Musical Recollections*, 39.

[74] "Sie nahm jedesmal, wenn sie von ihren Gastspielen nach Dresden zurückkehrte, wiederum Uebungsstuden bei dem altbewährten Chordirektor Miksch ... Auch hat sie sich später beim Zusammentreffen mit bemüht, ihren Kollegen und Kolleginnen von der italienischen Oper das nach Möglichkeit abzulernen, was ihr selbst fehlte." Hagemann, *Wilhelmine Schröder-Devrient*, 28.

[75] "[Wilhelmine Schröder-Devrient] wunderte sich nicht wenig, als Miksch sie auf diesen Mangel aufmerksam machte. Sie machte darauf bei Miksch diese *erste Tonbildung* durch und wird sich noch wohl des alten Meisters erinnern und seiner außerordentlichen Praxis darin. Miksch lernte es von Caselli, dem Schüler Bernacchi's." Friedrich Wieck, *Klavier und Gesang: Didaktisches und Polemisches*, 3rd edn. (Leipzig: F. E. C. Leuckart, 1878), 76.

[76] One example, cited in Meyer, of the simplification of coloratura would be the Dresden parts for *La Juive*, Sächsische Landesbibliothek Mus. 4895-F-504A.

sopranos were unflattering; in her memoirs of the German stage, the Biedermeier singer and actress Karoline Bauer recalls that Schröder-Devrient was "far-surpassed by [Nannette] Schachner in the rich metallic ring of her wonderful voice, and by the perfect technique of [Henriette] Sontag's singing."[77] And, as Meyer observes, later in her career, many arias also had to be transposed down to accommodate her ailing ability.[78] If Wagner took Schröder-Devrient as a vocal-melodic idol, it seems he chose a singer whose stage talents extended to everything but *Gesang* and *bel canto*, leading to a farcical situation in which critical orthodoxy pointed to a composer who could not write "melodies," composing for a singer with "no voice." For present purposes, the key question is why Schröder-Devrient's weakness as a singer should make her attractive for, and amenable to, appropriation as "German opera". What was it that defined her vocally ambivalent status?

The answer concerns different ways of hearing texted opera. A vigorous or exaggerated utterance conveys a non-verbal meaning whether or not we grasp its verbal content. This might be the case when listening to quick-fire recitative in a foreign language, or if the text becomes obscured in arioso passages by melodic elongation that causes verbal fragmentation. In this sense, Mladan Dolar is right that "singing is bad communication. It prevents a clear understanding of the text."[79] Most of Schröder-Devrient's perform-ances were in German, either as translations of foreign librettos or as German originals, but the special character of her delivery appeared to transcend the need for verbal comprehension, making the language less important than the manner of its performance, far more so, at least, than was customary in opera. While even her first critic had recorded her "pure and simple"[80] elocution as a fifteen-year-old actress, the Parisian *Journal des débats* articulates something of her supralinguistic quality in a review of *Fidelio* from 1830, commenting that the soprano "occupied herself just as carefully with dialogue as with singing, and her pronunciation is so pure that its *magic* does not escape even for the people who only have a distant idea of German."[81]

---

[77] Bauer, *Memoirs*, 4: 93.   [78] Meyer, "*Das wilde Herz*," 24.

[79] Mladan Dolar, *A Voice and Nothing More* (Cambridge, MA: MIT Press, 2006), 20ff.

[80] Quoted in Bauer, *Memoirs*, 4: 101. This was partly a maternal gift, for her mother, Sophie Schröder, was an actress whose declamatory expression in tragedy lifted her to national fame. A sketch from 1845 describes her accordingly: "one of Germany's greatest tragic actresses, so far as declamation and expression are concerned." See "Wilhelmine Schröder-Devrient: A Sketch," *The United States Democratic Review* (March 1845), 262. Wagner himself also speaks briefly of "the genius of the great Sophie Schröder," SSD 9: 230. Cf. PW 5: 228.

[81] "sie beschäftigt sich ebenso sorgfältig mit dem Dialog als mit dem Gesang, und ihre Aussprache ist so rein, daß der Zauber derselben sogar denjenigen Personen, welche von dem Deutschen nur einen

What these critical responses to Schröder-Devrient are picking up on is the power of an *intent to communicate*, whether the language sung is known or unknown. The struggle to form words amid the athleticism of operatic singing is perceived as the flinty expression of will, and as such is allied to both the linguistic and the performative.

Linguistic: as Paul Robinson once pointed out, we won't tolerate hours of pure vocalise, but we do listen contentedly to hours of staged singing where the words are consistently obscured or unfamiliar to us, and we take something away from this experience because the very presence of words "identifies the singer as a human actor with specific feelings, giving voice to specific thoughts."[82] In other words, it matters that the intent to communicate is embedded within the linguistic phenomenon, even when we have no idea what is being communicated;

Performative: the very practice of "acting" and "expressing" – rather than just emitting sounds without engagement or emotion – indicates the performer's acknowledgement that there is an audience listening, and that his / her utterance is not solipsistic, not mere meaning in a vacuum.

On the basis of these tacit assumptions, then, what the *Journal des débats* called Schröder-Devrient's "magic" pronunciation encapsulates a consistent theme in her reception, and leads to a subdivision within the critically self-serving, symbolic usage made of her performance of vocal melody, one that hinges on the distinction between language and music, speech and song, and ultimately between semantics and sensation, which is to say between the nineteenth-century disciplines of *Philologie* and *Physiologie*. In this context, modes of hearing sung melody can be divided into at least two types.

(Philology) First, what I will term "expressive melody" is that which says what voices say with their words; it is a signified of melody conditioned by the assumption of an *a priori* poetic content, whether or not this exists as text. Imagine hearing text sung in your mother tongue where the remaining voice, as a kind of surplus by-product to the linguistic message, has no inherent significance, becoming at best a material texture recalcitrant to meaning, without analogical or symbolic relationship to its verbal platform. Based precisely on what *can* be said, expressive melody thus relies on the hermeneutic category of an embedded meaning. It is coded by language, not physical sensation. Given the embeddedness of this

---

ganz entfernten Begriff haben, nicht entgangen ist." From "Chronique musicale," in *Journal des débats* (May 8, 1830). Cited in Wolzogen, *Wilhelmine Schröder-Devrient*, 152. Emphasis added.

[82] Paul Robinson, *Opera, Sex, and Other Vital Matters* (University of Chicago Press, 2002), 50–51.

meaningful content, however, it requires an act of listening *for* on the part of the observer – wilfully or instinctively – and therefore is neither intuitively comprehensible (Wagner's *gefühlsverständlich*) nor embodied in the "cavities, the muscles, the membranes, the cartilages" of Barthes' vocal grain.[83] An illustrative example would be Telramund's breathless recitations in act 2 scene 1 of *Lohengrin* or Wotan's monologue in act 2, scene 2 of *Die Walküre*: exact pitches are not important here compared to relative intonation and closely determined rhythm; it is essentially melodramatic speech written as recitative, where any and all "melody" is in the service of expressing the sonorous word, rather than the body of vocal sound.

(Physiology) Second, what I term "iconic melody" means melody as sounding material that signifies nothing but the singing voice, where this is non-symbolic, non-expressive of any prior lexical substance. Imagine hearing an unfamiliar tune sung movingly in a language that shares no etymological roots with those familiar to you. The wordless, sometimes unnotated screams, shouts, laughter, and cries that pervade Wagner's oeuvre would fall into this latter category because they transcend text, but are not the exclusive constituents of the concept (Sieglinde's melismatic reaction to mention of her unborn son in *Die Walküre* – Wagner's "glorification of Brünnhilde" – would come close to iconic melody in the sense of a maternal *cri de coeur* whose meaning is precisely the passion of its delivery, wherein various factors conspire to obscure the text: "O hehrstes Wunder!").[84] Iconic melody connotes an infinitely self-referential vocal sound, it is melody *qua* melody, which is to say, an icon of itself: redolent of a pre-linguistic utterance, but formulated (ahistorically) as a logical short circuit that cancels distinctions between meaning and medium. Iconic melody places an emphasis on *hearing* texted melody as sheer vocal sonority rather than a constituent of some content that is only embodied by aural presence. Rather than an act of listening *for*, iconic melody requires an intuitive surrender *within* the

---

[83] Roland Barthes, "The Grain of the Voice," in *Image–Music–Text*, trans. Stephen Heath (New York: Hill & Wang, 1978), 181.

[84] There are three unnotated screams in *Lohengrin*, for example. Singers often omit these in performance due to a lack of definite notation, but they are nevertheless written into the stage directions of act 1, scene 3 "Hier hat Elsa sich ungewandt und schreit bei Lohengrin's Anblick laut auf," and act 3 during the wedding chamber scene "nach einem Schrei." At the close of the final act, Ortrud too "sinkt bei Gottfrieds Anblick mit einem Schrei zusammen." Furthermore, the nonsense cries of the Valkyries, as well as the shrieks and laughter of Kundry, are perhaps more familiar instances. The most direct study of this in English is Friedheim, "Wagner and the Aesthetics of the Scream," 63–70.

sonority, having already "sensualized away" the *a priori* of any semantic content.

In keeping with Wagner's "understanding ear," this distinction between expressive and iconic melody is explicitly listener-oriented and defines two ways of hearing mid-century opera rather than two discrete compositional categories. (Such ways of hearing are not mutually exclusive, of course, while, equally, the same vocal-melodic event could be heard in different categories by different people.) To an extent, the contemporary rationale for such a division had been summarized decades earlier in Wilhelm von Humboldt's celebrated "dual nature" of language. This cleared the way for the concept of a sensuous vocal sound that could stimulate intuitive "thoughts" in auditors, thoughts which no verbal language would be able to stimulate. (Wagner's schema for communication in *Oper und Drama* ascribes this to humanity's "instinctive power of feeling" [*unwillkürliche Gefühlsvermögen*], as the faculty of "inner understanding" triggered by a build-up of sensory feeling within melodicized language.[85]) By recognizing coexisting sensual and semantic qualities in speech, Humboldt was led to acknowledge a mutually reversible relation between thought and sound. Though for him, the capacity for logical thought in any given nation resulted primarily from a symbiotic development of the particular grammatical structure of its language and an essential nature, sound itself also influenced thought, he claimed: "the delicate alertness which lets tuning through sound give thought a multiplicity of forms ... the mind alone, coming from above, would never have been able to produce through any process of logical distinction."[86] The complementarities of each side of this "dual nature" lend weight to iconic listening and Wagner's implicit belief in a unified mode of verbal–vocal-melodic expression, considerably reducing the erstwhile gap between his philology and Schröder-Devrient's reception. Humboldt articulates the theory most clearly:

language forms concepts, introduces the rule of thought into life, and achieves this through sound. The mental stimulus it brings about can lead to the position where, responding primarily to thought, one attempts to grasp this equally by some other, more direct means, either more sensuously, or more purely, more independently of what may appear *arbitrary sound*; in such a case the word will be treated only as an auxiliary device. But, on the other hand, it is precisely thought, clothed in sounds,

---

[85]   SSD 4: 143. Cf. PW 2: 246–47.
[86]   Wilhelm von Humboldt, *Essays on Language*, trans. John Wieczorek and Ian Roe, ed. T. Harden and D. Farrelly (Frankfurt am Main and New York: P. Lang, 1997), 80.

which can have the greatest effect on the mind, and precisely sound, formed into a word, which can *fill with inspiration*.[87]

The slippage between "what may appear arbitrary sound" and that which can "fill with inspiration" is synonymous with Wagner's belief in the aboriginal communicative agency of Old High German root syllables that needed to be reawakened through the sensual sounding of language: a particular word may have conceptual content, but is "forced upon [the poet] by his feeling," and within this chosen word, Wagner posits a "constraining force in the root," where he locates its "original truth." Thus Wagner reverses the direction of Humboldt's thesis – i.e. from sonic sensations to intuitive concept – arguing that understanding dramatic expression begins with the "sensuous substance of our *roots of speech*" which in turn rises to an older, purified, conscious idea, or "original truth."[88]

Before interrogating any such propositions in detail (a project reserved for Chapter 5), suffice to say the claim I am making is not that Wagner mimicked or codified an extant practice that he observed through Schröder-Devrient's performances, but that she became for him the embodiment of a successful concept of intuitively comprehensible German melodic sound that subsumed both French and Italian (particularly Bellini's) traditions by performing their vocal lines in her unique manner. She was not, in other words, the origin of Wagner's specific desire to bridge what he termed *Wortsprache* and *Tonsprache* as Avenarius' second-hand anecdote purports, rather her very existence demonstrated that the performance of "Germanicized" melodic expression was independent of other national models. Her innate incapacity for *bel canto* foregrounded the perception of her complementary ability for "truthful" dramatic expression *qua* German by an international cast of critics, reinscribing a dialectical model of operatic singing between artful tone and truthful declamation that effectively denied "melody" in the strong sense to German self-identity.[89]

---

[87] *Ibid.*, 79. Emphasis added.   [88] SSD 4: 127, 129. Cf. PW 2: 266, 264.

[89] A French critic reviewing *Norma* from 1836 put the condition politely: "she does not sing as other artists sing . . . she sings more with the soul than with the voice, her tones come more from the heart than from the throat, she forgets the public, she forgets herself, and enters completely into the character that she portrays." ["Sie singt nicht, wie andere Künstler singen . . . Sie singt mit der Seele noch mehr als mit der Stimme; ihre Töne entquellen mehr dem Herzen als der Kehle; sie vergißt das Publikum, sie vergißt sich selbst, um ganz in dem Wesen aufzugehen, das sie darstellt."] Cited in Wolzogen, *Wilhelmine Schröder-Devrient*, 148. Karoline Bauer made an identical observation in her memoirs using a comparison with Sontag and Schechner: "Both these highly famous songstresses sang, it is undoubted, with their brilliant throats – Wilhelmine Schröder-Devrient sang with her burning soul." And Hagemann parroted essentially the same

It is worth bearing in mind that in any act of listening – whether iconic or expressive – Wagner insists on the importance of cognizing a poetic idea. In 1852 he likened listening to pure "speech sound" (*Sprachklang*) in a language that neither the reciter nor the listener understands to modern conductors who comprehend only the letter of a Beethoven score and miss its "poetic content." In their anti-rational isolation, purely sensuous phonemes voided of their historical etymological basis remained uncommunicative – incomprehensible, as Wagner opined to Theodor Uhlig.[90] An anecdote about Wagner's own, decidedly informed reading of *Die Walküre* a year later suggests that it was a combination of non-verbal expression and half-intuited speech sounds that enabled the kind of iconic listening described above. Marie zu Hohenlohe (the daughter of Liszt's long-term partner, Carolyn zu Sayn-Wittgenstein) recalls: "I was only sixteen and *understood little* ... but Wagner's vibrant voice affected me deeply, and I gained an inkling of [the work's] underlying poetry ... [W]hen he finished reading ... I was barely able to suppress my tears."[91] Here, Wagner's vocal pathos is explicitly non-verbal. In latching onto the emotion of the occasion rather than the verbal message, Marie's response suggests the extent to which (Wagner's) inflected vocal sonorities could elicit powerful emotional reactions by opening up what we might call a pre-semantic channel of communication.

This is why Schröder-Devrient's status is significant for Wagner. She was widely celebrated as "expressing" poetic content through her melody even if her audience did not actually understand the words; her reception also suggests that she was heard as an iconic voice whether in French, Italian, English, or German. That is, she bridged the gap between these categories by potentially rendering expressive melody iconic in any language – sensualizing the linguistic component into an alternative medium – which is to say, she allowed semantic expression and plastic melody to blend within the moment of an unconventional vocal utterance which listeners heard as

idea when summing up Schröder-Devrient's ideological reception for German drama in 1904: "For her there was always only one question, and that is: what is truth? What is truth for the interpretation of just this artistically conceived character?" See Bauer, *Memoirs*, 4: 93; and Hagemann, *Wilhelmine Schröder-Devrient*, 10.

[90] "Man urtheile nun, wie das Verständniß eines Dichters ausfallen müßte, wenn vom Deklamirenden, wie vom Zuhörer, nur der Sprachklang wiedergegeben und vorgenommen würde, wie dieß gar nicht anders der Fall sein könnte, wenn das Gedicht in einer Sprache zum Vorschein käme, die weder der Deklamator (der sie eben nur dem Klange nach auswendig gelernt hätte) noch der Zuhörer verstünden." Wagner to Theodor Uhlig, February 15, 1852, Zurich, SB 4: 286.

[91] Marie Fürstin zu Hohenlohe, *Erinnerungen an Richard Wagner* (Weimar: Herm. Böhlaus Nachf., 1938), 13–14; cited in Spencer, *Wagner Remembered*, 79–80. Emphasis added.

sheer sonority (her "magic" locution). Ironically, therefore, for listeners in the iconic mode, her half-spoken, half-voiced, dramatized sounds came to define melody in its German aspirations for true expression.

But what did it sound like? Less than a year after Schröder-Devrient's singing persuaded Wagner – as he explains – of Bellini's melodic value, Julius Epstein gave a revealingly detailed account of her singing in the *Breslauer Zeitung*:

She regarded singing as nothing but a translation of speech into a higher language and modulated the sound to the freest echo of her feeling. While other, even the most famous, prima donnas understand no nuance other than singing now with full voice, now with half, our artist decided on the momentary emotion of every content, the qualitative volume of tones. So she gained a true *speaking* expression, quite apart from the content of the words; so they became an interpreter of her soul; a single accent often painted an entire order of feelings. Her performance won therewith such a manifold color and gradation, such a soulful inwardness, such a magical intensity of expression that one did not miss the metal timbre of the voice at all.[92]

Such rhetoric essentially came to define Schröder-Devrient as German in a debate between German and Italian style. While Epstein ostensibly credits Schröder-Devrient with epitomizing an expressive–iconic merger ("a translation of speech into a higher language"), his description indicates that, even for Germans, her vocal lines were heard as intuitively comprehensible ("true *speaking* expression, *quite apart from the content of the words*"). What he venerates as the "magical intensity of [her] expression" and what the *Journal des débats* in 1830 called the "magic" of her pure pronunciation, could surely refer only to its meaning *beyond* language. The key point is that, in contrast to *gesangvoll* performances of untranslated foreign opera in Germany which might comfortably be more iconic (in German singers) or more expressive (in native voices), blending iconic and expressive melody became associated above all with German sounds for an international audience, and by extension (for Wagner), with German melody.

---

[92] "Sie betrachtete den Gesang nur wie eine Übersetzung der Rede in eine höhere Sprache und modulierte den Ton zum freiesten Widerhall ihres Gefühls. Während andere, selbst hochberühmte Sängerinnen keine andere Nuancirung verstehen, als daß sie bald mit ganzer, bald mit halber Stimme singen, bestimmte bei unserer Künstlerin die momentane Empfindung den jedesmaligen Gehalt, das qualitative Volumen des Tons. So gewann derselbe einen wahrhaft *sprechenden* Ausdruck, ganz abgesehen vom Inhalt der Worte; so ward er zum Dolmetscher ihrer Seele; so oft ein einzelner Accent eine ganze Reihenfolge von Gefühlen. Dadurch gewann ihr Vortrag eine so mannigfaltige Färbung und Abstufung, eine so seelenhafte Innigkeit, eine so bezaubernde Intensität des Ausdrucks, daß man den Metallklang der Stimme gar nicht vermißte." Julius Epstein, *Breslauer Zeitung* 122 (1835). Quoted in Wolzogen, *Wilhelmine Schröder-Devrient*, 114.

Though there is less evidence than one might expect to suggest that Schröder-Devrient's manner of enunciating was identified openly with being German, Friedrich Tietz spoke of the "strangely emotional effect" that her "truly German singing style"[93] created in Weigl's *Schweizerfamilie*, indicating that this was variously cast at least in opposition to extant Italian traditions. Reports suggest that Schröder-Devrient was decidedly patriotic in this respect,[94] and she became acutely aware of her own national associations, confessing that her artistic standing was indivisible from her ambassadorial role for nothing less than German opera itself. "I had not only my own reputation," she recalls of her Paris debut, "I had to represent *German music*; if this artist failed to please, then Mozart, Beethoven, Weber had to suffer."[95] The sentiment was beyond modesty; other German sopranos such as Henriette Sontag and Nannette Schechner rivalled her in this capacity, but it was the particular link of declamatory enunciation with realist acting, resulting in a merger of expressive and iconic melody, that cemented Schröder-Devrient's association with "truthful" expression, which in a liberal *Vormärz* context, as mentioned above, translated with increasing clarity into "German" melodic expression.[96]

---

[93] Quoted in Bauer, *Memoirs*, 4: 109.

[94] Evidence suggesting that the simmering national tensions in Wagner's Dresden opera were personal exists principally at the level of anecdote. Glümer records that Kapellmeister Francesco Morlacchi became angry with the chorus: "The passage was bad"; he shouted, "the chorus sang like pigs, like German pigs!" Most onlookers were terrified, Glümer continues: "Only *Wilhelmine Schröder-Devrient* stepped forward with blazing eyes from the background. 'If you speak but once of pigs,' she cried, 'I will only say to you that you can sing your Italian pig-music yourself!' With that she threw her score at the Kapellmeister, turned her back on him and went home," in Glümer, *Erinnerungen an Wilhelmine Schröder-Devrient*, 120–21.

 Whether or not this diva fit actually happened as Glümer reports, its circulation is indicative of German sensitivities to the perception of Italian operatic hegemony, an inequality traceable particularly through attitudes towards language and pay. See Meyer, *Carl Maria von Weber and the Search for a German Opera* (Bloomington and Indianapolis: Indiana University Press, 2003), 25ff.

[95] "Ich [Schröder-Devrient] hatte nicht allein meinen eigenen Ruf, ich hatte die *deutsche Musik* zu vertreten; wenn die Künstlerin nicht gefiel, so mußte Mozart, Beethoven, Weber darunter leiden." Quoted in Wolzogen, *Wilhelmine Schröder-Devrient*, 145. That Schröder-Devrient was aware of her own continued patriotism is evident in a letter she wrote to an anonymous benefactor from Berlin who sent her a sum of money in 1848 after her divorce proceedings with her second husband (von Döring) left her almost bankrupt: "You are the only person who, in our great German fatherland, has thought that a German artist could be in need. Certainly you are a great exception, for I have not yet experienced that Germans consider it a national matter not to allow their native artists to sink, an example often given to us by other countries, but which has found no imitation in Germany." Cited in Glümer, *Erinnerungen an Wilhelmine Schröder-Devrient*, 194.

[96] Chorley reports unabashedly that "Madame Schröder-Devrient resolved to be *par excellence* 'the German dramatic singer,'" and as the unofficial creator of Leonore (*Fidelio*), and an

Critics such as Wolzogen did not associate Wagner and the concepts of *Worttonsprache* or *Versmelodie* with Schröder-Devrient's declamatory vocal manner because they remained unappealing to writers versed in French and Italian melodic idioms: "Of course, we absolutely cannot think of Wagner here," he cautions backhandedly, "for what little there is to *sing* in his music ... is not clear to us."[97] But over and above the debates about Wagner's tuneless melodies, the vocabulary of criticism surrounding Schröder-Devrient nevertheless bears a striking resemblance to that of Wagner's description of his ideal *Melodik* in parts 2 and 3 of *Oper und Drama*. The Parisian *Feuilleton* reviewed her performance of *Fidelio* stating – in Wolzogen's translation – that her "dramatic action harmonizes so well with her *Wortsprache* and *Tonsprache*,"[98] while Wagner theorizes (apparently in the abstract) that "*Tonsprache* is the beginning and end of *Wortsprache*,"[99] later emphasizing implicitly what Schröder-Devrient embodies, namely "the endless capacity for enhancement through interaction between the inner expression of the voice and the outer expression of gestures."[100] While Wagner's point of contrast – pure voice with no accompanying gestures – is a woodland bird rather than a virtuosic Italian soprano,[101] his description of *Tonsprache* as "the most spontaneous expression of inner feeling"[102] closely echoes the many accounts of Schröder-Devrient singing "more from the soul than from the throat." With such a close mapping at hand, there is good reason to pursue Wagner's actual melodic composition during the later 1840s in light of descriptions surrounding Schröder-Devrient's iconic–expressive vocal manner. In particular, his tendency in *Lohengrin*, written between August 3, 1845 and April 28, 1848, toward recitational melody over static accompaniment, sits well with descriptions of a performance aesthetic in which "a single accent often painted an entire order of feelings." The notation of such "melodies" would seem to provide a musical setting that allowed for those very half-enunciated emotional utterances that characterized Schröder-Devrient's aptitudes.

internationally successful exponent of Agathe (*Freischütz*), Euryanthe (*Euryanthe*), Rezia (*Oberon*), Emmeline (*Schweizerfamilie*), Emmy (*Vampyr*), Rebecca (*Templer*), Pamina (*Zauberflöte*), among others, she had good reason to consider herself the *de facto* voice of German opera. See Chorley, *Modern German Music*, 1: 342.

[97] "an Wagner ist natürlich hier gar nicht zu denken, denn was an seiner Musik überhaupt zu *singen* sei, es wäre denn der 'Holde Abendstern' und der 'Liebe Schwan,' will uns bis auf den heutigen Tag nicht recht einleuchten." Wolzogen, *Wilhelmine Schröder-Devrient*, 151 (fn).

[98] "Die dramatische Action der Madame Devrient harmonirt so gut mit ihrer Wort- und Tonsprache," in *Le Feuilleton de Paris: journal de littérature amusante* (May 10, 1830). Cited in Wolzogen, *Wilhelmine Schröder-Devrient*, 156.

[99] SSD 4: 91. Cf. PW 2: 224.   [100] SSD 4: 92. Cf. PW 2: 225

[101] See Wagner's footnote in *Ibid.*   [102] SSD 4: 91. Cf. PW 2: 224.

PART 2

The *Lohengrin* recitatives

The final role that Wagner composed with the expectation that Schröder-Devrient would create it was Elsa.[103] *Lohengrin* had been advertised in January 1849 as a coming "brilliant production" in Dresden, but Wagner's participation in the May uprising and his rapid escape to Switzerland put paid to that.[104] If he composed the work with her expressive caliber in mind, what exactly in *Lohengrin* relates to the nexus of breath, utterance, and *Gesang* that characterized Schröder-Devrient's international reception?

Most revealing are Wagner's suppositions about what went wrong at the eventual premiere under Liszt in Weimar on August 28, 1850. Though absent from the performance, he initially received an unfavorable report from Baron von Zigesar (Intendant at Weimar's Hoftheater) about its length and execution on a small stage and with an undermanned chorus: slow, meandering, inarticulate singing – particularly from the tenor (and former pastry chef) Carl Beck who created the title role – was the principal reason, he surmised, for the performance lasting about seventy-five minutes longer than anticipated.[105] In tandem with Franz Dingelstedt's uncomprehending review in the *Augsburger Allgemeine Zeitung*,[106] this persuaded him that the first performance had bored the audience, had been theatrically weak, and must have lacked adequate declamation without Schröder-Devrient or the "peculiarly sharp 'speaking' tone" of Tichatschek.[107] He responded frantically to Zigesar:

---

[103] Richard Pohl corroborates this in a review article from 1873 of a performance of *Lohengrin* in Mannheim, stating: "[*Lohengrin*] kam in Dresden, wo doch *Rienzi, Holländer* und *Tannhäuser* unter des Meisters eigner Leitung zuerst zur Aufführung gelangt waren, in Dresden, für dessen damals eminente Opernkräfte (Schröder-Devrient, Johanna Wagner, Tichatschek und Mitterwurzer) *Lohengrin* zunächst gedacht und bestimmt war . . ." See Pohl, "*Lohengrin* in Mannheim," in *Richard Wagner: Studien und Kritiken* (Leipzig: Bernhard Schlicke, 1883), 69–70. Johanna Wagner sang Ortrud in the 1859 Berlin production of *Lohengrin*, indicating that this, not Elsa, was her intended role.

[104] "Nächstens soll hier Kapellmeister *Wagner's* Oper 'Lohengrin' mit brillanter Ausstattung in Scene gehen," *Kleine Musikzeitung* 10 (1849), 19. Cited in Helmut Kirchmeyer, *Situationsgeschichte der Musikkritik und des musikalischen Pressewesens in Deutschland: IV. Theil. Das zeitgenössische Wagner-Bild. Dritter Band: Dokumente 1846–1850* (Regensburg: Gustav Bosse, 1968), 3: 531.

[105] Wagner to Liszt, September 8, 1850; and to Zigesar, September 9, 1850, Zurich, SB 3: 384–401.

[106] Franz Dingelstedt, "Weimarischer Festkalender," *Augsburger Allgemeine Zeitung* 247 (September 4, 1850), 3947b–3949a; rpt. Kirchmeyer, *Situationsgeschichte der Musikkritik und des musikalischen Pressewesens in Deutschland. IV. Teil*, 3: 691–97.

[107] ML 368.

the actors remained far behind their task ... If in future the so-called recitatives are sung as I have asked Liszt to insist upon their being sung, the halting and freezing impression of whole, long passages will disappear, and the duration of the perform-ance will be considerably shortened ... I can imagine, for instance, that the speeches of the king and the herald may have made a fatiguing impression ... this was the case because the singers sang them in a limp, lazy manner, without real utterance ... Art and artists will be equally benefitted only if those singers are earnestly requested to perform those speeches with energy, fire, and determined expression.[108]

Wagner's choice of terms – "real utterance ... energy, fire, and determined expression" – could easily have been plucked from a review of Schröder-Devrient's Leonore or Agathe. The occasion lays bare Wagner's personal prejudices about German voices; the restrained fury of his letters after the premiere speaks from the perspective of a composer–listener *in absentia*, who theorizes the faults of execution through information gleaned from second-hand reports (Zigesar and Dingelstedt). The content of these revealing and understudied letters – later to be expanded upon in the final section of *Oper und Drama* – thus reflects more the composer's own presuppositions and imagi-nation than the reality of the Weimar premiere. (It was only after Karl Ritter arrived in Zurich with a rather different report on September 10 that Wagner conceded Liszt had in fact maintained tempo in the recitatives and sought to marshal the singers' delivery accordingly.[109]) As his later correspondence with Liszt shows, however, he remained uneasy about his "recitatives" in *Lohengrin*, which he feared would continue to be badly served by German singers. This anxiety, that German voices are inept on stage, is the central message that emerges from Wagner's response to *Lohengrin*'s premiere, making Schröder-Devrient all the more symbolic for his ambitions at this time.

Like A. B. Marx in 1826,[110] he had complained early on that Germans lacked a natural aptitude for declamation and dramatic song. They should train vocally, he had urged in 1837, to compensate for their congenital "deficiency" instead of blathering "so much muddle and vulgarity" about the aesthetics of singing.[111] At that time, Wagner was a young man infatuated with Schröder-Devrient's

---

[108] Wagner to Baron von Zigesar, September 9, 1850, Zurich, SB 3: 398–99.

[109] Wagner to Liszt, September 11, 1850, Zurich, SB 3: 401–03.

[110] Marx's treatise *Die Kunst des Gesanges* (Berlin: A. M. Schlesinger, 1826) was conceived as part of an attempt to raise the standard of German vocal music, both in composition and performance, and to respond – as the opening of the preface explains – to the perceived "end of a musical age in which Italian music preoccupies all countries, even Germany, and almost makes us forget what German art is, and what music is for Germans" (iv).

[111] SSD 12: 15.

stage talents;[112] but he would maintain essentially the same sentiment fourteen years later in his first communication after the premiere of *Lohengrin*. The following comment to Liszt is typical in laying the problem squarely at the doorstep of bad German translations grafted onto foreign melodies:

Owing to the deplorable fact that at our German theatres scarcely anything but operas translated from a foreign language are given, our dramatic singers have been most unspeakably demoralized. The translations of French and Italian operas are generally made by blunderers . . . The result has been in the course of time that singers have got into the habit of neglecting altogether the connection between word and tone, of pronouncing an unimportant syllable on an accented note of the melody, and of putting the important word to a weak part of the bar. In this way they gradually became accustomed to the most absolute nonsense to such an extent that it was often quite immaterial whether or not they pronounced at all. Recitative has fared worst.[113]

Native Italian and French speakers formed the antithesis of Wagner's complaint. Lacking real fluency in either French or Italian, he most likely heard those voices as more iconic but perceived them as expressive in their semantic vigor, emphasizing what the Weimar premiere of *Lohengrin* lacked: "the distinctness and energy wherewith [Italian and French singers] speak out their words . . . especially in the drastic phrases of the recitative."[114] Wagner unabashedly idealized such foreign voices by virtue of their birth ("a natural instinct prevents them from ever disfiguring the spoken sense through false delivery"),[115] bringing into sharp focus the congenital void he was attempting to fill. By the 1840s, the specter of poor translation and correspondingly inept performance preoccupied Wagner throughout the early stages of *Lohengrin*, so how exactly did he imagine such foreign "energy, fire, and determined expression" could be written into a *German* score? For present purposes, pursuing this outside of Wagner's original composition may be most revealing.

Late in 1845, Wagner had to postpone his plan to arrange Gluck's *Iphigénie en Aulide* (1774) because of his "horror at the translation"[116] in his Berlin score (F. Brissler, 1839), which passed from "grossest offences against the sound" of the verse to a "complete distortion of its sense."[117] On December 15, Wagner

---

[112] Over and above vocal–theatrical talent, Laurence Dreyfus has interpreted Wagner's infatuation within the erotic sphere, arguing that it extended to Schröder-Devrient's "dominant femininity," where Wagner projects onto her an "erotic of his own passivity . . . to relinquish and submit to sexual control." See Dreyfus, *Wagner and the Erotic Impulse*, 60–61.

[113] Wagner to Liszt, September 8, 1850, Zurich, SB 3: 386–87. Wagner's caustic complaints about foreign translations and the negative effects this had on German singers occur throughout his early writings, and reach something of a climax in part 3 of *Oper und Drama*. See SSD 4: 212–13. Cf. PW 2: 359–60.

[114] SSD 4: 212. Cf. PW 2: 359.   [115] *Ibid.*   [116] ML 337.   [117] SSD 4: 213. Cf. PW 2: 360.

requested a French edition (unadorned by instrumental additions) from Gottfried Anders in Paris,[118] and duly revised the translation "to get the vocal stress right."[119] While he later explained in *Mein Leben* that his main aim was to shorten Gluck's opera and make it cohere, bringing it closer to Euripides' drama, Wagner's modifications to the text and rhythm reveal what exactly he means by "correct" declamation at the very time he was working on *Lohengrin* (the Gluck arrangement dragged on from December 1845 to at least January 1847).[120] Modifying recitative became something of a habit for Wagner at this time; he also reworked a German translation of *Don Giovanni* during 1850, adding his own recitative for Donna Anna and Don Ottavio as well as other "small things."[121] This arrangement was performed at the Aktientheater in Zurich on November 8, 1850, though details of Wagner's interventions are scarce: only two small manuscript fragments survive of this self-styled "patchwork [*Flickarbeit*]."[122]

Returning to Gluck's *Iphigénie*, Wagner's copy of the Berlin piano score contains his many handwritten alterations, inserts, and cuts, most of which were incorporated into the printed vocal score issued by Breitkopf in 1858.[123] Example 4.1 illustrates the changes that Wagner introduced to Gluck's translated recitative, where formerly "short syllables occurred on lengthy notes, with longer syllables on the shorter notes; on the musical 'ridge' there came the verse's 'hollow,' and vice versa."[124]

[118] Wagner to Gottfried Engelbert Anders, December 15, 1845, Dresden, SB 2: 467.

[119] ML 337.

[120] In the *Annalen* and in *Mein Leben*, Wagner indicates that the arrangement was completed by the end of 1846. The full *Orchesterskizze* for *Lohengrin*, however, bears the following text: "Nach 2 monatlicher Unterbrechung am 11. Februar 1847 hier fortgefahren," suggesting that it lasted into the beginning of 1847 (Musik III). Furthermore, a letter to Eduard Devrient on January 18, 1847 reveals that Wagner's reply to an invitation was delayed by "eine sehr dringende Arbeit" which most likely refers to his Gluck arrangement. See Wagner to Devrient, January 18, 1847, Dresden, in SB 2: 539. Further information on WWV 77 is given in John Deathridge, Martin Geck and Egon Voss (eds.), *Wagner-Werk-Verzeichnis: Verzeichnis der musikalischen Werke Richard Wagners und ihrer Quellen* (Mainz, New York: B. Schott's Söhne, 1986), 330–35.

[121] Wagner's fullest account of his arrangement of Mozart's score is given in a letter to Theodor Uhlig postmarked February 26, 1852, SB 4: 298.

[122] See Chris Walton, "'Flickarbeit' oder Bearbeitung? Ein neuer Wagner-Fund in der Zentralbibliothek Zürich," *Neue Zürcher Zeitung* (December 12, 1996), 70.

[123] Wagner owned a copy of the piano score by F. Brissler (Berlin), which he annotated extensively. This is now held at the National Archive in Bayreuth (B I i 2 b), while a printed piano score of Wagner's arrangement of the opera was published in 1858 by Breitkopf & Härtel. Its title page reads: "Iphigenia in Aulis / Oper in drei Akten / von / J. C. Von Gluck / Nach Richard Wagner's Bearbeitung / von Jahre 1847 / Klavierauszug / von / Hans von Bülow." The critical edition of Wagner's arrangement of Gluck's score (WWV 77), edited by Christa Jost, appeared as *Samtliche Werke 20, IV* in 2010.

[124] SSD 4: 213. Cf. PW 2: 360.

Example 4.1a Wagner's arrangement of Iphigénie's recitative "Vous essayez envain" compared with Friedrich Brissler's Berlin edition (1839); act 2, scene 1, *Iphigénie en Aulide*, transcribed from NA B I i 2 b, *Nationalarchiv der Richard-Wagner-Stiftung*, Bayreuth.

Example 4.1b Wagner's arrangement of Achilles' recitative "Mais vous qui m'avez fait" compared with Brissler's edition, act 2, scene 6, *Iphigénie en Aulide*, transcribed from NA B I i 2 b, *Nationalarchiv der Richard-Wagner-Stiftung*, Bayreuth.

(*RW*, 1858) (*F. Brissler*, 1839)

Three examples show Wagner's remedy: in Example 4.1a he follows Gluck's original melodic contour and harmonic outline rather loosely, and with rather different, entirely idiomatic German text. His arrangement gives rhythmic accentuation and a descending subsequent syllable to "Sorgen" (m. 2), "Beleidigt" (mm. 2–3), and "klein" (m. 6) which contrasts with Brissler's unidiomatic emphasis on "ihr" (m. 2), "nicht" (m. 4), and "wenn" (m. 5) in the "blundering" translation. Example 4.1b illustrates a similar degree of intervention, where – with the exception of the first phrase – Wagner simply modifies Gluck's rhythm as necessary to accommodate his German, while largely retaining his pitches. Finally, Example 4.1c shows an unusual case of Wagner retaining Gluck's rhythm (and Brissler's translation), while altering the pitches purely to better inflect the German intonation.

Such care for German pitch inflection, agogic, rhythmic declamation, and above all correct locution, indicates that – in between drafting the *Kompositionsskizze* and *Orchesterskizze* for *Lohengrin* – Wagner's interest in spoken language was bound to a translation of idiom, both melodic and linguistic, in which his German verse could be "correctly" set with the "fire

Example 4.1c Wagner's re-inflection of Achilles' "votre fille est à moi," while retaining Brissler's German translation; act 2, scene 6, *Iphigénie en Aulide*, transcribed from NA B I i 2 b, *Nationalarchiv der Richard-Wagner-Stiftung*, Bayreuth.

and determined expression" of proto-Bellinian melody in passages from *Lohengrin*, while Gluck's melodies (and French) could similarly be made to accommodate idiomatic German. Speaking retrospectively about the repertoire at the Dresden Hoftheater in 1841–49, the theater historian Robert Prölss cites Gluck's operas as "undisputedly the most significant events in whose great triumphs were celebrated Wagner's conducting talent, the power of the band, and the dramatic, embodying talent of Schröder-Devrient."[125] It may be less than coincidence that Schröder-Devrient sang the role of Klytemnestra in the premiere of Wagner's arrangement on February 24, 1847. As it turns out, this was her last performance for him.[126]

Neither she nor any of Wagner's favored singers at Dresden were on hand for *Lohengrin*'s premiere, of course, and in addition to blaming a predominance of incompetent translations of foreign opera, Wagner cannot conceal

[125] "Die bedeutendsten Erscheinungen waren unstreitig die Opern Gluck's, in denen das Directionstalent Wagner's, die Kraft der Kapelle und das dramatische Gestaltungstalent der Schröder-Devrient gemeinsam grosse Triumphe feierten." Prölss, *Geschichte des Hoftheaters zu Dresden*, 542.

[126] Prölss reports that the end of Schröder-Devrient's contract at the Dresden Hoftheater in 1847 was precipitated by her increasing demands for holiday, higher pay, and her increasingly restricted repertoire. With each passing year, she received 100 Thalers more in her annual pension, and in 1846, having sung thirty times that year with a princely salary of 4,500 Thalers, was effectively paid 150 Thalers per appearance. Baron August von Lüttichau, the Intendant of the Dresden Hof-Theater, considered whether it might be more appropriate to hire Schröder-Devrient for a particular number of roles per year, but his request was denied by royal decree. On March 23, 1847 Schröder-Devrient gave an ultimatum, however, requesting a six-month vacation owing to "physical and mental agitation," or her release from contract. On July 1, her contract was not renewed, and her prior request to sing Valentine (*Les Huguenots*) as her final role at Dresden is tinged with allegorical bitterness, for in Meyerbeer's narrative, the Count of Saint-Bris unwittingly orders the execution of his own daughter. The opera is not listed as having been performed at Dresden in that year. See Prölss, *Geschichte des Hoftheaters zu Dresden*, 540ff.

his frustration – in the same letter to Liszt – at the corollary effect this has brought about: undisciplined singers.

When in opera the recitative commences, it means to [German singers], "The Lord be praised, here is an end to that bloody tempo, which every so often compels us to a kind of rational rendering; now we can float about in all directions, dwell on any note we like until the prompter has given us the next phrase; now the conductor has no power whatsoever over us, and we can take revenge for his pretensions by commanding *him* to give us the beat when it suits us," etc.[127]

To be sure, certain German singers were in fact contracted shortly before Wagner's tenure at the Dresden Hoftheater solely to sing Italian opera.[128] This speaks to their aptitude in delivering foreign recitative, even if better paid native Italians continued to be engaged on an *ad hoc* basis.[129] But Wagner's skepticism shines through his correspondence. Lamenting the arbitrary tempos and bad training of German singers, he discloses that he had wanted to overcome such problems:

Nowhere in the score of *Lohengrin* have I written above a vocal phrase the word "recitative"; the singers ought not to know that there are any recitatives in it; on the other hand, I have endeavored to weigh and indicate the verbal emphasis of speech so surely and so distinctly that the singers need only sing the notes *exactly, according to their value in the given tempo* to get purely by that means the declamatory expression.[130]

So what had gone wrong in Weimar? Liszt's conducting score of *Lohengrin* is filled with markings that offer a glimpse of his approach to directing Wagner's more declamatory passages (see Figures 4.1a–c). As the markings in Figure 4.1a reveal, he stopped beating time during "recitatives" over tremolo chords, i.e. he did not try to micromanage the articulate delivery of each singer, and simply gestured for each change of chord or gave the four beats for brief orchestral fanfares. Where the arioso accompaniments had more rhythmic interest, Liszt tended to beat them in time, though this evidently altered bar by bar as the back-and-forth between one and four beats in Figure 4.1b indicates. For much of the

---

[127] Wagner to Liszt, September 8, 1850, Zurich, SB 3: 387. Again, the selfsame sentiment would later appear in *Oper und Drama*. See SSD 4: 214. Cf. PW 2: 361.

[128] Examples include Johannes Miksch, Fräulein Hunt, Frau von Biedenfeld. See Prölss, *Geschichte des Hoftheaters zu Dresden*, 45ff.

[129] See "Verzeichnis des Personals der Oper und des Schauspiels des Königl. Hoftheaters zu Dresden vom 1. Oktober 1816 bis 1. Januar 1862. II. Italiänische Oper. B. Sängpersonal," in Prölss, *Geschichte des Hoftheaters zu Dresden*, 659–60. The income discrepancy between the German actor Carl Devrient (who married Wilhelmine Schröder in 1823 but divorced her in 1828) and the Italian soprano Matilde Palazzesi in 1831 was 2,200 Thalers: Devrient was paid 1,800; Palazzesi 4,000. See *Ibid.*, 662–63.

[130] Wagner to Liszt, September 8, 1850, Zurich, SB 3: 387–88.

4.1a Liszt's conducting score of *Lohengrin*, act 1, scene 1, mm. 64–75. Goethe- und Schiller-Archiv, Weimar (GSA 60/Z 19). Photo: Klassik Stiftung Weimar.

score, the libretto text is underlined in red pencil, suggesting that Liszt followed it closely, and wanted to have quick reference to it during performance. In Figure 4.1c, the emphatic vertical lines, numerical counting, and frequent underlining of accented syllables as well as the attempt to align syllables with the orchestral accompaniment using arrows indicate that achieving coordination during these passages was an enormous problem. (No fewer than seven exclamation marks accompany the fourth beat of measure three in Figure 4.1c).

It is unlikely Liszt would have felt he was neglecting his duty by not continually delineating the beat. The frequent underlining of syllables

4.1b Liszt's conducting score of *Lohengrin*, act 2, scene 5, mm. 2030–47. Goethe- und Schiller-Archiv, Weimar (GSA 60/Z 19). Photo: Klassik Stiftung Weimar.

corresponds to the beats in each measure, suggesting that Liszt coached singers to keep these in time, even if he did not beat them in performance. In 1881, a treatise on conducting by the musical polymath and Wagner enthusiast Hermann Zopff explains that recitative is the "most difficult" musical material to direct, and its success depends upon "following the singers exactly."[131] Irrespective of Liszt's efforts to mediate between following the

---

[131] "Am Schwierigsten ist u. a. das Dirigiren von *Recitativen*. Hier kommt es vor Allem darauf an, dem Sänger genau zu *folgen*." Hermann Zopff, *Der angehende Dirigent* (Leipzig: Merseburger, 1881), 93.

4.1c Liszt's conducting score of *Lohengrin*, act 2, scene 1, mm. 182–89. Goethe- und Schiller-Archiv, Weimar (GSA 60/Z 19). Photo: Klassik Stiftung Weimar.

singers and Wagner's demand to keep them in time, Wagner's remarks above reveal *Lohengrin's* melodies to be intentionally declamatory in their construction, and highlight a latent paradox in part 3 of *Oper und Drama*: German actors and singers, who – for Wagner – lack any competitive aptitude for dramatic recitation, were to be the vessels – in body, throat, and national tongue – of an ideal synthesis of drama and music that would communicate its universality more directly to the senses than any previous conception since Aeschylus and Sophocles. The venture seems unlikely and almost counterintuitive when set against such complaints about German theater.

The contemporary critic Friedrich Meyer captured something of the ambivalence surrounding Wagner's aspirations when he equivocated of *Lohengrin* in 1859: "Admittedly, [Wagner] declaims the text correctly, often very *sensitively*," but qualified that "the whole nevertheless becomes increasingly tiresome towards the end." After lamenting an overall lack of lyrical moment in the score, Meyer continues that even in the attempt to mimic speech "[Wagner] does not achieve the impression of ease made by the, as it were, winged speech of *Recitative*."[132] Writing less sympathetically in 1854, the archeologist and philologist Otto Jahn declared Wagner's inscribed declamation "already exaggerated ... [and] very often driven to extremes, which violates the musically educated ear, just as when actors recite absolutely correctly, but exaggerate accent and articulation."[133] In these historically self-aware readings, Wagner's attempt at poetic realism had fallen squarely between two stools: it seemingly displayed neither genuine spoken verisimilitude nor lyrical points of rest; that is, it was neither realist nor poetic. Meyer's critique represents a body of criticism in labeling the result simply as "a *ponderous, impassioned, dramatic–declamatory style* interspersed with short self-enclosed melodic thoughts."[134]

Of course, it was the Weimar performers – Wagner believed initially – who had crippled *Lohengrin*. Highlighting the need for tutored declamation after the unsatisfactory premiere, Wagner recommended to the stage manager, Eduard Genast, that the singers undertake a "reading rehearsal" in which to "*read* their parts together, distinctly and expressively, from the printed libretto ... [while Genast himself should] explain ... the meaning of the situations and their connections with the music bar by bar."[135] Wagner's emergency technique deliberately mimicked Goethe's practice for the first rehearsals of spoken drama in Weimar half a century earlier. In his *History of German Acting* (1848) Eduard Devrient reveals that Goethe and Schiller in

---

[132] "Das Ganze aber ermüdet dennoch gegen das Ende mehr und mehr ... Er declamirt zwar die Worte des Textes richtig, oft sehr *fein*, aber den Eindruck der Leichtigkeit, den die gleichsam beflügelte Rede des freien *Recitativs* macht, erreicht er nicht." Friedrich Meyer, *Richard Wagner und seine Stellung zur Vergangenheit und "Zukunft"* (Thorn: Ernst Lambeck, 1859), 43.

[133] "Übertrieben ist schon seine Declamation, die, obgleich im Allgemeinen lobenswerth genau und scharf, doch sehr häufig auf die Spitze getrieben ist, was ein musikalisch gebildetes Ohr ebenso verletzt, wie wenn ein Schauspieler zwar richtig recitirt, aber im Betonen und Articulation übertreibt." Jahn, "*Lohengrin*. Oper von Richard Wagner," 146.

[134] "So bewegt sich den der Styl des Werkes fast fortwährend in einem *schwerfälligen, pathetischen, dramatisch-deklamatirischen Styl*, mitunter allerdings unterbrochen durch kurze in sich abgeschlossenere melodische Gedanken." Meyer, *Richard Wagner und seine Stellung zur Vergangenheit und "Zukunft,"* 45.

[135] Wagner to Liszt, September 8, 1850, Zurich, SB 3: 393.

fact began rehearsals in this way, establishing a tone of declamation before any roles had been assigned.[136] But for Wagner (who penned a favorable review of Devrient's book in 1848, which was not accepted for publication by the *Augsburger Allgemeine Zeitung*),[137] such a read-through was a desperate measure that hinted at the need for a Devrientesque "true *speaking* expression" in which singing – to recapitulate Epstein's phrase – was "nothing but a translation of speech into a higher language." It reveals furthermore the extent to which Wagner believed he was composing for "empty" performers who brought little understanding to the score, and needed a composer to fix, control, even ventriloquize the singer's expression from the score.

This was both a deliberate and consistent strategy. As we saw above, Wagner impelled Liszt's singers in 1850 to "sing the notes *exactly, according to their value in the given tempo* to get purely by that means the declamatory expression," while as late as 1882, Cosima records his comments that unlike the effectiveness of Italian melody, "in our country everything must be locked in . . . it must all be locked in."[138] This is nothing less than freedom in chains. Wagner wants "freedom" in the sense of an *impression* of freedom that is closely scripted and managed, via compositional text. The reason? He believes he was writing declamatory music in *Lohengrin* for singers he knows are unable to do what he wants them to do with it in performance, so he feels compelled to over-script, and control even more.

The flipside of such determinism is Wagner's praise for the "sublime illusion" of actors who can fully divest themselves of ego. The "whole essence" of an actor and singer "is reproductiveness," he asserted in 1872, yet this carries its own danger:

the rather gifted, perfect mime appears in that act of self-divestment to sacrifice his consciousness of self to such a degree that, in a sense, he never recovers it even in daily life, or never completely . . . Whoever can stand with him on the brink of that abyss, will shudder at the peril of playing with one's personality, that a given moment may turn to raving madness.[139]

If Wagner had been aware since the 1830s that he was composing for "empty" performers in this sense, the melodic lines he composed in

---

[136] Eduard Devrient, *Geschichte der deutschen Schauspielkunst* [1848], 2 vols. (Munich and Vienna: Langen Müller 1967), 1: 630.

[137] SSD 12: 230–32.   [138] CT (April 25, 1882).

[139] SSD 9: 217–19. Cf. PW 5: 216–17. Wagner hints that the danger of going mad through such complete self-divestment is not real, however. It is mere acting. Predictably, it was his stage heroine who alerted him to this reality: "Through [Schröder-Devrient] I became acquainted, in a truly startling manner, with the saving return of a consciousness lost in fullest self-divestment to the sudden remembrance that it was nothing but acting." SSD 9: 219. Cf. PW 5: 218.

Example 4.2 Friedrich von Telramund's melodic speech, *Lohengrin*, act 2, mm. 178–83.

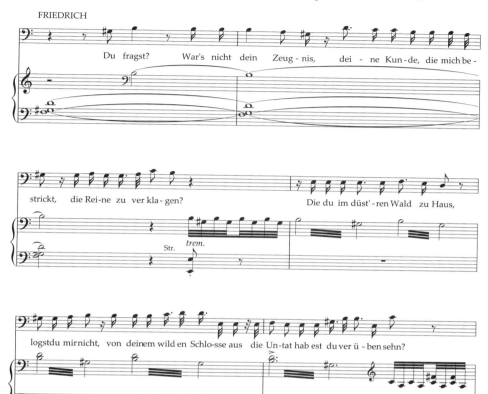

Lohengrin surely aspired to "fill" that expressive gap. But how did this work in practice?

An example from act 2 of *Lohengrin* illustrates the extent to which Wagner's melodic composition "locked in" expression. When Friedrich asks Ortrud whether she denies having lied to him, his question (blank verse, without a fixed number of feet) fills in the gaps of intonation that connect different recitational pitches, as Example 4.2 shows. Over a sustained diminished seventh, the inflections are written into the melodic line as recitative through delicate grades of rhythm and pitch. The extent to which this kind of melodic writing differs from Wagner's more familiar earlier composition is made clear by comparing it with a passage from *Rienzi*, which – as Examples 4.3a–d show – conforms to the use of more generic melodic shapes in recitative, ones shared by Mozart, Bellini, and even symphonic Beethoven.

Example 4.3a Wagner's *Rienzi*, act 1, no. 1 *Introduktion*, mm. 126–32
(Cosima-version, 1898–99).

Zur Ru_____ he!　　Und ihr,　　habt ihr ver-ges - sen　was ihr mir geschwo-ren

Example 4.3b Mozart's *Don Giovanni*, act 1 scene 5, Leporello's rectative, mm. 41–43.

ve - ra-men - te　　in que sto　mon-de　　con cios-sia co - sa quan do fos-se　obe...

Example 4.3c Bellini's *I Capuleti e i Montecchi*, act 1 scene 2, Capellio's
recitative mm. 1–2.

Van - ne　　Lo - ren - zo　　e tuobe'il　pu - oi

Example 4.3d Beethoven's 9th Symphony, iv: *Presto*, mm. 56–62

By way of contrast, the sung dialogue between Ortrud and Friedrich seventy measures later offers performers the freedom to inflect – tonally, phonetically – the melodic material. It alternates between iambic pentameter and free speech as they quarrel over the past lies that had cajoled Friedrich into spurning Elsa and marrying Ortrud. When the pagan sorceress finally persuades the ambitious nobleman that he may yet become Duke of Brabant and turns him to her prophecy of revenge, the vocal melody is oddly monochromatic, intoned to recitational pitches that are neither inflected nor melodic. As Example 4.4a shows, such expression is hardly "locked in."

Why would Wagner, given his interest in "correct" declamation, set a pivotal moment in the narrative with such apparent lack of vocal interest? Friedrich's gently rising and falling exclamation at the "crazy seer" is accompanied by the stepwise descent of a complete chromatic octave, which – in its abundance of pitches – is the opposite of Ortrud's subsequent phrases: psalmic intonations of the text with only one note per measure. In the hermeneutic tradition, several nineteenth-century commentators hung narrative ideas on this chromatic scale, including the transformation of

Example 4.4a *Lohengrin*, act 2, mm. 254–72.

Friedrich's allegiance and the doubtful wavering of his reason, though the transfer of "melodic" line from voice to orchestra, the switching of media, would seem the more post-hermeneutic reading today.[140]

In fact, Wagner's *Kompositionsskizze* (completed July 30, 1846) for Ortrud's phrase show a yet more extreme application of the psalmic

[140] See Albert Heintz, "Sie [the descending chromatic scale] soll das zweifelnde Schwanken seines Sinnes ausdrücken, der sich bereits wieder den ränkevollen Anschlägen der Gattin nähert." Heintz, *Richard Wagner's Lohengrin* (Berlin: Allgemeine Musik-Zeitung, 1894), 40.

principle; the original setting of mm. 266–67 was a full two-measure recitation on A with only a B$\sharp$ inflection on "da." Numerous instances of monotone recitations exist in this dialogue, and at least one contemporary critic felt that the scene "makes truly *enormous* demands on our ears."[141] Marx, speaking of such deliberate melodic monotony back in 1826, made the telling observation that "the main expression is entrusted to the spoken recitation."[142] It invites an improvisatory freedom, in other words, where singers are treated more as actors. Based on the reviews quoted above, were this sung by a Schröder-Devrient, such a passage would probably not have sounded like the uninspired monotony that several of Wagner's critics heard. (Performance traditions documented by the earliest surviving recordings of *Lohengrin* do indeed suggest a considerable degree of rhythmic flexibility vis-à-vis Wagner's notation, particularly among Italian singers such as Emilia Corsi, Linda Cannetti, and Celestina Boninsegna, as Stephen Meyer's research has shown.[143])

The visual impression of the score is misleading in this sense, and by replacing the note heads with pitchless crosses, as Example 4.4b shows, the potential for license in the declamation becomes clearer. This, then, is a critique of notation as much as performance, and I would speculate that, despite professing that his "singers need only sing the notes, exactly" for the desired effect, in such passages Wagner may not have been able to transfer into visual composition – the "eye of hearing" – those nuanced aspects of declamation that inspired him, that he could not capture the kind of *sinnlich* performance aesthetic for this passage he may have imagined. Drawing on Carlo Gozzi two decades later, Wagner recommended actor–singers practice improvisation regularly, alluding to this as a legitimate means of escaping the impossibility of transcribing a performance of character: "the ingenious Gozzi declared it clean impossible to write out certain of his

---

[141] "Eine Szene . . . beim Beginn des zweiten Aktes macht an unsre Ohren wahrhaft *unerhörte* Ansprüche." Meyer, *Richard Wagner und seine Stellung zur Vergangenheit und "Zukunft,"* 43.

[142] "der Hauptausdruck hier [ist] dem Sprachvortrage anvertraut." Marx, *Die Kunst des Gesanges*, 181.

[143] See Stephen C. Meyer, "Sound Recordings and the End of the Italian *Lohengrin*," *Cambridge Opera Journal* 20 (2008), 1–24, here 10, 12. There are two complete broadcasts of *Lohengrin* from the mid-1930s: Maurice de Abravanel's direction of the Metropolitan Opera on March 27, 1937 is available on Walhall Eternity Series (WLCD 0011); Fritz Busch's direction from Buenos Aires on September 17, 1936 is available on Archipel Desert Island Collection (ARPCD 0182–3). The famous new production at Bayreuth from 1936, conducted by Wilhelm Furtwängler, survives in fragments only. These are available on the Archipel Desert Island Collection (ARPCD 0284).

Example 4.4b Ortrud's suggestively intoned melodic lines, *Lohengrin*, act 2, mm. 261–67.

characters in prose, still less in verse, and contented himself with a mere sketch of their scenes for the performers to fill up."[144] Wagner's awareness that character is not always determinable (and writable) in this sense would seem very much to the point.

[144] SSD 9: 263. Cf. PW 5: 261.

We may wonder at the different approaches to notating the voice here: locking in the expression on the one hand, and leaving a limited freedom for improvising performers on the other. Why the discrepancy? Speaking of *Tannhäuser* in 1852 – the very work whose "locked in" notation Schröder-Devrient had criticized to Wagner's face – the composer obliquely explains his two alternatives. Echoing comments above about *Lohengrin*, he talks of having "labored to denote [vocal-melodic] phrasing in exact rhythmic accordance with the 'aim' of my expression" but goes on to add, perhaps with Schröder-Devrient in mind, that if and when the singers "feel" and adopt his directions "correctly," then:

the strictness of the musical beat must be almost totally abandoned, which up to then was a mere mechanical aid for agreement between composer and singer. When that agreement has been completely attained, however, it is to be discarded as a worn-out, useless tool that has become annoying. From the moment the singer fully absorbs my intentions for the delivery, let him give the freest play to his natural sensibility, even to the physical necessity of his breath in the more agitated phrases; the more creative he himself can become through the fullest freedom of feeling, the more delightedly grateful I will be.[145]

Such freedom is latent in the under-determined notation of Example 4.4, I would argue, though, as per the recurring hypocrisy of Wagner's "freedom in chains," a lot depends on what "correctly" feeling his prescribed intentions means here. It may seem contradictory that he asked at times for strict adherence to his rhythmic notation, and at other times for singers to abandon the beat, yet, as he would argue in 1871, it is precisely the dialectic between an unconscious, improvising *Volksgeist* (collectively embodied in the improvising mime) and a consciously notated artistic production that gives rise to the artwork of the future.[146] It is in this mindset, moreover, that Wagner credits the works of his two most canonic forebears, both Shakespeare's plays and Beethoven's late quartets, as fixed improvisations.[147]

Wagner's naïvety in seeking to erase the difference between writing and speaking media prompts two further observations: first, the score he used when he first conducted *Lohengrin* (in Frankfurt am Main on September 12 and 17, 1862) contains numerous pencilled notes, other marginalia, and calls to

---

[145] SSD 5: 129. Cf. PW 3: 175.

[146] See particularly Dieter Borchmeyer's enlightening discussion in *Richard Wagner: Theory and Theater*, trans. Stewart Spencer (Oxford University Press, 2002), 250–86.

[147] SSD 5: 143. Cf. PW 5: 144. See also CT (December 4, 1870).

reinstate passages in his hand. As Figure 4.2a shows, for this dialogue in act 2 he highlights the need for adequate performance, writing: "Everything is to be performed here [i.e. not cut] except when suitable singers are not available, in which case the entire opera should not be performed."[148] Elsewhere, he writes simply *Herzustellen!* (Reinstate!) or "If the chorus is good, this must be performed complete. RW,"[149] though later in the second act – given in Figure 4.2b – he iterates a similar condition for Friedrich's interruption on the Minster steps as he had for Ortrud's recitation: "Whether the following passage can be performed depends entirely on the energy [*Kraft*] of the singers."[150] In other words, though the right singers are essential for any performance of *Lohengrin*, Wagner imagined that Ortrud's and Friedrich's recitational melodies would suffer more than most if the singers were inadequate.

Second, both Wagner's aborted musical sketches for *Siegfrieds Tod* (1850) and his Lied *Der Tannenbaum* (1838) indicate that Ortrud's "reciting tones" were clearly more than a passing experiment. The former is similar to Ortrud's chanting in its psalmic pitches within the Norns scene, suggesting that, on the brink of writing *Oper und Drama*, Wagner pursued this recitational style as a means of seeking a drama-driven, declamatory verisimilitude in performance. Example 4.5a, taken from Werner Breig's transcription, illustrates the principle where, except for the first interval, the chromatically ordered pitches divide each sub-clause almost entirely by single pitches, forming a rising, speaking intensity. Similarly, Wagner's short *Tannenbaum* Lied requires the singer to recite almost as though the tonic and flat supertonic were psalm tones defining a church mode. Examples 4.5b and 4.5c illustrate the periodically mono-tonal expression. We even find this kind of writing in *Das Rheingold*, scene 3 (1854) – Example 4.5d – where Alberich sings seventeen consecutive Bs as he relates the fabrication of the Tarnhelm to Wotan and Loge (cf. Mime's version of the same in Example 1.3b). Of course, highlighting the risk of affectation here is the *ne plus ultra* of vocal monotones, Peter Cornelius' Lied "Ein Ton" (op. 3, no. 3), which also appeared in 1854, and consists of no fewer than eighty Bs wherein the virtuosic harmonization

---

[148] "Hier ist alles auszuführen, außer wenn die geeigneten Sänger nicht vorhanden, in welchem Fall dann die ganze Oper nicht gegeben werden möge. RW." This comment occurs right after Friedrich's line "Du fürchterliches Weib!" For a brief discussion of Wagner's comments see Rüdiger Pohl, "Zum neuen Bayreuther Lohengrin: 'Gieb die Oper, wie sie ist, streiche nichts!'" *Mitteilungen der Deutschen Richard-Wagner Gesellschaft* 30/31 (1999), 1. The score is housed in the Stadt- and Universitätsbibliothek Frankfurt am Main (Mus Wf 22/Mus Hs Opern 595 [1]).

[149] "Wenn der Chor gut ist, muß dies vollständig gegeben werden. RW."

[150] "Von der Kraft des Sängers hängt es allein ab, ob die folgende Stelle gegeben werden kann."

4.2a Wagner's conducting score for performances of *Lohengrin* in Frankfurt am Main on September 12–17, 1862; act 2 scene 1 dialogue. Universitätsbibliothek, Frankfurt am Main (Mus Wf 22). Transcription: *Hier ist alles auszuführen, außer wenn die geeigneten Sänger nicht vorhanden, in welchem Fall dann die ganze Oper nicht gegeben werden möge* [Everything is to be performed here except when suitable singers are not available in which case the entire opera should not be performed] RW.

4.2b Wagner's conducting score for performances of *Lohengrin* in Frankfurt am Main on September 12–17, 1862; Telramund's speech on the Minster steps, act 2, scene 3. Universitätsbibliothek, Frankfurt am Main (Mus Wf 22). Transcription: *Von der Kraft des Sängers hängt es allein ab, ob die folgende Stelle gegeben werden kann* [Whether the following passage can be performed depends entirely on the energy of the singers] RW.

Example 4.5a From Wagner's aborted sketches for *Siegfrieds Tod* (1850), mm. 11–16.

Example 4.5b From Wagner's Lied *Der Tannenbaum* (1838), mm. 13–17.

evokes a heritage of melodic games dating back at least to Purcell's "Fantasia upon one note" (Z. 745).

In the troublesome *Lohengrin* "recitatives," the potential of performance is what is at stake in any imagined elision between Wagner's composition and the echo of Devrient's voice: her "beautiful breath" literally in-spired this German melody, breathing life and spirit – musical *pneuma* (πνευμα) – into the will to be melodic *and* beautiful, yet self-consciously non-Italian, non-French. The slippage between metaphoric inspiration and literal inhalation is Wagner's own, for he argues in *Oper und Drama* that emotionally heightened speech accents are entirely "governed by [literal] breath,"[151] while critiquing the etymological investigations of German linguistics with the call to vivify:

[151] SSD 4: 120. Cf. PW 2: 257.

Example 4.5c From Wagner's Lied *Der Tannenbaum* (1838), mm. 27–43.

Example 4.5d Alberich chants a series of Bs over the Tarnhelm motif in *Das Rheingold* (1854), scene 3, mm. 2601–07.

the organism of speech ... by healing up the wounds with which the anatomical scalpel has gashed the body of speech, and by breathing into it the [metaphorical] breath that may ensoul it into living motion.[152]

In this sense, Schröder-Devrient's "beautiful breath" was the positive kiss of life for a negatively determined concept. It resuscitated a tired theory of inflected speech that both informed and elevated Wagner's vocal melody. In celebrating the articulate voice with its "infinite variety that comes from its characteristic play of vowels and consonants" as "the oldest, truest, and most beautiful organ of music, the organ to which our music exclusively owes its being," it is hard to imagine that he had anyone else in mind.[153]

Towards language: gas-light and candle-lamps

> Music can only ever be language developed to its fullest potential.
> Richard Wagner (1851)[154]

Breath, as Wagner's construction of Schröder-Devrient indicates, is connected to the production of speech as much as singing. As we have seen, these were permeable categories that Schröder-Devrient's declamatory aesthetic exploited, and that critics perceived as oddly hyperemotional utterances which did not fit cleanly within the comfort zones of either (spoken) theater or (sung) opera. By outlining a melodic theory in *Oper und Drama* that drew on his experience of an emergent practice of such dramatic singing, and was defined almost entirely in the absence of pitch sequences, melodic contour, or normative phrase structure, Wagner avoided the paralyzing inhibition that had dogged melody pedagogy for thirty years.[155] It was a solution that, as it were, moved the goalposts: rather than seeking to match the prestige of metaphysical speculation or outmaneuver Bellinian *bel canto* within its own stylistic bounds, he explained a desire to communicate "purely human" emotional content by redefining "melody" without reference to pitch or normative music theory; instead, the speaking of the German language – considered by Humboldt (after Herder and Hamann) as the formative substance of thought within the realm of the ideal

---

[152] SSD 4: 127. Cf. PW 2: 265.   [153] SSD 4: 166–7. Cf. PW 2: 309; and SSD 4: 4. Cf. PW 2: 122.

[154] Wagner to Adolph Stahr, May 31, 1851, Zurich, in SB 4: 59.

[155] The famous "poetic–musical period" Wagner describes in part 3 of *Oper und Drama* was conceived as a successor to eighteenth-century periodic syntax. For an excellent critique of Wagner's concept of the poetic–musical period, see Thomas Grey's chapter "The 'poetic–musical period' and the 'evolution' of Wagnerian form," *Wagner's Musical Prose*, 181–241, as well as his translation of Wagner's own description of the concept, 375–77.

(which cannot therefore be disembodied)[156] – would itself need to be sensualized as a mode of emotional expression.

This move effectively refined Wagner's vocal "melody" from a musical to a linguistic concept, shifting it from *Melodik* to *Philologie*, and – by implication – dismissing the non-linguistic identity of melody as "absolute." In its new guise, melody sought to function as a delivery system for distinctive poetic emotion, communicating its sensory load via inflected, alliterated consonants and the vowels of speech roots to the ears of imagined transnational listeners. In this sense, *Oper und Drama* created a gap and filled a void, for Wagner expounded a lengthy treatise on melody apparently without direct application (there is no Stabreim in *Lohengrin*), answering decades of melodic composition in the absence of any lasting melodic–theoretical basis.

While there is no shortage of writing about Wagner's politicized mid-century texts, relatively little attention has been paid to the contemporary commentators who received his ideas first-hand. Since *Melodik* had posed problems for German composers long before 1851, it was only to be expected that the earliest critiques of Wagner's treatise voiced continuing skepticism on the matter. The Königsberg-based, Polish-American composer Eduard Sobolewski likened Wagner's philologically prestigious but musically almost vacant theory to Mozart's ambitious proposition about aleatoric melody in *Ein musikalisches Würfelspiel*, paraphrasing incorrectly that "those persons who in vain racked their brains for melodies should have recourse to a game of dice, in which each person should be allowed only two or three throws, and immediately receive a theme for a cantata, symphony, air, or galop."[157] Wagner's plan to derive melody from words and syntax "is a more sensible one," Sobolewski admits, though it must ultimately fail, for:

Words, like tones, are capable of producing sensations by themselves; but if they are both united, the former pale like candle-lamps before gas-light. The former may aid in diffusing light, but it is from the latter that all the rays seem to proceed . . . in this manner we shall have no suns shining, but, at most, candle-lamps. *Trop raffiner c'est dénaturer.*[158]

---

[156] "Das Denken ist aber nicht bloss abhängig von der Sprache überhaupt, sondern, bis auf einen gewissen Grad, auch von jeder einzelnen bestimmten." See Wilhelm von Humboldt, *Gesammelte Schriften*, ed. Albert Leitzmann (Berlin: Deutsche Akademie der Wissenschaft, 1903–36), 4: 21.

[157] Eduard Sobolewski, *Reaktionäre Briefe aus dem Feuilleton der Ostpreuss. Zeitung* (Kotnigsberg: Schultzschen Hofbuchdruckerei, 1854); Eng trans. "Reactionary Letters. No. II," *TMW* 33 (1855), 45.

[158] *Ibid.*

Granted, Sobolewski's gas-powered melodies may outshine the dim alternative from a Franco-Italian perspective; but the reason for shunning the brighter option is that these candles were made wick and wax – vowel and consonant – in Germany (while the gas was imported through foreign "pipes" from Rome and Paris). Sobolewski's concluding *bon mot* ironically illustrates the point.

If Wagner's aim was to achieve – in this multinational context – a characteristically German mode of melodic expression, it was a lofty endeavor that would equally be criticized for banality. We should keep in mind that the idea of a national autochthony was always ancillary, and Wagner's "archaic" language can be seen in these terms as a means to an end that was essentially modern and progressive: he uses the archaic form to justify a musical language that is just as outlandish as its literary basis, which raised the suspicion of at least one musically educated German speaker in Wagner's circle:

Wagner came across the unfortunate idea in his most recent speculations of reawakening an archaic form of diction (alliterative poetry) and is all but writing a grammar book (as well as a lexicon, of course) in which one could find ready formed the musical expression after the corresponding linguistic expression. Through this, one would effectively be in a position to sing as to speak, i.e. every word receives well-nigh its typical musical setting, and finally one would be in a most comfortable position one morning to sight sing the Prussian *Staatsanzeiger* without any difficulties.[159]

Joachim Raff's ironic whim of droning through the Prussian *Staatsanzeiger* "at sight" is a logician's fantasy, a droll exaggeration of Wagner's *Worttonmelodie* in opposition to *bel canto* demonstrating that, as so often with Wagner, *Reductio* can be unhelpfully *ad absurdum*. The dreamt-of operatic newspaper would depend on the composer's undocumented "unfortunate idea" of establishing a lexicon of musical gestures corresponding to all known grammatical inflections. Raff probably inferred (rather than witnessed) Wagner's encyclopaedic intentions in this direction; far from an arbitrary quip, however, such an inference hinted at Wagner's debt to the burgeoning tradition of *Philologie*, in particular to Jacob Grimm, though it is unclear whether Raff is referring to the ongoing *Deutsches Wörterbuch*

[159] "Wagner ist in seinen letzten Speculationen auf die unselige Idee verfallen, eine archaistische Art der Diction (die Alliterationspoesie) wieder aufzuwecken und macht nicht übel Miene, eine Grammatik (natürlich auch ein Lexikon) zu schreiben, worin man den musikalischen Ausdruck nach dem so gestalteten sprachlichen fertig vorfinden könnte. Man würde dadurch bald in Stand gesetzt sein, zu singen wie zu sprechen, d. h. jedes Wort erhielte nachgerade seine typische musikalische Betonung, und schliesslich würde man eines Morgens den preußischen Staatsanzeiger ohne Schwierigkeiten abzusingen in der höchst angenehmen Verfassung sein." Raff, *Die Wagnerfrage*, 100–01.

project, or the *Deutsche Grammatik* (1819), part 1 of whose third edition (1840) was contained in Wagner's Dresden library.[160]

Raff's failure to distinguish between a grammar and lexicon reveals an ambiguity over the locus of signification in language: do intoned words acquire meaning exclusively by their context and proximity to other words (whether alliteration, assonance, or grammatical relationship), or do they still possess an original sound, a "language of feeling"[161] that predates the division Herder registered between sign and referent in his celebrated 1772 essay? Raff interprets Wagner's treatise as the latter, but jokes about the boredom of the former: recitational melody as a mind-numbing grammar book. This was not a new question in 1854; Humboldt had suggested back in 1822 that such a division was irrelevant in any case because the two cannot be separated in speech:

Words and their grammatical relationships are imagined as two entirely separate things. The former are the actual objects in the language, the latter merely the links, but speech is only possible through a combination of the two.[162]

In contrast to vocal pedagogy, Grimm furnished Wagner with an entirely different lens through which to focus his ideal *Melodik*, and in this respect, his theoretical work can indeed be seen as a continuation of the *Grammatik* by other means, bringing it into the realm of music. If there were any doubt, Raff's later aside makes the connection clear: "Shame that Wagner didn't unify his material with that of the Brothers Grimm from the very start."[163]

In one sense, Wagner was merely deepening a furrow that had already been ploughed. The eighteenth-century link between rhetoric and music maintained that speech and melody shared syntactical structure and punctuational functions: "This is a fact," Koch asserted in 1787 "which has never yet been called into question and therefore requires no further proof."[164] But Wagner's turn away from an overtly Italianate melodic idiom, I am arguing, demanded a historically "German" alternative that was embodied not in rhetorico–syntactical correspondence between *Gänge* or *Perioden*, but in language and Wagner's much-debated concept of "musikalische Prosa."

---

[160] Raff appears to refer to both, except that the *Grammatik* (unlike the *Wörterbuch*) was not a joint project between both Grimm brothers, but was completed entirely by Jacob. See Curt von Westernhagen, *Richard Wagners Dresdener Bibliothek*, 91.

[161] J. G. Herder and J. J. Rousseau, *On the Origin of Language*, trans. John H. Moran and Alexander Gode (University of Chicago Press, 1986), 88.

[162] See Wilhelm von Humboldt, "On the Grammatical Forms and their Influence on the Development of Ideas," *Essays on Language*, 29.

[163] "Schade, daß Wagner sein Material nicht von Haus aus mit dem der Gebrüder Grimm vereinigt hat." Raff, *Die Wagnerfrage*, 101.

[164] H. C. Koch, *Introductory Essay on Composition: The Mechanical Rules of Melody* [1787], trans. Nancy K. Backer (New Haven and London: Yale University Press, 1983), 1.

Notation: "entirely insufficient"[165]

But this linguistic turn posed the challenge of establishing a means of inscription that would enable future performance. The apparent disappointment of Wagner's recitatives in *Lohengrin* was a blow to the composer, who had sought to write the "energy, fire" of his declamation into the score through a dialectic of over- and under-determined pitch and rhythm. This, he confessed, was still not a foolproof treatment of melody. Shortly after the Weimar premiere, Wagner ceased defending the work and actively dissociated himself from it. His future-oriented perspective and recent, public coupling of liberal politics and artistic reform saw him condemn his fairy-tale opera only seven months after the premiere: "I glanced through my score of *Lohengrin*; it filled me absolutely with disgust, and my intermittent fits of laughter were not of a cheerful kind."[166]

Inspired by Wagner's Zurich writings, however, several contemporaries reversed his shift from music theory to linguistics. By scrutinizing the musical detail in speech inflection, their ostensibly supportive approach only revealed weaknesses of his claims in their practical application, most obviously by highlighting the limits of notation. A prominent case is Louis Köhler, a Königsberg-based Wagner acolyte who advocated quarter-tones to support a broader concept of *Versmelodie* within the sphere of acoustic curiosity. He first spoke of how "refreshing" *Lohengrin* was in this respect, "how harmonically effective the text alone is as a *poem*, this human speech in music."[167] Yet what is vocally most expressive – whimpers, cries and screams – remains untranscribable:

Such expressions of feeling cannot be captured authentically in notation . . . the actor, the singer must fill in such gaps of signification, he must know that *true* expression first begins *there* where the possibility of notation ends – he must know that a thousand more scale steps come into use than are contained by our compositional apparatus.[168]

The point for Wagner's linguistic turn is that literalists such as Köhler inserted Wagner's theory into a long-standing German discourse on speech melody, where, without any qualification, he could interpret speech itself as infinitely delicate music:

---

[165] Wagner to Liszt, June 29, 1851, Enge/Zurich, SB 4: 67.

[166] Wagner to Liszt, April 28, 1851, Zurich, SB 3: 543.

[167] "Wie erquickend, wie harmonisch wirkt allein schon der Text als *Gedicht*, und diese Menschensprache in der Musik – – !" Köhler, "Aus Königsberg," *NZfM* 36 (February 13, 1852), 75–76, here 76.

[168] "Solche Gefühlsäußerungen lassen sich nicht getreu in Noten geben . . . Der Darsteller, der Sänger muß solche Zeichenlücken ausfüllen, er muß wissen, daß der *wahre* Ausdruck erst *da* enfängt, wo die Möglichkeit der Bezeichnung aufhört, – er muß wissen, daß allerdings tausendmal mehr Tonstufen in Anwendung kommen, als unser Kompositionsapparat enthält." Köhler, *Die Melodie der Sprache* (Leipzig: J. J. Weber, 1853), 24.

Audible speech itself is sound … Thus song lies in speech, in its original essence it is only more musical speech … In speech, not only with an outcry of pain … are two tones attached to one syllable, but the tone wave of speech … is understood so that rather than each syllable being joined to a sharply differentiated tone, there are tonal connections [*Tonverbindungen*] – crossings in speech tone … a syllable often occurs, without the awareness of the speaker or listener, through a quantity of sound atoms [*Tonatome*] each one of which trickles into the next; one can pursue these as little as the course of a single drop in a waterfall, but one *feels* it – one notices it, if one *wants*, in the declamation of unselfconscious speakers; if one had apparatuses, one could perhaps measure and calculate it like the thousands of air waves that a single tone brings about, that in turn make the tone possible.[169]

In fact, only four years later, an apparatus did emerge to measure and calculate the voice by producing a graphic trace of the "most delicate details of the motion of sound waves."[170] On October 28, 1857 in a talk entitled "The Graphic Fixation of the Voice," the Parisian scientist Édouard-Léon Scott de Martinville unveiled his phonautograph technology for the assembled members of the *Société d'encouragement pour l'industrie nationale*. His device detailed what he called the "natural stenography" of "acoustic writing," a cutting-edge technology that mimicked the double membranous structure of the inner ear to inscribe raw waveforms into smoke-blackened paper, and sought thereby to "preserve for future generations some features of the diction of one of those eminent actors, those grand artists who die without leaving behind them the faintest trace of their genius."[171] Martinville described the resulting waveform graphs coolly as an "analysis of the elements of the speaking voice" – defined as a function of tonality, intensity and timbre – and declared confidently: "the invention of the writing of sound and of its fixing is, so to speak, consummated; nothing more remains than to perfect and extend the

---

[169] "Die hörbare Sprache selbst ist Ton … Der Gesang liegt also in der Sprache, er ist in seiner Urwesenheit nur tonvollere Sprache … in der Sprache nicht allein bei Ausrufen des Schmerzes … zwei Töne auf eine Sylbe kommen, sondern daß die Tonwelle der Rede … begriffen ist, – so, daß nicht etwa mit jeder neuen Sylbe auch ein vom vorigen scharf abgeschiedener Ton kommt, sondern daß es auch noch *Tonverbindungen*, – *Uebergänge* im Sprachetone giebt … So zieht sich oft eine Sylbe, ohne daß der Sprechende oder Hörende es weiß, durch eine Menge Tonatome, deren einer *aus* dem andern in den andern rieselt; man kann dies so wenig verfolgen wie den Lauf einzelner Tropfen im Wasserfalle, aber man *fühlt* es, – wenn man *will*, bemerkt man es in der Deklamation des Unbefangenen; wenn man Apparate besäße, könnte man es vielleicht auch messen und berechnen, wie die Tausende von Luftwellen, die ein einziger Ton bewirkt, die wiederum den Ton ermöglichen." Köhler, *Die Melodie der Sprache*, 3, 62–63.

[170] Édouard-Léon Scott de Martinville, "Principles of Phonautography" (January 26, 1857) in *The Phonautographic Manuscripts of Édouard-Léon Scott de Martinville*, ed. and trans. Patrick Feaster, www.firstsounds.org/publications/articles/Phonautographic-Manuscripts.pdf, 7.

[171] *Ibid.*, 5.

4.3a Édouard-Léon Scott de Martinville, "Fixation Graphique de la Voix" (1857), *Société d'encouragement pour l'industrie nationale*, archives, CEC 8/54–19(1). Transcription: *Déclamation écrite par la voix même: s'il faut qu'âce rival . . . terribles mains!* [Declamation written by the voice itself: if it must be that to this rival . . . terrible hands!] L. Scott, 1857.

4.3a The same image with inverted colors to show Martinville's text and etched lines more clearly.

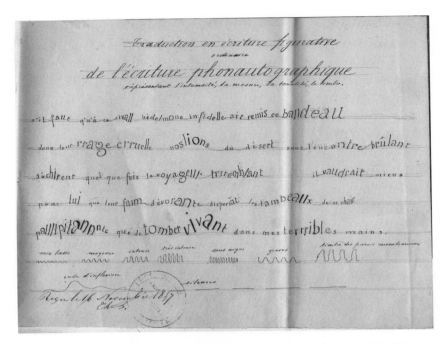

4.3b Édouard-Léon Scott de Martinville, "Fixation Graphique de la Voix" (1857), *Société d'encouragement pour l'industrie nationale*, archives, CEC 8/54–19(3).

process, to apply it to the sciences and to the arts."[172] But this proved difficult because, as Figure 4.3a shows, the zigzags and jagged lines of phonautographic script were illegible to human eyes, and attempts at providing alphabetic transcriptions, complete with a legend for deciphering the waveforms (Figure 4.3b), never gained currency within a practicable compositional sphere. Phonautography also lacked a playback mechanism at the time, leaving its runic script mysteriously silent. Despite these shortcomings, its precise transcription offered a scientific paradigm for capturing the minute fluctuations of an utterance wherein the materialization of any vocal sound meant that what was to be read or declaimed was no longer qualitatively distinct from that which should be sung or vocalized, resolving for Wagner the apparent contradiction of writing poetry to be enunciated as prose.[173]

---

[172] Martinville, "Fixation graphique de la voix" (October 28, 1857) in *Ibid.* 30, 37.

[173] A monistic paradigm for vocal sound had emerged much earlier from the extentsive discourse on melodic speech in German aesthetics. Typically, this was advanced on a scientific basis that drew on the intensity of vibrations and the shapes of waveforms; see, respectively, Gustav von Seckendorff, *Vorlesungen über Deklamation und Mimik. Erster Band, nebst einem Heft Musik-Beilagen* (Brunswick: Vieweg, 1816), 33ff. and Rötscher, *Die Kunst der dramatischen Darstellung*, 1: 137ff.

After clothing his singular interpretation of Wagner's linguistic theory in musical notation, Köhler's resulting compositional method is perhaps the weakest element in his treatise. To intone text correctly (i.e. as he mistakenly imagines Wagner must do), he argues, one simply recites a poetic phrase several times and "eavesdrops" on the "inner echo" after the final repetition, taking down the residual melodic contour through dictation. This is precisely composition as the stenography of original performance, exacting a role reversal of performer and composer, but one which ultimately annihilates the composer.[174] As a compositional tool this was far from an exclusively German practice, of course.[175] But here, Köhler's notational means is mechanical enough for him to claim that, if published, his notated declamation of Goethe's "Kennst du das Land" should be entitled "Lied, composed by itself."[176] (To underscore the kinship with Martinville, he too would entitle his transcriptions: "the sung voice written by itself at 50 centimeters" or "declamation written by the voice itself."[177]) Though hard to credit as "self-composed" without a lot of extra-poetic help, Köhler's Lied is broken down into its constituent stages of graphic notation that captures his lyrical declamation, which he subsequently harmonizes and finally rhythmicizes into a Lied. Figure 4.4 gives the graphic contour, Example 4.6a inserts this into a musical stave, while Example 4.6b shows the resulting "self-composed" work.

Not surprisingly, such methodology split critical opinion along party lines; it was ridiculed by Ludwig Bischoff, the anti-Wagnerian editor of the

---

[174] Köhler illustrates his method by setting Wagner's Stabreim archetype "Die Liebe bringt uns Lust und Leid, doch in ihr Weh auch webt sie Wonnen" to music in a "natural" version, but compares it to his three caricatured settings in the "absolute" style of Meyerbeer, Rossini, and "French." These rather amusing parodic compositions are reproduced in Grey, *Wagner's Musical Prose*, 192–94.

[175] A letter purporting to be from Bellini to Agostine Gallo describes Bellini composing with Romani in precisely the same way: "I begin by declaiming each character's lines with all the heat of passion, and I closely observe the inflection of my voice, the speeding up and slowing down of the declamation in each situation, the overall accent and the expressive tone that characterizes a man in the grip of passion." This first appeared in 1843 within a pamphlet entitled *Sull'estetica di Vincenzo Bellini – Notizie communicate da lui stesso al Gallo*, and was variously reprinted. This letter is a proven forgery, however, and despite several attempts to authenticate its basic claims, John Rosselli recently dismissed the matter in light of Bellini's documented practice of composing melodies with neither text nor poetic context: "The notion of Bellini as a bard driven by verbal afflatus is absurd." See John Rosselli, *The Life of Bellini* (Cambridge University Press, 1996), 43.

[176] "So würde ich nun kaum wagen, obiges Lied für meine Komposition auszugeben, denn ich habe *nichts* daran gethan, als sie erlauscht, und die Sprachmelodie bekleidet; ließe mann solche Lieder drucken, so sollte der Titel heißen: 'Lied: komponiert durch sich selbst.'" Köhler, *Die Melodie der Sprache*, 65.

[177] Martinville, "SEIN 8/54–18" in www.firstsounds.org/publications/articles/Phonautographic-Manuscripts.pdf, 48, 51.

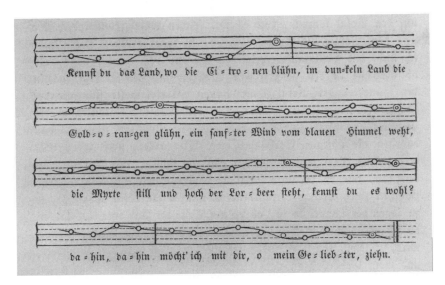

4.4 Louis Köhler's graphic notation of Goethe's poem "Kennst du das Land" from *Die Melodie der Sprache* (1853), p. 64. Reproduced by permission of the Eda Kuhn Loeb Music Library of the Harvard College Library.

Niederrheinische Musik-Zeitung,[178] but taken altogether more seriously by Franz Brendel and Liszt, who viewed the young Köhler as something of a firebrand.[179] Wagner privately dismissed him as a "mad crank" (*ein närrischer Kauz*) with an inexplicable enthusiasm for "artistic form without content,"[180] though responded more politely to the author himself, speaking of a book "I had read even before you sent me a copy," but which would more profitably have demonstrated that modern verse cannot be set to modern melodies, while simply intoning speech as "musical prose" results in

---

[178] Bischoff concludes his terse review dismissively: "Wahrlich! Nach diesem Buche liesse sich ein humoristisches Bild der Musikmacherei im zwanzigsten oder dreissigsten Jahrhundert entwerfen, bei dessen Anschauung die Thränen, welche der Genius der Kunst jetzt über die wahnwitzigen Verirrungen seiner Jünger weint, von unbändigem Lachen erstickt werden müssten." See Bischoff, "Die Melodie der Sprache," *Niederrheinische Musik-Zeitung* 14 (1853), 105–09, here, 109.

[179] Franz Brendel explains that "Diese Schrift ist, nach *Wagner's* Vorgang, der erste Schritt auf der neuen Bahn." He argues further that the development of art has now led to a point where "*die Melodie der Sprache ist die Aufgabe der Gegenwart und Zukunft, die bisherige Gesangsmelodie aber hatte damit äußerst wenig, meist gar nichts zu schaffen.*" Brendel, "Die Melodie der Sprache," *Anregungen für Kunst, Leben und Wissenschaft* 1 (1856), 10–28, here 11, 21.
  Liszt's appreciative letter to Köhler congratulates him on theorizing what Liszt does unawares in composition. See Liszt to Köhler, July 5, 1860, see *Franz Liszt's Briefe*, ed. La Mara (Leipzig: Breitkopf & Härtel, 1893), 1: 358–59.

[180] Wagner to Theodor Uhlig, March 22–25, 1852, Zurich, SB 4: 324–25.

Example 4.6a Louis Köhler's intonation of "Kennst du das Land" inserted into a musical stave (*Die Melodie der Sprache*, 1853), pp. 64–5.

Example 4.6b Köhler's "Kennst du das Land" as a Lied "composed by itself" (*Die Melodie der Sprache*, 1853), p. 65.

"unmelodic formlessness."[181] The scientific curiosity latent in Köhler's claims also engaged physiologists. Speaking from a materialist perspective, the Leipzig-based professor of medicine Karl Merkel shared Wagner's pessimism, but lumped him together with Köhler as fancifully pursuing a futile end:

---

[181] Wagner to Louis Köhler, July 24, 1853, St. Moritz, SB 5: 370–72.

Example 4.7 Karl Merkel's alternative to Louis Köhler's setting of Wagner's archetypal Stabreim (*Physiologie der Sprache*, 1866).

(a) Köhler.

Die Lie - be bringt Lust   und Leid,   doch in ihr Weh   auch webt sie   Won - nen.

(b) Merkel.

Die Lie - be   bringt Lust und Leid,   stets   in   ihr weh mischt sie auch Won-ne.

We *cannot talk of the melody of speech* here, and in all declamatory notation – even were it to be carried out with all the technical expedients of music, as Wagner and Köhler etc. have done – we find no actual trace of melody or of actual, intrinsic music.[182]

While the techniques Köhler espouses are perhaps only relevant as neo-Wagnerian arcana, then, his essentializing interpretation of audible speech as pure sound, and his belief in the tonal gradations of every enunciation, situate his aesthetics midway between song and speech, arguably at the apex of an iconic–expressive merger.

But the reality of fully aligning melodic shape with either lexical or grammatical structure appeared nonsensical to most contemporaries. Merkel is one of many who challenged Köhler's melodic setting of Wagner's exemplary music–poetic period with his own, verbally tweaked *Versmelodie*, complete with alternative intonations (Example 4.7). In his *Fliegende Blätter*, moreover, Lobe dismissed the entire enterprise with the deductive argument that if words and tones are conflated inwardly with one another:

(i) *every text must have only one true melody;* and consequently

(ii) to such a melody, *only one text will fit properly* ...

Or would the words "I love you" have to be set to the same melody regardless of whether Elsa or Lohengrin, Telramund or Ortrud sings them; is it only the grammatical accent that would determine the tonal and rhythmic contour and figure, not the character, feeling, and situation of the people, which can be totally different?[183]

---

[182] "In dieser Hinsicht kann also *nicht von Melodie der menschliche Sprache die Rede* sein, und es ist auch wirklich in allen den deklamatorischen Notirungen, und wären sie noch so sehr mit allen technischen Hülfsmitteln der Musik ausgeführt, wie es *Wagner, Köhler* u. a. m. gethan, keine Spur von Melodie oder von wirklicher, specifischer Musik aufzufinden." Karl Ludwig Merkel, *Physiologie der menschlichen Sprache* (Leipzig: O. Wigand, 1866), 391.

[183] "Wären Wort und Ton so innig miteinander verschmolzen, als die Verehrer der 'Melodie der Sprache' uns einreden wollen, so müßte es (a) für *jeden Text eine wahre Melodie* geben; und folglich könnten (b) zu einer solchen Melodie auch *keine andern Worte untergelegt werden* ... Oder müßten die *Worte*: 'Ich liebe dich' dieselbe Melodie erhalten, gleichviel ob sie Elsa, oder

Lobe is protesting about musical character on the basis of experience, though what he describes as an absurd (in fact, a falsified Wagnerian) theory was not unprecedented; it resonates with Conrad Beissel's (1691–1768) belief that every German sentence has a unique pitch structure determined by master and slave words.[184] If a grammar – in theory at least – inflected words to predefined pitches, the suspicion for skeptical nineteenth-century commentators was that this not only restricts musical characterization, but abdicates compositional responsibility to a mechanical process of dictation: "we should then be able to compose a Drama of the Future in a few hours," Sobolewski quipped.[185]

A brief examination of the *Kompositionsskizze* of *Lohengrin* reveals the extent to which this is wrong-headed. In addition to the structural alterations that would distinguish this from the later *Orchesterskizze*, Wagner's numerous recastings of his melodic material – in terms of declamation, intonation, agogic – illustrate his struggle with notation, as well as the strikingly diverse alternatives that exist within his second thoughts, reconsiderations, and revisions that characterized his process of melodic composition (sharpened, no doubt, by his preoccupation with a Germanic rendering of Gluck's *Iphigénie* at that time). Not surprisingly, therefore, Wagner's documented equivocation over alternatives suggests that his setting of *Lohengrin's* text was far from a stenographic tracing of speech: in fact, he toiled over the *richtige Deklamation*.

At the very outset of the opera, Example 4.8a shows the Heerrufer's call to the assembled Brabantines. Between *Kompositionsskizze*, *Orchesterskizze* and printed score, there is a progressive transfer of accent and more exalted pitch (e^1 rather than c^1) to emphasize "Deutschen König" rather than "Deutschen König," as well as "Freie von Brabant!" rather than "Freie von Brabant!" Similarly, Example 4.8b shows Ortrud's prophecy that, if any part of Lohengrin's body were severed, he would become powerless; within the *Kompositionsskizze* Wagner shifted the accent from "ohnmächtig" to "ohnmächtig," just as he altered Lohengrin's cry (Example 4.8c) to express an

---

Lohengrin, Telramund oder Ortrud sängen; nur der grammatikalische Accent bestimmte die tonliche und rhythmische Biegung und Gestalt, nicht der Charakter, das Gefühl und die Situation der Personen, die ja total verschieden sein können?" Lobe, "Briefe über Rich. Wagner an einen jungen Komponisten. Zwölfter Brief," *FBfM* 2 (1855), 30.

[184] See Lloyd George Blakely, "Johann Conrad Beissel and Music of the Ephrata Cloister," *Journal of Research in Music Education* 15 (1967), 120–38.

[185] Sobolewski's full comment invokes literal mechanical stenography and is worth quoting at length: "If the system of word-melody maintains its ground, it will not be difficult in this inventive age – which has already invented an instrument that immediately marks down every note a person sounds, as well as one that imitates all the instruments of an orchestra – to invent another that will set down musically whatever a person declaims. We should then be able to compose a Drama of the Future in a few hours." See *Reaktionäre Briefe aus dem Feuilleton der Ostpreuss*, 45.

Example 4.8a *Lohengrin*, act 1 scene 1, mm. 19–26 (King's Herald).

Example 4.8b *Lohengrin*, act 2 scene 1, mm. 327–28 (Ortrud).

emphatic double accent (rather than only one), after Elsa submits to forbidden desire and asks after his provenance. Finally, one instance of Wagner altering tonal inflection without changing his text rhythm is Friedrich's question (Example 4.8d), which becomes a more urgent inquiry in its open rising minor sixth, than in its original falling minor third (to the local tonic, a).

With no knowledge of these equivocations, Köhler implicitly discounts a Wagnerian lexicon of phonetically fixed sentiments by analyzing both how the

Example 4.8c *Lohengrin*, act 3, scene 2, mm. 1299–1300 (Lohengrin).

Example 4.8d *Lohengrin*, act 2 scene 1, m. 183 (Telramund).

Example 4.9a Köhler's setting of "Ei" (*Die Melodie der Sprache*, 1853), p. 25.

same monosyllables can be intoned differently according to character, and where notation ceases to be able to differentiate vocal delivery in performance: "Wie" as both question and surprise, in contrast to "Ei!" as exclamation. He conjures dramatic scenarios that determine how text should be enunciated differently. Example 4.9a sets "Ei!" as that of an elder sister responding sympathetically to a younger sibling's joy over a new puppy. (He may have had Mozart's three ladies from *Die Zauberflöte* in mind, where monosyllables are differentiated similarly by melodic interval and tonic / dominant context, see Example 4.9b.) Example 4.9c reproduces Köhler's setting of "Wie?" as a question that expects an answer, while Example 4.9d presents "Wie!" as that of a General's anger over a subordinate's contumacy (which expects no answer).

Example 4.9b Mozart's *Die Zauberflöte*, act 1, scene 1.

Example 4.9c Köhler's "Wie?".   **Example 4.9d** Köhler's "Wie!".

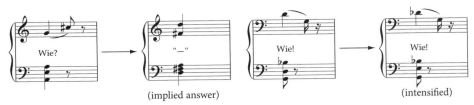

Completing his dissociation with lexical fixity, Köhler further argued that accent in performance distinguishes both settings of "Wie" (the questioner draws out the sound slowly, while the General's anger is violent and short). Without explaining his harmonization, Köhler concludes: "the external similarity between this 'Wie' and 'Ei' shortly before it lies only in the *notes* for our eyes, while the uninscribable *performance* together with the *harmony* marks the difference strongly enough."[186] Of course, Köhler's approach remains fundamentally different from Wagner's in that Wagner writes declamation to be performed, while Köhler literally declaims text aloud, later to be written; both are transcriptions of a kind, but Wagner's is prescriptive, Köhler's descriptive.[187]

Wagner had expressed similar frustrations over notation to Liszt in 1850, and given that – with Schröder-Devrient's utterances in mind – he

---

186 "Die äußerliche Aehnlichkeit dieses 'Wie' mit dem 'Ei' von vorhin liegt nur in den *Noten* fürs Auge, indem der nicht zu schildernde *Vortrag* vereint mit der *Harmonie* den Unterschied stark genug geben." Köhler, *Die Melodie der Sprache*, 26.

187 See Charles Seeger's classic account of this dichotomy in "Prescriptive and Descriptive Music-Writing," *The Musical Quarterly* 44 (1958), 184–95.

Example 4.10a *Lohengrin*, act 1, scene 1, mm. 90–97 (King Heinrich der Vogler).

4.5 Wagner's *Kompositionsskizze* for *Lohengrin* (showing revisions in Example 4.10a), NA A II B 2, 1 recto. Reproduced by permission of the *Nationalarchiv der Richard-Wagner-Stiftung*, Bayreuth.

equivocated between over- and under-determined notation, his revisions to spoken emphasis bear most on the present argument. I offer a relatively large sampling of six examples to illustrate his ongoing struggle with vocal prescription.

In Example 4.10a, the King's rallying cry for military power to defend the German realm rises in pitch (d^1 to f^1) and agogic accent (dotted quarter to dotted half note on "deutsche"), as well as gaining emphasis through syncopated metrical placement. Wagner's manuscript is given as Figure 4.5.

Similarly, when Lohengrin finally reveals his parentage to the awed Brabantine crowd (Example 4.10b), Wagner reversed the direction of his

Example 4.10b *Lohengrin*, act 3, mm. 1276–77 (Lohengrin).

Example 4.10c *Lohengrin*, act 3, mm. 1637–46 (Ortrud). Wagner's earlier harmonizations are indicated by roman numerals in square brackets.

original line between *Kompositionsskizze* and *Orchesterskizze*, further adding an appoggiatura on "Krone"; the resulting proclamation is a more glorified, forthright exertion that Parzifal "wears his crown."

At the close of the opera, Ortrud's fury at the departing knight is likewise far more emphatic with her sustained high 'A's in the *Orchesterskizze* (Example 4.10c). This is partly to do with the absence of Ortrud's original

Example 4.10d *Lohengrin*, act 2, scene 2, mm. 491–93 (Elsa).

continuation against Lohengrin (in the *Kompositionsskizze*) which in the later version turns her initial phrase into her final and only utterance at the end of act 3. Wagner's reinterpretation of this text is nevertheless a decisive enhancement of Ortrud's valedictory declamation, illustrating how the same visceral statement can receive radically different melodic settings.

Modifications of inflection on a lower lever can be equally revealing in Wagner's treatment of syntactical *minutiae*. Over different diminished triads, Elsa's reaction to Ortrud's unexpected appearance in act 2, scene 2 (Example 4.10d) is changed to accommodate a more urgent setting of "what <u>are</u> you doing here?"

In 1968, Robert Bailey identified a similar discrepancy between Wagner's 1850 setting of the duet between Brünnhilde and Siegfried in *Siegfrieds Tod*, and the same from 1869 for *Götterdämmerung*, commenting that this is a rare instance in which Wagner made two independent settings of almost exactly the same text, albeit "separated by a crucial interval of nineteen years."[188] As Bailey's comparison demonstrates, to the extent that the words prefigure a musical setting, they prefigured two quite different settings equally well. The radical implication here is the possibility that there is no one perfect, not-to-be-improved-on musical end point in Wagner's "energy, fire, and determined expression." Multiple competing melodic settings for any one text undermine the authority of a single "locked in" expression, elevating the aforementioned

---

[188] Robert Bailey, "Wagner's Musical Sketches for *Siegfrieds Tod*," in *Studies in Music History: Essay for Oliver Strunk*, ed. Harold Powers (Princeton University Press, 1968), 459–94, here 477. We might also think of *Tristan* here, where the same lines are set in act 1, scenes 3–4 between Isolde and Brangäne with slight differences: "Kennst du der Mutter / Künste nicht? / Wähnst du, die alles / klug erwägt, / ohne Rat in fremdes Land / hätt' sie mit dir mich entsandt? / . . . Für Weh und Wunden / gab sie Balsam, / für böse Gifte / Gegengift."

motifs of freedom, improvisation, and performing the same text in different ways to a new level of importance for Wagner's operas of this period. Wagner came close to admitting as much in 1871 when he said that viewers equate actors' activity with the "only reality of the artistic show," hence:

The *artistic* share in theatrical performances must simply be ascribed to the performers, whereas the author of the piece has no more to do with the actual "art" than insofar as he has planned his poem by calculating the effect it is to produce when acted.[189]

In perceptually rendering actors the only "reality" (*Wirklichkeit*) of an artistic event, this, for Wagner, taps the "aim of true art in general," suggesting that had Wagner been contented with existing performance traditions in Saxony, there would have been less need for such closely composed vocal melody.[190]

Returning to *Lohengrin*, his evident difficulty over notating revisions caused him in some instances to cede plastic melody from the voice to the orchestra in favor of freer vocal recitation. One of the more extended melodic revisions in the *Orchesterskizze* was to Lohengrin's stanzaic Grail Narration (Example 4.10e). In fact, Wagner's only authorized cut for the Weimar premiere had been the third verse; in his *Kompositionsskizze* he had set the first verse to the grail theme from the Prelude, though he modified portions of this in a second pen sketch; in the *Orchesterskizze* he changed these entirely so that Lohengrin recites his text to triadic pitches behind the upper string melody in the orchestra. There may be several reasons for this: first, the initial setting required unusual emphasis and melodic length on relatively insignificant, short words such as "mitten" (m. 1228), "drin" (m. 1231), and "dort" (m. 1233) which are set to correspondingly lowly pitches and metrical placement in the revision; second, the instrumental grail theme itself falls into the category Wagner would later dismiss as "absolute melody," and his attempt in 1846–47 to merge this with spoken inflection results in the kind of anomalous emphasis seen on "Reinste" (m. 1236), or the unusual rhythm of "ni-cht bekannt" (m. 1230). The recitational freedom of Wagner's setting in the *Orchesterskizze* provided him with an altogether more speech-*like* rhythm and tonal inflection; the contrast between the two melodies is emblematic of Wagner's frustrations – voiced in *Oper und Drama* – at the two "faults" of modern dramatic song, namely: "ignoring the determinative nature of poetic song–melody, for which an absolute melody drawn from instrumental music was substituted;

---

[189] SSD 9: 159. Cf. PW 5: 160.   [190] *Ibid.*

Example 4.10e Earlier versions of Lohengrin's Grail Narration, *Lohengrin*, act 3, mm. 1227–42.

Example 4.10e (cont.)

and second, ignoring the thorough difference in timbre between the human voice and orchestral instruments."[191] His comments seem tailor-made for the alterations to Lohengrin's narration. In this respect, Wagner was being truly autodidactic, which is to say, self-reflexive in his mid-century criticism.

Lurking in the background to such revisions is the Wagnerian process of stratifying dramatic dialogue, of absorbing "melody" into the orchestral texture as "orchestral speech," while the voice utters words in the direct narrative through tonally inflected pitches. Ostensibly, Wagner explains this theoretical innovation – outlined in the final pages of *Oper und Drama* – as a necessity resulting from his dissatisfaction with settings by Weber and

---

[191] SSD 4: 170. Cf. PW 2: 313.

Example 4.10f *Lohengrin*, act 3, mm. 307–10 (Lohengrin).

Meyerbeer. The melodic revisions to *Lohengrin* suggest equally that insert-ing melodic material into the orchestra while leaving voices to their inflected pitches may also result from a compositional strategy to better inflect the text after an initial *frustration* with notating the "melody." The theory of orchestral speech, in other words, may have been born in part from a failed vocal-melodic practice. In addition to Example 4.10e, one of the clearest illustrations of this is a brief revision to Lohengrin's comment to Elsa "we are alone" shortly before she asks the forbidden question in act 3. Here (Example 4.10f), the original vocal melody was doubled in the orchestra, but is altered so that the new recitational vocal line fits the old (now orchestral) melody without carrying its pitches.

On different levels, then, German locution was evidently a guiding specter throughout Wagner's composition of *Lohengrin*. But as Hermann Danuser reminded us in 1975, Wagner's musical prose does not – *pace* Köhler – mean the aperiodic setting of speech, but the setting of prosaically accented verses (i.e. from poetry) in which only speech accent, and not regular meter or end rhyme, is valid.[192] Wagner's revisions indicate the considerable flexibility this entailed in practice, where freedom from external meter – poetic or periodic – was merely a corollary of elevating speech to the status of poetry. In short, the potential for sentient expressivity in national speech led him to dismantle international poetic frames.

Pronouncing the homeland

This shift toward prose in the guise of poetry emphasizes what melodic analysts tend to forget, namely that the speaking voice was no longer innocent; with "musical speech" it acquired artistic responsibility. Just as one would not blow

---

[192] Hermann Danuser, *Musikalische Prosa* (Regensburg: G. Bosse, 1975), 68.

through the reed of an English Horn or into a trumpet but to make musical sound, after the quasi-verbal utterances of Schröder-Devrient, enunciating text was itself a musical endeavor of sorts for this particular aesthetic; elocution became not merely regulative, but – theoretically, at least – constitutive of texted artworks, if only for German aestheticians within Wagner's orbit.[193]

But unlike language, speech behaves as an idiolect; its character as performative melody varies with each exponent. The need for "correct" pronunciation in the singing of any operatic libretto had never been in question, of course. For the English critic Chorley, one of Schröder-Devrient's greatest professional mistakes was her attempt to sing in English "without having mastered the language."[194] The Austrian singer and pedagogue Ferdinand Sieber outlined the general problem in his 1854 aphorisms for the *Berliner Musik-Zeitung Echo*:

Complete knowledge of one's mother tongue is an indisputable prerequisite for the trained singer. If suddenly in the middle of the most beautiful and most delightful song a *speech impediment* or *provincialism* reaches our ear, it would have about the same disagreeable effect on us as when we see the proudly sailing swan that rises from the water level and stands on its ugly legs, or we suddenly hear vulgar speech from the mouth of a truly beautiful person, on whose physical beauty we just feasted our eyes.[195]

Sieber's avian metaphor taps into a long discourse on German declamation that required impeccable pronunciation from actors and singers alike. In 1774, Johann Georg Sulzer had required that, in addition to beauty of sound, pronunciation must be "agreeable";[196] the

---

[193] The literature on speech melody among nineteenth-century theorists of drama is vast. Three seminal contributions are Seckendorff, *Vorlesungen über Deklamation und Mimik*; Pius Alexander Wolff, "Bemerkung über die Stimme und ihre Ausbildung zum Vortrag auf der Bühne," in Karl Holtei, *Beiträge zur Geschichte dramatischer Kunst und Literatur* (Berlin: Haude und Spener, 1827); and Rötscher, *Die Kunst der dramatischen Darstellung*. Recent scholarly investigations of this tropic include Ulrich Kühn, *Sprech-Ton-Kunst: musikalisches Sprechen und Formen des Melodrams* (Tübingen: Niemeyer, 2001); and David Trippett, "Bayreuth in Miniature: Wagner and the Melodramatic Voice," *The Musical Quarterly* 95 (2012), 71–138.

[194] Chorley, *Thirty Years' Musical Recollections*, 40.

[195] "Die vollkommenste Kenntniß seiner Muttersprache ist ein unerläßliches Erforderniß für den gebildeten Sänger. Wenn inmitten des schönsten und entzückendsten Gesanges plötzlich ein *Sprachfehler* oder *Provinzialismus* an unser Ohr dringt, so wird das ungefähr denselben widerwärtigen Eindruck auf uns machen, als wenn wir den Stolz dahin segelnden Schwan mit einem Male dem Wasserspiegel entsteigen und auf seinen häßlichen Füßen stehen sehen, oder aus dem Munde eines wahrhaft schönen Menschen, an dessen Wohlgestalt wir uns eben weiden, plötzlich *gemeine Reden* erschallen hören." Ferdinand Sieber, "Aphorismen über Gesang," *Berliner Musik-Zeitung Echo* 21 (1854), 166.

[196] "*Vortrag (Redende Künste)*: Der Wohlklang hängt nicht blos von der Annehmlichkeit der Stimme ab, auch die Aussprache muß angenehm sein." Sulzer, *Allgemeine Theorie der schönen Künste in einzeln*, 4: 765–66.

Goethe-protégé Pius Alexander Wolff amplified this in 1827, claiming that diction assumes a didactic function, i.e. "to educate [both] natives and foreigners";[197] while Marx, writing in 1854 after decades of philological research, finds vocal beauty fully synonymous with pronunciation: "an ideal of purity *and* sonority . . . [is] indispensable, and the foundation of all artistic enunciation."[198] As Eric Hobsbawm reminds us, however, the idea of a national language is a chimera of the nineteenth century, wherein the attempt was made to raise one "dialect" to the status of a norm, to which other verbal idioms were then subjugated.[199] Such instability of verbal idiom could only be multiplied by the still greater variability of idiolect, with its wealth of alternative spoken delivery. Where Sieber's serenely gliding swan alludes to an ill-defined notion of received *hochdeutsch* pronunciation against which to measure the provincialisms of dialect, more was at stake for Wagner's intoned-speech, which straddled Humboldt's dualism of language where sensuous sound delicately implied immaterial thought. In this way, not only enunciation but also inflected text setting could belie spoken dialect, and it was probably with this in mind that Carl Stumpf alluded to Wagner's own provinciality, remarking in his study of musical origins: "I even believe that with Richard Wagner . . . echoes of his Saxon speech are clearly discernible in the phrasing of tones."[200] Stumpf was onto something, it seems, for Wagner's contemporary Robert von Hornstein corroborates his suspicion: "When [Wagner] was really high-spirited, he spoke the earthiest Saxon dialect. He always had a Saxon accent. Even French . . . he intoned in a Saxon way."[201] If Wagner was "locking in" a declamatory aesthetic into his vocal melodies to fill an "empty" performer, at least one commentator heard this as German dialect, i.e. ugly legs rather than a sailing swan.

---

[197] "Man hat das Recht, von dem Schauspieler alle Eigenschaften einer reinen, richtigen, makellosen Aussprache zu fordern, und der Vortrag auf der Bühne sollte als eine Schule desselben für Eingeborene und Fremde gelten können." Wolff, *Bemerkungen über die Stimme und ihre Ausbildung zum Vortrag auf der Buhne*, 295. Cited in Irmgard Weithase, *Die Geschichte der deutschen Vortragskunst im 19. Jahrhundert* (Weimar: H. Böhlau, 1940), 27ff.

[198] A. B. Marx, *The Music of the Nineteenth Century and Its Culture*, 268. Emphasis added.

[199] Eric J. Hobsbawm, *Nations and Nationalism Since 1780: Programme, Myth, Reality*, 2nd edn., rpt. (Cambridge University Press, 2012), 54ff.

[200] "Ich glaube sogar, daß bei Richard Wagner, der . . . sich Anklänge seines sächsischen Sprechens in den Tonwendungen deutlich bemerkbar machen." Carl Stumpf, *Die Anfänge der Musik* [1911], rpt. (Hildesheim and New York: G. Olms, 1979), 83.

[201] "Wenn er recht ausgelassen wurde, sprach er den derbsten sächsischen Dialekt. Sächsischen Akzent hatte er immer. Auch sein Französisch . . . sprach er in sächsischem Tonfall." Robert von Hornstein, "Memoiren," *Süddeutsche Monatshefte* 3 (1907), 166. I take this translation from Spencer, *Wagner Remembered*, 98.

So the universalized "feeling" communicated by *Worttonsprache* ("musical expression ... conditioned by the speaking-verse")[202] was potentially vulnerable to the indeterminability of "correct" pronunciation. Yet in Wagner's theory, at least, the aesthetic concept of Old High German alliteration exceeded its execution. In *Lohengrin*, he sought to replicate in iambic prose the experience of hearing French and Italian singers in their native tongue, or hearing Schröder-Devrient in any language. Revisions to his *Kompositionsskizze* effectively document the attempt to "dramatize" through declamation, bringing the opera closer to realist spoken theater in an eminently pragmatic way. It may well have been the suspected failure of these declamatory "recitatives" in Weimar that finally persuaded Wagner – on the brink of penning *Oper und Drama* – of the need that would have been satisfied by Stabreim, whose rhyming sonorities, we recall, the ear will intuitively understand.

* * *

Though Wagner's project for German melody in the 1840s was intricately bound to its expression through the German language, it seems he had already decided by December 1849 that his melodies were missing the vital ingredient. Less than perfect reports of the *Lohengrin* premiere merely confirmed this in what seems to have become a self-fulfilling prophecy. Consequently, Wagner's confidence in the ineluctable power of language (and erstwhile hope for German expression) waned, and under extreme financial pressure, he tells Liszt rather unconvincingly of his plan to compose an opera in French for Paris while determining "to remain as I am in my own character to speak to the French comprehensibly."[203] In the same letter, Wagner subsequently regarded the language of *Lohengrin* with indifference, tentatively agreeing to Liszt's suggestion from July 1849 that *Lohengrin* be translated into English for a world premiere in London.[204]

Whether or not this sentiment was sincere, Wagner took no such action. His comments nevertheless mark a point of departure from what Susan

---

[202] SSD 4: 216. Cf. PW 2: 363.   [203] Wagner to Liszt, December 5, 1849, Zurich, SB 3: 187–88.

[204] See Wagner to Liszt, December 5, 1849, Zurich, SB 3: 188. I infer Liszt's suggestions about an English *Lohengrin* from his earlier correspondence with Wagner. Liszt's letter of *ca.* July 6, 1849 survives only as a fragment, and closes with a statement of concern about performing *Lohengrin*: "I fear at the performance the superideal color which you have maintained throughout ... my sincere friendship may authorize me to tell you. . ." What follows must have concerned a possible performance in London because Wagner later refers back to Liszt's suggestion about this, a suggestion which is not otherwise to be found in Liszt's letters.

Bernstein enigmatically terms the "rigid identification with the typeface of an 'I,'" i.e. that which enacts an audio-visual identification "with one's language or words as one's 'own.'"[205] During his first few months in exile, Wagner's authorial position, in other words, became temporarily unmoored from an otherwise staunchly defended bond to the sound of spoken German. It may be no coincidence that this was also a time he lost faith as a German revolutionary, so much so that, upon his return to Germany in 1860, he could write to Liszt of "a sense of surprise at the silliness and unmannerliness [*Albernheit und Ungezogenheit*] of the language that was being spoken all around me. Believe me, we have no fatherland!"[206]

Wagner's earlier impetus toward spoken expression as *Versmelodie* appears now only to have been his first reaction to experiences of witnessing Schröder-Devrient. She was for him the verification of a specifically Germanicized *Melodik* that allowed for a melodic theory to absorb elements of language intrinsically into its body of sound. In the modes of listening I termed iconic and expressive, expressive melody was altogether more philosophically acceptable to Wagner at mid-century – as the realization *of* a semantically conditioned poetic idea. But iconic melody, with its emphasis on communicating emotion intuitively through the sensuous substance of sound, offered precisely the element he sought to harness in *Worttonsprache*. Schröder-Devrient appealed to both modes of listening, and – returning to the adolescent ear with which we started – by appealing to his "listeners" in *Oper und Drama*, Wagner went beyond his initial composition of speech that had preoccupied him throughout the later 1840s; in intuitively comprehensible sound he sought a guarantor for dramatic understanding, that is, he sought finally to compose a way of being heard.

---

[205] Susan Bernstein, "In Formel: Wagner und Liszt," *New German Critique* 69 (1996), 91.
[206] Wagner to Liszt, September 13, 1860, Paris, SB 12: 260.

5 | Vowels, voices, and "original truth"

Wagner's *Sinnlichkeit*

> I conceive that Ideas in the Understanding are coeval with Sensation; which is such an Impression or Motion, made in some part of the Body, as makes it be taken notice of in the Understanding.
>
> John Locke (1690)[1]

> We were all Feuerbachians for a moment.
>
> Friedrich Engels (1886)[2]

The topic of Wagner's poetic language often raises a smile. Back in 1911, the *Encyclopaedia Britannica* gave official sanction to widespread incredulity:

> the archaic alliteration of the *Niebelungenlied* is not allied with any sense of beauty in verbal sound or verse–rhythm; and [Wagner's] ways of expressing emotion in language consist chiefly in the piling-up of superlatives ... [demonstrating] the affectations of the amateur author.[3]

As early as 1854 Joachim Raff had declared the "great error" in *Oper und Drama* to be blind faith in alliterative poetry: "Does Wagner seriously believe that the chains of his Stabreim, precisely because they are freshly forged, will deaden less than the old, sometimes somewhat defective end rhyme?"[4] Few challenged this skepticism after Nietzsche had punctured the Teutonic aura of Wagner's linguistic designs ("today we laugh at that"):[5] Ernest Newman judged Wagner to be "elaborately absurd over his vowels

---

[1] John Locke, *An Essay Concerning Humane Understanding* (London: Edward Mory, 1690), 44.

[2] Friedrich Engels "Ludwig Feuerbach und der Ausgang der klassischen deutschen Philosophie" [1886], Eng. trans. *German Socialist Philosophy*, ed. Wolfgang Schirmacher (New York: Continuum, 1997), 190.

[3] *Enclaopedia Britannica*, 11th edn. (1911): www.1911encyclopedia.org/ Wilhelm_Richard_Wagner.

[4] "Oder glaubt Wagner im Ernste, daß die Kette seines Stabreims deswegen, weil sie wieder frisch geschmiedet ist, weniger drücken werde, als die alte, hie und da etwas schadhafte des Endreims?" Joachim Raff, *Die Wagnerfrage: kritisch beleuchtet* (Brunswick: F. Viewig, 1854), 103.

[5] Nietzsche, "Human, all too Human," in *The Portable Nietzsche*, ed. and trans. Walter Kaufmann (New York: Penguin, 1976), 668.

and consonants";[6] Jack Stein cautioned that his mid-century project with language "borders on the ludicrous";[7] and Pierre Boulez, in his detailed writings on Wagnerian aesthetics, simply deemed his linguistic preoccupations unworthy of mention.[8] If aligning historical opinion within opera studies is like herding cats, the consistency with which Wagner's beleaguered philology has been dismissed is *sui generis*. The implication is that his Stabreim was a mere indulgence, something to occupy the composer's inquisitive mind – bolstering his confidence – in vocal-melodic expression. Viewed as an authentic component of opera, it has the pale glow of illusion, which is to say something that vanishes under the scrutiny of cold reality. Over and above Wagner's considerable influence on Symbolist poetics,[9] even today there seems to be a consensus that the opera poems are at best a minor irritation, an idiosyncratic appendage that we tolerate, whereas for Wagner they were supposedly fundamental. This incongruity is worth exploring; in short, because it masks a shift in the conception of how sound carries meaning. Wagner's theory of communication in *Oper und Drama* was conceived straight-forwardly at the level of sensation, anterior to ideation; but this required language itself to become physiologically tangible. Wagner alludes to this physical immediacy in response to an article by Theodor Uhlig, perhaps his closest musical confidant at the time, wherein Wagner protests the practical necessity of his project: "In my view [Stabreim] is the only point on which I cannot make myself completely clear to others because this is only possible through the *deed*."[10] Although the *frisson nouveau* produced by Wagner's "ludicrous" poetry is long past, it still forms the nexus through which we can best access this discourse on the phonology of vocal expression and its effects. In Chapter 4 we examined the relationship between the importance Wagner placed on Schröder-Devrient's enunciations and the sensory power he would ascribe to language as a musical tool. Following this line of argument, we now consider the basis

---

[6] Ernest Newman, *Wagner as Man & Artist* (New York: Alfred Knopf, 1924), 213.

[7] Jack Stein, *Richard Wagner and the Synthesis of the Arts* (Detroit: Wayne State University Press, 1960), 71.

[8] Pierre Boulez, *Orientations*, trans. Martin Cooper (Oxford University Press, 1986), 223–91.

[9] A recent English summary of Wagner's influence on French Symbolism is given by Annegret Fauser in "Wagnerism," *The Cambridge Companion to Wagner*, 229–34. See also Janos Riesz, "Mallarmés *Richard Wagner, rêverie d'un poète français* und sein *Hommage à Wagner*," in *Von Wagner zum Wagnérism: Musik, Literatur, Kunst, Politik*, ed. Annegret Fauser and Manuela Schwartz (Leipzig: Leipziger Universitätsverlag, 1999), 445–58.

[10] Wagner to Theodor Uhlig, May 6–7, 1852, Zurich, SB 4: 356. Emphasis added. Uhlig's serialized article "Richard Wagners Schriften über Kunst" for the *Neue Zeitschrift für Musik* turned to *Oper und Drama* on January 1, 1851, though he was unable to complete his critique of part 3 before his death on January 3, 1853. See SB 4: 197, note 670.

for a shift in the conception of melodic and speech sound in Wagner's writings around the 1848 revolution, a shift, that is, between aesthetics and acoustics.

It may be no coincidence that the tipping point between these two perspectives is what Wagner called *Sinnlichkeit*. We have met this term before: it is directly implicated in the very qualities which drew Wagner to Bellinian melody, to Schröder-Devrient's "beautiful breath," and by extension, to his erotic metaphors for the interrelation of dramatic meaning with musical expression. During the late 1840s, *Sinnlichkeit* is both an arbiter and an actor in the decline (but survival) of idealism and the rise of the natural sciences. The Grimm brothers' *Deutsches Wörterbuch* (1854) lists ten shades of meaning, of which the third – "faculty of sensory perception" (*fähigkeit der sinnlichen wahrnehmung*) – is the most extensively supported by quotation;[11] this includes Johann Georg Hamann's solid opposition: "sensuality in our faculty of cognition (the faculty of perceiving experience) contains two parts: the senses and the power of imagination. The former is the capability of perceiving an object in the present; the latter is the same in the absence of the present."[12] When Wagner's Zurich essays were reprinted in 1872 he clarified his earlier use of the word *Sinnlichkeit* likewise as the antithesis of "ideality" (*"Gedanklichkeit"*), echoing Hamann's dualism closely – "the contrasts of intuitive and abstract perception and their results" – in formulating his own definition: "the sensory power of perception" (*sinnliches Anschauungsvermögen*).[13] Beyond the fleshy reality of the physical body, then, *Sinnlichkeit* emerges for Wagner as a means of recipient gratification that fuses, for the receiver, an attitude of critical appraisal for the art object with the sensation of pleasure in the hearing and viewing of that object. "The sovereign might of physical sensation and emotions of the heart," he declared, "breaks down the pride of intellect as soon as these proclaim their sway as something that all men must obey in common, as that of sensations and emotions *of the species*."[14] With this allusion to phylogeny, Wagner's urge to communicate to his audience at the level of biology – "feeling" as a sensory principle – aims for universality drawn from

---

[11] See J. / W. Grimm, *Deutsches Wörterbuch,* "Sinnlichkeit" § 3, http://woerterbuchnetz.de/DWB/?sigle=DWB&mode=Vernetzung&lemid=GS29575.

[12] "die sinnlichkeit im erkenntniszvermögen (das vermögen der vorstellungen in der anschauung) enthält zwei stücke: den sinn und die einbildungskraft, das erstere ist das vermögen der anschauung in der gegenwart des gegenstandes, das zweite auch ohne die gegenwart desselben." *Ibid.*

[13] SSD 3: 4–5.   [14] SSD 3: 66. Cf. PW 1: 94. Emphasis added.

our common anatomy, and finds a stable basis when tied to the capacity for pleasure in a modern sensorium.

But where did this particular conception of *Sinnlichkeit* come from? In addition to Wagner's literary and cultural preoccupations, this chapter's guiding thread is a certain watershed in idealist philosophy from the figure to whom Wagner dedicated *Das Kunstwerk der Zukunft*. Back in 1941 Jacques Barzun first posited Wagner as a pivotal figure in the impulse toward philosophical materialism,[15] and it is a curious fact that *Lohengrin* was completed only sixty-six days after the *Manifesto of the Communist Party* appeared, both of which, it could be argued, document a coalescing of *humanism* and *materialism*, both of which selected and reinterpreted ideas from Ludwig Feuerbach.

In his *Principles of the Philosophy of the Future* (1843), Feuerbach's notion of "sensuality" (*Sinnlichkeit*) held that man's conception of nature was dependent on acts of sensory experience that are equally as primary as self-consciousness. "What is light ... without the eye? It is nothing," he states, "Only the consciousness of seeing is the reality of seeing or real seeing."[16] Essentially, the concept of *Sinnlichkeit* points out the failure of speculative philosophy to acknowledge the integrity of sensation. In Hegelian philosophy, within which Feuerbach was educated, the senses were being subordinated to the intellect, he argued, and sense experience was being treated as a purely intellectual phenomenon: "[i]ts objects are only determinations of thought. They dissolve completely into it and keep for themselves nothing that would have remained outside the thought process."[17] By intellectualizing the experience of sensation, the idealist tradition had severed sensation's roots in the real world and made it possible to bestow upon sensation an illusory, false, and merely imagined foundation, one that existed only in the mind:

The recognition of the light of reality in the darkness of abstraction is a contradiction ... the reality of the idea is sensation. But reality is the truth of the idea; thus, sensation is the truth of the idea ... Because, however, one starts

---

[15] "[H]ow can art – particularly music – fit into the Marx-and-Darwin system? The answer is that Wagner too has a system, and ... it is basically materialistic and mechanical." Jacques Barzun, *Darwin, Marx, Wagner: Critique of a Heritage* [1941], rpt. (New York: Doubleday Anchor books, 1958), 12–13. Building on Barzun's work, Richard Justin presents a specifically Marxian study of the *Ring* as the internal corruption of an economic order in "Darwin, Marx, Wagner: Dialectical Materialism in the *Ring*," *New Studies in Richard Wagner's The Ring of the Nibelung*, ed. Herbert Richardson (Lewiston, NY: Edwin Mellen Press, 1991), 89–126.

[16] Ludwig Feuerbach, *Principles of the Philosophy of the Future*, trans. Manfred Vogel (Indianapolis: Hackett Publishing Co., 1986), 27.

[17] *Ibid.*, 15.

consciously with the truth of the idea, the truth of sensation is expressed only afterwards . . . we save ourselves from this contradiction only if we make the real, that is, the sensuous, into its own subject and give it an absolutely independent, divine, and primary meaning which is not first derived from the idea.[18]

A decisive embrace of sensation and corresponding rejection of what Isaiah Berlin once called "the fatal doctrine of Descartes"[19] resonates with Wagner's incessant distrust of the "impotent . . . abstract intellect,"[20] and treatment of feeling as a barometer calibrated according to sensuous truth, where "truth, reality, and sensation are identical."[21] Moreover, it was a distrust that went back to the nationalist leanings of the pietist Lutheran Hamann (Herder's teacher, cited above), whom Berlin paraphrases lucidly:

Such distinctions as we draw between thought and feeling (and their "objects"), physical sensation and intellectual or moral or aesthetic awareness, are, according to Hamann . . . an attempt to draw attention now to this, now to that facet of a single experience; a tendency which, pushed too far, tends to separate and abstract one facet from another and, pushed further still, to lead to the invention of imaginary abstract objects, or idealized entities – to transform reality into a collection of artificial figments. This . . . kills the sources of the true sense of reality.[22]

Feuerbach embraced Hamann's doctrine for the *Young Germans*, but rejected its basis in Christian mysticism (essentially by replacing the sacrament with the scalpel). Within this context, a suspicious division of heart and mind even acquired political overtones, not irrelevant to Wagner's Dresden: "How many are republicans in their heart and by their disposition," Feuerbach asked, "but in their minds, cannot detach themselves from the monarchy?"[23] Wagner publicly rejected the view that humanity must be subordinated to immaterial strictures or "external, imaginary . . . power[s]" that he saw vested in the church and the monarchy.[24] Mental illusion

---

[18] *Ibid.,* 49–51.

[19] Isaiah Berlin, *Three Critics of the Enlightenment: Vico, Hamann, Herder* (Princeton University Press, 2000), 189. While Berlin is paraphrasing J. G. Hamann, see also Maurice Merleau-Ponty, who speaks for himself: "it is I who read Descartes' text, I who recognize in it an underlying truth, so that finally the Cartesian *cogito* acquires its significance only through my own *cogito*, and I should have no thought of it, had I not within myself all that is needed to invent it. It is I who assigns to my thought the objective of resuming the action of the *cogito*, and I who constantly verify my thought's orientation towards this objective, therefore my thought must forestall itself in the pursuit of this aim, and must already have found what it seeks, otherwise it would not seek it." Merleau-Ponty, *Phenomenology of Perception*, trans. Colin Smith (London and New York: Routledge, 2002), 431–32.

[20] SSD 3: 145. Cf. PW 1: 179.   [21] Feuerbach, *Principles*, 51.

[22] Berlin, *Three Critics of the Enlightenment*, 190.   [23] Feuerbach, *Principles*, 29.

[24] SSD 3: 44. Cf. PW 1: 71.

enslaved people to Christianity, he protested, whose modern, subjugating doctrine "is patiently to sacrifice this miserable world for a better afterlife."[25] A cloistering of the mind, isolated from tangible reality, was solely responsible for the persistent hegemony of what he called "hypocritical absolutism."[26] The synonymy of social and aesthetic questions in Wagner's Zurich essays is effectively enabled, at a philosophical level, by his belief that sensation governs all perception, further tying him to Feuerbach's trust in a non-abstract, sensory relation to objects of contemplation, irrespective of whether they were political, aesthetic, or social–historical. It would seem the composer found this aspect of Feuerbach's writing attractive not only because it represented a kind of avant-garde of the German left, but also because his immersion in the sensory experience of opera preceded his political awakening during the 1840s.

It is not surprising, then, that Wagner's mid-century artistic leanings appear to emanate from Feuerbach's statement that the essence of the modern era was "materialism, empiricism, realism, humanism."[27] Wagner admired Feuerbach for his "human" perspective, in contrast to the intellectual apparatus of men of letters. This effectively made him a role model for *Young German* living: "Nowhere have I found the natural healthy process so clearly and so consciously expressed as by Feuerbach."[28] Beyond Wagner's familiar borrowings from him in the narrative sphere – a pantheistic characterization of the *Ring* gods as projections of human need,[29] the contradictions of belief and love in *Lohengrin*, a forthright renunciation of Christian dogma – Feuerbach seems also to have provided part of the scholarly impetus for the sensory content of vowels in Wagner's conception of *Versmelodie*, and for a belief in vocal–verbal sounds that are intuitively comprehensible at a sentient level (*gefühlsverständlich*).[30]

When Siegfried tells Mime of his hopes for a better companion in act 1 of *Siegfried*, he explains how he put this specific question to the forest inhabitants by means of a horncall: "In the depths of the forest I let my horn ring out clangorously: is there a faithful friend to accompany me? That I asked

---

[25] SSD 3: 27. Cf. PW 1: 50.   [26] SSD 3: 16. Cf. PW 1: 39.   [27] Feuerbach, *Principles*, 22.

[28] Wagner to Karl Ritter, November 19, 1849, Zurich, in *SLRW*, 180–81.

[29] Materialism's flexibility, as a set of changeable attitudes to physical matter, is attested by Max Horkheimer's remark a century later that bodily affectivity is a necessary condition of human knowledge. Hence, *pace* Feuerbach: "[A] god is incapable of knowing anything because it has no needs." Horkheimer, *Between Philosophy and Social Science: Selected Early Writings*, trans. G. Frederick Hunter, Matthew S. Kramer, and John Torpey (Cambridge, MA: MIT Press, 1993), 242.

[30] See Raff, *Die Wagnerfrage*, 27ff.

with sound!"[31] The channel of communication was not verbal but acoustically intuitive, raising the possibility in Wagner's thinking of sub-lexical sonorities that carry an inherent meaning.[32] A similar instance in *Tristan und Isolde* sees the shepherd's "old, sad tune" (*alte, ernste Weise*) not only signalling the news of the death of Tristan's parents, but asking him articulately of himself: "for what fate was I born at that time?" And answering: "to yearn, and to die!"[33] Whether the sensation of pure instrumental sound is merely a prompt to psychological interiority here or carries a more coherent sub-lexical message remains an open question.[34] Ironically, Wagner's orientation becomes most clear in his articulation of the concept of verbal thought as a derivative of somatic stimuli. His account implicates the study of etymologies alongside Feuerbach's material *Sinnlichkeit* in an attempt to serve a *coup de grâce* to the concept of disembodied ideas:

Everything for which we find an expression is also something real, and we recognize its reality if we decipher the expression which we *instinctively* employ for the thing. The expression: *thought*, is very easily explicable, if only we go back to its sensuous speech-root. A "thought" [*Gedanke*] is the "imagined" picture in our mind [*das im 'Gedenken' uns 'dünkende' Bild*], of a real "thing" that is non-present. Because of the thought's origin, this non-present "thing" is a real, physically apprehended object, which has made a definite impression on us in another place or at another time: this impression has seized upon our sensation [*Empfindung*], and, to communicate the latter to others, we have been forced to invent an expression which shall convey the object's generic impression in terms of the sentience of humanity at large. We thus could only apprehend the object internally according to the impression which it made upon our senses ... a "thought" is the image impressed upon our sensory

---

[31] "im tiefen Walde mein Horn / liess ich hallend da ertönen: ob sich froh mir gesellte / ein guter Freund, / das frug ich mit dem Getön!" *Siegfried*, act 1, scene 1.

[32] Edward T. Cone raised the intriguing possiblity in this scene that characters comprehend the vocabulary of leitmotifs *a priori*, see Cone, *Hearing and Knowing Music*, ed. Robert P. Morgan (Princeton University Press, 2009), 82.

[33] "zu welchem Los erkoren, / ich damals wohl geboren? . . . Die alte Weise / sagt mir's wieder: mich sehnen – und sterben!" *Tristan und Isolde*, act 3, scene 1.

[34] Thomas Grey has pointed out instances where Brangäne and Isolde mishear musical signs, noting how such signs, occurring within the frame of the drama (as opposed to orchestral leitmotifs), "are even more prone to subjective distortion or misreading" than visual signs. Despite the evident unreliability of such musical signs, this leaves the problem of how they can ask and answer articulate questions for individuals within Wagner's narrative. I would suggest the general role of subjective listening is to be regarded separately from the few specific occasions on which the sounds are explicitly intended as messages, and yet can only be based on qualities of sensation. See Thomas Grey, "In the realm of the senses: sight, sound and the music of desire in *Tristan und Isolde*," in *Richard Wagner: Tristan und Isolde*, ed. Arthur Groos (Cambridge University Press, 2011), 69–94, here 77.

faculty by an object ... brought back to re-arouse the sensation itself into a recreation of the sense impression.[35]

Historically, for Wagner, communication was exclusively channelled through physical sense impressions; this antique network is traceable through etymologies, a situation which requires us to accept that the words of modern language are just mnemonics for this sensory heritage. Precisely the same process of emotional transfer between sentient beings regulates Wagner's *Melodik* in *Oper und Drama*, and effectively enables the plausibility – for him – of a motif-driven, musico–dramatic fabric based on a correspondence of emotional–poetic sensations: "the emotion manifested in this melody is a thing which now belongs as much to us, to whom it has been imparted, as to him who has imparted it."[36]

In a striking case of historical equivalence, Marx and Engels' 1845 essay on *The Material Basis of Morality* also reflected this inversion of idealist priorities by asserting that "the phantoms formed in the human brain are also, necessarily, sublimates of their material life-process, which is empirically verifiable and bound to material premises."[37] Perhaps Wagner's most abiding "revolutionary" activity during these years was not the repulsion of monarchist troops from the barricades as part of a push to eradicate class antagonism, but a shift of perspective only partly documented in the Zurich writings: Wagner was intuiting how his own "phantoms" of mind could possibly be sublimates of a material process in music, and moreover how they could become materially expressive for his audiences across all class boundaries.

At the center of this hypothesis was language (the most articulate medium of poetic communication), and we must go back to the expansion of historical studies in Saxony and Prussia in order to see how the methodologies of historical linguistics helped to prepare the ground for a materialist conception of verbal and musical sound. In particular, the keystone of German *Philologie* was a belief in national identity as distinct from individual state identities. Notable skeptical voices, typified by the eminent historian Leopold von Ranke, doubted the validity of any such claims:

---

[35] SSD 4: 182. Cf. PW 2: 325–27. Michel Foucault offers a very similar account in his examination of the "designation" and "derivation" of language in *The Order of Things* [1966] (New York: Vintage Books, 1994), 104–15.

[36] SSD 4: 183. Cf. PW 2: 327–28.

[37] Karl Marx and Friedrich Engels, "The Material Basis of Morality," from *Die Deutsche Ideologie* [1845], cited in *Ethics*, ed. Peter Singer (Oxford University Press, 1994), 42.

Who will be able to grasp in a word or a concept what is German? Who will call it by name, the genius of our centuries, of the past and of the future? It would only be another phantom to lure us on one more false road.[38]

Despite such cynicism, notions of language and literature – as it were, the documents documenting the history of verbal communication – did increasingly form the basis of a sense of collective self-identity for a Germanic *Bildungsbürgertum* in the early nineteenth century. While there is no shortage of books devoted to this topic, it will be worth uncovering Wagner's specific interest in this discourse as it overlaps with the continuing appeal of *Sinnlichkeit* among the ageing members of *Young Germany*.

Speaking nationally

> And you German alone, returning from abroad,
> Wouldst greet your mother in French?
> O spew it out before your door
> Spew out the ugly slime of the Seine
> Speak German, O you German!   Johann Gottfried von Herder[39]

> Where does the *German* begin? Where does he end? May a German
> smoke? The majority say no. May a German wear gloves? Yes, but
> only of buffalo hide . . . But a German may drink beer, indeed as a true
> son of Germanias he should drink beer.
>
> Heinrich Heine[40]

A deep-seated connection between language and cultural identity – fermenting in earnest within the German states since the last quarter of the eighteenth century – functions as a starting point for this inquiry. German linguistic patriotism dates back at least to the early seventeenth century with Martin Opitz (1597–1639), and subsequently with Otto

---

[38] "Wer will jemals in den Begriff oder in Worte fassen was deutsch sey? Wer will ihn bei Namen nennen, den Genius unserer Jahrhunderte, der vergangenen und der künftigen? Es würde nur ein anderes Phantom werden, das und nach andern falschen Wegen verführte." Leopold von Ranke, "Über die Trennung und die Einheit von Deutschland," *Historisch-politische Zeitschrift* (Hamburg: Friedrich Perthes, 1832), 1: 388.

[39] J. G. von Herder, *An die Deutschen*, in HSW 27: 128–30. I take this translation from E. Kedourie, *Nationalism*, 3rd edn. (London: Hutchinson 1966), 59.

[40] Heinrich Heine, "Über Ludwig Börne" (1840), in *Werke*, 2 vols., ed. M. Greiner (Berlin and Cologne: Kiepenhever & Witsch, 1962), 2: 752–53.

Mencke, J. M. Moscherosch, F. F. von Logau, and Andreas Gryphius, among others, who resisted the domination of French and Latin with a Lutheran prerogative. Figures of the eighteenth-century counter-Enlightenment are perhaps more familiar, such as Hamann and Lessing, Leibniz and Thomasius, who continued to plough the ground of *Germanistik* that had been furrowed a century earlier. In their twenties, Herder spent more than double the time in Riga that Wagner had (1764–69 and 1837–39 respectively), and in this Russian-owned, German-colonized, Latvian town where the local rural population spoke Slavic or Baltic languages, Herder's experiences as a Lutheran preacher arguably prompted him to reflect on the value of the frail local Lettish culture (while Wagner's comparable professional concern was the locution of German and Italian on stage). Herder despised the unnatural welding together of disparate cultures because of what was destroyed[41] and – from his first essay on the philosophy of history, *Another Philosophy of History* (1774) – consistently denounced ancient Roman conquerors as sinister, lustful, and bloody for this reason, later likening the "holy" inheritors of their empire to a monstrous amalgam of arbitrary cultures.[42] Accordingly, in his immensely influential writings about language, nation, and history, numerous statements link national spirit and mother tongue.[43]

What Herder saw as the inhumanity of colonial rule (Rome remained his paradigm)[44] was to some extent visited by Napoleon on the German states themselves with their diverse dialects, laws, sovereignties, and identities, though ruling princes were kept in place, and local culture was not forcibly neutralized. Nevertheless, amid a consolidation of French military and political strength in continental Europe, Fichte's patriotic *Addresses to the German Nation*, given at the Science Academy building in French-occupied Berlin, echoed almost exactly the same message about *Nationalsprache*, but amplified Herder's intellectual observations, bringing them into a more urgently nationalist frame:

[41] "whom nature separated by language, customs, character, let no man artificially join together by chemistry," Herder, HSW 18: 206.

[42] Herder: "a lion's head with a dragon's tail, an eagle's wing, a bear's paw [glued together] in one unpatriotic structure of a State." *Ibid.,* 13: 385.

[43] Herder's comment from *Materials for the Philosophy of the History of Mankind* (1784) is typical: "Has a people anything dearer than the speech of its fathers? In its speech resides its whole thought-domain, its tradition, history, religion, and basis of life, all its heart and soul. To deprive a people of its speech is to deprive it of its one eternal good . . . With language is created the heart of a people." Johann Gottfried von Herder, *Materials for the Philosophy of the History of Mankind* [1784], see: www.fordham.edu/halsall/mod/1784herder-mankind.html.

[44] "the Roman eagle . . . pecked out [the] eyes [of foreign people], devoured their innards, and covered [their] wretched corpses with its feeble wings." Herder, HSW 14: 201.

Those who speak the same language are joined to each other by a multitude of invisible bonds by nature herself, long before any human art begins; they understand each other and have the power of continuing to make themselves understood more and more clearly; they belong together and are by nature one and an inseparable whole.[45]

At once defiant and uplifting, the belief that language is "the embodied and articulated Spirit of the Race"[46] as Coleridge put it, found expression in many forms: the metaphor in Schiller's fragment on *German Greatness* (1797) hinted at a national physiognomy where "language is the mirror of a nation, if we look into this mirror, a great, splendid image of ourselves emanates from it";[47] and half a century later, the philologist Jacob Grimm drew a direct link between language and literary works in the preface to his *Deutsches Wörterbuch* (1854), regarding this as the nation's cohesive, sustaining element in the absence of political unity, especially after 1848: "What else have we in common but our language and literature."[48] With different motives but a similar rationale, Wagner stated the case for a communal linguistic heritage most aggressively in *Das Judenthum in der Musik* (1850): "A language, with its expression and its evolution, is not the work of scattered units, but of a historical community: only he who has unconsciously grown up within the bond of this community also takes any share in its creations."[49] Nationhood and linguistic identity were quite simply two sides of the same ideological coin.

While the search for German identity was a "burning political issue" for *Vormärz* litterati, it remained ideology – never a reality – for neither language nor geography was constitutive of actual boundaries within which "Germany" could be defined in the late eighteenth and early nineteenth century.[50] Wagner's interest in what Eric Hobsbawm calls

---

[45] Johann Gottlieb Fichte, *Addresses to the German Nation*, trans. R. F. Jones and G. H. Turnbull (Westport, Connecticut: Greenwood Press, 1979), 223–24.

[46] S. T. Coleridge, *Aids to Reflection* [1825], ed. Henry Nelson Coleridge (New York: Swards, Stanford & Co.: 1839), fn. 183.

[47] "Die Sprache ist der Spiegel einer Nation, wenn wir in diesen Spiegel schauen, so kommt uns ein grosses treffliches Bild von uns selbst daraus entgangen," in "Deutsche Grösse" (Fragment), *Kleinere* from Friedrich Schiller, *Sämtliche Gedichte*, ed. Jochen Golz (Frankfurt am Main: Insel, 1992), 556ff.

[48] "Was haben wir denn gemeinsames als unsere sprache und literatur." Jacob Grimm, *Kleinere Schriften*, 8 vols. (Berlin: F. Dümmler, 1864–71), 8: 304.

[49] SSD 5: 70–71. Cf. PW 3: 84.

[50] Leaving aside the unifying opposition to Napoleon, this situation continued at least until 1815, as James Sheehan explains: "*Within* the German lands, there was a rich variety of dialects and cultural distinctions. *Between* Germans and other language groups, it is very hard to draw sharp lines. Border regions are often wide belts of mixed settlement; and even when divisions can be established, islands of linguistic minorities exist on either side of them. There was, in short, no terrain, no place, no

philological nationalism ("the insistence on the linguistic purity of the national vocabulary")[51] thus partakes in the artificially constructed or "virtually invented" status of a *Nationalsprache*, which amounted to little more than the attempt "to devise a standard idiom out of a multiplicity of actually spoken idioms, which are thereafter downgraded to dialects."[52] The logical problem in this process, however, is that within such constructed valuing of one's own language and culture is the virtual necessity to disparage that of others. By defining linguistic identity in terms of what is personally at stake, the collective assumptions within the statement "my language" become political and hierarchical.

Does this undermine the validity of German objections to being infiltrated by "foreign" language? It is tempting to dismiss such protectivism as the credo of a tiny literate elite rather than the illiterate majority. While it would be risky to assign the groundswell of anti-French rhetoric between 1808 and 1814 and the uprising of 1813 to philologically or intellectually motivated patriotism,[53] such texts as Fichte's *Addresses* nevertheless reflect a certain mode of thinking. They gave voice to the loathing of foreign elements in Germany, though intrinsically this has little to do with the value of the German language.

If Germany's musical–operatic antagonist was Italy, her political–military adversary was France. In both cases, Germany, splintered into culturally diverse feudal states, formed the weaker. Yet the position of language in this somewhat reductive master–slave formula was not quite so simple, because French is, of course, mere "neo-Latin" and has lost its authentic roots. This explains why, for Wagner, the French "speaking accent has become the absolute antithesis of an intonation of root syllables."[54] Nevertheless, as

---

region which we can call 'Germany'." Sheehan, "'What is German History?' Reflections on the Role of the *Nation* in German History and Historiography," *The Journal of Modern History* 53 (1981), 5.

[51] Eric J. Hobsbawm, *Nations and Nationalism since 1780: Programme, Myth, Reality* (Cambridge University Press, 1992), 56.

[52] *Ibid.*, 54.

[53] J. Christopher Herold, for example, has claimed it had almost nothing whatsoever to do with Fichte's *Addresses to the German Nation*, for relatively few people attended lectures and still fewer actually read philosophical texts. Rather, as Herold argues, it was sheer loathing of the oppressors by the oppressed. Germans took up arms against Napoleon in 1813 not because they had read Fichte, but "because they hated the French, because the French had given them ample cause for hating them, and because it seemed safe to do so after Napoleon's Russian disaster." J. Christopher Herold, *The Age of Napoleon* (New York: American Heritage Pub. Co., 1963), 279. Writing contrariwise during the Second World War, Alan John Percivale Taylor structured Franco–Prussian relations in 1806–15 along an axis of power and resentment: "the defeat of Austria was not crushing and the resentment at it [was] therefore limited; the defeat of Prussia was complete and Prussian resentment [was] therefore beyond all bounds." Alan John Percivale Taylor, *The Course of German History: A Survey of the Development of German History since 1815* [1945] (London and New York: Routledge, 2005), 32–33.

[54] SSD 4: 109. Cf. PW 2: 245.

Eduard Sobolewski illustrates as late as the early 1850s, French cultural transfer was far from unpopular in the German states, and – in a discourse of *Nationalsprache* – seemingly sapped the indigenous culture:

the French School of modern times ... has had injurious effects in Germany. Germans have, from the bad translations they are in the habit of hearing every day, learned to undervalue the text. In garden concerts, and in the streets, we hear mostly French airs ... The present tendency of public feeling in Germany is one that, for every *German*, is *contrary to nature*, and *forced upon* him by Paris. On this account it does not flourish, like a southern plant in a northern soil, but is cultivated from a dearth of indigenous produce. Paris sets the fashion. This should not be the case.[55]

Being well-versed in French taste was something of a pan-cultural phenomenon (even Baron Freiherr vom Stein, the Prussian Prime Minister under Frederick Wilhelm III and first hero of the anti-French German Nationalists, continued to write to his wife and converse in French).[56] Ironically, it was only after the Congress of Vienna and the triumphalism surrounding the dissolution of Bonaparte's France as a military opponent that this began to assume widespread negative political connotations within (pre-unified) Germany. The defensive rhetoric of German liberalism increasingly attacked the use of French as an unacceptable encroachment on vernacular identity. Since the argument was philological rather than economic or demographic, it was put forward primarily by men of letters. One such is Theodor Mundt:

German science expressed in Latin, German social life that converses in Italian and French, the poetic heart of the German people that now irreverently lets sounds of the homeland well up, now again becoming silent as [though] forgetting, these were the embarrassing conditions of a national culture that are only possible as long as a nation remains incapable of having a peculiar sum-total of an original worldview.[57]

To an extent, the entrenched pluralism of a French-speaking Germany is emblematic of a deeper cultural discontinuity and disunity (Sobolweski was of Polish descent and ultimately left his Königsberg theater for Milwaukee

---

[55] Eduard Sobolewski, "Reactionary Letters. No. II," *TMW* 33 (1855): 45.

[56] See Taylor, *The Course of German History*, 35.

[57] "Die deutsche Wissenschaft, die sich lateinisch ausdrückte, das deutsche Gesellschaftsleben, das italienisch und französische redete, das poetische deutsche Volksherz, das die heimathlichen Laute bald keck hervorquellen ließ, bald auch wieder wie stumm werdend verlernte, dies waren verlegene Zustände einer Nationalbildung, die nur so lange möglich sind, als eine Nation noch nicht eine eigenthümliche Summe origineller Weltanschauung in ihrem Vermögen hat." Theodor Mundt, *Die Kunst der deutschen Prosa: Aesthetisch, literargeschichtlich, gesellschaftlich* (Berlin: Veit und Comp., 1837), 4.

in 1859,[58] and Wagner was a Saxon in *Züritüütsch*-speaking Zurich). Yet this did not prevent the majority of academic and artistic liberals from defining their "Germanness" negatively, in opposition to foreign power. The philologist and historian Georg Gottfried Gervinus, for instance, complained bitterly in his 1834 *History of German Literature* that, following a surge of post-Napoleon national euphoria, the German youth were slipping back treacherously into French ways:

And who has not witnessed with astonishment and great disbelief the political movements of recent years; how the same young people who eighteen years ago [1815] wanted to wear only German national costume [a reference to "Turnvater" F. L. Jahn], wanted to sing its songs [a reference to E. M. Arndt], wanted to return to its simple virtues, and who no longer wanted to speak French – how these young people today prefer to incline towards the very same nation, whose whole nature forms a hostile element to ours that is never agreeable and reconciliatory.[59]

Wagner too was drawn stylistically to the *Opéra* and its culture, even setting a French translation of *l'adorable Heine* – "Les deux grenadiers" – complete with thematic borrowing from the *Marseillaise* shortly after he arrived in Paris in 1839.[60] Yet his well-documented failure to secure a Parisian success with *Rienzi* during 1839–42 dissuaded him from continuing to cultivate French elements. Without a firm grasp of Italian, and professing a sustained dislike of French,[61] Wagner would introduce a

---

58 Robert T. Laudon, "Eduard Sobolewski, Frontier Kapellmeister: from Königsberg to St Louis," *Musical Quarterly* 73 (1989), 94–118.

59 "Und wer wird es in den politischen Bewegungen der letzten Jahre nicht mit Staunen und grossen Unwillen beobachtet haben, wie dieselbe Jugend, die vor achtzehn Jahren [1815–16] nur der alten Deutschen Tracht tragen, ihre Lieder singen, ihre einfache Tugend zurückführen, und nicht mehr französisch sprechen wollte, wie dieselbe Jugend heute nach derselben Nation mit Vorliebe hinneigt, deren ganze Natur gegen die unsere ein feindseliges und niemals verträgliches und versöhnliches Element bildet!" Georg Gottfried Gervinus, *Zur Geschichte der deutschen Literatur* (Heidelberg: C. F. Winter, 1834), 3.

60 Wagner was commissioned to set a French translation of Heine – "Les deux grenadiers" – shortly after he arrived in Paris in 1839. Like Schumann's (German) setting of the same text, Wagner quotes a simple rendition of the *Marseillaise* in the closing section of the accompaniment (*un peu plus vite*). But his urge to appeal to French culture went a step too far, it seems, for he reports in *Mein Leben* that a "very popular concert singer and teacher" Monsieur Geraldy declared the song could only be sung "in the streets of Paris to the accompaniment of cannons and gunshots." Accordingly, Schott later published Wagner's Francophile setting in the original German (as *Grenadiere*) without changing any aspects of the melody, much to Wagner's dismay. See ML 174, 185.

61 "the reason why for a long time I could not warm to the idea of writing an opera for Paris was a certain dislike of the French language which is peculiar to me. You [Liszt] will not understand this, being at home in all Europe, while I came into the world in a specifically Teutonic manner." Wagner to Liszt, December 5, 1849, Zurich, in SB 3: 187. Fully thirty years later, Cosima reports:

renovating agenda for vocal melody that involved co-opting the current trends in *Philologie*, as we shall see.

Writing to Samuel Lehrs, Wagner hints at a solution to the difficulty of *Nationalsprache* that implicates a linguistic resolution of the problem of "German" operatic melody:

> I note with alarm to what depths our national sense of honor has sunk with respect to dramatic music, too: the long period during which our theaters were exclusively open to French and Italian music continues to have repercussions even today, when the French and Italians have been utterly discredited . . . since I know where the root of the problem lies, I am not down-hearted but shall strive all the more vigorously to bring about *a radical cure* in due course. It will be a slow process! This is something I must now leave behind me forever: we opera composers cannot be *European*, – so the question is – either *German* or *French*![62]

This, of course, was something of a Hobson's choice for Wagner as he assumed his post as royal Kapellmeister at the court of Dresden that year; his sensitivity here towards nationalities would seem to indicate, moreover, that the "radical cure" he proposes is linguistic. But Mundt later offers one reason why Wagner's subsequent attempt to mobilize antique German may have been received squeamishly by educated opera audiences: the language was not ready to equate with its nation's identity. "German spirit and German language always stand in strange counteraction to each other," he professed, "and have for a long time not yet achieved a satisfactory mutual relation."[63] Despite intellectual rhetoric to the contrary from such luminaries as Humboldt and Fichte, Mundt's warning would prove prescient for Wagner's project.

Philologie: "a radical cure"[64]

The burgeoning discipline of German *Philologie* (historical linguistics) gave voice to the most profound explosion of a national historical imagination in the story of European nationalism. In 1822, Wilhelm von Humboldt lectured in Berlin "On the National Character of Languages," and argued that

---

"the French language is causing R. increasing difficulties – not only speaking it, but also listening to it." CT (October 22, 1880).

[62] Wagner to Samuel Lehrs, April 7, 1843, Dresden, in SLRW, 107–08. Emphasis added.

[63] "Deutsche Geist und deutsche Sprache standen immer in einer seltsamen Gegenwirkung, und haben noch nicht seit lange ein befriedigendes Wechselverhältniß zu einander erreicht," Mundt, *Die Kunst der deutschen Prosa*, 4.

[64] Wagner to Samuel Lehrs, April 7, 1843, Dresden, in SLRW, 108.

character "is to be found primarily and in its most complete and pure form in the living use of speech." Since this disappears with transient speakers and listeners, the only option, Humboldt claimed, was to rely on a language character "preserved in its works of literature," that is, a discourse network.[65] His sentiment was widely echoed.[66] Correspondingly, the psychological impulse to *preserve* – character, nation, security, language – found expression in both scholarly and military forums. Jacob Grimm famously viewed language not as innate but learned, raising the alarming possibility that birth did not guarantee national character, that nationality (defined by language) could thus be forcibly usurped:

Let's submit that if the newborn child of a French or Russian mother on the battlefield were taken up and reared in Germany, he will not begin to speak French or Russian, but German like all the other children with whom he grows up.[67]

Grimm's admission that there is a difference between *ius sanguinis* and language meant that if a single mother tongue was essential to determining a modern German cultural identity, this would need to be protected, even openly defended.

The most appropriate medium on hand for this task was of course the printed word. Accordingly, etymological dictionaries, source compilations, and dictionaries of root words appeared in abundance after 1816, when Franz Bopp's epoch-making contribution to comparative grammar – *On the*

---

[65] Wilhelm von Humboldt, "On the National Character of Languages" [1822], in *Essays on Language*, 57.

[66] A major contribution to German historical consciousness during the early nineteenth century is the *Monumenta Germaniae Historica*, an ongoing project to collect German historical sources initiated by Freiherr vom Stein's (1757–1831) Society for the Study of Older German History. On the individual level, Eberhard Gottlieb Graff (1780–1841), a professor of philology at Königsberg University, relates an anecdote about losing irreplaceable manuscripts in the preface to his *Diskuta* (1826–29). The experience, he explains, illustrated the danger of losing unique literature, and the corresponding need to preserve everything multiply in print. "Mit der Herausgabe während meiner Reise zu eilen, bestimmte mich ein Unfall, der mich im vorigen Sommer traf. Auf dem Wege von Nancy nach Strassburg gingen meine Papiere beim nächtlichen Umpacken der Diligence verloren. Obgleich ich sie durch das Einschreiten des Hrn. Präfekten Grafen v. Choiseul nach drei Tagen wieder erhielt, so brachte mich doch die Gefahr ihres Verlustes, der für mich unersetzlich wäre, auf den Entschluss, jeden freien Augenblick zur Bearbeitung und Ordnung meiner Sammlungen anzuwenden und das Wichtigste derselben so rasch als möglich durch den Druck zu sichern." E. G. Graff, *Diskuta: Denkmäler deutscher Sprache und Literatur aus alten Handschriften*, 3 vols. (Stuttgart: J. S. Cotta, 1826), 1: vii.

[67] "Wir wollen . . . einmal setzen, daß auf einem schlachtfeld das neugeborne kind einer französischen oder russischen mutter aufgenommen und mitten in Deutschenland erzogen würde; es wird nicht französisch, nicht russisch, sondern gleich allen andern kindern, unter welchen es erwächst, deutsch zu sprechen anheben." Grimm, *Über den Ursprung der Sprache* (Frankfurt am Main: Insel, 1985), 17–18.

Conjugation System of Sanskrit Compared to those of Greek, Latin, Persian, and German – effectively inaugurated the study of language as a science.[68] Modern editions and modern language editions of Middle High German literary works became increasingly available, often going through multiple editions.[69] But the other side of Grimm's statement about kidnapped orphans is a political-turned-military campaign – to name but one contemporary with Wagner's *Lohengrin* – that was waged over the Schleswig–Holstein Question between 1846 and 1851, where the Danish King Friedrich VII sought to forcibly annex Danish speakers from Schleswig in northern Germany.[70] This desired congruence between territory and cultural–linguistic boundaries resulted in a policy of territorial assimilation.[71] Where monolingualism and cultural homogeneity are taken to be synonymous, the urge to preserve national character in academia and Aceldama was a battle on two very different fronts.

While Wagner only ever took up military arms against his fellow Germans, his melodic theory does arguably adopt German as a "weapon

---

68 *Über das Conjugationssystem der Sanskritsprache in Vergleichung mit jenem der griechischen, lateinischen, persischen und germanischen Sprache* (Frankfurt am Main: Andreäische Buchhandlung, 1816), rpt. (Hildesheim: Georg Olms, 1975). Bopp's later publications are indicative of the drive within comparative linguistics to reconstruct earlier periods by cross-referencing known syntactical and phonological structures. See particularly: *Vergleichende Grammatik des Sanskrit, Zend, Griechischen, Lateinischen, Litthauischen, Altslawischen, Gotischen und Deutschen* (Berlin: F. Dümmler, 1833–52); *Vocalismus, oder sprachvergleichende Kritiken über J. Grimm's Deutsche Grammatik und Graff's Althochdeutschen Sprachschatz, mit Begründung einer neuen Theorie des Ablauts* (Berlin: Nicolai, 1836); *Über die Sprache der alten Preußen in ihren verwandschaftlichen Beziehungen* (Berlin: F. Dümmler, 1855).

69 This was the case for Jacob Grimm's *Deutsche Grammatik* (1819; 2nd edn., rpt. Wilhelm Scherer (Berlin: Ferdinand Dümmlern, 1870), rpt. (Hildesheim, New York: Olms, 1989), *Deutsche Rechtsaltertumer* (1828; 1854), *Deutsche Mythologie* (1835; 1844; 1854; 1875), *Geschichte der deutschen Sprache* (1848; 1853; 1868); and the Grimm brothers' *Kinder- und Hausmärchen* (1812–15) and *Deutsche Sagen* (1816–18; 1865–66).

70 Briefly, the Danish King Christian VIII sought to absorb the duchy of Schleswig into Denmark under a liberal constitution that regarded the river Eider as its natural boundary, and demanded protection of the Danish language from German encroachment. His son, Friedrich VII, enacted the war his father promised, against which the outraged Frankfurt *Parlament* was unable to muster adequate military opposition. A popular insurrection by German confederate sympathizers "spread over the whole province . . . Volunteers from all parts of Germany rushed to the northern frontier," as the contemporary writer and historian Edwin Emerson Jr. recounted, but "the untrained volunteer army of Schleswig–Holsteiners suffered defeat at Bov. A corps of students from the University of Kiel was all but annihilated." Edwin Emerson, *A History of the Nineteenth Century, Year by Year*, 3 vols. (New York: P. F. Collier and Son, 1901), 2: 1061.

71 See Sue Wright, *Community and Communication: The Role of Language in Nation State Building* (Clevedon: Multilingual Matters, 2000), 33ff. See also Eric J. Hobsbawm, *Nations and Nationalism Since 1780*, 47ff.; and Ernest Gellner, *Nations and Nationalism* (Malden: Blackwell, 2006), 42ff..

of exclusion"[72] against the idioms of what he dismissed as "European" opera. We can begin to substantiate this claim through an analogue to the Schleswig–Holstein question in *Lohengrin*. Consider King Heinrich's recitational monologues, the first of which warns the assembled Brabantines[73] of threats to Germany from abroad, and bids them take up arms against foreigners: "now is the time to preserve the realm's honor,"[74] adding a rallying cry in act 3: "For Germany the German sword! Protect the kingdom's strength therewith!"[75] This was remarkably close to the attitude of the then Prussia foreign minister, Baron Heinrich von Arnim, who viewed strong military support for the provisional, pro-German government in Schleswig–Holstein as an acid test of the new Frankfurt assembly in 1849.[76]

Before exploring the nature of Wagner's debt to Grimm as the standard-bearer for early nineteenth-century *Philologie*, it may be helpful to outline his compositional theory in relation to language, as given in *Oper und Drama*. Several summaries of this text are available,[77] but in what follows I isolate those elements pertaining specifically to vocal–linguistic melodic expression.

Wagner's *Melodik*

In 1851, Wagner defined melody as "the redemption of the poet's endlessly conditioned thought into a deep-felt consciousness of emotion's highest freedom."[78] This formulation brings together the protean strands of his age: Hegel's doctrine of "progress in the consciousness of Freedom,"[79] redemption of art by revolutionary progress, synthesis of the arts (*Naturphilosophie*), and the healing of emotion between thought and

---

[72] This is Sue Wright's description of language in the specific context of linguistic nationalism. *Ibid.*, 8.

[73] To be sure, the dutchy of Brabant in the Netherlands was not German, and was never considered for incorporation into eastern Germany.

[74] "Nun ist es Zeit des Reiches Ehr' zu wahren" (*Lohengrin*, act 1, scene 1).

[75] "Für deutsches Land das deutsche Schwert! So sei des Reiches Kraft bewährt!" (*Lohengrin*, act 3, scene 3).

[76] Hajo Holborn, *A History of Modern Germany, 1840–1945* (Princeton University Press, 1982), 65.

[77] Thomas Grey's extensive critique of the Zurich essays in relation to the composition of the *Ring* is the most comprehensive account in English. See *Wagner's Musical Prose*. Other notable texts include Arne Stollberg, *Ohr und Auge – Klang und Form* (Munich: Franz Steiner: 2006), 111–242; Hermann Danuser & Herfried Münkler (eds.), *Zukunftsbilder: Richard Wagners Revolution und ihre Folgen in Kunst und Politik* (Schliengen: Argus, 2002); and Stefan Kunze, *Der Kunstbegriff Richard Wagners* (Regensburg: Bosse, 1983).

[78] SSD 4: 142. Cf. PW 2: 281.

[79] Hegel, *Philosophy of History*, trans. John Sibree (New York: Wiley Book Co., 1900), 19.

sensation, *Geist* and *Sinnlichkeit*. The principle through which he proposed to enact this idealist definition of melody was essentially a progression from poetic impulse to the emotive response of a listener, albeit linguistically conditioned. First, the poet strips away modern linguistic "disfigurements"[80] from his emotional utterance – which contains an underlying historical residue – leaving only the "purely human core."[81] He then identifies the sympathetic relationships between speech roots: etymologically derived, fossilized units of utterance (codified in the vast lists of Grimm's *Deutsche Grammatik*), and whose indivisibility promised – for Sanskritists – the origin of all meaning. Like concepts have like roots, and by coordinating these roots in alliterative verse, Wagner the poet effectively creates *Versmelodie*; by accenting the roots while leaving the surrounding "unemphatic, unimportant words"[82] unaccented, the singer's breath rhythmicizes the root syllables into organic phrase groupings without recourse to the "monotonous rhythm"[83] of iambic meter, thereby communicating their intuitive "sense" for Wagner: "*this breath is – Music*."[84] Over and above the poetic task, the specific linkage to music begins with his interest in the vowels within speech roots.

Ancient Teutonic or imported speech roots function as Wagner's indivisible poetic atoms, his historical units of emotional meaning in any verbal-melodic construction. Interpreting the claims by comparative linguists about Sanskrit, he also requires that they bear an inexplicable primal force – "original truth" – that remains philosophically indistinct as that which is either "invented or found":

> If the poet pries into the nature of the word which is forced upon him by his feeling, as the only word to fit an object or an emotion woken by that object, he discovers this constraining force in the *root* of this word, which has been invented or found [*erfunden oder gefunden*] through the necessity of man's earliest emotional stress . . . he perceives at last the origin of that [emotion-swaying] force in the purely *sensuous* body of this root, whose primal substance is the *sounding vowel* . . . the embodied inner feeling . . . which manifests itself . . . through the sounding vowel of the root.[85]

In a clear allusion to Herder's notion of "the original wild mother [tongue] of the human race . . . those howling and wailing tones,"[86] the slippage between

---

80 SSD 4: 118. Cf. PW 2: 255. Wagner defined these both culturally and syntactically, implying first why they existed, then outlining what they were, namely: "historico–social and state-religious relations and conditionings," and the "mechanical apparatus of qualifying words." SSD 4: 119. Cf. PW 2: 256.
81 SSD 4: 118. Cf. PW 2: 255.   82 SSD 4: 120. Cf. PW 2: 257.   83 SSD 4: 106. Cf. PW 2: 241.
84 SSD 4: 127. Cf. PW 2: 265.   85 SSD 4: 128–29. Cf. PW 2: 266.
86 Herder, *On the Origin of Language*, trans. John Moran and Alexander Gode (University of Chicago Press, 1986), 91.

enunciated vowel and musical tone is the crucial bridge along which Wagner blends the ostensibly separate sonorities of music and poetry into a unified mode of melodic expression. But as inherently musical units, *spoken* vowels cannot – in this schema – communicate the relationships latent in Stabreim:

> Since *all the vowels are primarily akin to one another,* [our "understanding" of a vowel] is based on *disclosing this primeval kinship* by giving full value to the vowel's *emotional content,* by *means of a musical tone.* The vowel itself is nothing but *a condensed tone.*[87]

Elsewhere Wagner applied precisely the same need for musical tone to Schröder-Devrient's *spoken* utterances, claiming: "[her] whole achievement must have issued from the element of music."[88] This justification for musical tone ultimately refers back to Wagner's pragmatic concern for the need to persuade the listener's ear. He puns that only when the sounding vowel ("tönender *Laut*") becomes a meaningful tone ("lautender *Ton*") is it "in a position to satisfy [*erfüllen*] the infinite capacity of the 'ear.'"[89]

As the load-bearers of musico–syntactical "sense," root vowels outrank consonants in Wagner's hierarchy of expressivity. His interest in the latter is therefore entirely relative to their capacity to modify the former. He outlines two main functions in this respect: determination of length and color, and tonal gradation. First, consonants "raise the sounding vowel of the root to a definite characterization [*Charakteristik*], by firmly hedging-in its infinitely fluid element, and through the lines of this delimitation [they] bring to the vowel's color, in a sense, the design [*Zeichnung*] which makes it into an exactly distinguishable shape."[90] Second, consonants also bind "the vowel within: i.e. [they] determine the specific nature of the vowel's manifestation through the roughness or smoothness of its inward contact therewith."[91] The specific application of this to singing is of course as much a pedagogical as a philological question, and Wagner interprets the evidence according to his experience, acknowledging that strengthened terminals ("nd, rt, st, ft") attached to roots make the latter sound "brief and brisk," and are best adapted to assonance such as "Hand und Mund," rather than rhyme *per se.*[92]

Given that *Versmelodie* is conceived with the listener in mind, Wagner's continual pleas for willing auditors are only to be expected. That these pleas require a change in the way people hear – a purification from socio-political

---

[87] SSD 4: 137. Cf. PW 2: 275.   [88] SSD 9: 140. Cf. PW 5: 141.

[89] SSD 4: 135–6. Cf. PW 2: 273. In modern parlance at least, Wagner's linguistic pirouette is not an equal exchange, for "lautender" carries a stronger sense of "meaning" than the English "sound."

[90] SSD 4: 129. Cf. PW 2: 267.   [91] SSD 4: 133–34. Cf. PW 2: 271.

[92] SSD 4: 134n. Cf. PW 2: 271n.

"dogmas" – invites skepticism over Wagner's self-justifying logic. A number of comparative philologists advocated a similar kind of linguistic paleon-tology that could undo what Sanskritist and Indologist Max Müller called the "disease of language." This referred to a process where words pass from an original to a metaphorical meaning; it risked, for Müller, the danger of lexical "mythology," in which myth transforms denotative words into beings and stories.[93] Though the claim of reaching back to linguistic origins resonates with Wagner's documented anxiety about composing original melodies (i.e. those with "highest artistic individuality"),[94] the two have entirely different meanings in this context: "original truth" appeals to historically Teutonic authority, while an original or "artistically individual" melody (as opposed to the *Rousseauean* concept of *première mélodie*, which also refers to the melodiousness of the very earliest languages) is a signifier, for Wagner, of compositional ability. The critical link is that Wagner was openly appealing to a communal pride in German language, while less overtly claiming his seat as its musical standard-bearer.

The resulting communicative model is dialectical; it traces a path from what is essentially an inner musical vowel to the outer world of syntactical expression and back to the musical tone, unifying the two in a higher syn-thesis of *Worttonsprache*. It was a Hegelian template Wagner understood more broadly: "The language of music [*Tonsprache*] is the beginning and end of the language of words [*Wortsprache*], just as emotion is the beginning and end of the intellect, myth the beginning and end of history."[95] Of course, the purpose of *Oper und Drama* was not didactic, but exegetical, and Wagner's recourse to personal necessity – "it was dire compulsion alone that wrung [my treatises] from me"[96] – has become the accepted explanation for his principal mid-century theoretical texts. In 1924, Newman described his effort at theory as a "needed purgation of the intellect,"[97] and even borrowed Oscar Wilde's (non-Wagnerian) barb to dismiss the philology in *Oper und Drama* as the composer's pursuit of "the obvious, hunting it down … with the enthusiasm of a short-sighted detective."[98] This continues part of the

---

[93] Max Müller, *Lectures on the Science of Language: Delivered at the Royal Institution of Great Britain in April, May, and June 1861* (London: Elibron Classics, 2005), 11ff.

[94] See Wagner to Mathilde Wesendonck, June 9, 1862, Biebrich, SB 14: 176–77.

[95] SSD 4: 91. Cf. PW 2: 224.

[96] "Meine Schrifstellerischen Arbeiten waren Zeugnisse für diese meine Unfreiheit als künstlerischer Mensch: nur im höchsten Zwange verfasste ich sie." Wagner to August Röckel, September 12, 1852, Zurich, in *Briefe an Röckel*, ed. La Mara (Leipzig: Breitkopf und Härtel, 1894), 10.

[97] Newman, *Wagner as Man and Artist*, 191.   [98] *Ibid.*, 213.

late-nineteenth-century reaction against Wagner's "scholarly prejudice . . . held up as something Teutonic," that Nietzsche first mocked as "so-called 'national' sense."[99] From a historically archeological perspective, however, the scholarly tradition of privileging the "musico–poetic period" and the leitmotif while dismissing the pedantic philology in *Oper und Drama* fails to ask certain vital questions about the myopic investigator and his innocently "obvious" vowels and consonants: where did this conception of a sophisticated linguistic melodic line originate? Why was Stabreim suddenly relevant to the problems of German melodic theory in 1850–51?[100] (Wagner had, after all, employed it in his very earliest verses for *Leubald* in 1826–28.[101]) The fact that Wagner virtually abandoned alliterative verse after the *Ring* (employing rhymed verse in *Meistersinger*, and rhymed, unrhymed, and alliterative verse in *Tristan*), indicates the concept's historical contingency rather than any transcendental character. (John Milton's return to rhyme in *Samson Agonistes*, after denouncing it in *Paradise Lost*, is oddly comparable.)

It was not long before the historical pedigree of speech roots and onomastics (the study of proper names, their history and origin) started to ring hollow. Martin Heidegger was also disposed to trace these roots in his labyrinthine quest for lexical specificity, yet became suspicious of etymological essentialism, that is, the blind tendency to ascribe authority to etymology in this way. Though he was not referring to Wagner in his probing of the essence of *Dinge* during the mid-1920s, he did warn against such methodology as "accidents of an etymological game . . . [played by] merely using the dictionary." This could never achieve understanding of the nature of things as such, he argued, though he later qualifies his dismissal in terms implicitly more favorable to the reception of Wagner's project: "etymology has the standing mandate first to give thought to the essential content involved in what dictionary words, as words, denote by implication."[102]

---

[99] Nietzsche, "Nietzsche contra Wagner," *The Portable Nietzsche*, 668.

[100] Stabreim emerged as relevant to nineteenth-century German culture following Jacob and Wilhelm Grimm's publication of an edition of the *Hildebrandslied* in 1812. Though originally written in Old High German, this short poem only survives in an Old Saxon manuscript. The alliterative principle was not rediscovered so much as revived, for the Icelandic and Anglo-Saxon traditions of epic poetry already had numerous well-known works such as *Beowulf* (Anglo-Saxon), and *Sir Gawain and the Green Knight* (Middle English). It was Old High German, in fact, that had the fewest examples of Stabreim in its historical literature.

[101] "Woher um mich dies wonnigliche Wehen." Quoted in Peter Branscombe, "The Dramatic Texts," *Wagner Handbook*, ed. Ulrich Müller and Peter Wapnewski, translation edited by John Deathridge (Cambridge, MA: Harvard University Press, 1992), 270.

[102] Martin Heidegger, "The Thing," in *Poetry, Language, Thought*, trans. Albert Hofstadter (New York: Perennial Classics, 2001), 172–73.

While Wagner believed speech roots harbored an unchanging physical reality, Heidegger did not. Over and above any opportunistic appropriation or historical Procrusteanism on Wagner's part, the original purpose of inquiries into the history of the German language – that is, the stated purpose of those Germanists motivated to undertake the painstaking research – remained focused on what Chaim Gans has termed the "adherence thesis" to cultural nationalism, namely that individuals have an interest in adhering to their cultures.[103] But, as we have seen, beyond preservation and adherence, the study of ancient languages sought to circumscribe and embolden a cultural identity in the present precisely in order to stimulate and orient progress in the future from the original source in the past. There can be little doubt, therefore, that it was essentially an invented tradition that stretches the evidence to give a new idea the legitimizing veneer of age and antiquity.

Speaking for both brothers, Wilhelm Grimm summarized the philological project as regenerative:

> these studies embrace our country, they always have their own attraction for indigenous people, which nothing foreign can replace ... the knowledge of our past, of its poetry, its law, its customs, aims at explaining our history, enlivening, refreshing, and adorning it. It wants to water the tree of German life from its fountain.[104]

But back in 1812, even Jacob Grimm implicitly agreed that resurrecting archaic language for current usage was impossible (recalling the famous, if spurious, "Gesichtserker" [literally: "face gable"] instead of the Latinate "Nase"),[105] and frowned on attempts by Joseph Görres and Ludwig Tieck to modernize old chapbooks or medieval love poetry.[106] Years later, Grimm's *History of the German Language* (1848) described ancient languages as physically perfect in contrast to modern ones, and regarded the opposition between the linguistic present and past as a universal, timeless truth.[107] History, for Grimm, was "a band which joins antiquity to the

---

[103] Chaim Gans, *The Limits of Nationalism* (Cambridge University Press, 2003), 39.

[104] "diese studien umfassen das vaterland, sie haben den eigenen reiz, den das heimische für jeden immer besitzt, den nichts fremdes ersetzen kann ... das erkenntnis unseres alterthums, seiner poesie, seines rechts, seiner sitte will die geschichte erklären, beleben, erfrischen und schmücken, will den baum des deutschen lebens tränken aus eigenem quell," in Grimm, *Kleinere Schriften*, 8: 465.

[105] See William J. Jones, *Images of Language: Six Essays on German Attitudes to European Languages from 1500 to 1800* (Amsterdam, Philadelphia: John Benjamins Publishing Co., 1999), 50.

[106] See Gunhild Ginschel, *Der junge Jacob Grimm* (Berlin: Akademie, 1967), 107ff.

[107] "Aus der geschichte der sprachen geht zuvorderst bedeutsame bestätigung hervor jenes mythischen gegensatzes: in allen findet absteigen von leiblicher vollkommenheit statt aufsteigen zu gelang als jene nicht zu weit vorgeschritten war: sie vermählten das milde gold ihrer poesie

present, necessity to freedom."[108] Though he never clarified the nature of its telos, he conceived its path as irreversible, in terms of a living organism's growth.[109] While remaining one of the most ardent philologists, he thus valued modern literature precisely for its contemporariness:

Modern poetry has the advantage that it stimulates and interests us more, like everything which is close to our life and customs, that its force and warmth is much more obvious and impressive. For this reason it is far more difficult to tear oneself away from one of Goethe's novels than from reading Homer.[110]

Wagner memorably lamented the "natural, mongrel shape"[111] of modern drama, where Tieck, Goethe, and Schiller were all fenced uncomfortably between the "extremes" of Shakespeare and Racine. If, as Stein and others assert, Wagner's corrective project for resurrecting archaic language in the *Ring* drama was "ludicrous," the conditions that first created the plausibility of this aspiration against Germany's literary giants, allowing it to crystallize in a spectacular instance of Wagnerian arrogance (his tendency to judge older artists in terms of idiosyncratic modern values), bear further scrutiny.

Reintroducing Jacob Grimm

> That I was never very thorough with my language studies probably explains why it was so easy for me to drop them later. It was not until a much later period that I gained an authentic interest in the study of languages, when I grasped their physiological and philosophical aspects, as revealed to modern Germanists by the pioneering work of Jacob Grimm.
>
> Richard Wagner[112]

Wilhelm and Jacob Grimm's *German Sagas* (1816–18) and *German Mythology* (1835) provided the sources for almost all of Wagner's plots

---

noch mit eisernen gewalt ihrer prosa," in Jacob Grimm, "Zeitalter und Sprachen," *Geschichte der deutschen Sprache*, 4.

[108] "ein band, welches alterthum und gegenwart, nothwendigkeit und freiheit mit einander verschmilzt." See Grimm, *Kleinere Schriften*, 8: 547.

[109] See Grimm to Friedrich Karl von Savigny, May 20, 1811 and October 29, 1814, *Briefe der Brüder Grimm an Savigny*, ed. W. Schoof and I. Schnack (Berlin: Schmidt, 1953), 105, 172.

[110] "dass die neue Poesie den Vortheil vor der alten hat, dass sie viel stärker reizt und an sich fesselt, wie alles was unserm Leben und unserer Sitte nah ist, dass ihre Kraft und Wärme viel offenbarer und eindringender ist, daher wir uns vom Lesen eines göthischen Romans viel weniger losreissen können, als vom Homer." Jacob Grimm to Arnim, October 29, 1812. See Reinhold Steig, *Achim von Arnim und Jacob und Wilhelm Grimm* (Stuttgart: J. G. Cotta, 1904), 237.

[111] SSD 4: 15. Cf. PW 2: 134.   [112] ML 14.

from *Tannhäuser* onward. But Wagner's engagement with their brand of philology went deeper than mythic figures and events. "I won my only breath of freedom by plunging into the ancient world," he wrote to Nietzsche in 1872 (then chair of Classical Philology at Basel), "however much I was crippled by having lost virtually all memory of its speech."[113] Speech, more than language, was the crucial link between the putative expressivity of ancient literature and the present. In the absence of an audio-cultural "memory," the imagination of historical-sounding languages proved a wellspring for Wagner. Indeed, this was central to his melodic composition in *Das Rheingold*, as he willingly explained:

From my studies of J. Grimm I once borrowed an Old German word *Heilawac* and, in order to make it more adaptable to my own purposes, reformed it as *Weiawaga* (a form which we may still recognize today in *Weihwasser* [holy water]); from this I passed to the cognate linguistic roots *wogen* [to surge] and *wiegen* [to rock], finally to *wellen* [to billow] and *wallen* [to seethe], and in this way I constructed a root-driven, syllabic melody for my watermaidens to sing.[114]

Jean-Jacques Nattiez's analysis of the progression through different vowels, semivowels, fricatives, and spirants in the opening scene from *Rheingold* leads him to conclude: "it is thus the birth of language that we witness."[115] This is certainly plausible as Wagner's expressive remainder, but it was precisely an attitude of freedom and flexibility towards old linguistic sonor-ities – speech roots as clay in the composer's hands – that enabled Wagner to build the Rheinmaidens' song from finely graded lexical–phonological relations.

Wagner evidently read Grimm's work closely, but treated his analysis of historical utterance loosely. Grimm's most significant contribution to the study of historical phonology and phonemic contrast was perhaps the *Deutsche Grammatik* (1st edn. 1819; 2nd edn. 1822; 3rd edn. 1840). Its radically revised and expanded second edition contained a 600-page discourse on phonology that performed an unprecedented archeology of historical speech sounds, charting those indivisible vocal units whose capture promised to provide privileged access to the powerfully communicative sonorities of historical speech. Grimm's chief concern from this second edition onwards was comparing speech sounds across geographic and temporal boundaries. The industry in producing such a work must have been immense; in its main body, he charted the vast phonological landscapes of Gothic, Old High

---

[113] SSD 9: 296. Cf. PW5: 293.   [114] SSD 9: 300. Cf. PW 5: 297.

[115] Jean-Jacques Nattiez, *Wagner Androgyne: A Study in Interpretation* (Princeton University Press, 1993), 60.

German, Anglo-Saxon, Old Frisian, and Old Norse; he compared this with later Middle High German, and Middle English; which he followed with his descriptions of the sounds of modern German, Dutch, English, Swedish, and Danish. The basis of the study was thus a comparison of sound, and sound shifts imbued with – or organized according to – national character.

At least one German contemporary sarcastically recognized Grimm's achievement with a musical simile. Heine compared the *Deutsche Grammatik* to a Gothic cathedral where the Germanic nations join forces in a gigantic choir. Erecting the edifice must have been the result of a Faustian pact, he balks, for there could have been no other way for one individual to gather all the materials for such an immense structure.[116]

Here, as Michel Foucault observed, language was being treated as a totality of phonetic elements for the first time: "A whole mystique is being born ... that ... of the pure poetic flash that disappears without a trace, leaving nothing behind it but a vibration suspended in the air for one brief moment."[117] Grimm, ever mindful of the historicity of such sonic moments, introduced two concepts into Indo-European linguistics that would particularly impact Wagner's so-called "Wigalaweia music": vowel gradation (*Ablaut*; apophony), and the consonant sound shift (*Lautverschiebung*). *Ablaut* refers to vowel alternation normally based on grammatical categories; *Lautverschiebung* refers to sound change among consonants: the former is synchronic, structured by conjugation (*singen, sang, gesungen*; see also *Burg, Berg* from b^herg^h meaning "high"); the latter occurs incrementally over time, as Grimm explains:

Ablaut: "the regulated substitution of one root vowel for another; a noble and
    fundamental asset of the German language."[118]
Lautverschiebung: "the shift of rows of consonants in German, initially with
    respect to primordial cognates, then also *a propos* Standard High German with
    respect to Low German dialect and Nordic."[119]

From these concepts, Wagner understood that the smallest lexical units are malleable yet intrinsically related by their putatively "original" meaning in

---

[116] Heinrich Heine, *Sämtliche Werke*, 10 vols., ed. O. Walzel (Leipzig: Insel, 1910–15), 7: 358.
[117] Michel Foucault, *The Order of Things* (New York: Random House, 1994), 286.
[118] "geregelter übergang des vocals der wurzel in einen andern; ein edles und ihr wesentliches vermögen der deutschen sprache." J./W. Grimm, *Deutsches Wörterbuch* [1854], see http://woerterbuchnetz.de/DWB/?sigle=DWB&mode=Vernetzung&lemid=GA00837
[119] "verschiebung von consonantenreihen in den deutschen sprachen, zunächst gegenüber den urverwandten, dann auch in bezug auf das hochdeutsche gegenüber dem niederdeutschen und nordischen." *Ibid.*, http://woerterbuchnetz.de/DWB/?sigle=DWB&mode=Vernetzung&lemid=GL02547

Sanskrit. While he got the wrong end of the stick with *Ablaut* (which he thought of as terminal consonants that modify a vowel),[120] he justifies the unity of dance, music, and poetry in 1849 through a *Lautverschiebung* between D and T – *Tanz-, Ton-, und* [T]*ichtkunst* – which Grimm traces between Greek, Gothic, and Old High German. Wagner hails this as "a beautifully descriptive sensual picture [*sinnliches Bild*] of the nature of this trinity of sisters, namely a perfect Stabreim, such as is native to the spirit of our language."[121] Grimm had justified the shift of consonants according to their etymology, which served in 1850 to underwrite Wagner's fantasy of the artwork of the future:

Yet more astounding than the accord of the liquids and the spirants is the variation of the lip, tongue, and throat sounds, not only from the Gothic, but also the Old High German arrangement . . . Gothic is related to Latin exactly as is Old High German to Gothic. The entire twofold sound shift, which has momentous consequences for the history of language and the rigor of etymology, can be so expressed in a table:[122]

Greek	P.	B.	F.	T.	D.	TH.	K.	G.	CH.
Goth.	F.	P.	B.	TH.	T.	D	-.	K.	G.
OHG	B. (V)	F.	P. (V)	D.	Z.	T	G.	CH.	K.

The same dental sound shift between T and D is also evident in Wagner's adoption of the Old High German spelling of "Wodan" in *Lohengrin*, and "Wotan" in *Das Rheingold* and *Die Walküre*. (During the English restoration, John Dryden also invokes the deity with a d: "To wodan thanks we render" for Purcell's *King Arthur*.) All in all, Grimm lists thirteen basic variants for "the highest and supreme deity" in his expansive exploration of its etymology,[123] remarking elsewhere that "our consonant sound shift bears witness to the deepest, innermost agility of the language."[124]

---

[120] Wagner contrasts this with an initial consonant, or *Anlaut*; see SSD 4: 129–30. Cf. PW 2: 267.

[121] SSD 3: 102. Cf. PW 1: 132.

[122] "Noch merkwürdiger als die einstimmung der liqu. und spir. ist die abweichung der lippen- zungen- und kehllaute nicht allein von der gothischen, sondern auch der alth. einrichtung . . . Das goth. verhält sich zum lat. gerade wie das alth. zum goth. Die ganze für die geschichte der sprache und strenge der etymologie folgenreiche zweifache lautverschiebung stellt sich tabellarisch so dar": Grimm, *Deutsche Grammatik*, 2nd edn., 498.

[123] "Die höchste und oberste gottheit." Grimm, *Deutsche Mythologie*, 2 vols., 2nd edn. (Göttingen: Dieterichsche Buchhandlung, 1844), 1: 120. Variants to the name include Gothic *Vôdans*; Old High German *Wuotan*; Longobarden *Wôdan / Guôdan*; Old Saxon *Wuodan / Wôdan*; Westfalen *Guôdan / Gudan*; Anglo-Saxon *Vôden*; Friesian *Wêda*; Nordic *Odînn*; Saxon *Othinus*; Faeröisch *Ouvin*. See *Wuoten* in *Ibid.*, 1: 120–50.

[124] "Von der tiefsten innersten regsamkeit der sprache zeugt aber unsere lautverschiebung." Grimm, *Deutsche Grammatik*, 2nd edn., 4: vi.

The importance of this concept for Wagner lends a degree of credence to its adoption by later commentators as a tool for interpreting Wagner's works. Claude Lévi-Strauss famously spoke of Wagner as "the undeniable originator of the structural analysis of myth."[125] He justified his view, in part, by the linguistic principle of sound shifts, likening the common root shared by the myths of Tristan and Isolde, and Siegfried and Brünnhilde, to Grimm's *Lautverschiebung*: "Just as in languages, a sound shift often produces two apparently different words from one and the same original, so two apparently differing relationships had evolved from this single mythic relationship as a result of a similar shift or transmutation."[126] While the structural reading of Wagner's mythic material in terms of linguistic principles may appear overly schematic, its elevation of philological method to a determining factor in Wagner's thinking rings true, at least at the level of metaphor.

Shortly before Wagner died, Cosima recorded his comment relating German works organically and systematically to each other in the manner that Grimm's sound shifts related seemingly disparate words between languages: "Herr Rub. plays us some fugues from the 48 Preludes and Fugues: 'They are like the roots of words,' R. says, and later, 'In relation to other music it is like Sanskrit to other languages.'"[127] The comment, if taken to be reliable, sums up much of Wagner's linkage to Grimm: preoccupation with the origins of expression, etymological essentialism, precedence of speech roots, and a less than rigorous methodology supporting the construction of cultural authority.

Linguistic relativity

Numerous authors expanded upon Grimm's *Lautverschiebung* as a scientific principle for tracing etymology, seemingly demonstrating greater coherence between the dialects behind *Neuhochdeutsch*.[128] But Germany's political and linguistic disunity stubbornly contradicted Humboldt's 1822 hypothesis about a national worldview:[129] that we experience the world

---

[125] Claude Lévi-Strauss, *The Raw and the Cooked* [1964], trans. John and Doreen Weightman (London: Jonathan Cape, 1970), 15.

[126] Cited in Nattiez, *Wagner Androgyne*, 237.   [127] CT (June 26, 1880).

[128] The most prominent case, sanctioned by Grimm, was Rudolf von Raumer, *Die Aspiration und die Lautverschiebung: Eine Sprachgeschichtliche Untersuchung* (Leipzig: F. A. Brockhaus, 1837).

[129] Following the Congress of Vienna, the constitution of the German Confederation retained the geographical boundaries of the old Reich, which were not linguistically determined, but included non-German-speaking Bohemia and Polish lands in West Prussia and the Duchy of Posen, not to mention Switzerland. See Taylor, *The Course of German History*, 47. As John

through our mother tongue (once known as the Whorf–Sapir hypothesis).[130] The Herderian correlate between language and thought on which Humboldt's assertion was based is very specific; it articulated a kinship between the grammatical structure of a language and its bearer's thought processes, effectively telescoping theoretical syntax into cognitive function, and thereby circumscribing the common element that binds a nation's constituents together.[131] Whether speech is caught in the grid of thought or vice versa, each is woven into the very fabric the other is unrolling: "The spiritual singularity of a people and the structure of their language are so inwardly conflated in each other that, if [only] one were given, the other would have had to be completely derived from it."[132] If the organization of our language determines our way of thinking, thereby directly effecting

Edwards points out, however, not all languages require possession of an original group language for their national identity (Irish – Celtic; Austrian – German). See "Language and Nation", *Encyclopaedia of Nationalism*, ed. Athena S. Leoussi (New Brunswick, NJ: Transaction Publishers, 2001), 171.

[130] "In every language there lies a characteristic worldview." ["So liegt in jeder Sprache eine eigenthümliche Weltansicht."] *Wilhelm von Humboldts Gesammelte Schriften*, 17 vols., ed. Albert Leitzmann (Berlin: B. Behr, 1903–36), 7: 60. For an examination of the distinction between cultural *Weltansicht* and ideological *Weltanschauung* in Humboldt's writings, see Elsina Stubbs, *Wilhelm von Humboldt's Philosophy of Language, its Sources and Influence* (Lewiston, Queenston, Lampeter: Edwin Mellen Press, 2002), 261–63. See also John B. Carroll (ed.), *Language, Thought, and Reality: Selected Writings of Benjamin Lee Whorf* [1957] (Cambridge, MA: MIT Press, 1997), esp. 246–70.

[131] Isaiah Berlin points out that Herder derived the notion that words and ideas are one from his teacher, J. G. Hamann. "Men do not think, as it were, in thoughts and ideas and then look for words in which to 'clothe' them, as one looks for a glove to fit a fully formed hand. Hamann taught that to think was to use symbols, and that to deny this was not so much false as unintelligible, because without symbolism one was led fallaciously to divide the aspects of a single experience into separate entities – the fatal doctrine of Descartes." Berlin, *Three Critics of the Enlightenment*, 189.

[132] "Die Geisteseigenthümlichkeit und die Sprachgestaltung eines Volkes stehen in solcher Innigkeit der Verschmelzung in einander, daß, wenn die eine gegeben wäre, die andere müßte vollständig aus ihr abgeleitet werden können. "*Über die Kawi-Sprache*, quoted in Mundt, *Die Kunst der deutschen Prosa*, 9. In contrast to Wagner's metaphorical usage, Humboldt argued that correspondences between the grammatical structure of language and its national culture can be determined still more precisely: "If there is an exact correspondence between logic and grammatical relationships," he asserted, "man's thinking gains in incisiveness, and the intellect is attracted even more strongly to formal and consequently pure thought, if, as a result of the language, it grows accustomed to making precise distinctions between grammatical forms." And in a different essay ("On the National Character of Languages" [1822]), he repeated his claims for a direct reciprocity between language character and national identity (defined by mentality), citing the latter as self-evidently proof of the former in what amounts to circular logic: "what primarily renders the differences in the character of languages visible is the intellectual mentality and therefore the mode of thinking and feeling." See particularly Humboldt's essay "On the Origin of Grammatical Forms and their Influence" (1822), in *Wilhelm von Humboldt: Essays on Language*, ed. T. Harden and D. Farrelly, trans. John Wieczorek and Ian Roe (Frankfurt am Main: Peter Lang, 1997), 23–51, here 32, 66.

the development and shaping of our ideas, its mode of expression – "material" speech – communicates that unique relationship beyond the realm of thought. It is speech that becomes *ex-pressive* (in Derrida's sense of imparting "to a certain outside a sense which is first found in a certain inside").[133] For this reason, Humboldt regarded speech as "material" in contrast to thought which was ideal. Speech is "the consequence of an actual need [and] directly concerned with the denotation of things" whereas thought is concerned with the abstractionism of form.[134] The key point in this excursus is to underscore the legitimacy of *spoken* expression as a constitutive element of present, outwardly perceptible identity. This was not "speech in its transcendental flesh," as Derrida put it, the phenomenological voice that would continue "to speak and be present to itself – *to hear itself* – in the absence of the world."[135] It was precisely with the sonorous texture of a physical voice, with the body of speech in the world, that perceptions of the different sounding physiology could function as a social marker, circumscribing its sound as qualitatively different from the speakers of other "nations."

This signifying quality had of course been linked to singing styles centuries before Wagner. The seventeenth-century theorist Vincenzo Giustiniani, for example, famously discussed "new arias pleasing to the ear" in the Roman Madrigals of Marenzio and Giovannelli, adding:

Besides these changes in the manner of singing, it may be observed that each nation, each province, almost each city has a way of singing entirely different from the others. And from this comes the old saying: *the French sing, the Spaniards howl, the Germans shout, the Italians cry*.[136]

And in the early twentieth century, the French ethnomusicologist André Schaeffner explicitly elevated such music to the identifying criterion for social groups, claiming that "the music of a group of humans is the voice of that group, and it is the group itself."[137] Reading a continuous (sonic) relationship between language and music clarifies the relevance of this belief for Wagner. Back in 1878, Cosima recorded his remark to this effect: "It is as

---

[133] Jacques Derrida, *Speech and Phenomena* (Evanston: Northwest University Press, 1973), 32.

[134] Humboldt, "On the origin of grammatical forms and their influence on the development of ideas" [1822], in *Essays on Language*, 43.

[135] Derrida, *Speech and Phenomena*, 16.

[136] "Si vede per esperienza che ogni nazione, ogni provincia, anzi ogni citta', ha un modo di cantare differentissimo ciascuno dall'altro, e di qui viene quel dettato volgare *Galli cantant, Hispani ululant, Germani boant, Itali plorant*," in Vincenzo Giustiniani, *Discorso sopra la musica* [1628, first published 1878], trans. Carol MacClintock (Rome: American Institute of Musicology, 1962), 72.

[137] "La musique d'un groupe humain, c'est la voix de ce groupe, et c'est ce groupe même," in André Schaeffner, *Origine des instruments de musique* (Paris: Payot, 1936), 322.

impossible to write music without melody, as to speak without [verbal] thoughts: melody is musical thought."[138] As we have seen, Humboldt believed this direct correlate applied equally to language and national identity, thereby completing an extended triad between melody, language / worldview, and nationality. Nineteenth-century discourses of language permit that speech, melody, and national identity, in other words, were not qualitatively distinct layers within a construction of culture, not discrete film casings adhering to an ill-defined national "body," duplicating it on the outside. On the contrary, they were the continuous moments of a single body. Their uninterrupted relationship on the plane of pure sound acquired a scholarly pedigree beyond mere metaphor, though metaphor played a part in its rhetoric. If the perception of sound defines the characteristic, communicative agency of nationality, it makes sense to tackle this through the physiology of sound perception itself. For, following Wagner's logic, it was precisely "sounding physiology" – musically, linguistically – that *de facto* constituted and differentiated nationality.

This suited his newly Francophobic outlook in Dresden. But whereas the gradations between melody, language / worldview, and nationality pertain to language in the present of the 1840s, Wagner was concerned with languages in the past. A bevy of philologists also held the same correlate (of language / worldview) to be valid in medieval speech, though here the historical imagination is invoked to justify the claim, where analysis of *modern* German had drawn on metaphor and assessment of alphabetic and national character. Grimm, for one, believed affirmatively that "the essence and history of our people is mirrored in the characteristics and destiny of our language,"[139] adding in 1851 that "the oldest history of the human race lies hidden, like that of its language, and only linguistic research will cast some light upon it."[140] For pioneering philologists, then, linguistic paleontology promised to reveal the sedimented cultural past, becoming nothing less than "the science of their dreams," as Maurice Olender put it.[141]

Grimm used this historical correlate to explain a syntactical shift that articulates two broad phases in the growth of Teutonic literature; it was a

---

[138] CT (March 13, 1878).

[139] [D]as wesen und die geschichte unseres volks [spiegeln sich] in den eigenschaften und schicksalen unserer sprache [ab]." Grimm, *Deutsche Grammatik*, 2nd edn., 4: v.

[140] "des menschengeschlechts älteste geschichte lagert verborgen gleich der seiner sprache, und nur die sprachforschung wird lichtstrahlen darauf zurückwerfen." Grimm, *Über den Ursprung der Sprache*, 58–59.

[141] Maurice Olender, *The Languages of Paradise: Race, Religion, and Philology in the Nineteenth Century*, trans. Arthur Goldhammer (Cambridge, MA: Harvard University Press, 1992), 8.

shift vital for Wagner's concept of *Worttonsprache*, the shift after Middle High German from poetry to prose:

One can compare the inner strength of the old language with the keen sense of sight, hearing, smell of savages, even our shepherds and hunters who simply live among nature. By contrast, the rational concepts of more recent language grew increasingly clearer and more distinct. [Naïve] poetry is replaced by [intellectual] prose (not the vulgar but the spiritual kind), the medium appropriate to our own age.[142]

Unlike Coleridge or Wordsworth, Grimm believed that poetry belonged to the historical rather than the transcendental realm. Accordingly, he borrowed Schiller's distinction to separate a naïve popular poetry created collectively and anonymously by *das Volk*, from a sentimental body of literature written by more recent, individual poets. Grimm's understanding of this split saw early poetry as epic and mythical, while later poetry addresses the experiences and feelings of the author's own actual world, tending towards prose. For him, this succession corresponds exactly to the development of language from its concrete beginnings to abstraction and intellectualism.

Wagner's fear of a degeneration from original linguistic perfection tacitly assumes variable levels of a sound's communicative power. He distinguished modern speech from "older, poetic speech" in that the former "needs a far more copious use of words and clauses than did the other," because it is out of touch with the meaning of the speech roots and hence "estranged from our feeling."[143] Here, Wagner is probably drawing on the Classicist Karl Otfried Müller's influential comments about ancient Doric – "the object seems to have been to convey as much meaning in as few words as possible"[144] – but Wagner's viewpoint is selective, for Grimm's preoccupation with the course of a language's development led him to believe in the incessant growth and development of that language. In an age steeped in organic theory, a living language could not be stunted or reined in; it was best understood as progressing from uncomplicated material perfection to complete rational maturity. Of course, the flipside of organic growth is deformity and, hence,

---

[142] "Man kann die innere Stärke der alten Sprache mit dem scharfen Gesicht, Gehör, Geruch der Wilden, ja unserer Hirten und Jäger, die einfach in der Natur leben, vergleichen. Dafür werden die Verstandesbegriffe der neueren Sprache zunehmend klarer und deutlicher. Die Poesie vergeht, und die Prosa (nicht die gemeine, sondern die geistige) wird uns angemessener." Quoted in Mundt, *Die Kunst der deutschen Prosa*, 20.

[143] SSD 4: 117. Cf. PW 2: 254.

[144] Karl Otfried Müller, *The History and Antiquities of the Doric Race*, trans. Henry Tufnell and George C. Lewis (Oxford: S. Collingwood, 1830), 393. For an assessment of Müller's influence on Wagner, see Daniel Foster, *Wagner's* Ring *Cycle and the Greeks* (Cambridge University Press, 2010), 2ff.

degeneration. Thus, a developmental process was not incongruous with Grimm's belief that German words before the time of Luther retained greater plastic designation, i.e. a more tangible connection with the raw action or object a word designated. It celebrates a closer proximity to the primitive treasury of vocables that so fired up Wagner's interest in a *Versmelodie* and would realize their primal communicative agency.

The preface to Grimm's *Deutsches Wörterbuch* (1854) is far from nostalgic in this respect:

Whoever has studied our language and with an observant soul become aware of the advantages it has over that of today finds himself initially imperceptibly attracted to all monuments of earlier times and repelled by those of the present. The higher he can ascend, the more beautiful and the more perfect the language in its physical form [*leibliche Gestalt*] seems to him, the nearer he steps to its present form, the more it pains him to find that power and eloquence of form in decline and decay. The harvest to be reaped also grows and rises with such purity and perfection of the language's external constitution, because that which is transparent yields more than that which has already become dulled and confused. Even when I read through books from the sixteenth, indeed even the seventeenth century, the language – all its primitiveness and rawness which belongs to its age notwithstanding – seems to me in many of its features to remain enviable and *more powerful* [*vermögender*] than our language today.[145]

It is tempting to consider Grimm's comments here and those as far back as the introduction to the second edition of his *Grammatik* (1822) as particularly informative for Wagner, namely that modern German language – Luther's *Neuhochdeutsch* – had deviated from the "noble, almost wonderful purity" of its medieval incarnation to the detriment of its power of expression.[146] (People like William Barnes and Gerard Manley Hopkins were soon

---

[145] "Wer nun unsere sprache erforscht und mit beobachtender seele bald der vorzüge gewahr wird, die sie gegenüber der heutigen auszeichnen, sieht anfangs sich unvermerkt zu allen denkmälern der vorzeit hingezogen und von denen der gegenwart abgewandt. Je weiter aufwärts er klimmen kann, desto schöner und vollkommner dünkt ihn die leibliche gestalt der sprache, je näher ihrer jetzigen fassung er tritt, desto weher thut ihm jene macht und gewandtheit der form in abnahme und verfall zu finden. Mit solcher lauterkeit und vollendung der äuszeren beschaffenheit der sprache wächst und steigt auch die zu gewinnende ausbeute, weil das durchsichtigere mehr ergibt als das schon getrübte und verworrene. Sogar wenn ich bücher des sechzehnten ja siebenzehnten jahrhunderts durchlas, kam mir die sprache, aller damaligen verwilderung und roheit unerachtet, in manchen ihrer züge noch beneidenswerth und vermögender vor als unsere heutige." Translation adapted from Christopher Young and Thomas Gloning, *A History of the German Language through Texts* (London and New York: Routledge, 2004), 265–66.

[146] "Luthers sprache, deren grammatik gleichwohl eigentlich dargestellt zu werden verdiente, gehört nicht in diesen kreis, sie muß ihrer edlen, fast wunderbaren reinheit, auch ihres gewaltigen einfluß halber, für kern und grundlage der neuhochdeutschen sprachniedersetzung gehalten werden, wovon bis auf den heutigen tag nur sehr unbedeutend, meistens zum schaden der kraft und des ausdrucks abgewichen worden ist. "Grimm, *Deutsche Grammatik*, 2nd edn., xi.

speaking of English in exactly these terms: Barnes wished to extirpate all Latinate forms, and said that instead of degrees of comparison we should speak of pitches of suchness.)[147] Wagner's deep engagement with *Melodik* was, in part, to take advantage of, and remedy this situation for drama as much as music. My claim, inasmuch as this complex interaction of theories permits one, is that Wagner's commitment to philology led him to conceive of a cultural language – the very structures of German thought (after Humboldt) – etymologically, as "melodic echoes" of an imagined past.

Sound *qua* immanent meaning

Hence, the appeal for Wagner of this historic language – in addition to its national status – was pragmatic: the professed communicative agency inherent in its physical constitution. Grimm had asserted a directly proportional relationship between a language's age and its communicative potency, even stating that he would gladly have given up Gottfried von Strassburg, Wolfram von Eschenbach and all the poetry of the thirteenth century for the lost parts of a *Wulfina*, a translation of the New Testament into Gothic, and the earliest surviving evidence of any Germanic language (for Germanic languages, Gothic plays a role similar to that of Sanskrit in the Indo-European family).[148]

Wagner took this historicism to heart. As late as 1873, he read sections from Grimm's *History of the German Language* (1848) to Cosima:

[R. says] the only language which can be recognized as really beautiful is the one which is still attached to its roots, and it is a false optimism which induced Grimm to say that the mixing of the Latin and Germanic languages had produced perfection; such mixtures, R. says, are an evil, and the purer a language remains as it develops, the more significant it is. "Of course," he concludes, "Grimm [in 1848] had given up all hope of a German culture (and one can't blame him)."[149]

A silent continuation of this in 1873 would seem to be: "because he didn't live to see the day." Without seeking to ventriloquize Wagner's thoughts at two steps removed, his dismay at an adulterated national language is

---

[147] See William Barnes, *A Philological Grammar* (London: John Russell Smith, 1854).

[148] "Welchen abstand aber auch von ihnen stelle die edle, freie natur der mittelhochdeutschen dichtungen dar ... es gab stunden, wo für abhanden gekommene theile des ULFILAS ich die gesamte poesie der besten zeit des dreizehnten jahrhunderts mit freuden ausgeliefert haben würde." See Christopher Young and Thomas Gloning (eds.), *A History of the German Language through Texts*, 265.

[149] CT (June 7, 1873).

perhaps more understandable two years after the defeat of France and the long-awaited unification of Bismarck's Germany, when political institutions finally mirrored the "cultural" cohesion that a truly Germanic language had seemed to promise decades earlier, i.e. when the infrastructure of *Staatsnation* finally caught up with an existing sense of *Kulturnation*.[150] Ironically, the very concept of *Nationalsprache* allowed for aspirations towards political unity; once this was achieved institutionally and militarily, it confirmed the linguistic project (for Wagner at least) in a self-endorsing sequence.

Over and above the familiar mythological texts, Grimm turns out to be the unwitting source for Wagner's prejudices against modern speech, end rhyme, and iambic meter, as well as his interest in vowel sounds, speech roots, and sound shifts (as noted earlier). Wagner did not parrot Grimm without reflection, though; the evidence suggests that he absorbed and partially digested certain ideas, reformulating them to his own ends, where they functioned as a scholarly authorization of his approach to *Melodik*.

Grimm offered a balanced view of the historical importance of alliteration and rhyme, but claims that these ultimately degraded root syllables through time:

> Rhyme hindered only bad poets, [while it] served true poets to reveal their power of speech and of thought. There are times, however, when the art of rhyme dies out because the sensual tenderness of the root-impoverished language hardens itself and newly formed composites by nature have stiffer movement; so meter became obsolete earlier according to the laws of quantity and alliteration.[151]

Similarly, Wagner speaks of the same modern alienation from the original sense of speech roots, which "have become altered or newly accommodated to our social relations and views, and in any case estranged from our feeling."[152] The aim of Wagner's expressive poetic melody is predicated on a revival of (if not a nostalgic return to) this original state, which he sought through the dialectical model outlined earlier, namely a path from

---

[150] Friedrich Meinecke's distinction between a common political history built on overtly formal characteristics, and a shared cultural heritage including language and literature, respectively. See Meinecke, *Weltbürgertum und Nationalstaat*, ed. H. Herzfeld (Munich: Oldenbourg, 1969).

[151] "Der reim hat nur schlechte dichter gezwängt, wahren gedient, ihre gewalt der sprache und des gedankens zu enthüllen. Es gibt aber zeiten, wo die kunst des reimes ausstirbt, weil sich die sinnliche zartheit der wurzelärmeren sprache verhärtet und neugebildete zusammensetzungen eine von natur steifere bewegung haben; so sind früher die metra nach dem gesetz der quantität . . . und der alliteration untergegangen." Grimm *Deutsche Grammatik*, 2nd edn., viii.

[152] SSD 4: 117. Cf. PW2: 254.

what is essentially an inner musical vowel to the outer world of syntactical expression and back to the musical tone.

On the other hand, Grimm advocated rhyme and alliteration as pre-servers of language against its natural mutability, and the only means by which historical sounds become knowable for modern listeners:

Just as the laws of classical meter have revealed a wealth of rules of grammar, so the observance of alliteration and rhyme is extraordinarily important to German. Without rhyme there would be almost no history of our language to carry out. Poetry should not only please the listeners and singers of the *Lied*, it should also restrain the power of language, secure its purity and bring knowledge of it to future generations. Free prose allows the content to die away from memory, it makes the *true ensounding* [*belautung*] of words doubtful to the organs [ear and mouth].[153]

Wagner, while embracing (Buch)stabreim, dismissed end rhyme as some-thing that postdates a schism of original artistic unity, and merely "fluttered at the loose end of the ribbons of melody."[154] Grimm's appreciation of rhyme was also limited to its archaic forms, and thirty years before Wagner, he had similarly castigated modern rhyme, lamenting that "The coarser, careless rhyme of our best contemporary poets prophesies the gradual death of even this form."[155]

Finally, a practical instance of Wagner adopting Grimm's working prac-tices is his drafting of the *Lohengrin* libretto and the first prose scenario for the *Ring* (1848) without capitalization of substantives or common nouns. This even extended to Wagner's correspondence – somewhat inconsis-tently – between January 2, 1849 and November 27, 1852. Grimm printed the second edition of the *Deutsche Grammatik* without capitals and in Roman type (rather than Fraktur), advocating consistent use of lower case as the only "correct" orthography for German. In the preface to the *Deutsches Wörterbuch* he further criticized "the silly custom" of

---

[153] "So wie diesen die gesetze classischer metrik eine fülle grammatischer regeln offenbart haben, ist in den deutschen denkmählern die beachtung der alliterationen und reime von außerordentlichem gewicht. Ohne den reim wäre fast keine geschichte unserer sprache auszuführen. Das band der poesie soll nicht allein die hörer und sänger des lieds erfreuen, es soll auch die kraft der sprache zügeln, ihre reinheit sichern und kunde davon auf kommende geschlechter bringen. Ungebundene prosa läßt dem gedächtnis den inhalt verhallen, den organen die wahre belautung der worte zweifelhaft werden." Grimm, *Deutsche Grammatik*, 2nd edn., vii. Emphasis added.

[154] SSD 4: 97. Cf. PW2: 230. In the context of Wagner's early melodrama *Gretchen* (WWV 15; 1831), which matches the end rhyme to periodic phrase terminations, his later attack on precisely this practice can also be read as a self-reflexive criticism.

[155] "Der gröbere nachläßige reim unserer besten neueren dichter weissagt selbst dieser form einen allmähligen tod." Grimm, *Deutsche Grammatik*, 2nd edn., viii.

distinguishing substantives with capitals which he linked with the use of Gothic type (Fraktur).[156] Liszt crowed supportively about how, in *Lohengrin's* oasis of lower case, "this simple plan strikes the eye,"[157] but reviewers of the first fascicules of the *Deutsches Wörterbuch* were less kind, at least until Grimm's explanatory preface was published in 1854.[158]

Vowels: from speech physiology to material sound

What do these connections to Grimm amount to? Wagner, we recall, regarded vowels in speech roots as the most primitive units of language; Grimm found them unpredictable, volatile and hence far harder to study than consonant gradations, which were stable and traceable, by contrast.[159] Wagner again appears to have taken his cue from Grimm's cautious appreciation of vowels: "One may view the vowels as the necessary coloring or animation of all words, as the breath without which they would not even exist. The real individuality of the word rests on the vowel sound; it affords the finest relationships."[160] Grimm's observation is more a fact of speech than language, and the parallelism here to Wagner's ascription of the "most beautiful breath" to Schröder-Devrient is surely no coincidence. Significantly for Wagner's belief in language's basis in sensation, a number of writers felt this "necessary coloring of words" was not abstract, but

---

[156] "[Vulgarschrift] ist es, die den albernen gebrauch groszer buchstaben für alle substantiva veranlaszt hat." Grimm, "Vorrede" [§19], *Deutsches Wörterbuch*, http://woerterbuchnetz.de/cgi-bin/WBNetz/wbgui_py?sigle=DWB&mainmode=Vorworte&file=vor01_html#abs20

[157] "Diese schlichte Detail fällt schon beim bloßen Durchblättern des Textbuches auf." Liszt, "Lohengrin, Große romantische Oper von R. Wagner, und ihre erste Aufführung in Weimar bei Gelegenheit der Herder- und Goethe-Feiern 1850," in SS 4: 83.

[158] See John L. Flood, "'es verstand sich fast von selbst, dasz die ungestalte und häszliche schrift . . . bleiben mußte.' Jacob Grimm's Advocacy of Roman Type," in *"Das unsichtbare Band der Sprache." Studies in German Language and Linguisitc History in Memory of Leslie Seiffert*, ed. John Flood, Paul Salmon, Olive Sayce, and Christopher Wells (Stuttgart: Hans-Dieter Heinz, 1993), 279–312, here 280–81.

[159] "If a thoroughly grounded statement is ascertained and accepted for [consonants], then perhaps some insights might also be gained into the history of the vowels . . . in Germanic dialects with the same consonantal gradation we encounter such varying and manifold vowels." ["Läßt sich für diese eine gegründete bestimmung ermitteln und annehmen, so werden dadurch vielleicht auch einige blicke in die geschichte der vocale vergönnt . . . wir [begegnen] in deutschen dialecten derselben consonantenstufe so schwankenden und manigfaltigen vocalen."] Grimm, *Deutsche Grammatik*, 2nd edn., 497, 505.

[160] "Man kann die vocale als die nothwendige färbung oder belebung aller wörter betrachten, als den athem, ohne welchen diese gar nicht bestehen würden. Die eigentliche individualisierung des worts beruht auf dem vocallaut; er gewährt die feinsten beziehungen." *Ibid.*, 495.

physiologically conditioned: "Every sound has its natural value and future use founded upon the organ producing it," Grimm rationalized in 1851.[161] A professor of medicine at Leipzig, Karl Merkel, extended this supposition in 1866 to postulate a complete mapping of all possible vocal sounds – from characteristic noise to tone and vowel sound – based on the physical movements of the larynx: "in this way we want to become acquainted with the mechanism of human vocal and verbal sounds . . . On this physiological path we obtain the *natural alphabet* that must be valid for all languages, and which must contain all speech sounds used by the peoples of the earth for intellectual communication."[162] (Unlike Wagner, though, Merkel doesn't connect the corporeal medium of vocal production with its ostensive message.)

Yet Grimm had cautioned contrariwise that the vast phonological landscape of the *Grammatik* was descriptive rather than didactic, and cannot lead to physiological laws that govern enunciation:

If one only attributes a purely physiological function to speech sounds [*lauten*] and establishes an unproven and unprovable system of pronunciation, this becomes too tenuous for me at least, and I am not able to stand by it.[163]

Such views did little to dampen interest in the physical properties of speech, however, and Merkel publicly disparaged Grimm, even arguing that his theory of sound was in fact a theory of letters.[164] As early as 1830, moreover, a Cambridge professor of mechanics, Robert Willis, had claimed that vowel colors were "not inseparably connected to human organs." This view was based on the prior assumption that physiological properties of the larynx and vocal cords in tandem with the modification of the oral cavity determined vowel sound, and that these could be replicated. Accordingly Willis constructed a reed organ that, by varying the position of the reed in relation

---

[161] "Jeder laut hat seinen natürlichen, im organ das ihn hervorbringt gegründeten und zur anwendung kommenden gehalt." Grimm, *Über den Ursprung der Sprache*, 42.

[162] "Wir wollen auf diese Weise die Mechanik der menschlichen Stimm- und Sprachlaute kennen lernen . . . Wir erhalten auf diesem physiologischen Wege das *natürliche Alphabet*, das für alle Sprachen seine Gültigkeit haben muss, und in welchem alle Sprachlaute, welche von den Völkern der Erde zur geistigen Mittheilung gebraucht werden, enthalten sein müssen." Merkel, *Physiologie der menschlichen Sprache* (Leipzig: Otto Wigand, 1866), 2.

[163] "Nur wenn man den lauten reinphysiologische functionen unterschiebt und darauf ein unerwiesnes und unbeweisbares system der aussprache gründet . . . wird mir wenigstens die luft allzu dünn, und ich vermag nicht darin zu leben." Grimm, *Deutsche Grammatik*, 3rd edn. (Göttingen: Dieterichsche Buchhandlung, 1840), xv.

[164] Merkel, *Physiologie der menschlichen Sprache*, iv–v.

to the pipe, could produce tone qualities approximately equivalent to the vowel sequence: U–O–A–E–I.[165]

It is revealing that comparative anatomy arose at precisely the same time as comparative grammar within central European universities. In tandem with Grimm's chronology of historical sounds, *physical* speech seemed to offer another means of accessing what he called the "mysterious and miraculous"[166] nature of language, namely by treating speech as material substance in the present. In 1836, the Tübingen philologist Moritz Rapp published *Towards a Physiology of Language*, in which his stated aim was to design a natural history of speech as "the only secure basis" for all grammatical disciplines. Speech, for him, was now "physiology above all," and its "amphibious organ" (capable of singing and speaking) was governed by only two sets of laws: physiological and historical–etymological.[167]

Wagner effectively came of age during the historical emergence of physiological speech–sound as a mainstay of language studies. He knew of Rapp's work: the first edition of the *Physiology* was contained in his Bayreuth library (though this of course cannot confirm he read it thoroughly). While Wagner's belief in the "original truth" within root vowels was predicated on *historical* research, such sounds required a physical manifestation to exist. The dependence was not mutual, and Rapp's interest in vocal speech–sounds (*Laute*) of the here and now is only tangentially related to a theory of historically original sound; instead, he adduces an ahistorical predicate – *Urlaut* – from which all modern vowels are derived. He elaborates this hypothetical concept (*Urlaut*) as the "primary vowel sound," suggesting that, like primary colors, there must be a physiologically primal *sound*, which by definition would precede speech consciousness in a cognitive rather than temporal realm.[168] *Urlaut* is, in essence, Rapp's rhetorical term for the unvoiced, physical impulse to communicate vocally. By nature, it lacks a defining quality, and is most apparent in modern German, he suggests, through the sound of "tired" speech, indicating that

---

[165] See Robert Willis, "On the Vowel Sounds and on Reed Organ-Pipes," *Transactions of the Cambridge Philosophical Society* 3 (1830), 231–68, here 233.

[166] "Traun geheimnisvoll und wunderbar ist der sprache ursprung, doch rings umgegeben von andern wundern und geheimnissen." Grimm, *Über den Ursprung der Sprache*, 58.

[167] "Auf solche Leistungen sich stützend, unternahm es der Verfasser, eine Naturgeschichte der Sprache zu entwerfen, welche die einzige sichere Basis für alle grammatische Disciplin abgeben kann, und als Physiologie überhaupt die eine Hälfte der Gesetze nach seiner Überzeugung umfast, welche das doppellebige Organ der menschlichen Sprache bedingen." Moritz Rapp, *Versuch einer Physiologie der Sprache nebst historischer Entwicklung der abendlaendischen Idiome nach physiologischen Grundsätzen* (Stuttgart & Tübingen: J. G. Cotta, 1836), vi.

[168] *Ibid.*, 20.

it is ever latent and concealed rather than revived anachronistically: "it is that sound [*Laut*] around which the others, the developed vowels, sink back during flagging powers of production."[169] By inadvertently stripping away the rational, conceptual accretions of articulate modern language (whether through speaking "fatigue," or archaic verse composition), this predicate mirrors Wagner's aspirations towards an expression of raw feeling, an ahistorical "purely human core"[170] of utterance which forms the other side of his attraction to vowel sounds in *Oper und Drama*.

For Rapp, the vowel system is a living organism with an inner urge to change its auditory expression; hence its volubility in dialect. Purest *a* – as the sound closest to a theoretically prior *Urlaut* – is the sound most equidistant between *o* and *e*, he argues, again invoking color to clarify: reddest red is precisely equidistant between yellow and blue.[171] Together these three vowels make up a fundamental triad because they commune directly with, and first transform, the *Urlaut*.[172] For Grimm too, *a* was the central organizing point: "Of the vowels *a* holds the clear middle point; *i* the heights; *u* the depths. *a* is pure and fixed, *i* and *u* are liquid and capable of being restricted by a consonant."[173] Rapp expanded this beyond Grimm's straight shift between vowels, and postulates an infinite number of physiological stages – and hence, applied meanings – in contemporary speech between the poles – *i* and *u* – of the vowel system, creating a continuum that "until it arrives at the poles of *i* or *u* can be thought of as an unending and continuous row of middle steps."[174] Here is the liquid motion Rapp assigns three rows:

$$a - \ddot{u} - e - i$$
$$\H{o} - \ddot{o} - \ddot{u}$$
$$a - \mathring{a} - o - u^{175}$$

[169] "Der Urlaut wird sich gleichsam rückwärts so entdecken, er wird derjenige Laut seyn, um den die andern, die enwickelten Vocale, bei erlahmender Productionskraft zurücksinken." *Ibid.*, 21.

[170] SSD 4: 118. Cf. PW 2: 255.

[171] "Welches übrigens das allerreinste *a* sey, das sich am fernsten von *e* und *o* erhalte, darüber gibt er eben so wenig ein untrügliches Kennzeichen, als die Farbenlehre ein absolut reinstes Roth vorweisen kann, das dem Gelb und Blau gleich ferne steht." Rapp, *Versuch einer Physiologie der Sprache*, 22.

[172] *Ibid.*, 23.

[173] "Von den vokalen hält *a* die reine mitte, *i* höhe, *u* tiefe; *a* ist rein und starr, *i* und *u* sind flüssig und der konsonantierung fähig." Grimm, *Über den Ursprung der Sprache*, 43.

[174] "die beiden polaren Richtungen des Vocalsystems lassen sich von der Indifferenz *a* aus, als ein Continuum betrachen, das, bis es zur Spitze des *i* und *u* angelangt ist, eine unendliche Reihe von Mittelstufen durchlaufend gedacht werden kann." Rapp, *Versuch einer Physiologie der Sprache*, 23.

[175] *Ibid.*, 31–32.

With the exception of its outermost points these steps are fixed arbitrarily, for the cycle "does not consist in absolute phenomena." Vowels can either become lighter or darker, and as if to quantify a mysterious, inscrutable property inherent in this claim for a "living scale," Rapp further claims that "no human organ [ear] is able to follow the small deviations,"[176] describing the resulting "medial sounds" (*Zwischenlaute*) that characterize the system's undetectably minute gradations as having an "indecisive character, obscure, dark and mysterious like all 'between' states or half-natures."[177]

Thinking again of the opening vocal melody of *Rheingold*, the point for Wagner in seeking to utilize these "dark" *Zwischenlaute* was that each sound had a putatively fixed physiological designation, which implied an essentialized signification between sound, essence, and origin. It implied, in other words, a condition of absolute naming where sound and essence were identical. Novalis, for one, had famously termed the alphabet a *TonSchriftkunst*, reinscribing a cultural yearning to regain lost expression from the punishment of oblivion. The means of achieving this, his vocabulary implies, concern music above all:

> Our language – it was initially far more musical and only gradually become prosaic – is voided of tone [*enttönt*]. It has now become more like *noise – sound* [*Laut*], if one wants to humble this beautiful word. It must become song again.[178]

In this reading, true expression of thought depended on a musically latent sound understood as belonging to language: "as soon as one has but the right name, one has the inner idea."[179] This synchronic, physiological

---

[176] I have partly paraphrased, partly quoted from the following: "kein menschliches Organ wird aber die kleinen Abweichungen verfolgen können, nach welchen jeder einzelne Buchstabe je nach dem Wechsel der Landstriche um ein Minimum nach oben und unten variiren kann, und es ist genug, wenn wir uns die Ueberzeugung gewonnen haben, der Vocalcyclus besteht nicht in absolut gestellten Erscheinungen, sondern er ist eine lebendige Scala, die sich nur problematisch nach angenommenen Punkten theilen und fixiren läßt." *Ibid.*, 24.

[177] "Ihrem Charakter nach haben sie etwas Unentschiedenes, Clärobscüres, Düsteres und Mysterioses an sich, wie alle Zwischenzustände oder Halbnaturen." *Ibid.*, 24. Arguing that such gradations are beyond a perceptible realm and therefore above all questions is a deft rhetorical move, for it requires that readers take on faith Rapp's assertion, which itself is not grounded on quantifiable scientific evidence.

[178] "Unsre Sprache – sie war zu Anfang viel musicalischer und hat sich nur nach gerade so prosaisirt – so *enttönt*. Es ist jetzt mehr *Schallen* geworden – *Laut*, wenn man dieses schöne Wort so erniedrigen will. Sie muß wieder *Gesang* werden." Novalis, *Schriften. Die Werke Friedrich von Hardenbergs*, 5 vols., ed. Richard Samuel, 3rd edn. (Stuttgart: W. Kohlhammer, 1960–1988), 3: 283ff., No. 245.

[179] "Sobald man nur die rechten Namen hat, so hat man die Idee inne." Novalis, *Schriften. Die Werke Friedrich von Hardenbergs*, 2: 560, No. 164.

connection has no recourse to etymologically primitive roots. It was for this reason that Paul de Man – in reference to Hölderlin – drew attention to the inherent illusion of nature apparently creating itself in the act of naming, which he termed: "to originate anew."[180] If the sound structures of language carry physiologically innate meanings – which was the basis of Wagner's interest in Stabreim – how extensive were the attempts by philologists to chart his putatively "natural" vocal–physiological territory?

Musical vowels

In contrast to the dominant eighteenth-century view that language originated as musical wailing, only later to crystallize within the realm of logos, Grimm argued contrariwise that language is an *a priori* condition for music:

For singing and song originated from the intoned, measured recitation of words. From the song came the other poetic art, and from singing through heightened abstraction came all other music . . . Music could much rather be called a sublimation of language, than language a precipitate of music.[181]

A year after Rapp's *Physiologie* was published, August Kahlert – a regular contributor to Schumann's *Neue Zeitschrift für Musik* – similarly derided as "nice" but "fairly useless" the origin theory that claimed "the language of the first people was song."[182] His article is striking in prefiguring Wagner's musical scrutiny of vowels and consonants, and in borrowing the concept of a vowel continuum from Rapp, but uncomplicatedly, in terms of a spontaneous division:

The sound [*Klang*] of vowels was more varied [historically], they merged more into one another. A progressive culture – demanding order and thus laws everywhere – first separated the vowels and so speech–sound color [*Lautfarbe*] first emerged in the world. I would not know how to differentiate the vowels differently. The vowel in itself is still certainly not a sound [*Klang*], for even if only spoken we do not think

---

[180] Paul de Man, "Intentional Structure of the Romantic Language," in *Romanticism and Consciousness. Essays in Criticism*, ed. Harold Bloom (New York: Norton, 1970), 66.

[181] "Denn aus betonter, gemessener rezitation der worte entsprangen gesang und lied, aus dem lied die andere dichtkunst, aus dem gesang durch gesteigerte abstraction alle übrige musik . . . Viel eher dürfte die music ein sublimat der sprache heißen als die sprache ein niederschlag der music." Grimm's lecture to the Prussian Academy of sciences was delivered on January 9, 1851, See Grimm, *Über den Ursprung der Sprache*, 58.

[182] "Dies hat die alte Behauptung, die Sprache der ersten Menschen sey Gesang gewesen, oftmals unterstützen sollen. Allein diese schöne Hypothese ist ziemlich unnütz." August Kahlert, "Das musikalische Element in der Sprache," *NZfM* 46 (June 9, 1837), 181.

of particular pitches, and yet the ear is affected by separating our five vowels into diphthongs.[183]

But particular pitches were latent. A decade later, Helmholtz would build a vowel synthesizer, using eight electromagnetically vibrated tuning forks to designate fixed empirical identities for each vowel by varying the relative volume of different partials to simulate the different vowel qualities (other German researchers took different approaches to the same end of scrutinizing the material reality of vowel identities, notably Rudolph König and Karl Merkel).[184] Before this empiricism, however, Kahlert first hypothesized simply that infinite shades of *Lautfarbe* emerge only after a rational division of "more varied" sound into five vowels. Without those points of reference, the gradations would have nothing to deviate from. With this in mind, he offers a useful set of definitions for the multifarious German words for "sound" based on the principle of pitch deviation.

Schall: everything audible in a wide sense, "noise"
Laut: modification of noise [*Schall*] through speech, therefore
Laute: sounds that constitute speech,
Klang: noise [*Schall*] with recognizable pitch
Ton: sound [*Klang*] of a previously known pitch[185]

---

[183] "Der Klang der Vocale war mannigfaltiger, dieselben verschwammen mehr in eindander. Die vorschreitende Cultur, die überall Ordnung und daher Gesetz erfordete, schied erst allmählich die Vocale, und so entstand in der Welt die *Lautfarbe*. Anders wüßte ich nähmlich den Unterschied der Vocale nicht zu bezeichnen. Der Vocal an sich ist ja noch kein Klang, denn eben nur ausgesprochen, ist von bestimmbarer Höhe nicht die Rede, und doch wird das Ohr durch unsere fünf Vocale sammt Doppellauten verschieden berührt." *Ibid.*, 180–81.

[184] Hermann von Helmholtz, "Klänge der Vokale," in *Die Lehre von den Tonempfindungen* [1863], 2nd edn. (Brunswick: Friedrich Vieweg und Sohn, 1865), 163–181; and *Science and Culture: Popular and Philosophical Essays*, ed. David Cahan (University of Chicago Press, 1995), 68ff. The most recent contextual study of Helmholtz's study of vowels is Benjamin Steege, *Helmholtz and the Modern Listener* (Cambridge University Press, 2012), 178–92. See also David Pantalony, "Seeing a Voice: Rudolph König's Instruments for Studying Vowel Sounds" *The American Journal of Psychology* 117 (2004), 425–42; and Merkel, *Physiologie der menschlichen Sprache*, 109.

[185] "Der Ausdruck *Laut* . . . bezeichnet die Modificationen des *Schalles* durch die Sprachwerkzeuge . . . Alles hörbares im weitesten Sinne nennt man *Schall* . . . Auch ich nenne einen Schall von *erkennbarer* Höhe einen *Klang*, und einen Klang von *erkannter* Höhe einen *Ton* . . . Wir haben also in der Sprache es nur mit *Lauten* zu thun, d. i. mit dem Schalle, der sich zum Klange oder Tone runden kann, diese Vervollkommnung jedoch noch nicht erfahren hat." Kahlert, "Das musikalische Element in der Sprache," 180. National rather than physiological criteria determine the "wealth of sounds" inherent in Kahlert's typology, which rehearses a simplistic correlate between feeling, vowel, and national character that had been familiar for decades: "Die unmusikalischeste Nation Europa's, die Engländer haben fast nur Zisch- und Gurgellaute. Herrscht bei ihnen nicht der Begriff, dagegen bei den Italienern das Gefühl vor?" (page 183). The gap opening between *echt* philology and its selective appropriation by writers on

Wagner was an avid reader of Schumann's *Neue Zeitschrift*. While the extent to which he absorbed musical opinions about philology in this way during the 1830s–40s is open to debate, his correspondence certainly indicates he tried to keep abreast of all contributions.[186] But if *Oper und Drama* was far from unprecedented in its music–philological leanings, we may wonder how the more notable writers sought to map specific attributes of traditionally disembodied "feeling" onto the material of sound, connecting with what Wagner called our "sensory power of perception."

Two of the most prominent theorists were Heinrich August Kerndörffer (1769–1846) and Heinrich Theodor Rötscher (1803–81). In his *Handbook of Declamation* (1813), Kerndörffer – one of the most musically inspired writers on declamation – argued that "tonic keys" (*Grundtöne*) were inherent in verbal speech and could be used to establish a "correct and particular musical scale" for the human voice.[187] Not coincidentally, these vocal "keys" were based on the five vowel sounds, and Kerndörffer assigned the five principal notes in his scale to vowels on the assumption that each "tonic" is understood as an *Urlaut* insofar as "it belongs to five particular natural points in the throat [*Kehlpunkte*] germane to every human voice."[188] That is: vowel color was deemed wholly physiological.

While it is not possible to "modulate" between "keys" within a poem, one can mix the overtones of one key with those of another to create the desired "harmonic mixture," he explains.[189] As quasi-physiological qualities that seek to bridge the Cartesian divide, each tonic vowel is assigned a specific expressive quality by Kerndörffer:

U: a terrible shrinking back (like "uh!" or "huhu!"), otherwise known as a "sound of spirits" which means that, on stage, it is the sound adopted for the appearance of ghosts

---

music is made clear by comparing this statement with Grimm's view – penned during the same winter as Wagner's *Oper und Drama*: "Denn an reichtum, vernunft und gedrängter fuge läßt sich keine aller noch lebenden sprachen ihr [the English language] an die seite setzen, auch unsre deutsche nicht, die zerrissen ist wie wir selbst zerrissen sind, und erst manche gebrechen von sich abschütteln müßte ehe sie kühn mit in die laufbahn träte." See Grimm, *Über den Ursprung der Sprache*, 54.

[186]   See Wagner to Schumann, December 3, 1836, Leipzig: "Endlich erhielt ich letzthin wieder eine Lieferung der mus. Zeitschrift; durch meine Reisen war bis jetzt die Verbindung unterbrochen; ich habe jetzt die Blätter bis uhngefähr [*sic*] Ende Juli; wären Sie wohl so gut, und besorgten 'mal gelegentlich, daß mir endlich die übrigen auch zukommen?" in SB 1: 319.

[187]   "eine richtige und bestimmte Tonleiter." Heinrich August Kerndörffer, *Handbuch der Declamation* (Leipzig: Fleischer, 1813), 16.

[188]   "sie auf fünf besondere, jeder menschlichen Stimme eigene Kehlpunkte des Gemüths angehören." *Ibid.*, 21.

[189]   "obertönig mitschwingenden Akkordton." *Ibid.*, 27.

O: celebratory, sublime emotion, otherwise known as a "sound of worship," which means it is appropriate for odes, prayers, or for the portrayal of male deities

A: free sigh of relief

I: exaggerated effect, which is suitable for portraying female deities[190]

As the so-called central vowel or middle tone, E lacks a specific indicative quality and is not therefore assigned a particular place in the row. Such ambitious claims for vocal–tonal specificity were disputed by at least one fellow theorist.[191] But in his later *Manual for a Thorough Training in Public Oratory* (1833), Kerndörffer actually deepened his claim for the inherent connection between physiology and emotion in each vowel, and arranges their different sounds according to what he terms "different capabilities of the soul."[192] The expression of emotions and feelings is realized through tones as a "language of the heart," forming a "generally comprehensible primal language of nature,"[193] while the organizing framework, the "capabilities of the soul," are given as follows:

U rationality [*Vernunft*]
O the power of judgment [*Urteilskraft*]
E reason [*Verstand*];
A the power of imagination [*Einbildungskraft*];
I fantasy [*Phantasie*][194]

On the basis of this monistic connection between sound, physiology and soul, Kerndörffer situates declamation as the great nexus linking the human system together, whose principle consists "in every general language of nature, of *Tonsprache* or the language of feelings, from which the essential fundamental laws of declamation are to be divined."[195] Thus, more than three decades before Wagner would posit "objective sensations" that

---

[190] *Ibid.*, 21–24ff.

[191] In 1841 Emil Thürnagel questioned Kerndörffer's belief in a uniform "scale" of vocal vowels on the basis that they were undifferentiable in musical terms. "Da die Töne welche ihr [der Sprechstimme] zu Gebote stehen, ungleich näher beisammen liegen, als beim Gesange, so ist die Aufstellung einer vollkommenen, deklamatorischen Tonleiter etwas Unmögliches." Emil Thürnagel, *Theorie der Schauspielkunst* (Heidelberg: August Oswald's Univ.-Buchh., 1836), 55.

[192] "unterschiedliche Seelenvermögen" Kerndörffer, *Anleitung zur gründlichen Bildung der öffentlichen Beredsamkeit. Ein Compendium für Schulen, Gymnasien und akademische Vorlesungen* (Leipzig: Steinacker, 1833), 141.

[193] "allgemein verständliche Ursprache der Natur." *Ibid.*, 121.   [194] *Ibid.*, 141ff.

[195] "in jener allgemeinen Sprache der Natur, der Tonsprache oder der Sprache der Empfindungen enthalten, wonach die wesentlichen Grundreglen der Declamation zu entnehmen sind." *Ibid.*, 127.

designate particularities in speech roots, Kerndörffer had envisaged a linguistic–melodic means of immanent sounding signification, which made Wagner's claims all the more credible by 1851.

A second theorist I am briefly introducing, Heinrich Theodor Rötscher, also developed a monistic vowel theory in his *Art of Dramatic Representation* (1841) and also believed in a liquid vowel scale,[196] arguing that vowels were "urges" (rather than "capabilities") of the soul, dependent on pronunciation:

In vowels, the voice emerges in its original freedom, it is the direct outpouring thereof . . . Perfect pronunciation will bring the [significance of each soulful urge] into being as much as possible. There is no doubt that different emotions will be aroused through these [urges]. The purer they ring out in their pronunciation, the more clearly their significance will penetrate the ear . . . The clearer and more purely their sound is heard, the more they appear to the listener as music of speech, the clearer the torrent of emotions rushes towards them.[197]

Like Kerndörffer he lacked any empirical method, but believed in a direct connection between physical vibrations acting on a receptive anatomy, expressive impulse, and the perception of emotion.[198] Two decades later, Kahlert would situate this in a musical context, likewise asserting a purposive correspondence between vowels and a particular emotion, in which the individual quality of vowels attains a daring specificity: "A world of delight often lies in an 'O,' indescribable astonishment lies in an 'I,' a fear that almost paralyzes language lies in 'U'."[199]

What, though, is the significance of such eccentric theories for Wagner? While most writers introduced *different* specific "meanings" for each vowel, they consistently posited a connection between physiology, sensation, sound, and signification (all of which Wagner subsumed under the term *die Gefühle* in the broader context of *Sinnlichkeit*: "the

---

[196] "Der reine Vokal entsteht durch den bis zum Laut anschwellenden Hauch und bildet eine auf- und absteigende Scala." Rötscher, *Die Kunst der dramatischen Darstellung*, 1: 128.

[197] "Im Vokale erscheint also die Stimme in ihrer ursprünglichen Freiheit, er ist der unmittelbare Erguß derselben . . . Die Vokale haben aber, als vom Drange der Seele erzeugte Elemente, ihre *Bedeutsamkeit*. Eine vollkommene Aussprache wird dieselben daher so viel als möglich zur Erscheinung bringen. Daß durch sie unterschiedene Empfindungen angeregt werden, unterliegt keinem Zweifel. Je reiner sie in der Aussprache ertönen, desto klarer dringt sich die Bedeutsamkeit derselben an das Ohr . . . Je heller und reiner ihr Klang vernommen wird, desto gesteigerter erscheint dem Hörer die *Musik der Sprache*, desto klarer rauscht ihm der Strom der Empfindungen entgegen." *Ibid.*, 1: 123–26.

[198] *Ibid.*, 1: 137–38.

[199] "In einem 'O' liegt oft eine Welt von Entzücken, in einem 'I' eine unausprechliche Verwunderung, in einem 'U' eine Furcht, die fast die Sprache lähmt." Kahlert, "Das musikalische Element in der Sprache," 180.

sensory power of perception"). Indeed, Wagner's numerous statements about the expressive primacy of the human voice in his *Melodik* would appear to draw directly on the kind of aesthetic platform provided by theorists such as Kerndörffer and Rötscher, where liminal structures for pure phonetics (rather than linear sequence, tonal opposition, or predefined characteristic shape) become a new means of organizing the elements of vocal-melodic expression.

Consonants, being cast in opposition to vowels, played very little part in this (the antithesis of vowel–consonant was variously interpreted through gender,[200] Cartesian dualism,[201] and music).[202] For Novalis they simply turned tone into noise,[203] and could best be likened to fingers that alter the pitch on a metaphorical violin (actually a kind of mono-vocal cord):

> Consonants are the fingerings and their succession and alternation belongs to *Aplicatur*. Vowels are the resonating strings, or *rods of air*. The lungs are the *moving bow*. The multiple strings on an instrument are merely for comfort – they are abbreviations. It is actually only *one string*.[204]

A singing–speaking monochord implies a parallelism between pitch and vowel continuum, but *Lautfarbe* was more commonly compared to color because, unlike pitch frequencies, there was no octave equivalency in the wavelengths of the color spectrum.[205] Beyond paraphrases of

---

[200] "Offenbar muß den vokalen insgesamt ein weiblicher, den konsonanten insgesamt ein männlicher grund beigelegt werden." Grimm, *Über den Ursprung der Sprache*, 42.

[201] "Wie Denken und Sein, Seele und Leib, Erkennen und Begehren den Dualismus der menschlichen Natur ausdrücken, so liefert davon das *Wort* in seinen Bestandtheilen, Vocale und Consonanten ein niederes Abbild. Der Vocale allein giebt uns keinen Begriff; was ihn bindet, begränzt, beseelt ist der Consonant." Kahlert, "Das musikalische Element in der Sprache," *NZfM* 46 (June 9, 1837), 180.

[202] "der Mitlauter aber ist ein Feind der Klanges, ist antimusikalisch." *Ibid.*, 183.

[203] Novalis, *Schriften. Die Werke Friedrich von Hardenbergs*, "Das philosophische Werk II," 283ff., No. 245.

[204] "Die Consonanten sind die Fingersetzungen und ihre Folge und Abwechselung gehört zur *Aplicatur*. Die Vocale sind die tönenden Saiten, oder *Luftstäbe*. Die Lunge ist der *bewegte Bogen*. Die mehreren Sayten auf einem Instrument sind nur zur Bequemlichkeit – es sind Abbreviaturen. Es ist eigentlich nur *Eine Sayte*." *Ibid.*

[205] See Rudolph Hermann Lotze's view that "the ascending scale, which is just as clearly an ascent as is the number of waves and yet is quite unlike that increase, repeats in its own specific form the progress in the series of stimuli. Wherever this series attains, through the doubling of a previous number of waves, a marked import, there the sensation follows with the marked impression of the octave of the key-note, and thus again in its own particular way represents sensuously the likeness and difference of the two series. On the other hand the colours, though their prismatic order rests on a similar increase in the number of waves, gives no one who is unprejudiced the impression of a similar progress; and the reason for this possibly lies in the peculiar nature of the nervous process which intervenes between the stimulus and sensation, and which we cannot take into consideration because we do not know it." Lotze, *Metaphysic in Three Books: Ontology,*

Enlightenment origin theories that connected vowel to emotion, consonant to concept, no nineteenth-century music theorist I have encountered comes closer than those quoted above to mapping the infinite canvas of feeling onto correspondingly infinite vocalic shades; most writers – not least Wagner – made the tacit assumption, however, that such a link is operative, traceable, and primal.[206]

* * *

For Wagner himself it was the multi-volume, etymological dictionaries, grammars, and monographs on historical linguistics filling his libraries in Dresden (see Appendix A) and Wahnfried (see Appendix B),[207] that seemed to offer a key, a kind of historical cipher to release what could be termed the latent primal feeling within the "physical form" or "'objective' sensation" of root syllables that seemed tantalizingly within reach. "The physiognomic

Cosmology, and Psychology, trans. and ed. Bernard Bosanquet (Oxford: Clarendon Press, 1884), §257. Jacob Grimm had noted precisely the same phenomenon in 1851, and proceeded to draw a direct comparison between vowel color and pitch: "Every sound is produced by a movement of stirring air . . . The necessary range and the measure of these sounds and noises are naturally conditioned as are the scale in music and the spectrum and shades of the colors. To their law nothing can be added. For besides the seven basic colors which offer endless mixtures no others are imaginable, and just as little can the least thing be added to the three vowels, *a, i, u*. From these originate *e* and *o* together with all the remaining diphthongs and their formulations into mere length." Grimm, *Über den Ursprung der Sprache*, 19–20.

[206] Outside the rigorous methodologies of natural science and philology, the Wagner-influenced French symbolist Arthur Rimbaud – and speaking of vowels in his sonnet *Voyelles* (1871) – prophesied that "one day I will tell your latent birth," ["Je dirai quelque jour vos naissances latentes."] and further proposed (after Wagner) that "I have invented the color wheel of vowels!" which he gives as: "*A* black, *E* white, *I* red, *O* blue, *U* green. – I have decided upon the form and the movement of each consonant and, with instinctive rhythms, I have flattered myself to have invented a poetic word accessible, one day, to all senses." Rimbaud's first comment is taken from Rimbaud, *Complete Works, Selected Letters / A Bilingual Edition*, trans. Wallace Fowlie (University of Chicago Press, 2005), 140. The poem: "J'inventai la couleur des voyelles! – *A* noir, *E* blanc, *I* rouge, *O* bleu, *U* vert. – Je réglai la forme et le mouvement de chaque consonne, et, avec des rythmes instinctifs, je me flattai d'inventer un verbe poétique accessible, un jour ou l'autre, à tous les sens" is from Rimbaud's cynical "Une Saison en enfer" in *Une Saison en enfer & Le bateau ivre: A Season in Hell & The Drunken Boat*, trans. Louise Varèse (Norfolk, CT: J. Laughlin, 1961), 50.

[207] While Wagner only rarely left comments and other marginalia to indicate whether he actually read the books in his library, he indicated to Karl Gaillard the personal importance to him of reading: "I plan to idle away the whole of the coming year, i.e. devouring the contents of my library without producing any work, although I regret to say that I do once again feel the urge to write something . . . but I intend to resist that urge, by force if necessary, first because there are a number of new things I should like to learn about, and second because I have come to the conclusion that if a dramatic work is to possess concentrated significance and originality, it must be the result of a certain step upwards in an artist's life and of a certain important period in his development . . . it takes several years to produce such concentrated maturity." Wagner to Gaillard, June 5, 1845, Dresden, in SB 2: 435–36.

likeness of the root words," Wagner's oft-quoted rationale for Stabreim maintains:

shows [the sense of language] in a kinship which is not only swiftly seizable by the sensory organ, but is in truth indwelling also in the *sense* of the root. / The *sense* of a root is the 'objective' sensation embodied therein ... A sensation such as can vindicate its own expression through the Stabreim of root words which call instinctively for emphasis is comprehensible to us beyond all doubt.[208]

This, in short, was a historically sanctioned methodology for encoding meaning through sensualized language. Wagner's radical turn to an artwork as "*immediate physical portrayal ... the liberation of thought into sensuousness*"[209] can be seen in media theoretical terms as canceling the distinction between a spectator's reflections and physically lived experience, i.e. sound as immanent meaning. The widespread treatment of vowels as expressing a kind of physiology of the soul among *Vormärz* theorists actually gestured towards a fully objectified poetry, that is, a material channel wherein listeners are physically connected to phonetic structures at the level of sensation – a media transmission defined "not by what it means, but by the difference between meaning and non-meaning, information and noise."[210] Wagner's intense and short-lived adoption of Stabreim simply formed a methodical way of converting Grimm's vast lists of monosyllabic root syllables into a more potently communicative German opera. It was in effect a new way of solving the problems of German melodic expression discussed in Chapters 1–3.

Though the etymological essentialism in Wagner's theory was borrowed, his aspiration to realize its logical premise – that meaning (signification) is phonetically innate – was new. As we have seen, Grimm felt that modern poetry was altogether more appealing to modern readers, and Wagner's archaisms have tended to be viewed as a flight from reality. In the context of philological research that drew upon theories of physiological communication, Wagner's description of melodic communication may sound more plausible to us than perhaps it did before:

We ... are able, through our hearing, to hold that now merely imagined emotion secure *in all its purely melodic manifestation* [*Kundgebung*]: it has become the property of pure music, and, then made perceptible to the senses by the

---

[208] SSD 4: 131. Cf. PW 2: 269.   [209] SSD 3: 46. Cf. PW 1: 73.
[210] David Wellbery, "Foreword" to Kittler, *Discourse Networks* (Stanford University Press, 1990), xiv.

orchestra's appropriate expression, it appears to us as *the realization in the present of what the actor has just told us as a mere thing of thought*. Such a melody, once imparted to us by the actor as the outpouring of an emotion, and now expressively delivered by the orchestra at an instant when the person represented merely nurses that emotion in his memory – *such a melody materializes for us this personage's thought*.[211]

Wagner's claims, however outlandish, rest on an edifice of philological research, becoming essentially a form of applied linguistics. Instead of opera as the fixing of melodic shape around language, now there was to be language as a melodizing of lexical fixity, construed as physiologically innate. If linguistic paleontology was the "science of ... dreams," Wagner too was a dreamer, albeit one who disparaged the toil of dry research in favor of tangible poetic urges: "a need [*Not*], such as the poet feels when he is driven to impart himself . . . to the senses."[212] Driven by such urges, it seems the promise of a physical, sensory language came full circle.

---

[211] SSD 4: 184. Cf. PW 2: 328. Emphasis added.   [212] SSD 4: 127. Cf. PW 2: 264–65.

6 | Wagner's material expression

PART 1

Oper und Drama is a crash site. Aesthetic theory and a materialist concern for the senses converge in a single vision for communication whose contortions of logic can deter all but the most sympathetic readers. Wagner himself needed time to recover from drafting it. During five weeks of hydrotherapy at Albisbrunn, he impressed the salutary effects of ice baths upon Theodor Uhlig, adding: "it was freakish how theory and abstraction still tortured me during the first eight days: it was this – like a mental illness, a perpetual crossfire of abstract art-theoretical thoughts – that I wanted to tell you about ... It is gradually disappearing now more and more like gray clouds from the brain ... my senses are gradually being satisfied ever more by the present, and by that which they perceive directly."[1] Wagner's proto-medical vocabulary bears traces – aftershocks? – of the collision between idealism and materialism in his book. We tend not to think of Wagner as a materialist. But his pronouncements that "all art reaches us exclusively through the definiteness of a universally sensory outlook [*universell sinnlichen Anschauung*],"[2] and that music "can actualize [*verwirklichen*] thought," certainly open this door.[3]

An awareness of our biological frame turns out to be central to Wagner's outlook for his melodic material in part 3 of *Oper und Drama*:

> So we call the most perfect unity of artistic form that in which a widest conjuncture of the phenomena of human life – as content – can impart itself to our feeling [*Gefühl*] in so completely intelligible an expression that in all its moments this content shall completely stimulate, and completely satisfy, our feeling [*Gefühl*].[4]

Here, as elsewhere in his writings, Wagner's use of the word *das Gefühl* connotes both feeling and sensation, i.e. both a psychological quality and a somatic stimulus. As such it reflects a broader parallelism between a metaphysics of musical rapture and a view of music where "sound has no existence but in the excitement of a quality of the auditory nerve," which led to the uneasy dance of speculative philosophy and "hard" natural science in Germany during

---

[1] Wagner to Theodor Uhlig, September 30, 1851, Albisbrunn, SB 4: 122.
[2] SSD 4: 11. Cf. PW 2: 129–30.   [3] SSD 4: 184. Cf. PW 2: 329.   [4] SSD 4: 202–03. Cf. PW 2: 349.

the mid-nineteenth century.[5] In the context of Wagner reception, we can think of this accommodation in terms of the aesthetic application of "psychophysics," a mid-century scientific orientation defined by its founder, Gustav Fechner, as "an exact science of the relationships between mind and body."[6] Fechner, an experimental psychologist, argued in 1851 that mind and body are two aspects of the same reality, hence mental and physical *processes* are also "basically the same" but are interpreted from different, if necessarily simultaneous, perspectives: bodily–organic or mental–psychological. "Try as he will, the scientist cannot directly perceive even the tiniest bit of psychical phenomena in another person; yet these processes are perceptible as mental processes, namely as feelings, sensations, ideas, desires, and so forth, as soon as self-perception occurs within them."[7] But just as the perceived reality of a circle differs depending on whether you are inside or outside it, it remains just as impossible to stand on the plane of a circle and view both the convex and concave lines, as it is to perceive the dual aspect of human existence.[8] Against this mid-century double vision, the final stage in our journey through Wagnerian *Melodik* examines the materialist idea that the effects of Wagner's music on listeners could be explained physiologically, and that melodic expression could be objectified in this way, where categories such as feeling and meaning become reified as empirical objects. My approach to this centers on a development, a parallelism, and a metaphor. The development concerns the burgeoning natural sciences, the parallelism is that between physics and metaphysics, and the metaphor that unlocks this for a study of melody relates to water and wave forms. As a way into this territory, let us first reconsider Lohengrin's swan as an interface between willful fantasy and empirical reality.

The "real" swan

> In those days Darwin and Helmholtz were the real fathers of the Church.
> George Bernard Shaw (1898)[9]

---

[5] Johannes Müller, *Elements of Physiology*, trans. William Baly (Philadelphia: Lea and Blanchard, 1843), 588.

[6] "eine exacte Lehre von den Beziehungen zwischen Leib und Seele." Gustav Fechner, *Elemente der Psychophysik*, 2 vols. (Leipzig: Breitkopf & Härtel, 1860), 1: v.

[7] Gustav Fechner, *Zend-Avesta oder über die Dinge des Himmels und des Jenseits. Vom Standpunkt der Naturbetrachtung*, 3 vols. (Leipzig: Leopold Voß, 1851), 2: 320. Cited in Michael Heidelberger, *Nature from Within: Gustav Theodor Fechner and His Psychophysical Worldview*, trans. Cynthia Klohr (University of Pittsburg Press, 2004), 97.

[8] Fechner, *Elemente der Psychophysik*, 1: 2–3.

[9] George Bernard Shaw, *The Perfect Wagnerite* (Kessinger: Whitefish, 2004), 4.

Gaps between the Middle High German epic of *Lohengrin* recorded by the Grimm brothers and Wagner's own libretto highlight a graceful collision between mythic possibilities and historical images. The swan is either imaginary or fake; either it carries Lohengrin fully 400 miles in the blink of an eye and later transcends avian form, or it symbolizes an impossibly voiceless (i.e. soulless)[10] anatomy that metamorphoses between human and animal as per pantomime and fantasy literature. But in the Grimms' summary of the late thirteenth-century tale, the journey from Monsalvat to Brabant is putatively real, i.e. a different class of "miracle." It takes fully five days and nights, and the swan even dives its head into the sea to catch a fish, which it shares with its armored passenger as sustenance for their journey.[11] By speeding up the swan's passage to an instantaneous act of envisioning, Wagner rendered it both medieval and modern: either "a mysterious miracle" or a technological medium that breaks the sound barrier.[12] The perspectival conflict between occult mysticism and empirical reality, Romantic fantasy and comical prop was the reason Adorno felt *Lohengrin* had become "objectively uninterpretable" by the 1940s.[13] But his assumption that the "illusory reproduction" of operatic miracles was truly "possible at that time," that audiences were "still able to conceive the spirit world without any empirical reality, while today it would only be tolerable as a 'fact,'" is wide of the mark. In a milestone biography, *Hegel and his Era* (1857), Rudolf Haym regarded the 1850s as a period "which has learned to renounce poetic illusions and Romantic confusions . . . [one that] sees itself surrounded by unresolved contradictions."[14] His distinctly post-Hegelian perspective in 1848 meant that the "seams with which Idealism contained us are now tearing."[15] These contradictions can be seen in an aesthetics of melody no less than in the socio-political sphere, and in what follows we

---

[10] Friedrich Kittler, in a post-hermeneutic approach to literature, co-opts a group of Romantic authors to designate the voice as "the one signified, or trademark, of the soul." See Kittler, *Gramophone, Film, Typewriter* trans. G. Winthrop-Young and M. Wutz (Stanford University Press, 1990), 70.

[11] See "Lohengrin in Brabant," [*ca.* 1280] trans. Stewart Spencer, in *Lohengrin* (London: John Calder, 1993), 41.

[12] "Welch ein seltsam Wunder!" *Lohengrin*, act 1, scene 2.

[13] "Denn der Gehalt . . . ist das geschichtliche Bild . . . Das an sich interpretierbare Werk ist zugleich . . . das objektiv uninterpretierbare." Adorno, *Zu einer Theorie der musikalischen Reproduktion* (Frankfurt a. M.: Suhrkamp, 2005), 66–7.

[14] "In einer Zeit, die den poetischen Illusionen und den romantischen Unklarheiten entsagen gelernt hat, in einer Zeit, die sich von ungelösten Widersprüchen . . . umringt sieht, giebt es von hier aus nur Einen Schritt." Rudolf Haym, *Hegel und seiner Zeit: Vorlesungen über Entstehung und Entwicklung, Wesen und Wert der Hegelschen Philosophie* (Berlin: Gaertner, 1857), 466.

[15] Haym, "Philosophie," in *Allgemeine Encyklopädie der Wissenschaften und Künste*, ed. J. S. Ersch and J. G. Gruber, 26 vols. (Leipzig: Johann Friedrich Gleditsch, 1846–48), 24: 183–84.

shall examine some of the tearing seams in detail. (George Steiner's vener-
able argument that the seventeenth century marks the "great divide" in the
history of tragedy, after which the rationalism of the Enlightenment spelled
the genre's impossibility, is oddly parallel.)[16]

Adorno's postulate of an age of fantasy neglects the scrutiny of "empirical
reality" implicit in the professionalization and growing institutionalization of
the natural sciences during the middle decades of the nineteenth century. In
1826, the Berlin anatomist Johannes Müller published *On the Comparative
Physiology of Vision in Men and Animals*, in which he conceived his law of
specific sense energies. Following his investigations into the nervous system
across multiple species, he established that nerves do not passively conduct
external stimuli, for the same stimulus is perceived differently – as sound,
taste, light etc. – by different sense organs. So all external affects on the optic
nerve produce the sensation of light, for instance. Müller formulated this
principle most clearly in his landmark *Handbook of Human Physiology*
(1833–40), published as he took up the professorship in anatomy and physiology at Berlin University: "sensation is not the conduction to our consciousness of a quality or circumstance outside our body, but the conduction to our
consciousness of a quality or circumstance of our nerves which has been
caused by an external event."[17] This meant that the mind is not aware of
objects as such, but only the electrical stimulation in the brain conveyed by
sensory nerves. It had radical implications for theories of sentient communication, latent in *Oper und Drama*, for it effectively proved that we perceive the
world according to the structure of our nervous system.[18] Müller's more
illustrious students (including Hermann von Helmholtz and Emil du Bois-
Reymond) cited his rigorous empiricism in dissection and comparative
anatomy as the key to advancing modern understanding: "a skeptical shaking
of everything long since believed in; time-honored problems were assailed
with a boldness of research unheard-of till then."[19] Seven months before
Wagner began his prose sketch for *Lohengrin*, the *Berlin Physical Society* was
founded by Gustav Karsten, Bois-Reymond, and E. W. von Brücke. At one of

---

[16] George Steiner, *The Death of Tragedy* (London: Faber, 1961).

[17] Johannes Müller, *Handbuch der Physiologie des Menschen*, 3rd edn. (Coblenz: Hölscher, 1838), 780.
Cited in Laura Otis, *Müller's Lab* (Oxford University Press, 2007), 9. An English translation by
William Baly, otherwise used in this chapter, was published as *Elements of Physiology* in 1842–43.

[18] Müller, *Elements of Physiology*, 588. See also Olaf Breidbach, "Zur Argumentations- und
Vermittlungsstrategie in Müller's *Handbuch der Physiologie des Menschen*," *Annals of the History
and Philosophy of Biology 10/2005* (Göttingen: University of Göttingen, 2006), 3–30.

[19] Emil du Bois-Reymond, "Gedächtnissrede auf Johannes Müller, gehalten in der Akademie der
Wissenschaften am 8. Juli 1858," in Estelle du Bois-Reymond (ed.), *Reden von Emil du Bois-
Reymond*, 2 vols. (Leipzig: Veit, 1912), 2: 215.

the first weekly meetings, members foreswore talk of vital forces in their practice of physiology, instating instead the pre-eminence of mechanical and chemical laws.[20] It was in effect an elimination from their worldview of transcendence and fantasy. While it is hard to gauge quite how aware an educated, concert-going public would have been of these matters, the advent of public science lectures and accessible, serialized letters on chemistry[21] and physiology[22] would have helped to popularize scientific research before a curious *Bildungsbürgertum*, for whom daily telegrams, inoculations, and train travel only served to galvanize the disseminating process. Adorno's belief in the "death of fantasy" much later in the Wilhelmine period conveniently supports the intriguing notion of an "uninterpretable" opera for a post-fantastical age (a diagnosis synchronized with Max Weber's social process of *Entzauberung*);[23] but the key point is that it is also in danger of ascribing *too much fantasy* to nineteenth-century audiences.

Extrapolating from this, the swan – as an "unresolved contradiction" – is far from anomalous in Wagner's *oeuvre*: he would continue to require credulity, fantasy, and suspended disbelief *in excelsis* from his audiences for the *Ring* and *Parsifal*. And yet, Wagner's definition of a "poetic" (as opposed to a "Judeo-Christian" or "dogmatic")[24] miracle explains that this phenomenon "shuts its own . . . magic within itself, and is in no way taken by the spectator *for a miracle* but is apprehended as the *most intelligible* representation of reality."[25] His "poetic" miracles, in other words, connote a belief in the putatively real within an axiology of poetic / Christian, real / unnatural.[26]

Such tensions are not helped by the fact that the anthropomorphic Gottfried (swan) in act 3 was originally to have sung a melodic line in A major (akin to Lohengrin's Grail Narrative), which would have confirmed his loss of avian form and instated his true dramatic identity (Example 6.1).[27]

---

[20] See Timothy Lenoir, *Instituting Science* (Stanford University Press, 1997), 139ff.

[21] Justus Liebig, *Chemische Briefe* (Heidelberg: C. F. Winter, 1844); Jacob Moleschott, *Der Kreislauf des Lebens: Physiologische Antworten auf Liebigs Chemische Briefe* (Mainz: Zabern, 1852).

[22] Carl Vogt, *Physiologische Briefe für Gebildete aller Stände* (Stuttgart and Tübingen: J. G. Cotta, 1847); Rudolph Wagner, *Physiologische Briefe* [1851–52], rpt. (Göttingen: Klatt, 1997).

[23] Max Weber, *Wissenschaft als Beruf 1917–1919, Politik als Beruf 1919* (Tübingen: Siebeck, 1994), 1–24.

[24] These are based, Wagner explains, on a "*fundamental negation of understanding*" and require blind belief in divine power because it rips apart "the connection of natural phenomena"; SSD 4: 82. Cf. PW 2: 213.

[25] SSD 4: 84. Cf. PW 2: 216.

[26] Berthold Hoeckner argues accordingly that while Lohengrin's arrival in act 1 is supposed to be a "poetic" miracle in this sense, it actually "has come to represent something entirely real: a true miracle," in Hoeckner, *Programming the Absolute* (Princeton University Press, 2002), 137.

[27] This was first recorded by A. Naubert in "Ein bisher ungedrucktes Stückchen Lohengrin," *AmZ* 6 (February 10, 1893), 72–73.

Example 6.1 Gottfried's original utterance, which Wagner cut from act 3 of *Lohengrin*. Translation: *Farewell, untamed tide that has carried me so far, / Farewell, pure and shining waves on which my white feathers have glided. / My dear sister awaits me on the shore; by me she shall be consoled.*

By cutting Gottfried's only "human" utterance, Wagner curiously marginalized the amphibious creature as a real character, rendering him all the more fantastical. From the vantage point of the natural sciences, the mute swan-child's anatomical impossibility – like that of Max's ghostly mother in *Der Freischütz* or Undine's water spirit in *Undine* – forces *Lohengrin* to rely on technologies of phantasmagoria or else alienates the audience's suspended disbelief. Few would argue that this clash of German empirical science and Romanticism needs any further explanation; one can no more resolve a collision than anatomize mythic hybrids. It presents a kind of parallax view of musical aesthetics, where perspective constantly shifts between two points that cannot be synthesized, much like the convex and concave lines of Fechner's circle. To take another simile, fantasy and empirical science become as opposite sides of an operatic Möbius strip: perspectives that exist in parallel but never meet.

To what extent did Wagner think of science in this way? Right at the outset of *Das Kunstwerk der Zukunft*, he suggests he was neither ignorant of nor opposed to the natural sciences, setting out his qualified appreciation of their rigor as something capable of banishing unwelcome illusions: "The path of [empirical] science lies from error to knowledge, from appearance to reality, from religion to nature."[28] The sciences seemed to offer a means of accessing the physical nature of things (so prized by Feuerbach, Wagner's dedicatee), but should not be pursued arrogantly, as an end in themselves. "Life" is infinite vis-à-vis a finite "knowledge of nature," he continues, and the greater goal of modern understanding will be attained through the unmediated, sensory experience of art:

That alone is true and living which is sentient, and hearkens to the terms of physicality [*Sinnlichkeit*] … The highest victory of science is … the

---

[28] SSD 3: 45. Cf. PW 2: 72.

acknowledgement of the teaching of the senses. / The end of science is the justifying of the unconscious, the giving of self-consciousness to life, the reinstatement of the senses in their perceptive rights, ... As science melts away into recognition of the ultimate and self-determinate reality, of actual life itself, so this avowal gains its frankest, most direct expression in art, or rather in the *work of art*.[29]

Art thus evinces the process of synthesizing science and life. For Wagner, the one merges into the other: sentient reality becomes intrinsic, not incidental, to art, and science completes a circuit with *Lohengrin*.

But Wagner never entered a laboratory in his life. He once dismissed Humboldt and Helmholtz as "Schopenhauerian 'donkeys,'" and it remains unclear to what extent he even knew of Müller's anatomical work. No wonder, then, that his knowledge of science has proved a prickly topic: it was publicly debated in a bad-tempered exchange by Guido Adler and Richard Bakta in 1903, the former dismissing Wagner's views on science as "irrelevant," the latter proclaiming them significant, nuanced, and informed.[30] Back in 1851, Wagner himself was forced to address the matter in a heated altercation with a Swiss politician, Jakob Sulzer, about the chemical benefits and detriments of hydrotherapy and alcohol, respectively. Wagner followed up the argument in writing, wherein he suggested chapters that Sulzer might read,[31] and defended himself against the accusation that he makes claims about things of which he has no professional knowledge by arguing that: (a) he had read literature by respected hydrotherapists; and (b) the expectation that he should want first to study chemistry or even medicine is tantamount to saying he would need to study theology before being able to justify his views about God, or read Hegel's *Aesthetics* before being able to make artistic assertions.[32] This defensive retort confirms Wagner was not so much interested in the detail of scientific research as its broader enterprise, and in this (familiar) spirit of dilettantism he certainly socialized with scientists, receiving the Dutch physiologist Jacob Moleschott in Zurich and Rome several times over a twenty-year period, and he kept abreast

---

[29] SSD 4: 45. Cf. PW 1: 72–73.

[30] Guido Adler, "Richard Wagner und die Wissenschaft," *Neue Freie Presse* (May 10, 1903), 12–13, here 13; Richard Bakta, "Richard Wagner und die Wissenschaft," *Bohemia* (May 13, 1903), 17. A helpful summary of this debate and its context is given in Kevin Karnes, *Music Criticsm and the Challenge of History* (Oxford University Press, 2008), 135–43.

[31] Wagner procured several books by J. H. Rausse (a pseudonym for the hydrotherapist Heinrich Friedrich Franke) via Theodor Uhlig from the Royal State Library in Dresden, including: *Beschreibung der Wasserheilanstalt Lehsen bei Wittenburg in Meklenburg* (Parchim: Ludwigslust, 1847); *Über die gewöhnlichsten ärztlichen Mißgriffe beim Gebrauch des Wassers als Heilmittel. Nebst einer Abhandlung über die Aufsaugung und Ablagerung der Gifte und Medikamente im lebenden animalischen Körper und einer Kritik der Kurmethode des Vincenz Prießnitz* (Zeitz: Schieferdecker, 1847). See SB 4: 21–24, 99.

[32] Wagner to Jacob Sulzer, Zurich, December 15, 1851, SB 4: 223–25. See also ML 476.

of technological developments, recommending Theodor Uhlig travel to Zurich on the "barbaric railway" followed by a steamer: "you'll get here fastest."[33] As Gundula Kreuzer reminds us, moreover, Wagner was in close contact with stage technologists, such as Carl Brandt, in procuring the use of modern locomotive boilers for producing steam to create fog, vapour, mist, and smoke effects during the *Ring* premiere in 1876.[34] His staunch opposition to the ethics of experimental medicine, documented in his open letter against vivisection, indicates that he was also aware to some degree about research practices.[35] His position was occasionally inconsistent, however. While he would later label all doctors "vivisectors," he continued to medicate, taking prescribed bromine as a sedative.[36]

The range of meanings in Wagner's use of *das Gefühl*, noted above, is a critical bridge in this context. Eduard Hanslick actually had great sympathy for Wagner's qualified embrace of scientific frontiers. While the Viennese critic urgently distinguished feeling (*Gefühl*) from sensation (*Empfindung*) in the opening sentences of *On the Musically Beautiful* (1854), he went on to advocate a "scientific knowledge of things" for his topic, adding that "this investigation will have to approach the method of the natural sciences, at least to the point of attempting to get alongside the thing itself and seeking whatever among our thousandfold flickering impressions and feelings may be enduring and objective."[37] The concepts of instrumental *Klangfarbe* and vocal *Lautfarbe* can be understood physiologically, as well as aesthetically, in this sense, and the implication is that composing an opera – which "wills to become a fully manifest deed, to seize people by their every fiber of sensation, to invade them," as Wagner maintained[38] – becomes primarily a manipulation of the nervous system, after Müller:

Once it is established that an integral part of the emotional change produced by music is physical, it follows that this phenomenon, as encountered in our neural activity, ought also to be investigated on this, its corporeal side ... If we trace the pathway which a melody must follow in order to act upon our state of feeling, we find that it

---

[33] Wagner to Theodor Uhlig, Enge/Zurich, June 18, 1851, SB 4: 65.

[34] CT (January 25, 1882); see Gundula Kreuzer, "Wagner-*Dampf*: Steam in *Der Ring des Nibelungen* and Operatic Production," *Opera Quarterly* 27 (2011), 179–218.

[35] SSD 10: 194–210. Cf PW 6: 193–210. In writing his open letter, Wagner was reacting to a request from Ernst von Weber, author of *Die Folterkammern der Wissenschaft* (Berlin: Voigt, 1879).

[36] CT (August 6 and 8, 1880).

[37] Hanslick, *On the Musically Beautiful*, trans. G. Payzant (Indiana: Hackett, 1986), 1. Two recent studies of Hanslick's treatise in light of the discourse of materialism, formalism, and idealism during the 1840s are Barbara Titus, "The quest for spiritualized form: (Re)positioning Eduard Hanslick," *Acta Musicologica* 80 (2008), 67–97; and Mark Burford, "Hanslick's Idealist Materialism," *19th-Century Music* 30 (2006), 166–81.

[38] SSD 9: 291. Cf PW 5: 288.

goes from vibrating instrument to auditory nerve … the whole process of tonal sensation is now physiologically comprehensible … Physiology tells us that what we experience as tone is a molecular motion in neural tissue … [T]he basis of every feeling aroused by music must lie first of all in a particular manner of affecting the nerves by an auditory impression. But how an excitation of the auditory nerve, which we cannot even trace to its origins, is perceived as a particular sense quality; how the bodily impression becomes a mental state; finally, how sensation becomes feeling: All that lies on the other side of the mysterious divide which no investigator has crossed.[39]

Melody, defined simultaneously according to the differing epistemologies of aesthetics and physiology, constitutes a particularly rich nexus during the 1850s, and a discourse network that addresses the way these perspectives confront one another is traceable, particularly in the debate Hanslick identifies over how physical sensation "becomes" psychological feeling.

At this point, it is worth taking a general, rather than a specifying, view of the character of the materialism at hand. One assumption that Hanslick makes, along with several writers cited in this chapter, is that, when an individual is affected by art, mental change is always acompanied by physical change. This follows from Fechner's argument we encountered earlier, that mind and body are one entity whose dual aspect is as two sides of a coin, where change visited upon one side (by pliers, for instance) is also visited upon the other side. Fechner called this "the basic law of psycho-physics" where "nothing can exist, develop, or move within the mind, without there being something in the body that exists, develops, or moves, whose effects and consequences reach into the present and future physical world. In short: all that is mental is borne by or exessed in something physical and by this means has physical effects and consequences."[40] The key question for materialists, and particularly – for our purposes – those interested in sound, was whether purely somatic stimuli could *cause* or evoke particular mental states or feelings, whether this is potentially what Fechner meant by psychological activity "borne by" physical effect.[41]

---

[39] Hanslick, *On the Musically Beautiful*, 53–56.

[40] "Das allgemeinste Gesetz ist dieses: daß nichts im Geiste bestehen, entstehen, gehen kann, ohne daß etwas im Körper mit besteht, entsteht, geht, was seine Wirkungen und Folgen in den Umkreis und die Zukunft der Körperwelt hinein erstreckt. Man kann es kurz so ausdrücken, daß alles Geistige seinen Träger oder Ausdruck in etwas Körperlichem und hierdurch seine weiteren Wirkungen und Folgen im körperlichen hat." Fechner, *Ueber die Seelenfrage. Ein Gang durch die sichtbare Welt, um die unsichtbare zu finden* (Leipzig: C. F. Amelang, 1861), 221. Translation modified from Heidelberger, *Nature from Within*, 98.

[41] James Kennaway has investigated the historical claim that musical sounds have physical effects that are noxious, serving as a pathogen, and can induce actual illness in its listeners, where heart attack, arousal-related arhythmia, musico–genetic epilepsy, and musical hallucinations

Extrapolating to Wagner, could the sensory experience of music drama bypass the mental deliberation of audience members completely in the creation of a meaningful artistic experience? Philosophically, the crux of the matter is whether qualities of sensation can be equated with semiotic units of communication that are not arbitrary (unlike Saussure's linguistic sign).[42] Fechner thought not. As Michael Heidelberger points out, Fechner's law is asymmetrical; while mental change brings about physical change in an individual, "the reverse is not necessarily true."[43] Commentators on Wagner's music, freed from the rigorous constraints of empirical science, were less cautious, as we shall see.

Hitherto we have considered how Wagner escaped the imbroglio of nineteenth-century melodic theory by sublimating normative melody to language, which – based on his adopted philological ideas – he believed could encode an intuitive emotional content sensualized into sound, thereby bypassing an audience's need for verbal comprehension. The immanent specificity of this emotional content was to be harnessed etymologically through the "physiognomic resemblance" of speech roots in Stabreim. As we have seen, prominent philologists even argued that the emotion-bearing vowels therein operated at a pre-linguistic level in the "soul," expressing inherent human qualities. As fanciful as this may sound, the principles on which such a vocal-melodic strategy was based were derived from *bona fide* research. The dream espoused by such research, in short, was precisely the establishment of a *science of feeling*.

This is the implied knowledge guiding our final chapter, which interweaves mid-century discourses of philology, medical physiology, and Wagner's melodic theory in *Oper und Drama*. I script a historical dialogue about German culture between contemporary voices in which Wagner is merely a participant. The broader horizon informing this historical topic, though, is a more recent turn towards "materialities of communication" in academic discourse. At its most basic, this is a critique of infinitely reflexive theorizing that, on the one hand, warns of "the risk implied in the boundless abstraction of losing contact with the concrete and sensual dimensions of our experience" in Hans Ulrich Gumbrecht's words[44] and, on the other, predicts the demise of philosophical questions – the mind's never-ending

---

constitute "a number of ways in which music can have a malign impact on the health of listeners and performers." See Kennaway, *Bad Vibrations* (Farnham: Ashgate, 2012), 5.

[42] See Christopher Hill's study of the semantic properties of sensations and "sensation concepts" in *Sensations: A Defense of Type Materialism* (Cambridge University Press, 1991), 159ff.

[43] Heidelberger, *Nature from Within*, 98.

[44] See Hans Ulrich Gumbrecht and K. Ludwig Pfeiffer (eds.), *Materialities of Communication*, trans. William Whobrey (Stanford University Press, 1994).

deferral of concrete answers – by scheduling the explosion of the sun in 4.5 billion years: "death of the sun is a death of mind, because it is the death of death as the life of the mind," Jean-François Lyotard taunts: "there's no sublation or deferral if nothing survives."[45] The mid-nineteenth-century knowledge that sound is material, that the body is, at one level, a receptacle of sound waves, and the suspicion that the sensation of listening is merely the final stage in a transmission determined by physical laws becomes a historical "materiality" of communication, in this sense.

The human "language machine"[46]

"Mine is a different kind of organism," Wagner protested to Eliza Willa, a novelist near Zurich who reported his private words of frustration in 1864; "I have sensitive nerves, I must have beauty, radiance and light ... I can't live the miserable life of an organist like your Master Bach!"[47] The necessity of sentient fulfillment in Wagner's hedonistic complaint points – among other things – to his presupposition of corporeality, a pathos of the body and its sufferance. Wagner's sensitivity to nervous stimulation was personal: in pleasure, he notoriously sought out reams of richly colored silk from his milliners for lining the walls of his Penzing villa and for making clothes, stuffing his slippers and satin garments with cotton to keep warm, while lining his boots with fur. "Wagner loved everything soft," one supplier reported.[48] And in pain, he suffered from a lifelong allergy to wool (which caused blotches on his skin),[49] and from various bowel problems since his late 20s – his constipation meant he was living in real discomfort for a time in 1851: "I am very annoyed: my haemorrhoids are wreaking havoc in my body."[50] Such bodily fragility puts Wagner's assertions about the sensory perception of art in a more immediate context. It was an altogether different kind of "meaning" – but equally physical. If musical philologists sought to probe the objective content of melodicized speech–sounds, it is a small step to consider the extent to which materialist and

---

[45] Jean-François Lyotard, "Can Thought go on without a Body?" in *Posthumanism*, ed. Neil Badmington (Basingstoke: Palgrave, 2000), 129–40, here 130.

[46] "Die sprachmachine," Grimm, *Über den Ursprung der Sprache*, 57.

[47] Cited in Spencer, *Wagner Remembered*, 157.

[48] Ludwig Karpath, *Zu den Briefen Richard Wagners an eine Putzmacherin: Unterredungen mit der Putzmacherin Berta* (Berlin, 1906), 22.

[49] See Wagner to Minna Wagner, October 12 and 17, 1851, Zurich, SB 4: 132–33, 134–35.

[50] Wagner to Theodor Uhlig, Zurich, October 19, 1851, SB 4: 137. See also Chris Walton, *Richard Wagner's Zurich: The Muse of Place* (Woodbridge; Camden House, 2007), 95ff.

musical writers believed meaning could be physiologically fixed in sound, that is, corporeal, or: *beautiful, radiant and light.*

Etymological essentialism enabled Wagner's assumption that speech roots embodied an "objective sensation." But was there an assumed reciprocal relation in language between vocal physiology and historical thought embodied physiognomically in its roots? Since a root syllable can be traced to its rawest, most "expressive" form, and this divulges a physiologically specific sound, the suspicion arose that an ahistoric sound in the present could be connected to an equally expressive designation, i.e. root syllables may not only be expressive because of their historical etymology but also by virtue of their innate physiognomy (as Wagner seemed to imply). Jacob Grimm thought that the *a, i, u* vowels are primal, innately human sounds precisely because they "are conditioned by the organs of our body, either forced out of a full chest and throat or produced with the help of the palate, the tongue, teeth, and lips."[51] So physiologically comprehensible are the conditions under which these sounds are produced, he continued, that they could reasonably be imitated, indeed plausibly produced by synthetic mechanical devices.[52]

Eighteenth-century speaking machines (notably that of Wolfgang von Kempelen from 1780) had already changed the perception of voice from an organic unity to a technical assemblage.[53] This became a reciprocal pattern, for beyond the attraction of curious automata, the possibility of mechanical speech now reformulated language's self-conception for modern philology. Grimm says that:

[t]he natural basis of sound . . . is nothing but an instrument upon which language is played . . . The instrument itself is indeed more attractive to the physiologist; its playing however attracts the philologist . . . The language machine . . . developed from the idea of imitating human language less in the thought than in the sound of words. In a physiological sense it seeks to get beyond the mechanism of the basic sounds.[54]

[51] "Diese urlaute sind uns angeboren, da sie durch organe unseres leibs bedingt entweder aus voller brust und kehle gestoßen und gehaucht, oder mit hilfe des gaumens, der zunge, zähne und lippen hervorgebracht werden." Grimm, *Über den Ursprung der Sprache*, 20.

[52] "Einige ihrer bedingungen sind auch so greif- oder faßbar, daß es nicht völlig mißlingen konnte, sie durch künstliche mechanische vorrichtungen bis auf einen gewissen grad nachzuahmen und scheinbar darzustellen." *Ibid.*

[53] For a detailed history of technological mimicry of the voice before the phonograph, see Hankins and Silverman, "*Vox Mechana*: The History of Speaking Machines," in *Instruments and the Imagination* (Princeton University Press, 1995), 178–220.

[54] "Die natürliche lautgrundlage . . . ist nichts als das instrument, auf dem die sprache gespielt wird . . . Den physiologen wird doch mehr das instrument selbst, den philologen das spiel darauf anziehen . . . Die sprachmaschine . . . ging davon aus die menschensprache weniger im gedanken als im wortschall nachzuahmen und physiologisch hinter den mechanismus der grundlaute zu kommen." Grimm, *Über den Ursprung der Sprache*, 22, 57.

The significance of this viewpoint is that a colorful continuum of vowel gradations, whose primal etymology assured Wagner of their intuitively comprehensible sound, had now seemingly developed a physiological basis.

The intellectual current that led Wagner to believe in the "physiognomic" properties of root syllables was almost certainly driven by comparative anatomy. Its driving force was Müller, mentioned earlier, who knew Grimm personally (he once sought advice from the philologist on naming the mass of micro-organisms welling around in sea water: together they decided on "ocean swelling" [*pelagischer Auftrieb*]; the modern term is plankton).[55] Müller's wide-ranging *Handbook of Human Physiology* became the leading textbook in physiology for much of the nineteenth century,[56] and included a section on vocal production in humans and animals. Its opening sentence announces that:

the sounds of the voice and speech are [the] . . . result of . . . the vibrations of a peculiar apparatus which may be compared to a musical instrument: the tension of the instrument necessary for the product of sound, and the height and succession of tones, are . . . determined by the contraction of muscles, the physiology of the voice and speech.[57]

That is unequivocal materialism. The so-called aesthetics of singing, of speech, of regional accent and its identifying *Klangfarbe* is reified and its quantifiable physiological basis revealed.[58]

In one of his final physiological investigations, *On the Compensation of Physical Forces in the Human Voicebox* (1839), Müller used a severed head, and his wife's piano, to study the way that the human larynx produces particular tones.[59] "One is amazed that the means we admire in the modulation of the singer can be accounted for physically to such an extent," he remarked after calculating the range of ways to manipulate pitch and timbre by applying graded forces to regions of the vocal cords, larynx, epiglottis, laryngeal ventricle, membranous walls, and even thyroid cartilage.[60] "The head of a cadaver is severed in such a way that the whole hangs on a small area of the trachea"

---

[55] See Otis, *Müller's Lab*, 38.

[56] See Brigitte Lohff, "Johannes Müllers Rezeption der Zellenlehre in seinem *Handbuch der Physiologie des Menschen*," *Medizinhistorisches Journal* 13 (1978), 247–58, here 247.

[57] Müller, *Elements of Physiology*, 637.

[58] At a push, we might even interpret Hans Sachs' observation that "The bird that sang today / has a well-formed beak" in this context as a commentary on the physiological conditioning of a good singer. ["Das merkt' ich ganz besonders. / Dem Vogel, der heut' sang, / dem war der Schnabel hold gewachsen."] Hans Sachs in act 2 of *Die Meistersinger*.

[59] Müller, *Über die Compensation der physischen Kräfte am menschlichen Stimmorgan* (Berlin: A. Hirschwald, 1839), 5–37.

[60] "Man erstaunt, dass die Mittel, welche wir in der Modulation der Sänger bewundern, bis so weit sich physikalisch am Stimmorgan nachweisen lassen." *Ibid.*, 32.

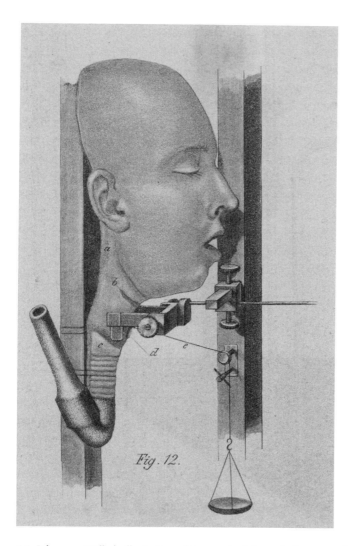

6.1 Johannes Müller's illustration of the manipulation of a human cadaver to produce artificial tones. From Müller, *Über die Compensation der physischen Kräfte am menschlichen Stimmorgan* (Berlin: August Hirschwald, 1839), figure 12.

(Figure 6.1), he continues, and "by moving the lips we can even proceed to forming a few consonants, M and W are very easy, as are the vowels U and A through the requisite modifications of the opening of the mouth."[61]

---

[61] "Bei Bewegung der Lippen kann man selbst zur Bildung einiger Consonanten schreiten, M und W gelingen sehr leicht, auch die Vocale U und A durch die nöthigen Veränderungen der Mundöffnung." *Ibid.*, 34.

Intriguingly, this morbid ventriloquism transcended its artificiality by extending the range of male voices considerably compared to living singers (reaching $d\sharp^3$ in one experiment). Turning to animals, by contrast, Müller asserts a fully physical prosopopeia: "if air is blown into the bronchi of a duck, a sound exactly similar to the natural cry of the bird is produced; the same result is obtained by blowing into the trachea of the duck or goose, even when the bronchi have been cut away."[62] His experiments on the throats of songbirds likewise offered a physical explanation for what causes and generates their characteristic singing at a consistent pitch.[63] Literary fiction was also on the brink of a material voice, and a year before Wagner had dramatized a singing contest in *Tannhäuser*, Hans Christian Andersen had pitted two nightingales against each other, a bejeweled, mechanical automaton and a biologically ensouled creature, where "everyone agreed that [the mechanical bird's] song was just as beautiful as the real nightingale."[64] This tale was allegedly inspired by soprano Jenny Lind – the "Swedish Nightingale" – and Müller's research led Grimm to ask whether similar dissections of the cultivated throats of human singers might furnish signs of their more developed singing ability, adding: "to ask a still stronger question, would the anatomist succeed in exhibiting pertinent external traces in the speech organs of those people who used decidedly harsh gutturals, or who have, like the Slavs, used strong sibilant combinations."[65]

Müller's work implied this possibility, and Grimm's skepticism on the matter was not shared by physiologist Otto Ule, whose 1852 article "The Voice as Inner Expression" argued contrariwise that the *Klangfarbe* of a human voice was exclusively physiologically determined:

The sound of a voice, as with musical instruments, is determined especially by the toughness of the larynx cartilage. This is flexible and soft in children and women; it is hard and often almost ossified in men and many women whose voices sound manly. Mouth, pharynx and nasal passage, ultimately the resonance cavities of the human voice, palate, teeth, tongue and lips form – by their multifarious position and

---

[62] Müller, *Elements of Physiology*, 2: 1040.   [63] *Ibid.*, 2: 703.

[64] Hans Christian Andersen, "The Nightingale" [1844], *The Complete Fairy Tales and Stories*, trans. and ed. Erik Christian Haugaard (New York: Anchor Books, 1983), 208.

[65] "oder um noch stärkeres zu fragen, ob es dem anatom gelänge, in den sprachorganen solcher völker, die entschieden harter guttural pflegen oder wie die Slaven schwere zischlautverbindungen eingeübt haben, äußere spuren davon aufzuweisen." Grimm, *Über den Ursprung der Sprache*, 21.

movement – the tones of those particular sounds from which human language is put together.[66]

Ule is explicit, and the title of his article essentially rewords Wagner's assertion that "true melody is . . . itself the utterance of an inner organism."[67] Thus, material sound or the esteemed physiognomic properties of monosyllabic roots in Wagner's *Melodik* were understood by some as belonging to the world of objects, the human corpus. This was an uncomfortable conclusion for idealists such as Wagner, and even today, post-Lacanian commentators continue to rebuff the demystifying aspirations of vocal physiology: "an unbridgeable gap separates forever a human body from 'its' voice," Slavoj Žižek retorts. "The voice displays a spectral autonomy, it never quite belongs to the body we see . . . it is as if the speaker's voice hollows him out and in a sense speaks 'by itself' through him."[68] Such comments remind us that the drive to examine and speculate on the material aperture of vocalic production expressed nothing but the deepest desire of mid-century scientists like Ule, namely to establish a pure physics of vocal–emotional content.

The ambiguous category of "feeling" had long been at the center of a debate over music expression. While for Wagner, "feeling grasps nothing but the actual [*das Wirkliche*], what is physically enacted, perceivable by the senses,"[69] the deterministic imperative is perhaps most evident in Herbert Spencer's argument that "all feelings – pleasurable or painful, sensations or emotions – . . . are muscular stimuli."[70] Based on Müller's dictum that muscles can only respond to stimuli by contracting, Spencer argues the principle governing all production of and response to music is nothing but a kind of motor reflex action. (Darwin initially endorsed this view a year before publishing *On the Origin of Species*, though came to doubt it a decade later.[71]) Since, for Spencer, "all music is originally vocal," he applies this biological reductionism to the singing voice

---

[66] "Der Klang der Stimme aber wird, ähnlich wie bei musikalischen Instrumenten, besonders durch die Härte der Kehlkopfknorpel bestimmt. Bei Kindern und Frauen sind diese Knorpel biegsam und weich, bei Männer und vielen Frauen, deren Stimme männlich klingt, hart und oft fast verknöchert. Mund-, Rachen-, und Nasenhöhle endlich die Resonanz-höhlen der menschlichen Stimme, Gaumen, Zähne, Zunge und Lippen bilden die Töne durch ihre mannifaltige Stellung und Bewegung zu jenen bestimmten Lauten, aus denen die menschliche Sprache sich zusammensetzt." Otto Ule, "Die Stimme als Ausdruck des Innern," *Die Natur* 30 (July 24, 1852), 233–36, here 235.

[67] SSD 3: 314. Cf. PW 2: 108.   [68] Slavoj Žižek, *On Belief* (London: Routledge, 2001), 58.

[69] SSD 4: 69. Cf PW 2: 198.   [70] Spencer, "The Origin and Function of Music," 403.

[71] Drawin's tentative support reads: "Your article on Music has also interested me much, for I had often thought on the subject & had come to nearly the same conclusion with you, though unable to support the notion in any detail. Furthermore . . . I most entirely agree with you that all expression has some biological meaning." Charles Darwin to Herbert Spencer, November 25, 1858, Kent, see *Darwin Correspondence Project:* www.darwinproject.ac.uk/darwinletters/

in particular, thereby establishing a basis on which Wagner's theory of "*speech itself as the indispensable basis of a perfect artistic expression*"[72] finds a materialist rationale and endorsement. As with Müller's cadaver and Andersen's nightingale, Spencer describes the voice as a mechanism for expression voided of mystery:

All vocal sounds are produced by the agency of certain muscles. These muscles, in common with those of the body at large, are excited to contraction by pleasurable and painful feelings. And therefore it is that feelings demonstrate themselves in sounds as well as in movements ... The muscles that move the chest, larynx, and vocal cords, contracting like other muscles in proportion to the intensity of the feelings; every different contraction of these muscles involving, as it does, a different adjustment of the vocal organs; every different adjustment of the vocal organs causing a change in the sound emitted; – it follows that variations of voice are the physiological results of variations of feeling. It follows that each inflection or modulation is the natural outcome of some passing emotion or sensation; and it follows that the explanation of all kinds of vocal expression must be sought in this general relation between mental and muscular excitements.[73]

In this reading, vocal composition required less a music-theoretical, more an anatomical–biological knowledge. Indicating his distaste for such trends, Wagner had rejected the inference in 1849 that "life itself could be made dependent upon scientific speculation,"[74] and in any case, most writers were far more skeptical than Spencer about a directly causal connection between sensation and feeling. Hanslick said we "know nothing" about it,[75] while Müller observed that entirely different groups of facial nerve fibers are excited according to the kind of feeling aroused, but confessed: "Of the cause of this we are quite ignorant."[76] The unavoidable deduction in Spencer's account of music, however, was a redefinition of expression, one recognized by Friedrich von Hausegger – a Wagnerite – in his tome on the subject for the *Bayreuther Blätter*: "Bodily motion or utterance of speech sounds, in which an emotional state [*Gemüthszustand*] becomes recognizable to others, is called *expression*."[77]

---

calendar/entry-2373.html. But he later qualifies: "The cause of widely different sounds being uttered under different emotions and sensations is a very obscure subject. ... [Spencer's] explanation appears to me too general and vague to throw much light on the various differences [of potential vocal expression], with the exception of that of loudness, between ordinary emotional speech, or singing." See Darwin, *The Expression of the Emotions in Man and Animals* [1872], ed. Joe Cain and Sharon Messenger (London: Penguin, 2009), 86–87.

[72] SSD 4: 210. Cf. PW 2: 357.   [73] Spencer, "The Origin and Function of Music," 403–04.

[74] SSD 3: 46. Cf. PW 1: 74.   [75] Hanslick, *On the Musically Beautiful*, 56.

[76] Müller, *Elements of Physiology*, 2: 934

[77] "Eine Köperbewegung oder Lautäusserung, in welcher ein Gemüthszustand Anderer erkennbar wird, heisst *Ausdruck*," in Friedrich von Hausegger, "Die Musik als Ausdruck," *Bayreuther Blätter* 2 (1884), 37.

6.2 The emblem for Otto Ule's journal *Die Natur* (1852).

Nietzsche agreed, judging four years later that "one never communicates thoughts, one communicates movements, mimics signs, which we then trace back to thoughts."[78] In other words, immaterial feeling, like immaterial sound, no longer existed for music by 1884. Communication was physical. To what extent, though, can this verdict be seen earlier in the century in the wake of *Oper und Drama*?

Ule's article from 1852, whose premise would be applied to vocal music by Spencer, appeared in the newly founded journal for natural sciences, *Nature: Journal for the Dissemination of Knowledge about the Natural Sciences and an Outlook on Nature for Readers of all Levels*.[79] The identifying emblem for each issue aptly captures the extraordinary impact of the new way of thinking (Figure 6.2). It showed a volcano eruption throwing up clouds of ash and stardust, amid leaves, fruit, and branches, all of which – in addition to depicting a "mysterious" natural phenomenon – neatly allegorized the stunning power of the epistemological shift that had occurred in this field, even if it did not exactly interlock with the metaphor Ule used for this shift in his standpoint article: "to illuminate the darkness of our present, that is the first task of the natural sciences."[80]

---

[78] Friedrich Nietzsche, *The Will to Power*, trans. Walter Kaufmann and R. J. Hollingdale (New York: Vintage Books, 1968), 428.

[79] "Die Natur: Zeitung zur Verbreitung naturwissenschaftlicher Kenntniß und Naturanschauung für Leser aller Stände." See Figure 6.2.

[80] "Das Dunkel der Gegenwart zu erleuchten, das ist die erste Aufgabe der Naturwissenschaft" in Otto Ule, "Die Aufgabe der Naturwissenschaft," *Die Natur* 1 (January 3, 1852), 2.

In this shift, our bodies had not exactly been reduced to an arbitrary bio-logical machine.[81] Whereas speech sounds were innate, language was not. Back in 1837, August Kahlert was clear in his definition of poetry (*Dichtkunst* with a *d*) that disembodied thought preceded utterance, where speech was a sensual embodiment of thought, and thought itself was boundless, requiring words as mere tools.[82] Ule likewise dislocated and isolated the word, though from feeling rather than thought: "[it] has nothing to do with feelings, and if it is a child of feeling, then it was born after the death of its father."[83] Wagner's *Versmelodie*, however, was predicated precisely on a healing of these dislocated elements. His concept of sound that is intuitively comprehensible by our feeling as the basis for poetry (*Dichtkunst* with a *t*) posited words as sensuous units that were bidden by feeling (*das Gefühlsnothwendige*). This aspiration elevated sense and sensation to the exclusion of intellect and ideation, where the poet's task is to "impart his subject unconditionally to the feeling [*Gefühl*] and nothing else,"[84] which required the melodicization of anaphoric, alliterative speech, as we saw in Chapter 5. The question as to whether this was manifest physically touches on a much broader psychophysical discourse of the age: the "one ancient riddle" as Hanslick put it. "How the body is connected to the soul."[85]

Musical monism *qua* science of feeling

If the eyes reveal one's inner soul, melody, correspondingly, is "the most perfect expression of the inner being of music."[86] Wagner's loose equation was old fashioned for 1851 – melody as the tangible point of access to music's "soul." Yet for all his wielding of scalpels, Müller too argued that the organizing unity of each animal he dissected was dependent on their

---

[81] La Mettrie's Enlightenment conception of man as "a self-winding . . . immense clock" was not mentioned in the discourse, but by the mid-nineteenth century technological innovation in steam and understanding of thermodynamics gave credence to the metaphor. Helmholtz, for instance, declared in 1854 that "the animal body . . . does not differ from the steam engine as regards the manner in which it obtains heat and force, but . . . in the manner in which the force gained is to be made use of." See Helmholtz, *Science and Culture*, 37; see also Julien Offray de La Mettrie, *L'homme machine* [1748], trans. Richard Watson and Maya Rybalka as *Man a Machine* (Indianapolis and Cambridge: Hackett, 1994), 32, 70.

[82] "Die Kunst insofern sie zur Lösung ihrer Aufgabe das Schöne hervorzubringen, sich der Sprache als ihrem Mittel, und insofern die Sprache wieder die sinnliche Erscheinung unseres Denkens ist, sich unserer Begriffe und Gefühle als ihrem Stoffe bedient, heißt die Dichtkunst . . . Das Reich der Dichtkunst ist . . . das unermeßliche des Gedankens, nur ihr *Werkzeug* ist das Wort." August Kahlert, "Das musikalische Element in der Sprache," *NZfM* 46 (June 9, 1837), 183.

[83] "Das Wort hat mit dem Gefühle nichts zu schaffen, und wenn es ein Kind des Gefühls ist, so ward es nach dem Tode seines Vaters geboren." Ule, "Die Stimme als Ausdruck des Innern," 233.

[84] SSD 4: 119. Cf. PW 2: 256.   [85] Hanslick, *On the Musically Beautiful*, 56.

[86] SSD 3: 309. Cf. PW 2: 104.

soul.[87] This disembodied object presented a challenge to mid-century physiologists. Did the profound feelings traditionally ascribed to it have an anatomical basis or not? Ule describes the "mechanism" of muscular movement that determines speech sounds with materialist relish,[88] yet proceeds to modify, rather than sever, a connection between "soul" and "sense." His premise is that voice is the externalized utterance of inwardness, but even for the physical scientist, this inwardness ("feeling") remains mysterious and explicable only by conceit.[89] For metaphysicians, the question was too important to permit such evasiveness, however. The Leipzig polymath Rudolf Hermann Lotze was well placed to tackle the problem, having gained a medical degree alongside his philosophy dissertation on Descartes and Leibniz. The fruits of his dual studies were published a year after *Oper und Drama*, as *Medical Psychology: Physiology of the Soul* (1852), an extensive treatise that sought to unravel the mystery of how to heal philosophy's Cartesian divide. Accordingly, he explained how material stimuli leading to "feelings" can possibly be linked to a disembodied soul:

Admittedly an immaterial substance, lacking any dimensions, cannot fill a stretch of space; nothing prevents it from occupying a particular *place* within [this space], however, from which adjacent particles of matter are set in motion directly by its force, and right up to which every excitation from external nature must travel [*fortpflanzen*] in order to have any effect on it at all.[90]

This dislocation gave rise to another. Lotze dismisses the idea that the failure to explain reciprocal actions of soul and body is an "inconvenient exception,"[91] arguing – after Müller's law – that our intuitions of sense are not to be identified with the real qualities as they are physically propagated: "The sensations of color tells nothing of the ether's oscillations, the tone nothing of the air's vibrations; both sensations betray nothing about the form of neural stimulation

---

[87] Müller, *Elements of Physiology*, 32.

[88] "Der Laut ist das Erzeugnis einer Muskelbewegung, die einem Mechanismus in Bewegung setzt, durch den früh und spät unwillkürlich, was uns bewegt, Lust und Unlust, wie sie an der Seele vorüberzieht, zur lauten Aeußerung wird." Ule, "Die Stimme als Ausdruck des Innern," 234.

[89] "Die Stimme ist der Laut des Innern, ist ein Ausdruck des Gefühls." *Ibid.*, 233.

[90] "Eine immaterielle Substanz, aller Ausdehnung entbehrend, kann freilich nicht eine gewisse Strecke des Raums erfüllen, aber Nichts hindert, dass sie einen bestimmten Ort in ihm habe, von welchem aus ihre Kraft unmittelbar die benachbarten Theilchen der Materie in Bewegung setzt, und bis zu welchem hin, um überhaupt zu Einwirkung auf sie zu gelangen, alle aus der äussern Natur stammenden Erregungen sich fortpflanzen müssen." Lotze, *Medicinische Psychologie: Physiologie der Seele* (Leipzig: Weidmann, 1852), 115–16. The question of whether forces can act over a distance across cells (implicitly modeled on Michael Faraday's principle of a magnetic field) was vigorously debated among anatomists during the 1840s–50s. See Otis, *Networking*, 53ff.

[91] Rudolf Hermann Lotze, *Outlines of Psychology* [1881], trans. George T. Ladd (Boston: Ginn & Company, 1886), 98.

by which they arise."[92] As he later put it: "they are consequences, not copies of their stimuli. Thus they are internal phenomena in the soul."[93] By uncoupling the essence from the effects of sensation, Lotze was able to declare that sense stimuli are "no doubt only motions" and create the property of a given sensation in the soul without actually conveying any material substance to it:

All the intuitions of sense, which at first appear to set before us with exactness what is in itself real, are merely secondary phenomena in which the results of the reciprocal actions of elements, in themselves wholly supersensible, reach our perception. / Accordingly it is not the conception of *immaterial*, but that of *material* being, which is to be scrupled at; and the gap does not exist, which appears to us at first to separate body and soul as two perfectly heterogeneous elements, and to render their reciprocal action impossible.[94]

This delicately balanced view from 1881 was not limited to the university elite (Wagner, for his part, used telling turns of phrase such as "all the nerves of my soul").[95] The concept of soul as a disembodied object was also consistent across Lotze's writings: "like sensations, feelings are not *mappings* of the processes, whose *consequences* they are," he concluded as early as 1852.[96]

This willful embrace of paradox can be identified with what Andreas Daum has termed "strategies for enchantment" in the discourse of nineteenth-century science, for it presents a counternarrative to the view of man's desacralization as a linear process against the rise of atheistic materialist thought and the rapid growth and popularization of science education alongside industrial progress.[97] Yet it also promoted a split worldview. The contemporary historian Friedrich Lange dubbed this Germany's "materialist controversy," adding that:

[t]he old creative impulse will not rest … Germany is the only country in the world where the apothecary cannot make up a prescription without being conscious of the relation of his activity to the constitution of the universe … Outside the daily habit of

---

[92] "Die Farbenempfindung erzählt nichts von Oscillationen des Aethers, der Ton nichts von Luftschwingungen, beide Empfindungen verrathen nichts über die Form der Nervenerregungen, durch sie die entstehen." Lotze, *Medicinische Psychologie*, 235–36.

[93] Lotze, *Metaphysic in Three Books*, trans. B. Bosanquet (Oxford: Clarendon Press, 1884), 255.

[94] Lotze, *Outlines of Psychology*, 103–04.

[95] Wagner to Theodor Uhlig, July 27, 1850, Zurich, SB 3: 364.

[96] "Wie die Empfindungen, so sind auch die Gefühle keine *Abbildungen* der Processe, deren *Folgen* sie sind." Lotze, *Medicinische Psychologie*, 236.

[97] Andreas Daum, "Science, Politics, and Religion: Humboldtian Thinking and the Transformation of Civil Society in Germany, 1830–1870," *Osiris* 17 (2002), 116. This strategy is ongoing in many respects; see also George Levine's recent attempt to dispel the notion that "disenchantment" is the only possible outcome of Darwinian thought, in *Darwin Loves You: Natural Selection and the Re-enchantment of the World* (Princeton University Press, 2006), 7ff.

labor and experiment, there lies still an infinite realm, to wander through which refreshes the mind and ennobles the soul.[98]

Within musical discourse, this cognizance of scientific law in tandem with traditional metaphysics tended to promote speculation more than empirical investigation. The only New German writer with documented expertise in the natural sciences was Richard Pohl – a powerfully articulate essayist – who anonymously authored eight "Acoustic Letters" in the *Neue Zeitschrift* during 1852–53, the first of which declared its aim to "explain the necessity of an ordered connection between natural phenomenon and mental activity [*Geistigthätigkeit*] in the context of music, as the most sensory and unmediated of all the arts, even if it will not be possible accurately to pursue this connection itself."[99] The most pregnant connection for Wagnerian aesthetics concerned the voice and emotion (or: speech and melody), which – as we saw in Chapter 4 – was treated most analytically from within Wagner's circle by Louis Köhler. His expressly "dark and distant aim" pivots between the psychological and physiological in seeking to "find the natural basis of a way of feeling that lies very deep in people's minds, but is only *recognized*, not *explained*."[100] *In nuce*, his discussion aims to pinpoint the effects of feeling on vocal sound production. But predictably inadequate scientific knowledge led him, like Pohl, to defer the potential of establishing a science of feeling, that is, the ability to quantify the production of emotion: "psychologists and physicists should, along with mathematicians and philologists, go hand in hand with the composer and poet, then progress of a considerable kind could be made."[101] Despite his admiration for Wagner, Köhler must have known the composer was inadequate to all of these professions; his call to arms therefore reaches out unequivocally through his treatise (and, by implication, its model: *Oper und Drama*) to qualified voices within the broader scientific discourse.

But such cautious indecision from Pohl and Köhler was mirrored even by trained scientists such as Ule, who was also attempting to quantify vocal

---

[98] Lange, *History of Materialism and Criticism of its Present Importance*, 263–64.

[99] "Dennoch ist der letzte Zweck dieser Briefe gerade der, die *Nothwendigkeit* eines gesetzlichen Zusammenhangs zwischen Naturerscheinung und Geistesthätigkeit in Bezug auf die Musik – als der sinnlichsten und unmittelbarsten unter den Künsten – darzulegen, wenn gleich es nicht möglich sein wird, diesen *Zusammenhang* selbst genau verfolgen zu können." Richard Pohl, "Akustische Briefe: Erster Brief," *NZfM* 1 (July 2, 1852), 3.

[100] "Sollte hierin nicht ein Schritt weiter erkannt werden dürfen zu dem so fernen, dunkeln Ziele, Geheimes offenbar werden zu sehen, den Natur*grund* einer Fühlsweise zu finden, die so tief im Menschengemüthe liegt, und doch *anerkannt*, nicht *erklärt* war?" in Köhler, *Die Melodie der Sprache in ihrer Anwendung besonders auf das Lied und die Oper* (Leipzig: J. J. Weber, 1853), 83.

[101] "Die Psychologen und Physiker sollten, wie auch die Mathematiker und Philologen, Hand in Hand mit dem Dichter in Ton und Wort gehen, dann könnte ein Fortschritt erheblicher Art werden." *Ibid.*

expression as a function of feeling. Without elucidating a physics of cause and effect, stimulus and sensation, Ule posits just such a mechanism in the soul, which – problematically – was the very seat of untouchable being. In speculating, however, his incomplete, partial materialism indicates the relative powerlessness of this approach in 1852 when confronting the paradox of soul and its "connection" with inanimate, dissected muscle tissue:

Deep in the soul a second, murkier order often draws behind a veil of transparent thoughts, which is conveyed to us only by a dark feeling. These are moods of the spirit ... everyone feels them in himself without being able to explain them ... Feeling connects thoughts into a unity, it is the surging sea on which thought – like a sailing ship – emerges and submerges. But the waves of feeling strike the shore and alter its forms. Mime and gesture spontaneously accompany those stirrings of inner life, and the voice is the reverberation of the breaking waves.

Mime and speech sound are based not on agreement, but on natural compulsion. They are movements, contractions of individual parts of our multi-structured muscle apparatus ... finally we try intentionally to produce the signals and speech sounds that we have learned as forms of certain feelings in order to share them with others. Thus speech sound becomes word, becomes language. But the word is again inferior to thought, and muscle movements rarely reach such a degree of freedom and ease that the spoken thought enters from the darkness of feeling into the clear light of cognition. Then, of course, speech begins to display that entire wealth of forms of mental [*geistiger*] motion, and the poet's imagination, the researcher's depth, the energy will affect thousands of people through the word and will do so for centuries to come. In that case, language is an expression of the entire inner human being because it no longer sensualizes thoughts alone, but its content.[102]

---

[102] "Tief in der Seele zieht hinter einem Schleier durchsichtiger Gedanken oft eine zweite trübere Reihe, von der uns nur ein dunkles Gefühl Kunde gibt. Das sind jene Stimmungen des Geistes ... Jeder fühlt sie in sich, ohne sie erklären zu können ... Das Gefühl verkettet die Gedanken zur Einheit, ist das wogende Meer, auf dem wie segelnde Schiffe die Gedanken auf und niedertauchen. Aber die Wogen der Gefühle schlagen an das Ufer und verändern seine Formen. Mienen und Gesten begleiten unwillkürlich jene Regungen des innersten Lebens, und die Stimme ist der Nachhall der brandenden Wogen ... Nicht auf Übereinkunft also, sondern auf einem natürlichen Zwange, beruhen Mienen und Laute. Sie sind Bewegungen, Zusammenziehungen einzelner Theile unsres vielgegliederten Muskelapparates ... wir versuchen es endlich, absichtlich jene Zeichen und Laute hervorzubringen, die wir als Formen gewisser Gefühle kennen gelernt haben, um sie Andern mitzutheilen; und so wird der Laut zum Worte, zur Sprache. Aber das Wort bleibt hinter dem Gedanken zurück, und selten erreichen die Muskelbewegungen jenen Grad von Freiheit und Leichtigkeit, daß der gesprochene Gedanke aus dem Dunkel des Gefühls in das klare Licht der Erkenntniß tritt. Dann freilich entfaltet sich in der Sprache jene ganze Formenfülle geistiger Bewegung, und die Phantasie des Dichters, die Tiefe des Forschers, die Energie des Willens wirken durch das Wort auf Tausende von Menschen und auf Jahrhunderte fort. Dann wird die Sprache ein Ausdruck des ganzen

By reinforcing an inscrutable link between sonic expression and pre-linguistic feeling, Ule decisively reduces language to an intermediary medium between "soul" and body, even as he lays bare the physical mechanisms of vocal expression, and defines the content of communication as sensation.

Possibilities for exploding the Cartesian divide were pursued still further in an unpublished treatise entitled "Microcosm: Outline of a Physiological Anthropology" written by Roland Daniels in 1851, a monist medical doctor from Cologne, whose lively conclusion was entitled "Ridiculousness of the Dualistic System."[103] Like Lotze, he refuted the burden placed on physical scientists to establish causal, physical connections between tissue, nerve, cartilage, and an immaterial "soul," where the physical voice was its vehicle of expression. Instead, he lambasted the project, as Wagner formulated it, when the composer characterized the power to communicate as an intuitive faculty of sense perception, wherein humanity's sentient capacity (*Gefühlsvermögen*) is the "bearing organ" (literally: uterus) of understanding.[104] If the soul is dependent on the body for its expression, Daniels maintained with tongue in cheek, it requires literal "bodily organs" and therefore, the greater or lesser perfection of these organs will result in corresponding degrees of perfection in expression, presumably in both reception as well as production. The organs essentially become "instruments" in this reading (cf. Novalis and Grimm), and he who works with better instruments works more perfectly. The more "normal" the process of nourishing one's brain, Daniels continues, the more freely the soul is allowed to reveal itself through this principal organ: "The difference between mental functions of different people would be based, according to this explanation, on the greater or lesser perfection of their instrument, their body," he concludes.[105]

Of course, Diderot had long since led the eighteenth-century debate over monism in France;[106] Daniels' statement in 1851 is nevertheless ironic, however, because his larger authorial strategy is to defeat this (longer

---

innern Menschen, weil sie nicht mehr die Form des Gedankens allein, sondern seinen Inhalt versinnlicht." Ule, "Die Stimme als Ausdruck des Innern," 234.

[103] "Lächerlichkeit der dualistischen System," in Roland Daniels, *Mikrokosmos: Entwurf einer Physiologischen Anthropologie* [1851], ed. Helmut Elsner (Frankfurt a. M.: Peter Lang, 1988), 127–39.

[104] SSD 4: 111. Cf. PW 2: 247.

[105] "Der Unterschied in den geistigen Funktionen verschiedener Menschen beruhte nach dieser Erklärung auf der größeren oder geringeren Vollkommenheit ihrer Instrumente, ihrer Körper." Daniels, *Mikrokosmos*, 129–30.

[106] See Mark W. Wartofsky, "Diderot and the Development of Materialist Monism" [1953], in *Models: Representation and the Scientific Understanding* (Dordrecht and Boston: D. Reidel, 1979), 297–337.

surviving German) idealist dualism *in extenso* without articulating a coherent substitute; hence, it is a protest rather than a delayed discourse on monism. "How bored good souls must become in the body of a child," he quips, "or even a soul that has only the honky-tonk instrument of an idiot to play on!"[107] While teasing that "bad singers" must still basically have been "good people," he isolates the concept of muscle power (*Muskelkraft*) to illustrate the flaws in this dualistic perspective, which in turn also denies the division of conceptual phenomena from their individual manifestation:

We see that a muscle contracts under different stimuli. We call this characteristic of the muscle its power [*Kraft*], we speak of muscle power. Now – in order to talk in the sense of those who personify the soul – I would have to say: this muscle power is a single essence, which itself uses the muscle for its expressions [*Äußerungen*]. Now we know that it all depends on how large or small the muscle is, which depends on how well or badly it has been nourished etc., which determines how strong or weak the contractions are, translated into dualistic style: the same muscle power expresses itself better through the one muscle than through the other, better through a well-nourished than through a scrawny muscle, better or worse depending on the quality of the material etc. According to this, the power of an old man would basically be equal to that of a youth – a well-intentioned theory that does not, however, pass muster in practice. It's like saying that the appearance of light is actually just as intense when burning a tallow candle as a wax candle, only that the light can express itself better with the latter material; or the warmth of a hot oven and that of my hand are equally great, but my hand is a worse instrument than the oven.[108]

Such ridicule was the final nail in the coffin of an idealist dualism (though Nietzsche felt the need to strike yet another hammer blow on behalf of

---

[107] "Wie sehr muß sich die gute Seele langweilen in dem Körper eines Kindes oder gar eine Seele, welche nur das verstimmte Instrument eines Blödsinnigen zu spielen hat!" Daniels, *Mikrokosmos*, 130.

[108] "Wie sehen, daß ein Muskel sich auf verschiedene Reize zusammenzieht. Wir nennen diese Eigenschaft des Muskels seine Kraft, wir sprechen von Muskelkraft. Jetzt würde ich, um im Sinne derjenigen zu reden, welche die Seele personifizieren, sagen müssen: diese Muskelkraft ist ein eigenes Wesen, welches sich zu seinen Äußerungen des Muskels bedient. Nun wissen wir, daß, je nachdem der Muskel größer oder kleiner ist, je nachdem er besser oder schlechter ernährt wird usw., je nachdem sind auch seine Kontraktionen starker oder schwächer. Ins Dualistische übersetzt: die gleiche Muskelkraft äußert sich besser durch den einen mageren, besser oder schlechter, je nach der verschiedenen Qualität der Materie usw. Die Kraft eines Greises wäre demnach im Grunde dieselbe wie die Kraft eines Jünglings, – eine Theorie des guten Willens, welche aber in der Praxis nicht stichhält. Es heiße dasselbe sagen, als wenn ich behauptete, die Lichterscheinung beim Verbrennungsprozesse eines Talglichtes u. eines Wachslichtes sei eigentlich gleich groß, nur könne das Licht sich an der letzteren Materie besser äußern als an der ersteren; oder die Wärme eines heißen Ofens u. die meiner Hand seien gleich groß, aber meine Hand sei für sie ein schlechteres Instrument als der Ofen." *Ibid.*

Wagner in 1872).[109] For despite Wagner's dualistic outlook in his gendered allegory for drama and music, word and voice, intellect and sensation, *ratio* and *anima*, his purpose is, of course, to effect an historical reconciliation of these in the neo-Grecian concept of music drama. Without engaging the detail of brain fibers and neural networks, in other words, Wagner's implicit understanding of melodic expressivity appears to be that at moments of peak intensity dualities collapse; he defined art itself, after all, in these terms precisely as the collapsing of life and science.[110] And if there were any doubt, he publicly ridiculed the Cartesian alternative.[111]

But his position vis-à-vis monism was arguably reaching. He aims for a mutual "understanding" (*Verständnis*) between composer and listener at the level of sensory feeling – in Lotze's terms, physically mediated psychological agreement:

Only when the whole capacity of man's feeling [*Gefühlsvermögen*] is completely excited to interest in an object conveyed to it through a recipient sense does that object win the force to expand its concentrated essence again, in such a way as to bring it to our understanding as infinitely enriched and flavored nourishment.[112]

Even Franz Brendel was suspicious of this. He responded with tentative support: "while even an intuitive understanding [*Gefühlsverständnis*] of *Lohengrin* is not given immediately to everyone, the difficulties nevertheless grow and multiply as soon as it concerns *conscious* insight."[113] The trouble was a lack of theoretical explanation. How exactly Wagner's brand of monism relates to anatomical processes remains undetermined in *Oper und Drama*, which goes some way to explaining his repetitious predicate of sensuous feeling as both a medium and currency of communication.

---

[109] He writes: "the popular and entirely false opposition of soul and body does nothing, of course, to explain the difficult relationship between music and drama, and does everything to confuse it," adding with disdain that "the unphilosophical crudeness of that opposition seems to have become a readily accepted article of faith among our aestheticians." Friedrich Nietzsche, *The Birth of Tragedy*, 104.

[110] SSD 3: 44–46. Cf. PW 1: 72–73.

[111] "[T]he dissociation of the artist from his person is as foolish as the divorce of the soul from the body." SSD 4: 231. Cf PW 1: 270.

[112] SSD 4: 110. Cf. PW 2: 246.

[113] "Ist doch schon das *Gefühlsverständnis* des *Lohengrin* nicht sofort Jedem gegeben; die Schwierigkeiten aber wachsen und vermehren sich, sobald es sich um *bewußte* Einsicht handelt." Franz Brendel, "Einige Worte über *Lohengrin* zum besseren Verständnis desselben," *NZfM* 8 (February 18, 1859), 90.

Physical *Mitleid*

> The sensation [*Empfindung*] manifested in this melody . . . is a
> phenomenon which now belongs as much to us, to whom it has been
> imparted, as to him who has imparted it.
>
> Richard Wagner[114]

While Wagner took a keen interest in the development of the natural
sciences, he resisted their perspective. Works of genius would soon be
explained away, he cautioned in 1878, "once chemistry has finally laid
hold of logic . . . [E]very mystery of being [would be exposed] as mere
imaginary secrets," while the faddish "*act of knowing*" would exclude all
"intuitive knowledge."[115] Wagner evidently resented the idea that knowledge emanating from the academic corridor might reify or undermine his
personal convictions. During the first year of the *Bayreuther Blätter* he
chastised the unnamed representatives of "science" who "haughtily look
down upon us artists, poets, and musicians, as the belated progeny of an
obsolete worldview."[116] The target here was Nietzsche, whose book *Human,
All too Human* – Wagner sensed – sought to undermine his self-conception
of artistic genius. "It is believed," Nietzsche writes in the anonymous
passive:

that the more profoundly man thinks, the more exquisitely he feels . . . the more he
appears as a genius . . . the nearer he gets to the true nature of the world and to
comprehension thereof: this, indeed, he really does through science, but he thinks he
does it far more adequately through his religions and arts.[117]

Wagner's reaction was almost compassionate: "a long dreaded and not
entirely unpredictable catastrophe [has] now overtaken [Nietzsche]," he
wrote to Karl Overbeck, adding "I have retained sufficient friendship for
him *not* to read his book."[118]

But compassion is an ambiguous concept here, for Nietzsche's claim
that worldly comprehension is achieved through science trickles into

---

[114] SSD 4: 183. Cf. PW 2: 327–28.   [115] SSD 10: 84. Cf PW 6: 75.

[116] SSD 10: 79. Cf. PW 6: 70.

[117] Friedrich Nietzsche, *Human, All too Human*, trans. A. Harvey (Chicago: C. H. Kerr &
Co., 1915), 58.

[118] Wagner to Franz Overbeck, May 24, 1878, Bayreuth, in SLRW, 884. In the event, Wagner
did read *Menschliches, Allzumenschliches*; his essay "Publikum und Popularität," written later in
1878, offers a rebarbative reply to the growing prominence of nineteenth-century
Darwinism and the natural sciences, and protests particularly against the annulment of the
genius concept. SSD 10: 84. Cf. PW 6: 75.

Wagner's own "obsolete worldview" ironically. Wagner wrote to Mathilde Wesendonck of his compassion as a projection of fatally sympathetic nerves: "the question here is not what the other person suffers but what *I* suffer when I know him to be suffering . . . how *I* imagine it is how it is for *me* . . . So my fellow-suffering makes the other person's suffering a reality."[119] In his dramatization of antivivisectionism in *Parsifal*, "compassion" forms the recurring motto: the hunted swan is real (unlike *Lohengrin's* Gottfried) and dies by the iron and wood of Parsifal's arrow, becoming a faint introduction – via his mother's pain – to the searing wound Amfortas must suffer, and for which Parsifal, ultimately, will feel physical compassion. Hausegger duly raised the question of compassion as a function of expression – i.e. how we comprehend the expression of others – two years after the premiere of *Parsifal*. "The expression 'compassion' [*Mitleid*]," he explains:

is also applicable in a purely physiological sense. The similarity of someone in sympathy goes so far that we even feel affected in the same organs and in a similar way as the sufferer . . . Not only pain, however, but also other physical conditions are felt sympathetically and arouse similar phenomena in others. Thus the conditions of sneezing, yawning, laughing, crying and especially conditions of deep excitement.[120]

This sympathetic reactivity on the level of biological organs offers a new shading of knowledge through compassion (*durch Mitleid wissend*), and the gulf between Parsifal's spiritual revelation and Hausegger's yawning encapsulates the parallax view of musical expression at this time; this, after all, is Hausegger's explanation for the "purely physiological" mechanism through which we understand musical experience. It is unintentional and unconscious, he maintains, and works as a kind of instinctual receptivity or "congenital *attentiveness*."[121]

At the center of this corporeal *Weltanschauung*, the belief that vocal emissions born of emotion manifest in a net of muscular tensions will elicit sympathetic reactions from auditors – essentially in the way Amfortas' wound affects Parsifal – is a striking claim, but one that has a clear, deductive basis.

---

[119] Wagner to Mathilde Wesendonck, October 1, 1858, Venice, in SLRW, 423.

[120] "Der Ausdruck 'Mitleid' ist auch in rein physiologischem Sinne zutreffend. Die Aehnlichkeit des Mitempfindens geht so weit, dass wir uns sogar in den gleichen Organen und in ähnlicher Weise, wie der Leidende, affizirt fühlen . . . Aber nicht nur Schmerzen, sondern auch andere körperliche Zustände werden mit-empfunden und erregen ähnliche Erscheinungen in Andern. So die Zustände des Niesens, Gähnens, Lachens, Weinens und namentlich auch Zustände tiefer Erregung." Friedrich von Hausegger, "Die Musik als Ausdruck," *Bayreuther Blätter* 1 (1884), 39.

[121] "eine angeborene *Aufmerksamkeit*." *Ibid.*

"Irritation or excitement of the auditory nerve is capable of giving rise to movements in the body, and to sensations in other organs of sense," Müller had explained in his *Handbook*. "[A] sudden noise excites in persons of excitable nervous system an unpleasant sensation, like that produced by an electric shock, throughout the body ... Various kinds of sounds ... cause in many people a disagreeable feeling in the teeth, or, indeed, a sensation of cold trickling through the body. Intense sounds are said to make the saliva collect in the mouth in some people."[122] This, it would seem, is the rational platform on which opera would become a contact sport, and on which commentators such as Heinrich Klein could complain of:

the wild Wagnerian corybantic orgy ... with orchestral accompaniment slapping you in the face ... Hence, the secret fascination that makes it the darling of feeble-minded royalty ... who need this galvanic stimulation by massive instrumental treatment to throw their pleasure-weary frog's legs into violent convulsion.[123]

Satire notwithstanding, the topos of galvanism in Wagner reception could be surprisingly anatomically accurate. "Bliss of the spinal cord" is one description of experiencing the last act of *Tristan*, reported by Henri Laujol in 1883.[124] Such stimulation was by definition non-conscious, and – allusions to orgasm aside – Müller's *Handbook* explained that these reflex motions of the animal system (whether natural, such as the contraction of the iris from irritation of the optic nerve; or artificial, such as Klein's galvanism) were indeed exclusively controlled at a non-conscious level by the "cerebro-spinal nerves."[125]

There is no evidence Wagner *consciously* pursued the connection of feeling and sensation at the level of physiology. Indeed, he writes privately in 1852 of being "astonished by the tremendously violent effect" a performance of his *Tannhäuser* overture had had on some women whose "effective symptoms" caused intense paroxysms: "so moved were they that they had to find relief by sobbing and crying."[126] But Wagner's description arguably reconfigured a currency of ideas, for such reactions are classified by Müller as reflected motions of the organic system, i.e. involuntary spasms or convulsive motions of the muscles supplied by the respiratory and facial nerves, but in response to mental excitement – i.e. psychological

---

[122] Müller, *Elements of Physiology*, 2: 1311.

[123] Julius Leopold Klein, *Geschichte des Dramas*, 8 vols. (Leipzig: 1871), 8: 738–39. Cited in Nicolas Slonimsky, *Lexicon of Musical Invective* (New York: Coleman-Ross, 1853), 237.

[124] Henri Laujol, "Villiers de l'Isle-Adam," *Jeune France* (April 1883); adapted from Jean Pierrot, *The Decadent Imagination: 1880–1900*, trans. Derek Coltman (University of Chicago Press, 1981), 50.

[125] Müller, *Elements of Physiology*, 2: 927.

[126] Wagner to Theodor Uhlig, March 20, 1852, Zurich, SB 4: 319.

sympathy – not purely physical stimulation.[127] Suffice to conclude that even by the 1850s, the effects of Wagner's sensuous sound – whether *Versmelodie*, *Stabreim*, or *Klangfarbe* – were believed by some to be decidedly real: more physics than metaphysics.

Popular supporters of Wagner's haptic music tacitly took this for granted. Without actually understanding the nature of any putative link between psychology and physiology that bears the burden of Wagner's theory, it remained possible for them to use this link to repulse complaints about Wagner's "lack" of melody. "The emotions of the mind have also their equivalents in sound," declared Jonathan Jones, a self-styled "Musical Student and Neophyte of the Order of St. Wagner." His defensive article on *Lohengrin* appeared in the *Musical World* shortly after the London premiere at Covent Garden (May 8, 1875), and telescopes Wagner's theoretical assumptions into a few sentences, which by the mid-1870s seemed surprisingly unproblematic:

The emotions of the mind have also their equivalents in sound. Every feeling of the heart has its natural utterance, and every passion of the soul its voice. A feeling or passion, when partially and moderately excited, imparts to speech an appropriate color and force of sound ... The musical poet is he who can realize the grades of passion, and has the Prospero-like power over the realms of sound to express them ... Herein is Wagner's excellence.[128]

In a physiologically deterministic context, Hausegger took precisely this reading of Wagner's talent and used it to reframe the composer's achievement. If muscular tensions and cerebral impulses were constitutive of the feeling and experience of musical expression, the capacity to understand these as artistic means, and to convey an emotional state to others through them, becomes the "creative power of the artist."[129] Ultimately, however, this merely recapitulates the old mystery of artistic genius, fo   assumed psychophysical laws governing physiological expression, feeling, as it were, remained safely out of reach for compos

---

[127] Müller, *Elements of Physiology*, 2: 933.

[128] Jonathan Jones, "Lohengrin," *TMW* 53 (July 3, 1875), 438.

[129] "In der Fähigkeit, sich der Mittel der Kunst in der Art zu bedienen, dass und durch sie Gemüthszustande auf andere übertragen werden, beste Künstlers." Hausegger, "Die Musik als Ausdruck," *Bayreuther Blätte*

[130] "The artist creates unconsciously, and all the surprising coincidenc governing motions of the apparatuses of expression are not the r product of direct urge toward *expression* that has grown in him. unbewusst, und alle die überraschenden Übereinstimmungen s Ausdrucks-Apparaten herrschenden Bewegungen sind nicht E Produkt eines unmittelbaren in ihm wach gewordenen Dran

It appears that there was never a serious debate over Wagner's potential mastery of sound or fraudulence in these material terms: experimentation could not dissolve the utopia. Doctors such as Daniels were evidently uninterested in, or unaware of, an artistic rationale for the medical approach to "soul," describing the dualism between sense and thought as "pure artifice."[131] Hence, the veracity one ascribes to Jones' description of Wagner's "excellence" remains largely rhetorical: an enthusiastic, majority endorsement in lieu of empirical alternatives.

PART 2

A comparative physiognomy: vowels and colors

> One can only speak of reaching a conclusion [about *Lohengrin*] . . . if one has really taken in the new phenomena, experienced them . . . without that one speaks like a blind man about color.[132]
>
> Franz Brendel (1859)

> Tone [*Ton*] lies in everything audible . . . There is a parallelism with color in its genetic development . . . commonly noted, but which physicists do not yet appear to have recognized comprehensively.[133]
>
> August Kahlert (1837)

> I myself believe that sound is identical in its nature with light. Sound is light, perceived under another form; each acts through vibrations to which man is sensitive and which he transforms, in the nervous centers, into ideas.[134]
>
> Honoré de Balzac (1838)

Beyond the expressive human voice, what about Wagner's ambitions for an instrumental speech faculty? Having established the discourse on

---

[131] "Der Dualismus von Sinnen u. Gedanken ist ein rein künstlicher, in der Wirklichkeit sind sie immer vereinigt." Daniels, *Mikrokosmos*, 133.

[132] "Nur dann erst [kann] von einem Abschluß die Rede sein . . . wenn man die neuen Erscheinungen wirklich in sich aufgenommen, durchlebt . . . Ohne das spricht man wie der Blinde von der Farbe." Brendel, "Einige Worte über *Lohengrin* zum besseren Verständniß desselben," 90.

[133] "Der Ton liegt in allem hörbaren . . . Es liegt in seiner genetischen Entwicklung ein Parallelismus mit der der Farbe, – eine oft und . . . angeregte Bemerkung, die aber die Physiker noch nicht in ihrem ganzen Umfange gewürdigt zu haben scheinen." Kahlert, "Das musikalische Element in der Sprache," 180.

Honoré de Balzac, *Gambara* (Kessinger Publishing, 2004), 19.

material expression, and its implications for Wagner's *Melodik* as part of a broader monistic turn, we may wonder to what extent the knowledge that expression is, in part, physiological – movements of matter – can be applied to Wagner's actual composition. Did the linguistic specificity of vowels within speech roots extend to Wagner's orchestral motifs and *Klangfarben*? His celebrated claim that "the orchestra indisputably possesses a *faculty of speech* . . . [which is] something quite real and palpable"[135] would appear to suggest so, but how far did the ambition of this sonic communication go? If his orchestra was to provide commentary on the dramatic action, as most Wagner commentators remind us, what level of literalism can be ascribed to this process? In philological terms, surely the ideal of instrumental *Sprachvermögen* is entirely metaphorical. An orchestral melody – without any basis in etymological essentialism, without a physical larynx – cannot really *speak*, can it?

Amid garrulous debates in the German press over Wagner's melodies, the composer was consistently lauded for his use of instrumental *Klangfarbe*. His treatment of the orchestra in *Lohengrin* is praised in this respect by Hanslick,[136] held up for emulation by J. C. Lobe,[137] evidenced as compositional process by Henry Finck,[138] and enviously analyzed by Joachim Raff.[139] Indeed, it is perhaps Wagner's only compositional parameter to escape ridicule during a decade shot through with partisan criticism. Berlioz even claimed that *Klangfarbe* expiated Wagner's difficulties over melody:

---

[135] SSD 4: 173. Cf. PW 2: 316.

[136] "[In der] Behandlung des Orchesters . . . leistet Wagner nicht blos Ausgezeichnetes, sondern auch theilweise Neues . . . Wagner . . . ist somit der Erste, der den Zauber neuer und kühner Orchester-Effecte in vollster Ausdehnung für *dramatische* Zwecke benützt hat. Wagners Instrumentirung ist in ihrer geistreichen Verwendung der Klangfarben, und dem elastischen Anschmiegen an den Text, interessant für den Musiker, hinreißend für den Laien." Hanslick, HSS I/4: 345.

[137] "Kein Sachverständiger wird Wagner die Kenntniß der Instrumentationsgesetz̸ seine Opern enthalten viele interessant und wirkungsvoll kolorirte Stellen," Lob̶ Wagner an einen jungen Komponisten, *FBfM* 1 (1853), 456.

[138] "A great part of his [Wagner] genius lay in producing with colors effects photograph can possibly reproduce. Wagner *thought out* his operas in or̸ ideas are often conceived in colors and instrumental combinations wh̛ more reproduce than it could have suggested them to the composer." *and his Works* [1893], 2 vols. (New York: Haskell House, 1968), 2: 2

[139] "Es ist bei der Wiederkehr [of the Swan's A major music] schön ge̶ der Vocale zeugt in demselben von einer Kenntniß und Berechnu· aus der Lage und der Mischung der Stimmen zu ziehen ist, die zu̶ sowie er den Pinsel zur Hand nimmt, ist er der größte Meister. ᐧ einen Coloristen zur Seite zu stellen. Berlioz gleicht ihm auf sei̶n Instrumentale, hinsichtlich des Gesanges aber nicht von Weit̶ *Kritisch Beleuchtet* (Brunswick: Friedrich Vieweg und Sohn,

"true, there is no *phrase*, properly speaking, but . . . [the *Lohengrin* prelude] is a marvel of orchestration, in the gentle shadings no less than in the brilliant colors."[140] And Liszt argued as early as 1851 that Wagner uses instrumental color structurally as a form-building device.[141] By visualizing the sound a decade later, Charles Baudelaire aims to make explicit through sensory perception of the *Lohengrin* Prelude what was arguably implicit in Liszt's analysis: "I experienced the sensation of heightened brightness, of an intensity of light increasing so quickly that no shades of meaning furnished by the dictionary could suffice to express this constant increase of burning whiteness."[142] Whether or not Baudelaire had read Pohl's "Acoustic letters," he was confident enough to invert the onus of proof in his review of *Tannhäuser*: "what would be really surprising," he countered, "is that a sound *could not suggest* a color, that colors *could not* give the idea of a melody, and that sound and color would be unsuitable for translating ideas."[143]

The gulf between conscious knowledge and inexplicable sensation in these accounts is telling. In Pohl's discourse on music and natural science, *Klangfarbe* sits at the intersection of a dualism between mind and matter – one of those "large interference points in nature" that delivers "the unity, the inseparability of spirit [*Geist*] and matter."[144] It offers a way of framing, in other words, the very site at which acoustic vibrations and human perception converge. His fourth letter from 1852 is seemingly torn between the two ideas – inspired by Wagner's sensations of speech physiognomy, yet informed by acoustic science, i.e. vibrations transmitted across the ether:

I hear in the tone of voice whether hate or love speaks to me, whether joy or pain moves the heart. Both can smudge the color – the voice can become toneless, indeed it can be snuffed out [*verlöschen*], suffocated in the highest moment of bliss or of pain. These last instances are nothing but changes of vibration and tension of

---

[140] Hector Berlioz, *The Art of Music and Other Essays*, trans. Elizabeth Csicsery-Róney (Bloomington: Indiana University Press, 1994), 205.

[141] See Franz Liszt, "*Lohengrin*, Grand opéra romantique de R. Wagner, et sa première représentation à Weimar aux Fêtes de Herder et Goethe 1850," SS 4: 86.

[142] Charles Baudelaire, *Selected Writings on Art and Literature*, trans. P. E. Charvet (London: Penguin, 1972), 331.

[143] Baudelaire, *Les Fleurs du mal et oeuvres choisies*, trans. Wallace Fowlie (New York: Dover, 1992), 227.

[144] "Hier ist einer jener großen Interferenzpunkte in der Natur, die uns die Einheit, die Untrennbarkeit von Geist und Materie predigen." Pohl, "Vierter Brief: Schallentstehung. Geräusch und Ton. Grenzen der Hörbarkeit. Höhe, Intensität, Klangfarbe," *NZfM* 9 (August 27, 1852), 88.

molecules – but who wants to deny that here there are still purely mental elements that move, that govern?[145]

This weakening dichotomy is reflected slightly differently in contemporary Wagner criticism. Raff – author of one of the most articulate critiques of Wagnerian aesthetics from the 1850s – argues that, in his theories of future works of art, the composer wants it both ways: with the deepest concern for the color of vocal (*Lautfarbe*) and instrumental (*Klangfarbe*) expression, he tries to countermand subjectivity, even specifying the "objects" of instrumental music in drama in order to inform (by way of hermeneutic clues) judgment of his material.[146] The motivation of premonitions, of memories, the preparation of atmosphere, the interpretation of gesture all become orchestral "objects" in Raff's science of expression.

A sampling of writers indicates that this was less far fetched for a musical mind during the middle third of the century than one might think. In the post-*philosophe* sphere of French literature, Balzac's fictional composer, Gambara, put the case in all its Leibnizian brevity in 1837: "Music is at once a science and an art. Its roots in physics and mathematics make it a science; it becomes an art by inspiration which unconsciously employs the theorems of science."[147] Similarly, Pohl characterized a disconnect between physics and aesthetics as that which appeared to bifurcate the substance of music, and which he felt could only be bridged through physiology: "The physicist concerned with sensory impression fails to ask where he is going . . . the composer with facts of harmony fails to ask where he is coming from."[148] Raff likewise disavows the contented equilibrium that Balzac's composer appears to espouse. Ironically, his aesthetic traditionalism prompts him to view Wagner as a progressive composer in this respect, dismissing as a red herring Gambara's "mathematical and physical laws" that would seem to underpin the basis of harmonic motion:

---

[145] "Ich höre am Klang der Stimme, ob Haß oder Liebe zu mir spricht, ob Freude oder Schmerz die Brust bewegt. Beide können die Farbe sogar ganz verwischen – die Stimme kann tonlos werden, ja sie kann im höchsten Moment der Luft oder des Schmerzes ersticken, verlöschen. Das sind in letzter Instanz wohl Nichts als Schwingungs- und Spannungsänderungen der Molecule – aber wer will läugnen, daß hier noch rein geistige Elemente die bewegenden, die herrschenden sind?" *Ibid.*, 88.

[146] Raff, *Die Wagnerfrage*, 165.   [147] Balzac, *Gambara*, 19.

[148] "Dies veranlaßt den Physiker, sich mit dem sinnlichen Eindruck zu begnügen, ohne zu fragen, wohin er führt, und den Musiker, die Harmonie als Thatsache zu ergreifen, ohne zu fragen, woher sie kommt." Pohl, "Akustische Briefe: erster Brief," *NZfM* 2 (1852), 13.

I am not of the opinion that the means of musical expression should be jammed into the region of mathematically grounded harmonic sound phenomena, and must disavow the pretensions of such theorists, even when they set out with such grandiose formal justification as [Moritz] Hauptmann, because with the increase of objects that become attributed to music and of the elastic material that music subjectively necessitates, more and more is to be freed from nature into the spirit.[149]

Raff's views are notable for binding idealist and materialist traditions together. The implied connection between what he terms "objects that become attributed to music" and "elastic material that music subjectively necessitates" is that of growing compositional means (chords, intervals, timbre etc. as well as newly developed instruments) and the composer's ability to express his subjectivity. Raff's twenty-first letter reveals that *Klangfarbe* and the notion of an orchestral speech capacity are directly implicated in this coupling. One must find the right point of view from which to observe the material nature (*Materiatur*)[150] of the orchestra, he explains, citing the two "essential differences" therein as formal–dynamic (pitch, duration) and density–derivative (sound color).[151] The latter is his chief concern, for he sees it as germane to Wagner's linguistic aesthetic.

Identifying the density of sound color as material expression in this way transgresses two important Wagnerian boundaries: voice and instrument, form and material. Raff posits a dialectical relation in Wagner's orchestra between formal content and real material nature (*reale Materiatur*), which is embodied approximately in the strings and brass, respectively. He argues that the body of orchestral strings is closest to the formal (non-vocal) content of an artwork, while the brass is more defined and particular in its (quasi-vocal) articulation. These conditions are due to the strings' chameleon capacity for poetic "assonance" through articulation that mimics speech but remains linguistically indistinct, so that "in a way [the strings] form the transition to real [vocalized] material" while the brass' less mimetic "assonance" compares

---

[149] "Ich bin nicht der Meinung, daß das musikalische Ausdrucksvermögen sich in den Bereich der mathematisch ergründeten harmonischen Klangphänomene einzuzwängen habe, und muß die diesseitigen Prätensionen der Theoretiker, selbst wenn sie mit so großer formaler Berechtigung auftreten, wie *Hauptmann*, desavouiren, weil mit Zunahme der der Musik zuwachsenden Objecte und der subjectiven Bedürfnisse das elastische Material der Musik mehr und mehr aus der Natur in den Geist zu befreien ist." Raff, *Die Wagnerfrage*, fn. 58.

[150] Raff adopts Hegel's term *Materiatur*, first employed by Hegel in his "Differenz des Fichteschen und Schellingschen Systems der Philosophie" (1801), and formerly by Carl Leonhard Reinhold. The term connotes the material nature or inner material composition of an entity.

[151] Raff, *Die Wagnerfrage*, 166.

to vocalization more directly because it draws real breath and its "colors are more differentiated." Such claims were bold. Speaking of the violin's versatile voice, Raff speculates that:

> its assonance can be graded from loveliest, almost inaudible [consonants] up to grating consonants, which the bow easily produces. The same is the case in vocalizing ... Finally, the violin easily assimilates the colors of other instruments. A passage painted [*angestrichen*] sonorously in a high register on the G string, for example, will come very close to a horn color. Play notes on the D string using the fingerboard somewhat loosely, and you achieve the color of the flute in a low register.[152]

Such mimesis is part of Raff's broader telos for the symphonic orchestra's body, where orchestral speech capacity is discussed in terms of becoming subject to both lyric and epic modes of "recitation," whose objects are too concrete for poetry and too abstract for visual arts, and which idealize the material of reasoned speech spatially, and that of painting temporally.[153] The former fits into meter and periodic construction, the latter is "made liquid with regard to time," which leaves, for Raff, only the division of shadow and light, which already concerns the number of instruments and their dynamic capacity, while physiological "*complexion* actually brings into consideration color in particular."[154]

Accordingly (and parallel to the vowel–soul ratios of Chapter 5), Raff does not shy away from specifying "shadow and light" in material sound, and lists the different colors of Wagner's instruments, underscoring the importance of their comprehensibility for his works: "Evidently, the configuration of instruments for each musical phrase must be such as to enable its complete sensory representation,"[155] he states unequivocally.

---

[152] "Ihre Assonanz kann vom lieblichsten, fast unhörbaren, bis zum rauhesten Consonanten abgestuft werden, da der Bogen dies leicht hergiebt. Dasselbe ist mit der Vocalisirung der Fall ... Endlich assimilirt sich die Violine auch in der Farbe sehr leicht anderen Instrumenten. Eine Passage z. B. auf der G-Saite in höherer Lage sonor angestrichen, wird sich sehr der Hornfarbe nähern. Streicht man Töne auf der D-Saite am Griffbrett etwas locker an, so erzielt man die Farbe der tiefen Flötenlage." *Ibid.*, 167.

[153] *Ibid.*, 168.

[154] "Bei Vertheilung von Schatten und Licht kommen das dynamische Vermögen und die Zahl der Instrumente schon in Betracht, bei dem *Colorit* selbst jedoch die Farbe speciell." *Ibid.*, 169.

[155] "Die Zusammenstellung von Instrumenten muß evident für jeden musikalischen Satz so sein, daß seine vollendete sinnliche Darstellung dadurch ermöglicht wird." *Ibid.*, 170.

flute = light and colorless air to blue air
oboe = light yellow to grass green
clarinet = pink to violet / blue
bassoon = gray to black
horn = forest green to brown
trumpet = intense red (scarlet) to purple / violet
trombone = from purple / red to brown / violet[156]

Though Raff admits these are only "approximate analogies," he is adamant that "exact knowledge of this palette demands serious study otherwise the purposeful individual application and mixture of colors is impossible."[157] The closest Wagner himself came to such stipulation was the orthography for his overture in B-flat major in 1830 (WWV 10; since lost). In his first (1843) and third (1865–80) autobiographies, the composer is at pains to illustrate the dilettantism of his early attempts at composition, recalling how he wanted to distinguish three "mystical elements" in the orchestra by their color so as to be immediately visually distinguishable: "I wanted to reserve black ink for the brass instruments alone; the strings were to be scored in red, and the woodwind green."[158] While this is not "writing" *Klangfarbe* as such, the composer-as-painter was never a more literal concept.

Regardless of the extent to which such a public revelation was purposive self-fashioning on Wagner's part, it functioned in this way, for Liszt drew on Wagner's words in all seriousness to confirm the deliberate coloristic division of Wagner's orchestra into strings, wind, and brass. An explicit, multi-colored precursor to *Lohengrin* was "no surprise," he declared.[159] Wagner himself harked back to these junior days in act 1 of *Die Meistersinger* when David cites color as a distinguishing feature of melody in the rules of mastersinging to Walther, referring, among other things, to "the 'writing-paper' and 'black ink' melodies . . . the 'red,' 'blue,' and 'green' tones,"[160] indicating his sustained engagement with the literalized concept.

Common-sense objections were readily forthcoming. In an extended review of Raff's book in the *Neue Berliner Musik-Zeitung*, Carl Kossmaly

---

[156] "Man findet selbige gemäß die Flöte von heller und farbloser bis zu blauer Luft, die Hoboe von hellem Gelb bis zu Saftgrün, die Clarinette von rosa bis zu violettblau, das Fagott von grau bis zu schwarz, das Horn von waldgrün bis zu braun, die Trompete von hochroth (scharlach) bis zu purpurviolett, die Posaune von purpurroth bis zu braunviolett farbhaltig." *Ibid.*, 169.

[157] "die genaue Kenntniß jener Palette auch ein ernstes Studium erfordert, da sonst die zweckmäßige Einzelverwendung und Mischung der Farben unmöglich ist." *Ibid.*

[158] ML 51.   [159] Liszt, SS 4: 89.

[160] "die 'Schreibpapier'-, 'Schwarz-Tinten-Weis'; / der 'rote,' 'blau,' und 'grüne' Ton." From *Die Meistersinger*, act 1, scene 2.

pointed out the obvious scruple that *Klangfarbe* cannot be inherent in an instrument that different people hear and "see" differently:

Given this distinction it is quite plausible that the tone of one and the same instrument, the clarinet for example, seems to one person to be *pink* or *violet-blue*, while to someone else, particularly in the instrument's lower register, it seems perhaps decidedly *dark brown* or even *deep red*.[161]

Accordingly, when applied to programmatic interpretation of instrumental portions of Wagner's works, Vienna's *Allgemeine Musik-Zeitung* was quick to lambast the kind of physiological precision Raff intimates as "glorified nonsense" in *Tannhäuser*, complaining that "the essence of this music, as even a naïve reader admits, lies in *not* being music; it is only fed to the imagination as a means of generating [visual] figures, in the process of which one never enjoys the freedom to imagine what one wants."[162] Importantly, neither critic denied that sound colors existed, only that these were not universal and so could not be pinpointed objectively.

Thus, the flipside of Raff's call to bring sensations of instrumental color to a listener's perception is the fixing of that listener's response by reconciliation of the dialectic between form and material;[163] it produces a kind of guaranteed physiological judgment in the listener (as suggested by the monistic discourse cited earlier), which effectively turns E. T. A. Hoffmann's concept of *Werktreue* from the responsibility of performance into a fact of reception. Here, the listener becomes at least implicated, and potentially even encoded in a sensory economy where "galvanic" listening – feelings convulsed as frogs' legs – is only the most extreme characterization. André Gill's 1869 caricature (Figure 6.3) of Wagner drawing blood from a collective, oversize ear by hammering a physical quarter note directly into the ear drum captures something of the literalism of this material mode of communication (as well as mocking Wagner's capacity for massed sonorities); and it was Nietzsche who famously recognized that Wagner had thereby reconciled the physical and intellectual components of sensual experience which had been separated in Western culture under the influence of Hellenistic philosophy.

---

[161] "bei dieser Verschiedenheit [ist] gar wohl denkbar ... dass der Ton ein und desselben Instruments – z.B. der *Clarinette* – den Einen als '*rosa*' oder '*violett-blau*' anmuthet, während er dem Andern, namentlich in den tiefern Regionen des Instrument's vielleicht entschieden *dunkelbraun* oder gar *tiefroth*." Carl Kossmaly, "Die Wagnerfrage von Joachim Raff," *Neue Berliner Musik-Zeitung* 21 (May 21, 1856), 161.

[162] Cited in Lobe, "Letters to a Young Composer about Wagner," trans. David Trippett in Thomas Grey (ed.), *Richard Wagner and his World* (Princeton University Press, 2009), 274.

[163] Raff, *Die Wagnerfrage*, 170.

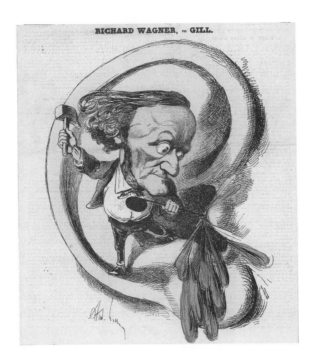

RICHARD WAGNER, ᴘᴀʀ GILL.

6.3 André Gill's caricature of Wagner in the newspaper *L'Eclipse* (April 18, 1869), frontispiece.

Recent commentaries in the realm of media theory have put this reconciliation with more acerbity, extrapolating from Nietzsche's trope of later nineteenth-century Wagner criticism: "*Wagner est une nervose!*" or simply *Nervenmusik*.[164] In 1990, Norbert Bolz proceeds from the assumption that the physiological *a priori* of thought response is not hermeneutic but media-technological, writing provocatively: "Wagner's is the first music to get on your nerves. All we need do is to hook up the [audience's] bared nerve ends with electronic wires to enter into the world of the new media."[165] (Adorno had made essentially the same point about Schoenberg's immediate, electroencephalographic expression in *Erwartung*,

---

[164] Nietzsche's comments on Wagner's art as neurosis are explicitly physiological. See *A Nietzsche Reader*, trans. R. J. Hollingdale (London: Penguin, 1977), 142. For an examination of the phenomenon of *Nervenmusik* in which (over)stimulation is viewed as the basic cause of sickness, see James Kennaway, "From Sensibility to Pathology: The Origins of the Idea of Nervous Music around 1800," *Journal of the History of Medicine and Allied Sciences* 65 (2010), 396–426.

[165] "Wagners Musik ist die erste, die auf die Nerven geht. Man muß nur noch die bloßgelegten Nervenfasern durch Elektrokabel technisch implementieren, um in die Welt der neuen Medien einzutreten." Norbert Bolz, *Theorie der neuen Medien* (Munich: Raben, 1990), 44.

though in less provocative terms.)[166] It is not as far fetched as we might first assume: Hanslick saw nerves (poetically) as agents of "the imperceptible telegraph service between body and soul,"[167] while even by the early 1850s, Helmholtz drew analogies between "neural telegraphy" and the process of perception, viewing the nervous system's sensory organs as media apparatus: "the eye was a photometer, the ear a tuning-folk interrupter with attached resonators," as Timothy Lenoir puts it.[168] But Wagner's "Prospero-like power" to summon control over, and transmit the grades of passion in vocal expression implied neither the fantasy of electrodes nor Bolz's Valhalla voltage, which must ultimately remain an underdeveloped facet of post-structuralist reception history. The contemporary theory of expression rests – as Raff put it – on shadings of light and shadow, though its subsequent appropriation as applied physics by writers such as Bolz testifies to its position at an intersection between materialist inquiry and philosophy of mind.

Physiological colors

> We have called [colors] physiological because they belong to the sound eye.
>
> Johann Wolfgang von Goethe[169]

> Goethe is a physicist become poet.
>
> Richard Wagner[170]

So what, if anything, was the theoretical foundation for Raff's colorful claims? In 1810, the polarity of light and shadow, to which he referred,

---

[166] Adorno claims that rather than mimicking the passion he sought to express, Schoenberg finds the route of direct access to agitate the auditory nerve as per electroencephalography: "the truly subversive moment for him lies in the change in the function of musical expression. No longer are passions feigned, but in the medium of music there are registered undissembled the incarnate motion of the unconscious – shocks, traumata." Cited in Daniel Albright, *Beckett and Aesthetics* (Cambridge University Press, 2003), 143.

[167] Hanslick, *On the Musically Beautiful*, 51.

[168] Timothy Lenoir, "Helmholtz and the Materialities of Communication," *Osiris* 9 (1994), 184–207, here 184. Later in the century, Ernst Kapp would articulate the first philosophy of technology that attempted to understand human organs in terms of media prosthesis. See Kapp, *Grundlinien einer Philosophie der Technik: zur Entstehungsgeschichte der Cultur aus neuen Gesichtspunkten* (Brunswick: G. Westermann, 1877).

[169] Goethe, *Theory of Color*, trans. Herb Aach (New York: Van Nostrand Reinhold, 1971), 78–95, here 78.

[170] SSD 12: 281. Cf. PW 8: 380.

had formed the basis of Goethe's *Farbenlehre*: "Colors are acts of light ... Light and its absence are necessary for the production of color."[171] While there is not space here for a detailed examination of Goethean theory, let me summarize its relevance for the present discussion. For Goethe, white light did not contain the complete color spectrum (*pace* Newton), but had progressed beyond the lightest color – yellow – into a colorless state. Similarly, black was not the absence of color in a Newtonian sense, but a progression beyond the darkest color – blue – into colorlessness. White and black are thus merely positive and negative affections of the eye, between which grays or σκιερόν (cloudiness) – strictly the nature of color – pass in a continuum of shading: "colors in general are to be considered as half-lights, as half-shadows, particularly if they are so mixed as to reciprocally destroy their specific hues, and produce a shadowy tint, a gray."[172]

When under Goethe's influence, the young Schopenhauer published his own treatise *On Vision and Colors*, in which, among other things, he expanded on Goethe's σκιερόν (cloudiness) as the seat of color differentiation. Unlike Goethe, Schopenhauer sought a physiological explanation for the "bright and cheerful impression of [shaded] color" in contrast to the "somber ... dismal" quality of the color gray. When perceiving the latter, he argues, the retina is partially "*intense*" in its activity; the perception of colors as manifestations of Goethe's cloudiness, by contrast, are determined by "*qualitatively* partial" activity of the retina. The former employs only one part of the retina "*intensively*," the latter depends on a balance whereby "the activity of the one half that appears has the inactivity of the other as its essential and necessary condition ... [creating] a chemical combination and an intimate permeation of light and darkness ... [which is] the phenomenon of color."[173] However imaginatively fallacious, this recourse to chemical reasoning is indicative of the belief that the perception of color (a property of sound as much as of light) must be physically explicable.[174] The question remained as to whether comparable "*qualitatively* partial" activity was thought to be ascribable to the auditory cortex in the perception

---

[171] Goethe, *Theory of Color*, 71, 75.   [172] *Ibid.*, 75.

[173] Schopenhauer, *On Visions and Colors* [1816], trans. E. F. J. Payne (Oxford and Providence: Berg, 1994), 36–7.

[174] Schopenhauer was speculating, of course. Actual scientific observation of the retina was first reported in 1823 by the Czech anatomist and physiologist Johannes Purkinje (1787–1869). The retina became an object of detailed scrutiny in 1847 when the English mathematician and engineer Charles Babbage devised an Ophthalmoscope. It was Helmholtz, however, who popularized his own Ophthalmoscope in 1850–51, demonstrating that light entering the pupil is reflected back to its source. See Nicholas J. Wade, *A Natural History of Vision* (Cambridge: MIT Press, 1998).

of *Klangfarbe*, and the extent to which this could then be said to be intuitively comprehensible.

Just as Wagner placed (sensible) art above (theoretical) science, Goethe's premise for his *Farbenlehre* was its intuitive usefulness for art. He rejected Newton's optical spectrum as unintelligible to the artist who already sensed in color the conditions of warmth and coldness, proximity and distance.[175] Appealing to accepted polarities in nature (magnetism, electricity), he bolstered his anti-abstract position with claims for what could be observed with the eye, that is, the appearance (analogy) rather than essence (identity) of color. These polarities essentially allowed him to structure his influential color wheel in opposition to Newton's rainbow spectrum.

How does this concern vowel color and *Klangfarbe*? Analogy (to Goethe) was precisely what structured Moritz Rapp's model for vowel gradation in his *Outline of a Physiology of Language* (1836), which we encountered in Chapter 5. Goethe's color wheel, variously synthesized into a hexagon of two superimposed triangles, is the template for Rapp's organization of an *Urlaut* that precedes a vowel continuum. When set beside Rapp's own vowel triangle, the analogy becomes clear (Figure 6.4). Furthermore, Goethe agreed that sound and color were "referable to a universal formula,"[176] but remained indirectly related: "They are like two rivers which have their source in one and the same mountain, but subsequently pursue their way under totally different conditions in two totally different regions."[177] (Might he have had *Faust* in mind: "Zwei Seelen wohnen, ach! in meiner Brust"?) Beyond the original kinship of sound and color, Goethe also believed – like Raff's *Klangfarbe* and Kerndörffer's vowels – that each color produced a "distinct impression" on the mind, thereby addressing both our ocular sense and feeling. This particularity could be employed for "sensual, moral and aesthetic ends," he suggests, adding that the primordial relations embodied in color "may be made use of as a language," to amplify those same relations in other phenomena.[178] Like Raff's instrumental colors, it was on the cusp of a theory of material communication that I am ascribing to Wagner.

Rapp's borrowing from Goethe is explicit. The three main vowels, *a, e, o*, emerge from the *Urlaut* in the same way that "gray makes the primal cause and mediation for yellow, blue, and red. Gray must first be conceived, it must proceed to the color element in its trinity. So in the *Urlaut* we have the

---

[175] Goethe's corresponding approach is "to present this theory in a way that is useful and intelligent to the artist." See "The Pure Phenomenon" [1798], in *Theory of Color*, 67.
[176] *Ibid.*, 166.　　[177] *Ibid.*　　[178] *Ibid.*, 189–90.

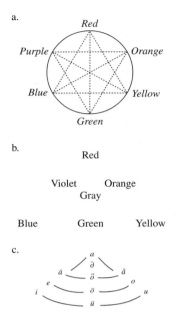

6.4 A comparison of Goethe's color triangle with Rapp's vowel triangle.
(a) Goethe's "ancient mysterious hexagon" (*Theory of Color* [1810], 1971, p. 190).
(b) Rapp's representation of Goethe's color triangle (*Physiologie der Sprache*, 1836, p. 19).
(c) Rapp's physiological triangle for vowels (*Physiologie der Sprache*, 1836, p. 30).

condition of all vowels, to which, however, belongs a further potency to actually produce them."[179] Goethe's σκιερόν – as the undeveloped difference between his three main colors – thus became the analogue to the undifferentiated, primal sound or *Urlaut*, from which all other shades of vowel – most clearly the primary three – emanate in a continuum between *i* and *u*.[180] Like Raff's sensory fixing of instrumental color, then, Rapp's

[179] "Es ist ganz dasselbe wie in der Farbenlehre das Grau den Urgrund und die Vermittlung für Gelb, Blau und Roth macht; Grau muß zuerst gedacht werden, er muß aber das Element der Farbe in seiner Dreiheit hintreten. So haben wir im Urlaut die Bedingung aller Vocale, es gehört aber eine weitere Potenz dazu, sie wirklich zu produciren." Rapp, *Versuch einer Physiologie der Sprache* (Stuttgart & Tübingen: J. G. Cotta, 1836), 31.

[180] Rapp begins his inquiry into the concept of a vowel by asking rhetorically why such a comparison should not be made: "Wenn man das Grau die unentwickelte Indifferenz zwischen den drei Farben Gelb, Roth, Blau nennen kann, weil sie in ihm noch nicht actuell enthalten, wohl aber potenziell bedingt sind, so fragt sich, gibt es einen diesem Standpunkt entsprechenden Sprach- order Vocallaut, und wenn es ihn gibt, so dürfen wir nicht anstehen, diesen Laut mit dem Namen des Urlauts oder Urvocals zu bezeichnen." *Ibid.*, 20.

appropriation of Goethe's color theory as the basis for vowels lends the *-farbe* in *Lautfarbe* a more literal character; viewed in terms of a spectrum of light waves, it also lends credence to Wagner's notion of intuitive comprehensibility through instrumental "vowels" as a physiological concept.

Two decades later, Lotze also sought to establish the physiology of color by, on the one hand, claiming that colors should be compared to timbral differentiation (rather than pitch) – particularly in the pronunciation of vowels on the same pitch – while, on the other hand, substituting "liveliness" (*Lebendigkeit*) for Goethe's polarity of light and dark as the organizing criterion.[181] But Lotze's vowel physiology went further than Rapp's when he suggested a parallelism between the sensation of particular muscular contractions and the feeling of the different vowels: "it would not be impossible that the feelings of [different] muscle contractions distinguish themselves in the same way as do vowels on the same pitch."[182] Elsewhere, however, his attempts to posit causal connections between material form, "wave motion," and soul become more evasive.[183] Not until 1926 would an empirical case be made for the total synonymy of vowel identities and instrumental timbres. Carl Stumpf, the Berlin-based psychologist and comparative musicologist, was able to verify empirically Helmholtz's characteristic frequency zones for vowels, and concluded:

a more detailed study always leads to the view that [vowel or instrumental sounds] are just parts of the infinite diversity of possible sound colors caused by the chance form of the hole of our mouth and the construction of our musical instruments, and that these chance parts are never sharply distinguished. Rather, they flow over into each other.[184]

---

[181] Lotze, *Medicinische Psychologie*, 216.

[182] For clarity, I quote Lotze's statement in full: "Zwar werden wir voraussetzen, dass Contraction überall an sich dieselbe Empfindung veranlasse, so wie die Wärme überall als dieselbe Wärme empfunden wird; da jedoch kein Muskel dem andern an Gesammtlänge und Dicke, an Zahl, Länge und Richtung der einzelnen Fasern völlig gleich, so wäre es nicht unmöglich, dass auch ihre Contractionsgefühle sich etwa in derselben Art, wie Vocale bei gleicher Tonhöhe unterschieden." *Ibid.*, 306.

[183] "The physical causes of the differing sounds are not known exactly; they would not easily lend themselves to a clear analysis, for they certainly consist of innumerable characteristics and in part irregularities of structure and the form of the sounding body ... it is not difficult to see that all these modifications of spatial wave motion could become useful passage for the soul." ["Die physischen Ursachen der abweichenden Klänge sind weniger genau bekannt; auch würden sie eine übersichtliche Analyse schwer gestatten, da sie gewiss in unzähligen Eigenthümlichkeiten und zum Theil Unregelmässigkeiten des Gefüges und der Form schallender Körper bestehen ... Es ist nicht schwer zu sehen, dass alle diese Modificationen räumlicher Wellenbewegung für die Seele zu nutzbaren Reisen werden können."] *Ibid.*, 214.

[184] "immer führt doch eine eingehendere Untersuchung zu der Anschauung, daß beide nur Ausschnitte aus der unendlichen Mannigfaltigkeit möglicher Klangfarben sind, bedingt durch

With the right equipment and a little "pretense" (*Verstellungen*), the sound of a trumpet flows readily into "A," a horn into "O," he concludes. It would seem, empirically, that an orchestra *could*, were Wagner's theory pushed over the edge, actually speak in human vowels (surely German?) – though such hypothetical realism has remained hypothetical rather than real.

Wagner's melodic triangle

Pace Stumpf, the difference between instrument and human voice, between Raff's and Rapp's color scheme, is decisive for Wagner: media, for him, remain untranslatable. In *Oper und Drama*, he suggests that the ineffectiveness of melodic theory hitherto rests mainly on the practice of cutting melodic pitches out of the harmonic accompaniment. This supposedly eradicates pitch duplication, but it ignores the "great distinction between the sensuous *Klangfarbe* of the instruments and that of the human voice," which we instinctively distinguish, resulting only in incomplete harmony.[185] In view of the transgression of this "hard" division by medical theorists such as Lotze and Daniels, it is possible finally to posit a "melodic triangle" for Wagner (Figure 6.5) that summarizes the spatial and sequential relationships of his materiality of melodic communication. This is modeled after the preceding examination of sensory perception of color through both instrumental and vowel timbres, yet here, the concept of melody is primal, a close analogue to the *Urlaut* or red-as-synthesis; it splits into a polarity of sound and vowel color, analogous to Goethe's white (–yellow) and black (–blue), or Rapp's *i* and *u*. The theoretical axiom is based equally on a radial motion outward from the central concept of musical color or *Tonfarbe* (just as Wagner's

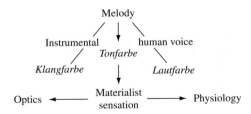

6.5 A Wagnerian "melodic triangle."

die zufällige Gestalt unserer Mundhöhle und die Konstruktion unserer Musikinstrumente, und daß diese zufälligen Ausschnitte nicht einmal scharf gescheiden sind, sondern fließend ineinander übergehen." Carl Stumpf, "Sprachlaute und Instrumentalklänge," *Zeitschrift für Physik* 38 (1926), 745–58, here 757.

[185] SSD 4: 168. Cf. PW 2: 310.

vowels must merge with musical tone to "redeem" their poetic expression, and Goethe's shades of gray form the mobilizing element in his theory), and a progressive movement from melody, through *Tonfarbe* and sensation, to the relevant branches of the life sciences: physiology and optics.

In placing melody at the apex of a schema progressing from aesthetics to science, I risk raising more questions than I answer. This, however, was precisely the problem characterizing a discourse among music theorists around the middle of the century who, in the wake of Helmholtz's popular lectures on the physiology of harmonic consonance and dissonance,[186] remained skeptical about a comparable theory for melody. Such would seem to have been the gifted legacy which the volumes of speculative physiology concerning vocal expression appeared to have promised earlier in the century, and which Wagner – however distantly, and in his own way – sought to appropriate: "if we trace the pathway which a melody must follow in order to act upon our state of feeling," Hanslick mused, "we find that it goes from vibrating instrument to auditory nerve, as is made amply clear in Helmholtz's epoch-making *On the Sensations of Tone*."[187] Yet two prominent writers who, like Hanslick, doubted the possibility of an exclusively physiological melodic theory were August Wilhelm Ambros and Lotze. The former weighs into this debate in 1856 with caution, stating:

> Even if harmony admits in any case of an additional explanation through agreeable or disagreeable convulsions of the auditory nerves by means of consonances or dissonances, yet in the case of the third element of music, which is almost the most essential one, namely, *melody*, a physiological theory for explaining its charm would hardly be so easy to establish.[188]

Back in 1852, Lotze had already expressed pessimism about the likelihood of a profitable relationship between acoustics and melody in his *Medical*

---

[186] Helmholtz gave his lecture "On the Physiological Causes of Harmony in Music," on January 9, 1857 at Bonn Univeristy, where he was Professor of anatomy and physiology. See Helmholtz, *Science and Culture: Popular and Philosophical Essays*, 46–75. Helmholtz later incorporated the material from this lecture into his monograph on the physics, physiology, and aesthetics of music, *On the Sensations of Tone as a Physiological Basis for the Theory of Music*, which was first published in 1863.

[187] Hanslick, *On the Musically Beautiful*, 54.

[188] "Läßt die Harmonie allenfalls auch noch eine physiologische Erklärung durch angenehme oder widrige Erschütterung der Gehörnerven durch Consonanzen oder Dissonanzen zu, so dürfte bei dem dritten Elemente der Musik, das beinahe das wesentlichste ist, der *Melodie* eine physiologische Theorie zur Erklärung ihres Zaubers schwerlich so leicht aufzustellen sein." Wilhelm August Ambros, *Die Grenzen der Musik und Poesie: Eine Studie zur Aesthetik der Tonkunst* (Leipzig: Heinrich Matthes, 1855), 40–41. Eng. trans. J. H. Cornell, *The Boundaries of Music and Poetry* (New York: G. Schirmer, 1893), 39–40.

Psychology. While he may not have read Wagner's texts, his own were carefully studied by Hanslick, who cited Lotze's judgment in his ultimate refutation of any direct referentiality between melodic stimulus and feeling perceived in a putatively sensory economy of musical expression:

Reflection upon melodies would lead to the admission that we know nothing at all about the conditions under which a transition of the nerves from one kind of excitation to another provides a physical basis for powerful aesthetics feelings which follow the change of tones.[189]

Yet precisely the opposite view was expressed later in the century by Hausegger, a staunch Wagnerian, whose emphatic optimism preceding his "physiological" analysis of Donna Anna's aria "Or sai che l'onore" (from *Le nozze di Figaro*) is an isolated attempt of its kind, but nevertheless allows him to conclude:

I therefore believe, despite the absence of detailed results of research, I am able to assert that unshakable laws or prohibitions of melodic succession can be explained by laws or limitations of sound expression with reference to the human organism.[190]

Detailed results of research did follow, as Fechner had predicted in 1860.[191] Part of the difficulty hindering a "physiological" *Melodik* in the 1850s was that the mechanism of sensation remained elusive for empirical research. Nobody believes any more that physical stimulation results directly in our experience of the world, Lotze argued, putting forward instead a six-part chain of signification from external stimulus to internal perception. If we perceive color from the oscillation of the ether, or melodic sounds from the vibration of the air, he continued, "we can only find the source of these sensory perceptions within ourselves," not within "physical

[189] Lotze, *Medicinische Psychologie*, 237. I take this reference from Hanslick, *On the Musically Beautiful*, 55.

[190] "[S]o viel glaube ich, trotz dem Abhandensein detaillirter Erforschungsresultate, behaupten zu dürfen, daß unumstößliche Gesetze der Melodieführung oder absolute Unzulässigkeiten in derselben sich auf Gesetze des Lautausdruckes oder Grenzen desselben im menschlichen Organismus zurückführen lassen," in Hausegger, "Die Musik als Ausdruck," *Bayreuther Blätter* 10 (1884), 312.

[191] See Fechner, *Elemente der Psychophysik*, 14. In 1910, the American psychologist Walter Bingham proposed a "motor theory of melody" based on a literal (muscular) reading of tension and resolution in musical form. He measured listener responses to short melodic sequences through movements of their right index finger – taken as a register of motor activity – and found that both sensory and associative forces organize corporeal response as a function of expectation, intervallic patterning, and prolongation. See Walter van Dyke Bingham, *Studies in Melody* (Baltimore: Review Publishing Company, 1910), esp. 43–88, here 82. Subsequent studies ensued, see also L. L. Thurstone, "The Problem of Melody," *Musical Quarterly* 4 (1920), 426–29.

processes" that may induce the soul to produce those perceptions, but do not cause them as such.[192] For all Wagner's theorizing over root vowel sensations in a poetic–melodic synthesis, his reluctance to engage with concrete concepts, such as pitch and rhythm, is perhaps indicative of this lack of clarity within medical anatomy.

The theorist J. C. Lobe represents nineteenth-century common sense in disputing flatly that one could "really *see* with the ears."[193] Yet the notion that the transmission between wave motion and sensation was an inexplicable or "miraculous" coupling makes it, ironically, not all that implausible, for similarly inexplicable phenomena are commonplace within the narrative sphere of opera – Wagner's *Tarnhelm* being the paradigmatic means of transmuting one physical reality into another. The device's magic, paradoxically, becomes a way of interpreting inexplicable scientific processes. Needless to say, Wagner's predilection for mythic subjects and personal fictions lends itself to the discourse in this sense. Hence, if the ears could see color, then the orchestra could pronounce different vowels, and the auditor's eyes could hear them.

After our earlier swan, another example from *Lohengrin* may help to underscore the latent materialism in this perspective. Consider Elsa's "slow scream"[194] into the foreground for Lohengrin to defend her honor; this commands the swan knight over a distance of some four hundred miles, the distance between her duchy in Brabant and his holy mountain at Monsalvat. For Friedrich Kittler, this is "an impossible exploit unless ... the medium were not the message ... barely audible sounds, freed from the speaker's mouth and will, have grown to an absolute sound that travels through space and time," that is, via radio waves.[195] For Alexander Rehding the feat of acoustic transmission even conjures the spectacle of the telephone.[196]

---

[192] "Folgt nun der Oscillation des Aethers eine Farbenempfindung in uns, der Luftschwingung ein Ton, so haben wir die Quelle dieser qualitativen Sinnesempfindungen nur in uns selbst zu suchen, dürfen aber in den äussern Reizen nichts sehen, als physische Vorgänge irgend welcher Art, zwar geeignet, die Seele zur innerlichen Erzeugung jener Anschauungen zu veranlassen, nicht aber, sie ihr als schon fertige zuzuführen." Lotze, *Medicinische Psychologie*, 174–75.

[193] Lobe is quoting a review from the *Augsburger Allgemeine Zeitung*, see "Letters to a Young Composer about Wagner," 274.

[194] Wagner's stage directions read: "Elsa tritt auf ... dann schreitet sie sehr langsam und mit großer Verschämtheit der Mitte des Vordergrundes zu," *Lohengrin*, act 1, scene 2.

[195] Friedrich Kittler, "*Weltatem*: On Wagner's Media Technology," in *Wagner in Retrospect*, ed. Leroy R. Shaw, Nancy R. Cirillo, and Marion Miller (Amsterdam: Rodopi, 1987), 206.

[196] Alexander Rehding, "Magic Boxes and Volksempfänger," in *Music, Theater and Politics in Germany: 1848 to the Third Reich*, ed. Nikolaus Bacht (Aldershot: Ashgate, 2006), 266.

This insight is less dependent on post-structuralist methodology than it might seem: in 1848 – just in time for the finished score of *Lohengrin* – *Punch* advertised a *Telakouphanon* or "speaking trumpet" that purported to carry the human voice across great distances, so that a priest may give his sermon simultaneously in three different churches, or that by laying down a number of these devices "domestic establishments [such as Lohengrin's castle] might be served with the liquid notes of Jenny Lind [singing Elsa] as easily as they are with soft water, and could be supplied with music as readily as they can with gas."[197] Beyond the fad for such eccentric theories, Nietzsche later relished this clash of technology and metaphysics when describing music's new Schopenhauerean empowerment: it symbolized "a priest . . . a sort of mouthpiece of the 'in itself' of things, *a telephone from the beyond.*"[198]

The assumption of a medium based on sense stimuli underpins these speculations, and finds an uncanny analogue in Lotze's description from 1883 of the telegraphic process by which sound, color, or taste is transmitted and perceived. As in *Medical Psychology*, he separated the stimulus and transmission of sensation from its effect – "there is nothing in the redness of red, the blueness of blue, or the sound of the heard tone, which suggests a larger or smaller number of vibrations of a medium"[199] – and in doing so, likened the transformative transmissions of this effect – tantamount to the unseen physical structure between a performer and an audience – to the electric telephone:

Effects or actions, which proceed from [things themselves] and are sense stimuli to us, are no doubt only motions and themselves neither red nor sweet; but what is there to prevent our supposing that, by acting through our nerves, they make that same redness or sweetness arise, as our sensation, in our souls, which also attaches as a quality to the things themselves? Such a process would be no more wonderful than the telephone, which receives waves of sound, propagates them in a form of a motion quite different, and in the end conducts them to the ear retransformed into waves of sound.[200]

Elsa's scream, in other words, reaches the listener's "soul" in precisely the same way that it reaches Lohengrin at Monsalvat, it is transmitted and retransformed as sound via motion along nerves or "electric cable,"

[197] "The Opera Telakouphanon," *Punch* (1848), 275.

[198] Friedrich Nietzsche, *On the Genealogy of Morals*, trans. Carol Diethe (Cambridge University Press, 2007), 73. Emphasis added.

[199] Lotze continues: "yet science has indirectly discovered such vibrations to be the occasion of these sensations." Lotze, *Metaphysic in Three Books*, 448–49.

[200] *Ibid.*, 449.

underscoring a parallelism between music and physics, or what could almost be called the melodic technology of music drama.

Suggestive metaphors: water and sound waves

> Light, as well as sound, is [a wave motion]; the name is derived from the analogy of waves on the surface of water ... When a point in a surface of still water is agitated – as by throwing in a stone – the motion thus caused is propagated in the form of waves, which spread in rings over the surface of the water. The circles of waves continue to increase even after rest has been restored at the point first affected.
>
> Hermann von Helmholtz (1857)[201]

> The ocean binds and separates the land: so does music bind and separate the two opposite poles of human art, dance and poetry.
>
> Richard Wagner (1849)[202]

> By symbol I mean, not a metaphor or allegory or any other figure of speech or form of fancy, but an actual and essential part of that, the whole of which it represents.
>
> Samuel Taylor Coleridge (1816)[203]

When Schopenhauer's treatise *On Vision and Colors* failed to create a sensation, he complained to Goethe that it was "like [throwing] a stone in a bog – no ripples."[204] Wagner too held out little hope that his essay *Das Kunstwerk der Zukunft* would make waves.[205] Water metaphors are some of Wagner's most consistent figures of speech in the Zurich writings. He acknowledges them cheerfully and openly ("we can't give up our simile of the ocean yet"),[206] but his prolix language is vulnerable to an interchange between literal and metaphorical meanings, such as when he signed off "Wassermann" in letters to his wife during five weeks of hydrotherapy in 1851, a literalism, but also a poetic complement to his "Wasserfrauen," or

---

[201] Helmholtz, "On the Physiological Causes of Harmony in Music" [1857], in David Cahan ed., *Hermann von Helmholtz, Science and Culture*, 52.

[202] SSD 3: 81. Cf. PW 1: 110.

[203] Samuel Taylor Coleridge, *The Statesman's Manual*, in *Lay Sermons*, ed. R. J. White, *The Collected Works of Samuel Taylor Coleridge*, 16 vols., ed. Kathleen Coburn, Bollingen Series, 75 (Princeton University Press, 1972), 6: 79.

[204] Schopenhauer to Goethe, June 23, 1818, in Schopenhauer, *Gesammelte Briefe*, ed. Arthur Hübscher (Bonn: Herbert Grundmann, 1987), 35.

[205] Wagner to Theodor Uhlig, July 27, 1850, Zurich, SB 3: 362.   [206] SSD 3: 83. Cf. PW 2 112.

Rhine maidens as they would later be called.[207] Given that "all language is metaphorical" at some level, the capacity for simultaneously metaphorical and literalized signification is impossible to reconcile in Wagner's writings.[208] In a way, this irreconcilability is precisely the value of their artistic purpose: to retain the instability of signification against the clear mnemonic recurrence of musical material in Wagner's dramas. Rather than searching for a weak compromise between these viewpoints, this closing section will use the ambiguity of "water" images in Wagner's rhetoric to clarify his irreconcilable relationships for us as part of a reflexive methodology that returns the ambiguity to Wagner himself, thereby strengthening the case for a literal, materialist reading of Wagner's sounds as set against the customary metaphorical fare.

Why is water similarly ambiguous? Its wetness conducts vibration just as well as air does, yet it also constitutes a vivid poetic metaphor.[209] Wagner's recurring image of "rising and sinking waves of melody"[210] pivots delicately between allegory and symbol in mid-century writings about sound, giving rise to a playful ambiguity that – far from teasing apart – draws together the very qualities the clarifying image purports to separate, namely acoustic symbol (sound waves) and aesthetic allegory (sea of harmony). This connecting process is probably what Roland Barthes had in mind when he defined the picture or image as "the organization of the various readings that can be made of it: a picture is never anything but its own plural description."[211] No intentional signification is invoked in this slippage between aesthetics and acoustics; it rests on the intriguingly flexible identity of musical sound at the time: at once material and metaphysical. Wagner, as we have seen, resisted the perspective offered by natural science, but his language of metaphors undermines that stance.

Rather than dismissing the divergent watery images as overblown rhetoric that sustains the ambiguity of Wagner's "unmelodic" art, let us ask what might be constant in them. Waves are always in motion, and cannot be

---

[207]   Wagner to Minna, September 28, 1851, Albisbrunn, SB 4: 121ff.

[208]   Michael McCanles, "The Literal and the Metaphorical: Dialectic or Interchange," *PMLA* 91 (1976), 279–90, here 279.

[209]   Practices of transmitting music through water, technologies for subaqueous sound production, and hydrophonic listening are now reasonably well established. For an overview, see Stefan Helmreich, "Underwater Music: Tuning Composition to the Sounds of Science," *Oxford Handbook of Sound Studies*, ed. Trevor Pinch and Karin Bijsterveld (Oxford University Press, 2012), 151–75.

[210]   SSD 3: 83. Cf. PW 1: 112.

[211]   Roland Barthes, "Is Painting a Language?" *The Responsibility of Forms*, trans. Richard Howard (New York: Hill and Wang, 1988), 150.

frozen; they simply become calm sea or adopt a constant amplitude of zero (i.e. no distortion). In 1808, when the Danish physician Hans Christian Ørsted examined the natural "acoustic figures" of fine powder that appeared on glass plates after several vigorous strokes of a violin bow caused each plate to vibrate, a principle of motion resulted:

The most perfect and internally harmonious motion of bodies is also the one which, through the ear, produces the deepest impression on our internal sense of beauty [symmetrical images]. With this, I believe that the first physical definition of the various kinds of sounds has been given.[212]

From the outset of a material conception of sound, then, regular motion and symmetrical imagery have been interrelated. A *Naturphilosoph*, Ørsted argued that this kind of kinship went some way to demonstrating the "great fundamental unity [that] pervades the whole of nature."[213] Ambiguity arose, however, as soon as the image itself was not produced by the vibrating, resonating body, but acquired metaphorical layers of signification for sound, layers abstracted from any physical connection to the original source. This divorce of meaning from appearance is based on the assumption of an originary unity and constitutes something of a secular fall in the story of sound images in the nineteenth century. It also unleashed the metaphorical richness of wave motion.

Back in 1816, Samuel Taylor Coleridge offered one of the clearest distinctions between allegory and symbol in *The Statesman's Manual*. Though he balances this heavily in favor of the symbol (which he connects to the universal through the particular), his articulation will nevertheless be useful for interrogating Wagner's unstable aquatic imagery: "An Allegory is but a translation of abstract notions into a picture-language which is itself nothing but an abstraction from objects of the senses."[214] Coleridge's "picture-language" that abstracts from sensation is an apt description of the most straightforward reading of Wagner's imaginative process in his writings; sensation is abstracted into image which informs idea, rather than vice versa. "On the other hand," Coleridge continues, "a Symbol is characterized by a translucence of the Special in the Individual or of the General in the Especial or of the Universal in the General. Above all by the translucence of the Eternal through and in the

[212] Hans Christian Ørsted, "Experiments on Acoustic Figures," *Selected Scientific Writings of H. C. Ørsted*, trans. and ed. Karen Jelved, Andrew D. Jackson, and Ole Knudsen (Princeton University Press, 1998), 274.

[213] Johannes Carsten Hauch, *H. C. Ørsted's Leben. Zwei Denkschriften von Hauch und Forchhammer*, trans. H. Sebald (Spandau: Vossische Buchhandlung, 1853), 13.

[214] Coleridge, *The Statesman's Manual*, 30.

Temporal. *It always partakes of the Reality which it renders intelligible.*"[215] In sum, whereas an allegory bears no traceable connection to the notion it translates into image, a symbol harbors an essential element of that which it represents. Allegories are phantasmal, while symbols are microcosmic; the one gestures toward the abstract, the other, to the concrete.

Wagner's music most explicitly evoking surging water, however, immediately blurs this distinction. The first scene of *Das Rheingold* takes place underwater, and was even apparently to be premiered on conjoined barges afloat lake Lucerne until safety concerns forced Wagner to abandon the plan.[216] The opening 136 measures of the Prelude are remarkable in being a paradigm of isosonorous musical representation. The passage is both allegorical and symbolic in that it both represents the birth of the world as a dramatic notion of beginning, and actualizes it through the gradual unfolding of the natural overtone series: the literal, concrete birth of the acoustic world. It is thus an "actual and essential part" of that which it represents, and its "wave motifs" translate – or allegorize – the aquatic sound of primal creation into abstract images. Here, in other words, "water" connects the symbolic overtone series to the allegorical, abstracted image of the surging Rhine.

Several modern scholars have responded to this duality (albeit indirectly). Kittler views this representation of the birth of the world as a "musico–physiological dream" that effects "a historical transition from intervals to frequencies, from a logic to a physics of sound,"[217] where Thomas Grey interprets it as "nothing less than a compact *mise-en-scène* of the mutual origins of language and melody"[218] and Jean-Jacques Nattiez similarly argues that the music "is born from primordial sound."[219] Kittler reorients the aural field from music to media, from a theory to a physics of sound, while Grey and Nattiez sublimate Wagner's instrumental overtones for a vocally undifferentiated *Urlaut*. More than sixty years earlier, Thomas Mann made heirs of all the above when he stated that Wagner's music for the flowing Rhine waters is "*the beginning of music itself*. And it was not just the music of myth that he, the poet–composer, would give us but the very myth of music itself, a mythical philosophy and a musical poem of Creation."[220] Thematizing the origin of Wagner's lofty music dramas

---

[215] *Ibid.* Emphasis added. Goethe had made a similar distinction using the same terms in his theory of color. See § 916 (symbol) and § 917 (allegory) in Goethe's *Theory of Color*, 350–51.

[216] See Max Fehr, *Richard Wagners Schweizer Zeit*, 2 vols. (Aarau: H. R. Sauerlander, 1934–54), 2: 21.

[217] Kittler, *Gramophone, Film, Typewriter*, 24. He is, of course, alluding to Wagner's account of conceiving the Prelude during a feverish night's sleep in La Spezia, Italy.

[218] Grey, *Wagner's Musical Prose*, 266.   [219] Nattiez, *Wagner Androgyne*, 54.

[220] Thomas Mann, *Pro and Contra Wagner*, trans. Allan Blunden (Univeristy of Chicago Press, 1985), 189.

through *Rheingold* is attractive by virtue of being a tidy – if problematic – allegory; as physical overtones, the music becomes a metaphor for itself (i.e. a symbol), a soundtrack to its own existence. But Mann's chiastic use of "myth" is double-edged; it connotes both Wagner's mythic origins of the musical world, and the "myth" of Wagner as the subject of his own "poem of creation" in which speech and music are conceived as equally apportioned shareholders in a singular economy of sound.

In fact, this Wagnerian myth of sonic origins dates back to Ørsted's 1808 experiment, though – appropriately – its circulation in Germany (in recycled form) is roughly coeval with the composition of *Rheingold* itself (November 1853): it dates from 1852, specifically from Pohl's "Acoustic Letters" in the *Neue Zeitschrift* we encountered earlier, in which he auspiciously dubbed the fantasy of original, physical sound "the Siren of our century."[221] Though iconic, the "physiological dream" of *Rheingold* is not unique in this regard. In *Lohengrin*, the first five partials of the overtone series are also symbolically regulative: another sounding beginning – daybreak in act 2, scene 3 – contains a 54-measure fanfare exploration of the D major triad, which gradually extends across three and a half octaves (from A to d^3), rising note by note in a 2-measure rhythmic ostinato (twenty-nine measures of which are underpinned by a sustained drone in the lower strings, thereby inverting the orchestration of *Rheingold's* opening, from m. 45). Liszt admired this realist mapping of sound image explicitly onto a narrative of daybreak,[222] and Wagner even thematizes geographic distance through contrasting frequencies: watchmen sound the *réveille* from a tower, and are answered by a distant tower, all in D major (54mm.); when the king's four trumpeters then appear immediately outside the banqueting hall to sound the summons, the fanfare pitch drops to C major for fifteen measures – bringing the sound symbolically closer by the perception of pitch.[223] The realist echoes of the sailors in *Tristan* and *Der fliegende Holländer* also point to elementary physics, and could one not also think of the *Lohengrin* Prelude's opening in terms of overtones? Like the "physiological dream" of *Rheingold*, the ethereal A major triad could be construed as the third, fourth, and fifth partials over a missing fundamental,

---

[221] "Das ist die *Syrene* unseres Jahrhunderts." Pohl, "Akustische Briefe: Vierter Brief," *NZfM* 8 (August 20, 1852), 74.

[222] "Die Ruhe der Nacht tritt ein, bis der Tag anbricht. Man hört, wie die Wachen sich von der Höhe der Türme ihre Signale geben . . . was einen sehr glücklichen Echo-Effekt hervorbringt . . . während welcher das immer bewegter Crescendo dem Glanze des nahenden Morgens entspricht." Liszt, SS 4: 55.

[223] See *Lohengrin*, act 2, scene 3, mm. 870–937.

in which the gradual descent to harmonic security (and fundamental resonance) inverts the ascent of act 3, scene 2, and of *Rheingold*. That all three
passages thematize a beginning or origin (of day, of the world, of the Holy
Grail on earth) is perhaps no coincidence. The beginning of sound itself –
Pohl's "Siren" – is heard, symbolically, in terms of pure overtones. By thinking
in terms of wave motion rather than poetics, Pohl asked rhetorically in 1852,
"does [sound] appear any the less magical?"[224]

Picturing vibrations

The idea of acoustic origins does not distinguish between language, voice,
vowel, melody, instrument, or sound color, still less between physics and
aesthetics; the undefined remainder rests on imag(in)ing pure "vibrations"
or waves of sound (a synaesthetic agent also adopted by such modernists as
Kandinsky and Klee to collapse pictorial and sonic media into each other).
If the acoustic symbolism of the opening of Wagner's Prelude seems far
fetched, consider Pohl's fourth "Acoustic Letter" in which this *Ur*-vibration
is given form as a fantastical vision of Heinrich Dove's (non-metaphorical)
siren of 1851,[225] i.e. a throbbing rod producing sound waves in the dark:

The vibrations of the rod increase more and more. The explosions occur faster and
faster, they always become stronger. There comes a point when my ear can no
longer separate them; they flow together into one in my awareness; I still only hear a
whistling – and suddenly a deep bass tone hits my ear. It is of such deafening
intensity that nothing could be heard, neither of a voice, nor of the sound of any
musical instrument, not even that of the organ. This sound rises in pitch continually. It runs through all middle steps up to the highest shrillest sound that cuts into
our ear with unbearable intensity.[226]

[224] "Ist sie auch weniger poesiereich – denn sie ist ja nur eine 'Maschine' – erscheint sie darum
weniger zaubervoll?" Pohl, "Akustische Briefe: Vierter Brief," *NZfM* 8 (August 20, 1852), 74.

[225] For a history of the siren, see Ernst Robel, *Die Sirenen: Ein Beitrag zur Entwicklungsgeschichte
der Akustik. Part II: Die Arbeiten deutscher Physiker über die Sirene im Zeitraume von 1830–
1856* (Berlin: R. Gaertner, 1894).

[226] "Die Schwingungen des Stabes vermehren sich aber fort und fort. Die Explosionen erfolgen
rascher und rascher, sie werden immer stärker. Es tritt ein Moment ein, wo sie mein Ohr nicht
mehr zu trennen vermag; sie fließen im Bewußtsein in Eins zusammen; ich vernahme nur noch
ein Sausen – und plötzlich schlägt ein tiefer Baßton an mein Ohr. Er ist von so betäubender
Intensität, daß weder von meiner Stimme, noch von dem Tone irgend eines musikalischen
Instruments, selbst nicht von dem der Orgel, das Geringste gehört werden könnte. Diese Ton
erhöht sich fortwährend. Er durchläuft alle Mittelstufen, bis zum höchsten schrillenden Ton,
der in unser Ohr mit unerträglicher Intensität einschneidet." See Pohl, "Akustische Briefe," 73.

By situating this primal sound in darkness, Pohl alerts us to the potent effect of visualizing the (sound) waves; his putative science is not supposed to be symbolic, still less allegorical, but in darkness it requires the same act of envisioning that Wagner's vocabulary does. By denying the reader a clearly defined image (in daylight), Pohl's description shares with Wagner's Prelude more than the "deafening intensity" of an inhumanly "deep bass tone" (*Rheingold* at 16 Hz), it also shares with it the sensory distance (and cognitive insertion) required by picturing something we cannot actually see.

Another reason for the pitch black context is that, as the rod's vibrations continue to speed up, Pohl's fantastical acoustic spectrum transmutes into Newton's color spectrum: "A weak red light becomes visible, it becomes more lively, the rod glows. First red, then it becomes yellow, then blue. It runs through all colors until after violet everything sinks back again to night."[227] As mentioned above, the original, less dramatic version of this scientific vision was penned by Ørsted,[228] and irrespective of whether we want to consider this or Pohl's text in any way an exemplar for *Rheingold avant la lettre*, the philosophical roots of this belief in a unified cosmos wherein the "octave" equivalency between senses (contiguous wavelengths separating the perception of sound and light) is engineered to demonstrate Ørsted's belief in natural unity, a single "grand scale of sensations," can be traced most directly to Schelling's *Naturphilosophie*, espousing a "system of nature [that] is at the same time the system of our mind."[229] In this way, synaesthetic observations of Wagner's music attain a basis in putative reality, at least from the perspective of monistically inspired natural science.

On this basis, the Dresden acoustician August Seebeck – who had first determined that pitch was based on periodicity – could assume that longitudinal (sound) and transverse (light) waves behave similarly. This led him to propose an optical analogue to acoustical resonance in 1844, wherein he explained the mechanism of brightness as the resonance of spectral colors with vibrating molecules in groups of nerves in the retina.[230] Drawing together the physiological and analogic strands of this discourse, furthermore,

---

[227] "Ein schwaches rothes Licht dämmert auf, es wird immer lebhafter, der Stab glüht. Erst roth, dann wird er gelb, dann blau. Er durchläuft alle Farben, bis nach dem Violett Alles wieder in Nacht versinkt." *Ibid.*

[228] Hans Christian Ørsted, "Experiments on Acoustic Figures," in *Selected Scientific Writings of H. C. Ørsted*, 280.

[229] Schelling, *Ideas for a Philosophy of Nature*, 30.

[230] August Seebeck, "Bemerkungen über Resonanz und über Helligkeit der Farben im Spectrum," *Annalen der Physik* 62 (1844) 62: 571–76. See also the reverse theory where color is treated in relation to acoustic resonance by Macedonio Melloni, "Beobachtung über die Farbung der Netzhaut und der Krystall-Linse," *Annalen der Physik* 56 (1842), 263–302.

Helmholtz only accepted Thomas Young's tricolor receptor theory (where the retinal structure comprised three receptors sensitive principally to wavelengths of red, green, and violet ranges) when he realized it formed a conceptual basis for understanding the organ of Corti in the ear; that is, where primary colors (objectively based in particular nerve endings of rods and cones) become analogous to simple tones (objectively based on the organ of Corti), and color mixtures to combination tones.[231] To be sure, such analogies between the physical properties of waveforms and of different organs of sensory perception remain inspirational rather than empirical; they nevertheless betray a common way of thinking during the mid-century, and lay bare the influence – even within the natural sciences – of the romantics' fervent desire to find a grand foundation for unity.

While Helmholtz's research from the 1860s (and later that of Alexander Graham Bell)[232] offered detailed explanations for the wave formations that produced different vowels' sound color, Eduard MacDowell demonstrates that writers on music continued to draw as late as 1912 on the enticing specter of a spectrum vibrating between sound and color to explain Wagner's compositional skill:

In the Prelude to *Lohengrin*, Wagner pictures his angels in dazzling white. He uses the highest vibrating sounds at his command. But for the dwarfs who live in the gloom of Niebelheim he chooses deep shades of red, the lowest vibrating color of the solar spectrum.[233]

---

[231] "In the cochlea of the internal ear, the ends of the nerve fibers, which lie spread out regularly side by side, are provided with minute elastic appendages (the rods of Corti) arranged like the keys and hammers of a piano. My hypothesis is that each of these separate nerve fibers is constructed so as to be sensitive to a definite tone, to which its elastic fiber vibrates in perfect consonance . . . Its analogy with Young's theory of colors is obvious." Hermann von Helmholtz, "Die neueren Fortschritte in der Theorie des Sehens," in Hermann von Helmholtz, *Selected Writings*, ed. Russell Kahn (Middleton: Wesleyan University Press, 1971), 181. For a contextual examination of Helmholtz's realization, see Timothy Lenoir, "Helmholtz and the Materialities of Communication," 184–207.

[232] Alexander Graham Bell, "Vowel Theories," in *The Mechanism of Speech: Lectures Delivered Before the American Association* (New York and London: Funk & Wagnalls Co., 1907), 117–29.

[233] Eduard MacDowell, "Origin of Song vs. Origin of Instrumental Music," in *Critical and Historical Essays: Lectures delivered at Columbia University* (Boston, Leipzig, New York: A. P. Schmidt, 1912), 21. MacDowell's ideas are almost identical to attempts at scientific explanations for comparative "octaves" across different senses, such as Alexander Wilford Hall's in 1878: "as the auditory nerve recognizes the octaves of sound by their *pitch*, from the slowly pulsating bass to the rapidly throbbing soprano, so the optic nerve recognizes its single octave of light in its vermilion and crimson, through the middle register of green and yellow, up to the highest tints of blue and violet: and as the gustary nerve recognizes its octaves of taste by variety of flavor, from the low and shuddering notes of aloes and wormwood, through the mean register of acids, up to the purest and highest tones of nectarous sweets, – so the olfactory nerve recognizes and analyses its

Back in 1852, however, Pohl declared the gap between sound and light to be too great to bridge with "*one* of our inadequate means,"[234] and we may suppose that the inherently ambiguous images of sound and light waves went a long way to assuaging this scientific lack, as it did for MacDowell even though explanations concerning waveforms existed long before 1912.

The crucial step taken by writers who treated music as the result of vibrations, i.e. a sounding medium, is to present an essentialist perspective in which vibrating air (ether) is considered a material reality rather than a secondary product of aesthetic theory; here, an abstract *idea* behind music recedes against the physiological pleasure of experiencing its emotional content, which was precisely Wagner's hope in 1851 for the "immediate physical portrayal" of art as an "immediate vital act."[235] Put more abstractly, an *a priori* retreats in favor of a *presence*; the vibrations mean nothing but the perception of their sensation (as Lotze argued in 1852), which Wagner wanted to be intuitively comprehensible on his terms.

Watery emblems: the harmonic sea

For both physiologist and music theorist, the "material reality" most comparable to vibrating air seems to have been water: the quintessential *fluidum vitale*. Köhler's fantasy of acoustic scrutiny is a case in point:

The silent, low-limbed fish in the deep regions of its fluid element feels every stirring of the water's surface above … We humans don't perceive anything in the constantly revolving, surging air waves; the delicate body of tones is not yet more than letters to the young schoolboy, its form appears like an Egyptian hieroglyph to the first-year elementary student.[236]

Less than four years later, Helmholtz used the same simile not to lament our poor understanding of sound, but precisely to explain wave motions to a non-scientific audience. The ocean was an instructive spectacle that illustrated what otherwise could only be "recognized by the mind's eye of the

---

numerous octaves of odour by their variety of *scent*." A. W. Hall, *Evolution of Sound: Part of the Problem of Human Life and Hereafter* (New York: Hall & Co., 1878), 228–29.

[234] "Die Kluft zwischen Ton und Licht ist zu groß, um sie mit *einem* unserer unzureichenden Mittel zu überbrücken." Pohl, "Akustische Briefe: Vierter Brief," *NZfM* 8 (August 20, 1852), 74.

[235] SSD 3: 46. Cf. PW 1: 73.

[236] "Der stumme, gliederarme Fisch auf tiefem Grunde seines flüssigen Elements fühlt jede Regung der obern Wasserfläche … Aber wir Menschen nehmen nichts wahr in den stets kreisenden, wogenden Luftwellen; der zarte Körper des Tones ist uns noch nicht mehr, wie dem Schulbübchen ein Buchstabe, dessen Form dem A-B-C Schützen eine ägyptische Hieroglyphe ist." Köhler, *Die Melodie der Sprache*, 78, 83.

mathematical thinker," namely a mass of air traversed in all directions by waves of sound:

We can watch it from the parapet of any bridge spanning a river, but it is most complete and sublime when viewed from a cliff beside the sea. It is then rare not to see innumerable systems of waves, of various lengths, propagated in various directions. The longest come from the deep sea and dash against the shore. Where the boiling breakers burst shorter waves arise and run back again toward the sea. Perhaps a bird of prey darting after a fish gives rise to a system of circular waves which, rocking over the undulating surface, are propagated with the same regularity as on the mirror of an inland lake. And thus, from the distant horizon, where white lines of foam on the steel-blue surface betray the coming trains of wave, down to the sand beneath our feet, where the impression of their arcs remains, there is unfolded before our eyes a sublime image of immeasurable power and unceasing variety which, as the eye at once recognizes its pervading order and law, enchains and exalts without confusing the mind.[237]

What this has in common with Wagner's theoretical writings is compelling. Both illustrate by literary representations of waves and water. Both draw on the concept of unknowably wide and powerful waters, i.e. a sublime ocean (though without recourse to "the voice of nature," i.e. the notion of natural sounds from thunder claps to Aeolian harps). Most revealingly, both adopt the ocean to say what it is they want to say about the functioning of musical sound, though ostensibly for different reasons. (The only evidence of Wagner's awareness of swirling sound waves in his "sea of harmony" is his reference to good music written according to "tone vibrations,"[238] and a glimmer of double meaning in his summary protest to Uhlig: "Ah, how ludicrous it would be if, with all our enthusiasm for art, what we were fighting over were simply thin air [*leere Luft*]!"[239])

Recall that this connection is specific to melody for A. F. Kanne – a leading critic for the *Allgmeine musikalische Zeitung* during the early decades of the nineteenth century. He argued that "morally the similarity [between the ocean and melody] is undeniable."[240] While historically melody has an audio–poetic association with water, Kanne's is kinetic. His view is based on the abstraction of a sine wave archetype for all melodic motion, which he sees infinitely replicated on the surface of the sea. By contrast, Wagner's symbolic use of water vocabulary is neither audio nor

---

[237] Helmholtz, "On the Physiological Causes of Harmony in Music" [1857], in *Science and Culture*, 57.

[238] SSD 3: 120. Cf. PW 1: 153.

[239] Wagner to Theodor Uhlig, January 12, 1852, Zurich, in SB 4: 249.

[240] "Moralisch wäre die Ähnlichkeit unläugbar." Kanne, "Der Zauber der Tonkunst," *AmZ* 63 (1821), 539.

kinetic, but sensory – pivoting between the disembodied idea of an oceanic expanse and the resonance of submerged vibrations. Throughout his writings, he reveals that he too thinks consciously in clarifying metaphors, the logic of which appears to be clinched only after images are formed. Such a thought process is, in a sense, a microcosm for Wagner's mantra that feeling and sensation precede understanding and knowledge. Consider the incongruities: the gap that must be traversed by daring sailor–composers – the sea of harmony – is comprised of "tinted waves of harmony" – water in its abundant vitality, in which melody is simultaneously the poet's "wave-born mirror image,"[241] as well as the droplets falling back to the "mountain lake" of the orchestra from the poet's oar aboard the boat of the dramatic singer's *Versmelodie*;[242] elsewhere, ringing sounds flow as breast milk (where melody is its "nursing mother").[243]

Wagner's potent tangle of images allied to the ocean is new neither in metaphor nor in subject. He tapped into a web of established metaphors relating to the Beethoven mythology, where the venturesome composer navigates uncharted, stormy waters according to his inner compass.[244] As early as 1799, Wackenroder had begun weaving this web by characterizing Germany – *Land der Musik* – as a "resonant ocean," which Wagner then localized in relation to a *Land / Meer der Harmonie*.[245] But his use of the metaphor in 1851, I am suggesting, is differentiated by the realism it had acquired by this time through proximity to the burgeoning natural sciences. His critics responded accordingly: Hanslick's negative description of *unendliche Melodie* in *Meistersinger* as "the intentional dissolution of every fixed form into a shapeless, sensually intoxicating resonance" seems oddly

---

[241] SSD 4: 142. Cf. PW 2: 280.　　[242] SSD 4: 173. Cf. PW 2: 314.　　[243] SSD 4: 93. Cf. PW 2: 226.

[244] The following text has multiple correspondences to Wagner's classic accounts in *Das Kunstwerk der Zukunft* and *Oper und Drama*, and appeared in 1838: "*Beethoven* war und bleibt wohl unbestritten der kühnste Segler auf den Fluthen der Harmonie … Jede seiner Fahrten auf des Tonreiches gränzenlosen Ocean gestaltet sich zu einer Entdeckungsreise, von wannen er stets Neues, noch Ungekanntes aus weiter Ferne mit zurück in die Heimath bringt. Scheint es auch zuweilen, als sey der allen Meeresstürm ein hohnlachend trotzende Argonaut irgendwo verschlagen, an schroff entgegenstarrende Klippen, oder auf wüstes, unbewohntes Eiland; doch immer findet der Genius seines unbeugsamen Geistes sich wieder zurechte, denn er darf vertrauen mit Zuversicht dem inner, nie trügenden Compaß, und ihm leuchtet als treuester Führer der reinste, hellstrahlende Demantglanz des unbeweglich am Himmelszelte flammenden Polarsterns." See "Zweytes Concert spiritual," *Allgemeine Musikalischer Anzeiger* 10 (1838), 45. Quoted in Heike Stumpf, "… wollet mir jetzt durch die phantastisch verschlungenen Kreuzgänge folgen!" *Metaphorisches Sprechen in der Musikkritik der ersten Hälfte des 19. Jahrhunderts* (Frankfurt am Main: Bonner, 1996), 103. For discussion of Uhlig's essays on Beethoven, see Kropfinger, *Wagner and Beethoven*, 70–76.

[245] "tönendes Meer," in Wilhelm Heinrich Wackenroder, *Sämtliche Werke und Briefe*, 2 vols. (Heidelberg: C. Winter, 1991), 1: 206.

apt;[246] as does Nietzsche's criticism of the same as part allegory, part acoustic symbol: "One walks into the sea, gradually loses one's secure footing, and finally surrenders oneself to the elements without reservation: one must *swim*."[247] At the end of the century, Max Nordau humorlessly tied the metaphor to diatribes of degeneration where "weak-brain[ed]" listeners resurface from the opera house "with a merely sensual feeling of having enjoyed a hot, nervously exciting tone-bath."[248]

In these readings, Wagner's harmonic sea was nothing but a vast resonance chamber, in which the physiological immediacy of listening to an artwork defined by its *"immediate physical portrayal"*[249] provoked some wearied responses: "Wagner seems to mean business ... We simply groan under a weight of bare realism and amorphous sound," Moritz Hauptmann wrote of *Lohengrin*. "There is something wrong somewhere," he scoffed, "when a man comes away from a drama or an opera feeling as if he had been beaten."[250] In tandem with this proto-scientific protest, water was also a motif of nature's seemingly irresistible might, and feeds into a discourse that David Blackbourn has linked to the specifically modern project of conquering nature through science. In such a reading, the material landscape provides an entry point to access Germany's cultural past; marshaling water, reclaiming marshland as fields for agriculture, and replotting the course of the Rhine to prevent flooding and aid shipping, were instances of man's mastery of natural waters that, Blackbourn argues, became particularly relevant to the modernization of German culture.[251]

Like the sensory basis of *Lautfarbe* and *Klangfarbe*, therefore, there is a constant flavor of realism in Wagner's ostensibly fantastical, aquatic rhetoric. In his conceit about the harmonic "sea," he even applies a realist substitution test. Without an ocean to connect the various allegorical shores "no light-winged ship [may] carry anything from either continent" until some "machinery, perhaps a railway, is able to bridge the waste!"[252] Consider Wagner's joke: the *Bavarian Ludwigsbahn* had first journeyed on December 7, 1835, so Beethoven (the "most daring swimmer") could only have taken the train

---

[246] Hanslick, *Music Criticisms 1846–99*, trans. Henry Pleasants (Baltimore: Penguin, 1950), 119.

[247] Nietzsche, "Nietzsche contra Wagner," 666.

[248] Max Nordau, *Degeneration* [1892], (Lincoln and London: University of Nebraska Press, 1993), 211.

[249] SSD 3: 46. Cf. PW 1: 73.

[250] Moritz Hauptmann to Louis Spohr, February 9, 1853, in *The Letters of a Leipzig Cantor*, ed. Alfred Schöne and Ferdinand Hiller (London: Richard Bentley & Son, 1892), 2: 211.

[251] David Blackbourn, *The Conquest of Nature: Water, Landscape, and the Making of Modern Germany* (New York: Norton, 2006).

[252] SSD 3: 82. Cf. PW 1: 111.

between melody and rhythm anachronistically. By intuitively linking the overwhelming natural power of the ocean to that of musical expression, Wagner rejects modern technology – the specter of a nineteenth-century channel tunnel – as the equivalent of superficial art: meaningless short cuts, effects without causes (Wagner's poetic boat used oars, not steam).[253] From his "boundless sea of harmony" to the "waves of melody," the image of water thereby informs Wagner's ability to express through sound, and like Helmholtz, he held fast to a simile between the ocean and the "nature of tones":

If melody and rhythm are the shores on which musical art touches with fertilizing contact the two continents of its primally related arts, so sound itself is her very own, liquid element, and its immeasurable expanse of waters make out the sea of *harmony*. The eye knows but the surface of this sea; its depth the depth of the heart alone can fathom. Upwards from its nocturnal sea bed it extends to the sunlit surface; the ever-widening rings of rhythm cross over on it from one shore; from the shady valleys of the other shore arise the yearning gentle breezes that rouse this calm surface to gracefully rising and sinking waves of melody.[254]

Wagner's propagating ripples ("the ever-widening rings of rhythm") parallel Helmholtz's "innumerable systems of [circular] waves" confirming that harmony and water interact intuitively on more than one level. This rebus-like vocabulary of aquatic symbols provided a means of expressing the belief in an invisible, material substance. Implicit therein is the enveloping materiality of water. This never materializes as rain – whether element or ambience – with its disconnected droplets. In the Wagnerian imagination, water remains a continuous, enveloping quality capable of propagating waves. Like the Rhine waters that collapse Coleridge's distinction between allegory and symbol, Wagner's water imagery crystallizes into a more concrete phenomenon for the scientific (or scientifically curious) mind; its structural relation to Helmholtz's sound waves enters along a path where the "sea of harmony," in addition to being merely poetic metaphor, can be read as a claim for the plausible materiality of sound.

Of course, the signified of sound / ocean waves remained undetermined: if Nietzsche saw the paradox of willful freedom and mathematical order in a waterfall,[255] Helmholtz saw an illustration of material sound from his cliff-top vantage point. The tendency of water to provoke solipsistic reflections

---

[253] SSD 4: 172. Cf. PW 2: 315. Wagner's remarks against technology are not old-fashioned so much as critical of industrialized machinery's unnatural power and failure to engage "authentically" with its environment. See SSD 3: 82–83. Cf. PW 1: 111–12.
[254] SSD 3: 83. Cf. PW 1: 112.   [255] Nietzsche, *Human, All too Human*, 131.

was evident for Wagner himself when he was ambling alongside Cosima, Nietzsche, and Nietzsche's sister, who recounts that the party sat still:

looking out over the sea of glistening silver. As we listened to the soft lapping of the waves, each one of us heard the song of his own thoughts sounding out of this sweet monotonous melody as if some magic horn were sending forth a piercingly sweet echo.[256]

Such correspondences between solipsism and illusion were confronted by Raff, who was skeptical of the hypnotic effect Wagner's wave images had on a reader. "But what do I see, my friend?!" he balked, after quoting a passage from *Das Kunstwerk der Zukunft*:

You are staring straight forward, you appear not to hear me! Ah, I see . . . Wagner's attractive description arouses your memories from Heligoland. All the magic of seascape steps before you through a willing imagination supported by lively remembrance, wake up, my friend, wake up![257]

Ironically, this freedom of interpretive reflection is opposed to the physiological determinism that proto-scientific inquiries sought to establish through color and vowel, *Klang-* and *Lautfarbe*. As noted at the outset, however, Wagner's idea of recurring musical motifs tacitly holds their signification to be learned, not innately perceivable; as A. B. Marx put it in 1854, it is "an external reminiscence acting mnemonically, but not psychologically."[258] While vocal and instrumental sound color remained a universally respected parameter of Wagner's compositional practice, he played no role directly in the scientific debate about their perception. Regardless of the extent to which his works may have provoked contributions to this discourse, as prompts to the scientific imagination, the foregoing discussion indicates how thoroughly his writings can be read through the constellation of contemporary scientific thought.

---

[256] *The Nietzsche–Wagner Correspondence*, ed. Elizabeth Foerster-Nietzsche, trans. Caroline V. Kerr (New York: Boni and Liveright, 1921), 79.

[257] "Aber was muß ich sehen, mein Freund?! Sie starren vor Sich hin, Sie scheinen mich nicht zu hören! Ach, ich errathe. . . die reizende Schilderung Wagner's ruft Ihnen Erinnerungen aus Helgoland wach; alle Zauber der Seelandschaft treten vor Ihnen, durch ein williges Gedächtniß unterstützte lebhafte Phantasie. Erwachen Sie, Freund, erwachen Sie. . ." Raff, *Die Wagnerfrage*, 72.

[258] Marx, *The Music of the Nineteenth Century and its Culture*, 97.

Epilogue: Turning off the lights

It seems only fair that the last word should go to Wagner himself, whose voice has been somewhat less than authoritative in the preceding pages. In one of the more intriguing passages from *Lohengrin* – the opera that has pivoted, for us, between so many of the dualisms in this journey through *Melodik* – Ortrud eyes a solution to her intractable problem, her mysteriously invincible adversary (Lohengrin):

> One who possesses *magic strength*
> will, if the smallest of his limbs
> is torn from him, at once be seen
> stripped of his power, yes, exposed![1]

This famous prophecy is, in many respects, an apt metaphor for the problem of idealized melody that we have been probing because it captures the need to explode the illusory "magic strength" of a musical object by means of the simultaneously desirous and dangerous objectification of that object. "Cut a finger from this god, and he will no longer be a god" is Wagner's Feuerbachian message; its silent continuation, by extension, would be that by taking a pedagogue's pen or a physiologist's scalpel to melody, one expels its inscrutable powers of expression, for better or worse. As we have seen, Wagner and Franz Brendel interpreted Lohengrin as a model of genius in these terms, and appropriately, the composer implored Liszt to "cut nothing!"[2]

But the objectification of melody came in many flavors during the course of the nineteenth century, and Wagner's role as the poster boy of Germany's *Melodielosigkeit* makes him a thoroughly ambiguous figure in this respect. On the one hand, he espoused the phonological voice as the centerpiece of all melodic expression while, on the other hand, his dry, recitative-like stichomythia made him a laughing stock for Italianist listeners. He placed human "feeling" at the fountainhead of all sensory communication, yet stubbornly rejected its basis in scientific inquiry as the "exposure of every mystery of being

---

[1] "Jed' Wesen, das, durch *Zauber stark*, / wird ihm des Leibes kleinstes Glied / entrissen nur, muss sich alsbald / ohnmächtig zeigen, wie es ist!" *Lohengrin*, act 2, scene 1. Emphasis added.

[2] Wagner to Liszt, July 2, 1850, Thun, in *Correspondence of Wagner and Liszt* (vols. 1 & 2), trans. Francis Hueffer (Cirencestor: Echo library, 2005), 46.

as mere imaginary secrets."[3] These representative contradictions betray what I have termed the parallax perspective of mid-century aesthetics: one that views the same object simultaneously from two different positions, wherein the singular object appears not to be the same as itself, and one's perspective forever flits between the two viewpoints. As we saw in our study of Wagner's philological borrowings, it seems that because the one melodic "object" Wagner did adhere to rigorously (at least for a time) has been largely discredited, commentators have marginalized its importance for his *Weltanschauung*. Speech roots, Stabreim, and vowel sounds thus form a pressure point in the parallax perspective mentioned above. Their communicative power – or "magic strength" – was thought to be historically real, i.e. scientific: something Wagner felt he could harness, and yet the implications of this reality – the continuity between *Lautfarbe* and *Klangfarbe*, the materialism in any etymological "physiognomy" – remained beneath the surface of Wagner's composition for listeners, it remained speculative, acquiring only the semblance of scientific rigor through figures such as Pohl and Köhler. (The concept of realism is of course always relative in relation to its object, and in this case, we are reminded of the so-called Thomas theorum, that "if men define situations as real, then they are real in their consequences.")

By his autumn years Wagner had had enough of pseudo-scientific speculation, and shot down ideas of musical synaesthesia in an aphorism penned more than three decades after the shimmering *Lohengrin* prelude.

I have met – intelligent – people with no sense at all of music, and for whom tonal configurations [*Tongestaltungen*] had no expression, who tried to interpret them by analogy with color-impressions; but never have I met a musical person to whom sound conveyed colors, except by a figure of speech.[4]

Of course, the scientific basis for Goethe's "physiological colors," Ule's voice, or Lotze's muscle contractions that isolated the emotion sensation of a vowel, i.e. a mechanics of the "soul," were strongly supported at the time by the monist platform of Germany's liberal academy, and thus make a legitimate claim on historical assessments of Wagner's music. While these writers do not exactly provide an insight that completely shatters our latter-day perception of Wagner's music, they foreground the contemporary fear – very real for Nietzsche – that his music does work on the nerve fibers, muscle tissue, and skin cells of his auditors.[5] "After all," he claimed of

---

[3] SSD 10: 84. Cf. PW 6: 75.   [4] SSD 12: 280. Cf. PW 8: 375.

[5] The residue of this fear finds expression with writers such as Adorno, who argued in value-laden terms that Wagner's approach inverted Hegel's: "the Hegelian definition that art is the sensuous manifestation of the idea [no longer applies]. Instead, the sensuous is so arranged as to appear to

Wagner, "aesthetics is nothing but a kind of applied physiology." Like Hauptmann earlier, he was not being facetious when he observed: "I no longer breathe easily when this music begins to affect me," and his complaint need not be read as intended, simply a critique of psychological sickness.[6] It also betrays the anxiety among listeners that Wagnerian music *does* act physiologically, and that we cannot close our ears.

By taking this principle to an extreme, writers such as Spencer and Hausegger sought to reify the entire experience of emotion and feeling as the sensations of muscular contractions, i.e. Wagner's would-be scientific rationale for sound that is *gefühlsverständlich*. The fantasy of a composer's physiological power dominates this landscape of ideas, and while skeptical commentators have tended to formulate this negatively (where "style becomes the sum of all the stimuli registered by the totality of his senses"),[7] it can equally break through the barrier of cultural institutionalism; despite Wagner's passionate philology, in other words, his modes – or "materialities" – of communication reach the illiterate and uneducated just as powerfully as the privileged literati, as Kittler put it: "an aesthetics of applied physiology . . . required neither training nor elite culture."[8] So if, in Wagnerian sonorous melodies, we have not been learning about a *new* cultural "object," we have all the same been confronted with its own hidden presuppositions and become aware of another – disturbing – side of that object that we knew all along: cognitive surrender to the sheer materiality of sound.

In her celebrated essay on "Wagner's Fluids," Susan Sontag thought of *Tristan* act 3 as "a platform against lucidity" where not eroticism but the surrender of consciousness is the point: "they want the lights turned off. Isolde's last words . . . are a description of losing consciousness: *ertrinken, versinken / unbewusst höchste Lust!*"[9] In some ways, this observation establishes the narrative end point for Chapter 6. Neural networks, after all, require no consciousness when stimulated by acids or electrodes – the analogue of an objectified melodic expression. Correspondingly, in the search among German physiologists for a mechanical basis for sensory perception of melody, every movement towards emotional or physiological specificity became a hemming-in of interpretation in the realm of art, which – for music – entailed an act of listening that becomes ever more akin to an involuntary physical

be in control of the idea." T. W. Adorno, *In Search of Wagner*, trans. Rodney Livingstone (London and New York: Verso, 2005), 96.

[6] Nietzsche, "Nietzsche contra Wagner," *The Portable Nietzsche*, 664.
[7] Adorno, *In Search of Wagner*, 91.
[8] Friedrich Kittler, *Discourse Networks 1800–1900* (Stanford University Press, 1990), 189.
[9] Susan Sontag, "Wagner's Fluids," *London Review of Books* (December 10, 1987), 8–9.

reflex: the ultimate loss of contemplative freedom. The possibility that such control (or manipulation) could be transferred to musical sound – conceived as an experience of immersion in vibrating air masses where "to hear is to be touched, both physically and emotionally"[10] – constitutes a dark fantasy of Wagner reception and remains a specter over those writers who sought to uncover a "science of feeling": a traceable physiological link between stimulus, sensation, and emotion.

In 1854, Hanslick had cautiously predicted the future possibility of "an 'exact' science of music after the model of chemistry or physiology,"[11] though he later complained of being subject to irresistible chemical stimulation in just this manner when listening to Richard Strauss' *Don Juan*: "The composer may thus be compared with a routine chemist who well understands how to mix all the elements of musical–sensual stimulation to produce a stupefying 'pleasure gas.' For my part I prefer, with all due homage to such chemical skill, not to be its victim."[12] This quip is only a euphemism for music Hanslick didn't like; but if he presents one view, Nietzsche offered another: the decadent motive for seeking out stimuli, fearless of the results, in what amounted to artistic voyeurism. "The essential thing is the type of new desire, the wish to imitate and to experience the lives of others, disguise, dissimulation of the soul. Romantic art is only a make-shift substitute for a defective 'reality.'"[13] The implication is that artistic stimulation is artificial because neural excitement with no connection to (authentic) experience outside the grip of art is tantamount to galvanism – or, in the context of new media: virtual reality. One of the modern inheritances of this claim is Robert Nozick's "experience machine," a thought experiment in which individuals are given the choice whether or not to enter a machine that could simulate any pleasurable experience they wished – indistinguishable from reality – through cerebral stimulation. Nozick's second argument (of three) against entering the machine rhymes with Hanslick's dislike of "pleasure gas," namely that we want a unique identity: "someone floating in a tank is an indeterminate blob."[14]

Reflex functions flatten out the ground of individuality, presupposing a uniform response that is incapable of being misunderstood – the extreme

---

[10] Frances Dyson, *Sounding New Media: Immersion and Embodiment in the Arts and Culture* (Berkeley: University of California Press, 2009), 4.

[11] Hanslick, *On the Musically Beautiful*, 35.   [12] Hanslick, *Musical Criticisms 1846–99*, 292.

[13] Nietzsche, *The Will to Power*, 440.

[14] Robert Nozick, *Anarchy, State, and Utopia* (Oxford: Basil Blackwell, 1974), 43. The other two arguments Nozick gives against entering the machine are that "We want to do certain things, and not just have the experience of doing them . . . [and that] plugging into an experience machine limits us to man-made reality." *Ibid.*

edge of intuitively comprehensible melody. The historiography of Wagner studies has come to associate this control of the physically vulnerable subject with what, after the Second World War, is often called Wagner's proto-fascism (i.e. the Nietzschian trope of an overblown sensuality that keeps audiences pinned in their seats in order to subject them to "mytho-logical configurations" of feudal socialism).[15] But earlier figures like William James passionately refuted the theory that we are responsive automata, that "feeling is a mere collateral product of our nervous processes, unable to react upon them any more than a shadow reacts on the steps of the traveller whom it accompanies."[16] Common sense, he asserts, shows that even a live frog with an intact brain will not respond in predictable ways to stimuli: "The signal may be given, but ideas, emotions or caprices will be aroused instead of the fatal motor reply."[17]

Wagner, as we have seen, also rejected the deterministic logic of this strand of materialism, though for different reasons, even if the mid-century reception of his music and vocabulary was inevitably characterized to some extent by the intellectual currents of sensuality and physical stimuli ema-nating from Johannes Müller's Berlin.[18] In this context, Brünnhilde's plea that a chemically forgetful Siegfried "*forced* delight from me, and love" resonates provocatively.[19] But Wagner's music is not just erotic spasm, of course; it is precisely because anatomical excitation forms only one contrib-utory strand to the dense woof of his reception that he continues to elude reductive historical categories. What is lost, he protested, in a deterministic worldview based on the physical sciences is "spontaneity itself"; and this surely traverses the gamut of unpredictable reactions to *Laut-* and *Klangfarben* within his melodies, however contrary this may be to his urge to be understood precisely, and on his own terms. "Few puzzle any more," Sontag reflected, "about what Wagner's operas *mean*. Now Wagner is just enjoyed – as a drug."[20] Such deliverance from his political reception, though well-intentioned, can only sound ironic against the heritage of material incursion and artificial stimuli from which it originates.

Which brings us back to Ortrud's tuneless recitation about severing Lohengrin's finger – or the puncturing of idealism with a sharp scalpel.

---

[15] On this sizeable topic, see, most recently, Alain Badiou, *Five Lessons on Wagner* (London and New York: Verso, 2010), 9ff.; and Slavoj Žižek, "Why is Wagner Worth Saving?" in Adorno, *In Search of Wagner*, viii–xxvii.

[16] William James, "Are we Automata?" *Mind* 4 (1879), 1–22, here 1.

[17] *Ibid.*, 4. See also *Principles of Psychology* [1890] (New York: Cosimo, 2007) 1: 130ff.

[18] See Laura Otis, *Müller's Lab*, 6ff.

[19] "Er zwang mir Lust und Liebe ab" *Götterdämmerung*, act 2, scene 4.

[20] Sontag, "Wagner's Fluids," 9.

The double vision that pits the idealist viewpoint against the realism of a materialist perspective wears a Janus face. Germany's Wilhelmine future looked increasingly toward scientific materialism, and Wagner's recalcitrant emphasis on genius and the unscientific criteria of "feeling" and "intuitive knowledge"[21] makes him perhaps just as much a cultural reactionary as an artistic revolutionary during the 1850s. Another way of putting this is that, already in 1848, Ortrud's modernist observation cedes the final victory between idealism and materialism to the latter. And here, a final Wagnerian contradiction is exposed: the sorceress-turned-scientist lacks the proper word for the means by which Lohengrin will be undone; she intuits it, but cannot name it. Wagner similarly refused to move beyond historical linguistics for his "science" of melody that "actualizes thought," even while his ambiguously materialist metaphors and suggestive imagery pointed to that which he could not bring himself to name – the science of sound. It was easier simply to say: "we tersely sum up music's nature in the concept – Melody."[22]

[21] SSD 10: 84. Cf. PW 6: 75.   [22] SSD 3: 304. Cf. PW 2: 103.

Appendix A: Books on language in Wagner's Dresden library

Author	Title	Publication	Topics
Bemmel, Eugène van	*De la langue et de la poésie provençales*	Bruxelles: A. Vandale, 1846	historical linguistics
Gervinus, G. G.	*Geschichte der poetischen National-Literatur der Deutschen* (5 vols.)	Leipzig: Wilhelm Engelmann, 1840–44	historical linguistics and literature
Gervinus, G. G.	*Handbuch der Geschichte der poetischen National-Literatur der Deutschen*	Leipzig: Wilhelm Engelmann, 1842	historical linguistics and literature
Graff, E. G.	*Diskuta. Denkmäler deutscher Sprache und Literatur, aus alten Handschriften zum ersten Male theils herausgegeben, theils nachgewiesen und beschrieben.* (3 vols.)	Stuttgart u. Tübingen: J. G. Cotta, 1826–29	historical linguistics and literature
Grimm, Jacob	*Deutsche Grammatik* (vol. 1 only)	Göttingen: Heinrich Dieterich, 1840 [3rd edn.]	grammar, etymology, historical linguistics
Grimm, Jacob	*Geschichte der Deutschen Sprache* (2 vols.)	Leipzig: Weidmannsche Buchhandlung, 1848	historical linguistics
Grimm, Jacob	*Ueber den altdeutschen Meistergesang*	Göttingen: Heinrich Dieterich, 1811	historical linguistics
Hagen, Godefrit	*Des Meisters Godefrit Hagen, der Zeit Stadtschreibers, Reimchronik der Stadt Cöln aus dem dreizehnten Jahrhundert. Mit*	Cöln am Rhein: M. DüMont-Schauberg, 1834	dictionary, historical linguistics

Author	Title	Publication	Topics
	Anmerkungen und Wörterbuch nach der einzigen alten Handschrift zum erstenmale vollständig herausgegeben von E. von Groote, Stadtrath.		
Herder, Johann Gottfried von	*Ausgewählte Werke in Einem Bande*	Stuttgart u. Tübingen: J. G. Cotta, 1844	philosophy of language, philology
Hornig, C. August	*Glossarium zu den Gedichten Walthers von der Vogelweide nebst einem Reimverzeichniss.*	Quedlinburg: L. L. Franke, 1844	dictionary, historical linguistics
Lachmann, Karl u. Wilhelm Wackernagel	*Zu den Nibelungen und zur Klage. Anmerkungen von Karl Lachmann. Wörterbuch von W. Wackernagel*	Berlin: G. Reimer, 1836	dictionary, historical linguistics
Minnesinger	*Deutsche Liederdichter des zwölften, dreizehnten und vierzehnten Jahrhunderts, aus alten bekannten Handschriften und früheren Drucken gesammelt und berichtigt, mit den Lesarten derselben, Geschichte des Lebens der Dichter und ihrer Werke, Sangweisen der Lieder, Reimverzeichnis der Anfänge, und Abbildungen sämmtlicher Handschriften von Fr. Heinrich von der Hagen (2 vols.)*	Leipzig: J. A. Barth, 1838	historical linguistics and literature
Rühs, Friedrich	*Die Edda nebst einer Einleitung über nordische Poesie und Mythologie und einem Anhang über die historische Literatur der Isländer*	Berlin: Realschulbuch-handlung, 1812	historical linguistics and literature
Saxo Grammaticus	*Saxonis Grammatici Historia Danica. Recensuit et commen-tariis illustravit Petrus Erasmus Müller (2 vols.)*	Havniae: Gyldendal, 1839	historical linguistics

Author	Title	Publication	Topics
Vaulu-Spá	*Das älteste Denkmal germanisch-nordischer Sprache, nebst einigen Gedanken über Nordens Wissen und Glauben und nordische Dichtkunst von Ludwig Ettmüller*	Leipzig: Weidmann, 1830	historical linguistics
Volkslieder	*Alte, hoch- und niederdeutsche mit Abhandlung und Anmerkungen herausgegeben von Ludwig Uhland*	Stuttgart u. Tübingen, J. G. Cotta, 1844–45 [2nd edn.]	historical linguistics and literature
Ziemann, Adolf	*Mittelhochdeutsches Wörterbuch zum Handgebrauch. Nebst grammatischer Einleitung*	Quedlinburg u. Leipzig: G. Basse, 1838	dictionary, grammar, historical linguistics

Appendix B: Books on language in Wagner's Wahnfried library

Author	Title	Publication	Topics
Abel, Heinrich F.	*Die deutschen Personen-Namen*	Berlin: Herz, 1853	etymology
Apel, August	*Metrik* (2 vols.)	Leipzig: Weygand, 1834	linguistics
Becker, Karl F.	*Schulgrammatik der deutschen Sprache*	Frankfurt a. M.: Herrmann, 1835	grammar
Benecke, Friedrich G.	*Beyträge zur Kenntnis der altdeutschen Sprache*	Göttingen: Dieterich, 1810–32	literature of the Middle Ages
Bode, Georg, H.	*Geschichte der Hellenischen Dichtkunst* (3 vols.)	Leipzig: Heinrich Bode, 1840	historical linguistics
Bopp, Franz	*Vergleichende Grammatik des Sanskrit, Send, Armenischen, Griechischen, Lateinischen, Litauischen, Altslavischen, Gothischen und Deutschen* (3 vols.)	Leipzig: Dümmler, 1868–71 (3rd edn.)	linguistics, comparative grammar
Brandstätter, Franz A.	*Die Gallicismen in der deutschen Schriftsprache mit besonderer Rücksicht auf unsere neuere schönwissenschaftliche Literatur*	Leipzig: Hartknoch, 1874	linguistics, historical linguistics and literature
Braun, Julius	*Naturgeschichte der Sage: Rückführung aller religiösen Ideen, Sagen, Systeme auf ihren gemeinsamen Stammbaum u. ihre letzte Wurzel* (2 vols.)	Munich: Bruckmann, 1864–65	etymology, historical linguistics and literature

Author	Title	Publication	Topics
Braune, Wilhelm (ed.)	*Beiträge zur Geschichte der deutschen Sprache und Literatur*	Halle: Lippert, 1874	linguistics, historical linguistics
Colebrooke, H. T.	*Abhandlung über die heiligen Schriften der Indier*	Leipzig: Teubner, 1847	theology, Sanskrit
Diez, Friedrich	*Grammatik der romanischen Sprachen* (3 vols.)	Bonn: Diez, 1870	grammar
Düringsfeld, Ida von. (ed.)	*Sprichwörter der germanischen und romanischen Sprachen* (2 vols.)	Leipzig: Fries, 1872–75	linguistics
Geiger, Ludwig	*Ursprung und Entwicklung der menschlichen Sprache und Vernunft* (2 vols.)	Stuttgart: Cotta, 1868–72	linguistics and historical linguistics
Gerber, Gustav	*Die Sprache als Kunst*	Bromberg: Mittler, 1871	linguistics
Gley, Gérard	*Langue et littérature des anciens Francs*	Paris: Michaud, 1814	etymology and historical linguistics
Gobineau, Arthur	*Traité des écritures cunéiformes*	Paris: Didot, 1864	historical writing systems
Grimm, Jacob	*Kleinere Schriften* (8 vols.)	Berlin: Dümmler, 1864–71	historical linguistics, mythology
Grimm, Jacob	*Deutsche Grammatik* (4 vols.)	Göttingen: Dieterich, 1822–37 [2nd edn.]	grammar, etymology, historical linguistics
Grimm, Jacob	*Deutsche Grammatik* (1st vol. only)	Göttingen: Dieterich, 1840 [3rd edn.]	grammar, etymology, linguistics
Grimm, J./W.	*Deutsches Wörterbuch*	Leipzig: Hirzel, 1854–1961; ongoing project	etymological dictionary, historical linguistics
Grimm, Jacob	*Geschichte der deutschen Sprache*	Leipzig: Hirzel, 1868 [3rd edn.]	historical linguistics
Grimm, Jacob	*Reden und Abhandlungen*	Berlin: Dümmler, 1864	linguistics and historical linguistics

Author	Title	Publication	Topics
Grimm, Jacob	*Abhandlungen zur Litteratur u. Grammatik*	Berlin: Dümmler, 1866	linguistics, grammar
Grimm, Jacob	*Rezensionen und vermischte Aufsätze* (2 vols.)	Berlin: Dümmler, 1869–71	linguistics
Grimm, Wilhelm	*Ueber deutsche Runen*	Göttingen: Dieterich, 1821	historical linguistics
Hahn, Karl A.	*Althochdeutsche Grammatik mit einigen Lesestücken und Glossen*	Prag: Calve, 1852	historical grammar, dictionary
Hahn, Karl A.	*Mittelhochdeutsche Grammatik*	Frankfurt a. M.: Brönner, 1842–47	historical grammar
Hahn, Karl A.	*Mittelhochdeutsche Grammatik*	Frankfurt a. M.: Brönner, 1871 [2nd edn.]	historical grammar
Heyse, Johann C.	*Theoretisch–praktische Deutsche Grammatik oder Lehrbuch zum richtigen Sprechen, Lesen und Schreiben der deutschen Sprache, nebst einer kurzen Geschichte und Verslehre desselben* (2 vols.)	Hannover: Hahn, 1839–49	grammar
Hoefer, Albert (ed.)	*Zeitschrift für die Wissenschaft der Sprache* (vol. 1 only)	Berlin: Reimer, 1845	linguistics journal
Holtzmann, Adolf (ed.)	*Das Niebelungenlied*, vol. 1 "Die specielle Lautlehre"	Leipzig: Brockhaus, 1870	grammar, historical linguistics
Littré, Émile	*Histoire de la langue française: études sur les origin, l'étymologie, la grammaire, les dialectes, la versification, et les lettres au moyen âge* (2 vols.)	Paris: Dider, 1863	etymology, linguistics, historical linguistics
Matthiä, August	*Ausführliche griechische Grammatik* (2 vols.)	Leipzig: Vogel, 1825–27 [2nd edn]	historical grammar

Author	Title	Publication	Topics
Obermüller, Wilhelm	*Deutsche-Keltisches, Geschichtliche-Geographisches Wörterbuch: zur Erklaerung der Fluss- Gerb- Orts- Gau- Völker- und Personen-Namen Europas, West-Asiens und Nord-Afrikas im allgemeinen wie insbesondere Deutschlands nebst den daraus sich ergebenden Folgerungen für die Urgeschichte der Menschheit* (2 vols.)	Berlin: Denicke, 1872	comparative dictionary, historical linguistics
Pott, August F.	*Die Personennamen, insbesondere die Familiennamen und ihre Entstehungsarten, auch unter Berücksichtigung der Ortsnamen*	Leipzig: Brockhaus, 1853	etymology, linguistics
Pott, August F.	*Die Ungleichheit menschlicher Rassen: hauptsächlich vom sprachwissenschaftlichen Standpunkte, unter besonderer Berücksichtigung von des Grafen von Gobineau gleichnamigem Werke; mit einem Ueberblicke über die Sprachverhältnisse der Völker*	Lemgo u. Detmold: Meyer, 1856	theories of race
Pott, August F.	*Etymologische Forschungen auf dem Gebiete der Indo-Germanischen Sprachen: unter Berücksichtigung ihrer Hauptformen, Sanskrit, Zend–Persisch, Griechisch–Lateinisch, Litauisch–Slawisch, Germanisch und Keltisch* (6 vols.)	Lemgo u. Detmold: Meyer, 1859–76 [2nd edn.]	etymology, historical linguistics

Author	Title	Publication	Topics
Rapp, Moritz	*Versuch einer Physiologie der Sprache nebst historischer Entwicklung der abendländischen Idiome nach physiologischen Grundsätzen* (4 vols.)	Stuttgart u. Tübingen: Cotta, 1836–41	etymology, linguistics, physiology
Rapp, Moritz	*Grundriß der Grammatik des indisch-europäischen Sprachstammes* (2 vols.)	Stuttgart: Cotta, 1852–55	historical grammar, linguistics
Riecke, Carl F.	*Die Schichtung der Völker und Sprachen in Deutschland: auf Grund der vergleichenden Sprachforschung nachgewiesen an Orts-, Familien-, Their-Namen, Titeln und Idiotismen*	Gera: Strebel, 1872	German history, historical linguistics
Ritschl, Friedrich	*Canticum und Diverbium bei Plautus*	Bonn: Georgi, 1871	linguistics, Classical literature
Schlegel, Friedrich	*Ueber die Sprache und Weisheit der Indier: ein Beitrag zur Begründung der Alterthumskunde*	Heidelberg: Mohr u. Zimmer, 1808	linguistics, Indian literature and philosophy
Schmitthenner, Friedrich	*Ursprachlehre: Entwurf zu einem System der Grammatik mit besonderer Rücksicht auf die Sprachen des indisch-teutschen Stammes: das Sanskrit, das Persische, die pelasgischen, slavischen und teutschen Sprachen*	Frankfurt a. M.: Herrmann, 1826	historical linguistics, historical and comparative grammar
Schulze, Ernst	*Gothisches Glossar*	Magdeburg: Baensch, 1848	historical dictionary, linguistics
Stark, Franz	*Die Kosenamen der Germanen: eine Studie; mit drei Excursen: 1. Über Zunamen; 2. Über den Ursprung die zusammengesetzten Namen; 3. Über besondere*	Vienna: Tendler & Co., 1868	history of German names

Author	Title	Publication	Topics
	friesische Namensformen u. Verkürzungen		
Stephanius, Stephanus J.	*Saxonis grammatici historiae danicae libri XVI*	Sorae: Moltken, 1645	historical linguistics, historical grammar
Stephanius, Stephanus J.	*Stephani Johannis Stephanii notae ueberiores in historiam danicam Saxonis grammatici: una cum prolegomenis ad easdem notas*	Sorae: Crusius, n. d.	historical linguistics
Wack, Johann C.	*Kurze Anzeigung: wie nemlich die uralte Teutsche Sprache meistentheils Ihren Ursprung aus dem Celtisch-oder Chaldaeischen habe / und das Beyrische vom Syrischen herkomme*	Regenpurg: Hagen, 1713	historical linguistics, grammar
Westphal, Rudolph	*Philosophisch–historische Grammatik der deutschen Sprache*	Jena: Mauke, 1869	etymology, historical linguistics, grammar
Xylander, Josef von	*Das Sprachgeschlecht der Titanen: Darstellung der ursprünglichen Verwandtschaft der tatarischen Sprachen unter sich und mit der Sprache der Hellenen, und Andeutung der zunächst daraus hervorgehenden Folgen für die Geschichte der Sprachen und Völker*	Frankfurt a. M.: Sauerländer, 1837	historical linguistics
Zeuss, I. C.	*Grammatica Celtica: e moumentis vetustis tam hibernicae linguae quam Britannicarum dialectarum Cambricae Cornicae Aremorcae comparitis Gallicae priscae reliquiis*	Berlin: Wiedman-nos, 1871 [2nd edn.]	historical Celtic grammar, linguistics

Select bibliography

Abbate, Carolyn. *Unsung Voices: Opera and Musical Narrative in the Nineteenth Century*. Princeton University Press, 1991.

  In Search of Opera. Princeton University Press, 2002.

  "Music – Drastic or Gnostic?," *Critical Enquiry* 30 (2004): 505–36.

Abrams, M. H. *The Mirror and the Lamp*. Oxford University Press, 1971.

  Natural Supernaturalism: Tradition and Revolution in Romantic Literature. New York: Norton, 1973.

Adler, Guido. "Richard Wagner und die Wissenschaft," *Neue Freie Presse* (May 10, 1903): 12–13.

Adorno, Theodor W. *Musikalische Schriften*. 4 vols., edited by Rolf Tiedemann. Frankfurt am Main, 1982.

  Aesthetic Theory, translated by Robert Hullot-Kentor. London: Continuum, 2002.

  In Search of Wagner, translated by Rodney Livingstone. London: Verso, 2005.

  Zu einer Theorie der musikalischen Reproduktion. Frankfurt am Main: Suhrkamp, 2005.

Alberti, C. E. R. *Richard Wagner und seine Stellung in der Geschichte der dramatischen Musik*. Stettin: Müller, 1856.

Albright, Daniel. *Beckett and Aesthetics*. Cambridge University Press, 2003.

Allfeld, J. B. *Tristan und Isolde von Richard Wagner. Kritisch beleuchtet mit einleitenden Bemerkungen über Melodie und Musik*. Munich: C. Fritsch, 1865.

Ambros, Wilhelm August. *Die Grenzen der Musik und Poesie. Eine Studie zur Aesthetik der Tonkunst*. Leipzig: Heinrich Matthes, 1855. English translation by J. H. Cornell. *The Boundaries of Music and Poetry*. New York: G. Schirmer, 1893.

Andersen, Hans Christen. *The Complete Fairy Tales and Stories*, edited and translated by Erik Christian Haugaard. New York: Anchor Books, 1983.

Applegate, Celia. *A Nation of Provincials: The German Idea of Heimat*. Berkeley & Los Angeles: University of California Press, 1990.

Applegate, Celia and Pamela Potter (eds.). *Music and German National Identity*. University of Chicago Press, 2002.

Aristotle. *The Poetics*, translated by Stephen Halliwell. Cambridge MA: Harvard University Press, 1995.

Bacon, Francis. *The Essayes or Councele, Civil and Morall* (1597–1625), edited by Michael Kiernan. Oxford: Clarendon Press, 1985.

Badiou, Alain. *Five Lessons on Wagner*. London: Verso, 2010.

Bailey, Robert, "Wagner's Musical Sketches for Siegfrieds Tod," in *Studies in Music History: Essay for Oliver Strunk*, edited by Harold Powers, 459–94. Princeton University Press, 1968.

Bakta, Richard. "Richard Wagner und die Wissenschaft," *Bohemia* (May 13, 1903): 17.

Baragwanath, Nicholas. *The Italian Traditions and Puccini: Compositional Theory and Practice in Nineteenth-Century Opera.* Bloomington, IN: Indiana University Press, 2011.

Barnes, William. *A Philological Grammar.* London: John Russell Smith, 1854.

Barthes, Roland. *Image – Music – Text*, translated by Stephen Heath. New York: Hill and Wang, 1978.

The Responsibility of Forms, translated by Richard Howard. New York: Hill and Wang, 1988.

Barzun, Jacques. *Darwin, Marx, Wagner: Critique of a Heritage* [1941]. Rpt. New York: Doubleday Anchor books, 1958.

Bates, Jennifer Ann. *Hegel's Theory of Imagination.* State University of New York Press, 2004.

Baudelaire, Charles. *Baudelaire as a Literary Critic*, translated by Lois Boe Hyslop and Francis E. Hyslop. Pennsylvania State University Press, 1964.

Selected Writings on Art and Literature, translated by P. E. Charvet. London: Penguin, 1972.

Les Feurs du mal et oeuvres choisies, translated by Wallace Fowlie. New York: Dover, 1992.

Baudrillard, Jean. *Simulacra and Simulation*, translated by Sheila Faria Glaser. Ann Arbor: University of Michigan Press, 1994.

Bauer, Karoline. *Memoirs of Karoline Bauer.* London: Remington & Co., 1885.

Bayer, Josef. *Aesthetik im Umrissen: Zur allgemeineren philosophischen Orientierung auf dem Gebiete der Kunst.* 2 vols. Prague: Heinrich Mercy, 1856.

Becker, Julius. "Theorie: J. C. Lobe, 'Compositions-Lehre,'" *Neue Zeitschrift für Musik* 25 (1844).

Bekker, Paul. "Zum Gedächtnis K. Fr. Weitzmann," *Allgemeine musikalische Musik-Zeitung* 35 (1908): 577.

"Zum Gedächtnis K. Fr. Weitzmann," in *Wagner: Das Leben im Werke.* Berlin and Leipzig: Deutsche Verlags-Anstalt Stuttgart, 1924. English translation by M. M. Bozman. *Richard Wagner: His Life in His Work.* New York: Norton & Co., 1931.

Bergson, Henri. *Oeuvres*, edited by André Robinet. 3rd edn. Paris: Presses Universitaires de France, 1972.

Berlin, Isaiah. *Three Critics of the Enlightenment: Vico, Hamann, Herder.* Princeton University Press, 2000.

Berlioz, Hector. *Les Musiciens et la musique.* Paris: Calmann-Lévy, 1903.

A travers chants, edited by Léon Guichard. Paris: Gründ, 1971.

The Art of Music and Other Essays, translated by Elizabeth Csicsery-Ronay. Bloomington: Indiana University Press, 1994.

Critique musicale I: 1823–1834, edited by H. Robert Cohen and Yves Gérard. Paris: Bucht/Chastel, 1996.

Bernd, Clifford. "The Emergence of *Poetischer Realismus* as a term of Literary Criticism in German," in *Thematics Reconsidered*, edited by Frank Trommler, 229–36. Amsterdam: Rodopi, 1995.

Bernstein, Susan. "Fear of Music?" in *Nietzsche and the Feminine*, edited by Peter J. Burgard, 104–34. University of Virginia Press, 1994.

"In Formel: Wagner und Liszt," *New German Critique* 69 (1996): 85–97.

Berry, Mark. *Treacherous Bonds and Laughing Fire: Politics and Religion in Wagner's* Ring. Aldershot: Ashgate, 2006.

Bie, Oscar. "Melody" translated by Theodor Backer. *The Musical Quarterly* 2 (1916): 402–17.

Bingham, Walter van Dyke. *Studies in Melody*. Baltimore: Review Publishing Company, 1910.

Bischoff, Ludwig. "Die Melodie der Sprache," *Niederrheinische Musik-Zeitung* 14 (1853): 105–09.

"*Lohengrin*, Oper von Richard Wagner," *Niederrheinische Musik-Zeitung* 6 (1854): 33–36, 41–44.

"Stimmen der Kritik über Richard Wagner," *Niederrheinische Musik-Zeitung* 11–12 (1855): 81–84, 89–91, 276–79, 284–86.

"Richard Wagner's *Lohengrin* in Wien," *Niederrheinische Musik-Zeitung* 38 (1858): 285–86.

Blachard, Henri. "Mélodies de Meyerbeer," *Revue et Gazette Musicale de Paris* 68 (November 29, 1840): 580–81.

Blackbourn, David. *History of Germany, 1780–1918*. 2nd edn. Oxford: Blackwell, 2003.

The Conquest of Nature: Water, Landscape, and the Making of Modern Germany. New York: Norton, 2006.

Blakely, Lloyd George, "Johann Conrad Beissel and Music of the Ephrata Cloister," *Journal of Research in Music Education* 15 (1967): 120–38.

Bois-Reymond, Emil du. *Reden*. 2 vols. Leipzig: Veit, 1887.

Bolz, Norbert. *Theorie der neuen Medien*. Munich: Raben, 1990.

Bopp, Franz. *Vergleichende Grammatik des Sanskrit, Zend, Griechischen, Lateinischen, Litauischen, Gotischen und Deutschen*. Berlin, 1833–52.

Borchmeyer, Dieter. *Richard Wagner: Theory and Theater*, translated by Stewart Spencer. Oxford University Press, 2002.

"Critique as Passion and Polemic: Nietzsche and Wagner," in *The Cambridge Companion to Wagner*, edited by Thomas Grey, 192–202. Cambridge University Press, 2008.

Boulez, Pierre. *Orientations*, translated by Martin Cooper. London and Boston: Faber, 1986.

Bowie, Andrew. *Aesthetics and Subjectivity: From Kant to Nietzsche*. Worcester: Billing & Sons, 1990.

Brandt, Torstend. *Johann Christian Lobe*. Göttingen: Vadenhoeck & Ruprecht, 2002.

Branscombe, Peter. "The Dramatic Texts," in *The Wagner Handbook*, edited by Ulrich Müller and Peter Wapnewski, 269–86. Cambridge, MA: Harvard University Press, 1992.

Braun, Max. "Max 'versus' Marx: Critical Analysis of A. B. Marx's 'Musical Composition' with Additional Commentary on Music Training," *The New York Musical World* 18 (1857): 532–33, 566–67, 615–16.

Breidbach, Olaf. "Zur Argumentations- und Vermittlungsstrategie in Müllers Handbuch der Physiologie des Menschen," *Annals of the History and Philosophy of Biology* 10/2005 (2006): 3–30.

Breig, Werner. "Kompositionsentwürfe Richard Wagners zu 'Lohengrin' und 'Der Ring des Niebelungen,'" *Die Zeitschrift des Richard Wagner Verband International* 35 (2001).

Bremer, Thomas. "Charakter / charakteristisch," in *Ästhetische Grundbegriffe: Historisches Wörterbuch. 7 vols.*, edited by Karlheinz Barck, Martin Fontius, Dieter Schlenstedt, Burkhart Steinwachs, Friedrich Wolfzettel, 772–93. Stuttgart and Weimar: J. J. Metzler, 2000.

Brendel, Franz. "Zur Einleitung," *Neue Zeitschrift für Musik* 22 (1845): 6.

"Leipziger Musikleben," *Neue Zeitschrift für Musik* 18 (March 1, 1846).

"Das Bewußtsein der Neuzeit, das moderne Ideal," *Neue Zeitschrift für Musik* 30 (1849): 233ff.

Geschichte der Musik in Italien, Deutschland und Frankreich von den ersten christlichen Zeiten bis auf die Gegenwart. Leipzig: Bruno Hinze, 1852.

"Der Kampf des Alten und Neuen," *Anregungen für Kunst, Leben und Wissenschaft* 1 (1856): 45–47.

"Die Melodie der Sprache," *Anregungen für Kunst, Leben und Wissenschaft* 1 (1856): 10–28.

"Einige Worte über *Lohengrin* zum besseren Verständniß desselben," *Neue Zeitschrift für Musik* 8–10 (1859): 89–92, 109–111.

"Lohengrin als dramatischer Charakter," *Anregungen für Kunst, Leben und Wissenschaft* 4 (1859): 265–73.

"Zur Eröffnung des 50. Bandes der Zeitschrift," *Neue Zeitschrift für Musik* 50 (1859): 1–2.

Brinkmann, Reinhold. "Wunder, Realität und die Figur der Grenzüberschreitung," *Bayreuther Festspiele Programheft: Lohengrin* (1979): 1–105.

Bryson, Norman. "The Gaze in the Expanded Field," in *Vision and Visuality*, edited by Hal Foster, 87–113. Seattle: Bay Press, 1988.

Budden, Julian. *The Operas of Verdi.* 3 vols. Oxford: Clarendon Press, 1992.

Bull, Michael and Les Black (eds.) *The Auditory Culture Reader.* New York: Berg, 2003.

Burford, Mark. "Hanslick's Idealist Materialism," *19th-Century Music* 30 (2006): 166–81.

Burmeister, Johannes, *Musica autoschediastike.* Rostock: C. Reusnerus, 1601.

Musical Poetics [1606], translated by Benito V. Rivera. New Haven: Yale University Press, 1983.

Casillo, Robert. *The Empire of Stereotypes: Germaine de Staël and the Idea of Italy.* New York: Palgrave Macmillan, 2006.

Chorley, Henry. *Modern German Music: Recollections and Criticism.* 2 vols. London: Smith Elder & Co., 1854.

Thirty Years' Musical Recollections, edited by Ernest Newman. New York: Vienna House, 1972.

Clarke, Arthur C. *The Collected Stories of Arthur C. Clarke.* London: Gollancz, 2001.

Cohen, Mitchell. "To the Dresden barricades: the genesis of Wagner's political ideas," in *The Cambridge Companion to Wagner*, edited by Thomas Grey, 47–64. Cambridge University Press, 2008.

Coleridge, Samuel Taylor. *Aids to Reflection* [1825], edited by Henry Nelson Coleridge. New York: Swards, Stanford & Co., 1839.

The Collected Works of Samuel Taylor Coleridge. 23 vols. [projected]. Edited by J. Engell, W. J. Bate, J. R. D. J. Jackson, *et al.* Princeton University Press, 1972.

Biographia Literaria [1817], edited by George Watson. London: J. M. Dent & Sons, 1975.

Cooke, Deryck. "Wagner's Operatic Apprenticeship," *The Musical Times* 106 (1965): 103–05.

Cowen, Roy C. *Der Poetische Realismus: Kommentar zu einer Epoche.* Munich: Winkler, 1985.

Cramer, Alfred. "Of Serpentina and Stenography: Shapes of Handwriting in Romantic Melody," *19th-Century Music* 30 (2006): 133–65.

Cuéllar, David Pavón. *From the Conscious Interior to an Exterior Unconscious: Lacan, Discourse Analysis and Social Psychology.* London: Karnac, 2010.

Czolbe, Heinrich. *Neue Darstellung des Sensualismus.* Leipzig: Hermann Costenoble, 1855.

Dahlhaus, Carl. *Richard Wagner's Music Drama*, translated by Mary Whittall. Cambridge University Press, 1979.

Foundations of Music History, translated by J. B. Robinson. Cambridge University Press, 1983.

Die Musiktheorie im 18. und 19. Jahrhundert. 2 vols. Darmstadt: Wissenschaftliche Buchgesellschaft, 1984.

Klassische und romantische Musikästhetik. Laaber, 1988.

Nineteenth-Century Music, translated by J. Bradford Robinson. Berkeley and Los Angeles: University of California Press, 1989.

Dahlhaus, Carl and L. U. Abraham. *Melodielehre.* Cologne: Hans Gerig, 1972.

The Idea of Absolute Music, translated by Roger Lustig. University of Chicago Press, 1989.

Daniels, Roland. *Mikrokosmos: Entwurf einer Physiologischen Anthropologie* [1851], edited by Helmut Elsner. Frankfurt am Main: Peter Lang, 1988.

Danuser, Hermann. *Musikalische Prosa.* Regensburg: G. Bosse, 1975.

Danuser, Hermann and Herfried Münkler (eds.), *Zukunftsbilder: Richard Wagners Revolution und ihre Folgen in Kunst und Politik.* Schliengen: Argus, 2002.

Darcy, Warren. *Wagner's Das Rheingold*. Oxford University Press, 1993.

Darwin, Charles. *Darwin Correspondence Project:* www.darwinproject.ac.uk/
The Expression of the Emotions in Man and Animals [1872], ed. Joe Cain and Sharon Messenger. London: Penguin, 2009.

Daube, Johann Friedrich. *Anleitung zur Erfindung der Melodie und ihrer Fortsetzung*. Wien: Christian Gottlob Täubel, 1797.

Daude, Paul. *Lehrbuch des Deutschen litterarischen, künstlerischen und gewerblichen Urheberrechts*. Stuttgart: Ferdinand Enke, 1888.

Daum, Andreas. "Science, Politics, and Religion: Humboldtian Thinking and the Transformation of Civil Society in Germany, 1830–1870," *Osiris* 17 (2002): 107–40.

Davison, James William. "New Philharmonic Society," *The Times* (May 3, 1854).

Deathridge, John. *Wagner's Rienzi. A Reappraisal based on a Study of the Sketches and Drafts*. Oxford: Clarendon Press, 1977.
"Reminiscences of Norma," in *Das musikalische Kunstwerk: Geschichte – Ästhetik – Theorie: Festschrift Carl Dahlhaus zum 60. Geburtstag*, edited by Hermann Danuser, Helga de la Motte-Haber, Silke Leopold and Norbert Miller, 223–27. Laaber, 1988.
Wagner Beyond Good and Evil. Berkeley and Los Angeles: University of California Press, 2008.

Deathridge, John and Carl Dahlhaus. *The New Grove: Wagner*. New York: Norton, 1984.

Deathridge, John, Carl Dahlhaus, Martin Geck, Egon Voss, and Isolde Vetter (eds.). *Wagner-Werk-Verzeichnis: Verzeichnis der musikalischen Werke Richard Wagners und ihrer Quellen*. Mainz, New York, and Tokyo: B. Schott's Söhne, 1986.

Derrida, Jacques. *Speech and Phenomena*. Evanston: Northwest University Press, 1973.

Devrient, Eduard. *Geschichte der deutschen Schauspielkunst* [1848]. Rpt. Munich and Vienna: Langen Müller, 1967.

Dolar, Mladen. *A Voice and Nothing More*. Cambridge MA: MIT Press, 2006.

Draeseke, Felix. "Richard Wagner, der Componist," *Neue Zeitschrift für Musik* 13 (1856): 133, 145, 157, 169, 177.

Dreyfus, Laurence. *Wagner and the Erotic Impulse*. Cambridge, MA: Harvard University Press, 2010.

Dursch, Johann Georg Martin. *Aesthetik; oder die Wissenschaft des Schönen auf dem christlichen Standpunkte*. Stuttgart and Tübingen: J. G. Cotta, 1839.

Dyson, Frances. *Sounding New Media: Immersion and Embodiment in the Arts and Culture*. Berkeley: University of California Press, 2009.

Eagleton, Terry. *Figures of Dissent*. London: Verso, 2003.

Ebers, John. *Seven Years of the King's Theatre*. London: Cary, Lea & Carey, 1828.

Eco, Umberto. *The Search for the Perfect Language*, translated by James Fentress. London: Fontana, 1997.
On Ugliness, translated by Alastair McEwen. London: Harvill Secker, 2007.

Edwards, Arthur C. *The Art of Melody*. New York: Philosophical Library, 1956.

Eicke, Kurt-Erich. *Der Streit zwischen Adolf Bernhard Marx und Gottfried Wilhelm Fink um die Kompositionslehre*. Regensburg: Gustav Bosse, 1966.

Eisler, Rudolf. *Wörterbuch der philosophischen Begriffe*. 2nd edn. Berlin: Ernst Siegfried Mittler und Sohn, 1904.

Eliot, George [Mary Anne Evans]. *The George Eliot Letters*, edited by Gordon S. Haight. Oxford University Press, 1954.

Selected Critical Writings. Oxford University Press, 1992.

Emerson, Edwin. *A History of the Nineteenth Century, Year by Year*. New York: Collier and Son, 1901.

Erlmann, Veit (ed.). *Hearing Cultures: Essays on Sound, Listening and Modernity*. Oxford, New York: Berg, 2004.

Reason and Resonance. New York: Zone Books / Cambridge, MA: MIT Press, 2010.

Ersch, J. S. and J. G. Gruber (eds.). *Allgemeine Encyklopädie der Wissenschaften und Künste*. 26 vols. Leipzig: Johann Friedrich Gleditsch, 1846–48.

Fauser, Annegret. "Wagnerism," in *The Cambridge Companion to Wagner*, edited by Thomas Grey, 221–34. Cambridge University Press, 2008.

Fay, Amy. *Music-Study in Germany*. Chicago: A. C. McClurg, 1891.

Fechner, Gustav. *Zend-Avesta oder über die Dinge des Himmels und des Jenseits. Vom Standpunkt der Naturbetrachtung*. 3 vols. Leipzig: Leopold Voß, 1851.

Elemente der Psychophysik. 2 vols. Leipzig: Breitkopf & Härtel, 1860.

Ueber die Seelenfrage. Ein Gang durch die sichtbare Welt, um die unsichtbare zu finden. Leipzig: C. F. Amelang, 1861.

Fétis, François-Josef. *Traité élémentaire de musique*. Brussels, 1831–32. Rpt. *Biographie universelle*. Paris, 1863.

Biographie universelle des musiciens. 8th edn. Paris: 1865.

Feuerbach, Ludwig. *Principles of the Philosophy of the Future*, translated by Manfred Vogel. Indianapolis: Hackett Publishing Co., 1986.

Fichte, Johann Gottlieb. *Addresses to the German Nation*, translated by R. F. Jones and G. H. Turnbull. Westport, CN: Greenwood Press, 1979.

Filippi, Filippo, "Studio analitico sul *Don Carlos* di Giuseppe Verdi," *Gazetta musicale di Milano* 24 (1869): 33–35.

Finck, Henry T. *Wagner and his Works* [1893]. Rpt. New York: Haskell House, 1968.

Flaubert, Gustave. *Mémoires d'un fou* [1838], translated by Timothy Unwin. www.liv.ac.uk/soclas/los/madman.pdf

Flood, John L. "'Es verstand sich fast von selbst, dasz die ungestalte und häszliche schrift… bleiben muste.' Jacob Grimm's Advocacy of Roman Type," in *'Das unsichtbare Band der Sprache,' Studies in German Language and Linguisitc History in Memory of Leslie Seiffert*, edited by John Flood, 279–312. Stuttgart: Hans-Dieter Heinz, 1993.

Florimo, Francesco. *La Scuola musicale di Napoli e i suoi conservatorii, con uno sgardo sulla storia della musica in Italia*. Naples: Stabilimento tip. di V. Morano, 1881–82.

Fontane, Theodor. *Effi Briest* [1894]. Rpt. translated by Hugh Rorrison and Helen Chambers. London: Penguin, 2000.

Forstner, Alexander Freiherr von. *Der Psychograph oder Seelenschreiber des Herrn Musikdirektor A. Wagner in Berlin*. Berlin: A. Wagner, 1853.

Foster, Daniel. *Wagner's Ring Cycle and the Greeks*. Cambridge University Press, 2010.

Foucault, Michel. *The History of Sexuality: An Introduction*, translated by Robert Hurley. New York: Vintage Books, 1990.

   The Order of Things. New York: Vintage books, 1994.

   Abnormal: Lectures at the Collège de France 1974–1975, translated by Graham Burchel, edited by Valerio Marchetti and Antonella Salomoni. New York: Picador, 2003.

Freud, Sigmund. *Standard Edition of the Complete Psychological Works of Sigmund Freud*. 24 vols., edited by James Strachey. London: Hogarth Press, 1959.

Friedheim, Philip. "Wagner and the Aesthetics of the Scream," *19th-Century Music* 7 (1983): 63–70.

Gaillard, Carl. "Über das Eigenthum an einer musikalischen Composition," *Allgemeine Press-Zeitung* 7–8 (1841): 49–53, 57–60.

Galvani, Luigi. *De viribus electricitatis in motu musculari commentarius*. Bononiae: Ex Typographia Instituti Scientiarium, 1791.

Gans, Chaim. *The Limits of Nationalism*. Cambridge University Press, 2003.

Ganz, Peter. *Jacob Grimm's Conception of German Studies*. Oxford: Clarendon Press, 1973.

Garratt, James. *Palestrina and the German Romantic Imagination: Interpreting Historicism in Nineteenth-Century Music*. Cambridge University Press, 2002.

   Culture and Social Reform in the Age of Wagner. Cambridge University Press, 2010.

Gay, Peter. *The Naked Heart*. New York: Norton, 1995.

Gelbart, Matthew. *The Invention of "Folk Music" and "Art Music"*. Cambridge University Press, 2007.

Gellner, Ernest. *Nations and Nationalism*. Malden: Blackwell, 2006.

Gerard, Alexander. *Essay on Genius*. London: Strahan and Cadell, 1774.

   Essay on Taste [1759]. Rpt. edited by Walter J. Hipple, Jr. Gainesville: Scholars' Facsimiles & Reprints, 1963.

Gervinus, Georg Gottfried. *Zur Geschichte der deutschen Literatur*. Heidelberg: C. F. Winter, 1834.

   Handbuch der Geschichte der poetischen National-Literatur der Deutschen. Leipzig: Wilhelm Engelmann 1842.

Geyer, Flodoard. "Kann und soll die Melodie gelehrt werden?" *Neue Berliner Musik-Zeitung* 41 (1860): 321–23, 329–31, 337–39.

   Musikalische Compositions-Lehre. Berlin: A Vogel & Co., 1862.

Gibson, Mary. *Prostitution and the State in Italy, 1860–1915*. 2nd edn. Columbus, OH: Ohio State University Press, 2000.

Giger, Andreas. *Verdi and the French Aesthetic*. Cambridge University Press, 2008.

Ginschel, Gunhild. *Der junge Jacob Grimm*. Berlin: Akademie, 1967.

Giustiniani, Vincenzo. *Discorso sopra la musica* [1628], translated by Carol MacClintock. Rome: American Institute of Musicology, 1962.

Glasenapp, Carl Friedrich. "1834–1884. Ein Nachwort," *Bayreuther Blätter* 7 (1884): 343–47.

Das Leben Richard Wagners. 6 vols. Leipzig: Breitkopf & Härtel, 1876–1911. English translation by W. Ashton Ellis [*The Life of Wagner* 1894]. London: Kegan Paul, 1900.

Glümer, Claire von. *Erinnerungen an Wilhelmine Schröder-Devrient.* Leipzig: Johann Ambrose Barth., 1862.

Goehr, Lydia. *The Imaginary Museum of Musical Works: An Essay in the Philosophy of Music.* Oxford: Clarendon Press, 1992.

Goethe, J. W. von. *Goethes Sämmtliche Werke.* 15 vols., edited by Karl Goedeke. Stuttgart: J. G. Cotta, 1874.

Italian Journey, translated by W. H. Auden and Elizabeth Mayer. Middlesex: Penguin, 1962.

Theory of Color, translated by Herb Aach. New York: Van Nostrand Reinhold, 1971.

Goethe: The Collected Works. Essays on Art and Literature, edited by John Geary. Princeton University Press, 1994.

Gooley, Dana. *The Virtuoso Liszt.* Cambridge University Press, 2004.

"Hanslick and the Institution of Criticism," *Journal of Musicology* 28 (2011): 289–324.

Göpfert, Bernd. *Stimmtypen und Rollencharaktere in der deutschen Oper 1815–1848.* Wiesbaden: Breitkopf & Härtel, 1977.

Gossett, Phillip. "Verdi the Craftsman," *Revista Portuguesa de Musicologia* 11 (2001): 81–111.

Divas and Scholars. University of Chicago Press, 2006.

Graff, E. G. *Diutiska. Denkmäler deutscher Sprache und Literatur, aus alten Handschriften zum ersten Male theils herausgegeben, theils nachgewiesen und beschrieben.* 3 vols. Stuttgart and Tübingen: J. G. Cotta, 1826–29.

Gramit, David. *Cultivating Music: The Aspirations, Interests, and Limits of German Musical Culture, 1770–1848.* Berkeley and Los Angeles: University of California Press, 2002.

Green, Abigail. *Fatherlands: State-Building and Nationhood in Nineteenth-Century Germany.* Cambridge University Press, 2001.

Gregory, Frederick. *Scientific Materialism in Nineteenth Century Germany.* Boston: D. Reidel, 1977.

Gregory, John. *A Comparative View of the State and Faculties of Man with those of the Animal World.* 4th edn. London: J. Dodsley, 1767.

Grey, Thomas. *Wagner's Musical Prose: Texts and Contexts.* Cambridge University Press, 1995.

"Music as Natural Language in Wagner's Ring," in *Nineteenth-Century Music. Selected Proceedings of the Tenth International Conference*, edited by Jim Samson, and Bennett Zon, 39–59. Aldershot: Ashgate, 2002.

"Meister Richard's Apprenticeship: The Early Operas (1833–1840)," in *The Cambridge Companion to Wagner*, edited by Thomas Grey, 18–46. Cambridge University Press, 2008.

"In the realm of the senses: sight, sound and the music of desire in *Tristan und Isolde*," in *Richard Wagner: Tristan und Isolde*, edited by Arthur Groos, 69–94. Cambridge University Press, 2011.

Grimm, Jacob. *Deutsche Grammatik*. 3rd edn. Göttingen: Dieterichsche Buchhandlung, 1840.

Deutsche Mythologie [1822]. 2 vols. 2nd edn. Göttingen: Dieterichsche Buchhandlung, 1844. Rpt. Wilhelm Scherer. Berlin: Ferdinand Dümmler, 1870. Rpt. Hildesheim, New York: Olms, 1989.

Deutsches Wörterbuch [1854]. http://woerterbuchnetz.de/DWB/?sigle=DWB&mode=Vernetzung&lemid=GA00837

Geschichte der deutschen Sprache [1848]. 4th edn. Leipzig: S. Hirzel, 1880.

Kleinere Schriften. 8 vols. Berlin: F. Dümmler, 1864–90.

Briefe der Brüder Grimm an Savigny, edited by W. Schoof and I. Schnack. Berlin: Schmidt, 1953.

Über den Ursprung der Sprache [1851]. Frankfurt am Main: Insel, 1985.

Gumbrecht, Hans Ulrich. *The Production of Presence*. Stanford University Press, 2004.

Gumbrecht, Hans Ulrich, and K. Ludwig Pfeiffer (eds.). *Materialities of Communication*, translated by William Whobrey. Stanford University Press, 1994.

Gurney, Edmund. *The Power of Sound*. London: Smith, Elder & Co., 1880.

Hagemann, Carl. *Wilhelmine Schröder-Devrient*. Berlin and Leipzig: Schuster & Loeffler, 1904.

Hall, Alexander Wilford. *Evolution of Sound: Part of the Problem of Human Life and Hereafter*. New York: Hall & Co., 1878.

Hamann, Johann Georg. *Sämtliche Werke*. 6 vols., edited by Josef Nadler. Vienna: Thomas-Morus-Presse, 1949.

Hamilton, Kenneth. "Wagner and Liszt: Elective Affinities," in *Wagner and his World*, edited by Thomas Grey, 27–65. Cambridge University Press, 2009.

Hankins, Thomas, and Robert Silverman (eds). *Instruments and the Imagination*. Princeton University Press, 1995.

Hanslick, Eduard. *Die moderne Oper*. Berlin: A. Hofmann & Co. 1875.

Musikalisches und Litterarisches. Kritiken und Schilderungen, 2nd edn. Berlin: Allgemeiner Verein für Deutsche Litteratur, 1889.

Music Criticisms, translated by Henry Pleasants. London: Penguin, 1950.

Vienna's Golden Years, translated by Henry Pleasants. New York: Simon and Schuster, 1950.

On the Musically Beautiful, 8th edn., translated by Geoffrey Payzant. Indiana: Hackett, 1986.

Sämtliche Schriften: Historisch-kritische Ausgabe. 6 vols., edited by Dietmar Strauß. Vienna: Böhlau, 1993.

Hartford, Robert (ed.). *Bayreuth: the Early Years*. London: Victor Gollancz, 1980.

Hartman, Geoffrey H. "Romanticisim and Anti-Self-Consciousness," in *Romanticism and Consciousness: Essays in Criticism*, edited by Harold Bloom, 47–56. New York: Norton, 1970.

Hartmann, Eduard von. *Eduard von Hartmann's Ausgewählte Werke. 3, Die deutsche Ästhetik seit Kant: Historisch-Kritischer Theil*. Leipzig: Friedrich, 1886.

Hauch, Johannes Carsten. *H. C. Ørsted's Leben. Zwei Denkschriften von Hauch und Forchhammer*, translated by H. Sebald. Spandau: Vossische Buchhandlung, 1853.

Hauptmann, Moritz. *The Letters of a Leipzig Cantor*. 2 vols., edited by Alfred Schöne and Ferdinand Hiller. London: Richard Bentley & Son, 1892.

Hausegger, Friedrich von. "Die Musik als Ausdruck" *Bayreuther Blätter* 1–12 (1884): 9–15, 37–48, 78–82, 107–13, 142–52, 175–84, 214–19, 242–53, 305–16, 356–67, 381–93. Subsequently published as *Die Musik als Ausdruck*. Vienna: C. Konegen, 1885.

Haym, Rudolf. *Hegel und seine Zeit: Vorlesungen über Entstehung und Entwicklung, Wesen und Wert der Hegelschen Philosophie*. Berlin: Gaertner, 1857.

Hegel, Georg Wilhelm Friedrich. *Lectures on the Philosophy of World History. Introduction: Reason in History*, translated by J. Sibree. New York: Dover, 1956.

  The Science of Logic, translated by A. V. Miller. Atlantic Highlands: Humanities Press International, 1969.

  Philosophy of Mind, translated by A. V. Miller. Oxford: Clarendon Press, 1971.

  Aesthetics: Lectures on Fine Art. 2 vols., translated by T. M. Knox. Oxford: Clarendon Press, 1988.

Heidegger, Martin. *Poetry, Language, Thought*, translated by Albert Hofstadter. New York: Perennial Classics, 2001.

Heidelberger, Michael. *Nature from Within: Gustav Theodor Fechner and his Psychophysical Worldview* [1993], translated by Cynthia Klohr. Pittsburg University Press, 2004.

Heine, Heinrich. *Sämtliche Werke*. 10 vols., edited by O. Walzel. Leipzig: Insel. 1910–15.

  Werke. 2 vols., edited by Martin Greiner. Berlin and Cologne, 1962.

Heintz, Albert. *Richard Wagner's Lohengrin*. Berlin: Allgemeine Musik-Zeitung, 1894.

Helmholtz, Hermann von. *Die Lehre von den Tonempfindungen* [1863]. 2nd edn. Brunswick: Friedrich Vieweg und Sohn, 1865.

  Popular Lectures on Scientific Subjects, translated by E. Atkinson. New York: Dover, 1962.

  Selected Writings, edited by Russell Kahn. Middleton: Wesleyan University Press, 1971.

  Science and Culture: Popular and Philosophical Essays, edited by David Cahan. University of Chicago Press, 1995.

Helmreich, Stefan. "Underwater Music: Tuning Composition to the Sounds of Science," *Oxford Handbook of Sound Studies*, edited by Trevor Pinch and Karin Bijsterveld, 151–75. Oxford University Press, 2012.

Herder, Johann Gottfried von. *Sämtliche Werke*, edited by Bernhard Suphan. 33 vols. Hildesheim: Georg Olms, 1967–68.

Herder, Johann Gottfried and Jean-Jacques Rousseau, *On the Origin of Languages*, translated by John H. Moran and Alexander Gode. University of Chicago Press, 1986.

Herold, J. Christopher. *The Age of Napoleon*. New York: American Heritage Pub. Co., 1963.

Herzfeld, Michael. *Cultural Intimacy: Social Poetics in the Nation-State*. New York: Routledge, 1997.

Hess, Moses. *Jugement dernier du vieux monde social*. Geneva: F. Melly, 1851.

Hill, Christopher. *Sensations: A Defense of Type Materialism*. Cambridge University Press, 1991.

Hiltner, Beate. *Vollkommenes Stimmideal?: eine Suche durch die Jahrhunderte; wie sich die Ansichten über den Kunstgesang änderten*. Frankfurt am Main: Peter Lang, 1996.

Hindemith, Paul. *The Craft of Musical Composition*. Translated by Arthur Mendel. 2 vols. Revised edn. New York: Associated Music Publishers, 1941–45.

Hinrichs, Friedrich. *Richard Wagner und die neuere Musik. Eine Skizze aus der musikalischen Gegenwart*. Halle: Schrödel and Simon, 1854.

Hitzschold, August. "Zur Physiologie des musicalischen Drama's," *Niederrheinische Musik-Zeitung* 23 (1853): 161–78.

Hobsbawm, Eric J. *Nations and Nationalism since 1780: Programme, Myth, Reality*. Cambridge University Press, 1992; 2nd edn. 2012.

Hoeckner, Berthold. *Programming the Absolute*. Princeton University Press, 2002.

Hoffmann, E. T. A. *The Golden Pot and Other Tales*, edited and translated by Ritchie Robertson. Oxford University Press, 1992.

  Fantasiestücke in Callot's Manier. Werke. 1814, edited by Hartmut Steinecke. Frankfurt am Main: Deutscher Klassiker Verlag, 1993.

Hohenlohe, Marie Fürstin zu. *Erinnerungen an Richard Wagner*. Weimar: Herm. Böhlaus Nachf., 1938.

Holborn, Hajo. *A History of Modern Germany, 1840–1945*. Princeton University Press, 1982.

Holtei, Karl. *Beitraege zur Geschichte dramatischer Kunst und Literatur*. 3 vols. Berlin, Haude & Spener, 1827.

Holtmeier, Ludwig. "Von den Feen zum Liebesverbot. The Story of a Dilettante," in *Richard Wagner und seine Zeit*, edited by Eckehard Keim and Ludwig Holtmeier, 33–73. Laaber, 2003.

Horkheimer, Max. *Between Philosophy and Social Science: Selected Early Writings*, translated by G. Frederick Hunter, Matthew S. Kramer, and John Torpey. Cambridge, MA: MIT Press, 1993.

Hornstein, Robert von. "Memoiren," *Süddeutsche Monasthefte* 3 (1907): 30–60, 145–69, 289–316, 453–82, 551–77.

Hornung, D. *Heinrich Heine, der Unsterbliche: Eine Mahnung aus dem Jenseits. Nur Thatsächliches, keine Dichtung*. Stuttgart: J. Scheible, 1857.

Huber, Ernst Robert, ed. *Dokumente zur deutschen Verfassungsgeschichte.* 5 vols. 3rd edn. Stuttgart: Kohlhammer, 1978–97.

Hubig, Christoph. "Genie – Typus oder Original? Vom Paradigma der Kreativität zum Kult des Individuums," in *Propyläen-Geschichte der* Literatur. 6 vols., edited by E. Wischer, 4: 207–10. Berlin: Propyläen, 1983.

Hugo, Victor. *Oeuvres complètes. Actes et paroles.* 3 vols. Paris: Albin Michel, 1937–40. *Cromwell.* Paris: Garnier, 1968.

Humboldt, Alexander von. *Versuche über die gereizte Muskel- und Nervenfaser nebst Vermuthungen über den chemischen Process des Lebens in der Thier- und Pflanzenwelt.* 2 vols. Berlin: Heinrich August Rottmann, 1797–99.

Briefe von Alexander von Humboldt an Varnhagen von Ense aus den Jahren 1827–1858, 5th edn. Leipzig: F. A. Brockhaus, 1860.

Humboldt, Wilhelm von. *Gesammelte Schriften.* 17 vols., edited by Albert Leitzmann. Deutsche Akademie der Wissenschaft. Berlin: B. Behr, 1903–36.

Essays on Language, translated by John Wieczorek and Ian Roe, edited by T. Harden and D. Farrely. Frankfurt am Main: Peter Lang, 1997.

Huurdeman, Anton A. *The Worldwide History of Telecommunications.* Hoboken, NJ: Wiley, 2003.

Iser, Wolfgang. "The Reading Process: A Phenomenological Approach," in *Reader–Response Criticism: From Formalism to Post-Structuralism,* edited by Jane P. Tompkins, 50–69. Baltimore and London: Johns Hopkins University Press, 1980.

Jackson, Myles W. "Physics, Machines and Musical Pedagogy in Nineteenth-Century Germany," *History of Science* 42 (2004): 371–418.

Harmonious Triads: Physicists, Musicians and Instrument Makers in Nineteenth-Century Germany. Cambridge, MA: MIT Press, 2006.

Jadassohn, Salomon. *Das Wesen der Melodie in der Tonkunst.* Leipzig: Breitkopf & Härtel, 1899.

Jahn, Otto. *Gesammelte Aufsätze über Musik.* Leipzig: Breitkopf & Härtel, 1866.

Jakobson, Roman. *Selected Writings II: Word and Language.* The Hague: Mouton & Co., 1971.

Language in Literature, edited by Krystyna Pomorska and Stephen Rudy. Cambridge, MA: Harvard University Press, 1987.

James, William. "Are we Automata?," *Mind* 4 (1879): 1–22.

The Principles of Psychology [1890]. New York: Cosimo, 2007.

Jones, Jonathan. "Lohengrin," *The Musical World* 53 (July 3, 1875): 437–39.

Jones, William J. *Images of Language: Six Essays on German Attitudes to European Languages from 1500 to 1800.* Amsterdam, Philadelphia: John Benjamins Publishing Co., 1999.

Justin, Richard. "Darwin, Marx, Wagner: Dialectical Materialism in the *Ring*," in *New Studies in Richard Wagner's The Ring of the Nibelung,* edited by Herbert Richardson, 89–126. Lewiston, NY: Edwin Mellen Press, 1991.

Kahlert, August, "Das musikalische Element in der Sprache," *Neue Zeitschrift für Musik* 45–47 (1837): 179–81, 183–84, 187–88.

"Aus Breslau" *Neue Zeitschrift für Musik* 16 (1842): 116.

Kanne, Friedrich August "Der Zauber der Tonkunst," *Allgemeine musikalische Zeitung, mit besonderer Rüksicht auf den österreichischen Kaiserstaat* 35–89 (1821): 249–53, 257–62, 265–88, 273–75, 281–84, 313–15, 321–24, 329–31, 507–8, 513–16, 521–24, 529–33, 537–40, 545–8, 553–55, 561–63, 569–71, 577–79, 585–88, 593–95, 601–03, 609–13, 617–19, 625–27, 633–36, 641–44, 649–51, 657–59, 673–76, 693–97, 701–05.

Kant, Immanuel. *Kant's Werke*. 29 vols., edited by the Königlich-Preußische Akademie der Wissenschaften. Berlin: Reimer, 1910.

Critique of Judgment [1790], translated by J. H. Bernard. New York: Hafner Press, 1951.

Kanz, Roland, and Jürgen Schönwälder (eds.). *Ästhetik des Charakteristischen: Quellentexte zu Kunstkritik und Romantik*. Göttingen and Bonn: V&R Unipress / Bonn University Press, 2008.

Kapp, Ernst. *Grundlinien einer Philosophie der Technik: zur Entstehungsgeschichte der Cultur aus neuen Gesichtspunkten*. Brunswick: G. Westermann, 1877.

Karnes, Kevin. *Music Criticsm and the Challenge of History*. Oxford University Press, 2008.

Karpath Ludwig. *Zu den Briefen Richard Wagners an eine Putzmacherin: Unterredungen mit der Putzmacherin Berta*. Berlin: "Harmonie," Verlagsgesellschaft für Literatur und Kunst, 1906.

Kawohl, Friedemann. *Urheberrecht der Musik in Preussen (1820–1840)*. Tutzing: Hans Schneider, 2002.

Keiler, Allan. "Melody and Motive in Schenker's Earliest Writings," in *Critica Musica. Essays in Honor of Paul Brainard*, edited by John Knowles, 169–91. Australia: Gordon and Breach, 1996.

Kennaway, James. *Bad Vibrations: The History of the Idea of Music as a Cause of Disease*. Farnham: Ashgate, 2012.

Kerndörffer, Heinrich August. *Handbuch der Declamation. Ein Leitfaden für Schulen und für den Selbstunterricht zur Bildung eines guten rednerischen Vortrags*. Leipzig: Fleischer, 1813.

Anleitung zur gründlichen Bildung der öffentlichen Beredsamkeit. Ein Compendium für Schulen, Gymnasien und akademische Vorlesungen. Leipzig: Steinacker, 1833.

Kienzl, Wilhelm. *Die musikalische Deklamation, dargestellt an der Hand der Entwickelungsgeschichte des deutschen Gesanges; Musikalische-Philologische Studie*. Leipzig: H. Matthes, 1885.

Richard Wagner. 2nd edn. Munich: Kirchheim'sche Verlagsbuchhandlung, 1908.

Kierkegaard, Søren. *Either / Or*, translated by Alastair Hannay. London: Penguin Classics, 1992.

Kiesewetter, Raphael Georg. *Geschichte der europaeisch-abendlaendischen oder unserer heutigen Musik*. Leipzig: Breitkopf und Härtel, 1834.

Kimbell, David. *Norma*. Cambridge University Press, 1998.

Kirchmeyer, Helmut. *Situationsgeschichte der Musikkritik und des musikalischen Pressewesens in Deutschland: dargestellt vom Ausgange des 18. bis zum Beginn des 20. Jahrhunderts. IV: Das zeitgenössische Wagner-Bild*. 5 vols. Regensburg: Gustav Bosse, 1967–85.

Kittler, Friedrich. "*Weltatem*. On Wagner's Media Technology," in *Wagner in Retrospect. A Centennial Reappraisal*, edited by Leroy R. Shaw, Nancy R. Cirillo, and Marion Miller, 203–12. Amsterdam: Rodopi, 1987.

Discourse Networks 1800 / 1900, translated by Michael Metteer and Chris Cullens. Stanford University Press, 1990.

"The World of the Symbolic – A World of the Machine," in *Literature, Media, Information Systems*, edited by John Johnston. Amsterdam: G+B Arts International, 1997.

Gramophone, Film, Typewriter, translated by Geoffrey Winthrop-Young and Michael Wutz. Stanford University Press, 1999.

Kleist, Heinrich von. *Selected Writings*, edited and translated by David Constantine. Indianapolis and Cambridge: Hacket Publishing, 1997.

Knapp, Raymond. "Brahms and the Anxiety of Allusion," *Journal of Musicological Research* 18 (1998): 1–30.

Koch, Heinrich Christoph. *Versuch einer Anleitung zur Composition* [1782–93]. 3 vols. Rpt. Hildesheim: Georg Olms, 1969. English translation by Nancy K. Backer, *Introductory Essay on Composition*. New Haven and London: Yale University Press, 1983.

Köhler, Louis. *Die Melodie der Sprache in ihrer Anwendung besonders auf das Lied und die Oper*. Leipzig: J. J. Weber, 1853.

Kollek, Peter. *Bogumil Dawison: Porträt und Deutung eines genialen Schauspielers*. Kastellaun: A. Henn, 1978.

Kolocotroni, Vassiliki, Jane Goldman and Olga Taxidou (eds.). *Modernism: An Anthology of Sources*. University of Chicago Press, 1998.

Kondo, Koji. "Interview with a legend," http://uk.wii.ign.com/articles/772/772299p2.html

Konrad, Ulrich. "Friedrich Rochlitz und die Entstehung des Mozart-Bildes um 1900," in *Mozart – Aspekte des 19. Jahrhunderts*, edited by Hermann Jung, 1–22. Mannheim: Mannheim Hochschulschriften, 1995.

Korstvedt. Benjamin. "Reading Music Criticism beyond the Fin-de-siècle Vienna Paradigm," *Musical Quarterly* 94 (2011): 156–210.

Korsyn, Kevin. "Towards a New Poetics of Musical Influence," *Musical Analysis* 10 (1991): 3–72.

Koselleck, Reinhart. *Preußen zwischen Reform und Revolution. Allgemeines Landrecht, Verwaltung und soziale Bewegung von 1791 bis 1848*. Stuttgart: Klett, 1967.

Kossmaly, Carl. "Die Wagnerfrage von Joachim Raff," *Neue Berliner Musik-Zeitung* 33–51 (1855): 257–60, 265–68, 273–76, 281–84, 289–92, 297–300, 305–08,

377–78, 385–86, 393–94, 401–02; and *Neue Berliner Musik-Zeitung* 2–24 (1856): 9–10, 25–26, 161–63, 169–71, 177–79, 185–87.

Kretschmer, Andreas. "Einiges über das Lied," *Neue Zeitschrift für Musik* 55 (October 9, 1834): 218–19, 221–22.

Kreuzer, Gundula. *Verdi and the Germans.* Cambridge University Press, 2010.

　"*Wagner-Dampf*: Steam in *Der Ring des Nibelungen* and Operatic Production," *Opera Quarterly* 27 (2011): 179–218.

Kröll, Christina. *Gesang und Rede, sinniges Bewegen. Goethe als Theaterleiter.* Düsseldorf: Goethe-Museum, 1973.

Kropfinger, Klaus. *Wagner and Beethoven*, translated by Peter Palmer. Cambridge University Press, 1991.

Krüger, Eduard. "Zerstreute Anmerkungen zu Wagner's *Lohengrin*," *Niederrheinische Musik-Zeitung* 1 (1856): 2–6, 9–13.

Kühn, Ulrich. *Sprech-Ton-Kunst.* Tübingen: Niemeyer, 2001.

Kulke, Eduard. "*Semele* und *Lohengrin*. Eine Parallele," *Anregungen für Kunst, Leben und Wissenschaft* 6 (1861): 41–46, 77–90.

Kunze, Stefan. *Der Kunstbegriff Richard Wagners.* Regensburg: Bosse, 1983.

Kurth, Ernst. *Romantische Harmonik und ihre Krise in Wagners Tristan.* Berlin: Hesse, 1920.

　Ernst Kurth: Selected Writings, edited and translated by Lee A. Rothfarb. Cambridge University Press, 1991.

Kutsch, Karl-Josef, and Leo Riemens (eds.). *Großes Sängerlexikon.* 6 vols. Bern and Stuttgart: Franke 1987–94.

Lange, Friedrich Albert. *History of Materialism and Criticism of its Present Importance*, translated by Ernest Chester Thomas. London: Paul, Trench, Trübner, 1892.

Lardner, Dionysius. *Popular Lectures on Science and Art.* New York: Greely and McElrath, 1846.

Laube, Heinrich. "Wilhelmine Schröder-Devrient," *Zeitung für die elegante Welt* 6 (1833): 21.

Laudon, Robert T. "Eduard Sobolewski, Frontier Kapellmeister: From Königsberg to St Louis," *Musical Quarterly* 73 (1989): 94–118.

Lenoir, Timothy. *The Strategy of Life: Teleology and Mechanics in Nineteenth-Century German Biology.* University of Chicago Press, 1989.

　"Helmholtz and the Materialities of Communication," *Osiris* 9 (1994): 184–207.

　Instituting Science. Stanford University Press, 1997.

Leoussi, Athena (ed.). *Encyclopaedia of Nationalism.* New Brunswick, New Jersey: Transaction Publishers, 2001.

Lévi-Strauss, Claude. *The Raw and the Cooked* [1964]. Rpt. translated by John and Doreen Weightman. London: Jonathan Cape, 1970.

Liebig, Justus. *Chemische Briefe.* Heidelberg: C. F. Winter, 1844.

Lippmann, Friedrich. "Ein neuentdecktes Autograph Richard Wagners: Rezension der Königsberger 'Norma'-Aufführung von 1837," in *Musica scientiae collectanea:*

Festschrift Karl Gustav Fellerer zum siebzigsten Geburtstag, edited by Heinrich Hüschen, 373–79. Cologne: Arno Volk, 1973.

Liszt, Franz. *Franz Liszt's Briefe*, edited by Maria Lipsius [= La Mara]. 8 vols. Leipzig: Breitkopf & Härtel, 1893–1902.

Sämtliche Schriften. 9 vols. [projected] Detlef Altenburg general editor, edited by Rainer Kleinertz (vol. 1), Detlef Altenburg (vols. 3–4), Dorothea Redepenning and Britta Schilling (vol. 5). Wiesbaden: Breitkopf & Härtel, 1989–.

"Richard Wagner's *Lohengrin*. Mitgetheilet von Dr. Fr. Lißt," *Illustrirte Zeitung* 16 (April 12, 1851), translated by C. A. Barry and rpt. as "Franz Liszt's *Lohengrin*," edited by David Trippett. *The Wagner Journal* 4 (1–3) (2010): 4–21. 2: 28–40. 3: 43–57.

"Wagner's *Lohengrin*, translated from the French of F. Liszt," translated by Charles Ainslie Barry. *The Monthly Musical Record* (February 1–May 1, 1876) 19–22, 31–35, 51–54, 70–72.

Liszt, Franz, and Richard Wagner. *Correspondence of Wagner and Liszt (vols. 1 and 2)*, translated by Francis Hueffer. Cirencester: The Echo Library, 2005.

Lobe, Johann Christian. "Fortschritt," *Allgemeine musikalische Zeitung* 50 (1848): "Erster Artikel," 49–51, "Zweiter Artikel," 65–69, "Dritter Artikel," 169–73, "Vierter Artikel," 337–41, "Fünfter Artikel," 581–87, 598–601, 615–28, 641–46, 673–78.

Musikalische Briefe. Wahrheit über Tonkunst und Tonkünstler. Von einem Wohlbekannten. 2 vols. Leipzig: Baumgärtner, 1852.

"Aesthetische Briefe," *Fliegende Blätter für Musik* 1 (1853): 185–92; 2 (1854): 241–62, 325–32, 370–85, 476–86.

Aus dem Leben eines Musikers. Leipzig: J. J. Weber, 1859.

Musikalische Briefe. Wahrheit über Tonkunst und Tonkünstler. Von einem Wohlbekannten. 2nd edn. Leipzig: Baumgärtner, 1860.

"Bellini," *Fliegende Blätter für Musik* 1 (1854): 262–80. Rpt. "Vincenzo Bellini," *Musik-Konzepte* 46, edited by Heinz-Klaus Metzger and Rainer Riehn. Munich: Edition Text + Kritik, 1985: 109–16.

Compositions-Lehre oder umfassende Theorie von der thematischen Arbeit und den modernen Instrumentalformen. Weimar: Bernhard Friedrich Voigt, 1844. Rpt. Hildesheim: Georg Olms, 1988.

"Briefe über Richard Wagner an einen jungen Komponisten," *Fliegende Blätter für Musik* 1 (1854): 411–29, 444–65; 2 (1855): 27–48. English translation by David Trippett, "Letters to a Young Composer about Richard Wagner," in *Wagner and his World*, edited by Thomas Grey, 269–310. Princeton University Press, 2009.

Lohff, Brigitte. "Johannes Müllers Rezeption der Zellenlehre in seinem 'Handbuch der Physiologie des Menschen,'" *Medizinhistorisches Journal* 13 (1978): 247–58.

Lotze, Rudolf Hermann. *Medicinische Psychologie, oder, Physiologie der Seele.* Leipzig: Weidmann, 1852.

Metaphysic in Three Books: Ontology, Cosmology, and Psychology, translated by Bernard Bosanquet. Oxford: Clarendon Press, 1884.

Outlines of Psychology [1881], translated by George T. Ladd. Boston: Ginn & Company, 1886.

Ludwig, Otto. *Gesammelte Schriften*. 6 vols. Leipzig: Fr. Wilh. Grunow, 1891.

Lyotard, Jean-François. "Can Thought go on without a Body?," in *Posthumanism*, edited by Neil Badmington, 129–40. Basingstoke: Palgrave, 2000.

MacDowell, Eduard. *Critical and Historical Essays: Lectures Delivered at Columbia University*. Boston, Leipzig, New York: A.P. Schmidt, 1912.

Maguire, Simon. *Vincenzo Bellini and the Aesthetics of Early Nineteenth-Century Opera*. New York and London: Garland, 1989.

Mahony, Francis, "Moore's Plagiarisms," *The Musical World* 48–51 (1849): 764–65, 780–81, 797–98, 809–10; 1–26 (1850): 3–4, 42–43, 56–58, 62–63, 80–82, 105–06, 120–21, 169–70, 217, 281, 297, 361, 408.

Man, Paul de. "Intentional Structure of the Romantic Language," in *Romanticism and Consciousness. Essays in Criticism*, edited by Harold Bloom, 65–77. New York: Norton, 1970.

   Romanticism and Contemporary Criticism. Baltimore: Johns Hopkins University Press, 1996.

Mann, Thomas. *Doktor Faustus. Das Leben des deutschen Tonsetzers Adrian Leverkühn erzählt von einem Freunde*. Frankfurt am Main: S. Fischer, 1947.

   Essays of Three Decades, translated by H. T. Lowe-Porter. New York: Alfred A. Knopf, 1947.

   Pro and Contra Wagner, translated by Allan Blunden. London: Faber, 1985.

Marget, Arthur. "Liszt and Parsifal," *Music Review* 14 (1953): 107–24.

Marpurg, Friedrich, ed. *Historisch-Kritische Beyträge zur Aufnahme der Musik*. Berlin: J. J. Schützens selige Witwe, 1754.

Martinville, Édouard-Léon Scott de. "Principles of Phonautography" [January 26, 1857], in *The Phonautographic Manuscripts of Édouard-Léon Scott de Martinville*, edited and translated by Patrick Feaster, 4–12, www.firstsounds. org/publications/articles/Phonautographic-Manuscripts.pdf

   "Fixation graphique de la voix" [October 28, 1857], in *The Phonautographic Manuscripts of Édouard-Léon Scott de Martinville*, edited and translated by Patrick Feaster, 23–42, www.firstsounds.org/publications/articles/ Phonautographic-Manuscripts.pdf

Marx, Adolf Bernhard. "Andeutung des Standpunktes der Zeitung (Als Epiloge)," *Berliner allgemeine musikalische Zeitung* 1 (1824): 444–48.

   "Vollständige Singschule in vier Abtheilungen, mit deutschen, italienischen und französischen Vorbemerkungen und Erläuterungen," *Berliner allgemeine musikalische Zeitung* 20 (1825), 121–23, 158–59, 167–68, 173–76, 183–87.

   "Zusatz aus andrer Feder," *Berliner Allgemeine musikalische Zeitung* 2 (1825): 58–60, 65–67, 73–75.

   Die Kunst des Gesanges, theoretisch–praktisch. Berlin: A. M. Schlesinger, 1826.

   "Übersicht der verschiedenen wesentlichen Gattungen des musikalischen Drama," *Berliner allgemeine musikalische Zeitung* 25–26 (1828): 195–97, 203–06.

Die alte Musiklehre im Streit in unserer Zeit. Leipzig: Breitkopf & Härtel, 1841.

Die Lehre von der musikalischen Komposition, praktisch theorietisch. 3rd edn. Leipzig: Breitkopf & Härtel, 1868; *The School of Musical Composition.* 4th edn. English translation by Augustus Wehrhan. London: Robert Cocks and Co., 1852.

Die Musik des neunzehnten Jahrhunderts und ihre Pflege. Leipzig: Breitkopf & Härtel, 1855. English translation by August Heinrich Wehrhan and C. Natalia Macfarren. *The Music of the Nineteenth Century and Its Culture.* London: Robert Cocks & Co., 1854.

Musical Form in the Age of Beethoven. Selected Writings on Theory and Method, edited and translated by Scott Burnham. Cambridge University Press, 1997.

Mattheson, Johann. *Der Vollkommene Capellmeister,* edited by Friederike Ramm. Kassel: Bärenreiter, 1999.

McCanles, Michael. "The Literal and the Metaphorical: Dialectic or Interchange," *PMLA* 91 (1976): 279–90.

McClaine, William. *Between Real and Ideal: The Course of Otto Ludwig's Development as a Narrative Writer.* Chapel Hill: University of North Carolina Press, 1963.

McClatchie, Stephen. *Analyzing Wagner's Operas: Alfred Lorenz and German Nationalist Ideology.* University of Rochester Press, 1998.

McLuhan, Marshall. *Understanding Media: The Extensions of Man.* Cambridge, MA: MIT Press, 1994.

Meinecke, Friedrich. *Weltbürgertum und Nationalstaat,* edited by H. Herzfeld. Munich: Oldenbourg, 1969.

Melloni, Macedonio, "Beobachtung über die Farbung der Netzhaut und der Krystall-Linse," *Annalen der Physik* 56 (1842): 263–302.

Merkel, Carl Ludwig. *Anatomie und Physiologie des menschlichen Stimm- und Sprach-Organs (Anthropophonik): Nach eigenen Beobachtungen und Versuchen wissenschaftlich begründet und für Studierende und ausübende Ärzte, Physiologen, Akustiker, Sänger.* Leipzig: Abel, 1857.

Physiologie der menschlichen Sprache. Leipzig: O. Wigand, 1866.

Merleau-Ponty, Maurice. *Phenomenology of Perception,* translated by Colin Smith. London and New York: Routledge, 2002.

Meyer, Friedrich. *Richard Wagner und seine Stellung zur Vergangenheit und "Zukunft."* Thorn: Ernst Lambeck, 1859.

Meyer, Stephen. "*Das wilde Herz*: Interpreting Wilhelmine Schröder-Devrient," *Opera Quarterly* 14 (1997): 23–40.

Carl Maria von Weber and the Search for a German Opera. Bloomington and Indianapolis: Indiana University press, 2003.

"Sound recordings and the end of the Italian *Lohengrin*," *Cambridge Opera Journal* 20 (2008): 1–24.

Mill, James. *Analysis of the Phenomena of the Human Mind.* London: Baldwin and Cradock, 1829.

Mill, John Stewart. *Early Essays*, edited by J. W. M. Gibbs. London: George Bell & Sons, 1897.

The Logic of the Moral Sciences. London: Open Court, 1994.

Millington, Barry. *Wagner*. London: Dent, 1992.

Millington, Barry (ed.) *The Wagner Compendium*. London: Thames & Hudson, 1992.

Moleschott, Jacob. *Der Kreislauf des Lebens: Physiologische Antworten auf Liebig's Chemische Briefe*. Mainz: Zabern, 1852.

Mollison, David. *Melody: The Soul of Music*. Glasgow, 1798.

Mörike, Eduard. *Mozart's Journey to Prague and a Selection of Poems*, translated by David Luke. London: Penguin, 2003.

Morrow, Mary Sue. *German Music Criticism in the Late Eighteenth Century*. Cambridge University Press, 1997.

"Building a National Identity with Music: A Story from the Eighteenth Century," in *Searching for Common Ground: Diskurse zur deutschen Identität 1750–1871*, edited by Nicholas Vazsonyi, 255–69. Cologne: Böhlau, 2000.

Müller, Johannes. *Ueber die Compensation der physischen Kräfte am menschlichen Stimmorgan*. Berlin: A. Hirschwald, 1839.

Handbuch der Physiologie des Menschen. Coblenz: Höltscher, 1834–40. English translation by William Baly. *Elements of Physiology*, edited by John Bell. 2nd edn. Philadelphia: Lea and Blanchard, 1843.

Müller, Max. *Lectures on the Science of Language: Delivered at the Royal Institution of Great Britain in April, May, and June 1861*. London: Elibron Classics, 2005.

Müller, Ulrich, and Peter Wapnewski (eds.). *Wagner Handbook*. Edited and translated by John Deathridge. Cambridge, MA: Harvard University Press, 1992.

Mulvey, Laura. *Visual and Other Pleasures*. Basingstoke: Palgrave Macmillan, 2009.

Mundt, Theodor. *Die Kunst der deutschen Prosa: Aesthetisch, literargeschichtlich, gesellschaftlich*. Berlin: Veit und Comp., 1837.

Nattiez, Jean-Jacques. *Wagner Androgyne: A Study in Interpretation*. Translated by Stewart Spencer. Princeton University Press, 1993.

Nauenburg, Gustav. "Kritische Mischlinge," *Neue Zeitschrift für Musik* 7–8 (1843): 25–6, 29–30.

"Die Phrenologie in ihrer Beziehung zur Tonkunst," *Neue Zeitschrift für Musik* 2 (1851): 13–16.

Newcomb, Anthony. "The Birth of Music out of the Spirit of Drama," *19th-Century Music* 5 (1981): 38–66.

Newman, Ernest. *Wagner as Man and Artist*. New York: Alfred A. Knopf, 1924.

The Life of Richard Wagner. 4 vols. New York: Alfred Knopf, 1966.

Nietzsche, Friedrich. *The Nietzsche–Wagner Correspondence*, edited by Elizabeth Foerster-Nietzsche, translated by Caroline V. Kerr. New York: Boni and Liveright, 1921.

The Will to Power, translated by Walter Kaufmann and R. J. Hollingdale. New York: Vintage Books, 1968.

The Portable Nietzsche, edited and translated by Walter Kaufmann. New York: Penguin, 1976.

Sämtliche Briefe: Kritische Studienausgabe. 8 vols., edited by Giorgio Colli and Mazzino Montinari. Munich: Deutscher Taschenbuch Verlag, 1986.

Philosophical Writings, edited by Reinhold Grimm and Caroline Molina y Vedia, translated by Walter Kaufmann, and R. J. Hollingdale. New York: Continuum, 1995.

Basic Writings of Nietzsche, translated by Walter Kaufmann. New York: Vintage Books, 2000.

Unpublished Writings from the Period of Unfashionable Observations, translated by Richard T. Gray. Stanford University Press, 2000.

The Birth of Tragedy out of the Spirit of Music, translated by Shaun Whiteside. London: Penguin, 2003.

Nietzsche: The Anti-Christ, Ecce Homo, Twilight of the Idols and other writings, edited by Aaron Ridley and Judith Norman. Cambridge University Press, 2005.

On the Genealogy of Morals, translated by Carol Diethe. Cambridge University Press, 2007.

Human, All too Human, Beyond Good and Evil. Translated by Helen Zimmern and Paul V. Cohn. Ware: Wordsworth Classics, 2008.

Nisbet, Hugh Barr, ed. *German Aesthetic and Literary Criticism: Winckelmann, Lessing, Hamann, Herder, Schiller, Goethe*. Cambridge University Press, 1985.

Nissen, Georg Niklaus von. *Biographie W. A. Mozart's* [1828]. Rpt. Hildesheim and New York: G. Olms, 1972.

Nottebohm, Gustav. "Beethoven's theoretische Studien," *Allgemeine musikalische Zeitung* 41 (October 7, 1863): 685–91.

Ein Skizzenbuch von Beethoven. Leipzig: Breitkopf & Härtel, 1865.

Novalis. *Schriften. Die Werke Friedrich von Hardenbergs*. 5 vols., edited by Paul Kluckhohn and Richard Samuel. Stuttgart: W. Kohlhammer, 1960–88.

Nozick, Robert. *Anarchy, State, and Utopia*. Oxford: Basil Blackwell, 1974.

Olender, Maurice. *The Languages of Paradise: Race, Religion, and Philology in the Nineteenth Century*, translated by Arthur Goldhammer. Cambridge, MA: Harvard University Press, 1992.

Ørsted, Hans Christian. *Selected Scientific Writings of H. C. Ørsted*, edited and translated by Karen Jelved. Princeton University Press, 1998.

Otis, Laura. *Networking: Communicating with Bodies and Machines in the Nineteenth Century*. Ann Arbor: University of Michigan Press, 2001.

Müller's Lab. Oxford University Press, 2007.

Painter, Karen. "The Sensuality of Timbre: Responses to Mahler and Modernity at the 'Fin de siècle," *19th-Century Music* 18 (1995): 236–56.

Parker, Roger. *Leonora's Last Act: Essays in Verdian Discourse*. Princeton University Press, 1997.

Pasley, Brian, Stephen David, Nima Mesgarani, *et al.* "Reconstructing Speech from Human Auditory Cortex," *PLoS Biology* 10 (2012): 1001251.doi:10.1371/journal.pbio.1001251

Pastura, Francesco. *Bellini secondo la storia.* Parma: Guanda, 1959.

Pederson, Sanna. "A. B. Marx, Berlin Concert Life, and German National Identity" *19th Century Music* 18 (1994): 87–107.

"Enlightened and Romantic German Music Criticism, 1800–1850," PhD thesis. University of Pennsylvania, 1995.

"Defining the Term 'Absolute Music' Historically," *Music and Letters* 90 (2009): 240–62.

Petty, W. C. "Chopin and the Ghost of Beethoven," *19th-Century Music* 22 (1998): 281–99.

Picard, Timothée (ed.). *Dictionnaire Encyclopédique Wagner.* Arles: Actes Sud Editions, 2010.

Plato. *Ion*, translated by Benjamin Jowett at: http://classics.mit.edu/Plato/ion.html

Pohl, Richard. "Akustische Briefe," *Neue Zeitschrift für Musik* (1852). "Erster Brief," 1–3, 13–15; "Zweiter Brief," 21–24, 33–36; "Dritter Brief," 41–47; "Vierter Brief," 73–76, 85–88; "Fünfter Brief," 185–87, 193–96; "Sechster Brief: Physikalische und chemische Musik," 217–20, 249–51, 261–64; "Siebter Brief," *Neue Zeitschrift für Musik* 38 (1853): 53–57. Published separately as *Akustische Briefe für Musiker und Musikfreunde. Eine populäre Darstellung der Akustik als Naturwissenschaft in Beziehung zur Tonkunst.* Leipzig: Bruno Hinze, 1853.

"Die erste Aufführung des *Lohengrin* in Dresden," *Neue Zeitschrift für Musik* 7 (1859): 55–57, 64–65.

Pohl, Rüdiger. "Zum neuen Bayreuther *Lohengrin*: 'Gieb die Oper, wie sie ist, streiche nichts!'" *Mitteilungen der deutschen Richard-Wagner Gesellschaft* 30–31 (1999): 1–2.

Poriss, Hilary. *Changing the Score: Arias, Prima Donnas, and the Authority of Performance.* Oxford University Press, 2009.

Prince, Thomas. *Two Boston Puritans on God, Earthquakes, Electricity and Faith,* 1755–56. http://nationalhumanitiescenter.org/pds/becomingamer/ideas/text1/godlightningrods.pdf

Prinz, Gustav. "Musikalische Literatur," *Allgemeine Wiener Musik-Zeitung* 4 (1843): 547–48.

Pritchard, Matthew. "'The Moral Background of the Work of Art': 'Character' in German Musical Aesthetics 1780–1850," *Eighteenth-Century Music* 9 (2012): 63–80.

Prölss, Robert. *Geschichte des Hoftheaters zu Dresden von seinem Anfängen bis zum Jahre 1862.* Dresden: Wilhelm Baensch, 1878.

Proudhon, Pierre-Joseph. *What is Property?*, edited and translated by Donald R. Kelley and Bonnie G. Smith. Cambridge University Press, 2004.

Raff, Joachim. *Die Wagnerfrage. Kritisch beleuchtet.* Brunswick: Vieweg, 1854.

Ranke, Leopold von (ed.). *Historisch-politische Zeitschrift*. 2 vols. Hamburg: Friedrich Perthes, 1832–36.

Rapp, Moritz. *Versuch einer Physioloige der Sprache nebst historischer Entwicklung der abendlaendischen Idiome nach physiologischen Grundsaetzen*. Stuttgart & Tübingen: Cotta, 1836.

Raumer, Rudolf von. *Die Aspiration und die Lautverschiebung: Eine Sprachgeschichtliche Untersuchung*. Leipzig: F. A. Brockhaus, 1837.

Rehding, Alexander. *Hugo Riemann and the Birth of Modern Musical Thought*. Cambridge University Press, 2003.

"Magic Boxes and Volksempfänger," in *Music, Theatre, and Politics in Germany: 1848 to the Third Reich*, edited by Nikolaus Bacht. Aldershot: Ashgate, 2006.

"Unsound Seeds" (2007), unpublished paper.

Music and Monumentality: Commemoration and Wonderment in Nineteenth-Century Germany. Oxford University Press, 2009.

Reicha, Anton. *Treatise on Melody* [1814], translated by Peter M. Landey. Hillsdale: Pendragon, 2000.

Rellstab, Ludwig. *Musikalische Beurteilungen*. Leipzig: Brockhaus, 1848. Rpt. Leipzig: Brockhaus, 1861.

Reuterswärd, Patrik. *Studien zur Polychromie der Plastik. Griechenland und Rom*. Stockholm: Almqvist & Wiksell, 1960.

Reyna, Philippe. "Richard Wagner als Pariser Korrespondent 1841: Neun Pariser Berichte für die Dresdner Abend-Zeitung – Reportage oder Vorwand?" in *"Schlagen Sie die Kraft der Reflexion nicht zu gering an!" Beiträge zu Richard Wagners Denken, Werk und Wirken*, edited by Klaus Döge, Christa Jost, and Peter Jost, 21–31. Mainz: Schott, 2002.

Reynolds, Christopher. *Motives for Allusion: Context and Content in Nineteenth-Century Music*. Cambridge University Press, 2003.

Richards, Annette. "Automatic Genius: Mozart and the Mechanical Sublime," *Musik and Letters* 80 (1999): 366–89.

The Free Fantasia and the Musical Picturesque. Cambridge University Press, 2001.

Richter, Jean Paul. *Sämtlich Werke*. 4 vols., edited by Norbert Miller. Munich: Carl Hanser, 1974.

Riemann, Hugo. *Musik-Lexikon*. 1st edn. Leipzig: Bibliographisches Institut, 1882.

Riesz, Janos. "Mallarmés Richard Wagner, rêverie d'un poète français und sein Hommage à Wagner," in *Von Wagner zum Wagnérisme: Musik, Literatur, Kunst, Politik*, edited by Annegret Fauser and Manuela Schwartz, 445–58. Leipziger Universitätsverlag, 1999.

Riley, Matthew. *Musical Listening in the German Enlightenment*. Aldershot: Ashgate, 2004.

Rimbaud, Arthur. *Complete Works, Selected Letters*, translated by Wallace Fowlie. University of Chicago Press, 2005.

Robel, Ernst. *Die Sirenen: Ein Beitrag zur Entwicklungsgeschichte der Akustik*. Berlin: R. Gaertner, 1894.

Robinson, Paul. *Opera, Sex, and Other Vital Matters.* University of Chicago Press, 2002.

Rochlitz, Friedrich. "Schreiben Mozarts an den Baron von . . ." *Allgemeine musikalische Zeitung* 34 (1815).

"Mozarts gutter Rath an Componisten," *Allgemeine musikalische Zeitung* 22 (1820).

Rosen, Charles. "Influence: Plagiarism and Inspiration," *19th-Century Music* 4 (1980): 87–100.

Sonata Forms. New York and London: Norton, 1988.

The Romantic Generation. London: Fontana, 1999.

Rosenkranz, Karl. *Ästhetik des Häßlichen.* Königsberg: Gebrüder Bornträger, 1853. Rpt. Leizpig: Reclam, 1996.

Rosselli, John. *The Life of Bellini.* Cambridge University Press, 1996.

Rötscher, Heinrich Theodor. *Die Kunst der dramatischen Darstellung.* 3 vols. Berlin: Wilhelm Thome, 1841.

Rousseau, Jean-Jacques. *Oeuvres complètes.* 5 vols., edited by Bernard Gagnebin and Marcel Raymond. Paris: Gallinard, 1959–95.

Ruiter, Jacob de. *Der Charakterbegriff in der Musik: Studien zur deutschen Ästhetik der Instrumentalmusik 1740–1850.* Stuttgart: Franz Steiner, 1989.

Saint-Saëns, Camille. *On Music and Musicians,* translated by Roger Nichols. Oxford University Press, 2008.

Schaeffner, André. *Origine des instruments de musique.* Paris: Payot, 1936.

Schelling, F. W. J. *Philosophy of Art. Philosophie der Kunst. Vorlesung.* Darmstadt: Wissenschaftliche Buchgesellschaft, 1976, translated by Douglas W. Stott. Minneapolis: University of Minnesota Press, 1989.

Schiffer, Michael Brian. *Draw the Lightning Down: Benjamin Franklin and Electrical Technology in the Age of Enlightenment.* Berkeley and Los Angeles: University of California Press, 2006.

Schiller, Friedrich. *Sämtliche Gedichte,* edited by Jochen Golz. Frankfurt am Main: Insel, 1992.

Schilling, Gustav von (ed.). *Encyclopädie der gesammten musikalischen Wissenschaften.* 7 vols. Stuttgart: Franz Heinrich Köhler, 1837–42. Rpt. Hildesheim: Georg Olms, 2004.

Schirmacher, Wolfgang (ed.). *German Socialist Philosophy.* New York: Continuum, 1997.

Schlegel, August Wilhelm. *Vorlesungen ueber dramatische Kunst und Literatur,* edited by Eduard Böcking. 3rd edn. Leipzig: Weidmann, 1846.

Schlegel, Friedrich. *Literary Notebooks 1797–1801,* edited by Hans Eichner. London: Athlone Press, 1957.

Kritische Friedrich–Schlegel–Ausgabe, 35 vols., edited by Ernst Behler, Jean-Jacques Ansett and Hans Eichner. Munich: F. Schöningh, 1958–.

Kritische Schriften und Fragmente. 6 vols., edited by Ernst Behler, and Hans Eichner. Paderborn: F. Schöningh, 1988.

Schleiermacher, Friedrich. *Hermeneutics and Criticism*, edited by Andrew Bowie. Cambridge University Press, 1998.

Schleuning, Peter. "Die Fantasiermaschine. Ein Beitrag zur Geschichte der Stilwende um 1750," *Archiv für Musikwissenschaft* 27 (1970): 192–213.

Schmidt, Jochen. *Die Geschichte des Genie-Gedankens in der deutschen Literatur, Philosophie und Politik*. 2 vols. 3rd edn. Heidelberg: Universitätsverlag Winter, 2004.

Schoenberg, Arnold. *The Musical Idea and the Logic, Technique and Art of its Presentation*. Bloomington: Indiana University Press, 2006.

Schopenhauer, Arthur. *The World as Will and Representation*. 2 vols., translated by E. F. J. Payne. New York: Dover, 1969.

   Gesammelte Briefe, edited by Arthur Hübscher. Bonn: Bouvier Verlag Herbert Grundmann, 1987.

   On Visions and Colors [1816], translated by E. F. J. Payne. Oxford and Providence: Berg, 1994.

   Philosophical Writings, edited by Wolfgang Schirmacher. New York: The German Library, 1994.

Schreinert, Kurt (ed.). *Briefe an Wilhelm und Hans Hertz 1859–1898*. Stuttgart: Ernst Klett, 1972.

Schumann, Max. *Zur Geschichte des deutschen Musikalienbuchhandels seit der Gründung des Vereins der deutschen Musikalienhändler 1829–1929*. Leipzig: Verband der Deutschen Musikalienhändler, 1929.

Schumann, Robert. *Gesammelte Schriften über Musik und Musiker*, edited by Martin Kreisig. 2 vols. 5th edn. Leipzig: Breitkopf & Härtel, 1914. English translation by Paul Rosenfeld. *On Music and Musicians*, edited by Konrad Wolff. New York: Norton, 1969.

Schütze, Stephan. "Über Gefühl und Ausdruck in der Musik," *Caecelia* 12 (1830): 237–56.

Seckendorff, Gustav Freyherr von. *Vorlesungen über Deklamation und Mimik. Erster Band, nebst einem Heft Musik-Beilagen*. Brunswick: Vieweg, 1816.

Seebeck, August. "Bemerkungen über Resonanz und über Helligkeit der Farben im Spectrum," *Annalen der Physik* 62 (1844): 571–76.

Seedorf, Thomas. "'Deklamation und 'Gesangswohllaut' – Richard Wagner und der 'deutsche *Bel canto*,'" in *Vierzehn Beiträge (nicht nur) über Richard Wagner*, edited by Christa Jost, 181–206. Tutzing: Hans Schneider, 2006.

Seeger, Charles. "Prescriptive and Descriptive Music-Writing," *The Musical Quarterly* 44 (1958): 184–95.

Servières, Georges. *Richard Wagner: jugé en France*. Paris: Librairie illustrée, 1887.

Sharp, Lesley (ed.). *The Cambridge Companion to Goethe*. Cambridge University Press, 2002.

Shaw, George Bernard. *The Perfect Wagnerite*. Kessinger: Whitefish, 2004.

Sheehan, James. "What is German History? Reflections on the Role of the Nation in German History and Historiography," *The Journal of Modern History* 53 (1981): 5.

German History 1770–1866. Oxford University Press, 1994.

Sieber, Ferdinand. "Aphorismen über Gesang," *Berliner Musik-Zeitung Echo* 21 (1854): 157–58, 165–67, 261–62, 271–72.

Skokan, Isabel. *Germania und Italia: Nationale Mythen und Heldengestalten in Gemälden des 19. Jahnhunderts.* Berlin: Lukas 2009.

Slonimsky, Nicolas. *Lexicon of Musical Invective.* New York: Coleman-Ross, 1853.

Smart, Mary Ann. "In Praise of Convention: Formula and Experiment in Bellini's Self-Borrowings," *Journal of the America Musicological Society* 53 (2000): 25–68.

Mimomania. Berkeley and Los Angeles: University of California Press, 2004.

Spencer, Herbert. *Essays, Scientific, Political, and Speculative.* New York: D. Appleton & Co., 1907.

Spencer, Stewart (trans. and ed.). *Wagner Remembered.* London: Faber & Faber, 2000.

Spitzer, Michael. *Metaphor and Musical Thought.* University of Chicago Press, 2003.

Sobolewski, Eduard. "Phantasie," *Neue Zeitschrift für Musik* 5 (December 24, 1839): 201–03.

Reaktionäre Briefe aus dem Feuilleton der Ostpreuss. Zeitung. Königsberg: Schultzschen Hofbuchdruckerei, 1854, translated as "Reactionary Letters I–XI" in *The Musical World* 33 (1855): 19, 45, 49, 69–70, 81, 99–100, 113–14, 129, 146–47, 162, 179–80.

Sontag, Susan. "Wagner's Fluids," *London Review of Books* (December 10, 1987): 8–9.

Staël, Germaine de. *Corinne, or Italy*, translated by Avriel H. Goldberger. New Brunswick and London: Rutgers University Press, 1987.

Politics, Literature, and National Character, edited and translated by Morroe Berger. New Brunswick and London: Transaction, 2000.

Steege, Benjamin. *Helmholtz and the Modern Listener.* Cambridge University Press, 2012.

Steig, Reinhold. *Achim von Arnim und Jacob und Wilhelm Grimm.* Stuttgart: J. G. Cotta, 1904.

Stein, Jack. *Richard Wagner and the Synthesis of the Arts.* Detroit: Wayne State University Press, 1960.

Steiner, George. *The Death of Tragedy.* London: Faber, 1961.

Stelzig, Eugene L. *The Romantic Subject in Autobiography: Rousseau and Goethe.* Charlottesville and London: University of Virginia Press, 2000.

Stendhal. *Rome, Naples et Florence.* 2 vols. 3rd edn. Paris: Delaunay, Librairie Palais-Royal, 1826.

Vies de Haydn, de Mozart et de Métastase [1814], edited by Daniel Muller. Geneva: Slatkine, 1986.

Stoljar, Margaret Mahony. *Poetry and Song in Later Eighteenth-Century Germany: A Study in the Musical Sturm und Drang.* London: Routledge, 1985.

Stollberg, Arne. *Ohr und Auge – Klang und Form.* Munich: Franz Steiner: 2006.

Strahle, Graham (ed.). *An Early Music Dictionary.* Cambridge University Press, 2009.

Stubbs, Elsina. *Wilhelm von Humboldt's Philosophy of Language, its Sources and Influence.* Lewiston, Queenston, Lampeter: Edwin Mellen Press, 2002.

Stumpf, Carl. "Sprachlaute und Instrumentalklänge," *Zeitschrift für Physik* 38 (1926): 745–58.

  Die Anfänge der Musik. Leipzig: J. A. Barth, 1911. Rpt. Hildesheim and New York: G. Olms, 1979. English translation by David Trippett. *The Origins of Music.* Oxford University Press, 2012.

Stumpf, Heike. *". . . wollet mir jetzt durch die phantastisch verschlungenen Kreuzgänge folgen?" Metaphorisches Sprechen in der Musikkritik der ersten Hälfte des 19. Jahrhunderts.* Frankfurt am Main: Bonner, 1996.

Sulzer, Johann Georg. *Allgemeine Theorie der schönen Künste in Einzeln*, 5 vols. Leipzig: Weidmannschen, 1793–99.

Tappert, Wilhelm. "Percunos und Lohengrin," *Musikalisches Wochenblatt. Organ für Musiker und Musikfreunde* 35 (August 25, 1887): 413–15.

  Wandernde Melodien: eine musikalische Studie [1868]. 2nd edn. Berlin: Brachvogel & Ranft, 1889.

  Richard Wagner im Spiegel der Kritik. Leipzig: C. F. W. Siegel, 1915.

Taylor, Alan John Percivale. *The Course of German History: A Survey of the Development of German History since 1815* [1945]. London and New York: Routledge, 2005.

Teutonius. "Letters to a Music Student," *The Musical World.* "1. On the Tonal System," *TMW* 44 (1848): 689–91; "2. The Origin and Fundamental Laws of Harmony," *TMW* 45 1848): 709–11; "3. cont." *TWM* 46 (1848): 729–31; "4. The Study of Musical Composition," *TMW* 48 (1848): 762–64; "5. Melody and Melodious Combination," *TMW* 49 (1848): 773–75; "6. cont." *TMW* 50 (1848): 792–96.

Thissen, Paul. *Zitattechniken in der Symphonik des 19. Jahrhunderts.* Sinzig: Studio, 1998.

Thorau, Christian. *Semantisierte Sinnlichkeit: Studien zu Rezeption und Zeichenstruktur der Leitmotivtenik Richard Wagners.* Stuttgart: Steiner, 2003.

Thürnagel, Emil. *Theorie der Schauspielkunst.* Heidelberg: August Oswald's Universitäts-Buchhandlung, 1836)

Tiggelen, Philippe Van. *Componium: The Mechanical Musical Improvisor.* Louvain-la-Neuve: Institut supérieur d'archéologie er d'histoire de l'Art, 1987.

Tintori, Giampiero. *Bellini.* Milan: Rusconi, 1983.

Titus, Barbara. "The quest for spiritualized form: (Re)positioning Eduard Hanslick," *Acta Musicologica* 80 (2008): 67–97.

Todd, R. Larry. "Franz Liszt, Carl Friedrich Weitzmann, and the Augmented Triad," in *The Second Practice of Nineteenth-Century Tonality*, edited by W. Kinderman, and H. M. Krebs, 153–77. Lincoln: University of Nebraska Press, 1996.

Tomlinson, Gary. *Metaphysical Song: An Essay on Opera.* Princeton University Press, 1999.

Treadwell, James. "The Urge to Communicate," in *The Cambridge Companion to Wagner*, edited by Thomas Grey. Cambridge University Press, 2008.

Trippett, David. "Bayreuth in Miniature: Wagner and the Melodramatic Voice," *The Musical Quarterly* 95 (2012): 71–138.

"Defending Wagner's Italy," in *The Legacy of Richard Wagner*, edited by Luca Sala, 363–98. Turnhout: Brepols, 2012.

Ule, Otto. "Die Aufgabe der Naturwissenschaft," *Die Natur* 1 (January 3, 1852): 1–4.

"Die Stimme als Ausdruck des Innern," *Die Natur* 30 (July 24, 1852): 233–36.

Populäre Naturlehre (Physik), oder, Die Lehre von den Bewegungen in der Natur und von den Naturkräften im Dienste des Menschen. Leipzig: Ernst Keil, 1867.

Unger, Johann Friedrich. *Entwurf einer Maschine, wodurch alles was auf dem Clavier gespielt wird, sich von selber in Noten setzt*. Brunswick: Fürstl. Waisenhaus, 1774.

Vazsonyi, Nicholas. *Richard Wagner: Self-Promotion and the Making of a Brand*. Cambridge University Press, 2010.

Vischer, Friedrich Theodor. *Aesthetik oder Wissenschaft des Schönen. Zum Gebrauche für Vorlesungen*. 6 vols. Munich: Meyer & Jessen, 1923.

Vogt, Carl. *Physiologische Briefe für Gebildete aller Stände*. Stuttgart and Tübingen: J. G Cotta, 2nd edn., 1854.

Voltaire [= François-Marie Arouet]. *Oeuvres complètes de Voltaire*. 142 vols. Oxford: Taylor Institution, 1992.

Voss, Egon. *Richard Wagner und die Instrumentalmusik. Wagners symphonischer Ehrgeiz*. Wilhelmshaven: Heinrichshofen, 1977.

"Wagner und kein Ende": Betrachtungen und Studien. Zurich and Mainz: Atlantis, 1996.

Wackenroder, Wilhelm Heinrich. *Werke und Briefe*, edited by Lambert Schneider. Heidelberg: Lambert Schneider, 1967.

Confessions and Fantasies, edited and translated by M. H. Schubert. Pennsylvania State University Press, 1971.

Sämtliche Werke und Briefe. 2 vols., edited by Silvio Vietta and Richard Littlejohns. Heidelberg: C. Winter, 1991.

Wade, Nicholas J. *A Natural History of Vision*. Cambridge, MA: MIT Press, 1998.

Wadle, Elmar. "Das preußische Urheberrechtgesetz von 1837 im Spiegel seiner Vorgeschichte," in *Woher kommt das Urheberrecht und wohin geht es?*, edited by Robert Dittrich, 55–98. Vienna: Manz, 1988.

"Kontrolle und Schutz – Presserecht des 19. Jahrhunderts im Spannungsfeld von öffentlichem Recht und Privatrecht," in *Politischer Journalismus, Öffentlichkeiten und Medien im 19. und 20. Jahrhundert*, edited by Clemens Zimmermann, 61–77. Ostfildern: Jan Thorbecke, 2006.

Waeber, Jacqueline. *En Musique dans le Texte: Le Mélodrame, de Rousseau à Schoenberg*. Paris: Van Dieren, 2005.

Wagner, Cosima. *Cosima Wagner's Diaries*. 2 vols., edited by Martin Gregor-Dellin and Dietrich Mack, translated and introduced by Geoffrey Skelton. New York and London: Harcourt Brace Jovanovich, 1978–80.

Wagner, Richard. *Richard Wagner's Letters to His Dresden Friends*, translated by J. S. Shedlock. London: Grevel and Co., 1890.

Briefe an Röckel von Richard Wagner, edited by Marie Lipsius [= La Mara]. Leipzig: Breitkopf & Härtel, 1894.

Sämtliche Werke. 31 vols. [projected]. Mainz: B. Schott's Söhne / Schott Musik International, 1970–. [Individual titles, editors, and publication dates are given in footnotes for particular volumes.]

Three Wagner Essays, translated by Robert Jacobs. London: Eulenburg, 1979.

Dichtungen und Schriften, edited by Dieter Borchmeyer. 10 vols. Frankfurt am Main: Insel, 1983.

Mein Leben, edited by Martin Gregor-Dellin. Munich: List, 1976. English translation by Andrew Gray, edited by Mary Whittall. *My Life*. Cambridge University Press, 1983.

Selected Letters of Richard Wagner, edited and translated by Stewart Spencer and Barry Millington. New York and London: Norton, 1987.

Lohengrin. English National Opera Guide 47. London: John Calder, 1993.

Sämtliche Schriften und Dichtungen, 16 vols. Volks-Ausgabe (Leipzig: Breitkopf & Härtel and C. F. W. Siegel [R. Linnemann], 1911 [vols. 1–12], 1914 [13–16]). English translation by W. Ashton Ellis. *Richard Wagner's Prose Works*. 8 vols. London: Kegan Paul, Trench, Trübner & Co., 1892–99; rpt. Lincoln and London: University of Nebraska Press, 1995.

Sämtliche Briefe, edited by Gertrud Strobel and Werner Wolf (vols. 1–5), Hans-Joachim Bauer and Johannes Forner (vols. 6–8), Klaus Burmeister and Johannes Forner (vol. 9), Andreas Mielke (vol. 10), Martin Dürrer (vols. 11–13, 16), and Andreas Mielke (vols. 14–15). Leipzig: Deutscher Verlag für Musik, 1967–2000 [vols. 1–9]; Wiesbaden, Leipzig, and Paris: Breitkopf & Härtel, 2000– [vols. 10–].

Lohengrin, edited by John Deathridge and Klaus Döge. London and Mainz: Eulenburg, 2007.

"Wagner and Bellini's Norma." Translated by Stewart Spencer. *The Wagner Journal* 1 (2007): 33–37.

"Autobiographical Sketch (to 1842)." Translated by Thomas Grey. *The Wagner Journal* 2 (2008): 42–58.

Walker, Alan. *Franz Liszt*. 3 vols. London: Faber & Faber, 1989–97.

Walton, Chris. "'Flickarbeit' oder Bearbeitung? Ein neuer Wagner-Fund in der Zentralbibliothek Zürich," *Neue Zürcher Zeitung* 14–15 (December 12, 1996).

Richard Wagner's Zurich: The Muse of Place. Woodbridge: Camden House, 2007.

Ward, Seth. *Vindicae academiarum*. Oxford: Leonard Litchfield, 1654.

Wartofsky, Mark W. *Models: Representation and the Scientific Understanding*. Dordrecht and Boston: D. Reidel, 1979.

Wason, Robert. "Progressive Harmonic Theory in the Mid-Nineteenth Century," *Journal of Musicological Research* 8 (1988): 55–90.

Watkins, Holly. *Metaphors of Depth in German Musical Thought*. Cambridge University Press, 2011.

Weber, Gottfried. *Versuch einer geordneten Theorie der Tonsetzkunst*. 4 vols. 2nd edn. Mainz: B. Schotts Söhne, 1824.

Weinstock, Herbert. *Vincenzo Bellini: His Life and His Operas*. New York: Alfred Knopf, 1971.

Weithase, Irmgard. *Die Geschichte der deutschen Vortragskunst im 19. Jahrhundert*. Weimar: H. Böhlau, 1940.

Weitzmann, Carl Friedrich. *Der übermässige Dreiklang*. Berlin, 1853.
  Der verminderte Septimen-Akkord. Berlin, 1854.
  Geschichte des Septimen-Akkordes. Berlin, 1854.

Wellberry, David E. "Foreword," in Friedrich Kittler, *Discourse Networks 1800–1900*, vii–xxxiii. Stanford University Press, 1990.

West, Martin. *Indo-European Poetry and Myth*. Oxford University Press, 2007.

Westernhagen, Curt von. *Richard Wagners Dresdener Bibliothek 1842 bis 1849*. Wiesbaden: F. A. Brockhaus, 1966.

Whittall, Arnold. "Criticism and analysis: current perspectives," in *Wagner and his World*, edited by Thomas Grey, 276–89. Princeton University Press, 2008.

Wieck, Friedrich. *Klavier und Gesang: Didaktisches und Polemisches*. 3rd edn. Leipzig: F. E. C. Leuckart, 1878.

Wieland, Christoph Martin. *Sämmtliche Werke*. 52 vols. Leipzig: G. J. Göschen, 1824–28.

Willis, Robert. "On the Vowel Sounds and on Reed Organ-Pipes," *Transactions of the Cambridge Philosophical Society* 3 (1830): 231–68.

Winckelmann, J. J. *History of the Art of Antiquity*, translated by Harry Francis Mallgrave. Los Angeles: Getty Research Institute, 2006.

Wittgenstein, Ludwig. *Tractatus Logico-Philosophicus* [1921], translated by D. F. Pears and B. F. McGuinness. London and New York: Routledge, 2010.

Wittkau-Horgby, Annette. *Materialismus: Entstehung und Wirkung in den Wissenschaften des 19. Jahrhunderts*. Göttingen: Vandenhoeck & Ruprecht, 1998.

Wright, Sue. *Community and Communication: The Role of Language in Nation State Building*. Clevedon: Multilingual Matters, 2000.

Wolfson, Susan. "Revision as Form: Wordsworth's Drowned Man," in *William Wordsworth's The Prelude*, edited by Stephen C. Gill, 73–122. Oxford University Press, 2006.

Wolzogen, Alfred von. *Wilhelmine Schröder-Devrient*. Leipzig: F. A. Brockhaus, 1863.

Wolzogen, Hanz von. "Nachwort," *Bayreuther Blätter* 8 (1885): 365–67.

Young, Christopher, and Thomas Gloning, eds. *A History of the German Language through Texts*. London and New York: Routledge, 2004.

Young, Eduard. *Conjectures on Original Composition in a Letter to the Author of Sir Charles Grandison*. London: A. Millar, R. and J. Dodsley, 1759.

Zammito, John H. *The Genesis of Kant's Critique of Judgment*. University of Chicago Press, 1992.

Zellner, L. A. "Über Plagiat," *Blätter für Musik, Theater und Kunst* 1 (November 27, 1855).

Ziegler, Klaus. *Grabbes Leben und Charakter*. Hamburg: Hoffmann, 1855.

Zimmermann, Robert. *Geschichte der Aesthetik als philosophischer Wissenschaft*. Vienna: Wilhelm Braumüller, 1858.

Žižek, Slavoj. *On Belief*. London: Routledge, 2001.

Zopff, Hermann. "Zur Gesangcomposition," *Neue Zeitschrift für Musik* 11 (1859): 89–91, 97–98.

   Der angehende Dirigent. Leipzig: Merseburger, 1881.

Texts by editorial or otherwise unknown writers

W. B. L. Z. "Die Aufführung der Wagner'schen Opern auf dem Dresdner Hoftheater," *Berliner Musik-Zeitung Echo* 38 (1859): 297–300, 305–09, 313–16, 321–23.

W. M. S. "*Lohengrin* in Wien," *Monatschrift für Theater und Musik* (1858): 435–39.

Anon [falsely attributed to Wilhelmine Schröder-Devrient]. *Aus den Memoiren einer Saengerin*. Altona: n.p., 1862.

Anon. "The Melodies of Germany," *The Harmonicon* 5 (December, 1827): 242–3.

Anon. "Correspondence: Mr. J. B. Sale, and Mr. J. Dair," *The Musical World* 15 (February 18, 1841): 105.

Anon. "Über Reminiscenzenjägerei," *AmZ* 49 (1847): 561–66.

Anon. "The Opera Telakouphanon," *Punch* (1848): 275.

Anon. "Richard Wagner's *Lohengrin*," *Rheinische Musik-Zeitung für Kunstfreunde und Künstler* 164–65, 168, 170 (1853): 1282–84, 1286–88, 1297–98, 1304–07.

Anon. "Tannhäuser und der Sängerkrieg auf Wartburg. Romantische Oper und drei Akten von Richard Wagner. IX," *Rheinische Musik-Zeitung* 138 (1853): 1041–43, 1057–60, 1065–67, 1089–91, 1097–1100, 1113–17, 1145–48.

Anon. "Lohengrin," *Signale für die Musikalische Welt* 4 (1854): 25–27.

Anon. "Richard Wagner," *Niederrheinische Musik-Zeitung für Kunstfreunde und Künstler* 8 (1854): 57–61.

Anon. "Über Plagiate und Reminiscenzen," *Berlin Musik-Zeitung Echo* 7 (February 18, 1855): 49–51, 58–60.

Anon. *Patents for Inventions: Abridgements of Specifications*. Patent Office, Great Britain Patent Office, 1859.

Anon. "Mr Mill's Analysis of the Mind," *The Westminster Review* 36 (1869): 148–79.

Anon. "Wagner on Bellini," *The Musical Times and Singing Class Circular* 27 (1886): 66–68.

Index